CHILE

2ND EDITION

Where to Stay and Eat
for All Budgets

Must-See Sights
and Local Secrets

Ratings You Can Trust

Fodor's Travel Publications   New York, Toronto, London, Sydney, Auckland
www.fodors.com

FODOR'S CHILE

Editors: Deborah Kaufman, Lisa Dunford

Editorial Production: Ira-Neil Dittersdorf
Editorial Contributors: Gregory Benchwick, Michael de Zayas, David Dudenhoefer, Cheryl Stanton, Jeffrey Van Fleet.
Maps: David Lindroth, Inc., and Eureka Cartography, *cartographers;* Rebecca Baer and Bob Blake, *map editors*
Design: Fabrizio La Rocca, *creative director;* Guido Caroti, *art director;* Melanie Marin, *senior photo editor*
Production/Manufacturing: Colleen Ziemba
Cover Photo (Atacama Desert): Jorg Brockmann

SPECIAL SALES
Fodor's Travel Publications are available at special discounts for bulk purchases for sales promotions or premiums. Special editions, including personalized covers, excerpts of existing guides, and corporate imprints, can be created in large quantities for special needs. For more information, contact your local bookseller or write to Special Markets, Fodor's Travel Publications, 1745 Broadway, New York, New York 10019. Inquiries from Canada should be directed to your local Canadian bookseller or sent to Random House of Canada, Ltd., Marketing Department, 2775 Matheson Boulevard East, Mississauga, Ontario L4W 4P7. Inquiries from the United Kingdom should be sent to Fodor's Travel Publications, 20 Vauxhall Bridge Road, London SW1V 2SA, England.

IMPORTANT TIP & AN INVITATION
Although all prices, opening times, and other details in this book are based on information supplied to us at press time, changes occur all the time in the travel world, and Fodor's cannot accept responsibility for facts that become outdated or for inadvertent errors or omissions. So **always confirm information when it matters,** especially if you're making a detour to visit a specific place. Your experiences—positive and negative—matter to us. If we have missed or misstated something, **please write to us.** We follow up on all suggestions. Contact the Chile editors at editors@fodors.com or c/o Fodor's at 1745 Broadway, New York, New York 10019.

DESTINATION CHILE

I live now in a country as soft as the autumnal flesh of grapes," begins "Country," a poem by Pablo Neruda. With his odes to the place of his birth, the Nobel Prize winner sang Chile into being, inviting us to inhale the bouquet of its salty breezes and its soaring Andean peaks before we hold them to our lips and drink them down. Chile is as luminous and piquant, as rustic and romantic, as any of Neruda's poems describing it. It encompasses a bone-dry desert that blooms in a riot of color once or twice a decade, sprawling glaciers that bellow like thunder, and snow-covered volcanoes that perpetually smolder. You'll also find sprawling ranches and first-rate vineyards, mysterious geoglyphs and fascinating museums of pre-Columbian artifacts, sleepy fishing villages and glittery resorts by the sea—all this and more in one sliver of land squeezed between the Andes and the Pacific. So wherever your journey takes you through this exciting, enchanting, sumptuous country that so inspired Neruda, prepare to be intoxicated.

Karen Cure, Editorial Director

CONTENTS

ON THE ROAD WITH FODOR'S

A trip takes you out of yourself. Concerns of life at home completely disappear, driven away by more immediate thoughts—about, say, what marvels will beguile the next day, or where you'll have dinner. That's where Fodor's comes in. We make sure that you know all your options, so that you don't miss something that's around the next bend just because you didn't know it was there. Because the best memories of your trip might well have nothing to do with what you came to Chile to see, we guide you to sights large and small all over the region. You might set out to soak up the sun on Chile's miles of coastline, but back at home you find yourself unable to forget hiking through the haunting, barren landscape of the Valle de la Luna in the Atacama Desert. With Fodor's at your side, serendipitous discoveries are never far away.

Our success in showing you every corner of Chile is a credit to our extraordinary writers. Although there's no substitute for travel advice from a good friend who knows your style, our contributors are the next best thing—the kind of people you would poll for travel advice if you knew them.

A former editor for *The Bolivian Times*, Gregory Benchwick first fell in love with Latin America when he traveled via chicken bus from Costa Rica to Belize in 1995. Since then he has written extensively on traveling in the region. He covered the rugged, enchanting, and often inhospitable landscape of El Norte Chico and El Norte Grande for this book. Gregory now resides near Alicante, Spain, where he works as a freelance journalist.

Michael de Zayas, a twentysomething Cuban-American writer, has contributed to Fodor's guides to Argentina, the Caribbean, Central America, Cuba, Florida, Mexico, New York City, and Spain, among others. He covered the Southern Coast and Patagonia and Tierra del Fuego chapters of this book, and says the landscape is the most beautiful he's ever encountered. In between travels, Michael runs an Internet business.

According to David Dudenhoefer's mother, he has spent too long wandering around Latin America with too little to show for

it. He was based in San José, Costa Rica, for most of the 1990s, when he covered Central and South America as a freelance journalist and photographer. Though now based in Florida, he still spends most of his time south of Key West. His articles and photos have appeared in more than 30 publications on both sides of the Rio Grande, and he has contributed to half a dozen Fodor's guides. David updated the Central Coast and Central Valley chapters of this book.

Freelance writer Cheryl Stanton worked in an editorial capacity in London's magazine market for several years before moving to Santiago, Chile, in the mid-1990s. She now resides with her family in southern Chile. Cheryl has traveled extensively throughout the country and contributes articles to lifestyle and travel magazines in both the United Kingdom and the United States. She updated the Smart Travel Tips A to Z section and the Santiago and Easter Island chapters for this book.

Costa Rica–based freelance writer and pharmacist Jeffrey Van Fleet divides his time between Central America and Wisconsin, but always looks for opportunities to enjoy the more cosmopolitan ambience of South America's southern cone. He is a regular contributor to Costa Rica's English-language *Tico Times*. Jeff updated the Lake District and Chiloé chapters for this book.

ABOUT THIS BOOK

There's no doubt that the best source for travel advice is a like-minded friend who's just been where you're headed. But with or without that friend, you'll have a better trip with a Fodor's guide in hand. Once you've learned to find your way around its pages, you'll be in great shape to find your way around your destination.

SELECTION
Our goal is to cover the best properties, sights, and activities in their category, as well as the most interesting communities to visit. We make a point of including local food-lovers' hot spots as well as neighborhood options, and we avoid all that's touristy unless it's really worth your time. You can go on the assumption that everything you read about in this book is recommended wholeheartedly by our writers and editors. Flip to On the Road with Fodor's to learn more about who they are. It goes without saying that no property mentioned in the book has paid to be included.

RATINGS
Orange stars ★ denote sights and properties that our editors and writers consider the very best in the area covered by the entire book. These, the best of the best, are listed in the Fodor's Choice section in the front of the book. Black stars ★ highlight the sights and properties we deem Highly Recommended, the don't-miss sights within any region. Fodor's Choice and Highly Recommended options in each region are listed on the title page of the chapter covering that region. Use the index to find complete descriptions. In cities, sights pinpointed with numbered map bullets ❶ in the margins tend to be more important than those without bullets.

SPECIAL SPOTS
Pleasures & Pastimes focuses on types of experiences that reveal the spirit of the destination. Watch for Off the Beaten Path sights. Some are out of the way, some are quirky, and all are worth your while. If the munchies hit while you're exploring, look for Need a Break? suggestions.

TIME IT RIGHT
Wondering when to go? Check On the Calendar up front and chapters' Timing sections for weather and crowd overviews and best days and times to visit.

SEE IT ALL
Use Fodor's exclusive Great Itineraries as a model for your trip. (For a good overview of the entire destination, follow those that begin the book, or mix regional itineraries from several chapters.) In cities, Good Walks guide you to important sights in each neighborhood; ▶ indicates the starting points of walks and itineraries in the text and on the map.

BUDGET WELL
Hotel and restaurant price categories from ¢ to $$$$ are defined in the opening pages of each chapter—expect to find a balanced selection for every budget. For attractions, we always give standard adult admission fees; reductions are sometimes available for children, students, and senior citizens.

BASIC INFO
Smart Travel Tips lists travel essentials for the entire area covered by the book; city- and region-specific basics end each chapter. To find the best way to get around, see the transportation section; see individual modes of travel ("By Car," "By Train") for details. We assume you'll check Web sites or call for particulars.

ON THE MAPS	Maps throughout the book show you what's where and help you find your way around. Black and orange numbered bullets ❶ ① in the text correlate to bullets on maps.
BACKGROUND	In general, we give background information within the chapters in the course of explaining sights as well as in CloseUp boxes. The Spanish Vocabulary section at the end of the book can be invaluable.
FIND IT FAST	Within the book, chapters are arranged heading north and then south of Santiago. Chapters are divided into small regions, within which towns are covered in logical geographical order; attractive routes and interesting places between towns are flagged as En Route. Heads at the top of each page help you find what you need within a chapter.
DON'T FORGET	Restaurants are open for lunch and dinner daily unless we state otherwise; we mention dress only when there's a specific requirement and reservations only when they're essential or not accepted— it's always best to book ahead. Unless otherwise indicated, assume hotels have private baths, phones, TVs, and air-conditioning and operate on the European Plan (a.k.a. EP, meaning without meals). We always list facilities but not whether you'll be charged extra to use them, so when pricing accommodations, find out what's included.
SYMBOLS	

Many Listings

- ★ Fodor's Choice
- ★ Highly recommended
- ⊠ Physical address
- ✛ Directions
- ⌖ Mailing address
- ☎ Telephone
- 🖶 Fax
- ⊕ On the Web
- ✎ E-mail
- 💷 Admission fee
- ☾ Open/closed times
- ⚑ Start of walk/itinerary
- Ⓜ Metro stations
- ⊟ Credit cards

Outdoors

- 🏌 Golf
- ⚠ Camping

Hotels & Restaurants

- 🏨 Hotel
- ⇌ Number of rooms
- ♨ Facilities
- ¶◯¶ Meal plans
- ✕ Restaurant
- ⌣ Reservations
- 🎩 Dress code
- ↘ Smoking
- 🍷 BYOB
- ✕🏨 Hotel with restaurant that warrants a visit

Other

- ☾ Family-friendly
- 🖪 Contact information
- ⇨ See also
- ⊠ Branch address
- ☞ Take note

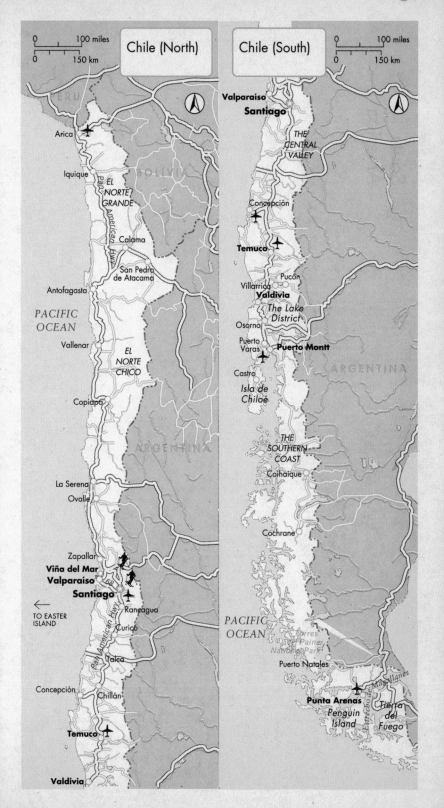

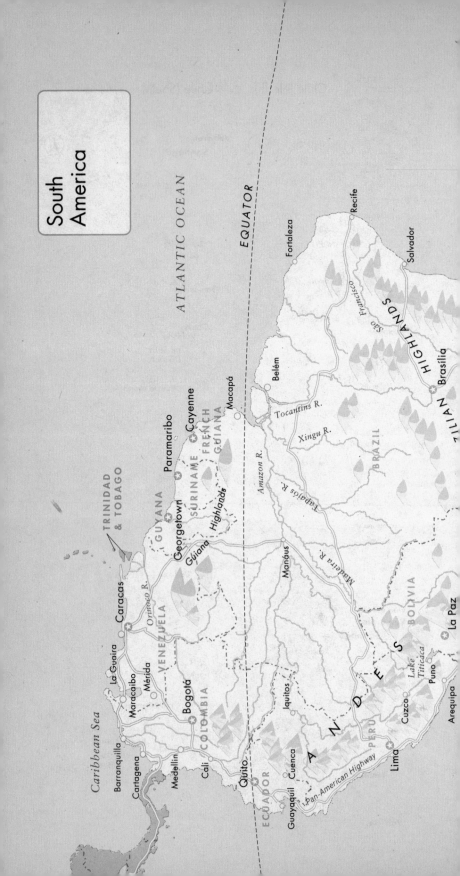

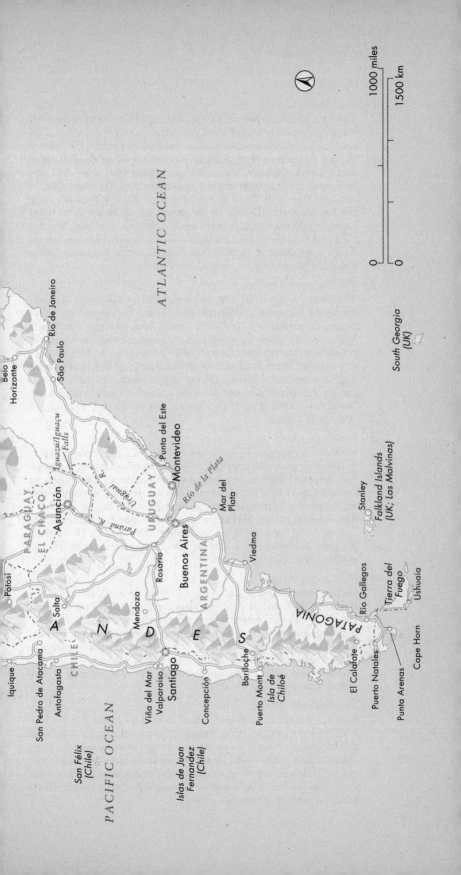

WHAT'S WHERE

(1) Santiago

There are 15 million people in Chile, and more than a third of them call the sprawling metropolis of Santiago, approximately in the center of the country, home. Ancient and modern stand side-by-side in the heart of the city—a common photograph on postcards is the neoclassical cathedral reflected in the windows of the nearby glass office tower. You may be amazed at the amount of green in a city so large. Downtown you're never far from leafy Plaza de Armas or the paths that meander along the Río Mapocho. To take in the entire city, climb up Cerro Santa Lucía, or take the funicular to the top of Cerro San Cristóbal. Not that the views from the ground are shabby—on a clear day you can see the Andes in the distance. Head in that direction for the hot springs of the Cajón del Maipo or skiing in the Valle Nevado.

(2) The Central Coast

The Central Coast is the summer playground for Santiago's vacationing masses. Valparaíso and Viña del Mar, the country's second- and third-largest cities, overlook the Pacific Ocean from adjacent bays. Gritty Valparaíso, the country's largest port, provides stunning views from the promenades atop its more than 40 hills. Glittery Viña del Mar has non-stop nightlife, streets lined with trendy boutiques, and the country's most popular stretch of shoreline. On the rugged beaches to the north you can get close to penguins and sea lions. In the south, pay homage to the Nobel Prize–winning poet Pablo Neruda, whose hillside house faces the ocean at Isla Negra.

(3) El Norte Chico

North of Santiago lies El Norte Chico, a land of dusty brown hills that stretches for some 700 km (435 mi) from Río Aconcagua to Río Copiapó. Some of Chile's most beautiful valleys cut through this region. In the lush Elqui Valley, just about everyone you meet is involved in growing the grapes used to make pisco, the heady brew that has become Chile's national drink. Inland lies Parque Nacional Nevado Tres Cruces, where four species of flamingos fly across dazzling white salt flats. On the coast is Parque Nacional Pan de Azúcar, home to sea lions, sea otters, and stunning beaches.

(4) El Norte Grande

Chile's northernmost region borders Peru to the north and Bolivia to the east. This is one of the driest places on earth, site of the Atacama Desert. The climate helped to preserve tantalizing clues of the indigenous peoples of the past, including the Chinchorro mummies near Arica. As you ascend into the Andes, the air becomes dramatically cooler. In Parque Nacional Lauca the landscape is dotted with a brilliant emerald-green moss called *llareta,* and llamas and groups of galloping vicuñas and alpacas make their homes here.

(5) The Central Valley

This region south of Santiago is where most of the grapes that produce Chile's finest wines are grown. An easy drive from the capital is the Valle de Colchagua, where you can sample vintages at many wineries. Also in the area are the beautiful manor houses of the sprawling farms once run by Chile's most powerful families. The region's many rivers, such as the Río Bío Bío in the southern Central Valley, are great for white-water rafting and other water sports.

6 The Lake District

Many visitors to the Lake District are surprised to find that the 400-km (250-mi) stretch of land between Temuco and Puerto Montt is bordered by a string of volcanoes. More than 50 snow-covered peaks, many of them still smoldering, offer splendid hiking. The region's forested foothills, long the home of the Mapuche people, are where you'll find popular summer resorts such as Pucón and Villarrica.

7 Chiloé

The rainy archipelago of Chiloé is made up of more than 40 islands sprinkled across the Golfo de Ancud. The largest by far, the appropriately named Isla Grande, measures 180 km (112 mi) long. The main draw here are the dozens of simple wood churches, a remnant of the colonial era, dotting the landscape. Dense forests cover the western half of Isla Grande, while gently rolling farmland dominates the eastern part where most of its 130,000 residents live.

8 The Southern Coast

This stretch of coastline between the Lake District and Patagonia is one of the most remote regions on earth. So much of the Southern Coast is a labyrinth of icy fjords that you're likely to take a boat or plane to wherever you want to go. The only town of any size, Coihaique, is in the middle of everything and therefore makes a good base for exploring the area. To the north is the privately owned Parque Pumalín, one of the last-remaining temperate rain forests in the world. The most popular attraction, and the hardest to reach, is the spectacular glacier that forms the centerpiece of Parque Nacional Laguna San Rafael.

9 Patagonia & Tierra del Fuego

Its impenetrable forests and impassable mountains meant that Chilean Patagonia, in the southernmost part of the country, went largely unexplored until the beginning of the 20th century. It's still sparsely inhabited. Here you'll find the colorful provincial city of Punta Arenas, which looks like it's about to be swept into the Strait of Magellan. Drive north and you'll reach Parque Nacional Torres del Paine, the country's most magnificent natural wonder. Its snow-covered peaks seem to rise vertically from the plains below. To the east is mythical Tierra del Fuego, the windswept island at the continent's southernmost tip. For the most intrepid travelers, this is literally the end of the world.

10 Easter Island

Known to locals as "the loneliest place on earth," Easter Island lies 3,700 km (2,295 mi) off the Chilean coast. The tiny island in the middle of the South Pacific was unknown to the outside world until a Dutch explorer happened across it in 1722. Jacob Roggeveen's crew at first thought the island was inhabited by giants, but soon realized they were looking at hundreds of stone idols standing along the coast. A century later, nearly all had been toppled. Who carved them? How were they raised? Why were they destroyed? Most of the mysteries surrounding these carvings have yet to be solved, and many people travel here hoping to come up with their own answers.

GREAT ITINERARIES

The number of wonderful natural and cultural attractions in Chile and the great distances between them mean that fitting all the highlights into one trip can be a challenge, especially with Santiago, the main point of entry by air into Chile, smack dab in the center of the country. It doesn't help that two of the country's most extraordinary natural attractions—the Atacama Desert in the north and Parque Nacional Torres del Paine in the south—are at extreme opposite ends of the country. Traveling by air is one way of moving around the country, but if you don't have a lot of time to spend in Chile, consider breaking your trip into Santiago and northern Chile or Santiago and southern Chile.

Santiago & Northern Chile
10 to 12 days

SANTIAGO 3 days. Take two days to explore the small neighborhoods that make up Chile's bustling capital. On the third day, head out to one or more of the nearby wineries, such as those in the Valle de Maipo.
⇨ *Exploring Santiago and Side Trips from Santiago in Chapter 1.*

VIÑA DEL MAR & VALPARAÍSO 2 or 3 days. Devote some time to meandering among Valparaíso's picturesque hills, cobbled streets, and many funiculars. Nearby, busier Viña del Mar, with its chic cafés and restaurants and its miles of beach, is also worth a visit. Overnight in either city.
⇨ *Viña del Mar and Valparaíso in Chapter 2.*

SAN PEDRO DE ATACAMA 2 or 3 days. This is one of the most visited towns in Chile, for good reason: it sits right in the midst of the Atacama Desert, with striking sights all around. You'll need at least two days here to do justice to the alpine lakes, ancient fortresses, Chile's largest salt flat, and the surreal landscape of the Valle de la Luna.
⇨ *The Nitrate Pampa in Chapter 4.*

IQUIQUE 2 days. There's not much of interest in the town itself, other than some nice white-sand beaches and the nearby ghost town of Humberstone, but Iquique makes a good base for visiting the hundreds of geoglyphs at the Cerros Pintados, in the Reserva Nacional Pampa del Tamarugal. Also nearby is the Gigante de Atacama, the world's largest geoglyph.
⇨ *Iquique Area in Chapter 4.*

ARICA 1 day. If you've come this far, you might as well head to Chile's northernmost city, with a temperate climate and a couple of creations by French architect Gustave Eiffel. The main attraction, however, is the nearby Museo Arqueológico de San Miguel de Azapa and its famed Chinchorro mummies, the oldest in the world, dating to 6,000 BC.
⇨ *Arica Area in Chapter 4.*

TRANSPORTATION Although it's quite easy, and even preferable, to explore Santiago, Viña del Mar, and Valparaíso by using public transportation, a car makes it easier to visit the other sights and towns, all of which are in El Norte Grande. That said, it is possible to get around using the bus, which connects most of the cities of El Norte Grande. Once in San Pedro de Atacama or Iquique, you can likely hook up with various tour agencies to visit sights not accessible by bus. From Arica, there are numerous flights back to Santiago.

Santiago & Southern Chile
16 days

SANTIAGO **2 days.** Take two days to explore Chile's sprawling capital, working in time to visit its many museums, shops, and green spaces. ⇨ *Exploring Santiago in Chapter 1.*

THE LAKE DISTRICT **4 days.** Base yourself in quiet, pleasant Villarrica or the flashier resort town of Pucón, both on the shore of Lago Villarrica, to enjoy the lake and surrounding national parks. Drive south through the region, stopping at the various resort towns, including the graceful old city of Valdivia, to Puerto Montt. Be sure to make time to relax in one of the region's many hot springs. ⇨ *La Araucanía and Los Lagos in Chapter 6.*

PARQUE NACIONAL LAGUNA SAN RAFAEL **5 days.** From Puerto Montt, take a five-day round-trip cruise through a maze of fjords down the coast to the unforgettable glacier in Parque Nacional Laguna San Rafael. If you're lucky, you'll see the huge glacier calving off pieces of ice that cause violent waves in the brilliant blue water. ⇨ *Parque Nacional Laguna San Rafael in Chapter 8.*

PARQUE NACIONAL TORRES DEL PAINE **5 days.** When you return to Puerto Montt, take a spectacular morning flight over the Andes to the Patagonian city of Punta Arenas. On the next day drive north to Puerto Natales, gateway to the Parque Nacional Torres del Paine. You'll need at least two days to wander through the wonders of the park's granite spires. On your final day head back to Punta Arenas, stopping en route at one of the penguin sanctuaries, and catch your flight back to Santiago.

TRANSPORTATION It would be exhausting to try to see all of the sights on this itinerary by car (and you wouldn't be able to visit Parque Nacional Laguna San Rafael at all), so a combination of flights, rental car, and boat works best. From Santiago, drive south through the various sights and towns of the Lake District. Take the boat cruise down to Parque Nacional Laguna San Rafael, and on your return to Puerto Montt fly into the city of Punta Arenas. From there drive north to Puerto Natales and to Parque Nacional Torres del Paine. Buses can also be used to visit most of the towns in place of a rental car.

WHEN TO GO

°C		°F
100		212
40		105
37		98.6
30		90
25		80
20		70
15		60
10		50
5		40
0		32
−5		20
−10		10
−15		0
−20		

Climate

Chile's seasons are the reverse of North America's—that is, June–August is Chile's winter. Tourism peaks during the hot summer months of January and February, except in Santiago, which tends to empty as most Santiaguinos take their summer holiday. Though prices are at their highest, it's worth braving the summer heat if you're interested in lying on the beach or enjoying the many concerts, folklore festivals, and outdoor theater performances offered during this period.

If you're heading to the Lake District or Patagonia and want good weather without the crowds, the shoulder seasons of December and March are the months to visit. The best time to see the Atacama Desert is late spring, preferably in November, when temperatures are bearable and air clarity is at its peak. In spring Santiago blooms, and the fragrance of the flowers distracts even the most avid workaholic. A second tourist season occurs in the winter, as skiers flock to Chile's mountaintops for some of the world's best skiing, available at the height of northern summers. Winter smog is a good reason to stay away from Santiago during July and August, unless you're coming for a ski holiday and won't be spending much time in the city.

📶 Forecasts **Weather Channel Connection** ☎ 900/932–8437, 95¢ per minute from a Touch-Tone phone ⊕ www.weather.com.

The following are the average daily maximum and minimum temperatures for Santiago, Arica, and Punta Arenas.

SANTIAGO

Jan.	85F	29C	May	65F	18C	Sept.	66F	19C
	53	12		41	5		42	6
Feb.	84F	29C	June	58F	14C	Oct.	72F	22C
	52	11		37	3		45	7
Mar.	80F	27C	July	59F	15C	Nov.	78F	26C
	49	9		37	3		48	9
Apr.	74F	23C	Aug.	62F	17C	Dec.	83F	28C
	54	7		39	4		51	11

PUNTA ARENAS

Jan.	58F	14C	May	45F	7C	Sept.	46F	8C
	45	7		35	2		35	2
Feb.	58F	14C	June	41F	5C	Oct.	51F	11C
	44	7		33	1		38	3
Mar.	54F	12C	July	40F	4C	Nov.	54F	12C
	41	5		31	0		40	4
Apr.	50F	10C	Aug.	42F	6C	Dec.	57F	14C
	39	4		33	1		43	6

ON THE CALENDAR

	Note that Chile's seasons are the reverse of North America's.
ONGOING	
Feb.–Apr.	February 9 is the beginning of the two-month-long Verano en Valdivia, a favorite celebration for those living in the Lake District. It culminates with a spectacular fireworks display.
SUMMER	
December	The Fiesta Grande (Big Festival), honoring the patron saint of miners, culminates in frenzied festivities on December 26 in Andacolla, a small town in El Norte Chico. More than 100,000 pilgrims come to watch the masked dancers.
January	The Festival Foclórico (Folklore Festival) is held in Santiago during the fourth week of January.
Jan.–Feb.	In late January and early February, Semanas Musicales (Music Weeks) in the Lake District town of Frutillar bring virtuoso performances of classical music. The Lake District town of Villarrica hosts the Muestra Cultural Mapuche (Mapuche Cultural Show) from January 3 to February 28. Here you'll find examples of the indigenous people's art and music. Look for the reproduction of a ruka, the Mapuche traditional dwelling. The pastoral quiet of Isla Huapi is broken in late January or early February with the annual harvest festival called Lepún. It's one of the Lake District's most interesting celebrations. The Fiestas Costumbristas, celebrating Chilote customs and folklore, take place over several weekends during January and February in the Chiloé towns of Ancud and Castro.
	The annual Tapati Rapa Nui festival, a two-week celebration of Easter Island's heritage, takes place every year in January and February. The normally laid-back village of Hanga Roa bursts to life in a colorful festival that includes much singing and dancing.
February	The Fiesta de la Virgen de la Canderlaria, a three-day romp that begins on February 2, is held in the tiny antiplano village of Parinacota in El Norte Grande. It includes music and traditional dancing. The annual Festival Internacional de la Canción (International Song Festival) takes place over a week in mid-February in Viña del Mar. The concerts are broadcast live on television.
AUTUMN	
March	The four-day Fiesta de la Vendimia, the annual grape harvest festival, takes place in the Central Valley town of Curicó the first weekend in March. It includes grape-stomping contests and the selection of a queen, whose weight is measured out in grapes on a massive scale. A similar celebration is held in nearby Santa Cruz.
April	Semana Santa, or Holy Week, is popular all over Chile. Different events are held each day between Palm Sunday and Easter Sunday. The Sunday after Easter is Fiesta de Cuasimodo, a celebration in which priests in decorated carriages ride through villages as parishioners cheer. The village of Colina, north of Santiago, has one of the largest gatherings.
May	The Fiesta de las Cruces (Festival of the Crosses) takes place in the tiny city of Putre in El Norte Grande on May 3.

WINTER	
June	In Valparaíso, colorful processions mark the Día de San Pedro (St. Peter's Day) on June 29. A statue of the patron saint of fisherfolk is paraded through town.
July	In honor of the Virgen del Carmen, the town of La Tirana in El Norte Grande hosts one of the country's most famous celebrations from July 12 to July 18. During this time some 80,000 dancing pilgrims converge on the central square.
SPRING	
September	On September 18 Fiestas Patrias (patriotic festivals) take place all over the country to mark National Independence Day. The most fun is around Rancagua, in the Central Valley, where you'll find hard-fought rodeo competitions.
October	The Fiesta Chica (Little Festival), honoring the Virgen del Rosario, is held in Andacolla in El Norte Chico on the first Sunday of October. In the Fiesta de San Francisco, held October 4 in the Central Valley town of Huerta de Maule, more than 200 cowboys gather from all over the country for a day of riding and roping.
November	November 1 is Todos los Santos (All Saints Day), when Chileans traditionally tend to the graves of relatives. It's followed on November 2 by Día de los Muertos (All Souls Day). In late November, the Chilean wine industry shows off the fruits of its hard labor at the annual Feria International de Vino del Hemisferio Sur in Santiago.

PLEASURES & PASTIMES

The Distinctive Cuisine

Kissing her shores from tip to toe, the Pacific Ocean is the breadbasket of Chile's cuisine, proffering delicacies like conger eel, sea bass, king crab, and *locos* (abalone the size of fat clams). But the Pacific isn't Chile's only answer to fine dining—European immigrants brought with them a love for robust country cooking. Indeed, many simple country dishes are among the best offerings of Chilean cuisine, including *cazuela*, a superb stew made of meat, potatoes, and corn on the cob in a thick broth; *porotos granados*, a thick bean, corn, and squash stew; and *humitas*, ground corn seasoned and steamed in its own husk. At markets all over the country, vendors try to woo you with the ubiquitous and delicious *pastel de choclo*, a corn pie that usually contains ground beef, chicken, and seasonings. Empanadas, pastries stuffed with meat or cheese, are popular everywhere.

Pork is another Chilean specialty, especially in *arrollados* (a stuffed pork roll encased in pork rind), *costillares* (ribs, often covered in chili, known here as *ají*), *lomo* (roast pork loin), and *pernil* (the whole leg, so make sure you're hungry).

Some Spanish-inspired dishes like *guatitas* (tripe) send Chileans into states of culinary bliss, as do blood sausage, *chunchules* (a spicy stew of beef or pork intestines), and other odds and ends of edible beasts. If you order a *parrillada* (a barbecue at your table), ask about the cuts being served so as to avoid those that are too peculiar for your taste.

Sports & the Outdoors

Chile's Lake District is legendary for its fly-fishing. You can stay in a rustic lodge and enjoy the icy lakes and streams jumping with trout and salmon. Opportunities also abound for hiking and mountain biking in Chile's national parks, over its mountain trails, and through its forests. If you're a serious mountaineer, you probably know about the challenging Volcán Ojos del Salado in El Norte Chico. The world's highest active volcano, it soars to 6,893 m (22,609 ft). There are dozens of other challenging climbs all along the eastern border of the country.

Since Chile's seasons are the opposite of those of North America, you can ski or snowboard from June to September. Most of Chile's ski resorts are in the Andes close to Santiago. With the top elevations at the majority of ski areas extending to 3,300 m (10,825 ft), you can expect long runs and deep, dry snow.

Shopping

Chile is one of only three countries in the world that mine lapis lazuli, so it's worth checking out the workshops and stores in Santiago. The city's artisans are increasingly sophisticated, and you can find earrings, rings, and necklaces to please virtually every taste. Handicrafts you'll find all over Chile include warm sweaters that are hand-dyed, -spun, and -knitted in the southern parts of the country (it's cheaper to purchase them there) and ponchos whose designs vary according to the region; the best are by the Mapuche artisans in and around Temuco and by the Chilote women on Chiloé. Thick wool blankets are woven in Chiloé but are heavy to carry, as are the figures of reddish-brown clay from Pomaire and the famous black clay ceramics of Quinchamalí. Purchase them at the end of your trip. Several towns specialize in wicker, particularly Chimbarongo (about an hour's drive from Santiago) and Chiloé, where baskets and woven effigies of that island's mythical figures abound.

The Pleasures of the Vine

Many vineyards in the valleys around Santiago have been producing wine for more than 100 years, some with French vinestocks that date to the middle of the 19th century. Chilean wines were introduced to the world in the 1980s, when formerly inexpensive California wines started to jump in price. Since that time, the Chilean wineries have been working furiously to keep pace with the broadening international demand while steadily trying to improve their product.

An oft-repeated fact about Chilean wine is that the best is reserved for the export market. Although you can find some good quality wines at upscale Chilean restaurants, the big vintners are still concentrating their energy on the international market. To that end, the best wineries are modernizing the growing and fermenting methods (with help from French and Californian oenological experts) to produce wines that are better suited for the European and North American markets. These changes have paid off in recent years with improved overall quality of Chilean wines. In fact, a small number of Chilean vintners are already turning out a few truly first-rate wines, including Concha y Toro's Don Melchor Reserve, Santa Rita's Casa Real, and Veramonte's Primus.

As a general rule, Chilean merlots and cabernet sauvignons are more likely to be the full-bodied wines that Americans and Europeans enjoy. Chardonnays and sauvignon blancs are usually not as pleasing to the palate. When you're considering these different varietals, keep in mind the name of Chile's largest winery, Concha y Toro. It has a number of different labels (some made exclusively for the Chilean market) that usually offer good value. At one end is the affordable and popular Casillero del Diablo label; at the other is the export-oriented Trio wines. Other reliable wineries that are strong in the domestic market include Errázuriz, Santa Carolina, and Santa Rita. Also, be on the lookout for the smaller Casa Lapostolle winery, whose reds are highly regarded but not as widely available.

FODOR'S CHOICE

The sights, restaurants, hotels, and other travel experiences on these pages are our editors' top picks—our Fodor's Choices. They're the best of their type in the area covered by the book—not to be missed and always worth your time. In the destination chapters that follow, you will find all the details.

LODGING

$$$$	**Hacienda Los Lingues, outside Rancagua.** Staying at this well-preserved colonial hacienda, with 17th- and 18th-century adobe buildings, is a bit like traveling back in time.
$$$$	**Hotel Del Mar, Viña del Mar.** With marble floors, spacious modern guest rooms, impeccable service, and a casino next door, this is one of Chile's most luxurious hotels.
$$$$	**Hotel Explora, Parque Nacional Torres del Paine.** Tucked away on the southeast corner of Lago Pehoé, this Scandinavian-style lodge is a luxurious alternative to roughing it in the national park.
$$$$	**Hotel José Nogueira, Punta Arenas.** Once the home of a wealthy wool baron's widow, this opulent 19th-century mansion retains the original crystal chandeliers, marble floors, and polished bronze accents that were imported from France.
$$$$	**Hotel Plaza San Francisco, Santiago.** This historic hotel across from the Iglesia San Francisco pampers you with unparalleled luxury.
$$$$	**Termas de Puyuhuapi, outside of Puerto Puyuhuapi.** Accessible only by boat, this world-class resort gives new meaning to the word "secluded." Its redwood structures have lots of windows to take full advantage of the gorgeous scenery.
$$$	**Hotel Pedro de Valdivia, Valdivia.** Lavish furnishings and peerless service are the hallmarks of this magnificent pink palace on the Río Calle Calle.
$$$	**Lodge Andino Terrantai, San Pedro de Atacama.** Wood-beam ceilings, river-stone walls, and rustic rooms bathed in light from the wide windows are among the many touches that make this hotel extraordinary.
$$–$$$	**Hostería de la Colina, Villarrica.** Arguably Chile's most attentive innkeepers will ply you with apple pie, homemade ice cream, and sound advice at their hillside lodge just south of town.
$$–$$$	**Isla Seca, Zapallar.** The place is chic, but it's the view of the rocky coast and the Pacific from some of the rooms that makes this hotel special.
$$–$$$	**La Fayette, Reñaca.** You can take in some of the best views of the Central Coast from this quiet hotel built onto a hillside overlooking the beach.

$$	**Hostería Ancud, Ancud.** Stately and dignified, Chiloé's best-known hotel stands watch on the bluff overlooking the Canal de Chacao, defending the island much as the nearby forts did centuries ago.

BUDGET LODGING

$	**Brighton B&B, Valparaíso.** This inexpensive bed-and-breakfast in a lemon-yellow Victorian-style house is one of the pretty port town's most recognizable landmarks.
$	**Hotel Rocas de Bahia, Bahía Inglesa.** This sprawling modern hotel right on one of El Norte Chico's prettiest beaches has fantastic views from the rooms and the rooftop pool.

RESTAURANTS

$$–$$$	**Aquí Está Coco, Santiago.** Flotsam and jetsam found on nearby beaches add a whimsical touch to this restaurant cooking up the best fish and shellfish in the capital.
$$–$$$	**Bristol, Santiago.** Innovative takes on traditional Chilean dishes make this downtown eatery a must for Santiago's movers and shakers.
$$–$$$	**Café Turri, Valparaíso.** Dine on seafood in an elegant 19th-century mansion high above the city before strolling along the hilltop promenades nearby.
$$–$$$	**Casino Español, Iquique.** Superb Moorish architecture that calls to mind the Alhambra in Granada makes this fine Spanish restaurant a sight in its own right.
$$	**Azul Profundo, Santiago.** Chileans favor heavy sauces on their fish dishes, but this Bellavista eatery serves unadorned seafood grilled to perfection.
$–$$	**Aquí Jaime, Concón.** Large windows let you watch the waves crashing against the rocky shore at this small seafood restaurant with one of the best reputations in the region.
$–$$	**Delicias del Mar, Viña del Mar and Reñaca.** Such delicacies as stuffed sea bass, the house's own version of paella, and cheesecake with a raspberry sauce round out the menu at both branches of this seafood restaurant.
$–$$	**El Chiringuito, Zapallar.** The seafood is always fresh here, whether you choose razor clams, scallops, or any of the various fish served with different sauces.
$–$$	**Los Ganaderos, Punta Arenas.** Spit-roasted lamb is the specialty at this restaurant resembling a rural ranch. To put you in the mood, the waiters dress as gauchos.

BUDGET RESTAURANTS

$	**El Rincón del Tata, Puerto Natales.** The friendly waiters are known to tango at this funky little spot while serving up the region's most succulent lamb.

$ **Rubén Tapío, Talca.** One of the best restaurants in the Central Valley, Rubén Tapío is renowned for its refined service and outstanding Latin cuisine, including excellent seafood dishes.

HISTORY

Casa-Museo Isla Negra, Isla Negra. A must-see for his ardent admirers, Pablo Neruda's seaside hideaway on the Central Coast is filled with mementos from the poet's fascinating life.

Iglesia Santa María de Loreto, Achao. Of the dozens of wonderful wooden churches on the archipelago of Chiloé, this one on the island of Achao is the most fascinating.

Ranu Raraku, Easter Island. When it comes to the famous stone heads, this is the mother lode. Researchers have counted 397 *moais*—nearly half of those found on the island—at the quarry in this long-extinct volcano.

MUSEUMS

Museo Arqueológico de San Miguel de Azapa, Arica. In an 18th-century olive-oil refinery, this museum houses an impressive collection of artifacts, including the Chinchorro mummies, which date to 6000 BC.

Museo Arqueológico Gustavo Le Paige, San Pedro de Atacama. This awe-inspiring collection of artifacts from the region traces the history of the Atacama Desert from pre-Columbian times through Spanish colonization.

Museo de Arte Precolombino, Santiago. Artifacts of Central and South America's indigenous peoples are on display here in the city's beautifully restored Royal Customs House.

Museo Regional de Castro, Castro. This museum of life on Chiloé holds everything from the farming and fishing implements of indigenous peoples to the looms, spinning wheels, and plows of European settlers.

Museo Regional de Magallanes, Punta Arenas. Lavish Carrara-marble hearths, English bath fixtures, and cordovan-leather walls are among the original accoutrements at this restored mansion providing an intriguing glimpse of a wealthy family's life at the beginning of the 20th century.

NATURAL WONDERS

Atacama Desert, El Norte Grande. The world's driest desert holds many natural wonders, such as La Cordillera de Sal, a mountain range composed almost entirely of salt.

Cerros Pintados, El Norte Grande. The largest group of geoglyphs in the world—more than 400—is here, in the Painted Hills, part of the Reserva Nacional Pampa del Tamarugal.

Parque Nacional Fray Jorge, El Norte Chico. Incongruously set in the middle of the region's dusty hills, northern Chile's only cloud forest makes a great retreat from the relentless sun.

Parque Nacional Laguna San Rafael, the Southern Coast. The Ventis-quero San Rafael, a spectacular glacier extending 4 km (2½ mi), is one of the country's greatest natural wonders.

Parque Nacional Torres del Paine, Patagonia. Glaciers that swept through the region millions of years ago created the ash-gray spires that dominate this unforgettable national park.

Parque Nacional Villarrica, The Lake District. The main draw at this national park is the 3,116-m-high (9,350-ft-high) perpetually smouldering Volcán Villarrica.

Parque Pumalín, the Southern Coast. An American conservationist purchased the 800,000 acres that make up this privately owned park in one of the world's last remaining temperate rain forests.

SMART TRAVEL TIPS

Finding out about your destination before you leave home means you won't squander time organizing everyday minutiae once you've arrived. You'll be more streetwise when you hit the ground as well, better prepared to explore the aspects of Chile that drew you here in the first place. The organizations in this section can provide information to supplement this guide; contact them for up-to-the-minute details, and consult the A to Z sections that end each chapter for facts on the various topics as they relate to Chile's many regions. Happy landings!

ADDRESSES

The most common street terms in Spanish are *avenida* (avenue) and *calle* (street). *Local,* which sometimes appears in an address, means the location is in a small room or office, quite often in an arcade or passageway. Numbering individual buildings isn't as popular in South America as it is elsewhere. In some listings in this guide, establishments have necessarily been identified by the street they're on and their nearest cross street—Calle Bolívar and Avenida Valdivia, for example. In extreme cases, where neither address nor cross street is available, you may find the notation "s/n," meaning "no street number." In these cases the towns are usually so small that finding a particular building won't be a problem.

AIR TRAVEL

Miami and New York are the primary departure points for flights to Chile from the United States, though there are also daily flights from Dallas and Atlanta. Other international flights often connect through other major South American cities like Buenos Aires and Lima.

Arriving from abroad, American, Canadian, and Australian citizens must pay a "reciprocity" fee (to balance out fees Chileans pay upon entering foreign countries) of $61, $55, and $30, respectively. Only cash, normally paid in the currency of your country, is accepted. A departure tax of $18 is included in the cost of your ticket.

BOOKING

When you book, **look for nonstop flights** and **remember that "direct" flights stop at least once.** Try to avoid connecting flights, which require a change of plane. Two airlines may operate a connecting flight jointly, so ask whether your airline operates every segment of the trip; you may find that the carrier you prefer flies you only part of the way. To find more booking tips and to check prices and make on-line flight reservations, log on to www.fodors.com.

CARRIERS

The largest North American carrier is American Airlines, which has direct service from Dallas and Miami; Delta flies from Atlanta. No Canadian airlines fly directly to South American destinations, though Canadian Airlines has a partnership with American.

The major Chilean airline is LanChile, which flies directly to Santiago from New York and Miami. Many South American airlines have connecting flights to Santiago: Aerocontinente connects through Lima, Peru; Aerolíneas Argentinas has connections in Buenos Aires, Argentina; Avianca flies through Bogota, Colombia; Lloyd Aéreo Boliviano (LAB) flies through La Paz and other Bolivian cities; Tam flies through Asunción, Paraguay; TAME connects through the Ecuadoran cities of Guayaquil and Quito; and Varig stops in the Brazilian cities of Fortaleza, Manaus, Rio de Janeiro, and São Paulo.

From the United Kingdom, British Airways flies from London Gatwick to Santiago. Aerolíneas Argentinas flies from London to Santiago via Buenos Aires. LanChile operates from London to Santiago via Frankfurt or Madrid. Iberia flies from London Heathrow to Santiago via Madrid. Lufthansa flies from London Heathrow via Frankfurt to Santiago. You can take American from London Heathrow and fly to South America via Miami or New York.

From Australia, LanChile flies directly from Sydney to Santiago via Auckland, New Zealand. From New Zealand, LanChile flies to Santiago via Tahiti or Easter Island.

To & From North America American Airlines ☎ 2/690-1090 in Chile; 800/433-7300 in North America. **Delta Airlines** ☎ 2/690-1551 in Chile; 800/221-1212 in North America. **LanChile** ☎ 2/565-2525 or 600/526-2000 in Chile; 800/735-5526 in North America.
To & From the U.K. Aerolíneas Argentinas ☎ 020/7494-1075. **American Airlines** ☎ 0845/

789-789. **British Airways** ☎ 0845/222-111. **Iberia** ☎ 0845/601-2854. **LanChile** ☎ 0129/359-6607. **Lufthansa** ☎ 0845/603-0747. **Varig** ☎ 0845/603-7601.
To & From Australia & New Zealand Air New Zealand ☎ 0396/703-700 in Australia; 0800/737-000 in New Zealand. **LanChile** ☎ 1300/361-400 in Australia; 09/309-8673 in New Zealand. **Qantas** ☎ 13-11-31 in Australia; 0800/808-767 in New Zealand.
Within Chile Aerocontinente ☎ 2/690-9399 in Chile; 888/586-9400 in North America. **Aerolíneas Argentinas** ☎ 2/690-1030 in Chile; 800/333-0276 in North America. **Aeromexico** ☎ 2/690-1028 in Chile; 800/237-6639 in North America. **Avianca** ☎ 2/690-1051 in Chile; 800/284-2622 in North America. **Lacsa** ☎ 2/690-1276 in Chile; 800/225-2272 in North America. **LanChile** ☎ 2/565-2525 or 600/526-2000 in Chile; 800/735-5526 in North America. **Lloyd Aéreo Boliviano** ☎ 2/671-2334 in Chile. **Tam** ☎ 2/690-1156 in Chile; 888/235-9826 in North America. **TAME** ☎ 2/630-1681 in Chile. **Varig** ☎ 2/690-1930 in Chile; 800/468-2744 in North America.

CHECK-IN & BOARDING

Always **ask your carrier about its check-in policy.** Plan to arrive at the airport about two hours before your scheduled departure time for domestic flights and 2½ to 3 hours before international flights. You may need to arrive earlier if you're flying from one of the busier airports or during peak air-traffic times. To avoid delays at airport-security checkpoints, try not to wear any metal. Jewelry, belt and other buckles, steel-toe shoes, barrettes, and underwire bras are among the items that can set off detectors.

Assuming that not everyone with a ticket will show up, airlines routinely overbook planes. When everyone does, airlines ask for volunteers to give up their seats. In return, these volunteers usually get a several-hundred-dollar flight voucher, which can be used toward the purchase of another ticket, and are rebooked on the next flight out. If there are not enough volunteers, the airline must choose who will be denied boarding. The first to get bumped are passengers who checked in late and those flying on discounted tickets, so **get to the gate and check in as early as possible,** especially during peak periods.

Always **bring a government-issued photo I.D. to the airport;** even when it's not required, a passport is best.

CUTTING COSTS

The least expensive airfares to Chile are priced for round-trip travel and must usually be purchased in advance. Airlines generally allow you to change your return date for a fee; most low-fare tickets, however, are nonrefundable. It's smart to **call a number of airlines and check the Internet;** when you are quoted a good price, **book it on the spot**—the same fare may not be available the next day, or even the next hour. Always **check different routings** and look into using alternate airports. Also, price off-peak flights, which may be significantly less expensive than others. Travel agents, especially low-fare specialists (⇨ Discounts and Deals), are helpful.

Consolidators are another good source. They buy tickets for scheduled flights at reduced rates from the airlines, then sell them at prices that beat the best fare available directly from the airlines. Sometimes you can even get your money back if you need to return the ticket. Carefully read the fine print detailing penalties for changes and cancellations, purchase the ticket with a credit card, and **confirm your consolidator reservation with the airline.**
🛈 Consolidators AirlineConsolidator.com ☎ 888/468-5385 ⊕ www.airlineconsolidator.com; for international tickets. Best Fares ☎ 800/576-8255 or 800/576-1600 ⊕ www.bestfares.com; $59.90 annual membership. Cheap Tickets ☎ 800/377-1000 or 888/922-8849 ⊕ www.cheaptickets.com. Expedia ☎ 800/397-3342 or 404/728-8787 ⊕ www.expedia.com. Hotwire ☎ 866/468-9473 or 920/330-9418 ⊕ www.hotwire.com. Now Voyager Travel ✉ 45 W. 21st St., 5th floor, New York, NY 10010 ☎ 212/459-1616 🖷 212/243-2711 ⊕ www.nowvoyagertravel.com. Onetravel.com ⊕ www.onetravel.com. Orbitz ☎ 888/656-4546 ⊕ www.orbitz.com. Pino Welcome Travel ☎ 800/247-6578. Priceline.com ⊕ www.priceline.com. Travelocity ☎ 888/709-5983 or 877/282-2925 in the U.S. or Canada; 0870/876-3876 in the U.K. ⊕ www.travelocity.com.

ENJOYING THE FLIGHT

Traveling between the Americas is usually less tiring than traveling to Europe or Asia because you cross fewer time zones. New York is one hour behind Santiago, and Los Angeles is four hours behind Santiago. London is three to five hours ahead of Santiago, depending on the time of year. New Zealand and Australia are 11 hours ahead.

If you have a choice of when to fly, **take a night flight.** You'll arrive the next morning with plenty of time to start exploring. Flying into Chile from the north you'll be treated to lovely sunrises over the mountains (assuming you're seated on the plane's left side).

State your seat preference when purchasing your ticket, and then repeat it when you confirm and when you check in. For more legroom, you can request one of the few emergency-aisle seats at check-in, if you are capable of lifting at least 50 pounds—a Federal Aviation Administration requirement of passengers in these seats. Seats behind a bulkhead also offer more legroom, but they don't have underseat storage. Don't sit in the row in front of the emergency aisle or in front of a bulkhead, where seats may not recline.

Ask the airline whether a snack or meal is served on the flight. If you have dietary concerns, **request special meals when booking.** These can be vegetarian, low-cholesterol, or kosher, for example. It's a good idea to pack some healthful snacks and a small (plastic) bottle of water in your carry-on bag. On long flights, try to maintain a normal routine to help fight jet lag. At night, **get some sleep.** By day, **eat light meals, drink water** (not alcohol), and **move around the cabin** to stretch your legs. For additional jet-lag tips consult *Fodor's FYI: Travel Fit & Healthy* (available at bookstores everywhere).

Smoking policies vary from carrier to carrier. Many airlines prohibit smoking on all of their flights; others allow smoking only on certain routes or certain departures. Ask your carrier about its policy.

FLYING TIMES

The major North American departure points for Santiago are New York (11½ hours), Miami (9 hours), and Atlanta (9 hours). If you're traveling from Canada and connecting in the United States, the Toronto–New York flight is just over an hour, while the flight to Miami is about 3 hours. From London to Santiago takes about 17 hours, including a stopover in a European or South American city; it's an 18-hour flight from Sydney, including a stopover in Auckland. Note that flight times may vary according to the size of the plane.

HOW TO COMPLAIN

If your baggage goes astray or your flight goes awry, complain right away. Most carriers require that you **file a claim immediately.** The Aviation Consumer Protection Division of the Department of Transportation publishes *Fly-Rights,* which discusses airlines and consumer issues and is available on-line.

⚑ Airline Complaints **Aviation Consumer Protection Division** ⊠ U.S. Department of Transportation, C-75, Room 4107, 400 7th St. NW, Washington, DC 20590 ☎ 202/366-2220 ⊕ www.dot.gov/airconsumer. **Federal Aviation Administration Consumer Hotline** ⊠ for inquiries: FAA, 800 Independence Ave. SW, Room 810, Washington, DC 20591 ☎ 800/322-7873 ⊕ www.faa.gov.

RECONFIRMING

Check the status of your flight before you leave for the airport. You can do this on your carrier's Web site, by linking to a flight-status checker (many Web booking services offer these), or by calling your carrier or travel agent. Always confirm international flights at least 72 hours ahead of the scheduled departure time. This is particularly true for travel within South America, where flights tend to operate at full capacity—often with passengers who have a great deal of baggage to process before departure.

AIRPORTS

Most international flights head to Santiago's Comodoro Arturo Merino Benítez International Airport (SCL), also known as Pudahuel, about 30 minutes west of the city. Domestic flights leave from the same terminal.

⚑ Airport Information **Comodoro Arturo Merino Benítez International Airport** ☎ 2/690-1900.

BIKE TRAVEL

Riding a bike will put you face to face with the people and landscapes of Chile. However, the rugged terrain and varying road conditions pose considerable challenges. **Consider a mountain bike,** since basic touring bikes are too fragile for the potholes on the best roads. Many tour operators in Santiago and other places offer bike trips—sometimes including equipment rental—that range in length from a half day to several days. Always remember to **lock your bike when you make stops,**

and **avoid riding in congested urban areas,** where it's difficult and dangerous.

BIKES IN FLIGHT

Most airlines accommodate bikes as luggage, provided they are dismantled and boxed; check with individual airlines about packing requirements. Some airlines sell bike boxes, which are often free at bike shops, for about $15 (bike bags can be considerably more expensive). International travelers often can substitute a bike for a piece of checked luggage at no charge. Otherwise, the cost is about $100. U.S. and Canadian airlines charge $40–$80 each way.

BOAT & FERRY TRAVEL

Boats and ferries are the best way to reach many places in Chile, such as Chiloé and the Southern Coast. They are also a great alternative to flying when your destination is a southern port like Puerto Natales or Punta Arenas. Navimag and Transmarchilay are the two main companies operating routes in the south. Further details on boat travel are discussed in the various chapter A to Z sections throughout this guide.

Keep in mind that most Chileans vacation in January and February, particularly the latter month. If you're traveling during this period, it's advisable to plan ahead and make a reservation for ferry service.

⚑ Boat & Ferry Information **Navimag** ⊠ Av. El Bosque Norte 0440, Piso 11, Las Condes, Santiago ☎ 2/442-3120 ⊠ Angelmó 2187, Puerto Montt ☎ 65/432-300 ⊕ www.navimag.cl. **Transmarchilay** ⊠ Av. Providencia 2653, Local 24, Providencia, Santiago ⊕ www.transmarchilay.cl. ⊠ Angelmó 2187, Puerto Montt ☎ 600/600-8687 or 600/600-8688.

BUS TRAVEL

Bus travel in Chile is relatively cheap and safe, provided you use one of the better lines. Intercity bus service is a comfortable, safe, and reasonably priced alternative for getting around. Luxury bus travel between cities costs about one-third that of plane travel and is more comfortable, with wide reclining seats, movies, drinks, and snacks. The most luxurious and expensive service offered by most bus companies is called *salon cama* or *semi-cama.*

Without doubt, the low cost of bus travel is its greatest advantage; its greatest drawback is the time you need to cover the distances involved and, in some outlying areas, having to allow for delays due to faulty equipment or poor road conditions. When traveling by bus, **pack light, dress comfortably,** and be sure to **keep a close watch on your belongings.**

For more information on local bus service, see the A to Z sections at the end of each chapter.

FARES

Bus fares are substantially cheaper than in North America or Europe. In Chile you'll usually pay up to 2,300 pesos, or $3, per hour of travel for a semi-cama; some ritzy sleeper buses cost more. Competing bus companies serve all major and many minor routes, so it can pay to **shop around.** Always speak to the counter clerk, as cut-throat competition may mean you can ride for less than the official fare.

Tickets are sold at bus-company offices and at city bus terminals. Note that in larger cities there may be different terminals for buses to different destinations, and some small towns may not have a terminal at all. You'll be picked up and dropped off at the bus line's office, invariably in a central location. Expect to pay with cash, as only the large bus companies such as Tur-Bus and JAC accept credit cards.

RESERVATIONS

Note that reservations for advance ticket purchases aren't necessary except for trips to resort areas in high season or during major holidays. You should **arrive at bus stations extra early for travel during peak seasons.** Companies are notoriously difficult to reach by phone, so it's often better to stop by the terminal to check on prices and schedules.

BUSINESS HOURS

Most retail businesses are open weekdays 10–7 and Saturday until 2; most are closed Sunday. Many businesses close for lunch between about 1 and 3 or 4, though this is becoming less common, especially in larger cities.

BANKS & OFFICES

Most banks are open weekdays 9–2. Casas de cambio are open weekdays 9–2 and 3–6 for currency exchange.

GAS STATIONS

Gas stations in major cities and along the Pan-American Highway tend to stay open 24 hours. Others follow regular business hours.

MUSEUMS & SIGHTS

Most tourist attractions are open during normal business hours during the week and for at least the morning on Saturday and Sunday. Most museums are closed on Monday.

SHOPS

Shops generally are open weekdays 10–7 and Saturdays 10–2. Large malls often stay open daily 10–10. In small towns, shops often close for lunch between 1 and 3 or 4.

CAMERAS & PHOTOGRAPHY

Chile, with its majestic landscapes and varied cityscapes, is a photographer's dream. Chileans seem amenable to having picture-taking tourists in their midst, but you should always **ask permission before taking pictures of individuals.** Be aware that photos shouldn't be taken in or around government or military areas. Photography of Chilean war ships docked in Valparaíso is not permitted.

To avoid the blurriness caused by shaking hands, **buy a mini tripod**—they're available in sizes as small as 6 inches. A small beanbag can be used to support your camera on uneven surfaces. If you'll be visiting the Andes, **get a skylight (81B or 81C) or polarizing filter to minimize haze and light problems.** The higher the altitude, the greater the proportion of ultraviolet rays. Light meters don't read these rays and consequently, except for close-ups or full-frame portraits where the reading is taken directly off the subject, photos may be overexposed. These filters may also help with the glare caused by white adobe buildings, sandy beaches, and so on. You may want to invest in a telephoto lens to photograph wildlife: even standard zoom lenses of the 35–88 range won't capture a satisfying amount of detail. **Bring high-speed film to compensate for low light in the rain forest.** The thick tree canopy blocks out more light than you might expect. The *Kodak Guide to Shooting Great Travel Pictures* (available at bookstores everywhere) is loaded with tips.

Photo Help Kodak Information Center ☎ 800/242-2424 ⊕ www.kodak.com.

EQUIPMENT PRECAUTIONS

Don't pack film and equipment in checked luggage, where it is much more susceptible to damage. X-ray machines used to view checked luggage are extremely powerful and therefore are likely to ruin your film. Try to **ask for hand inspection of film,** which becomes clouded after repeated exposure to airport X-ray machines, and **keep videotapes and computer disks away from metal detectors.** Always **keep film, tape, and computer disks out of the sun.** Carry an extra supply of batteries, and **be prepared to turn on your camera, camcorder, or laptop** to prove to airport security personnel that the device is real.

FILM & DEVELOPING

Remember to **bring plenty of film** if you are traveling to remote areas where your favorite brand may not be available. Plan on shooting a minimum of one 36-exposure roll per week of travel. If you don't want the hassle of keeping a shot log, **make a quick note whenever you start a new roll**—it will make identifying your photos much easier when you get home.

CAR RENTAL

On average it costs approximately 30,000 pesos (about $40) a day to rent the cheapest type of car, which usually includes unlimited mileage and insurance. To access some of Chile's more remote regions, it may be necessary to rent a four-wheel-drive vehicle, which can cost up to 70,000 pesos (about $90) a day. You can often get a discounted weekly rate.

It is by far easier to rent a car in Santiago, where all the international agencies have branches at the airport and in town. You'll find mostly local rental agencies in the rest of the country, except at airports, where many international companies often have small kiosks.

Always **give the rental car a once-over** to make sure that the headlights, jack, and tires (including the spare) are in working condition. Be sure to **alert the agency about any scratches and dents** before you set off on your trip or you may be held liable for damages you didn't cause.

Major Agencies Alamo ☎ 800/522-9696 ⊕ www.alamo.com. **Avis** ☎ 800/331-1084; 800/879-2847 in Canada; 0870/606-0100 in the U.K.; 02/9353-9000 in Australia; 09/526-2847 in New Zealand ⊕ www.avis.com. **Budget** ☎ 800/527-0700; 0870/156-5656 in the U.K. ⊕ www.budget.com. **Dollar** ☎ 800/800-6000; 0124/622-0111 in the U.K., where it's affiliated with Sixt; 02/9223-1444 in Australia ⊕ www.dollar.com. **Hertz** ☎ 800/654-3001; 800/263-0600 in Canada; 0870/844-8844 in the U.K.; 02/9669-2444 in Australia; 09/256-8690 in New Zealand ⊕ www.hertz.com. **National Car Rental** ☎ 800/227-7368; 0870/600-6666 in the U.K. ⊕ www.nationalcar.com.

CUTTING COSTS

For a good deal, **book through a travel agent who will shop around.** If you don't want to drive yourself, **consider hiring a car and driver** through your hotel concierge, or **make a deal with a taxi driver** for some extended sightseeing at a longer-term rate. Drivers charge an hourly rate regardless of the distance traveled. You'll often spend less than you would for a rental car.

Local companies are sometimes a cheaper option. El Automóvil Club de Chile is a reputable local company with offices in Santiago and all major southern cities.

Local Agency El Automóvil Club de Chile ☎ 2/431-1106 or 2/431-1107.

INSURANCE

When driving a rented car you are generally responsible for any damage to or loss of the vehicle. You also may be liable for any property damage or personal injury that you may cause while driving. Before you rent, see what coverage you already have under the terms of your personal auto-insurance policy and credit cards.

REQUIREMENTS & RESTRICTIONS

Your own driver's license and an International Driving Permit make it legal for you to drive. The minimum age for driving in Chile is 18. To rent a car you usually have to be 25, but a few companies let you rent at 22.

SURCHARGES

Before you pick up a car in one city and leave it in another, **ask about drop-off** charges or one-way service fees, which can be substantial. Note, too, that some rental agencies charge extra if you return the car before the time specified in your contract. To avoid a hefty refueling fee, fill the tank just before you turn in the car, but be aware that gas stations near the rental outlet may overcharge. It's almost never a deal to buy the tank of gas that's in the car when you rent it; the understanding is that you'll return it empty, but some fuel usually remains.

CAR TRAVEL

Certain areas of Chile are most enjoyable when explored on your own in a car, such as the wineries of the Central Valley, the ski areas east of Santiago, and the Lake District in the south. Some regions, such as parts of the Atacama Desert and the Carretera Austral highway, are impossible to explore without your own wheels.

Drivers in Chile are not particularly aggressive, but neither are they particularly polite. A certain amount of machismo is displayed by some male drivers. Some common-sense rules of the road: before you set out establish an itinerary. Be sure to plan your daily driving distance conservatively. Always obey speed limits and traffic regulations. And above all, if you get a traffic ticket, don't argue—and plan to spend longer than you want settling it.

Your driver's license may not be recognized outside your home country. International driving permits (IDPs) are available from the American and Canadian automobile associations and, in the United Kingdom, from the Automobile Association and Royal Automobile Club. These international permits, valid only in conjunction with your regular driver's license, are universally recognized; having one may save you a problem with local authorities.

AUTO CLUBS

El Automóvil Club de Chile offers low-cost road service and towing in and around the main cities to members of the Automobile Association of America (AAA).

🅵 In Chile El Automóvil Club de Chile ✉ Av. Andrés Bello 1863, Providencia, Santiago ☎ 2/431-1000.

GASOLINE

Most service stations are operated by an attendant and accept credit cards. They are open 24 hours a day along the Pan-American Highway and in most major cities, but not in small towns and villages. Attendants will often ask you to glance at the zero reading on the gas pump to show that you are not being cheated.

In Chile, gasoline is cheap. At press time a liter of gas cost about 450 pesos (61¢). To make sure you don't run out of gas, always ask about gas stations en route.

PARKING

Depending on the area, you can park on the street, in parking lots, or in parking garages in Santiago and large cities in Chile. Expect to pay anywhere from 600 to 800 pesos. There are parking meters for street parking, but more often a parking attendant will be there to direct and charge you.

ROAD CONDITIONS

Between May and August, roads, underpasses, and parks can flood when it rains. It's very dangerous, especially for drivers who don't know their way around. Avoid driving if it has been raining for several hours.

The Pan-American Highway runs from Arica in the far north down to Puerto Montt, in the Lake District. Much of it is now double lane, or in the process of being widened, and bypasses most large cities. The Carretera Austral, an unpaved road that runs for more than 1,000 km (620 mi) as far as Villa O'Higgins in Patagonia, starts just south of Puerto Montt. A few stretches of the road are broken by water and are linked only by car ferries. Some parts of the Carretera can be washed away in heavy rain; it is wise to consult local police for details.

Many cyclists ride without lights in rural areas, so be careful when driving at night, particularly on roads without street lighting. This also applies to horse- and bull-drawn carts.

RULES OF THE ROAD

Keep in mind that the speed limit is 60 kmh (37mph) in cities and 120 kmh (75 mph) on highways unless otherwise posted. The police regularly enforce the speed limit, handing out *partes* (tickets) to speeders.

Seat belts are mandatory in the front and back of the car, and police give on-the-spot fines for not wearing them. If the police find you with more than 0.5 miligrams of alcohol in your blood, you will be considered to be driving under the influence and arrested.

There are restrictions, depending on license-plate suffixes, on which days of the week you can drive in Santiago, and it applies to all vehicles. The car-rental agency can fill you in, or you can consult the national broadsheet *El Mercurio* or another daily paper.

In order to drive to Punta Arenas in Patagonia you will need to cross into Argentina at Chile Chico or at one of the international border crossings beforehand. If you plan to do this you must tell your car-rental company, which will provide notorized authorization—otherwise you will be refused permission to cross.

Plan to rent snow chains for driving on the road up to the ski resorts outside of Santiago. Police will stop you and ask if you have them—if you don't, you will be forced to turn back.

CHILDREN IN CHILE

Children are welcomed in most hotels and restaurants, especially on weekends, when families go out for lunch in droves. The *balnearios* (beach towns) along Chile's Central Coast expect you to bring the kids—the most common form of lodging is family-size bungalows. Children are also a common sight in the pine-covered mountains of the Lake District and the ski resorts of the Central Valley.

If you are renting a car, don't forget to **arrange for a car seat** when you reserve. For general advice about traveling with children, consult *Fodor's FYI: Travel with Your Baby* (available in bookstores everywhere).

FLYING

If your children are two or older, **ask about children's airfares.** As a general rule, infants under two not occupying a seat fly at greatly reduced fares or even for free. But if you want to guarantee a seat for an infant, you have to pay full fare. Consider flying during off-peak days and times; most airlines will grant an infant a seat without a ticket if there are available seats. When booking, **confirm carry-on allowances** if you're traveling with infants. In general, for babies charged 10% to 50% of the adult fare you are allowed one carry-on bag and a collapsible stroller; if the flight is full, the stroller may have to be checked or you may be limited to less.

Experts agree that it's a good idea to use safety seats aloft for children weighing less than 40 pounds. Airlines set their own policies: if you use a safety seat, U.S. carriers usually require that the child be ticketed, even if he or she is young enough to ride free, because the seats must be strapped into regular seats. And even if you pay the full adult fare for the seat, it may be worth it, especially on longer trips. Do **check your airline's policy about using safety seats during takeoff and landing.** Safety seats are not allowed everywhere in the plane, so get your seat assignments as early as possible.

When reserving, **request children's meals or a freestanding bassinet** (not available at all airlines) if you need them. But note that bulkhead seats, where you must sit to use the bassinet, may lack an overhead bin or storage space on the floor.

LODGING

Most hotels in Chile allow children under a certain age to stay in their parents' room at no extra charge, but others charge for them as extra adults; be sure to **find out the cutoff age for children's discounts.**

SIGHTS & ATTRACTIONS

There's plenty for kids to do in Chile. Santiago is filled with interesting museums that appeal to the entire family. Every town has public parks where parents can relax while their children romp. Kids are fascinated by the *ascensores* (funiculars) of Valparaíso. The ferries around Puerto Montt are a great way to see the coastline. And most children delight at the penguin colonies near Punta Arenas.

Places that are especially appealing to children are indicated by a rubber-duckie icon (🐤) in the margin.

COMPUTERS ON THE ROAD

If you're planning to bring a laptop computer into the country, check the manual first to see if it requires a converter. Newer laptops will only require an adapter plug.

Chile uses the same phone plugs as the United States, so plan accordingly if you'll be using a modem. Remember to ask about electrical surges before plugging in your computer. Note that South America's luxury hotels typically offer business centers with computers.

Carrying a laptop computer could make you a target for thieves; **conceal your laptop in a generic bag** and keep it close to you at all times.

CONSUMER PROTECTION

Whether you're shopping for gifts or purchasing travel services, **pay with a major credit card** whenever possible, so you can cancel payment or get reimbursed if there's a problem (and you can provide documentation). If you're doing business with a particular company for the first time, **contact your local Better Business Bureau and the attorney general's offices** in your state and (for U.S. businesses) the company's home state as well. Have any complaints been filed? Finally, if you're buying a package or tour, always **consider travel insurance** that includes default coverage (⇨ Insurance).

🗐 BBBs **Council of Better Business Bureaus** ✉ 4200 Wilson Blvd., Suite 800, Arlington, VA 22203 ☎ 703/276-0100 🖷 703/525-8277 ⊕ www.bbb.org.

CRUISE TRAVEL

Several international cruise lines, including Celebrity Cruises, Cruise West, Holland America, Princess Cruises, Royal Olympic, and Silversea Cruises, call at Chile or offer cruises that start in Chile, typically in Valparaíso, following the coastline to the southern archipelago and its fjords. Some companies, such as Cruise West, Holland America, and Orient Lines, have itineraries that include Antarctica. Victory Yacht Cruises and Adventure Associates operate in southern Chile and also have cruises to Antarctica.

You can spend a week aboard the luxury *Skorpios,* run by Cruceros Maritimos Skorpios, which leaves from Puerto Montt and sails through the archipelago to the San Rafael glacier. In the far south, you can board Navimag's *Terra Australis* and motor through the fjords to the Beagle Channel, stopping in Puerto Williams, Chile's most southerly settlement.

To learn how to plan, choose, and book a cruise-ship voyage, consult *Fodor's FYI: Plan & Enjoy Your Cruise* (available in bookstores everywhere).

🗐 Cruise Lines **Adventure Associates** ☎ 2/9389-7466 in Australia. **Celebrity Cruises** ☎ 800/722-5941. **Cruise West** ☎ 800/580-0072. **Cruceros Maritimos Skorpios** ☎ 2/231-1030. **Holland America** ☎ 877/932-4259. **Navimag** ☎ 2/442-3120. **Orient Lines** ☎ 800/333-7300. **Princess Cruises** ☎ 800/746-2377. **Royal Olympic** ☎ 800/872-6400; 020/7440-9090 in the U.K. **Silversea Cruises** ☎ 800/722-9955; 870/333-7030 in the U.K. **Victory Yacht Cruises** ☎ 61/621-010 in Chile.

CUSTOMS & DUTIES

When shopping abroad, **keep receipts** for all purchases. Upon reentering the country, **be ready to show customs officials what you've bought.** Pack purchases together in an easily accessible place. If you think a duty is incorrect, appeal the assessment. If you object to the way your clearance was handled, note the inspector's badge number. In either case, first ask to see a supervisor. If the problem isn't resolved, write to the appropriate authorities, beginning with the port director at your point of entry.

IN AUSTRALIA

Australian residents who are 18 or older may bring home A$400 worth of souvenirs and gifts (including jewelry), 250 cigarettes or 250 grams of cigars or other tobacco products, and 1,125 ml of alcohol (including wine, beer, and spirits). Residents under 18 may bring back A$200 worth of goods. Members of the same family traveling together may pool their allowances. Prohibited items include meat products. Seeds, plants, and fruits need to be declared upon arrival.

🗐 **Australian Customs Service** 🖅 Regional Director, Box 8, Sydney, NSW 2001 ☎ 02/9213-2000 or 1300/363263; 02/9364-7222 or 1800/803-006 quarantine-inquiry line 🖷 02/9213-4043 ⊕ www.customs.gov.au.

IN CANADA

Canadian residents who have been out of Canada for at least seven days may bring in C$750 worth of goods duty-free. If you've been away fewer than seven days but more than 48 hours, the duty-free allowance drops to C$200. If your trip lasts 24 to 48 hours, the allowance is C$50.

You may not pool allowances with family members. Goods claimed under the C$750 exemption may follow you by mail; those claimed under the lesser exemptions must accompany you. Alcohol and tobacco products may be included in the seven-day and 48-hour exemptions but not in the 24-hour exemption. If you meet the age requirements of the province or territory through which you reenter Canada, you may bring in, duty-free, 1.5 liters of wine *or* 1.14 liters (40 imperial ounces) of liquor *or* 24 12-ounce cans or bottles of beer or ale. Also, if you meet the local age requirement for tobacco products, you may bring in, duty-free, 200 cigarettes and 50 cigars. Check ahead of time with the Canada Customs and Revenue Agency or the Department of Agriculture for policies regarding meat products, seeds, plants, and fruits.

You may send an unlimited number of gifts (only one gift per recipient, however) worth up to C$60 each duty-free to Canada. Label the package UNSOLICITED GIFT—VALUE UNDER $60. Alcohol and tobacco are excluded.

Canada Customs and Revenue Agency ⊠ 2265 St. Laurent Blvd., Ottawa, Ontario K1G 4K3 ☎ 800/461-9999; 204/983-3500; 506/636-5064 ⊕ www.ccra.gc.ca.

IN CHILE

You may bring into Chile up to 400 cigarettes, 500 grams of tobacco, 50 cigars, two open bottles of perfume, 2.5 liters of alcoholic beverages, and gifts. Prohibited items include plants, fruit, seeds, meat, and honey. Spot checks take place at airports and border crossings.

Visitors, although seldom questioned, are prohibited from leaving with handicrafts and souvenirs worth more than $500. You are generally prohibited from taking antiques out of the country without special permission (⇨ Shopping).

Chilean Embassy ⊠ 1732 Massachusetts Ave. NW, Washington, DC 20036 U.S.A. ☎ 202/785-1746 ⊕ www.chile-usa.org.

IN NEW ZEALAND

All homeward-bound residents may bring back NZ$700 worth of souvenirs and gifts; passengers may not pool their allowances, and children can claim only the concession on goods intended for their own use. For those 17 or older, the duty-free allowance also includes 4.5 liters of wine or beer; one 1,125-ml bottle of spirits; and either 200 cigarettes, 250 grams of tobacco, 50 cigars, *or* a combination of the three up to 250 grams. Meat products, seeds, plants, and fruits must be declared upon arrival to the Agricultural Services Department.

New Zealand Customs ⊠ Head office: The Customhouse, 17–21 Whitmore St., Box 2218, Wellington ☎ 09/300–5399 or 0800/428–786 ⊕ www.customs.govt.nz.

IN THE U.K.

From countries outside the European Union, including Chile, you may bring home, duty-free, 200 cigarettes or 50 cigars; 1 liter of spirits or 2 liters of fortified or sparkling wine or liqueurs; 2 liters of still table wine; 60 ml of perfume; 250 ml of toilet water; plus £145 worth of other goods, including gifts and souvenirs. Prohibited items include meat products, seeds, plants, and fruits.

HM Customs and Excise ⊠ Portcullis House, 21 Cowbridge Rd. E, Cardiff CF11 9SS ☎ 0845/010–9000 or 0208/929–0152; 0208/929–6731 or 0208/910–3602 complaints ⊕ www.hmce.gov.uk.

IN THE U.S.

U.S. residents who have been out of the country for at least 48 hours may bring home, for personal use, $800 worth of foreign goods duty-free, as long as they haven't used the $800 allowance or any part of it in the past 30 days. This exemption may include 1 liter of alcohol (for travelers 21 and older), 200 cigarettes, and 100 non-Cuban cigars. Family members from the same household who are traveling together may pool their $800 personal exemptions. For fewer than 48 hours, the duty-free allowance drops to $200, which may include 50 cigarettes, 10 non-Cuban cigars, and 150 ml of alcohol (or 150 ml of perfume containing alcohol). The $200 allowance cannot be combined with other individuals' exemptions, and if you exceed it, the full value of all the goods will be taxed. Antiques, which the U.S. Bureau of Customs and Border Protection defines as objects more than 100 years old, enter duty-free, as do original works of art done entirely by hand, including paintings, drawings, and sculptures. This doesn't apply to folk art or handicrafts, which are in general dutiable.

You may also send packages home duty-free, with a limit of one parcel per addressee per day (except alcohol or tobacco products or perfume worth more than $5). You can mail up to $200 worth of goods for personal use; label the package PERSONAL USE and attach a list of its contents and their retail value. If the package contains your used personal belongings, mark it AMERICAN GOODS RETURNED to avoid paying duties. You may send up to $100 worth of goods as a gift; mark the package UNSOLICITED GIFT. Mailed items do not affect your duty-free allowance on your return.

To avoid paying duty on foreign-made high-ticket items you already own and will take on your trip, register them with Customs before you leave the country. Consider filing a Certificate of Registration for laptops, cameras, watches, and other digital devices identified with serial numbers or other permanent markings; you can keep the certificate for other trips. Otherwise, bring a sales receipt or insurance form to show that you owned the item before you left the United States.

🗊 **U.S. Bureau of Customs and Border Protection** ✉ for inquiries and equipment registration, 1300 Pennsylvania Ave. NW, Washington, DC 20229 🌐 www.customs.gov ☎ 202/354-1000 ✉ for complaints, Customer Satisfaction Unit, 1300 Pennsylvania Ave. NW, Room 5.5D, Washington, DC 20229.

DINING

The restaurants (all of which are indicated by a ✕ symbol) that we list are the cream of the crop in each price category. Properties indicated by a ✕⊡ are lodging establishments whose restaurant warrants a special trip. It is customary to tip 10% in Chile; tipping above this amount is uncommon among locals.

MEALS & SPECIALTIES

Chile serves an incredible variety of foods. With such a long coastline, it's no surprise that you can get wonderful seafood. Salmon is caught off the southern coast and raised in farms in the Lake District. Other popular catches include sea bass, conger eel, and reineta. Shellfish such as mussels and scallops are widely available, while *locos* (abalone) and *jaiba* (crab) are frequently prepared as *chupes* (stews) or *pasteles* (pies). Raw shellfish is best avoided, but cooked with cheese or white wine, lemon, and fresh coriander, it's an excellent introduction to Chilean cuisine. Awaken your palate with a seafood appetizer, such as *choritos al vapor* (mussels steamed in white wine), *machas a la parmesana* (similar to razor clams but unique to Chile, grilled with tomatoes and Parmesan cheese), or *chupe de centolla* (king crab). Simply seasoned grilled fish is a Chilean favorite, usually served with steamed potatoes or an *ensalada a la chilena* (sliced tomatoes and onions). Also worth tasting is the humble *merluza* (hake), which makes a delicious, cheap lunch.

But fish isn't all that's available. *Pastel de choclo* is a typical dish that you'll find just about everywhere in Chile. Served in a heavy, clay bowl, it's a mixture of minced beef, chicken, olives, hard-boiled egg, and sultanas, topped with a layer of creamy mashed corn. Then there are the tasty and filling *humitas,* mashed corn with chopped onion and basil served in the corn husk. Stews of vegetables with chicken, beef, or lamb are known as *cazuelas;* a hearty bean stew with chopped vegetables is known as *porotos granados.*

A *parrillada* is a platter of every cut of meat imaginable—often one order will serve many. Beefsteak *a la pobre* comes with a fried egg or two on top, plus onions and french fries. *Longanizas* are Spanish-style sausages.

For something lighter try an empanada, which you can order as a starter or a main course. These come most commonly stuffed with meat, olives, egg, and onions (*pino*), or with cheese (*queso*); occasionally they'll be stuffed with shellfish (*mariscos*). Toasted sandwiches are another option: a *barro luco* consists of slender steak topped with melted cheese, and a *barro jarpa* comes with ham and cheese.

Chileans know their sweets, with foamy meringues topping the list of indulgences, followed closely by *alfajor de manjar* (creamy, caramelized condensed milk smashed between wafers and bathed in chocolate). The German immigrants who came to the Lake District a century ago brought their tasty *küchen,* rich fruit-filled pastries. Spring and summer sunshine brings to life an unparalleled Chilean ice cream culture; parlors line almost every pedestrian walkway, and vats filled with exotic fruit flavors tempt even the most dedicated of dieters.

MEALTIMES

Lunch, which usually begins at 1 or 2, is the most important meal of the day. It can take two hours or more. Some Chileans forgo dinner, making do with an *once,* a light evening meal similar in style to a high tea. Many restaurants have once meals, which include a sandwich (often ham and cheese), fresh juice, tea, and a dessert. Once is served from 5 to 8; dinner is eaten later than in North America, usually starting anywhere from 8 to 10. Unless otherwise noted, the restaurants listed in this guide are open daily for lunch and dinner.

PAYING

Credit cards are widely accepted at restaurants in Santiago and most other cities in Chile. In small villages restaurants may not accept credit cards, so it's advisable to carry cash.

RESERVATIONS & DRESS

Reservations are always a good idea; we mention them only when they're essential or not accepted. Book as far ahead as you can, and reconfirm as soon as you arrive. (Large parties should always call ahead to check the reservations policy.) For the most part, the dress code for restaurants is fairly casual in Chile. We mention dress only when men are required to wear a jacket or a jacket and tie.

WINE, BEER & SPIRITS

The national drink is pisco, a brandy distilled from small grapes. A pisco sour, a tangy cocktail, is made from pisco, fresh lemon juice, ice, and sugar. It is sometimes topped off with a thin layer of whisked egg white. Several Chilean wines, especially cabernet sauvignons, are on par with top European and American counterparts. They are also a terrific value. Local beer labels include Escudo, Royal, Becker, and Kuntsmann, a tasty brew from Valdivia; Imperial, based in Punta Arenas, claims to be the world's most southerly brewery.

DISABILITIES & ACCESSIBILITY

Although international chain hotels in Santiago and a few other cities have some wheelchair-accessible rooms, Chile isn't very well equipped to handle travelers with disabilities. There are few ramps and curb cuts, and it takes effort and planning to negotiate cobbled city streets, get around museums and other buildings, and explore the countryside. Some regions, such as the Atacama Desert and Parque Nacional Torres del Paine, are a challenge for those with mobility problems. Valparaíso, with its hillside topography and unending staircases, could be unmanageable.

RESERVATIONS

When discussing accessibility with an operator or reservations agent, **ask hard questions.** Are there any stairs, inside *or* out? Are there grab bars next to the toilet *and* in the shower/tub? How wide is the doorway to the room? To the bathroom? For the most extensive facilities meeting the latest legal specifications, **opt for newer accommodations.** If you reserve through a toll-free number, consider also calling the hotel's local number to confirm the information from the central reservations office. Get confirmation in writing when you can.

SIGHTS & ATTRACTIONS

Few sights in Chile were designed with travelers who use wheelchairs in mind, and fewer still have been renovated to meet their needs. Newer destinations may have the necessary facilities, but don't count on it. Call ahead or ask someone who has visited before.

Complaints Aviation Consumer Protection Division (⇨ Air Travel) for airline-related problems. **Departmental Office of Civil Rights** ⊠ for general inquiries, U.S. Department of Transportation, S-30, 400 7th St. SW, Room 10215, Washington, DC 20590 ☎ 202/366-4648 🖷 202/366-9371 ⊕ www.dot. gov/ost/docr/index.htm. **Disability Rights Section** ⊠ NYAV, U.S. Department of Justice, Civil Rights Division, 950 Pennsylvania Ave. NW, Washington, DC 20530 ☎ ADA information line 202/514-0301, 800/514-0301, 202/514-0383 TTY, 800/514-0383 TTY ⊕ www.ada.gov. **U.S. Department of Transportation Hotline** ☎ 800/778-4838 or 800/455-9880 TTY for disability-related air-travel problems.

TRAVEL AGENCIES

In the United States, the Americans with Disabilities Act requires that travel firms serve the needs of all travelers. Some agencies specialize in working with people with disabilities.

Travelers with Mobility Problems Access Adventures ⊠ 206 Chestnut Ridge Rd., Scottsville, NY

14624 🕾 585/889-9096 ✍ dltravel@prodigy.net, run by a former physical-rehabilitation counselor. **CareVacations** ✉ No. 5, 5110-50 Ave., Leduc, Alberta, Canada, T9E 6V4 🕾 780/986-6404 or 877/478-7827 🖷 780/986-8332 ⊕ www.carevacations.com, for group tours and cruise vacations. **Flying Wheels Travel** ✉ 143 W. Bridge St., Box 382, Owatonna, MN 55060 🕾 507/451-5005 🖷 507/451-1685 ⊕ www.flyingwheelstravel.com.

DISCOUNTS & DEALS

Be a smart shopper and **compare all your options** before making decisions. A plane ticket bought with a promotional coupon from travel clubs, coupon books, and direct-mail offers or purchased on the Internet may not be cheaper than the least expensive fare from a discount ticket agency. And always keep in mind that what you get is just as important as what you save.

DISCOUNT RESERVATIONS

To save money, **look into discount reservations services** with Web sites and toll-free numbers, which use their buying power to get a better price on hotels, airline tickets (⇨ Air Travel), even car rentals. When booking a room, always **call the hotel's local toll-free number** (if one is available) rather than the central reservations number—you'll often get a better price. Always ask about special packages or corporate rates.

When shopping for the best deal on hotels and car rentals, **look for guaranteed exchange rates,** which protect you against a falling dollar. With your rate locked in, you won't pay more, even if the price goes up in the local currency.
🚺 Airline Tickets **Air 4 Less** 🕾 800/AIR4LESS; low-fare specialist.
🚺 Hotel Rooms **Accommodations Express** 🕾 800/444-7666 or 800/277-1064 ⊕ www.accommodationsexpress.com. **Steigenberger Reservation Service** 🕾 800/223-5652 ⊕ www.srs-worldhotels.com. **Travel Interlink** 🕾 800/888-5898 ⊕ www.travelinterlink.com. **Turbotrip.com** 🕾 800/473-7829 ⊕ www.turbotrip.com.

PACKAGE DEALS

Don't confuse packages and guided tours. When you buy a package, you travel on your own, just as though you had planned the trip yourself. Fly/drive packages, which combine airfare and car rental, are often a good deal. In cities, ask the local visitor's bureau about hotel packages that include tickets to major museum exhibits or other special events.

ELECTRICITY

Unlike the United States and Canada—which have a 110- to 120-volt standard—the current in Chile is 220 volts, 50 cycles alternating current (AC). To use an appliance from home, **bring a converter.**

If your appliances are dual-voltage—as many laptops are these days—you'll need only an adapter. Don't use 110-volt outlets, marked FOR SHAVERS ONLY, for high-wattage appliances such as hair dryers.

EMBASSIES

🚺 Australia **Chile** ✉ 10 Culgoa Circuit O'Malley, Monaco Crescent, ACT 2606 Australia 🕾 262/862-2430.
🚺 Canada **Chile** ✉ 50 O'Conner St., Suite 1413, Ottawa, Ontario, K1P 5A9, Canada 🕾 613/235-4402.
🚺 Chile **Australia** ✉ Isidora Goyenechea 3621, Piso 12-13, Las Condes, Santiago 🕾 2/550-3500. **Canada** ✉ Nueva Tajamar 481, Piso 12, Torre Norte, Las Condes, Santiago 🕾 2/362-9660. **New Zealand** ✉ El Golf 99, Oficina 703, Las Condes, Santiago 🕾 2/290 9800. **United Kingdom** ✉ Av. El Bosque Norte 0125, Piso 3, Las Condes, Santiago 🕾 2/231-3737. **United States** ✉ Av. Andrés Bello 2800, Las Condes, Santiago 🕾 2/232-2600.
🚺 New Zealand **Chile** ✉ 1-3 Willeston St., Willis Corroon House, 7th floor, Wellington, New Zealand 🕾 4/471-6270.
🚺 United Kingdom **Chile** ✉ 12 Devonshire St., London, W1G 7DS, England 🕾 020/7580-6392.
🚺 United States **Chile** ✉ 1732 Massachusetts Ave. NW, Washington, DC 20036 U.S.A. 🕾 202/785-1746.

EMERGENCIES

The numbers to call in case of emergency are the same all over Chile.
🚺 **Ambulance** 🕾 131. **Fire** 🕾 132. **Police** 🕾 133.

ENGLISH-LANGUAGE MEDIA

There is very little in the way of English-language media in Chile. *News Review,* which regurgitates some local and international news, is published weekly. It also lists English-language events and services. It's not easy to find on the newsstands, although it is available free in Santiago's airport.

GAY & LESBIAN TRAVEL

Although the government repealed its law banning gay sex in 1999, it's still difficult for many Chilean gay men and lesbians to be out of the closet. This may be why the gay scene remains very subdued. Still, while there are few open displays of same-sex affection in public, Chile is at least as tolerant of gays as most other South American countries. There are gay bars and clubs in Santiago and a few other cities, but they often can be difficult to find.

GAY & LESBIAN WEB SITES

For specific information about Chile's gay scene, try the online Gay Chile (www.gaychile.com). It lists all the local gay bars and clubs and gay-friendly hotels. The best site online for general information about gay travel is Out and About (www.outandabout.com). Here you can scour though the back issues for information on gay-friendly destinations. You also can try PlanetOut (www.planetout.com/travel) and Gay.Com (www.gay.com), two general-interest gay sites.

▪ Gay- & Lesbian-Friendly Travel Agencies **Different Roads Travel** ✉ 8383 Wilshire Blvd., Suite 520, Beverly Hills, CA 90211 ☎ 323/651-5557 or 800/429-8747 (Ext. 14 for both) ☎ 323/651-3678 ✉ lgernert@tzell.com. **Kennedy Travel** ✉ 130 W. 42nd St., Suite 401, New York, NY 10036 ☎ 212/840-8659 or 800/237-7433 ☎ 212/730-2269 ⊕ www.kennedytravel.com. **Now, Voyager** ✉ 4406 18th St., San Francisco, CA 94114 ☎ 415/626-1169 or 800/255-6951 ☎ 415/626-8626 ⊕ www.nowvoyager.com. **Skylink Travel and Tour** ✉ 1455 N. Dutton Ave., Suite A, Santa Rosa, CA 95401 ☎ 707/546-9888 or 800/225-5759 ☎ 707/636-0951; serving lesbian travelers.

HEALTH

From a health standpoint, Chile is one of the safer countries in which to travel. To be on the safe side, **take the normal precautions** you would traveling anywhere in South America.

In Santiago there are several large private *clinicas* (clinics; ⇨ Santiago A to Z *in* Chapter 1), and many doctors can speak at least a bit of English. In most other large cities there are one or two private clinics where you can be seen quickly. Generally, *hospitales* (hospitals) are for those receiving free or heavily subsidized treatment, and they are often crowded with long lines of patients waiting to be seen.

ALTITUDE SICKNESS

Altitude sickness—which causes shortness of breath, nausea, and splitting headaches—may be a problem when you visit Andean countries. The best way to prevent *soroche* is to **ascend slowly.** Spend a few nights at 6,000–9,000 ft before you head higher. If you must fly straight in, plan on doing next to nothing for your first few days. The traditional remedy is herbal tea made from coca leaves. Over-the-counter analgesics and napping also help. If symptoms persist, return to lower elevations. Note that if you have high blood pressure and/or a history of heart trouble, check with your doctor before traveling to the mountains.

DIVERS' ALERT

Scuba divers take note: **Do not fly within 24 hours of scuba diving.** Neophyte divers should have a complete physical exam before undertaking a dive. If you have travel insurance, **make sure your policy applies to scuba-related injuries,** as not all companies provide this coverage.

FOOD & DRINK

Visitors seldom encounter problems with drinking the water in Chile. Almost all drinking water receives proper treatment and is unlikely to produce health problems. If you have any doubts, stick to bottled water. Mineral water is good and comes carbonated (*con gas*) and noncarbonated (*sin gas*).

Food preparation is strictly regulated by the government, so outbreaks of food-borne diseases are very rare. But it's still a good idea to use the same common-sense rules you would in any other part of South America. Don't risk restaurants where the hygiene is suspect or street vendors where the food is allowed to sit around unrefrigerated. Always **avoid raw shellfish,** such as ceviche. Remember to **steer clear of raw fruits and vegetables** unless you know they've been thoroughly washed and disinfected.

MEDICAL PLANS

No one plans to get sick while traveling, but it happens, so **consider signing up with** a **medical-assistance company.** Members get doctor referrals, emergency evacuation or repatriation, hot lines for medical consultation, cash for emergencies, and other assistance.

🖪 Medical-Assistance Companies International SOS Assistance ⊕ www.internationalsos.com ✉ 8 Neshaminy Interplex, Suite 207, Trevose, PA 19053 ☎ 215/245-4707 or 800/523-6586 🖶 215/244-9617 ✉ Landmark House, Hammersmith Bridge Rd., 6th floor, London, W6 9DP ☎ 20/8762-8008 🖶 20/8748-7744 ✉ 12 Chemin Riantbosson, 1217 Meyrin 1, Geneva, Switzerland ☎ 22/785-6464 🖶 22/785-6424 ✉ 331 N. Bridge Rd., 17-00, Odeon Towers, Singapore 188720 ☎ 6338-7800 🖶 6338-7611.

OVER-THE-COUNTER REMEDIES

Mild cases of diarrhea may respond to Imodium (known generically as loperamide), Pepto-Bismol (not as strong), and Lomotil. Drink plenty of purified water or tea—chamomile (*manzanilla* in Spanish) is a good folk remedy.

You will need to visit a *farmacia* (pharmacy) to purchase medications such as Tylenol and *aspirina* (aspirin), which are readily available. Pharmacists can often recommend a medicine for your condition, but they are not always certain of the dosage. Quite often the packaging comes with no instructions unless the drug is imported, in which case it will cost two or three times the price of a local product.

SHOTS & MEDICATIONS

All travelers to Chile should get up-to-date tetanus, diphtheria, and measles boosters, and a hepatitis A inoculation is recommended. Children traveling to Chile should have current inoculations against mumps, rubella, and polio. Always **check with your doctor** about which shots to get.

According to the Centers for Disease Control and Prevention, there's no risk of contracting malaria, but a limited risk of cholera, typhoid, hepatitis B, dengue, and Chagas. While a few of these you could catch anywhere, most are restricted to jungle areas. The best way to avoid these diseases is to **prevent insect bites** by wearing long pants and long-sleeve shirts and by using insect repellents with DEET. If you plan to visit remote regions or stay for more than six weeks, **check with the CDC's International Travelers Hot Line.**

🖪 Health Warnings National Centers for Disease Control and Prevention (CDC) ✉ National Center for Infectious Diseases, Division of Quarantine, Travelers' Health, 1600 Clifton Rd. NE, Atlanta, GA 30333 ☎ 877/394-8747 international travelers' health line; 800/311-3435 other inquiries 🖶 888/232-3299 ⊕ www.cdc.gov/travel.

HOLIDAYS

New Year's Day (Jan. 1), Labor Day (May 1), Day of Naval Glories (May 21), Corpus Christi (in June), Feast of St. Peter and St. Paul (June 29), Independence Celebrations (Sept. 18), Discovery of the Americas (Oct. 12), Day of the Dead (Nov. 1), Immaculate Conception (Dec. 8), Christmas (Dec. 25).

Many shops and services are open on most of these days, but transportation is always heavily booked up on and around the holidays. The two most important dates in the Chilean calendar are September 18 and New Year's Day. On these days shops close and public transportation is reduced to the bare minimum or is nonexistent. Trying to book a ticket around these dates will be impossible unless you do it well in advance.

INSURANCE

The most useful travel-insurance plan is a comprehensive policy that includes coverage for trip cancellation and interruption, default, trip delay, and medical expenses (with a waiver for preexisting conditions).

Without insurance you'll lose all or most of your money if you cancel your trip, regardless of the reason. Default insurance covers you if your tour operator, airline, or cruise line goes out of business. Trip-delay covers expenses that arise because of bad weather or mechanical delays. Study the fine print when comparing policies.

If you're traveling internationally, a key component of travel insurance is coverage for medical bills incurred if you get sick on the road. Such expenses aren't generally covered by Medicare or private policies. U.K. residents can buy a travel-insurance policy valid for most vacations taken during the year in which it's purchased (but check preexisting-condition coverage). British and Australian citizens need extra medical coverage when traveling overseas.

Always **buy travel policies directly from the insurance company**; if you buy them from a cruise line, airline, or tour operator that goes out of business you probably won't be covered for the agency or operator's default, a major risk. Before making any purchase, **review your existing health and home-owner's policies** to find what they cover away from home.

Travel Insurers In the U.S.: **Access America** ✉ 6600 W. Broad St., Richmond, VA 23230 ☎ 800/284-8300 🖷 804/673-1491 or 800/346-9265 ⊕ www.accessamerica.com. **Travel Guard International** ✉ 1145 Clark St., Stevens Point, WI 54481 ☎ 715/345-0505 or 800/826-1300 🖷 800/955-8785 ⊕ www.travelguard.com.

In the U.K.: Association of British Insurers ✉ 51 Gresham St., London EC2V 7HQ ☎ 020/7600-3333 🖷 020/7696-8999 ⊕ www.abi.org.uk. In Canada: **RBC Insurance** ✉ 6880 Financial Dr., Mississauga, Ontario L5N 7Y5 ☎ 800/565-3129 🖷 905/813-4704 ⊕ www.rbcinsurance.com. In Australia: **Insurance Council of Australia** ✉ Insurance Enquiries and Complaints, Level 3, 56 Pitt St., Sydney, NSW 2000 ☎ 1300/363683 or 02/9251-4456 🖷 02/9251-4453 ⊕ www.iecltd.com.au. In New Zealand: **Insurance Council of New Zealand** ✉ Level 7, 111–115 Customhouse Quay, Box 474, Wellington ☎ 04/472-5230 🖷 04/473-3011 ⊕ www.icnz.org.nz.

INTERNET ACCESS

Although Chileans are generally savvy about the Internet, it is not as widely used as in the United States, which may be partly due to the sluggish connection speeds. Only the most expensive hotels have business centers with Internet-linked computer terminals. If your hotel doesn't have one, ask at the front desk or at a tourism office for directions to an Internet café. Connection fees are generally no more than $1 for a half hour. There is at least one Internet café in every city. Smaller towns may not have one, so make sure you check your e-mail before you leave urban areas.

LANGUAGE

Chile's official language is Spanish, so it's best to learn at least a few words and carry a good phrase book. Chilean Spanish is fast, clipped, and chock-full of colloquialisms. For example, the word for police officer isn't *policía*, but *carabinero*. Even foreigners with a good deal of experience in Spanish-speaking countries may feel like they are encountering a completely new language. However, receptionists at most upscale hotels speak English.

When giving directions, Chileans seldom use left and right, indicating the way instead with a mixture of sign language and *para acá, para allá* (towards here, towards there) instructions.

A phrase book and language-tape set can help you get started. *Fodor's Spanish for Travelers* (available at bookstores everywhere) is excellent.

LODGING

The lodgings (all indicated with a 🖭 symbol) that we list are the cream of the crop in each price category. We always list the facilities that are available—but we don't specify whether they cost extra: when pricing accommodations, always ask what's included and what costs extra. All hotels listed have private bath unless otherwise noted. Properties indicated by ✕🖭 are lodging establishments whose restaurant warrants a special trip.

It's always good to **look at any room before accepting it.** Expense is no guarantee of charm or cleanliness, and accommodations can vary dramatically within one hotel. If you ask for a double room, you'll get a room for two people, but you're not guaranteed a double mattress. If you'd like to avoid twin beds, ask for a *cama de matrimonio*. Many older hotels in Chile have rooms with wrought-iron balconies or spacious terraces; ask if there's a room *con balcón* or *con terraza* when checking in.

Hotels in Chile do not charge taxes to foreign tourists. Knowing this in advance can save you some cash. When checking the price, make sure to ask for the *precio extranjero, sin impuestos* (foreign rate, without taxes).

Also, note that you can always ask for a *descuento* (discount) out of season or sometimes midweek during high season.

Assume that hotels operate on the **European Plan** (EP, with no meals) unless we specify that they use either the **Continental Plan** (CP, with a Continental breakfast), **Breakfast Plan** (BP, with a full breakfast), **Full American Plan** (FAP, with breakfast, lunch, and dinner), or the **Modified American Plan** (MAP, with breakfast and dinner), or are **all-inclusive** (including all meals and most activities).

APARTMENT & VILLA RENTALS

If you want a home base that's roomy enough for a family and comes with cooking facilities, **consider a furnished rental.** These can save you money, especially if you're traveling with a group. Home-exchange directories sometimes list rentals as well as exchanges.

🏠 International Agents **Hideaways International** ✉ 767 Islington St., Portsmouth, NH 03802 ☎ 603/430-4433 or 800/843-4433 🖷 603/430-4444 ⊕ www.hideaways.com, membership $129. **Villas International** ✉ 4340 Redwood Hwy., Suite D309, San Rafael, CA 94903 ☎ 415/499-9490 or 800/221-2260 🖷 415/499-9491 ⊕ www.villasintl.com.

HOME EXCHANGES

If you would like to exchange your home for someone else's, **join a home-exchange organization,** which will send you its updated listings of available exchanges for a year and will include your own listing in at least one of them. It's up to you to make specific arrangements.

🏠 Exchange Club **HomeLink International** 📦 Box 47747, Tampa, FL 33647 ☎ 813/975-9825 or 800/638-3841 🖷 813/910-8144 ⊕ www.homelink. org; $110 yearly for a listing, on-line access, and catalog; $40 without catalog.

HOSTELS

No matter what your age, you can **save on lodging costs by staying at hostels.** Youth hostels in Chile are not very popular, perhaps due to the prevalence of *residenciales* and other low-cost lodging. Still, Hostelling International (HI), the umbrella group for a number of national youth-hostel associations, offers single-sex, dorm-style beds and, at many hostels, rooms for couples and family accommodations. Membership in any HI national hostel association, open to travelers of all ages, allows you to stay in HI-affiliated hostels at member rates; one-year membership is about $28 for adults (C$35 for a two-year minimum membership in Canada, £13.50 in the U.K., A$52 in Australia, and NZ$40 in New Zealand); hostels charge about $10–$30 per night. Members have priority if the hostel is full; they're also eligible for discounts around the world, even on rail and bus travel in some countries.

🏠 Organizations **Hostelling International–USA** ✉ 8401 Colesville Rd., Suite 600, Silver Spring, MD 20910 ☎ 301/495-1240 🖷 301/495-6697 ⊕ www. hiayh.org. **Hostelling International–Canada**

✉ 400-205 Catherine St., Ottawa, Ontario K2P 1C3 ☎ 613/237-7884 or 800/663-5777 🖷 613/237-7868 ⊕ www.hihostels.ca. **YHA England and Wales** ✉ Trevelyan House, Dimple Rd., Matlock, Derbyshire DE4 3YH, U.K. ☎ 0870/870-8808 🖷 0870/770-6127 ⊕ www.yha.org.uk. **YHA Australia** ✉ 422 Kent St., Sydney, NSW 2001 ☎ 02/9261-1111 🖷 02/9261-1969 ⊕ www.yha.com.au. **YHA New Zealand** ✉ Level 3, 193 Cashel St., Box 436, Christchurch ☎ 03/379-9970 or 0800/278-299 🖷 03/365-4476 ⊕ www.yha.org.nz.

HOTELS

Only Chile's larger cities and resort areas have hotels that come with all of the amenities that are taken for granted in North America and Europe, such as room service, a restaurant, or a swimming pool. Elsewhere you may not have television or a phone in your room, although you will find them somewhere in the hotel. Rooms that have a private bath may only have a shower, and in some cases, there will be a shared bath in the hall. In all but the most upscale hotels, you may be asked to leave your key at the reception desk whenever you leave.

🏠 Toll-Free Numbers **Best Western** ☎ 800/528-1234 ⊕ www.bestwestern.com. **Choice** ☎ 800/424-6423 ⊕ www.choicehotels.com. **Holiday Inn** ☎ 800/465-4329 ⊕ www.sixcontinentshotels.com. **Hyatt Hotels & Resorts** ☎ 800/233-1234 ⊕ www. hyatt.com. **Inter-Continental** ☎ 800/327-0200 ⊕ www.intercontinental.com. **Marriott** ☎ 800/228-9290 ⊕ www.marriott.com. **Quality Inn** ☎ 800/424-6423 ⊕ www.choicehotels.com. **Radisson** ☎ 800/333-3333 ⊕ www.radisson.com. **Ritz-Carlton** ☎ 800/241-3333 ⊕ www.ritzcarlton.com. **Sheraton** ☎ 800/325-3535 ⊕ www.starwood.com/sheraton.

RESIDENCIALES

Private homes that rent rooms, *residenciales,* are a unique way to get to know Chile, especially if you're on a budget. Sometimes residenciales are small, very basic accommodations and not necessarily private homes. *Hospedajes* are similar. Many rent rooms for less than $10. Some will be shabby, but others can be substantially better than hotel rooms. They also offer the added benefit of allowing you to interact with locals, though they are unlikely to speak English. Contact the local tourist office for details on residenciales and hospedajes.

MAIL & SHIPPING

The postal system is efficient, and, on average, letters take five–seven days to reach the United States, Europe, Australia, and New Zealand. They will arrive sooner if you send them *prioritaria* (priority) post, but the price will almost double. You can send them *certificado* (registered), in which case the recipient will need to sign for them. Vendors often sell stamps at the entrances to larger post offices, which can save you a potentially long wait in line— the stamps are valid, and selling them this way is legal.

OVERNIGHT SERVICES

Federal Express has offices in Santiago and operates an international overnight service. DHL, with offices in Santiago and most cities throughout Chile, provides overnight service. If you want to send a package to North America, Europe, Australia, or New Zealand, it will take one–four days, depending on where you're sending it from in Chile.

Chile's post office (*el correo*), in conjunction with TNT, can ship overnight parcels of up to 33 kilograms (73 pounds) within Chile and internationally. ChileExpress and LanCourier also offer overnight services between most cities within Chile. None of these companies operates out of resorts.
F Major Services **ChileExpress** ☎ 800/200-102. **DHL** ☎ 800/800-345. **Federal Express** ☎ 2/361-6000. **LanCourier** ☎ 2/699-2104. **TNT & Correos de Chile** ☎ 600/420-4020.

POSTAL RATES

Postage on regular letters and postcards to Canada and the United States costs 250 pesos and 230 pesos, respectively. The postage to Australia, the United Kingdom, and New Zealand is 290 pesos for letters and postcards.

RECEIVING MAIL

If you wish to receive a parcel in Chile and don't have a specific address to which it can be sent, then you can have it labeled poste restante and sent to the nearest post office.

SHIPPING PARCELS

A cheap, reliable method for sending parcels is to use the Chilean postal system, which although slow—up to 15 business days—is still reliable for sending packages weighing up to 30 kilograms (73 pounds). **Shipping** a small parcel of 2 kilograms (4 pounds) will cost 10,000 pesos to North America, 15,000 pesos to Europe, and 20,640 pesos to Australia and New Zealand. Express service is also available.

MONEY MATTERS

Credit cards and traveler's checks are accepted in most resorts and in many shops and restaurants in major cities, though you should **always carry some local currency** for minor expenses like taxis and tipping. Once you stray from the beaten path, you can often only pay with pesos.

Typically you will pay 700 pesos for a cup of coffee, 1,100 pesos for a glass of beer in a bar, 1,000 pesos for a ham sandwich, 600 pesos for a one-mile taxi ride in Santiago, and 800 pesos for an average museum admission.

Prices throughout this guide are given for adults. Substantially reduced fees are sometimes available for children, students, and senior citizens. For information on taxes, *see* Taxes.

ATMS

ATMs are widely available, and you can get cash with a Cirrus- or Plus-linked debit card or with a major credit card. Most ATMs in Chile have a special screen—accessed after entering your PIN code—for foreign-account withdrawals. In this case, merely selecting a "cash withdrawal" won't work—you need to access your account first via the "foreign client" option. Although ATM fees may be higher than back home, Cirrus and Plus offer excellent exchange rates because they are based on wholesale rates offered only by major banks.

Before leaving home, **make sure that your credit cards have been programmed for ATM use in Chile.** You may want to ask your bank about getting a debit card, which works like a bank card but can be used at any ATM displaying a MasterCard or Visa logo.
F ATM Locations **MasterCard Cirrus** ☎ 800/424-7787 ⊕ www.mastercard.com. **Visa Plus** ☎ 800/843-7587 ⊕ www.visa.com.

CREDIT CARDS

Credit cards are widely accepted in hotels, restaurants, and shops in most cities and tourist destinations. Fewer establishments accept credit cards in more rural areas. It may be easier to **use your credit card whenever possible.** The exchange rate only varies by a fraction of a cent, so you won't need to worry about whether your purchase is charged on the day of purchase or at some point in the future. Note, however that you may get a slightly better deal if you pay with cash.

Throughout this guide, the following abbreviations are used: **AE,** American Express; **DC,** Diners Club; **MC,** MasterCard; and **V,** Visa.

Reporting Lost Cards **American Express** ☎ 801/964-6665 in the U.S. **MasterCard** ☎ 1230/020-2012 in Chile (no carrier required). **Visa** ☎ 1230/020-2136 in Chile (no carrier required).

CURRENCY

The peso ($) is the unit of currency in Chile. Chilean bills are issued in 1,000, 2,000, 5,000, 10,000, and 20,000 pesos (some 500-peso bills are still in circulation); coins come in units of 1, 5, 10, 50, 100, and 500 pesos. Note that acquiring change for larger bills, especially from small shopkeepers, can be difficult. Make sure to **get smaller bills** when you exchange money. Always **check exchange rates** in your local newspaper for the most current information; at press time the exchange rate was approximately 463 pesos to the Australian dollar, 524 pesos to the Canadian dollar, 708 pesos to the U.S. dollar, 1,157 pesos to the British pound, and 411 pesos to the New Zealand dollar.

CURRENCY EXCHANGE

For the most favorable rates, **change money through banks.** Although ATM transaction fees may be higher abroad than at home, ATM rates are excellent because they're based on wholesale rates offered only by major banks. You won't do as well at exchange booths in airports or rail and bus stations, in hotels, in restaurants, or in stores. To avoid lines at airport exchange booths, **get a bit of local currency before you leave home.**

Exchange Services **International Currency Express** ✉ 427 N. Camden Dr., Suite F, Beverly Hills, CA 90210 ☎ 888/278-6628 orders 🖷 310/278-6410 ⊕ www.foreignmoney.com. **Thomas Cook Currency Services** ☎ 800/287-7362 orders and retail locations ⊕ www.us.thomascook.com.

TRAVELER'S CHECKS

Do you need traveler's checks? It depends on where you're headed. If you're going to rural areas and small towns, go with cash; traveler's checks are best used in cities. Lost or stolen checks can usually be replaced within 24 hours. To ensure a speedy refund, buy your own traveler's checks—don't let someone else pay for them: irregularities like this can cause delays. The person who bought the checks should make the call to request a refund.

Note that some banks will not convert traveler's checks in U.S. dollars into pesos (though this is usually not a problem at casas de cambio), so you may want to order your traveler's checks in pesos.

PACKING

For a trip to Chile you'll need to **pack for all seasons**—no matter what time of year you're traveling. For sightseeing and leisure, casual clothing and good walking shoes are both desirable and appropriate. Travel in the forests requires long-sleeve shirts, long pants, socks, sneakers, a hat, a light waterproof jacket, a bathing suit, and insect repellent. Light colors are best, since mosquitoes avoid them. If you're visiting Patagonia or the Andes, bring a jacket and sweater or a fleece pullover. A high-factor sunscreen is essential at all times, especially in the far south where the ozone layer is much depleted.

Other useful items include a screw-top water bottle that you can fill with bottled water, a money pouch, a travel flashlight and extra batteries, a Swiss Army knife with a bottle opener, a medical kit, binoculars, and a pocket calculator to help with currency conversions. A sarong or light cotton blanket can have many uses: beach towel, picnic blanket, and cushion for hard seats, among other things. You can never have too many large resealable plastic bags, which are ideal for storing film, protecting things from rain and damp, and quarantining stinky socks.

In your carry-on luggage, **pack an extra pair of eyeglasses or contact lenses and enough of any medication** you take to last a few days longer than the entire trip. You may also ask your doctor to write a spare prescription using the drug's generic name, as brand names may vary from country to country. In luggage to be checked, **never**

pack prescription drugs, valuables, or undeveloped film. And don't forget to carry with you the addresses of offices that handle refunds of lost traveler's checks. Check *Fodor's How to Pack* (available at on-line retailers and bookstores everywhere) for more tips.

To avoid customs and security delays, carry medications in their original packaging. Don't pack any sharp objects in your carry-on luggage, including knives of any size or material, scissors, and corkscrews, or anything else that might arouse suspicion.

To avoid having your checked luggage chosen for hand inspection, don't cram bags full. The U.S. Transportation Security Administration suggests packing shoes on top and placing personal items you don't want touched in clear plastic bags.

CHECKING LUGGAGE

You're allowed to carry aboard one bag and one personal article, such as a purse or a laptop computer. Make sure what you carry on fits under your seat or in the overhead bin. Get to the gate early, so you can board as soon as possible, before the overhead bins fill up.

Baggage allowances vary by carrier, destination, and ticket class. On international flights, you're usually allowed to check two bags weighing up to 70 pounds (32 kilograms) each, although a few airlines allow checked bags of up to 88 pounds (40 kilograms) in first class. Some international carriers don't allow more than 66 pounds (30 kilograms) per bag in business class and 44 pounds (20 kilograms) in economy. On domestic flights, the limit may be 50 pounds (23 kilograms) per bag. Most airlines won't accept bags that weigh more than 100 pounds (45 kilograms) on domestic or international flights. Check baggage restrictions with your carrier before you pack.

Airline liability for baggage is limited to $2,500 per person on flights within the United States. On international flights it amounts to $9.07 per pound or $20 per kilogram for checked baggage (roughly $640 per 70-pound bag) and $400 per passenger for unchecked baggage. You can buy additional coverage at check-in for about $10 per $1,000 of coverage, but it

often excludes a rather extensive list of items, shown on your airline ticket.

Before departure, **itemize your bags' contents** and their worth, and label the bags with your name, address, and phone number. (If you use your home address, cover it so potential thieves can't see it readily.) Include a label inside each bag and **pack a copy of your itinerary.** At check-in, **make sure each bag is correctly tagged** with the destination airport's three-letter code. Because some checked bags will be opened for hand inspection, the U.S. Transportation Security Administration recommends that you leave luggage unlocked or use the plastic locks offered at check-in. TSA screeners place an inspection notice inside searched bags, which are re-sealed with a special lock.

If your bag has been searched and contents are missing or damaged, file a claim with the TSA Consumer Response Center as soon as possible. If your bags arrive damaged or fail to arrive at all, file a written report with the airline before leaving the airport.

🔲 Complaints **U.S. Transportation Security Administration Consumer Response Center** ☎ 866/289-9673 ⊕ www.tsa.gov.

PASSPORTS & VISAS

When traveling internationally, **carry your passport** even if you don't need one (it's always the best form of I.D.) and **make two photocopies of the data page** (one for someone at home and another for you, carried separately from your passport). While traveling in Chile you might want to carry the copy of your passport and leave the original in your hotel safe. However, if you plan on paying by credit card you will often be asked to show identification. If you lose your passport, promptly call the nearest embassy or consulate and the local police.

U.S. passport applications for children under age 14 require consent from both parents or legal guardians; both parents must appear together to sign the application. If only one parent appears, he or she must submit a written statement from the other parent authorizing passport issuance for the child. A parent with sole authority must present evidence of it when applying; acceptable documentation includes the child's certified birth certificate listing only the applying parent, a court order specifically permitting this parent's travel with the child, or a death certificate for the non-applying parent. Application forms and instructions are available on the Web site of the U.S. State Department's Bureau of Consular Affairs (⊕ www.travel.state.gov).

ENTERING CHILE

Citizens of the United States, Canada, Australia, New Zealand, and the United Kingdom need only a passport to enter Chile for up to three months.

Upon arrival in Chile, you will be given a flimsy piece of paper that is your three-month tourist visa. This has to be handed in when you leave; because getting a new one involves waiting in many lines and a lot of bureaucracy, put it somewhere safe.

PASSPORT OFFICES

The best time to apply for a passport or to renew is in fall and winter. Before any trip, check your passport's expiration date, and, if necessary, renew it as soon as possible.

🇦🇺 Australian Citizens **Passports Australia** ☎ 13-12-32 ⊕ www.passports.gov.au.
🇨🇦 Canadian Citizens **Passport Office** ✉ to mail in applications: 200 Promenade du Portage, Hull, Québec J8X 4B7 ☎ 819/994-3500 or 800/567-6868 ⊕ www.ppt.gc.ca.
🇳🇿 New Zealand Citizens **New Zealand Passports Office** ☎ 0800/22-5050 or 04/474-8100 ⊕ www.passports.govt.nz.
🇬🇧 U.K. Citizens **U.K. Passport Service** ☎ 0870/521-0410 ⊕ www.passport.gov.uk.
🇺🇸 U.S. Citizens **National Passport Information Center** ☎ 900/225-5674 or 900/225-7778 TTY (calls are 55¢ per minute for automated service or $1.50 per minute for operator service); 888/362-8668 or 888/498-3648 TTY (calls are $5.50 each) ⊕ www.travel.state.gov.

SAFETY

Areas frequented by tourists are generally safe, provided you use common sense. Don't wear a money belt or a waist pack, both of which peg you as a tourist. Distribute your cash and any valuables (including your credit cards and passport) among a deep front pocket, an inside jacket or vest pocket, and a hidden money pouch. Do not reach for the money pouch once you're in public.

Wherever you go, **don't wear expensive clothing or flashy jewelry,** and **don't handle money in public. Keep cameras in a secure camera bag,** preferably one with a chain or wire embedded in the strap. Always **remain alert for pickpockets,** and **don't walk alone at night,** especially in the larger cities.

TRAVEL ADVISORIES

Before heading to Chile or any other country in South America, **get the latest travel warnings and advisories.** The U.S. State Department has a 24-hour hot line, a "fax on demand" (just dial the number and follow the instructions) number, and a Web site.

🇫 U.S. Government Advisories **U.S. Department of State** ✉ Overseas Citizens Services Office, Room 4811 N.S., 2201 C St. NW, Washington, DC 20520 ☎ 202/647-5225 for interactive hot line; 301/946-4400 for computer bulletin board 🖷 202/647-3000 for interactive hot line ⊕ www.travel.state.gov.; enclose a self-addressed, stamped, business-size envelope.

WOMEN IN CHILE

Many women travel alone or in groups in Chile with no problems. Chilean men are more subtle in their machismo than men in other South American countries, but it's still an aspect of the culture, and foreign women are considered fair game. Men are apt to misinterpret a casual, informal attitude or friendly behavior.

If you carry a purse, choose one with a zipper and a thick strap that you can drape across your body; adjust the length so that the purse sits in front of you at or above hip level. On buses and in crowded areas, hold purses or handbags close to the body; thieves use knives to slice the bottom of a bag and catch the contents as they fall out. Store only enough money in the purse to cover casual spending, and distribute the rest of your cash hidden on your person.

SENIOR-CITIZEN TRAVEL

There's no reason that active, well-traveled senior citizens (*tercera edad*) shouldn't visit Chile, whether on an independent vacation, an escorted tour, or an adventure vacation. Before you leave home, however, determine what medical services your health insurance will cover outside the

United States; note that Medicare doesn't provide for payment of hospital and medical services outside the United States. If you need additional travel insurance, buy it (⇨ Insurance).

Chile is full of good hotels and competent ground operators who will meet your flights and organize your sightseeing. Few museums and sights have discounts for senior citizens, but it's always worth asking. To qualify for age-related discounts, **mention your senior-citizen status up front** when booking hotel reservations (not when checking out) and before you're seated in restaurants (not when paying the bill). Be sure to have identification on hand. When renting a car, ask about promotional car-rental discounts, which can be cheaper than senior-citizen rates.

🎓 Educational Programs **Elderhostel** ✉ 11 Ave. de Lafayette, Boston, MA 02111-1746 ☎ 877/426-8056; 978/323-4141 international callers; 877/426-2167 TTY 🖷 877/426-2166 ⊕ www.elderhostel.org.

SHOPPING

Handicrafts and wine are probably the most popular purchases by visitors to Chile. Wine boutiques and supermarkets carry a tremendous selection of vintages. Handicrafts from across the country are available at craft markets around Santiago. Generally, most large cities have a craft market selling products from that region, and in summer many host open-air markets in which vendors gather from across Chile.

It's fine to bargain. Normally you can ask a vendor in a market if he or she will accept 10% less than the listed price, or maybe a little more than 10% if the figure is being rounded down to the nearest 1,000 pesos, especially if you're paying cash. This is also acceptable in shops, which are not averse to giving small discounts for cash (al contado/efectivo) sales.

KEY DESTINATIONS

Temuco, in the Lake District, is known for its Mapuche rugs, ponchos, and jewelry. South of Temuco, in Villarica, you can buy salad bowls, spoons, and other products carved from raulí wood. If it's a warm woolen sweater you're after, head to the island of Chiloé.

Rustic clay pottery in all shapes and sizes is sold along the streets of the small village of Pomaire, 70 km (43 mi) west of Santiago. In the city of La Serena, in El Norte Chico, you can buy Diaguita-style ceramics (often with intricate geometric patterns) and trinkets made from combabalita, a local marble.

Santiago, however, sells the best selection of Diaguita-style ceramics as well as lapis lazuli products and Chilean copper bowls and pewter ware.

WATCH OUT

Any item more than 100 years old is categorized as an antique, and though enforcement is spotty you are generally required to obtain special permission to remove antiques from the country. If you have purchased or wish to purchase something and are unsure as to whether it, be it a book, painting, or other item, could be considered an antique, you will need to contact the Biblioteca National, Museo Nacional Bellas Artes, or Monumentos Nacionales, respectively. They will provide the necessary authorization in order for you to take your purchase out of the country.

📚 **Biblioteca National** ☎ 2/360-5239. **Museo Nacional Bellas Artes** ☎ 2/633-0655. **Monumentos Nacionales** ☎ 2/420-2008.

STUDENTS IN CHILE

Although airfares to and within South America are high, you can take buses in Chile for mere dollars, and you can usually find safe, comfortable, affordable accommodations for a fraction of what it might cost back home. You can sometimes get student discounts at museums and sights, though you're usually required to show an I.D. Many cities, especially Santiago and Valparaíso, have vibrant student populations.

🎓 I.D.s & Services **STA Travel** ✉ 10 Downing St., New York, NY 10014 ☎ 212/627-3111 or 800/777-0112 🖷 212/627-3387 ⊕ www.sta.com. **Travel Cuts** ✉ 187 College St., Toronto, Ontario M5T 1P7, Canada ☎ 416/979-2406; 800/592-2887; 866/246-9762 in Canada 🖷 416/979-8167 ⊕ www.travelcuts.com.

TAXES

An 18% value-added tax (VAT, called IVA here) is added to the cost of most goods and services in Chile; often you won't notice because it's included in the price. When it's not, the seller gives you the price plus IVA. At many hotels you may receive an exemption from the IVA if you pay in American dollars or traveler's checks; some also offer this discount if you use an American Express card.

TELEPHONES

To dial a local or international number from any phone, you first dial the three-digit number of the carrier you want to use. Then dial 0, followed by the country code, the area or city code, and the phone number. Price differences among carriers can be large; to verify rates, dial the carrier's number, followed by 123.

Phone Carriers Bellsouth ☎ 181. **Carrier 120** ☎ 120. **Carrier 155** ☎ 155. **Chilesat** ☎ 171. **Entel** ☎ 123. **Mundo Telefónica** ☎ 188. **Telefónica del Sur** ☎ 121. **Transam** ☎ 113.

AREA & COUNTRY CODES

The country code for Chile is 56. When dialing a Chilean number from abroad, drop the initial 0 from the local area code. The area code is 2 for Santiago, 58 for Arica, 55 for Antofagasta and San Pedro de Atacama, 42 for Chillán, 57 for Iquique, 56 for La Serena, 65 for Puerto Montt, 61 for Puerto Natales and Punta Arenas, 45 for Temuco, 63 for Valdivia, 32 for Valparaíso and Viña del Mar.

From Chile the country code is 01 for the United States and Canada, 061 for Australia, 064 for New Zealand, and 044 for the United Kingdom.

DIRECTORY & OPERATOR ASSISTANCE

You can reach directory assistance in Chile by calling 103. English-speaking operators are not available.

INTERNATIONAL CALLS

An international call at a public phone requires anywhere from a 400- or 500-peso deposit (depending on the phone box), which will give you anywhere between 47 and 66 seconds of talking time. You can call the United States for between 39 and 76 seconds (depending on the carrier you use) for 200 pesos.

LOCAL CALLS

A 100-peso piece is required to make a local call in a public phone booth, allowing 110 seconds of conversation between the hours of 9 AM and 8 PM, and 160 seconds of talk from 8 PM to 9 AM. Prefix codes are not needed for local dialing.

To call a cell phone within Chile you will need to insert 200 pesos in a phone box.

LONG-DISTANCE SERVICES

AT&T, MCI, and Sprint access codes make calling long-distance relatively convenient, but you may find the local access number blocked in many hotel rooms. First ask the hotel operator to connect you. If the hotel operator balks, ask for an international operator, or dial the international operator yourself. One way to improve your odds of getting connected to your long-distance carrier is to travel with more than one company's calling card (a hotel may block Sprint, for example, but not MCI). If all else fails, call from a pay phone.

Access Codes AT&T Direct ☎ 800/225-288. **MCI Worldcom** ☎ 800/444-4444. **Sprint Express** ☎ 800/793-1153.

PHONE CARDS

If you plan to call abroad while in Chile, it's in your best interest to buy a local phone card (sold in varying amounts at kiosks and calling centers) or use a calling center (*centro de llamadas*). For calls to the United States, EntelTicket phone cards, available in denominations of 1,000, 3,000, and 5,000 pesos, are the best deal. Regular phone cards cost about a dollar a minute; the EntelTicket costs about 25¢ a minute.

PUBLIC PHONES

Having numerous telephone companies means that Chilean public phones all look different. Public phones use either coins (and require a 100-peso deposit) or phone cards. Telefónica and other companies sell telephone cards, but many locals continue to use coins. If you will only be making a few local calls, it's not necessary to purchase a phone card.

Most city areas have standing phone booths, but phones are also found at restaurants, calling centers, and even newsstands. You may have to wait several seconds after picking up the receiver before a steady humming sound signals that you may dial. After dialing, you'll hear a characteristic beep-beep as your call goes through; then there's a pause, followed by a long tone signaling that the other phone is ringing. A busy signal is similar but repeats itself with no pause in between. Most public phones allow you to make several calls in succession, provided you don't hang up in between: there's a special button to push—marked with an R—that cuts off one call and starts another. Some phones also include English-language instructions, accessed by pressing a button marked with a flag icon.

Instead of using a public phone, you can pay a little more and use a *centro de llamadas,* small phone shops divided into booths. The number is dialed for you. For this service you pay an additional charge.

TIME

Chile is one hour ahead of Eastern Standard Time and four hours ahead of Pacific Standard Time. Daylight savings time in Chile begins in October and ends in March.

TIPPING

The usual tip, or *propina,* in restaurants is 10%. Leave more if you really enjoyed the service. City taxi drivers don't usually expect a tip because most own their cabs. However, if you hire a taxi to take you around a city, you should consider giving a good tip. Hotel porters should be tipped at least 800 pesos. Also give doormen and ushers about 800 pesos. Beauty- and barber-shop personnel generally get around 5%.

TOURS & PACKAGES

Because everything is prearranged on a prepackaged tour or independent vacation, you spend less time planning—and often get it all at a good price.

BOOKING WITH AN AGENT

Travel agents are excellent resources. But it's a good idea to collect brochures from several agencies, as some agents' suggestions may be influenced by relationships with tour and package firms that reward them for volume sales. If you have a special interest, **find an agent with expertise in that area**; the American Society of Travel Agents (ASTA; ⇨ Travel Agencies) has a database of specialists worldwide.

Make sure your travel agent knows the accommodations and other services of the place being recommended. Ask about the hotel's location, room size, beds, and whether it has a pool, room service, or programs for children, if you care about these. Has your agent been there in person or sent others whom you can contact?

Do some homework on your own, too: local tourism boards can provide information about lesser-known and small-niche operators, some of which may sell only direct.

BUYER BEWARE

Each year consumers are stranded or lose their money when tour operators—even large ones with excellent reputations—go out of business. So **check out the operator.** Ask several travel agents about its reputation, and try to **book with a company that has a consumer-protection program.** (Look for information in the company's brochure.) In the United States, members of the National Tour Association and the United States Tour Operators Association are required to set aside funds to cover payments and travel arrangements in the event that the company defaults. It's also a good idea to choose a company that participates in the American Society of Travel Agents' Tour Operator Program; ASTA will act as mediator in any disputes between you and your tour operator.

Remember that the more your package or tour includes, the better you can predict the ultimate cost of your vacation. Make sure you know exactly what is covered, and **beware of hidden costs.** Are taxes, tips, and transfers included? Entertainment and excursions? These can add up.

Tour-Operator Recommendations American Society of Travel Agents (⇨ Travel Agencies). **National Tour Association** (NTA) ✉ 546 E. Main St., Lexington, KY 40508 ☎ 859/226-4444 or 800/682-8886 🖷 859/226-4404 🌐 www.ntaonline.com. **United States Tour Operators Association** (USTOA) ✉ 275 Madison Ave., Suite 2014, New York, NY 10016 ☎ 212/599-6599 or 800/468-7862 🖷 212/599-6744 🌐 www.ustoa.com.

TRAIN TRAVEL

Good train service is a thing of the past in Chile, though there is still limited service from Santiago to points south. For information on service from Santiago to Nos, Rancagua, San Fernando, Chillán, and other destinations, *see* Santiago A to Z *in* Chapter 1.

There are daily departures between Santiago and Temuco, but be prepared for frequent delays and a painfully slow journey—if the train runs according to schedule it should take around 12 hours. You can travel overnight in a dormitory car with old-fashioned beds or in a compartment that sleeps two. Reservations, which can be made in Santiago at the Estación Central or at the Estación Metro Universidad de Chile, are recommended.

TRANSPORTATION AROUND CHILE

Distances are great in Chile, so if you're just going to spend one or two weeks here, it's best to fly to your destinations. If you have more time to spare, consider using buses, which are both cheap and dependable.

However, if you really want to get to know Chile well—aside from Santiago, where you can get around on foot, hop on the excellent metro, or take any one of hundreds of taxis—then consider renting a car. If you plan to visit remote regions, such as the Carretera Austral, or a national park, then you'd be better off with a four-wheel-drive vehicle.

TRAVEL AGENCIES

A good travel agent puts your needs first. Look for an agency that has been in business at least five years, emphasizes customer service, and has someone on staff who specializes in your destination. In addition, **make sure the agency belongs to a professional trade organization.** The American Society of Travel Agents (ASTA)—the largest and most influential in the field with more than 20,000 members in some 140 countries—maintains and enforces a strict code of ethics and will step in to help mediate any agent-client disputes involving ASTA members if necessary. ASTA (whose motto is "Without a travel agent, you're on your own") also maintains a Web site that includes a directory of agents. (If a travel agency is also acting as your tour operator, *see* Buyer Beware *in* Tours and Packages.)

Local Agent Referrals **American Society of Travel Agents** (ASTA) 1101 King St., Suite 200, Alexandria, VA 22314 703/739-2782 or 800/965-2782 24-hr hot line 703/739-3268 www.astanet.com. **Association of British Travel Agents** 68-71 Newman St., London W1T 3AH 020/7637-2444 020/7637-0713 www.abtanet.com.

Association of Canadian Travel Agents 130 Albert St., Suite 1705, Ottawa, Ontario K1P 5G4 613/237-3657 613/237-7052 www.acta.ca. **Australian Federation of Travel Agents** Level 3, 309 Pitt St., Sydney, NSW 2000 02/9264-3299 02/9264-1085 www.afta.com.au. **Travel Agents' Association of New Zealand** Level 5, Tourism and Travel House, 79 Boulcott St., Box 1888, Wellington 6001 04/499-0104 04/499-0786 www.taanz.org.nz.

VISITOR INFORMATION

The national tourist office Sernatur (Servicio Nacional de Turismo) has branches in Santiago and in major tourist destinations around the country. Sernatur offices, often the best source for general information about a region, are generally open daily from 9 to 6, with lunch generally from 2 to 3.

Municipal tourist offices, often located near a central square, usually have better information about their town's sights, restaurants, and lodging. Many have shorter hours or close altogether during low season, however.

Learn more about foreign destinations by checking government-issued travel advisories and country information. For a broader picture, consider information from more than one country.

Tourist Information **Sernatur main office** Providencia 1550, Providencia, Santiago 2/731-8336 or 2/731-8337 www.sernatur.cl. Government Advisories **U.S. Department of State** Overseas Citizens Services Office, Room 4811, 2201 C St. NW, Washington, DC 20520 202/647-5225 interactive hot line or 888/407-4747 www.travel.state.gov; enclose a cover letter with your request and a business-size SASE. **Consular Affairs Bureau of Canada** 800/267-6788 or 613/944-6788 www.voyage.gc.ca. **U.K. Foreign and Commonwealth Office** Travel Advice Unit, Consular Division, Old Admiralty Building, London SW1A 2PA 020/7008-0232 or 020/7008-0233 www.fco.gov.uk/travel. **Australian Department of Foreign Affairs and Trade** 02/6261-1299 Consular Travel Advice Faxback Service www.dfat.gov.au. **New Zealand Ministry of Foreign Affairs and Trade** 04/439-8000 www.mft.govt.nz.

WEB SITES

Do check out the World Wide Web when planning your trip. You'll find everything from weather forecasts to virtual tours of famous cities. Be sure to **visit Fodors.com**

(⊕ www.fodors.com), a complete travel-planning site. You can research prices and book plane tickets, hotel rooms, rental cars, vacation packages, and more. In addition, you can post your pressing questions in the Travel Talk section. Other planning tools include a currency converter and weather reports, and there are loads of links to travel resources.

On Spanish-language sites, watch for the name of the country, region, state, or city in which you have an interest. The search terms for "look," "find," and "get" are *mirar* and *buscar* in Spanish. "Next" and "last" (as in "next/last 10") are *próximo* and *último/anterior* in Spanish. Keep an eye out for such words as *turismo* (tourism), *turístico* (tourist-related), *hoteles* (hotels), *hospedajes* (hotel-like accommodation), *residenciales* (guest houses),

restaurantes (restaurants), *gobierno* (government), *estado* (state), *región* (administrative region), *ciudad* (city), *carabinero* (police officer), and *municipalidad* (town hall).

The following sites are good places to start a search (unless otherwise noted, these sites have information in English): ⊕ www.gochile.cl has travel information and on-line booking, ⊕ www.chilnet.cl has business listings, ⊕ www.santiagotimes.cl is an on-line English-language newspaper, and ⊕ www.winesofchile.com is a site for true oenophiles. For Spanish speakers, ⊕ www.granvalparaiso.cl serves as a guide to Valparaíso with articles on current national issues. Also in Spanish, ⊕ www.emol.com is the on-line edition of the national newspaper *El Mercurio*.

SANTIAGO

(1)

FODOR'S CHOICE

Aquí Está Coco, restaurant in Providencia
Azul Profundo, restaurant in Bellavista
Bristol, restaurant in Santiago Centro
Hotel Plaza San Francisco, Santiago Centro
Museo de Arte Precolombino, Santiago Centro

HIGHLY RECOMMENDED

RESTAURANTS Anakena, Las Condes
Bice, Las Condes
Como Agua Para Chocolate, Bellavista
Donde Augusto, Santiago Centro
La Esquina al Jerez, Bellavista
Restorán Don Peyo, Nuñoa
El Venezia, Bellavista

HOTELS Carrera, Santiago Centro
City Hotel, Santiago Centro
Hotel Orly, Providencia
Hyatt Regency, Las Condes
Residencial Londres, Santiago Centro
Sheraton Santiago, Providencia

SIGHTS La Chascona, Pablo Neruda's house in Bellavista
Estación Mapocho, train station in Parque Forestal
Iglesia San Francisco, church in La Alameda
Museo Artequín, Parque Quinta Normal
Museo de Artes Visuales, Parque Forestal
Plaza de Armas, Santiago Centro
Plaza de la Constitución, La Alameda

Many other great hotels and restaurants enliven this area. For other favorites, look for the black stars as you read this chapter.

By Michael de Zayas

Updated by Cheryl Stanton

WHEN IT WAS FOUNDED by Spanish conquistador Pedro de Valdivia in 1541, Santiago was little more than the triangular patch of land embraced by two arms of the Río Mapocho. Today that area, known as Santiago Centro, is just one of 32 *comunas* that make up the city, each with its own distinct personality. You'd never mistake Patronato, a neighborhood north of downtown filled with Moorish-style mansions built by families who made their fortunes in textiles, with Providencia, where the modern skyscrapers built by international corporations crowd the avenues. The chic shopping centers of Las Condes have little in common with the outdoor markets in Bellavista.

Perhaps the neighborhoods have retained their individuality because many have histories as old as Santiago itself. Nuñoa, for example, was a hardworking farm town to the east. Farther away was El Arrayán, a sleepy village in the foothills of the Andes. As the capital grew, these and many other communities were drawn inside the city limits. If you ask Santiaguinos you meet today where they reside, they are just as likely to mention their neighborhood as their city.

Like many of the early Spanish settlements, Santiago suffered some severe setbacks. Six months after the town was founded, a group of the indigenous Picunche people attacked, burning every building to the ground. Undeterred, the Spanish rebuilt in the same spot. The narrow streets that radiated out then from the Plaza de Armas are the same ones that can be seen today.

The Spanish lost interest in Santiago after about a decade, moving south in search of gold. But fierce resistance from the Mapuche people in 1599 forced many settlers to retreat to Santiago. The population swelled, solidifying the city's claim as the region's colonial capital. Soon many of the city's landmarks, including the colorful Casa Colorada, were erected.

It wasn't until after Chile finally won its independence from Spain in 1818 that Santiago took the shape it has today. Broad avenues extended in every direction. Buildings befitting a national capital, such as the Congreso Nacional and the Teatro Municipal, won wide acclaim. Parque Quinta Normal and Parque O'Higgins preserved huge swaths of green for the people, and the poplar-lined Parque Forestal gave the increasingly proud populace a place to promenade.

Santiago today is home to almost 6 million people—nearly a third of the country's total population. It continues to spread outward to the so-called *barrios altos* (upper neighborhoods) east of the center. It's also growing upward, as new office towers transform the skyline. Yet in many ways, Santiago still feels like a small town, where residents are always likely to bump into an acquaintance along the city center's crowded streets and bustling plazas.

EXPLORING SANTIAGO

Pedro de Valdivia wasn't very creative when he mapped out the streets of Santiago. He stuck to the same simple grid pattern you'll find in almost all of the colonial towns along the coast. The city didn't grow much larger before the meandering Río Mapocho impeded these plans. You may be surprised, however, at how orderly the city remains. It's difficult to get lost wandering around downtown.

Running through the center is the city's major thoroughfare, Avenida Libertador Bernardo O'Higgins, better known as the Alameda. East of Plaza Baquedano, the Alameda turns into Avenida Providencia, where

If you have 3 days

Santiago is a compact city, small enough that you can visit all the must-see sights in a few days. Consider the weather when planning your itinerary—on the first clear day your destination should be Parque Metropolitano, where you'll be treated to exquisite views from Cerro San Cristóbal. After a morning gazing at the Andes, head back down the hill and spend the afternoon wandering the bohemian streets of Bellavista, with a visit to Nobel laureate Pablo Neruda's Santiago residence, La Chascona. Check out one of the neighborhood's colorful eateries.

The next day, head to Parque Forestal, a leafy park that runs along the Río Mapocho. Be sure to visit the lovely old train station, the Estación Mapocho. After lunch at the Mercado Central, uncover the city's colonial past in Santiago Centro. Requisite sights include the Plaza de Armas, around which you'll find the Casa Colorada and the Museo de Arte Precolombino. Stop for tea in the afternoon at a quaint café in Plaza Mulato Gil de Castro. On the third day explore the sights along the Alameda, especially the presidential palace of La Moneda and the landmark church, Iglesia San Francisco. For a last look at the city, climb Cerro Santa Lucía. That night put on your chicest outfit for dinner in the trendy neighborhood of Providencia or Las Condes.

If you have 5 days

In addition to the above itinerary, you may want to spend the good part of a day exploring the area around Parque Quinta Normal, where you can relax with a picnic while watching children scurry about flying kites. Ask your concierge to make reservations for a show that evening at the stunning Teatro Municipal. On the fifth day make a reservation for lunch at one of Chile's best wineries, Viña Santa Rita. If you're a fan of Chile's most famous export, spend the rest of the day touring the vineyards just south of Santiago. You'll undoubtedly find a few bottles to take back home. Treat yourself to dinner in Vitacura, where the dining district known as Borde Río offers just about every type of food imaginable.

If you have 7 days

With a few extra days, you have plenty of time to head to the hills. Skiers should hit the slopes of nearby Valle Nevado, or travel a little farther north to the more exclusive resort of Portillo. If you're visiting the area during the few months when there isn't any snow, take a drive through the Cajón del Maipo. Hike up to the glacier below the El Morado peak or soak in the hot springs of Baños de Colina, which, although not easy to reach, are worth the journey.

---

you'll find an upscale shopping district. After this it becomes Avenida Apoquindo, full of high-rise apartment blocks, and farther along it turns into Avenida Las Condes.

Much of the city, especially communities such as Bellavista and Providencia, is best explored on foot. The subway is probably the quickest, cleanest, and most economical way to shuttle between neighborhoods. To travel to more distant neighborhoods, or to get anywhere in the evening after the subway closes, you'll probably want to hail a taxi.

About the Restaurants

Dining is one of Santiago's great pleasures, and one of its most afford-able delectations. Everything from fine restaurants to informal *picadas,* restaurants that specialize in typical Chilean food, is spread across the city. Menus run the gamut of international cuisines, but don't miss the local bounty—seafood delivered directly from the Pacific Ocean. You can't beat a plate of fresh fish at Mercado Central, the city's bustling market.

Lunch and dinner are served later than in many places—2 PM for lunch, 8 or 9 PM for dinner. People do dress smartly for dinner, but a coat and tie are rarely necessary.

About the Hotels

Santiago has more than a dozen five-star hotels, many of them in the burgeoning Providencia and Las Condes neighborhoods. With the in-creased popularity of Chile as a travel destination, most major inter-national chains are represented here. You won't find better service than at newer hotels such as the lavish Sheraton Santiago. But don't write off the old standbys. The Carrera, which has been around for decades, is still one of Santiago's finest luxury hotels. Inexpensive small hotels, especially near the city center, are harder to find, but they do exist.

All the construction in the past decade means competition between ho-tels is heated. You can often find a room for considerably less than the advertised high-season rates.

Timing

Santiaguinos tend to abandon their city every summer during the school holidays that run from the end of December to early March. February is a particularly popular vacation time, when nearly everybody who's anybody is out of town. If you're not averse to the heat this can be a good time for walking around the city; otherwise spring and fall are bet-ter choices, as the weather is more comfortable. Spring and fall are also good times to drive through the Cajón del Maipo, when the scenery is at its peak. Winters in the city aren't especially cold—temperatures rarely dip below freezing—but days are gray and gloomy. Ski season, depending on the resort, runs mid-June through mid-September. Good weather conditions, however, mean six-month-long seasons beginning in May and ending in October.

Santiago Centro

Shiny new skyscrapers may be sprouting up in neighborhoods to the east, but Santiago Centro is the place to start if you really want to take the pulse of the city. After all, this is the historic heart of Santiago. All the major traffic arteries cross here—creating the usual traffic headaches—and all the subway lines converge here before whisking riders out to the suburbs. In Santiago Centro you'll find interesting museums, imposing government buildings, and bustling commercial streets. But don't think you'll be lost in a sprawling area—it takes only about 10 minutes to walk from one edge of the neighborhood to the other.

Numbers in the text correspond to numbers in the margins and on the Santiago Centro & La Alameda map.

a good
walk

To really know Santiago, get acquainted with the **Plaza de Armas** ① ▶. Across Calle Catedral is a block-long threesome of historic buildings, centered by the the Palacio de la Real Audiencia, at one time the coun-try's highest court and currently home to the **Museo Histórico Nacional** ②. To the west of the museum is the whitewashed **Correo Central** ③; to the

Shopping

In Santiago's markets you can easily find fresh produce, fine woolen items, and handicrafts from across the country. Trendy boutiques line the streets of Providencia and Vitacura, and luxury department stores in modern shopping malls lure dedicated shoppers to Las Condes. Keep an eye out for lapis lazuli—Chile is one of only three countries that produce this lovely stone, and the jewelers of Santiago show it off in every type of setting imaginable.

Wineries

Santiago nestles in the Maipo Valley, the country's oldest wine-growing district. Some of Chile's largest and best wineries—Concha y Toro, Cousiño-Macul, and Santa Rita—are within an hour's drive of the city. November to March is the best time to visit if you want to see the wine-making process. The *vendimia*, or annual harvest, takes place in late February and early March.

---

east is the **Municipalidad de Santiago** ④. The **Catedral** ⑤, twice destroyed by earthquakes and once by fire before the current neoclassical structure was completed in the 18th century, looms over the western end of the plaza. A motley assortment of commercial arcades completes the fringes of the square, adding a touch of modernity to one of the city's most traditional neighborhoods.

On the southeast corner of the Plaza de Armas on Calle Merced stands the attractive **Edificio Comercial Edwards** ⑥; just to the east along Calle Merced is a beautifully restored colonial mansion called the **Casa Colorada** ⑦. The **Museo de Arte Precolombino** ⑧ is two blocks west of Casa Colorada on the corner of Calle Compañía and Calle Bandera. Across the street stands Chile's lordly **Palacio de los Tribunales de Justicia** ⑨. Encompassing an entire city block to the north is the **Ex Congreso Nacional** ⑩ and its gated gardens, providing refuge from the hustle and bustle of Santiago Centro.

TIMING The walk itself should take less than an hour. If you explore a few museums, wander around the squares, and rest here and there, this itinerary could take a full morning. Each of the small museums on this route should take about 45 minutes to see thoroughly.

What to See

❼ **Casa Colorada.** The appropriately named Red House is one of the best-preserved colonial structures in the city. Mateo de Toro y Zambrano, Santiago's most prosperous businessman of the 18th century, once made his home here. The building today houses the Museo de Santiago, a modest but informative museum that makes an excellent place to dive into the city's history. For an explanation of the exhibits, ask for an English guidebook. ✉ *Merced 860, Santiago Centro* ☎ *2/633–0723* 🎫 *Tues.–Sat. 500 pesos, Sun. free* 🕐 *Tues.–Fri. 10–6, Sat. 10–5, Sun. 11–2* Ⓜ *Plaza de Armas.*

❺ **Catedral.** Conquistador Pedro de Valdivia declared in 1541 that a house of worship would be constructed at this site bordering the Plaza de Armas. The first adobe building burned to the ground, and the structures that replaced it were destroyed by the earthquakes of 1647 and 1730. The finishing touches of the neoclassical cathedral standing today were added in 1789 by Italian architect Joaquín Toesca. Be sure to see the

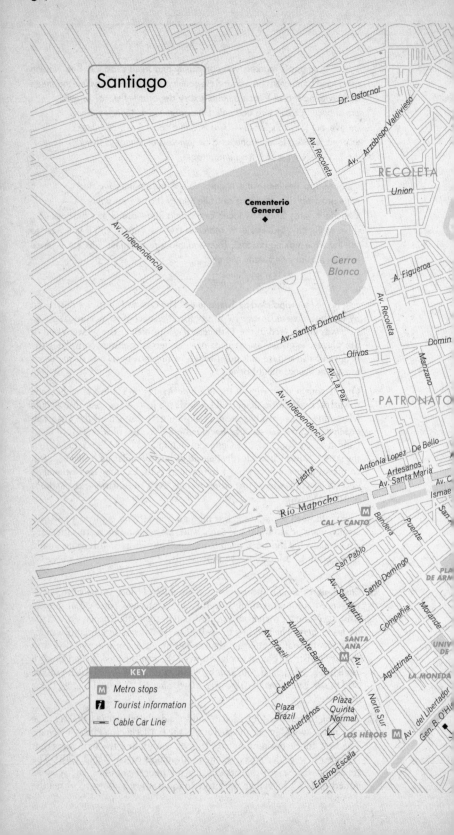

6

Santiago

Cementerio General ♦

Cerro Blanco

RECOLETA

Union

Dr. Ostornol

Av. Recoleta

Av. Arzobispo Valdivieso

A. Figueroa

Av. Recoleta

Av. Santos Dumont

Olivos

Av. La Paz

Domin

Manzano

PATRONATO

Av. Independencia

Av. Independencia

Antonia Lopez - De Bello

Artesanos

Av. Santa María

Av. C

Ismae

Lastra

Río Mapocho

CAL Y CANTO

Bandera

Puente

San

San Pablo

Santo Domingo

Av. San Martín

Compañia

Morande

PLA
DE ARM

Almirante Barroso

Av. Brazil

SANTA
ANA

Av.

Agustinas

UNIV
DE

LA MONEDA

Cathedral

Plaza
Brazil

Huerfanos

Plaza
Quinta
Normal

Norte Sur

Av. del Libertador

Gen. B. O'Hi

↓

LOS HÉROES

Erasmo Escala

KEY	
Ⓜ	Metro stops
🛈	Tourist information
▭▭	Cable Car Line

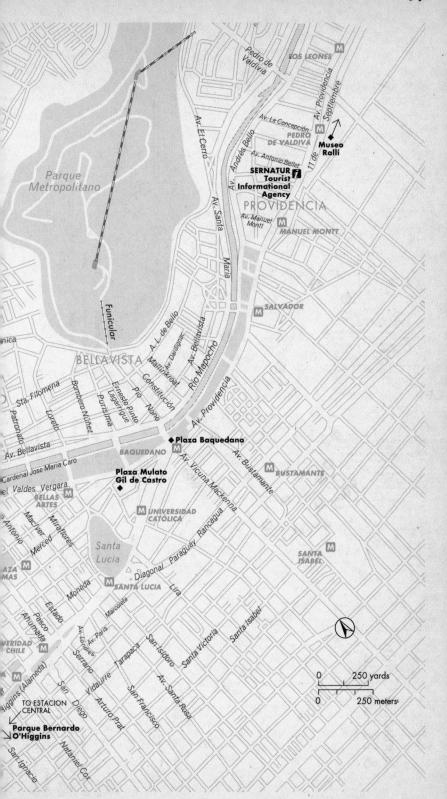

Pedro de Valdivia

LOS LEONES Ⓜ

Av. La Concepción

Av. Providencia

11 de Septiembre

PEDRO
DE VALDIVA

Av. Andrés Bello

Av. Antonio Bellet

**Museo
Ralli**

SERNATUR
Tourist
Informational
Agency

PROVIDENCIA

Av. El Cerro

Av. Manuel
Montt

Av. Santa
María

MANUEL MONTT Ⓜ

Parque
Metropolitano

SALVADOR Ⓜ

Funicular

A. L. de Bello

Av. Dardignac

Av. Bellavista

Río Mapocho

Av. Providencia

Mallinkroat

Constitución

Pío Nono

BELLAVISTA

Sta. Filomena

Ernesto Pinto
Lagarrigue

Purísima

Bombero Núñez

Loreto

Patronato

Av. Bellavista

◆ **Plaza Baquedano**

BAQUEDANO Ⓜ

Cardenal José María Caro

Av. Vicuña Mackenna

Av. Bustamante

BUSTAMANTE Ⓜ

el Valdés Vergara

Plaza Mulato
Gil de Castro
◆

BELLAS
ARTES

Ⓜ

Av. Antonio

MacIver

Miraflores

Merced

Ⓜ **UNIVERSIDAD**
CATÓLICA

Paraguay

Rancagua

Santa
Lucía

SANTA
ISABEL Ⓜ

△ Diagonal

AZA
MAS Ⓜ

SANTA LUCÍA Ⓜ

Moneda

Lira

Marcoleta

Estado

Ahumada

Paseo

△

San Isidoro

Santa Victoria

Santa Isabel

Av. Paris

Av. Londres

ERIDAD
CHILE Ⓜ

Serrano

Vidaurre

Tarapacá

San Diego

Arturo Prat

San Francisco

Av. Santa Rosa

Higgins (Alameda)

TO ESTACION
CENTRAL

↙ **Parque Bernardo**
O'Higgins

San Ignacio

Nataniel Cox

0   250 yards

0   250 meters

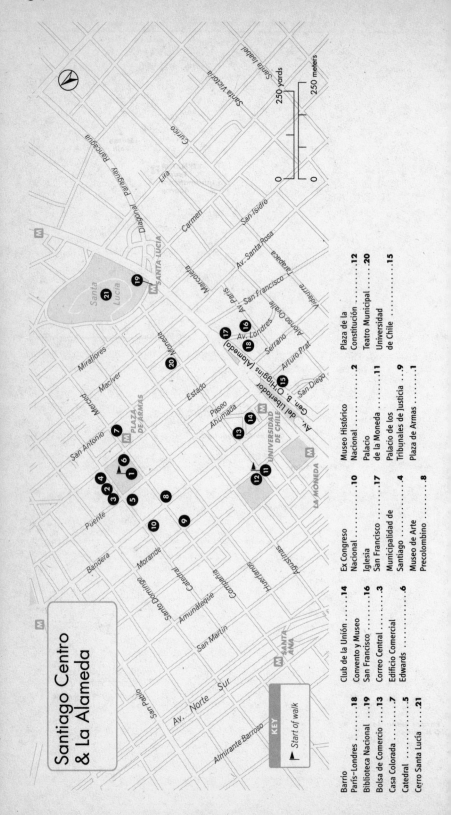

Santiago Centro & La Alameda

Barrio
Paris-Londres **18**

Biblioteca Nacional . . . **19**

Bolsa de Comercio **13**

Casa Colorada **7**

Catedral **5**

Cerro Santa Lucía **21**

Club de la Unión **14**

Convento y Museo
San Francisco **16**

Correo Central **3**

Edificio Comercial
Edwards **6**

Ex Congreso
Nacional **10**

Iglesia
San Francisco **17**

Municipalidad de
Santiago **4**

Museo de Arte
Precolombino **8**

Museo Histórico
Nacional **2**

Palacio
de la Moneda **11**

Palacio de los
Tribunales de Justicia . . . **9**

Plaza de Armas **1**

Plaza de la
Constitución **12**

Teatro Municipal **20**

Universidad
de Chile **15**

stunning interior—a line of gilt arches topped by stained-glass windows parades down the long nave. ⊠ *Plaza de Armas, Santiago Centro* ☎ *2/ 696–2777* ☉ *Daily 9–7* Ⓜ *Plaza de Armas.*

❸ **Correo Central.** Housed in what was once the ornate Palacio de los Gobernadores, this building dating from 1715 is one of the most beautiful post offices you are likely to see. It was reconstructed by Ricardo Brown in 1882 after being ravaged by fire and is a fine example of neoclassical architecture. The third story, which includes an attractive half dome, was added in the early 20th century. ⊠ *Plaza de Armas, Santiago Centro* ☎ *2/698–7274* ⊕ *www.correos.cl* ☉ *Weekdays 8–7, Sat. 8–2* Ⓜ *Plaza de Armas.*

❻ **Edificio Comercial Edwards.** Architect Eugenio Joannon sent the plans for his prized shopping emporium to Paris, where it was prefabricated in cast iron before being shipped back to Santiago and constructed in 1893. Its distinctive glass and blue metallic facades form the corner building on Calle Merced and Calle Estado, overlooking the Plaza de Armas. It still fulfills a commercial role as a shop selling children's clothes. ⊠ *Merced at Estado, Santiago Centro* Ⓜ *Plaza de Armas.*

❿ **Ex Congreso Nacional.** Once the meeting place for the National Congress (the legislature moved to Valparaíso in 1990), this palatial neoclassical building now houses the offices of the Ministry of Foreign Affairs. The original structure on the site, the Iglesia de la Compañía de Jesús, was destroyed by a fire in 1863 in which 2,000 people perished. Inside the peaceful gated gardens is a monument commemorating the victims. ⊠ *Bandera 345, at Morandé, Santiago Centro* Ⓜ *Plaza de Armas.*

❹ **Municipalidad de Santiago.** Today's governmental center for Santiago can be found on the site of the colonial city hall and jail. The original structure, built in 1552, survived until a devastating earthquake in 1730. Joaquín Toesca, the architect who also designed the presidential palace and completed the cathedral, reconstructed the building in 1785, but it was destroyed by fire a century later. In 1891, Eugenio Joannon, who favored an Italian Renaissance style, erected the structure standing today. On the facade hangs an elaborate coat of arms presented by Spain. The interior is not open to the public. ⊠ *Plaza de Armas, Santiago Centro* Ⓜ *Plaza de Armas.*

need a break?

You can shut out the bustle of Santiago Centro in the cool, dim, dark-wood-paneled bar of the **City Hotel** (⊠ Compañía 1063, Santiago Centro ☎ 2/695–4526), close to the Plaza de Armas. Order a coffee, cold beer, or sandwich and look for the regulars—dapper old Santiaguinos who sit at the hotel's well-stocked bar.

❽ **Museo de Arte Precolombino.** If you plan to visit only one museum in Santiago, it should be the Museum of Pre-Columbian Art, a block from the Plaza de Armas. The well-endowed collection of artifacts of Central and South America's indigenous peoples is displayed in a beautifully restored Royal Customs House dating to 1807. The permanent collection, on the upper floor, showcases textiles and ceramics from Mexico to Patagonia. Unlike many of the city's museums, the displays here are well labeled in Spanish and English. ⊠ *Bandera 361, at Av. Compañía, Santiago Centro* ☎ *2/688–7348* ⊕ *www.museoprecolombino.cl* ☞ *Tues.–Sat. 2,000 pesos, Sun. free* ☉ *Tues.–Sat. 10–6, Sun. 10–2* Ⓜ *Plaza de Armas.*

FodorśChoice ★

❷ **Museo Histórico Nacional.** The colonial-era Palacio de la Real Audiencia served as the meeting place of Chile's first Congress in September 1810. The building then functioned as a telegraph office before the museum moved here in 1911. It's worth the small admission charge to see the interior of the 200-year-old structure, where exhibits tracing Chile's history are arranged chronologically in rooms centered around a courtyard. Among the exhibits are large collections of coins, stamps, and traditional handicrafts, including more than 3,000 examples of native textiles. ✉ *Plaza de Armas, Santiago Centro* ☎ *2/633–1815* ⊕ *www. museohistoriconacional.cl* ✆ *Tues.–Sat. 600 pesos, Sun. free* ☉ *Tues.–Sun. 10–5:30* Ⓜ *Plaza de Armas.*

❾ Palacio de los Tribunales de Justicia. During Augusto Pinochet's rule, countless human-rights demonstrations were held outside the Courts of Justice, which house the country's Supreme Court. Protests are still held near this stately neoclassical building a block from the Plaza de Armas, including some in support of the former dictator. In front of the building, perhaps ironically, is a monument celebrating justice and the promulgation of Chile's civil code. ✉ *Bandera 344, Santiago Centro* Ⓜ *Plaza de Armas.*

off the beaten path	**Parque Bernardo O'Higgins.** Named for Chile's national hero, whose troops were victorious against the Spanish, this park has plenty of open space for everything from ball games to military parades. Street vendors sell *volantines* (kites) outside the park year-round; high winds make September and early October the prime kite-flying season. ✉ *Av. Jorge Alessandri Rodríguez between Av. Blanca Encalada and Av. General Rondizzoni, Santiago Centro* ☎ *2/556–1927* ✆ *Free* ☉ *Daily 8–8* Ⓜ *Parque O'Higgins.*

★ ▶ ❶ Plaza de Armas. This square has been the symbolic heart of Chile—as well as its political, social, religious, and commercial center—since Pedro de Valdivia established the city on this spot in 1541. The Palacio de los Gobernadores, the Palacio de la Real Audiencia, and the Municipalidad de Santiago front the square's northern edge. The dignified Catedral graces the western side of the square. Among the palm trees are distinctive fountains and gardens revealing the Chileans' pride about their history. Also here is a bronze well that once served as the city's main source of water. On any given day, the plaza teems with life—vendors selling religious icons, artists painting the activity around them, street performers juggling fire, and tourists clutching guidebooks. In the southern corner of the plaza you can watch people playing chess. ✉ *Calle Compañía and Calle Estado, Santiago Centro* Ⓜ *Plaza de Armas.*

La Alameda

Avenida Libertador Bernardo O'Higgins, more frequently called La Alameda, is the city's principal thoroughfare. Along with the Avenida Norte Sur and the Río Mapocho, it forms the wedge that defines the city's historic district. Many of Santiago's most important buildings, including landmarks such as the Iglesia San Francisco, stand along the avenue. Others, like Teatro Municipal, are just steps away.

a good walk	Unthinkable only a few years ago, today you can walk unescorted into the courtyard of the **Palacio de la Moneda** ⓫ ▶, the nerve center of the Chilean government. Across Calle Moneda you'll find **Plaza de la Constitución** ⓬, a formal square where you can watch the changing of the guard. Walk a block east along Calle Moneda to the cobblestone Calle La Bolsa. On this narrow diagonal street stands the ornate **Bolsa de Comercio** ⓭, the country's stock exchange. A block down, at a dainty fountain, the street turns into Calle Nueva York, where you'll find the **Club de la Unión** ⓮. Across the street is the main building, or casa central, of

the **Universidad de Chile** ⑮. Reach it by crossing under the Universidad de Chile Metro stop, which contains monumental murals depicting Chilean history painted by Mario Toral, part of the fine MetroArte series in all subway stops. Two blocks east are the **Convento y Museo San Francisco** ⑯ and the **Iglesia San Francisco** ⑰. Turn left after exiting Iglesia San Francisco onto Calle Londres and into the **Barrio París-Londres** ⑱. Enjoy a pleasant stroll through this charming area otherwise known as Little Europe. On returning to the Alameda, avoid the crazy drivers by crossing back to the other (north) side via the Santa Lucía Metro station. Directly ahead of you is the **Biblioteca Nacional** ⑲. After leaving the library make a left and then another left. Cross Calle Maciver and then turn right down pedestrian-only German Tenderini to the **Teatro Municipal** ⑳. Head east through Plaza Vicuña Mackenna to survey the entire city from **Cerro Santa Lucía** ㉑.

TIMING &
PRECAUTIONS

The walk itself is fairly short, but it's full of beautiful old buildings where you'll likely want to linger. You could spend an hour alone at the Palacio de la Moneda—try to time your visit with the changing of the guard, which takes place every other day at 10 AM. Across the Alameda, take at least an hour and a half to explore Iglesia San Francisco, the adjacent museum, and the Barrio París-Londres. You could easily spend a bookish half hour perusing the stacks at the Biblioteca Nacional. Plan for an hour or more at Cerro Santa Lucía—don't get here too late, as the hilltop park isn't safe after dark.

What to See

⑱ **Barrio París-Londres.** Many architects contributed to what is frequently referred to as Santiago's Little Europe, among them Alamos, Larraín, and Mönckeberg. The string of small mansion houses lining the cobbled streets of Calles París and Londres sprang up in the mid-1920s on the vegetable patches and gardens that once belonged to the convent adjoining Iglesia San Francisco. The three- and four-story town houses are all unique; some have redbrick facades or terra-cotta-tile roofs, and others are done in Palladian style. ✉ *Calles Londres and París, La Alameda.*

⑲ **Biblioteca Nacional.** Near the foot of Cerro Santa Lucía is the block-long classical facade of the National Library. With more than 3 million titles, this is one of the largest libraries in South America. The vast interior includes arcane collections. The attractive Sala Medina holds the most important collection of prints by native peoples in Latin America. ✉ *Av. O'Higgins 651, La Alameda* ☎ *2/360–5259* 🎫 *Free* ☉ *Weekdays 9–8, Sat. 9–3:30* Ⓜ *Santa Lucía.*

⑬ **Bolsa de Comercio.** Chile's stock exchange is housed in a 1917 French neoclassical structure with an elegant clock tower surmounted by an arched slate cupola. Weekdays you can watch the shouting of traders in the three buying and selling circles called *redondeles.* ✉ *Calle La Bolsa 64, La Alameda* ☎ *2/399–3000* ⊕ *www.bolsadesantiago.com* 🎫 *Free* ☉ *Weekdays noon–1:20 and 4–4:30* Ⓜ *Universidad de Chile.*

need a
break?

Alongside the Bolsa de Comercio runs the narrow cobbled street of La Bolsa. Here you'll find **Kebab, Kebab** (✉ La Bolsa 67, La Alameda ☎ 2/569–0642), a hole-in-the-wall Mediterranean eatery consisting of two tiny rooms, one at street level, the other up a spiral staircase. Sit at the horseshoe-shape bar and order a refreshing carrot juice, followed by a bowl of fresh salad garnished with sizzling kebab meat.

㉑ **Cerro Santa Lucía.** The mazelike park of St. Lucía is a hangout for souvenir vendors, park-bench smoochers, and photo-snapping tourists.

Walking uphill along the labyrinth of interconnected paths and plazas takes about 30 minutes. An elevator two blocks north of the park's main entrance is a little faster, but its schedule is erratic. The crow's nest, reached via a series of steep and slippery stone steps, affords an excellent 360-degree view of the entire city. Be careful near dusk, as the park also attracts the occasional mugger. ⊠ *Santa Lucía and Av. O'Higgins, La Alameda* 🕾 *no phone* ◷ *Oct.–Mar., daily 9–6.30; Apr.–Sept., daily 7–8* Ⓜ *Santa Lucía.*

⓮ **Club de la Unión.** The facade of this neoclassical building, dating to 1925, is one of the city's finest. The interior of this private club, whose roster has included numerous Chilean presidents, is open only to members. ⊠ *Av. O'Higgins at Calle Bandera, La Alameda* Ⓜ *Universidad de Chile.*

⓰ **Convento y Museo San Francisco.** This former convent next to Iglesia San Francisco functions as a religious and colonial art museum: inside is the best collection of 17th-century colonial paintings on the continent, with 54 large-scale canvases portraying the life of St. Francis and a plethora of religious iconography. Most pieces are labeled in Spanish and English. Fans of literature shouldn't miss a small exhibit devoted to Gabriela Mistral, who won the Nobel Prize in 1945 for her poetry about Chile. ⊠ *Londres 4, La Alameda* 🕾 *2/639–8737* 🎟 *1,000 pesos* ◷ *Tues.–Sat. 10–1 and 3–6, Sun. 10–2* Ⓜ *Santa Lucía, Universidad de Chile.*

★ ⓱ **Iglesia San Francisco.** Santiago's oldest structure, greatest symbol, and principal landmark, the Church of St. Francis is the last trace of 16th-century colonial architecture in the city. Construction began in 1586, and although the church survived successive earthquakes, early tremors took their toll and portions had to be rebuilt in 1698. Today's neoclassical tower, which forms the city's most recognizable silhouette, was added in 1857 by architect Fermín Vivaceta. Inside are rough stone-and-brick walls, marble columns, and ornate wood ceilings. Visible on the main altar is the image of the Virgen del Socorro (Virgin of Assistance) that conquistador Pedro de Valdivia carried for protection and guidance. ⊠ *Av. O'Higgins 834, La Alameda* 🕾 *2/638–3238* ◷ *Daily 7 AM–8 PM* Ⓜ *Santa Lucía, Universidad de Chile.*

▶ ⓫ **Palacio de la Moneda.** Originally the royal mint, this sober neoclassical edifice built by Joaquín Toesca in 1805 became the presidential palace in 1846 and served that purpose for more than a century. It was bombarded by the military in the 1973 coup, when Salvador Allende defended his presidency against the assault of General Augusto Pinochet. Allende's death is still shrouded in mystery—some say he went down fighting, others claim he took his own life before the future dictator entered the palace in triumph. The two central courtyards are open to the public, and tours of the interior can be arranged at the reception desk. ⊠ *Plaza de la Constitución, Moneda between Teatinos and Morandé, La Alameda* 🕾 *no phone* ◷ *Daily 10–6* Ⓜ *La Moneda.*

★ ⓬ **Plaza de la Constitución.** Palacio de la Moneda and other government buildings line Constitution Square, the country's most formal plaza. The changing of the guard takes place every other day at 10 AM within the triangle defined by 12 Chilean flags. Adorning the plaza are three monuments, each dedicated to a notable national figure: Diego Portales, founder of the Chilean republic; Jorge Alessandri, the country's leader from 1958 to 1964; and Don Eduardo Frei, president from 1964 to 1970. The plaza also serves as the roof of the underground bunker Pinochet had installed when he "redecorated" La Moneda. Pillars in each of the four corners of the square serve as ventilation ducts for the bunker, which is now a parking lot. Locals joke that these monoliths represent the four founding members of the military junta—they're made of stone, full of hot air, and no one knows their real function. One pillar has been converted into a memorial honoring President Salvador Allende. ⊠ *Moneda and Morande, La Alameda* Ⓜ *La Moneda.*

㉑ Teatro Municipal. The opulent Municipal Theater is the city's cultural center, with performances of opera, ballet, and classical music from April to November. Originally built in 1857, with major renovations in 1870 and 1906 following a fire and an earthquake, the Renaissance-style building is one of the city's most refined monuments. The lavish interior deserves a visit. Tours can be arranged with a week's notice. ⊠ *Plaza Alcade Mekis, Av. Agustinas at Av. San Antonio, La Alameda* ☎ 2/463–8888 Ⓜ *Universidad de Chile, Santa Lucía.*

⑮ Universidad de Chile. The main branch of the University of Chile, the country's largest educational institution, is a symmetrical ocher edifice completed in 1872, when it was known as the University Palace. It's not officially open to the public, but you are free to stroll through the grounds. ⊠ *Av. O'Higgins, La Alameda* Ⓜ *Universidad de Chile.*

Parque Forestal

After building a canal in 1891 to tame the unpredictable Río Mapocho, Santiago found itself with a thin strip of land that it didn't quite know what to do with. The area quickly filled with the city's refuse. A decade later, under the watchful eye of Enrique Cousiño, it was transformed into the leafy Forest Park. It was and still is enormously popular with Santiaguinos. Parque Forestal is the perfect antidote to the spirited Plaza de Armas. The eastern tip, near Plaza Baquedano, is distinguished by the Wagnerian-scale Fuente Alemana (German Fountain), donated by the Germanic community of Santiago. The bronze and stone monolith commemorates the centennial of Chilean Independence.

Numbers in white bullets in the text correspond to numbers in black bullets in the margins and on the Parque Forestal map.

a good walk

Near the park's western edge you'll find the wrought-iron **Mercado Central** ㉒ ☞, the city's fish market. Stroll in the park along the Río Mapocho a block west to reach the former train terminal, the **Estación Mapocho** ㉓. Cross the river and follow your nose to the flower market **Pérgola de las Flores** ㉔. After leaving the flower market, head east on Artesanos and walk until you see the lime-green entrance to the gritty **Vega Chica and Vega Central** ㉕ (the peach-color Vega Central is a full block to the north of Vega Chica).

Strolling east through the Parque Forestal will bring you to the jewel-like **Museo Nacional de Bellas Artes** ㉖ and the adjacent **Museo de Arte Contemporáneo** ㉗. Just south of the park, near where Calle Merced and Calle José Victorino Lastarria meet, is the Plaza Mulato Gil de Castro, a pleasant little nook with bookshops and cafés, as well as the **Museo Arqueológico** ㉘ and the **Museo de Artes Visuales** ㉙.

TIMING & PRECAUTIONS You can have a pleasant, relaxing day strolling through the city's most popular park, losing yourself in the art museums, and exploring the Mercado Central. In Plaza Mulato Gil de Castro, allot at least 30 minutes for the Museo Arqueológico and the Museo de Artes Visuales. You can easily spend a few hours in the Museo Nacional de Bellas Artes and the Museo de Arte Contemporáneo. Vega Chica and Vega Central are usually crowded, so keep an eye on your personal belongings. When the markets are closing around sunset, it's best to return to neighborhoods south of the river.

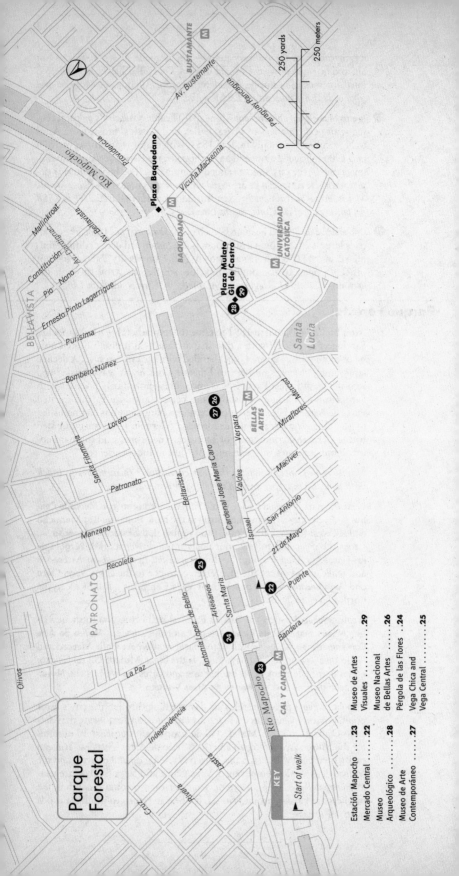

Parque Forestal

KEY

▲ Start of walk

Estación Mapocho **23**
Mercado Central **22**
Museo
Arqueológico **28**
Museo de Arte
Contemporáneo **27**

Museo de Artes
Visuales **29**
Museo Nacional
de Bellas Artes **26**
Pérgola de las Flores ..**24**
Vega Chica and
Vega Central **25**

What to See

Antiguedades Balmaceda. A taxi ride away or a good 20-minute walk from the Estación Mapocho on Balmaceda is a large warehouse-type building that houses the Antiguedades Balmaceda. If you like antiques then it's worth browsing among the corridors of stands for something that catches your fancy. On display is everything from furniture to books to jewelry. ⊠ *Av. Brasil at Balmaceda, Santiago Centro* ☎ *no phone* ⊙ *Daily 10:30–7.*

★ ㉓ **Estación Mapocho.** This mighty edifice, with its trio of two-story arches framed by intricate terra-cotta detailing, is as elegant as any train station in the world. The station was inaugurated in 1913 as a terminus for trains arriving from Valparaíso and points north, but steam engines no longer pull in here. A major conversion transformed the structure into one of the city's principal cultural centers. The Centro Cultural Estación Mapocho houses two restaurants, a fine bookstore and café, a large exhibition and arts space, and a handicrafts shop. The cavernous space that once sheltered steam engines now hosts musical performances and other events. ⊠ *Plaza de la Cultura, Independencia and Balmaceda, Parque Forestal* ☎ *2/361–1761* ⊕ *www.estacionmapocho. cl* ⊙ *Daily 9–6* Ⓜ *Puente Cal y Canto.*

▶ ㉒ **Mercado Central.** At the Central Market you'll find a matchless selection of creatures from the sea. Depending on the season, you might see the delicate beaks of *picorocos,* the world's only edible barnacles; *erizos,* the prickly shelled sea urchins; or shadowy pails full of succulent bullfrogs. If the fish don't capture your interest, the architecture may: the lofty wrought-iron ceiling of the structure, reminiscent of a Victorian train station, was prefabricated in England and erected in Santiago between 1868 and 1872. Diners are regaled by musicians in the middle of the market, where two restaurants compete for customers. You can also find a cheap, filling meal at a stand along the market's southern edge. ⊠ *Ismael Valdés Vergara 900, Parque Forestal* ☎ *2/696–8327* ⊙ *Mon.–Thurs. 5–5, Fri. 5–9, Sat. 5–7, Sun. 5–6* Ⓜ *Puente Cal y Canto.*

㉘ **Museo Arqueológico.** The little Archaeological Museum is devoted specifically to the indigenous peoples of Chile. Some 3,000 artifacts bring the country's Mapuche, Aymara, Fueguino, Huilliche, and Pehuenche cultures vividly to life. ⊠ *José Victorino Lastarria 307, 2nd floor, Parque Forestal* ☎ *2/664–9337* ✉ *Free* ⊙ *Weekdays and Sun. 10–2 and 3:30–6:30, Sat. 10–2* Ⓜ *Baquedano, Universidad Católica.*

The pleasant Plaza Mulato Gil de Castro, a cobblestone square off the colorful Calle José Victorino Lastarria, is an unexpected treat. In the midst of it is **R** (⊠ Plaza Mulato Gil de Castro, Parque Forestal ☎ 2/ 664–9844), a cozy café serving English teas and light fare. Weary travelers relax beneath the kettles and cups hanging from the ceiling.

㉗ **Museo de Arte Contemporáneo.** The Museum of Contemporary Art, on the opposite side of the building housing the Museo de Bellas Artes, showcases a collection of modern Latin American paintings, photography, and sculpture. The museum is run by the art school of the Universidad de Chile, so it isn't afraid to take risks; the rather dilapidated interior is a perfect setting for the edgier art. Look for Fernando Botero's pudgy *Caballo* sculpture gracing the square out front. ⊠ *Bounded by Jose M. de la Barra and Ismael Valdés Vergara, Parque Forestal* ☎ *2/639–6488* ⊕ *www.mac.uchile.cl* ✉ *400 pesos* ⊙ *Tues.–Sat. 11–7, Sun. 11–5* Ⓜ *Bellas Artes.*

★ ㉙ **Museo de Artes Visuales.** You'll never confuse this dazzling museum of contemporary art with the crumbling Museo de Arte Contemporáneo. Displaying the combined private holdings of Chilean construction moguls Manuel Santa Cruz and Hugo Yaconi, this gallery has one of the finest collections of contemporary Chilean art. The building itself is a masterpiece: six gallery levels float into each other in surprising ways. The wood floors and Plexiglas-sided stairways create an open and airy space for paintings and sculptures by Roberto Matta, Arturo Duclos, Roser Bru, José Balmes, and Eugenio Dittborn, among others. ⊠ *José Victorino Lastarria 307, Plaza Mulato Gil de Castro, Parque Forestal* ☎ *2/638–3502* ⌛ *1,000 pesos* ⊙ *Tues.–Sun. 10:30–6:30* Ⓜ *Bellas Artes.*

㉖ **Museo Nacional de Bellas Artes.** Paintings, drawings, and sculpture by 16th- to 20th-century Chilean and European artists fill the grand National Museum of Fine Arts. The elegant, neoclassical building, which was originally intended to house the city's school of fine arts, has an impressive glass-domed ceiling that illuminates the main hall. A theater on the second floor screens short films about the featured artists. ⊠ *Bounded by Jose M. de la Barra and Ismael Valdés Vergara, Parque Forestal* ☎ *2/633–0655* ⊕ *www.mnba.cl* ⌛ *Tues.–Sat. 600 pesos, Sun. free* ⊙ *Tues.–Sun. 10–6:45* Ⓜ *Bellas Artes.*

> **off the beaten path**

Parque de las Esculturas. Providencia is mainly a business district, but it has one of the city's most captivating—and least publicized—public parks. Here, the gardens are filled with sculptures by Chile's top artists. Because of its pastoral atmosphere, the park is popular with joggers and cuddling couples. In the center is a wood pavilion that hosts sculpture exhibitions. To get here from the Pedro de Valdivia Metro stop, walk a block north to the Río Mapocho and cross the bridge to Avenida Santa María. The park is on your right.

㉔ **Pérgola de las Flores.** Santiaguinos come to the Trellis of Flowers to buy wreaths and flower arrangements to bring to the city's two cemeteries. *La Pérgola de las Flores,* a famous Chilean musical, is based on the conflict that arose in the 1930s when the mayor of Santiago wanted to shut down the market. Find a chatty florist here and you may learn all about it. ⊠ *Corner of Av. La Paz and Artesanos, Recoleta* ☎ *no phone* ⊙ *Daily, sunrise–sunset* Ⓜ *Puente Cal y Canto.*

㉕ **Vega Chica and Vega Central.** From fruit to furniture, meat to machinery, these lively markets stock just about anything you can name. Alongside the ordinary items you can find delicacies like *piñones,* giant pine nuts found on monkey puzzle trees. If you're undaunted by crowds, try a typical Chilean meal in a closet-size eatery or picada. Chow down with the locals on *pastel de choclo,* a pie filled with ground beef, chicken, olives, boiled egg, and sultanas, and topped with mashed corn. ⊠ *Antonia López de Bello between Av. Salas and Av. Gandarillas, Recoleta* Ⓜ *Puente Cal y Canto.*

Bellavista & Parque Metropolitano

If you happen to be in Santiago on one of the rare days when the smog dissipates, head straight for Parque Metropolitano. In the center is Cerro San Cristóbal, a hill reached via cable car or funicular. A journey to the top of the hill rewards you with spectacular views in all directions. In the shadow of Cerro San Cristóbal is Bellavista. The neighborhood has but one sight—the poet Pablo Neruda's hillside home of La Chascona—but it's perhaps the city's best place to wander. You're sure to discover interesting antiques shops, bustling outdoor markets, and adventurous and colorful eateries.

Numbers in the text correspond to numbers in the margins and on the Bellavista & Parque Metropolitano map.

a good walk

Starting from Plaza Baquedano, cross the bridge over the Río Mapocho to Bellavista. Acacia trees line the streets here, which are filled with quaint cafés, trendy restaurants, and one-story homes painted in pinks, aquamarines, and blues. Walk three blocks north on Calle Pío Nono and turn right onto Calle Antonia López de Bello. Make a left onto Constitución and head north—you'll soon enter Santiago's most lively restaurant district. On Fernando Márquez de la Plata sits the house Pablo Neruda designed, **La Chascona** ㉚ ▶.

At the northern end of Calle Pío Nono is Plaza Caupolicán, the entrance to Parque Metropolitano. The funicular, housed in an old castlelike terminus, climbs up Santiago's highest hill, **Cerro San Cristóbal** ㉛. A quarter of the way up the hill, the funicular stops at the **Jardín Zoológico** ㉜, which you can also reach on foot by following the road. After reaching the summit, take in the expansive views, then follow the signs to the *teleférico* (cable car) and get out halfway at **Plaza Tupahue** ㉝. A short walk away is **Jardín Botánico Mapulemu** ㉞, an expansive botanical garden. A 15-minute walk east and slightly downhill will bring you to the authentic and well-kept **Jardín Japonés** ㉟.

TIMING & PRECAUTIONS

Plan on devoting an entire day to seeing Parque Metropolitano's major attractions. During the week the park is almost empty, and you can enjoy the views in relative solitude. Avoid walking down if you decide to watch the sunset from the lofty perch—the area is not well patrolled. Give yourself at least an hour to wander through Bellavista, and another hour for a tour of La Chascona.

What to See

❸❶ **Cerro San Cristóbal.** St. Christopher's Hill, within Parque Metropolitano, is one of the most popular tourist attractions in Santiago. From the western entrance at Plaza Caupolicán you can walk—it's a steep but enjoyable one-hour climb—or take the funicular. Either route leads you to the summit, which is crowned by a gleaming white statue of the Virgen de la Inmaculada. If you are coming from the eastern entrance, you can ascend in the cable car that leaves seven blocks north of the Pedro de Valdivia Metro stop. The ride, which seats two in a colored-glass bubble, can be terrifying for acrophobics. Tree branches whack at your lift as you glide over the park. ⊠ *Cerro San Cristóbal, Bellavista* ☎ *2/777–6666 for park administration; 2/735–2081 for lift information* ⊕ *www.parquemet.cl or www.funicular.cl* ⊠ *Park free; round-trip funicular 1,500 pesos; round-trip cable car 1,500 pesos* ☉ *Park: Sun.–Thurs. 8 AM–10 PM, Fri.–Sat. 8 AM–midnight. Funicular: Mon. 1–8, Tues.–Fri. 10–8, weekends 10–8:30. Cable car: Mon. 1–8:30, Tues.–Sun. 10–8:30* Ⓜ *Baquedano, Pedro de Valdivia.*

★ ▶ ㉚ **La Chascona.** This house designed by the Nobel-winning poet Pablo Neruda was dubbed the "Woman with the Tousled Hair" after Matilde Urrutia, the poet's third wife. The two met while strolling in nearby Parque Forestal, and for years the house served as a romantic hideaway before they married. The pair's passionate relationship was recounted in the 1995 Italian film *Il Postino.* Tours allow you to step into the extraordinary mind of the poet whose eclectic designs earned him the label "organic architect." Winding garden paths, stairs, and bridges lead to the house and its library stuffed with books, a bedroom in a tower, and a secret passageway. Scattered throughout are collections of butterflies,

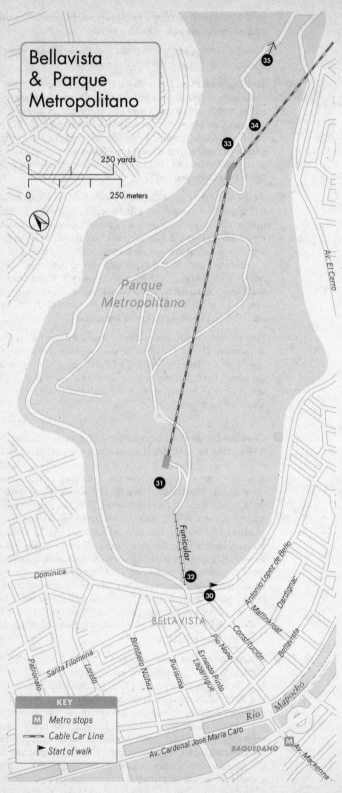

Bellavista
& Parque
Metropolitano

0   250 yards

0   250 meters

35

34

33

Av. El Cerro

Parque
Metropolitano

31

Funicular

Dominica

32

30

BELLAVISTA

Antonio Lopez de Bello

Dardignac

Mallinkroat

Constitución

Bellavista

Pío Nono

Ernesto Pinto
Lagarrigue

Purísima

Bombero Nuñez

Loreto

Santa Filomena

Patronato

Rio Mapocho

KEY

Ⓜ *Metro stops*

Cable Car Line

▶ *Start of walk*

Rio

Av. Cardenal Jose Maria Caro

BAQUEDANO

Ⓜ Av. Mackenna

seashells, wineglasses, and other odd objects that inspired Neruda's tumultuous life and romantic poetry. Neruda, who died in 1973, had two other houses on the coast—one in Valparaíso, the other in Isla Negra. All three are open as museums. Though it's not as magical as the other two, La Chascona can still set your imagination dancing. ⊠ *Fernando Márquez de la Plata 0192, Bellavista* ☎ *2/777–8741* ⊠ *La Chascona 1,800 pesos, tour 3,000 pesos* ☉ *Tues.–Sun. 10–6* Ⓜ *Baquedano.*

need a break?

A short walk from La Chascona is Calle Antonia López de Bello, a street overflowing with bars and restaurants. Here, the café **Off the Record** (⊠ Antonia López de Bello 0155, Bellavista ☎ 2/777–7710) has a decidedly bohemian air. The wooden booths, for example, seem to have been designed with witty conversation and artistic bonhomie in mind. Black-and-white photographs recall visitors from Pablo Neruda to Uma Thurman.

㉞ Jardín Botánico Mapulemu. Gravel paths lead you to restful nooks among acres of well-labeled local flora at the Mapulemu Botanical Garden. Some 80 native-Chilean species grow here, including the araucaria, canelo, and macci trees. The botanical star is the squat *jubea chilena,* the ubiquitous Chilean palm. Every path and stairway seems to bring you to better views of Santiago and the Andes. Sunday mornings there are tai chi, yoga, and aerobics free of charge. ⊠ *Cerro San Cristóbal, Bellavista* ☎ *2/777–6666* ⊠ *Free* ☉ *Daily 10–4* Ⓜ *Pedro de Valdivia, Baquedano.*

㉟ Jardín Japonés. The tranquil Japanese Garden affords a sumptuous view over the skyscrapers of Las Condes and Bellavista. Paths edged with bamboo and lit by Japanese lanterns lead past lily ponds and a gazebo beside a trickling fountain. ⊠ *Cerro San Cristóbal, Bellavista* ☎ *2/777–6666* ⊠ *Free* ☉ *Daily 10–6* Ⓜ *Pedro de Valdivia, Baquedano.*

㉜ Jardín Zoológico. The Zoological Garden is a good place to see examples of many Chilean animals, some nearly extinct, that you might not otherwise encounter. As is often the case with many older zoos, the creatures aren't given a lot of room. Be careful with children, as some of the cages aren't properly protected, and the animals can bite. A larger, modern zoo is being built outside the city near the Universidad de Chile. ⊠ *Cerro San Cristóbal, Bellavista* ☎ *no phone* ⊠ *1,700 pesos* ☉ *Tues.–Sun. 10–5* Ⓜ *Baquedano.*

㉝ Plaza Tupahue. The middle stop on the teleférico deposits you in the center of Parque Metropolitano. The main attraction here in summer is the delightful **Piscina Tupahue,** a 46-m (150-ft) pool with a rocky crag running along one side. Beside the pool is the 1925 **Torreón Victoria,** a stone tower surrounded by a trellis of bougainvillea. If Piscina Tupahue is too crowded, try the nearby **Piscina Antilén.** From Plaza Tupahue you can follow a path below to **Plaza de Juegos Infantiles Gabriela Mistral,** a popular playground. ⊠ *Cerro San Cristóbal, Bellavista* ☎ *2/777–6666* ⊠ *Park free, Piscina Tupahue 4,500 pesos, Piscina Antilén 5,000 pesos* ☉ *Piscina Tupahue: Nov.–Mar., Tues.–Sun. 10–7. Piscina Antilén: Nov.–Mar., Wed.–Mon. 10–7* Ⓜ *Pedro de Valdivia, Baquedano.*

Parque Quinta Normal Area

Just west of downtown is shady Parque Quinta Normal, a 75-acre park with three museums within its borders and another just across the street. This is an especially good place to take the kids, as all the museums were designed to stimulate eager young minds. The park was created in 1841 as a place to experiment with new agricultural techniques.

On weekdays it is great for quiet strolls; on weekends you'll have to maneuver around noisy families. Pack a picnic or a soccer ball and you'll fit right in.

Numbers in the text correspond to numbers in the margins and on the Parque Quinta Normal map.

a good walk

Take a cab or the subway to the Estación Central stop. Outside the Metro is the **Estación Central de Ferrocarriles** ㊱ ▶, a graceful colossus that is the city's only functioning train station. Across the street is the **Planetario** ㊲, on the southeast corner of the Universidad de Santiago. Walk five blocks north on Avenida Matucana to Avenida Portales. Half a block west is the colorful **Museo Artequín** ㊳. Across the street is the main entrance to Parque Quinta Normal, where you'll find the **Museo Ferroviario** ㊴. Avenida Las Palmas, a wide pedestrian path, leads through the park to the **Museo Nacional de Historia Natural** ㊵ and the **Museo de Ciencia y Tecnología** ㊶.

TIMING

You can visit the museums in and around the park, stroll along a wooded path, and even row a boat on a lake, all within a few hours. The hour-long presentation at the planetarium is shown only on weekends.

What to See

off the beaten path

Cementerio General. It may be an unusual tourist attraction, but this cemetery in the northern part of the city reveals a lot about traditional Chilean society. After passing through the lofty stone arches of the main entrance you'll find well-tended paths lined with marble mausoleums, squat mansions belonging to Chile's wealthy families. The 8- or 10-story "niches" farther along—concrete shelves housing thousands of coffins—resemble middle-class apartment buildings. Their inhabitants lie here until the rent runs out and they're evicted. Look for former President Salvador Allende's final resting spot. A map at the main entrance to the cemetery can help you find it. This is an emotionally charged place around September 11, the anniversary of the 1973 military coup. ⊠ *Av. Recoleta, Recoleta.*

▶ ㊱ **Estación Central de Ferrocarriles.** Inaugurated in 1897, Central Station is the city's last remaining train station, serving Concepción and points south. The greenish iron canopy that once shielded the engines from the weather is flanked by two lovely beaux arts edifices. A lively market keeps this terminal buzzing with activity. ⊠ *Av. O'Higgins 3170, Estación Central* ☎ *2/376–8500* ⊠ *Free* ☉ *Daily 6 AM–midnight* Ⓜ *Estación Central.*

★ ☺ ㊳ **Museo Artequín.** The resplendent Pabellón París houses this interactive museum that teaches the fundamentals of art to children, but the pavilion itself is the real jewel. It was designed by French architect Henri Picq to house Chile's exhibition in the 1889 Paris International Exposition (where Gustave Eiffel's skyline-defining tower was unveiled). After the show the structure was shipped back to Santiago. Its glass domes, Pompeiian-red walls, and blue-steel columns and supports make it a diaphanous box of exquisite beauty. Weekdays, school groups explore the two floors of reproductions of famous artworks, touch-screen computers, and didactic areas. On weekends there are more guides available to explain the pavilion's history. Call ahead to request an English-speaking tour. ⊠ *Av. Portales 3530, Parque Quinta Normal* ☎ *2/681–8687* ⊕ *www.artequin.cl* ⊠ *500 pesos* ☉ *Tues.–Fri. 9–5, Sun. 11–6* Ⓜ *Estación Central.*

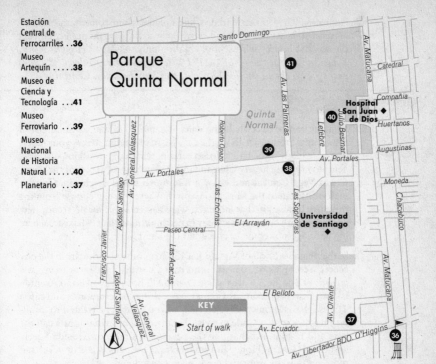

CB 41 **Museo de Ciencia y Tecnología.** This science and technology museum for children is rather unfocused but has a good collection of old phonographs and a dark and moody astronomy wing with exhibits that resemble overgrown science projects. It's worth a visit for its Internet room, which offers competitive connection rates. ⊠ *Parque Quinta Normal* ☎ *2/681–6022 or 2/689–8026* ⊕ *www.corpdicyt.cl* ✉ *800 pesos* ☉ *Tues.–Fri. 10–5:30, weekends 11–6* Ⓜ *Estación Central.*

CB 39 **Museo Ferroviario.** Chile's once-mighty railroads have been relegated to history, but this acre of Parque Quinta Normal keeps a bit of the romance alive. More than a dozen steam locomotives and three passenger coaches are set within quiet gardens with placards in Spanish and English. You can board two of the trains. Among the collection is the cross-Andes express, which operated between Chile and Argentina from 1911 until 1971. A re-creation of a typical station has photos and exhibits. ⊠ *Av. Las Palmas, Parque Quinta Normal* ☎☎ *2/681–4627* ⊕ *www.corpdicyt.cl* ✉ *750 pesos* ☉ *Tues.–Fri. 10–5:30, weekends 11–7* Ⓜ *Estación Central.*

CB 40 **Museo Nacional de Historia Natural.** The National Museum of Natural History is the centerpiece of Parque Quinta Normal. Paul Lathoud designed the building for Chile's first International Exposition, in 1875. After suffering damage from successive earthquakes, the neoclassical structure was rebuilt and enlarged. Though the exhibits are slightly outdated and there are no English texts to guide you, the large dioramas of stuffed animals against painted backdrops are still intriguing, as are the numerous stone heads from Easter Island. The skeleton of an enormous blue whale hangs in the central hall, delighting children of all ages. ⊠ *Parque Quinta Normal s/n* ☎ *2/680–4615* ⊕ *www.mnhn.cl* ✉ *Tues.–Sat. 600 pesos, Sun. free* ☉ *Tues.–Sat. 10–5:30, Sun. 12–5:30* Ⓜ *Estación Central.*

㉚ Planetario. The Universidad de Chile's planetarium dome mimics a universe of stars with a weekend show open to the general public. During the week it buzzes with school children only. ☒ *Av. O'Higgins 3349, Estación Central* ☏ *2/681–2171* ⊕ *www.planetariochile.cl* ☜ *2,000 pesos* ☉ *Weekend shows: 12, 3:30, and 5* Ⓜ *Estación Central.*

WHERE TO EAT

Santiago can be overwhelming when it comes to dining, as hundreds of restaurants are strewn about the city. No matter what strikes your fancy, there are likely to be half a dozen eateries within easy walking distance. Tempted to taste hearty Chilean fare? Pull up a stool at one of the counters at Vega Central and enjoy a traditional pastel de choclo. Craving seafood? Head to the Mercado Central, where you can choose from the fresh fish brought in that morning. Want a memorable meal? Trendy new restaurants are opening every day in neighborhoods like Bellavista, where hip Santiaguinos come to check out the latest hot spots.

In the neighborhood of Vitacura, a 15–20 minute taxi ride from the city center, a complex of 10 restaurants called Borde Río attracts an upscale crowd. El Bosque, an area along Avenida El Bosque Norte and Avenida Isidora Goyenechea in Las Condes, has a cluster of restaurants and cafés. The emphasis is on creative cuisine, so you'll often be treated to familiar favorites with a Chilean twist. Finally, *Suecia* is what locals call the bars and restaurants that line the pedestrian streets of Avenida Suecia and Calle General Holley in Providencia. The focus is less on food and more on fun: the priority here is people-watching.

One of the most pleasing aspects of the city's dining scene is the relatively low price of a fine meal. It's difficult to find an entrée in the city that tops $15. And many who assume that the best vintages have been exported are pleasantly surprised by extensive wine lists with good prices.

WHAT IT COSTS In pesos (in thousands)				
$$$$	**$$$**	**$$**	**$**	**¢**
AT DINNER	over 11	8–11	5–8	2.5–5	under 2.5

Prices are for a main course at dinner.

Bellavista

Chilean

$$$–$$$$ ✕ **El Camino Real.** On a clear day, treat yourself to the stunning views of the city through the floor-to-ceiling windows at this restaurant atop Cerro San Cristóbal. The menu lists such dishes as pork tenderloin in mustard sauce with caramelized onions, and warm scallop salad with quail eggs and asparagus. Oenophiles appreciate the 168-bottle wine list with many Chilean vintages. Neophytes can head across a central courtyard to Bar Dalí, where the servers can organize an impromptu *degustación* of a half dozen varietals. Downstairs is a small wine museum. ☒ *Parque Metropolitano, Bellavista* ☏ *2/232–3381 or 2/233–1238* ☒ *Reservations essential* ☐ *AE, DC, MC, V* Ⓜ *Pedro de Valdivia, Baquedano.*

★ **$$–$$$$** ✕ **Como Agua Para Chocolate.** Inspired by Laura Esquivel's romantic 1989 novel *Like Water for Chocolate*, this Bellavista standout is part restaurant, part theme park. It focuses on the aphrodisiacal qualities of food, so it shouldn't be surprising that one long table is actually an iron bed, with place settings arranged on a crisp white sheet. The food compares to the decor like the film version compares to the book: it's good, but not nearly as imaginative. *Ave de la pasión,* for instance, means Bird of

Passion. It may be just chicken with mushrooms, but it's served on a copper plate. ⊠ *Constitución 88, Bellavista* ☎ *2/777–8740* ▭ *AE, DC, MC, V* Ⓜ *Baquedano.*

$–$$ ✕ **Eladio.** At Eladio you can eat a succulent *bife de chorizo,* entrecôte steak, or any other cut cooked as you like; order a good bottle of Chilean wine; and even finish with a slice of *amapola* (poppy-seed) sponge cake—and you still wouldn't be much out of pocket. Come here any night but Friday, as the place fills up with office workers celebrating the arrival of the weekend. ⊠ *Pío Nono 251, Bellavista* ☎ *2/777–5083* Ⓜ *Baquedano* ⊠ *Avenida 11 de Septiembre 2250, 2nd floor, Providencia* ☎ *2/231–4224* Ⓜ *Los Leones* ⊠ *Avenida Ossa 2234, La Reina* ☎ *2/ 277–0661* ▭ *AE, DC, MC, V* ⊘ *Bellavista branch closed Sun.*

★ ¢–$ ✕ **El Venezia.** Long before Bellavista became fashionable, this bare-bones picada was where movie stars and TV personalities rubbed elbows with the hoi polloi. While gourmands now head a block or two in either direction to the latest hot spots, tacky El Venezia still fills to capacity each day at lunch. And what's not to like? The beer is icy, the waiters are efficient, and the food is abundant. The *congrio frito* (fried conger eel) is delicious, as are the *costillar de chancho* (pork ribs). What they accomplish here is nothing short of a miracle—while you can't pinpoint exactly why, you leave tremendously satisfied. ⊠ *Pío Nono 200, Bellavista* ☎ *2/737–0900* ▭ *AE, DC, MC, V* Ⓜ *Baquedano.*

Peruvian

$–$$ ✕ **Sarita Colonia.** Easily the most outrageous restaurant in Santiago, Sarita Colonia is a collection of colorful dining rooms, one more vibrant than the last. The food is authentic Peruvian—try the *cau cau* (scallops stewed with vegetables) or the *pollo al maní* (chicken with a spicy peanut sauce)—and the presentation is fun and fanciful. You can also stop by for a late-night cocktail in the second-floor lounge, but don't come here if it's quiet you seek—the music is often blaring. ⊠ *Av. Dardignac 50, Bellavista* ☎ *2/737–0242* ▭ *AE, DC, MC, V* ⊘ *No lunch weekends* Ⓜ *Baquedano.*

Seafood

$$ ✕ **Azul Profundo.** Not so many years ago, this was the only restaurant you'd find on this street near Parque Metropolitano. Today it's one of dozens of restaurants in trendy Bellavista, but its two-level dining room—with walls painted bright shades of blue and yellow, and racks of wine stretching to the ceiling—ensure that it stands out in the crowd. Choose your fish from the extensive menu—swordfish, sea bass, shark, flounder, salmon, trout, and haddock are among the choices—and enjoy it *a la plancha* (grilled) or *a la lata* (served on a sizzling plate with tomatoes and onions). ⊠ *Constitución 111, Bellavista* ☎ *2/738–0288* ⚫ *Reservations essential* ▭ *AE, DC, MC, V* Ⓜ *Baquedano.*

FodorśChoice ★

Spanish

$–$$ ✕ **La Bodeguilla.** This authentic Spanish restaurant is a great place to stop for a glass of sangria after a tour of Cerro San Cristóbal. After all, it's right at the foot of the funicular. The dozen or so tables are set among wine barrels and between hanging strings of garlic bulbs. Nibble on tasty tapas like Chorizo *riojano* (a piquant sausage), *pulpo a la gallega* (octopus with peppers and potatoes), and *queso manchego* (a mild white cheese) while perusing the long wine list. Then consider ordering the house specialty—*cabrito al horno* (oven-roasted goat). ⊠ *Av. Dominica 5, Bellavista* ☎ *2/732–5215* ▭ *No credit cards* ⊘ *Closed Sun.* Ⓜ *Baquedano.*

★ $–$$ ✕ **La Esquina al Jerez.** Iron lanterns and suits of armor decorate Bellavista's longtime favorite eatery, bringing to mind traditional Spanish restau-

Where to Stay & Eat in Santiago Centro & Bellavista

Restaurants ▼

Hotels ▼

rants, but the overall feeling here is contemporary, with billowing curtains and splashes of bright reds and yellows. Among the best dishes are *paella de mariscos* (seafood with rice) and tapas like *calamares fritos al alioli* (fried squid with garlic mayonnaise). There are zarzuela dance performances and live jazz weekends. ⊠ *Dardignac 0192, Bellavista* ☎ 2/777–4407 ⚑ *Reservations essential* ☰ *AE, DC, MC, V* ⊘ *Closed Sun.* Ⓜ *Baquedano.*

Centro

Chilean

$$–$$$ ✕ **Bristol.** The indefatigable Guillermo Rodríguez, who has commandeered the kitchen here for more than a decade, has won just about all the country's culinary competitions. No wonder he also serves as a private chef to Chilean president Ricardo Lagos. Besides the innovative takes on traditional Chilean dishes, the buffet includes unlimited access to a wine cart stocked with a dozen quality vintages. The expertise offered by the city's most prized sommelier, Alejandro Farias, is reason enough to visit. The restaurant's prime location in Hotel Plaza San Francisco makes it a good meeting point for Santiago's movers and shakers in politics and business. ⊠ *Av. O'Higgins 816, Santiago Centro* ☎ 2/639–3832 ☰ *AE, DC, MC, V* Ⓜ *Universidad de Chile.*

FodorsChoice ★

$$–$$$ ✕ **El Jardin Secreto.** Relax on a red-velvet-upholstered chaise lounge or sit back on an elegant dining-room chair in this stylish yet distinctly informal eatery. Large vases overflowing with hand-made ornamental foliage, Chinese cabinets, and small white-wood tables occupy a large section of the lobby restaurant in the Carrera Hotel. From here you can look through huge plate glass windows onto the Plaza de la Constitución as you tuck into a carefully prepared fresh fillet of *alfonsino* (an Easter Island fish) in a sauce of ginger and orange, or ravioli stuffed with *ostiones* (scallops). ⊠ *Teatinos 180, Santiago Centro* ☎ 2/698–2011 ☰ *AE, DC, MC, V* Ⓜ *La Moneda.*

$–$$ ✕ **Atelier del Parque.** In this vast orange building the menus come on palette boards along with their own paintbrushes. On offer are creations named for artists, such as the Da Vinci—fettucini in ink with squid—and the Warhol—salmon with caramelized almonds. The restaurant's quietly satisfying interior has lots of separate seating areas, including one in a large glass atrium and another filled with comfy armchairs. A connected gallery showcases temporary exhibits of art and sculpture. ⊠ *Casa Naranja, Santo Domingo 528, Parque Forestal* ☎ 2/639–5843 ☰ *AE, DC, MC, V* Ⓜ *Bellas Artes.*

French

$–$$ ✕ **Les Assassins.** Although this appears at first glance to be a rather somber bistro, nothing could be further from the truth. The service is friendly, and the Provence-influenced food is first-rate. The steak au poivre and crepes suzette would make a Frenchman's eyes water. If you want to practice your Spanish, you're in luck: there's always a line of talkative locals in the cozy ground-floor bar. ⊠ *Merced 297, Santiago Centro* ☎ 2/638–4280 ☰ *AE, DC, MC, V* ⊘ *Closed Sun.* Ⓜ *Universidad Católica.*

Indian

★ $–$$ ✕ **Majestic.** The dining area is a little cramped, but most people forgive this as soon as they taste what chef Haridas Chauhan, originally of the Sheraton in New Delhi, has to offer. Among his deliciously spicy dishes are *rogan josh* (hot lamb curry) and a pungent *murgh makhanwala* (chicken in a tangy butter sauce). The *kulfi de almendras,* made from evaporated milk, ice cream, walnuts, and almonds, is a sweet finish to a meal. Large copper base plates set on immaculate white tablecloths are a nice touch. ⊠ *Santo Domingo 1526, Santiago Centro* ☎ *2/695–8366* ♙ *Reservations essential* ⊟ *AE, DC, MC, V* Ⓜ *Santa Ana.*

Japanese

$–$$ ✕ **Japón.** Take off your shoes, settle onto a cushion, and prepare yourself for authentic flavors from the floating kingdom. Frequented by Santiago's small but growing Japanese community, this restaurant off Plaza Baquedano has a first-rate sushi bar and three comfortable dining rooms. The most patient waiters in town help you make a selection, and the chef is happy to custom-prepare a dish at your request. The *unagi* (eel) is fantastic, and the noodle soup is a meal in itself. ⊠ *Barón Pierre de Coubertin 39, Santiago Centro* ☎ *2/222–4517* ⊟ *AE, DC, MC, V* Ⓜ *Baquedano.*

$–$$ ✕ **Primado.** This self-service basement restaurant, accessible from Calle Agustinas or through the hotel lobby of the Carrera, is a new concept in fast food. A chalk board behind the long stainless-steel counter lists the day's choices, everything from sushi to baked *congrio* (conger eel). Serve yourself, pay at the end of the counter, and take your tray to a table in any one of several dining areas. Primado's light wood floors, soft illumination, and burlap screens have an instantly relaxing effect. ⊠ *Teatinos 180, Santiago Centro* ☎ *2/680–3600* ⊟ *AE, DC, MC, V* ✆ *No dinner* Ⓜ *La Moneda.*

Seafood

★ **$–$$** ✕ **Donde Augusto.** For the best value on seafood in town, head to this eatery within the bustling Mercado Central. If you don't mind the unhurried service and the odd tear in the tablecloth, you may have the time of your life dining on everything from sea urchins to ceviche. Placido Domingo eats here on every visit to Chile, attended to by the white-bearded Segovian Augusto Vasquez, who has run Donde Augusto for more than four decades. ⊠ *Mercado Central, Santiago Centro* ☎ *2/672–2829* ♙ *Reservations not accepted* ⊟ *AE, DC, MC, V* ✆ *No dinner* Ⓜ *Puente Cal y Canto.*

Vegetarian

¢–$ ✕ **Govinda's.** Cheap but hearty vegetarian lunches are prepared here by Hari Krishnas. Card tables and lawn chairs are the extent of the decor, but the fresh juices and homemade bread are delicious. Try the yogurt with mixed fruit and honey for dessert. ⊠ *Av. Compañía 1489, Santiago Centro* ☎ *2/673–0892* ⊟ *No credit cards* ✆ *Closed weekends. No dinner* Ⓜ *Santa Ana.*

Las Condes

Cafés

¢–$ ✕ **Cafe Melba.** Almost unheard of in Santiago, this small café-restaurant serves breakfast for as long as it's open, starting at 7:30 AM on weekdays and 8 AM on weekends. If you're particularly hungry, order The Works —baked beans, mushrooms, sausage, bacon, and more. Drink it down with a caffe latte, served in a large white bowl. The owner of Cafe Melba is hands-on, which may explain why this popular eatery continues to thrive. The interior is airy, with simple wood tables, black-metal chairs, light-wood floors, and whitewashed walls. ⊠ *Don Carlos 2898, off El Bosque Norte, Las Condes* ☎ *2/232–4546* ⊟ *AE, DC, MC, V* ✆ *No dinner* Ⓜ *Tobalaba.*

Italian

★ **$$$–$$$$** ✕ **Bice.** Bice has revolutionized Santiago's notion of elegant dining. The small, two-tiered dining room has soaring ceilings that lend a dramatic flair, while gleaming floors of alternating stripes of dark and light wood

Where to Stay & Eat in Providencia & Las Condes

add a touch of contemporary glamour. The service is a breed apart—white-jacketed waiters zip around, attending to your every need. The menu leans towards imaginatively prepared pastas, such as linguine with scallops, razor clams, shrimp, and mussels. Be sure to leave room for desserts such as the *cioccolatíssimo,* a hot, chocolate soufflé with melted chocolate inside, served with an exquisite *dulce de leche* ice cream. ✉ *Hotel Inter-Continental, Av. Luz 2920, Las Condes* ☎ *2/381–5500* ♠ *Reservations essential* ▤ *AE, DC, MC, V* Ⓜ *Tobalaba.*

$$–$$$$ ✕ **Le Due Torri.** For excellent homemade pastas, head to this longtime favorite. If you think the *agnolotti,* stuffed with ricotta cheese and spinach, resembles a feathered hat, you're right. The owner, who lived in Italy during World War II, intentionally shaped it like a Red Cross nurse's cap. The rear of the dining room, with its small cypress trees and a corner pergola, is traditional; seating in the front is more contemporary. The name of the restaurant, by the way, refers to the two towers erected by the dueling Garisenda and Asinelli families in the owner's native Bologna. ✉ *Av. Isidora Goyenechea 2908, Las Condes* ☎ *2/231–3427* ♠ *Reservations essential* ▤ *AE, DC, MC, V* Ⓜ *Tobalaba.*

Japanese

$–$$ ✕ **Matsuri.** With a sleek design that calls to mind Los Angeles as much as Tokyo, this restaurant in the Hyatt Regency is one of Santiago's most stylish eateries. The dining room's eclectic mix of materials includes porous stone from China and wood from Madagascar. Downstairs are a sushi bar and two tatami rooms (no shoes allowed, but slippers are provided) with sliding screens for privacy, while upstairs are two grill tables. Try the eight-piece dragon roll—cucumber and eel covered with avocado and smelt roe. ✉ *Av. Kennedy 4601, Las Condes* ☎ *2/363–3051* ▤ *AE, DC, MC, V* Ⓜ *Escuela Militar.*

Mexican

$ ✕ **Café Santa Fe.** Santiago's twentysomething crowd flocks to this Tex-Mex restaurant for its authentic guacamole, sizzling fajitas (with seafood or meat fillings), and frozen margaritas. Don't come here if you want a quiet meal, as the place is always noisy. Bright shades of blue, pink, and ocher decorate the restaurant. ✉ *Vitacura 9435, Las Condes* ☎ *2/325–5293* ▤ *AE, DC, MC, V* Ⓜ *Escuela Militar.*

Seafood

$–$$ ✕ **Isla Negra.** The sails flying from the roof let you know that Isla Negra means business when it comes to seafood. The restaurant takes its name from a coastal town south of Santiago that was Nobel laureate Pablo Neruda's last home. The poet's favorite dish was conger eel soup, and you'll find it served here as a starter. Don't miss the empanadas stuffed with everything from cheese to razor clams. The *chupe de marisco,* a delicious seafood chowder, comes in a quaint earthenware bowl. ✉ *Av. El Bosque Norte 0325, Las Condes* ☎ *2/231–3118* 🖷 *2/233–0339* ♠ *Reservations essential* ▤ *AE, DC, MC, V* Ⓜ *Tobalaba.*

Spanish

$$$–$$$$ ✕ **Gernika.** The Basque owners of this wood-and-stone restaurant have created a little slice of their homeland with black-and-white photographs of traditional scenes, tapestries bearing an ancient coat of arms, and even jai alai equipment. Head upstairs to the more intimate upper level, which has three well-decorated private dining salons. Chilean seafood is cooked with Spanish flair, as in the *congrio donostiarra* (conger eel coated in chili sauce and fried in olive oil). Fresh *centolla* (king crab) is brought in from Punta Arenas at the foot of Chile. Several selections from Spain's Rioja region appear on the wine list. ✉ *Av. El Bosque Norte*

0227, *Las Condes* ☎ *2/232–9954* ♨ *Reservations essential* 🖃 *AE,
DC, MC, V* ⊘ *No lunch Sat.* Ⓜ *Tobalaba.*

Thai

★ **$–$$** ✕ **Anakena.** This spacious Thai eatery in the Hyatt Regency serves some
of the finest spicy food in Santiago. You can tuck into the tastiest *pad
thai* (rice noodles, peanuts, egg, sprouts, and shrimp) or the spiciest green-
curry chicken while admiring the beautifully kept gardens and attractive pool. There's also a buffet with a terrific choice of dishes, including
pork with walnuts and celery in a tangy sauce, and tiger prawns with
lemongrass and cashews. ⊠ *Av. Kennedy 4601, Las Condes* ☎ *2/363–
3177* 🖃 *AE, DC, MC, V* Ⓜ *Escuela Militar.*

Vegetarian

¢–$ ✕ **El Naturista.** A green-and-white-checkered floor is the most prominent
feature of this large, airy restaurant, which has sidled away from run-
of-the-mill vegetarian fare. It conjures up such dishes as *fricasé de
cochayuyo* (seaweed stew)—a distinctly slimy but good dish that's typically Chilean in that seaweed is widely eaten throughout the country.
The scrumptious lasagne is made from home-grown eggplants. ⊠ *Vitacura 2751, Las Condes* ☎ *2/236–5140* 🖃 *AE, DC, MC, V* ⊘ *Closed
Sun.* Ⓜ *Tobalaba.*

Nuñoa

Chilean

★ **$** ✕ **Restorán Don Peyo.** For first-rate Chilean food, join the families that
flock to Don Peyo. The ceilings are low and the walls patched stucco,
but what this place lacks in aesthetics it more than makes up for in flavor. The hot sauce and the garlic spread are tasty, but meat dishes—especially a Chilean roast beef called *plateada del horno*—are what put
this restaurant on the map. ⊠ *Av. Grecia 448, Nuñoa* 🖃 *AE, DC, MC,
V* ⊘ *Closed Sun.* Ⓜ *Irrazaval.*

Providencia

Chilean

$$–$$$$ ✕ **El Cid.** Considered by critics to be among the city's top restaurants,
El Cid is the culinary centerpiece of the classic Sheraton Santiago. The
dining room, which overlooks the pool, is simple. All the excitement
here is provided by the food, which is served with a flourish. Don't miss
the famous *parrillada* of grilled seafood—king crab, prawns, squid,
and scallops with a sweet, spicy sauce. If you're new to Chilean cuisine,
you can't go wrong with the excellent lunch buffet, which includes ap-
petizers, entrées, desserts, and unlimited wine. ⊠ *Av. Santa María 1742,
Providencia* ☎ *2/233–5000* 🖃 *AE, DC, MC, V* Ⓜ *Pedro de Valdivia.*

$$ ✕ **El Parrón.** One of the city's oldest restaurants, dating from 1914, specializes in parrilladas, or meat platters, and serves just about every cut
you can imagine. The dining areas are large and slightly impersonal, but
the extensive wine list and menu make up for them. The congenial, wood-
paneled bar is the perfect place to sample the refreshing national aper-
itif—the pisco sour. For dessert try a popular Chilean street-trolley
offering, *mote con huesillos* (peeled wheat kernels and dried peaches).
⊠ *Providencia 1184, Providencia* ☎ *2/251–8911* 🖃 *AE, DC, MC, V*
⊘ *No dinner Sun.* Ⓜ *Manuel Montt.*

★ **$–$$** ✕ **Lomit's.** There's nothing particularly smart about Lomit's, a traditional
Chilean sandwich bar, but it unfailingly serves up some of the city's best
barro lucos, steak sandwiches with melted cheese. You can eat at the
long, central, diner-style bar and watch the sandwich maker at work,

or find a small table to the side. Black-trimmed red jackets are the everyday attire of the mature and slightly stern-faced waiters here. ⊠ *Providencia 1980, Providencia* ☎ *2/233–1897* ⊟ *AE, DC, MC, V* Ⓜ *Pedro de Valdivia.*

¢–$ ✕ **Liguria.** This extremely popular picada has four branches in the city where you can get reliable, typical Chilean food cheaply. A large selection of Chilean wine accompanies such favorites as *jardín de mariscos* (shellfish stew) and the filling *cazuela* (a stew of beef or chicken and potatoes). ⊠ *Av. Providencia 1373, Providencia* ☎ *2/235–7914* Ⓜ *Manuel Montt* ⊠ *Pedro de Valdivia 047, Providencia* ☎ *2/334–4346* Ⓜ *Pedro de Valdivia* ⊠ *Av. Providencia 2682, Providencia* ☎ *2/232–4918* Ⓜ *Los Leones* ⊠ *Av. Las Condes 12265, Las Condes* ☎ *2/243–6121* Ⓜ *Escuela Militar* ⊟ *No credit cards* ⊘ *Closed Sun.*

French

$–$$ ✕ **Le Flaubert.** You could be dining at home in this French tea room–restaurant with picture-filled walls, table lamps, magazine racks, and classical music. The menu of the day, written on a blackboard, might tempt you with such dishes as a traditional coq au vin or a *pastel de jaiba* (crab pie) cooked to perfection. Homesick Brits come here to reminisce over freshly baked scones and refreshing cups of tea. There's also a large, shady patio garden. ⊠ *Orrego Luco 125, Providencia* ☎ *2/231–9424* ⊟ *AE, DC, MC, V* Ⓜ *Pedro de Valdivia.*

Mediterranean

$–$$ ✕ **De Cangrejo a Conejo.** Don't bother looking for a sign because there isn't one—which seems to be the fashion for the hippest Santiago restaurants. From the outside this restaurant could be the house next door, an attractive beige period residence. You enter through tall, heavy wooden double doors into a large, high-ceilinged interior. Here, tables and chairs of light wood and steel have been thoughtfully arranged around a long curving bar, and flourishing greenery extends out into the patio garden. The menu is all encompassing, reflecting its name, with everything from crab pie to stewed rabbit. Try the lamb shanks on a bed of creamy mashed potatoes, or the sole with sautéed vegetables. ⊠ *Avenida Italia 805, Providencia* ☎ *2/634–4041 or 2/634–4064* ⊟ *No credit cards* ⊘ *Closed Sun.*

Mexican

$ ✕ **Los Geranios.** Maize, chile, and *refrijoles* (kidney beans) form the base of nearly all the dishes at this authentic Mexican restaurant in an attractive, dark red house with bright blue window frames. Stuffed peppers, enchiladas, and burritos are served with spicy rice and black beans. Dine at heavy wooden tables and chairs to the sounds of Mexican music. ⊠ *Santa Beatríz 93, Providencia* ☎ *2/236–6487* ⊟ *No credit cards* ⊘ *Closed Sun.* Ⓜ *Pedro de Valdivia, Manuel Montt.*

Seafood

$$–$$$ ✕ **Aquí Está Coco.** The best seafood in Santiago is served in a dining room
FodorsChoice where the walls are covered with flotsam and jetsam found on Chilean
★ beaches. Ask your waiter—or friendly owner "Coco" Pacheco—which fish was caught that day. This is a good place to try Chile's famous *machas* (clams), served with tomatoes and Parmesan cheese, or *corvina* (sea bass) grilled with plenty of butter. Don't miss the cellar, where you can sample wines from the extensive collection of Chilean vintages. ⊠ *La Concepción 236 Providencia* ☎ *2/235–8649* ⊕ *www.aquiestacoco.cl* ⌘ *Reservations essential* ⊟ *AE, DC, MC, V* ⊘ *Closed Sun.* Ⓜ *Pedro de Valdivia.*

Vegetarian

$ ✕ **Café del Patio.** The chef uses all organic produce, half of which is grown in the owner's garden, at this vegetarian eatery hidden in the back of quaint Galería del Patio. The chef's salad—with lettuce, tomato, hearts of palm, and Gruyère cheese—is exquisite, as is the vegetarian ravioli. The menu also includes a handful of dishes with an Asian flair. At night, Café del Patio turns into a bar. ✉ *Providencia 1670, Providencia* ☎ *2/236–1251* ▱ *AE, DC, MC, V* ☉ *Closed Sun. No lunch Sat.* Ⓜ *Pedro de Valdivia.*

$ ✕ **El Huerto.** In the heart of Providencia, this vegetarian eatery is a hangout for hip young Santiaguinos. Even the wood paneling and high windows here feel healthy. Simple dishes like stir-fried veggies (made with organic produce) and pancakes stuffed with asparagus and mushrooms are full of flavor, but it's the hearty soups and freshly squeezed juices that register the highest praise. Try the tasty *jugo de zanahoria* (carrot juice). Besides lunch and dinner, those in the know also drop by for afternoon tea. ✉ *Orrego Luco 054, Providencia* ☎ *2/233–2690* ▱ *AE, DC, MC, V* ☉ *No lunch Sun* Ⓜ *Pedro de Valdivia.*

Vitacura

French

$–$$ ✕ **Le Fournil.** Rumor has it that the French owners import even their flour from France at this café-boulangerie. The croissants and baguettes are excellent, but the *tarte tatin* steals the show—large, thick chunks of perfectly baked apple atop a thin layer of pastry, served with a scoop of creamy vanilla ice cream. The *plato del dia* (dish of the day) is always a tasty concoction, but equally good bets are the mixed green salad with grilled goat's cheese and the succulent entrecôte steak with chips. Wicker chairs, wooden tables, whitewashed walls, and large shady terraces make for comfortable dining. ✉ *Vitacura 3841, Vitacura* ☎ *2/228–0219* ✉ *Las Condes 7542, Las Condes* ☎ *2/212–5272* ✉ *Don Carlos 2879, Las Condes* ☎ *2/231–3583* ▱ *AE, DC, MC, V* Ⓜ *Tobalaba.*

Moroccan

$–$$ ✕ **Zanzibar.** Although you can order a tabouleh salad or lamb *tagine* (stew), this ostensibly Moroccan restaurant is more about conjuring up an exotic atmosphere than re-creating the cuisine of the region. (The first clue would be that Zanzibar isn't anywhere near Morocco.) The food is tasty, but the real reason to come is to glide across the multicolored mosaic floors and settle into a chair placed beneath dozens of silver lanterns. Tables are just as fanciful, with designs made from pistachio nuts, red peppers, and beans. It's all a bit over-the-top, but fun nonetheless. ✉ *Borde Río, Av. Monseñor Escrivá de Balaguer 6400, Vitacura* ☎ *2/218–0119* ⌂ *Reservations essential* ▱ *AE, DC, MC, V.*

Seafood

$$–$$$ ✕ **Europeo.** Whether you dine on the crisp white-linen tablecloths in the elegant dining room or under an umbrella in the open-air brasserie, you're in for a fine meal at this trendy yet relaxed eatery on Santiago's most prestigious shopping avenue. The menu leans towards fish: try the succulent parrillada *de pescado*, with scallops, squid, salmon, and crispy fried noodles; a lightly grilled smoked salmon steak on a bed of watercress; or the catch of the day. Juicy steaks, venison, and lamb are good choices for landlubbers. Save room for a dessert of crème brûlée *de lucuma* (lucuma is a fruit native to Peru) or chocolate mousse with almonds. ✉ *Av. Alonso de Cordova, Vitacura* ☎ *2/208–3603* ⌂ *Reservations Essential* ▱ *AE, DC, MC, V.*

$$–$$$ ✕ **Ibis de Puerto Varas.** Nattily nautical sails stretch taut across the ceiling, pierced here and there by mastlike wood columns, and the walls are a splashy blue at this seafood restaurant. Choose from appetizers such as baby eels with hot pepper and garlic or shrimp and squid with an orange sauce. *Panqueque Ibis* is a pancake stuffed with shrimp, calamari, and scallops; the whole thing is sautéed in butter, flambéed in cognac, and served with a spinach and cream sauce. ⊠ *Borde Río, Av. Monseñor Escrivá de Balaguer 6400, Vitacura* ☎ *2/218–0111* ⌕ *Reservations essential* ⊟ *AE, DC, MC, V.*

WHERE TO STAY

Santiago's accommodations range from luxurious *hoteles* to comfortable *residenciales*, which can be homey bed-and-breakfasts or simple hotel-style accommodations. The city also has more than a dozen five-star properties. Most newer hotels are in Providencia and Las Condes, a short taxi ride from Santiago Centro.

Although the official room rates are pricey, you'll undoubtedly find discounts. Call several hotels and ask for the best possible rate. It's a good idea to reserve in advance during the peak seasons (January–February and July–August).

Note that the 18% hotel tax is removed from your bill if you pay in U.S. dollars or with a credit card.

WHAT IT COSTS In pesos (in thousands)				
	$$$$	**$$$**	**$$**	**$**	**¢**
FOR 2 PEOPLE	over 105	75–105	45–75	15–45	under 15

Prices are for a double room in high season, excludig tax

Centro

$$$$ ▦ **Hotel Plaza San Francisco.** This central hotel facing the historic Iglesia
Fodor'sChoice San Francisco has everything corporate travelers need, from business services to a convention center. Between meetings there's plenty to do—take
★ a dip in the lovely pool, stroll through the art gallery, or select a bottle from the well-stocked wineshop. Bristol, the restaurant, serves Chilean food and has perhaps Chile's most talented chef. Large beds, lovely antique furniture, and marble-trim baths fill the hotel's cozy rooms. And while all these amenities are tremendous draws, one of the best reasons to choose this hotel is for its helpful, professional staff. ⊠ *Av. O'Higgins 816, Santiago Centro* ☎ *2/639–3832; 800/223–5652 toll free in the U.S.* 🖷 *2/639–7826* ⊕ *www.plazasanfrancisco.cl* 🖛 *155 rooms, 8 suites* ⌕ *Restaurant, room service, in-room data ports, in-room safes, minibars, indoor pool, gym, hot tub, massage, sauna, lobby lounge, piano bar, laundry service, Internet, business services, convention center, meeting rooms, free parking* ⊟ *AE, DC, MC, V* ⎱⎰ *BP* Ⓜ *Universidad de Chile.*

★ **$$$** ▦ **Carrera.** Santiago's oldest luxury hotel occupies a prominent corner of Plaza de la Constitución, and the rooftop restaurant here provides a matchless view of the country's most important square. Because it has been around for more than 60 years, the Carrera has the prestige that newer hotels lack. The opulent two-story lobby preserves its original art deco murals, and chintz draperies, prints of hunting scenes, and comfortable armchairs lend the suites overlooking the plaza an air of distinction. Live jazz performances are held in the dark-paneled bar, popular among business executives and politicians. ⊠ *Teatinos 180, Santiago Centro* ☎ *2/698–2011* 🖷 *2/672–1083* ⊕ *www.hotelcarrera.com* 🖛 *305* rooms, 22 suites ⚐ 4 restaurants, room service, in-room data ports, in-room safes, minibars, cable TV, in-room VCRs, golf privileges, pool, gym, hair salon, racquetball, piano bar, baby-sitting, laundry service, concierge, Internet, business services, meeting room, airport shuttle, car rental, travel services, free parking, no-smoking floor ▤ AE, DC, MC, V Ⓜ La Moneda, Plaza de Armas.

$$ 🏠 **Hotel Majestic.** Towering white pillars, peaked archways, and glittery brass ornaments welcome you to this Indian-inspired hotel, which also houses an excellent Indian restaurant. A welcoming staff and a location several blocks from the Plaza de Armas make the Majestic a good choice. Even though the bright, airy rooms have "soundproof" windows, ask for one facing away from the street. ✉ Santo Domingo 1526, Santiago Centro ☎ 2/695–8366 🖷 2/697–4051 ⊕ www.hotelmajestic.cl ⇒ 50 rooms ⚐ 2 restaurants, café, fans, in-room safes, minibars, cable TV, pool, bar, laundry service, free parking, no smoking rooms; no a/c in some rooms ▤ AE, DC, MC, V ⭘l BP Ⓜ Santa Ana.

★ $ 🏠 **City Hotel.** Suitably bedecked porters open the heavy front doors of this 70-year-old establishment, a former rival in its heyday of the upscale Carrera hotel. The City seems stuck in a time warp, but this is what gives the hotel its old-fashioned charm. The slightly dated rooms are spacious with high ceilings, and bathrooms still have the original large white tubs. Request one of the quieter rooms not facing the street. This place is a real bargain right in the heart of downtown, less than a minute from the Plaza de Armas. ✉ Compañía 1063, Santiago Centro ☎🖷 2/695–4526 ⇒ 72 rooms ⚐ Restaurant, room service, minibars, cable TV, bar, laundry service, meeting room, free parking; no a/c ▤ AE, DC, MC, V ⭘l CP Ⓜ Plaza de Armas.

$ 🏠 **Foresta.** Staying in this seven-story hotel across the street from Cerro Santa Lucía is like visiting an elegant old home. Cheery floral wallpaper, lovely antique furnishings, and bronze and marble accents decorate the guest rooms. The best ones are those on the upper floors overlooking the hill. A rooftop restaurant-bar is a great place to enjoy the view. The quaint cafés and shops of Plaza Mulato Gil de Castro are just around the corner. ✉ Victoria Subercaseaux 353, Santiago Centro ☎🖷 2/639–6261 ⇒ 35 rooms, 8 suites ⚐ Restaurant, room service, minibars, cable TV, piano bar, laundry service, Internet, meeting room, free parking; no a/c ▤ AE, DC, MC, V Ⓜ Bellas Artes.

$ 🏠 **Hostal Río Amazonas.** The narrow lobby of this small hostelry, overflowing with foliage, is painted a warm, welcoming orange. All the rooms have high ceilings and double doors, many of which open onto the table-filled lobby, where you can breakfast and sit around reading. Each evening, the friendly owner Fabian serves cocktails and cold beers to his crowd of foreign guests. ✉ Rosas 2234, Barrio Brasil ☎ 2/671–9013 or 2/698–4092 🖷 2/671–9013 ⊕ www.hostalrioamazonas.cl ⇒ 10 rooms ⚐ Bar, laundry service, Internet, parking (fee); no a/c, no room phones, no room TVs ▤ AE, DC, MC, V ⭘l CP Ⓜ Santa Ana.

$ 🏠 **Hotel Los Arcos.** Young foreigners on a budget flock to this modest hotel off Plaza Brasil. Rooms are simple but clean, and some have windows overlooking an interior courtyard and café. ✉ Agustinas 2173, Santiago Centro ☎🖷 2/699–0998 or 2/696–5602 ⇒ 20 rooms ⚐ Café, room service, fans, laundry service; no a/c ▤AE, DC, MC, V Ⓜ República.

$ 🏠 **Hotel Santa Lucia.** The rooms are on the small side and are a little tired looking—the hotel has been operating for more than 40 years—but they're spotlessly clean, and the hotel is central. The lobby is bright, airy, and spacious. The large terrace restaurant, unusually quiet given its location, serves nothing but typical Chilean fare. Each weekday, without fail, it plays host to the father of Marcelo Rios, who for a short time topped the world tennis rankings. ✉ San Antonio 327, Paseo Huérfanos 779,

Santiago Centro ☎ 2/639–8201 🖷 2/633–1844 ⟿ *70 rooms* ⚑ *Fans, in-room safes, minibars, cable TV, laundry service, Internet, meeting rooms, parking (fee); no a/c* ⊟ *AE, DC, MC, V* ⦿| *CP* Ⓜ *Plaza de Armas.*

$ 🖵 **Hotel Vegas.** This colonial-style building, adorned with a bullet-shape turret on the corner, is in the heart of the charming Barrio París-Londres. Minutes away is the stunning Iglesia San Francisco. Rooms here have plenty of windows—ask for one with a view of gently curving Calle Londres. ⊠ *Londres 49, Santiago Centro* ☎ 2/632–2498 *or* 2/632–2514 🖷 2/632–5084 ⊕ *www.hotelvegas.net* ⟿ *20 rooms* ⚑ *Café, room service, in-room safes, cable TV, bar, laundry service, Internet, free parking, no-smoking rooms; no a/c in some rooms* ⊟ *AE, DC, MC, V* Ⓜ *Universidad de Chile.*

$ 🖵 **El Marqués del Forestal.** A good budget choice for families, these small apartments sleep up to four people. The simply furnished rooms also have kitchenettes. The hotel overlooks Parque Forestal, not far from Mercado Central. ⊠ *Ismael Valdés Vergara 740, Santiago Centro* ☎ 2/633–3462 🖷 2/639–4157 ⟿ *15 apartments* ⚑ *Kitchenettes, laundry service, free parking; no a/c* ⊟ *AE, DC, MC, V* ⦿| *CP* Ⓜ *Puente Cal y Canto, Plaza de Armas.*

★ **$** 🖵 **Residencial Londres.** This inexpensive, 1920s-era hotel in the picturesque Barrio París-Londres is just a stone's throw from most of the city's major sights. Rooms are spacious, with high ceilings ringed by detailed moldings and expansive wood floors. The best rooms have stone balconies overlooking this charmingly atypical neighborhood. The hosts are friendly and helpful. ⊠ *Londres 54, Santiago Centro* ☎☎ 2/638–2215 ⟿ *27 rooms* ⚑ *Laundry service; no a/c, no room phones, no room TVs* ⊟ *No credit cards* Ⓜ *Universidad de Chile.*

¢–$ 🖵 **Hotel París.** In the heart of Barrio París-Londres stands this mansion-turned-hotel with a large lobby and a quaint courtyard garden. Rooms are old-fashioned and well furnished. Those in the more comfortable half, which you reach by a winding, marble staircase, are more spacious, come with cable TV, and are just a few thousand pesos extra. ⊠ *París 813, La Alameda* ☎ 2/664–0921 ☎☎ 2/639–4037 ⟿ *40 rooms* ⚑ *Dining room; no a/c* ⊟ *AE, DC, MC, V* Ⓜ *Universidad de Chile, Santa Lucía.*

Las Condes

★ **$$$$** 🖵 **Hyatt Regency.** The soaring spire of the Hyatt Regency leaves a lasting impression, especially if you're shooting up a glass elevator through a 24-story atrium. An architectural eye-catcher, the hotel has rooms that wrap around the cylindrical lobby, providing a panoramic view of the Andes. Executive suites in the upper-floor Regency Club include express check-in, a billiards room, and a private dining area. Duke's, the spitting image of an English pub, fills to standing capacity each day after work hours. The hotel's three restaurants—Tuscan, Thai, and Japanese—are all worth a visit. ⊠ *Av. Kennedy 4601, Las Condes* ☎ 2/218–1234 🖷 2/218–2513 ⊕ *www.santiago.hyatt.com* ⟿ *287 rooms, 23 suites* ⚑ *3 restaurants, room service, in-room data ports, some in-room faxes, in-room safes, minibars, cable TV, in-room VCRs, golf privileges, 2 tennis courts, pool, hair salon, health club, massage, sauna, bar, lobby lounge, shops, baby-sitting, laundry service, concierge, Internet, business services, convention center, meeting rooms, airport shuttle, free parking, no-smoking floor* ⊟ *AE, DC, MC, V.*

$$$$ 🖵 **Radisson Royal.** Santiago's most dynamic office building, the World Trade Center, is also home to the Radisson Royal, a combination that will make sense to many corporate travelers. The windows here are huge, with three wide glass panels for triptych perspectives of the city and the Andes beyond. The upholstered leather chairs and wood paneling in meeting rooms make it clear the hotel is serious in its attitude toward luxury. ⊠ *Av. Vitacura 2610, Las Condes* ☎ *2/203–6000; 800/333–3333 toll free in the U.S.* 🖷 *2/203–6001* ⊕ *www.radisson.com/santiagocl* 🖙 *159 rooms, 26 suites* ◊ *Restaurant, room service, in-room data ports, in-room safes, minibars, cable TV, indoor pool, gym, bar, lounge, library, baby-sitting, laundry service, concierge, Internet, business services, meeting rooms, helipad, free parking, no-smoking floors* ⊟ *AE, DC, MC, V* Ⓜ *Tobalaba.*

$$$$ 🏨 **Ritz-Carlton.** The redbrick exterior and glass atrium roof of this glitzy 15-story hotel, the first Ritz-Carlton in South America, make surrounding apartment blocks look dowdy in comparison. Mahogany-panel walls, cream marble floors, and enormous windows characterize the splendid two-story lobby, which faces a small leafy plaza just off busy Avenida Apoquindo. Elegant furnishings upholstered in brocade, and silk floral fabrics dominate the large guest rooms. Under a magnificent glass dome on the top floor you can swim or work out while pondering the panorama, smog permitting, of the Andes and the Santiago skyline. ⊠ *Calle El Alcade 15, Las Condes* ☎ *2/470–8500* 🖷 *2/470-8512* ⊕ *www.ritzcarlton.com* 🖙 *189 rooms, 16 suites* ◊ *Restaurant, room service, in-room data ports, in-room safes, minibars, cable TV, golf privileges, indoor pool, gym, hot tub, sauna, Turkish bath, 2 bars, lobby lounge, baby-sitting, laundry service, concierge, business services, convention center, meeting rooms, airport shuttle, car rental, travel services, free parking, no-smoking rooms* ⊟ *AE, DC, MC, V* Ⓜ *El Golf.*

$$$$ 🏨 **Santiago Marriott Hotel.** The first 25 floors of the tallest building in Santiago—40 stories in all—house the Marriott hotel. An impressive two-story, cream-marble lobby sprouts full-grown palm trees in and around comfortable seating areas. The hotel caters to those on business, and if you opt for an executive room you can breakfast in a private lounge while you scan the newspaper and marvel at the snowcapped Andes. You needn't venture out for entertainment either: there are tango evenings in the Latin Grill restaurant along with weekly wine tasting sessions. ⊠ *Av. Kennedy 5741, Las Condes* ☎ *2/426–2000; 800/228–9290 toll free in the U.S. and Canada* 🖷 *2/426–2001* ⊕ *www.santiagomarriott.com* 🖙 *280 rooms, 60 suites* ◊ *2 restaurants, in-room data ports, minibars, cable TV, indoor pool, health club, hot tub, sauna, bar, lobby lounge, shops, baby-sitting, laundry service, concierge, Internet, business services, convention center, meeting rooms, airport shuttle, travel services, free parking, no-smoking floor* ⊟ *AE, DC, MC, V.*

$$$–$$$$ 🏨 **Hotel Inter-Continental.** A two-story marble lobby announces that you have entered one of the city's top hotels; beyond the welcome desk there are comfortable lounges, including one next to an indoor waterfall. In the back is Bice, one of the city's most memorable restaurants. The rooms are sumptuous, with doors made from handsome panels of the native blond wood called *mañío* and a menu card listing five types of pillows, from "very soft" to "stiff." Five executive floors have express check-in, a sleek private dining area with open bar, and an elegant meeting room. ⊠ *Av. Vitacura 2885, Las Condes* ☎ *2/394–2000* 🖷 *2/394–2078* ⊕ *www.interconti.com* 🖙 *297 rooms, 9 suites* ◊ *2 restaurants, room service, in-room data ports, in-room safes, minibars, cable TV with movies and video games, indoor pool, gym, massage, sauna, 2 bars, lobby lounge, shops, baby-sitting, laundry service, concierge, Internet, business services, convention center, meeting rooms, travel services, free parking, no-smoking floors* ⊟ *AE, DC, MC, V* �ʘⅠ *BP* Ⓜ *Tobalaba.*

$$–$$$ 🏨 **Hotel Montebianco.** The four-floor Montebianco manages to combine a professional attitude that many larger places lack with an informal setting and a friendly, helpful staff. The rooms, which wind around a central staircase, are on the small side; the king-size beds take up most

of the space. A few dollars extra secures a room with more elbow room. The hotel is right on a popular dining thoroughfare. ⊠ *Av. Isidora Goyenechea 2911, Las Condes* ☎ *2/232–5034* 🖷 *2/233–0420* ⊕ *www. hotelmontebianco.cl* 🖘 *33 rooms* ⚒ *Cafeteria, dining room, in-room safes, some minibars, cable TV, bar, laundry service, Internet, business services, airport shuttle, travel services* ☰ *AE, DC, MC, V* ⅉ⃝ *BP* Ⓜ *El Golf, Tobalaba.*

$$ 🎛 **Hotel Tarapacá.** This smaller hotel may have a smudge here and there, but its location in fashionable Las Condes makes up for it. Rooms facing the commercial hub of Avenida Apoquindo are susceptible to traffic noise, so ask for one in the back. Better yet, pay a few extra dollars for one of two spacious suites on the 11th floor. The dormer windows make you feel that you're in a garret. ⊠ *Vecinal 40, at Av. Apoquindo, Las Condes* ☎ *2/245–1300* 🖷 *2/245–1440* ⊕ *www.hoteltarapaca.cl* 🖘 *52 rooms* ⚒ *Restaurant, room service, in-room safes, minibars, cable TV, sauna, bar, laundry service, Internet, business services, meeting rooms, free parking* ☰ *AE, DC, MC, V* ⅉ⃝ *BP* Ⓜ *El Golf, Tobalaba.*

Providencia

$$$$ 🎛 **Four Points Sheraton.** Río Mapocho and the heart of Providencia's shopping district are just steps away from this small luxury hotel. The cool rooftop terrace is a real pleasure in summer, when you can relax with a pisco sour and take in the city views. If you prefer a more active nightlife scene, you're in luck. The hotel is adjacent to one of the city's main party thoroughfares: Suecia, lined with pubs, restaurants, and discos. Rooms facing these streets can be noisy, even through double-paned windows. ⊠ *Av. Santa Magdalena 111, Providencia* ☎ *2/750–0300* 🖷 *2/750–0350* ⊕ *www.fourpoints.com* 🖘 *112 rooms, 16 suites* ⚒ *Restaurant, room service, in-room data ports, in-room safes, minibars, cable TV, golf privileges, pool, gym, sauna, bar, laundry service, Internet, business services, convention center, meeting rooms, airport shuttle, travel services, free parking, no-smoking rooms* ☰ *AE, DC, MC, V* Ⓜ *Los Leones.*

$$$$ 🎛 **Park Plaza.** It bills itself as a "classic European-style" hotel, and the receptionists that greet you from behind individual mahogany desks certainly call to mind the Continent. The refined decor, with rich burgundy and cream accents, extends to the adjoining Park Lane restaurant, whose chef masterfully combines international and Chilean cuisine. Although the glass-covered pool on the top floor is tiny, it has a great view. ⊠ *Av. Ricardo Lyon 207, Providencia* ☎ *2/233–6363* 🖷 *2/233–6668* ⊕ *www.parkplaza.cl* 🖘 *104 rooms, 6 suites* ⚒ *Restaurant, in-room data ports, in-room safes, minibars, cable TV, golf privileges, indoor pool, health club, sauna, bar, lobby lounge, shop, baby-sitting, laundry service, Internet, business services, convention center, meeting rooms, airport shuttle, travel services, free parking, no-smoking floor* ☰ *AE, DC, MC, V* ⅉ⃝ *BP* Ⓜ *Los Leones.*

★ **$$$$** 🎛 **Sheraton Santiago and San Cristóbal Tower.** Two distinct hotels stand side-by-side at this unrivaled resort. The Sheraton Santiago is certainly a luxury hotel, but the adjoining San Cristóbal Tower is in a class by itself, popular with business executives and foreign dignitaries who value its efficiency, elegance, and impeccable service. A lavish, labyrinthine marble lobby links the two hotels, three fine restaurants, and the city's largest hotel convention center. Pampering is not all that goes on at the San Cristóbal Tower—attentive staff members at the business center can provide you with everything from secretarial services to Internet access. ⊠ *Av. Santa María 1742, Providencia* ☎ *2/233–5000* 🖷 *2/234–1732* ⊕ *www. sheraton.cl* 🖘 *Sheraton Santiago: 379 rooms, 14 suites. San Cristóbal Tower: 139 rooms, 3 suites* ⚒ *3 restaurants, picnic area, in-room data* *ports, in-room faxes, in-room safes, minibars, tennis court, 2 pools, gym, hair salon, sauna, 2 bars, lobby lounge, shops, baby-sitting, laundry service, concierge, Internet, business services, convention center, meeting rooms, airport shuttle, car rental, helipad, travel services, no-smoking floors* ⊟ *AE, DC, MC, V* Ⓜ *Pedro de Valdivia.*

$$–$$$ 🏨 **Hotel Bonaparte.** Resembling a small château, this charming hotel on a corner of tree-lined Avenida Ricardo Lyon is often overshadowed by its flashier neighbors. The rooms with the most light are on the top floor, but all are tastefully decorated and have large baths. ⊠ *Mar del Plata 2171, at Av Ricardo Lyon, Providencia* ☎ *2/274–0621* ⊠ *2/204–8907* ⊕ *www.hotelbonaparte.com* ⤳ *25 rooms, 2 suites* ⚭ *Restaurant, room service, in-room data ports, minibars, cable TV, pool, gym, sauna, lobby lounge, baby-sitting, laundry service, Internet, business services, meeting rooms, free parking, no-smoking rooms* ⊟ *AE, DC, MC, V* ⦿ *BP* Ⓜ *Los Leones.*

★ $$–$$$ 🏨 **Hotel Orly.** This is a rare find—a moderately priced hotel with many of the comforts of those costing twice as much. That you can find a treasure like this in the middle of Providencia is nothing short of a miracle. The shiny wood floors, country-manor furnishings, and glass-domed breakfast room make this hotel as sweet as it is economical. Most of the credit can go to the owner, who decorated it herself. Rooms come in all shapes and sizes, so ask to see a few before you decide. Cafetto, the downstairs café, serves some of the finest coffee drinks in town. ⊠ *Av. Pedro de Valdivia 027, Providencia* ☎ *2/231–8947* ⊠ *2/252–0051* ⊕ *www.orlyhotel.com* ⤳ *25 rooms, 3 suites* ⚭ *Restaurant, café, room service, in-room safes, minibars, cable TV, laundry service, Internet, free parking* ⊟ *AE, DC, MC, V* ⦿ *BP* Ⓜ *Pedro de Valdivia.*

Vitacura

$$ 🏨 **Acacias de Vitacura.** The extraordinary location of this hotel—in the midst of towering eucalyptus and acacia trees thought to be more than a century old—is unforgettable. It's a pleasure to drink your morning coffee in the lush garden under one of the oversize umbrellas. The rooms here are simple but bright, and the owner's collection of old carriages gives the hotel a quirky personality. ⊠ *El Manantial 1781, Vitacura* ☎ *2/211–8601* ⊠ *2/212–7858* ⊕ *www.hotelacacias.cl* ⤳ *33 rooms, 2 suites* ⚭ *Restaurant, minibars, cable TV, pool, gym, baby-sitting, Internet, meeting room, travel services, free parking* ⊟ *AE, DC, MC, V* ⦿ *BP.*

$$ 🏨 **Hotel Kennedy.** This glass tower may seem impersonal, but the small details—such as beautiful vases of flowers atop the wardrobes—show the staff cares about keeping guests happy. Bilingual secretarial services and an elegant boardroom are among the pluses for visiting executives. The Aquarium restaurant serves international cuisine and has a cellar full of excellent Chilean wines. ⊠ *Av. Kennedy 4570, Vitacura* ☎ *2/219–4000* ⊠ *2/218–2188* ⊕ *www.hotelkennedy.cl* ⤳ *123 rooms, 10 suites* ⚭ *Restaurant, room service, in-room data ports, minibars, cable TV, pool, gym, massage, sauna, bar, laundry service, Internet, business services, meeting rooms, travel services, free parking, no-smoking floor* ⊟ *AE, DC, MC, V* ⦿ *BP.*

NIGHTLIFE & THE ARTS

Although it can't rival Buenos Aires or Rio de Janeiro, Santiago buzzes with increasingly sophisticated bars and clubs. Santiaguinos often meet for drinks during the week, usually after work when most bars have happy hour. Then they call it a night, as most people don't really cut loose until Friday and Saturday. Weekends commence with dinner beginning at 9 or 10 and then a drink at a pub. (This doesn't refer to an English beer hall; a pub here is a bar with loud music and a lot of seating). No one thinks of heading to the dance clubs until 1 AM, and they stay until 5 or 6 AM.

With dozens of museums scattered around the city, it's clear Santiaguinos also have a strong love of culture. Music, theater, and other artistic endeavors supplement weekends spent dancing the night away.

The Arts

Dance

The venerable **Ballet Nacional Chileno** (⊠ Av. Providencia 043, Providencia ☎ 2/634–4746), founded in 1945, performs from its repertoire of more than 150 pieces at the Teatro Universidad de Chile near Plaza Baquedano.

Film

Santiago's dozens of cinemas screen movies in English with Spanish subtitles. Movie listings are posted in *El Mercurio* and other dailies. Admission is generally 3,000 pesos; matinees often cost only 2,000 pesos. The newest multiplexes—with mammoth screens, plush seating, and fresh popcorn—are in the city's malls. Among the best theaters in town is the **Cinemark 12** (⊠ Av. Kennedy 9001, Las Condes ☎ 600/600–2463), in the Alto Las Condes mall. Its dozen screens show the latest releases. In the Parque Arauco mall, **Showcase Cinemas Parque Arauco** (⊠ Av. Kennedy 5413, Las Condes ☎ 2/224–7707) has the city's most modern facility. **Cine Hoyts Huérfanos** (⊠ Huérfanos 735, Santiago Centro ☎ 600/500–0400) has six screens. **Cine Hoyts San Agustín** (⊠ San Antonio 144, Santiago Centro ☎ 600/500–0400) has nine screens.

Most of the city's art cinemas tend to screen international favorites. The old standby is **El Biógrafo** (⊠ José Victorino Lastarria 181, Santiago Centro ☎ 2/633–4435), which shows foreign films on its single screen. It's on a colorful street lined with cafés. **Cine Arte Normandie** (⊠ Av. Tarapacá 1181, Santiago Centro ☎ 2/697–2979) is a popular theater south of Iglesia San Francisco. Affiliated with one of the city's universities, the **Centro de Extensión Universidad Católica** (⊠ Av. O'Higgins 390, Santiago Centro ☎ 2/686–6516) only screens the classics. **Tobalaba** (⊠ Providencia 2563, Las Condes ☎ 2/231–6630) shows arty and foreign films.

Galleries

Galleries are scattered around the city, and admission is usually free. The newspaper *El Mercurio* lists current exhibitions in its Saturday supplement *Vivienda Decoración*. **Galería del Cerro** (⊠ Antonía López de Bello 0135, Bellavista ☎ 2/737–3500 ⊕ www.delcerro.cl) features works by prominent local artists. At the foot of Cerro San Cristóbal, the bright and airy gallery is a short walk from Pablo Neruda's home of La Chascona. It's open weekdays 10:30–6:30 and Saturday 10:30–2. **Galería Isabel Aninat** (⊠ Alonso de Córdova 3053, Las Condes ☎ 2/263–2729) hosts exhibitions of international artists. It's open weekdays 10–2 and 4–8, Saturday 11–2 and 4–7, and Sunday 11–2. **Sala de Arte Fundación**

Telefónica (✉ Av. Providencia 111, Providencia ☎ 2/691–2000), near Plaza Baquedano, exhibits painting and sculpture in the lobby of the foundation's 32-story headquarters. It's open Tuesday–Sunday 10–8.

Temporary exhibitions of photography and paintings are frequently on display in *institutos culturales* or *centros de cultura*. Corporación Cultural de Las Condes and Instituto Cultural de Providencia, both open weekdays 9–5:30, lean toward contemporary art. **Corporación Cultural de Las Condes** (✉ Nuestra Señora del Rosario 30, at Av. Apoquindo, Las Condes ☎ 2/366–9382). **Instituto Cultural de Providencia** (✉ Av. 11 de Septiembre, Providencia ☎ 2/209–4341).

Music

Parque de las Esculturas (✉ Av. Santa María between Av. Pedro de Valdivia Norte and Padre Letelier, Providencia ☎ no phone) hosts numerous open-air concerts in the early evenings in summer. The **Teatro Municipal** (✉ Plaza Alcade Mekis, Av. Agustinas at Av. San Antonio, Santiago Centro ☎ 2/463–8888 ⊕ www.municipal.cl), Santiago's 19th-century theater, presents excellent classical concerts, opera, and ballet by internationally recognized artists from March to December. **Teatro Oriente** (✉ Av. Pedro de Valdivia, between the Costanera and Providencia, Providencia ☎ 2/335–0023) is a popular venue for classical concerts, including many performances of Beethoven's works. The Coro Sinfónico and the Orquestra Sinfónica, the city's highly regarded chorus and orchestra, perform near Plaza Baquedano at the **Teatro Universidad de Chile** (✉ Providencia 043, Providencia ☎ 2/634–5295).

Theater

Provided that you understand at least a little Spanish, you may want to take in a bit of Chilean theater. Its widely regarded to be among the best in Latin America. Performances take place all year, mainly from Thursday to Sunday at around 8 PM. In February the year's best plays are performed across the city in a program called *Teatro A Mil*, referring to the admission price of 1,000 pesos (less than $2). Contact the tourist office for details.

The following theaters produce a mix of Latin American comedies and dramas. **El Conventillo** (✉ Bellavista 173, Bellavista ☎ 2/777–4164). **Teatro Bellavista** (✉ Dardignac 0110, Bellavista ☎ 2/735–2395). **Teatro Lo Castillo** (✉ Candelaria Goyenechea 3820, Vitacura ☎ 2/244–5856). **Teatro San Ginés** (✉ Mallinkrodt 76, Bellavista ☎ 2/738–2159).

The well respected ICTUS theater company performs in the **Teatro la Comedia** (✉ Merced 349, Santiago Centro ☎ 2/639–1523).

Nightlife

Bars and clubs are scattered all over Santiago, but a handful of streets have such a concentration of establishments that they resemble block parties on Friday and Saturday nights. Try pub-crawling with all the well-heeled young locals on Avenida Suecia in the chic neighborhood of Providencia. Calle General Holley, which runs parallel to it, is also worth a try. Most establishments here try to lure you in with drink specials; it takes a while to get used to people bartering with you as you walk past. The crowd here is young, as the drinking age is 18. To the east in Las Condes, Paseo San Damián is an outdoor complex of bars and clubs. It's the newest and most fashionable of nighttime destinations. If you're looking for something a little more bohemian, head for Avenida Pío Nono, the main drag through the colorful neighborhood of Bellavista. Although slightly seedy, the web of streets is filled with cutting-edge clubs.

What you should wear depends on your destination. Bellavista has a mix of styles ranging from blue jeans to basic black. Avenida Suecia maintains a stricter dress code (sneakers might bar you from admission), as does Paseo San Damián. Note that establishments referred to as "night clubs" are female strip shows.

Bars & Clubs

BELLAVISTA   The **Libro Café** (⊠ Purísima 165, Bellavista ☎ 2/735–3901) is a late-night haunt for starving artists and those who wish they were. If you're hungry, head here for a tortilla *malageña* and a carafe of the house red. **Remix Restobar** (⊠ Antonía Lopez de Bello 94, Bellavista ☎ 2/777–8067) mixes food and music—sushi and tapas with deep house, down tempo, and bossa nova. While you sit back and relax, you can order something to nibble on and wash it down with a glass of Chilean wine. Reservations are advisable. Stop by for a drink in the evening at the sleek and stylish **Tantra** (⊠ Ernesto Pinto Lagarrigue 154, Bellavista ☎ 2/732–3287) and watch the restaurant transform itself into a disco at midnight. The beat goes on until 6 AM, unless one of the frequent after-hours parties keeps it open even later. Upstairs are king-size beds used as tables—reserve one for a memorable evening.

CENTRO   From the doorway, **Casa de Cena** (⊠ Almirante Simpson 20, Providencia ☎ 2/635–4418) looks like your average hole-in-the-wall, but it's actually a gem. Most nights a band wanders through the maze of wood-paneled rooms singing folk songs while the bartender listens to endless stories from inebriated regulars.

LAS CONDES   **Flannery's Geo Pub** (⊠ Encomenderos 83, Las Condes ☎ 2/233–6675), a few blocks up from Suecia and close to El Bosque Norte, is Chile's first real Irish drinking hole, a long-running establishment serving Irish food, beer, and occasionally Guinness on tap. **Publicity** (⊠ El Bosque Norte 0155, Las Condes ☎ 2/333–1214) is a large, popular, glass-fronted building permanently teeming with people in their 20s and early 30s.

PROVIDENCIA &   Most of the neighborhood's nightspots are found along the pedestrian
LAS CONDES   street of Avenida Suecia. One of the most popular is **Mister Ed** (⊠ Av. Suecia 0152, Providencia ☎ 2/231–2624), the best place to hear up-and-coming local bands. The **Green Bull** (⊠ Av. Suecia 0150, Providencia ☎ 2/334–5619), next door to Mister Ed, competes for pretty much the same crowd with live performances nightly. **Entre Negros** (⊠ Suecia 0188, Providencia ☎ 2/334–2094) might be the most popular of Avenida Suecia's discos. This longtime favorite also hosts live music on weekends.

Boomerang (⊠ General Holley 2285, Providencia ☎ 2/334–5081) is a raucous pub with a few pool tables. The **Phone Box** (⊠ Galería del Patio, Av. Providencia 1652, Providencia ☎ 2/235–9972) is a fairly convincing recreation of a British pub that serves steak-and-kidney pie to homesick Brits. You'll easily spot the entrance—it's through a red phone booth.

Gay & Lesbian Clubs

Once mostly underground, Santiago's gay scene is starting to assert itself. Although some bars are so discreet they don't have a sign, others are known by just about everyone. Clubs like Bunker, for example, are so popular that they attract a fair number of nongays. There's no real gay district, but a cluster of gay restaurants and bars are on the streets parallel to Avenida Pío Nono in Bellavista. There's not much for lesbians in Santiago, however, although some women can be found at most establishments catering to men.

On Bellavista's main drag, **Bokhara** (⊠ Pío Nono 430, Bellavista ☎ 2/732–1050 or 2/735–1271) is one of the city's largest and most popular gay discos. It has two dance floors playing house and techno. **Bunker** (✉ Bombero Nuñez 159, Bellavista ☎ 2/737–1716 or 2/777–3760), a mainstay of the gay scene, is in a cavernous space with numerous platforms overlooking the dance floor. Don't get here too early—people don't arrive until well after midnight. Note that it's only open Fridays and Saturdays.

The venerable **Fausto** (✉ Av. Santa María 0832, Providencia ☎ 2/777–1041), in business for more than 20 years, has polished wood paneling that calls to mind a gentlemen's club. The disco pumps until the wee hours. The friendly and unpretentious dance club **Naxos** (✉ Av. O'Higgins 776, Santiago Centro ☎ 2/639–9629), in a high-ceilinged basement, plays everything from techno to Latin rock.

If you're looking for a place to kick back with a beer, try **Pub Friend's** (✉ Bombero Nuñez 365, Bellavista ☎ 2/777–3979). Live music performances and karaoke take place on Thursdays, Fridays, and Saturdays. **Quasar** (✉ Coquimbo 1458, Santiago Centro ☎ 2/671–1267), frequented by men and women, has been around for more than 20 years and stages drag shows.

Salsa Clubs

Arriba de la Bola (✉ General Holley 171, Providencia ☎ 2/232–7965) shakes things up with a live Cuban band. It gets packed, so reservations are necessary. **Cimarrón** (✉ Av. Irarrázabal 1730, Nuñoa ☎ 2/225–1627), with salsa and tango classes on Wednesday and Thursday nights, is the perfect spot to learn how to shake to a tropical beat. On Fridays and Saturdays this *salsoteca* comes alive with sensuous salsa, merengue, and milonga. For salsa and merengue, try **Ilé Habana** (✉ Bucarest 95, Providencia ☎ 2/231–5711), where you can boogie to the beat of a live band. There are free salsa lessons Tuesday–Saturday at 9:30 PM.

SPORTS & THE OUTDOORS

Athletic Clubs & Spas

All of Santiago's larger hotels have health clubs on the premises, usually with personal trainers on hand to assist you with your workout. Even if you aren't staying at a particular hotel, you can usually pay to use the facilities for the day. **Balthus** (✉ Av. Monseñor Escrivá de Balaguer 5970, Vitacura ☎ 2/218–1831) is the city's top health club. This high-tech marvel has all the latest equipment. You feel healthier just by walking into the complex, a sleek series of riverside structures in concrete and glass designed by Santiago's ArchiPlan. There are eight tennis courts, spas, pools, and numerous fitness programs.

The modern **Spa Mund** (✉ Cardenal Belarmino 1075, Vitacura ☎ 2/211–2717) is a sprawling aquatic spa where you can relax in saunas and hot tubs. Better yet, pamper yourself with a facial. **Agua y Bién** (✉ Americo Vespucio Norte 1440, Vitacura ☎ 2/371–6554), a small club, offers massage, hydrotherapy, and other spa treatments.

Bicycling

Santiago has no shortage of public parks, and they provide good opportunities to see the city. If you're ambitious you can even pedal up Cerro San Cristóbal, the city's largest hill. You can rent mountain bikes for 9,000 pesos from **Lys** (✉ Av. Miraflores 537, Santiago Centro ☎ 2/633–7600).

Horse Racing

Betting on horses is popular in Santiago, which is the reason the city has two large racetracks. Races take place Mondays and alternating Thursdays at **Club Hípico** (⊠ Blanco Encalada 2540, Santiago Centro ☎ 2/693–9600), south of downtown. El Ensayo, an annual race that's a century-old tradition, is held here in early November. **Hipódromo Chile** (⊠ Hipódromo Chile 1715, Independencia ☎ 2/270–9270) is the home of the prestigious Gran Premio Internacional, which draws competitors from around South America. Regular races are held Saturdays and alternating Thursdays.

Soccer

Chile's most popular spectator sport is soccer, but a close second is watching the endless bickering among owners, trainers, and players whenever a match isn't going well. First-division soccer matches, featuring the city's handful of local teams, are held in the **Estadio Nacional** (⊠ Av. Grecia 2001, Nuñoa ☎ 2/238–8102), south of the city center. Soccer is played year-round, with most matches taking place on weekends. It was here in the Estadio that Pinochet's henchmen killed thousands of political opponents in 1973, including Chilean folk singer Victor Jara. To assure that he would never again provoke Chileans to action with his music, Jara's hands were mutilated before he was put to death.

SHOPPING

Providencia, the city's most popular shopping district, has boutiques, two department stores, and a small mall. Avenida Providencia slices through the neighborhood, branching off for several blocks into the parallel Avenida 11 de Septiembre. The shops continue east to Avenida El Bosque Norte, after which Avenida Providencia changes its name to Avenida Apoquindo and the neighborhood becomes Las Condes. In this chic district you'll find modern shopping malls filled with hundreds of specialty shops and international brands such as Tommy Hilfiger and Gucci. A stroll down the wide tree-lined Avenida Alonso de Cordova and La Nueva Costanera in Vitacura will take you past lots of exclusive shops.

Bohemian Bellavista attracts those in search of the perfect woolen sweater or the right piece of lapis lazuli jewelry. Santiago Centro is much more down-to-earth. The Mercado Central is where anything fishy is sold, while nearby markets like Vega Chica and Vega Central sell just about every item imaginable. Stores downtown usually face the street, which makes window-shopping more entertaining. Pedestrian streets around the Plaza de Armas are crowded with children licking ice-cream cones, older women strolling arm in arm, and business executives sitting under wide umbrellas having their shoes shined.

Shops in Santiago are generally open weekdays 10–7 and Saturdays 10–2. Malls are usually open daily 10–10.

Markets

Aldea de Vitacura (⊠ Av. Vitacura 6838, Vitacura ☎ 2/219–3161) is a pleasant outdoor market where you can browse among the various stands selling local and national craftwork. It's open Tuesday–Sunday 11–9.

Centro Artesanal Santa Lucía, an art fair at the base of Cerro Santa Lucía, is an excellent place to find Aymara and Mapuche crafts. It's open daily 10–7.

Bellavista's colorful **Feria Artesanal Pío Nono,** held in the park along Avenida Pío Nono, comes alive every night of the week. It's even busier on weekends, when more vendors gather in Parque Domingo Gómez to display their handicrafts.

Los Graneros de Alba (⊠ Av. Apoquindo 9085, Las Condes ☎ 2/248–2295), more commonly known as Pueblito Los Dominicos, is a "village" of more than 200 shops where you can find everything from fine leather to semiprecious stones and antiques. There's also a wonderful display of cockatoos and other live birds. It's a nice place to visit, especially on weekends when traveling musicians entertain the crowds. It's open Tuesday–Saturday 10:30–9:30 and Sunday 10:30–8. Next door is an attractive whitewashed church dating from the late 18th century.

Shopping Malls

In Santiago, the shopping malls are so enormous that they have become attractions in their own right. Some even provide free transportation from the major hotels.

Alto Las Condes (⊠ Av. Kennedy 9001, Las Condes ☎ 2/299–6999) has 245 shops, three department stores, a multiplex, and a seemingly endless food court. Also here is a supermarket, appropriately named Jumbo, where the staff members wear roller skates while restocking the shelves. It carries excellent Chilean wines.

Parque Arauco (⊠ Av. Kennedy 5413, Las Condes ☎ 2/299–0500) is a North American–style shopping center with an eclectic mix of designer boutiques, including clothing outlets like Benetton, Ralph Lauren, and Laura Ashley. Chile's three largest department stores—Falabella, Ripley, and Almacenes París—sell everything from perfume to plates.

The **Mall del Centro** (⊠ Puente 689, Santiago Centro ☎ 2/361–0011) is a smaller version of Parque Arauco, with fewer international brands but a more central location.

Specialty Shops

Handicrafts

You'll find replica Diaguita pottery, Mapuche rugs, and many other typical Chilean crafts in the **Centro de Artesanía** (⊠ Mall, Estación Central, Estación Central ☎ no phone). Shops of all sorts, selling local and national crafts, line the winding passageways of the **Centro de Artesanía Manquehue** (⊠ Av. Manquehue Sur at Apoquindo, Las Condes ☎ no phone), alongside the Apumanque Mall. **Cooperativa Almacén Campesino** (⊠ Torreón Victoria, Bellavista ☎ 2/335–4443), in the middle of Parque Metropolitano, is a cooperative of artisans from various indigenous cultures. This shop sells the best handicrafts from all over Chile.

Jewelry

Chile is one of the few places in the world where lapis lazuli, a brilliant blue mineral, is found in abundance. In Bellavista, a cluster of shops deals solely in lapiz lazuli, selling a range of products made from this semiprecious stone: paperweights, jewelry, and chess sets. Several larger shops selling lapis lazuli are dotted around the rest of the city. **Blue Stone** (⊠ Av. Costanera Norte 3863, Vitacura ☎ 2/207–4180). **Faba-Fina** (⊠ Av. Alonso de Cordova 4227, Vitacura ☎ 2/208–9526). **Rocco** (⊠ José Victorino Lastarria 53, Santiago Centro ☎ 2/633–4036).

Wine

Chileans have discovered just how good their vintages are, and wineshops are popping up everywhere. **El Mundo del Vino** (⊠ Isidora Goyenechea 2931, Las Condes ☎ 2/244–8888) is a world-class store with an international selection, in-store tastings, wine classes, and books for oenophiles. The store also provides sturdy boxes to protect your purchases on the flight home. **La Vinoteca** (⊠ Av. Isidora Goyenechea 2966, Las Condes

☎ 2/371–5942) proudly proclaims that it was Santiago's first fine wineshop. It offers personalized service and an excellent selection. **Vinopolis** (⊠ Av. El Bosque Norte 038, Las Condes ☎ 2/232–3814) stocks a top-notch selection and also has a shop at the airport for last-minute purchases.

SIDE TRIPS FROM SANTIAGO

For more than a few travelers, Santiago's main attraction is its proximity to the continent's best skiing. Three world-class ski resorts lie just outside the city, and another is only a little farther away. Others are curious to see the region where their favorite wines are produced. The wineries around Santiago provide the majority of the country's excellent exports. The Cajón del Maipo, deep in the Andes, is irresistible for those who want to soak in a natural hot spring, stroll through picturesque mountain villages where low adobe houses line the roads, or just take in the stark but majestic landscape.

It's also possible to take day trips to Pomaire, a craft village some 70 km (43 mi) west of Santiago, or to go farther afield to Valparaíso, Viña del Mar, or Isla Negra (⇨ Chapter 2).

Cajón del Maipo

The Cajón del Maipo, a stunning river valley southeast of Santiago, is so expansive that you can easily spend several days exploring the area. A narrow road runs parallel to the Río Maipo, the river that supplies Santiago with most of its drinking water, as it snakes up into the Andes. As you ascend, you'll see massive mountains of sedimentary rock, heaved up and thrown sideways millions of years ago when the Andes were formed. On a sunny day, the colors here are subtle but glowing, ranging from oranges and reds to ochers, buffs, beiges, browns, and even elusive greens. Locals in roadside stands sell homemade *chicha* (cider) and *miel* (honey). At the far end of the valley, you'll find an austere landscape where hot springs spill from the earth and the mountains display vibrant shades of blue and violet.

Whatever you do, don't hurry through the Cajón del Maipo. Any of the villages you pass is worth a visit. As the valley is a popular weekend getaway for Santiaguinos, most villages have small cafés providing basic meals and simple lodgings. There are also plenty of mercados where you can pick up supplies for a picnic. The canyon's main town, San José de Maipo, is a great place to get acquainted with small-town life in the Andes. Note that the going gets tougher shortly after you pass El Volcán, as the road is no longer paved. Make sure you have a four-wheel-drive vehicle if you want to venture farther, especially if there's rain in the forecast.

San José de Maipo

At the head of the Cajón del Maipo is the old colonial town of San José de Maipo, founded in the late 18th century when silver was discovered nearby. Rows of quaint, single-story adobe dwellings with thatched roofs line the streets. In the center of town is a large shady plaza where locals gather.

WHERE TO
STAY & EAT
$$

✕ **Trattoría Calypso.** The fresh homemade pasta couldn't be better in this small Italian-owned restaurant close to the Río Maipo. Vegetables from the garden are used to make an impressive selection of pastas with original sauces. The herb bread is delicious, and the wine list includes some good choices. ⊠ *Camino El Volcan 5247, El Manzano* ☎ *2/871–1498* ▭ *No credit cards* ☉ *Closed Mon.–Wed.*

$ ✕⊡ **La Petite France.** You can't miss this attractive pink hotel with its Tudor-style frontage sitting high on a hillside just before the village of San José de Maipo. The family that runs this small establishment, who returned to Chile after several years of living in France, keeps the hotel immaculate, including the inviting pool that fills one of the garden's many levels. The rooms are simple, spacious, and comfortable. Delight in unparalleled valley views from the restaurant's wide terrace while tucking into some delicious French-inspired cuisine like *caracoles* (snails). ⊠ *Camino al Volcan 16096, San José de Maipo* ☎☎2/861–1967 ↩*8 rooms* ⌂ *Restaurant, pool, bar* ☰ *AE, DC, MC, V* ⊘ *Restaurant closed Mon.*

San Alfonso

About 65 km (40 mi) south of Santiago is San Alfonso, a small but charming village with fantastic houses that look as though they've been stolen from a fairy tale. Just past San Alfonso is the abandoned mining town of **El Volcán,** where you can visit the old abandoned copper-mine shafts and peer into the decaying, cramped miners' quarters.

WHERE TO STAY
$–$$ ⊡ **Cascada de las Animas.** Set on its own 10,000-acre nature reserve in the foothills of the Andes, close to the village of San Alfonso, Cascada de las Animas affords breathtaking views in all directions. The huge restaurant terrace, for example, overlooks the river below. You likely won't want to sit still for long, as the family-run establishment has excellent guides that take you white-water rafting down the Río Maipo and horseback riding high up into the mountains. The whimsical wood cabins are rustic but spacious, with wood-burning fireplaces. Book ahead in the busy season. ⊠ *San Alfonson s/n* ✆ *(Casilla 57, San José de Maipo)* ☎2/861–1303 ╠2/861–1833 ⊕*www.cascada.net* ↩*9 cabins* ⌂ *Restaurant, kitchenettes, pool, sauna, hiking, horseback riding, Ping-Pong, bar, meeting room* ☰ *No credit cards.*

$ ⊡ **Hostería los Ciervos.** Rooms at this pleasant hostelry are simple and face a bright, plant-filled passageway. The two small cabin-style rooms are quieter and overlook a pretty, terraced garden with a tiny pool. At the restaurant you can enjoy a filling lunch of traditional Chilean dishes such as *pastel de choclo* (a pie filled with ground beef, chicken, olives, boiled egg, and sultanas, and topped with mashed corn) or *porotos granados* (a thick bean stew). ⊠ *Av. Argentina 31411, San Alfonso* ☎☎2/861–1581 ↩*7 rooms, 2 cabins* ⌂ *Restaurant, pool* ☰ *AE, DC, MC, V.*

Lo Valdés

Past El Volcán, the gravel road leads higher into the jagged mountains. Green slopes give way to sheer mountain cliffs of gray and purple. Here you'll be able to spot layer upon layer of sedimentary rock, packed with fossils from the time when this whole area was under the ocean. About 12 km (7 mi) beyond El Volcán you'll pass the tiny town of Baños Morales, where Santiaguinos go to soak their tired muscles in the hot springs. Beyond Baños Morales, take the right fork to reach Lo Valdés, a charming village that makes an excellent place to stop for the night.

In Baños Morales you'll find the entrance to the **Monumento Natural El Morado,** named after the impressive purple peak. If it's a clear day you'll be privy to some stunning views of the snowcapped Andean peaks from the park. An exhilarating 8-km (5-mi), 3-hour hike passes a glacier. There's an admission charge of 1,500 pesos.

About 11 km (7 mi) past Lo Valdés, along a poorly maintained road through an impressive moonscape of mauves, grays, and steely blues, are the isolated and picturesque **Baños de Colina.** These huge natural bowls, scooped out of the mountain edge, overflow with water from the hot springs. Here you can slip into a bathing suit (note, however, that there are no changing rooms) and choose the pool that has the temperature most to your liking. Let your body float gently in the mineral-rich waters and enjoy the view down the valley as your fellow soakers trade medical advice, offer salt and lemons to suck on, and speculate about the medicinal properties of the waters. Admission is 2,000 pesos.

WHERE TO STAY

$

☒ **Lo Valdés Mountain Center.** Santiago's German Alpine Club built this lodge, formerly the Refugio Alemán, in 1931 as a base camp for members scaling the Andes. The charming stone building looks as if it could be in the Alps. Wooden floors and walls exude a feeling of warmth, but accommodations are decidedly spartan. Its best selling point is its location at the base of the Andes. The restaurant terrace affords fabulous views. In summer this is a popular *paseo* (outing) for many Santiaguinos, who come to indulge not just in the clean air but also in the *küchen* (fruit pie). ☒ *Lo Valdés,* ☎ *9/220–8525* ⊅ *11 rooms with shared bath* ᗭ *Restaurant, mountain bikes, hiking, horseback riding* ▭ *No credit cards.*

Pomaire

You can easily spend a morning or afternoon wandering around the quaint village of Pomaire, a former settlement of indigenous people comprising nothing more than a few streets of single-story adobe dwellings. On weekends Pomaire teems with people who come to wander around, shop, and lunch in one of the picadas, which specialize in typical Chilean food such as empanadas.

Pomaire is famous for its brown *greda,* or pottery, which you'll likely come across in one form or another throughout Chile in crafts shops and restaurants. Order pastel de choclo or pastel de jaiba and it will nearly always be served in a round, simple clay dish—they're heavy and retain the heat, so the food is brought to the table piping hot.

The village bulges with bowls, pots, and plates of every shape and size, not to mention other objects such as piggy banks, plant pots, vases, and figurines. You can purchase these items at shops and open-air markets around town. An average bowl will set you back no more than 400 to 500 pesos; an oven dish might cost between 2,000 and 3,000 pesos. Workmanship varies, so it's worth taking a look around before you buy. Sometimes you'll even see craftspeople at work on their potter's wheels.

Pomaire, which lies 70 km (43 mi) west of Santiago, is easy to find. It's clearly signposted to your right off the Autopista del Sol. You can also take any of the buses that depart frequently from Terminal San Borja in downtown Santiago.

Where to Eat

★ $–$$

✕ **Los Naranjos.** An eclectic collection of gramophones could be reason enough to come and lunch here, but more than anything diners come back time and again for the excellent Chilean food. If you're hungry try the *pernil de chancho* (leg of pork)—it's succulent and fit for an army. This is also a good place to try one of the national staples such as pastel de choclo—a delicious concoction of minced beef, chicken, olives, sultanas, and boiled egg, topped with a creamy layer of mashed corn. Sundays there's often a traditional Chilean dance show to entertain you while you eat. ☒ *Roberto Bravo 44* ☎ *2/831–1791* ▭ *No credit cards.*

Ski Resorts

No wonder skiing aficionados from around the world head to Chile: the snowcapped mountains to the east of Santiago have the largest number of runs not just in Chile or South America, but in the entire southern hemisphere. The other attraction is that the season here lasts from June to September, so savvy skiers can take to the slopes when everyone else is hitting the beach.

There are three distinct ski areas within easy reach of Santiago—Farellones, La Parva, and Valle Nevado—with a total of 43 lifts that can carry you to the top of 1,260 acres of groomed runs. To reach these areas, follow Avenida Las Condes eastward until you leave Santiago. Here, you begin an arduous journey up the Andes, making 40 consecutive hairpin turns. The road forks when you reach the top, with one road taking the relatively easy 16-km (10-mi) route east to Valle Nevado, and the other following a more difficult road north to Farellones and La Parva.

About 160 km (100 mi) north of Santiago and close to the Argentine border is Portillo, the oldest ski area in South America. It's a three-hour drive from the city, so a day trip would be exhausting. The only accommodation is Hotel Portillo, which requires a minimum one-week stay. To reach Portillo from Santiago, head north on the Pan-American Highway, following signs to the town of Los Andes. From there take the International Highway (Ruta 60) east until you reach the resort.

Farellones & El Colorado

The closest ski area to Santiago is Farellones, at the foot of Cerro Colorado. This area, consisting of a couple of ski runs for beginners, is used mainly by locals out for a day trip. Facilities are scanty—just a couple of unremarkable restaurants and a few drink stands. Farther up the road is El Colorado, which has 568 acres of groomed runs—the most in Chile. There are 18 runs here: seven beginner, four intermediate, three advanced, and four expert. You'll find a few restaurants and pubs in the village. Ski season here runs mid-June to mid-October.

WHERE TO
STAY & EAT
★ $$$$

✕▣ **La Cornisa.** This year-round hotel on the road to Farellones is great if you want to get to the slopes early, as there's free shuttle service to and from the nearby ski areas. The quaint old inn, run by the same family for years, has 10 rooms with wood floors and heaters to keep out the chill. The best are the two corner rooms, which are a bit larger and have wide windows with excellent views. The rate includes breakfast and dinner in the small restaurant, warmed by a fireplace and looking directly down the mountain to Santiago. ⊠ *Av. Los Cóndores 636, Farellones* ☎ *2/321–1173* 🖷 *2/220–7581* ⊕ *www.lacornisa.cl* 🛏 *10 rooms* ⚲ *Restaurant, baby-sitting, laundry service* ▤ *AE, DC, MC, V* ¶⚬| *MAP.*

La Parva

La Parva, about 3 km (2 mi) up the road from Farellones, is a colorful conglomeration of private homes set along a handful of mountain roads. At the resort itself there are 14 ski runs, most for intermediate skiers. La Parva is positioned perfectly to give you a stunning view of Santiago, especially at night. The season here tends to be a little longer than at the neighboring resorts. The slopes usually open in May, meaning the season can sometimes last six months.

WHERE TO STAY
$$$$

▣ **Condominio Nuevo Parva.** The only place to stay in La Parva is this complex of apartments that sleep between six and eight people. You can rent only by the week, so plan for a lot of skiing. Valle Nevado and the other ski areas are a short drive away. ⊠ *Nueva La Parva 77,* ☎ *2/212–1363* 🛏 *32 apartments* ⚲ *Kitchenettes* ▤ *AE, MC, V* ⊘ *Closed Oct.–May.*

Valle Nevado

Valle Nevado, just 13 km (8 mi) beyond La Parva, is Chile's largest ski region—a luxury resort area with 11 ski lifts that take you up to 27 runs on more than 300 acres of groomed trails. More lifts are being built to provide skiing fanatics with even more options. There are a few slopes for beginners, but Valle Nevado is intended for skiers who like a challenge. Three of the extremely difficult runs from the top of Cerro Tres Puntas are labeled "Shake," "Rattle," and "Roll." If that doesn't intimidate you then you might be ready for some heliskiing. A Bell 407 helicopter whisks you to otherwise inaccessible peaks where you can ride a vertical drop of up to 2,500 m (8,200 ft).

A ski school at Valle Nevado gives pointers to everyone from beginners to experts. As most of the visitors here are European, the majority of the 50 instructors are from Europe. Equipment rental runs about 25,000 pesos a day. The ski season here runs mid-June–October.

WHERE TO STAY   Three hotels dominate Valle Nevado; staying at one gives you access to the facilities at the other two. The larger two—Puerta del Sol and Valle Nevado—are part of the same complex. The three hotels share restaurants, which serve almost every type of cuisine. Rates include lift tickets, ski equipment, and all meals. Peak season is July and August; you can often get the same room for half the price if you stay in June or September.

$$$$ ⊞ **Puerta del Sol.** The largest of the Valle Nevado hotels, Puerta del Sol can be identified by its signature sloped roof. Rooms here are larger than those at Tres Puntas, but still rather small. One good option are the "altillo rooms," which have a loft bed that gives you more space. North-facing rooms cost more but have unobstructed views of the slopes. Since all three hotels share facilities, Puerta del Sol is your best value. ⊠ *Valle Nevado* ☎ *2/206–0027; 800/669–0554 toll free in the U.S.* 🖷 *2/208–0697* ⊕ *www.vallenevado.com* ↪ *124 rooms* ♨ *2 restaurants, room service, in-room data ports, in-room safes, minibars, cable TV, gym, massage, sauna, Ping-Pong, downhill skiing, cinema, dance club, recreation room, baby-sitting, laundry service, airport shuttle* ⊟ *AE, DC, MC, V* ⊙ *Closed Oct.–June 14* ⍣ *MAP.*

$$$$ ⊞ **Tres Puntas.** It bills itself as a hotel for young people, and Tres Puntas may indeed remind you of a college dormitory. The closet-size rooms come with either bunk beds or two single beds and maybe a night table. And the tiny wooden balconies are just big enough for two people. In short, these rooms are for people who intend to be on the slopes all day. Inside is a pub and an American-style restaurant complete with a jukebox. ⊠ *Valle Nevado* ☎ *2/206–0027; 800/669–0554 toll free in the U. S.* 🖷 *2/208–0697* ⊕ *www.vallenevado.com* ↪ *89 rooms* ♨ *Restaurant, cable TV, billiards, downhill skiing, pub, recreation room, laundry service* ⊟ *AE, DC, MC, V* ⊙ *Closed Oct.–June 14* ⍣ *MAP.*

$$$$ ⊞ **Valle Nevado.** Valle Nevado's most expensive lodge provides ski-in/ski-out convenience. Rooms here are larger than at the other two hotels, and all have balconies. Off season, it's possible to trek by horse or on foot from here to the foot of El Plomo, which is more than 5,000 meters (16,400 ft) high. ⊠ *Valle Nevado* ☎ *2/206–0027; 800/669–0554 in the U.S.* 🖷 *2/208–0697* ⊕ *www.vallenevado.com* ↪ *53 rooms* ♨ *2 restaurants, room service, in-room data ports, in-room safes, minibars, cable TV, indoor pool, gym, massage, sauna, mountain bikes, hiking, horseback riding, downhill skiing, bar, lobby lounge, dance club, laundry service, Internet, business services, meeting rooms* ⊟ *AE, DC, MC, V* ⍣ *MAP.*

Portillo

This ski area north of Santiago is renowned for its slopes, where numerous world speed records have been recorded. It also has the best views of any of the area's ski resorts. The slopes here were discovered by engineers building the now-defunct railroad that linked Chile to Argentina. After the railroad was inaugurated in 1910, skiing aficionados headed here despite the fact that there were no facilities available. Hotel Portillo, the only accommodation in the area, opened its doors in 1949, making Portillo the country's first ski resort, and went on to host the World Ski Championships in 1966.

The facilities at the hotel are reserved for hotel guests, but you can dine in the *auto-servicio* (cafeteria-style) restaurant if you're here for the day. Ski season is mid-June to mid-October.

WHERE TO STAY

$$$$

☒ **Hotel Portillo.** Staying here feels a bit like going off to camp: every Saturday a new group settles in for a week's worth of outdoor activities. Besides skiing there's skating on the Laguna del Inca and even swimming in the heated outdoor pool. The hotel has almost as many employees as guests, which means service is excellent and the mood relaxed. Big windows in the guest rooms showcase mountain views or the more prized view of the lake. Family-style apartments come with bunk beds for children. ☒ *Los Andes* ☎ *2/361–7000 or 2/263–0606; 800/829–5325 toll free in the U.S.* 🖷 *2/361–7080* 🌐 *www.skiportillo.com* ➾ *150 rooms, 5 suites, 15 apartments* ⟁ *4 restaurants, in-room data ports, in-room safes, indoor-outdoor pool, gym, hair salon, massage, sauna, billiards, Ping-Pong, downhill skiing, ice-skating, ski shop, bar, dance club, recreation room, theater, baby-sitting, laundry service, Internet, business services, airport shuttle, helipad, travel services* ☰*AE, DC, MC, V* ⊘*All-inclusive.*

Wineries

The wineries in the valley below Santiago are some of the oldest in Chile. Here you'll find most of the biggest and best-known vineyards in the country. For years tourists were virtually ignored by these wineries, but they are finally getting attention. Now many wineries are throwing their doors open to visitors for the first time, often letting them see behind-the-scenes activities like harvesting and pressing.

Valle de Maipo

One of the most recognizable of Chile's wine appellations is the Valle de Maipo, an area that stretches south from Santiago. Viña Santa Rita is the only vineyard in the area with a restaurant, and it's a good one. Others worth a visit are Viña Concha y Toro, the country's largest wine maker; Viña Undurraga, known for its lovely grounds; and Viña Cousiño-Macul, which has been making wine in the region since 1856.

Chile's largest wine maker, **Viña Concha y Toro** produces 11 million cases annually. Some of its table wines—identifiable by the short, stout bottles—are sold domestically for about $2. The best bottles, however, fetch sky-high prices abroad. This is one of the oldest wineries in the region. Melchor de Concha y Toro, who once served as Chile's minister of finance, built the *casona,* or main house, in 1875. He imported vines from Europe, significantly improving the quality of the wines he was able to produce. Hour-long tours begin with an introductory video, a stroll through the vineyards and the century-old gardens, a look at the modern facilities, and a tasting. Reserve a week ahead for Saturday tours. ☒ *Virginia Subercaseaux 210, Pirque* ☎ *2/821–7069* 🌐 *www. conchaytoro.cl* 🎟 *Tour: 3,000 pesos* ⊘ *Weekdays 10:30–6, Sat. 10–12. English tours weekdays 11:30–3, Sat. 11 AM.*

Residential development keeps creeping closer to **Viña Cousiño-Macul**, a 625-acre estate where grapes have been grown since the mid-16th century. For the moment the venerable vineyard has managed to hang on. The Cousiño family home, set next to a beautiful 110-acre park, isn't open to the public, but you can visit the rest of the facilities. Especially interesting is the vaulted brick cellar, built in 1872, which can store more than 1 million bottles. ✉ *Av. Quilín 7100, Peñalolén Santiago* ☎ *2/284–1011* ⊕ *www.cousinomacul.cl* ✉ *Free* ◷ *Tours: Mon.–Sat. at 11 AM.*

Chile's third-largest winery, **Viña Santa Rita**, played an important historical role in Chile's battle for independence. In 1814, 120 soldiers led by revolutionary hero Bernardo O'Higgins hid here in the cellars. Paula Jaraquemada, who ran the estate, refused to let the Spanish enter, saving the soldiers. (Santa Rita's 120 label commemorates the event.) At the center of Santa Rita's Maipo Valley estate half an hour south of Santiago, the lovely colonial hacienda now serves as the winery's headquarters. Its restaurant, La Casa de Doña Paula, is a delightful place to have a bite after the tour.

Tours take you down into the winery's musty cellars, which are worthy of Edgar Allen Poe. Built by French engineers in 1875 using a lime-and-stone technique called *cal y canto,* the fan-vault cellars have been named a national monument. The wine was once aged in the barrels you'll see, which are more than 120 years old and are made of *raulí* wood; today the wine is aged in stainless-steel towers. Unfortunately, the wonderful gardens and the original proprietor's house, with its chapel steeple peeking out from behind a thick canopy of trees, are not part of the tour. Note that you must reserve ahead for these tours. ✉ *Camino Padre Hurtado 695, Alto Jahuel-Buín* ☎ *2/362–2594 or 2/362–2000* ⊕ *www. santarita.com* ✉ *Tours: 3,000 pesos; tastings cost extra* ◷ *Bilingual tours (English and Spanish): Tues.–Fri. at 10:30, 11:30, 12:15, 3, 4; weekends at 12:30 and 3:30.*

Don Francisco Undurraga Vicuña founded **Viña Undurraga** in 1885 in the town of Talagante, 34 km (21 mi) southwest of Santiago. The opulent mansion he built here has hosted various visiting dignitaries, from the queen of Denmark to the king of Norway. Today you can tour the house and the gardens—designed by Pierre Dubois, who planned Santiago's Parque Forestal—take a look at the facilities, and enjoy a tasting. Reserve ahead for a spot on the tour. ✉ *Camino a Melipilla Km 34, Talagante* ☎ *2/817–2346* ⊕ *www.undurraga.cl* ✉ *Free* ◷ *Tours: weekdays 9:30–4, Sat. 10–3.*

WHERE TO EAT ✕ **La Casa de Doña Paula.** A two-century-old colonial hacienda with thick
★ **$–$$** adobe walls houses Viña Santa Rita's restaurant. Under a peaked wood ceiling, the restaurant is decorated with old religious sculptures and portraits, including one of Paula Jaraquemada, who once ran the estate. If you plan to lunch here, it's a good idea to arrange to take the winery's 12:15 tour. Locally raised meats are the draw here; try the delicious *costillar de cerdo* (pork ribs). For dessert, the house specialty is *ponderación,* a crisp swirl of fried dough atop vanilla ice cream and caramel syrup. ✉ *Viña Santa Rita, Camino Padre Hurtado 695, Alto Jahuel-Buín* ☎ *2/821–4211* ⌕ *Reservations essential* ◷ *Closed Mon. No dinner* ▭ *AE, DC, MC, V.*

SANTIAGO A TO Z

To research prices, get advice from other travelers, and book travel arrangements, visit www.fodors.com.

AIR TRAVEL

Among the U.S. carriers, American serves Santiago from Dallas and Miami, while Delta connects from Atlanta. LanChile flies nonstop to Santiago from both Miami and Los Angeles and with a layover in Lima from New York. British Airways flies from London with a stop in Buenos Aires; LanChile connects London to Santiago with a stop in Frankfurt or Madrid. Most of the major Central and South American airlines also fly to Santiago, including Aerocontinente, Aerolíneas Argentinas, Aeromexico, Avianca, Lacsa, Lloyd Aéreo Boliviano, and Varig.

Lan Express, LanChile's domestic subsidiary, has daily flights from Santiago to most cities throughout Chile. Sky airline also flies to most large cities within Chile.

🛪 Carriers **Aerocontinente** ☎ 2/690-9399 in Chile. **Aerolíneas Argentinas** ☎ 2/690-1030 in Chile. **Aeromexico** ☎ 2/690-1028 in Chile. **American Airlines** ☎ 2/690-1090 in Santiago. **Avianca** ☎ 2/690-1051 in Chile. **British Airways** ☎ 0845/222-111. **Delta Airlines** ☎ 2/690-1551 in Santiago. **Lacsa** ☎ 2/690-1276 in Chile. **LanChile** ☎ 2/565-2525 or 600/526-2000 in Chile. **Lan Express** ☎ 2/565-2525. **Lloyd Aéreo Boliviano** ☎ 2/671-2334 in Chile. **Sky** ☎ 600/600-2828. **Varig** ☎ 2/690-1930 in Chile.

AIRPORT

Santiago's Comodoro Arturo Merino Benítez International Airport, often referred to simply as Pudahuel, is about a 30-minute drive west of the city.

🛪 Airport Information **Comodoro Arturo Merino Benítez International Airport** ☎ 2/690-1900.

TRANSFERS You have several options for getting to and from the airport. The most expensive is a taxi, which should cost you around 11,000 pesos for a trip downtown. Less expensive, especially if you are traveling alone, are the comfortable minibuses operated by Transfer. They whisk you from the airport to any location downtown for about 4,000 pesos.

Centropuerto, which runs buses every 10 minutes between the airport and Terminal Los Héroes, charges about 1,500 pesos. Tur-Bus has service between the airport and its own terminal near the Los Héroes Metro station; it departs every half hour and costs 1,200 pesos.

Alpha Service, Casual, and Transvip operate minibus service between the airport and various locations in the city. The cost is usually anywhere from 3,500 pesos to 4,500 pesos.

Note that there is no Metro service to the airport.

🛪 **Alpha Service** ☎ 2/555-8855. **Casual** ☎ 2/777-7707. **Centropuerto** ☎ 2/695-5958. **Transfer** ☎ 2/677-3000. **Transvip** ☎ 2/677-3000. **Tur-Bus** ☎ 2/270-7500.

BUS TRAVEL TO & FROM SANTIAGO

All the country's major highways pass through Santiago, which means you won't have a problem catching a bus to almost any destination. Finding that bus, however, can be a problem. The city has several terminals, each with buses heading in different directions. Terminal Los Héroes is on the edge of Santiago Centro near the Los Héroes Metro station. Several companies have buses to points north and south from this station. The other three stations are clustered around the Universidad de Santiago Metro station. The modern Terminal San Borja has buses headed north and west. Terminal Santiago is the busiest, with dozens of small companies going west to the coast and to the south. Terminal Alameda, which handles only Tur-Bus and Pullman Bus, is for coastal and southern traffic. Terminal Los Héroes and Terminal Santiago also handle a few international routes, heading to far-flung destinations such as Buenos Aires, Rio de Janeiro, and Lima.

Several bus companies run regularly scheduled service to the Andes in winter. Skitotal buses depart from the office on Avenida Apoquindo and head to all of the ski resorts except Portillo. Buses depart at 8:45 AM; a round-trip ticket costs 10,000 pesos. Also available for hire here are taxis— (65,000 pesos, including driver) and 12-person minibuses (90,000 pesos). Manzur Expediciones runs buses to Portillo on Wednesday, Saturday, and Sunday for about the same price. Buses leaves at 8:30 AM from the Plaza Italia in front of the Teatro Universidad de Chile.

Bus service to the Cajón del Maipo is frequent and inexpensive— Manzur offers a round-trip ticket to Lo Valdés Mountain Center for less than 8,000 pesos. Only the 8 AM bus makes the two-hour trek to Baños de Colina, however. Sit on the right side of the bus for a good view of the river.

🚌 Bus Companies **Manzur Expediciones** ⊠ Sótero del Río 475, Santiago Centro ☎ 2/777-4284. **Pullman Bus** ⊠ Terminal Alameda, Estación Central ☎ 2/779-2026. **Skitotal** ⊠ Av. Apoquindo 4900, Las Condes ☎ 2/246-0156. **Tur-Bus** ⊠ Terminal Alameda, Estación Central ☎ 2/270-7500.
🚌 Bus Depots **Terminal Alameda** ⊠ Av. O'Higgins 3750, Estación Central ☎ 2/270-7500. **Terminal Los Héroes** ⊠ Tucapel Jiménez 21, Estación Central ☎ 2/420-9900. **Terminal San Borja** ⊠ San Borja 184, Estación Central ☎ 2/776-0645. **Terminal Santiago** ⊠ Av. O'Higgins 3850, La Alameda ☎ 2/376-1755.

BUS TRAVEL WITHIN SANTIAGO
Bus service has improved, but it is still too confusing for most newcomers. (It's confusing for most residents, too.) For one thing, there are dozens of private companies operating on hundreds of routes around the city. For another, drivers almost invariably say they go where you want to go, whether they do or not. Bus fare is usually less than 300 pesos, paid upon boarding. Drivers are good about providing change for small bills.

CAR RENTALS
Renting a car is convenient in Santiago, as most companies have offices at the airport and downtown. The international agencies such as Avis, Budget, and Hertz generally rent compact cars with unlimited mileage and insurance coverage for about 38,000 pesos a day. They can provide ski-equipped vehicles for climbs to the Andes. Two reputable local agencies are Chilean Rent A Car and Diamond, whose rates can be as low as 26,000 pesos a day.

🚗 Agencies **Avis** ⊠ airport, ☎ 2/690-1382 ⊠ Av. Santa María 1742, Providencia ☎ 2/274-7621 ⊠ Av. San Pablo 9900, Pudahuel ☎ 2/601-9747. **Budget** ⊠ airport ☎ 2/690-1386 ⊠ Av. Francisco Bilbao 1439, Providencia ☎ 2/690-1489. **Chilean Rent A Car** ⊠ Bellavista 0183, Bellavista ☎ 2/737-9650. **Diamond** ⊠ Av. Manquehue Sur 795, Las Condes ☎ 2/212-1523. **Hertz** ⊠ airport, ☎ 2/690-1029 ⊠ Av. Costanera 1469, Providencia ☎ 2/420-5210.

CAR TRAVEL
You don't need a car if you're not going to venture outside the city limits, as most of the downtown sights are within walking distance of each other. To get to other neighborhoods, taxis are inexpensive and the subway system is safe and efficient. After you dodge a line of cars speeding through a red light or see the traffic snarls during rush hour, you may be glad you don't have to drive in the city.

A car is the best way to see the surrounding countryside, however. Although the highways around Santiago are generally well maintained, weather conditions can make them dangerous. Between May and August, rain can cause roads in low-lying areas to flood. Avoid driving if it has been raining for several hours. If you're headed north or south, you'll probably use the Pan-American Highway, also called Ruta 5. To reach Valparaíso, Viña del Mar, or the northernmost beach resorts on the Central Coast, take Highway 68; for the southern beaches, take Ruta 78.

It can take up to two hours to reach the region's three major ski resorts, which lie 48–56 km (30–35 mi) from Santiago. The road is narrow, winding, and full of Chileans racing to get to the top. If you decide to drive, make sure you have either a four-wheel-drive vehicle or snow chains, which you can rent along the way. The chains are installed for about 8,000 pesos. Don't think you need them? There's a police checkpoint just before the road starts to climb into the Andes, and if the weather is rough they'll make you turn back. To reach Valle Nevado, Farellones, and La Parva, take Avenida Kennedy or Avenida Las Condes east. Signs direct you once you get into the mountains. Portillo is three hours north of Santiago. Call the hotel there ahead of time to find out about road conditions.

To reach Cajón del Maipo, head south on Avenida José Alessandri until you reach the Rotonda Departamental, a large traffic circle. There you take Camino Las Vizcachas, following it south into the valley.

EMERGENCIES
🖪 Emergency Numbers **Ambulance** ☎ 131. **Fire** ☎ 132. **Police** ☎ 133.
🖪 Hospitals **Clinica Alemana** ✉ Av. Vitacura 5951, Las Condes ☎ 2/210-1334. **Clinica Las Condes** ✉ Lo Fontecilla 441, Las Condes ☎ 2/210-4000. **Clinica Santa María** ✉ Av. Santa Maria 0410, Providencia ☎ 2/461-2000.

ENGLISH-LANGUAGE MEDIA
The Instituto Chileno-Norteamericano de Cultura has a selection of books in English, as well as English-language periodicals. Librería Books sells secondhand English books. Librería Inglesa sells new books, but the prices are high. For popular newspapers and magazines in English, check the kiosks on the pedestrian mall of Paseo Ahumada in Santiago Centro or the kiosk on the top floor of the Parque Arauco Mall (Avenida Kennedy 5413) in Las Condes.
🖪 Bookstores **Instituto Chileno-Norteamericano de Cultura** ✉ Moneda 1467, Santiago Centro ☎ 2/696-3215. **Librería Books** ✉ Av. Providencia 1652, Local 5, Providencia ☎ 2/235-1205. **Librería Inglesa** ✉ Av. Pedro de Valdivia 47, Providencia ☎ 2/231-6270 ✉ Vitacura 5950, Vitacura ☎ 2/219-3080 ✉ Huérfanos 669, Local 11, Santiago Centro ☎ 2/638-7118.

HEALTH
In terms of food, Santiago is one of the safest cities in South America. Because of strict health codes, you shouldn't worry too much about the food in most restaurants. If you decide to sample something from a street vendor, make sure it has been thoroughly cooked. The tap water in Santiago and most of Chile is quite safe, but if you have any concerns you can always drink the bottled water available everywhere.

Altitude sickness—which is marked by difficulty breathing, dizziness, headaches, and nausea—is a danger when heading to the Andes. The best way to ward off altitude sickness is to take it slowly. Try to spend a day or two acclimatizing before any physical exertion. When skiing, rest often and drink as much water as possible. If symptoms continue, return to a lower altitude.

INTERNET

In Santiago there are plenty of Internet cafés; you're likely to find several around your hotel. Most larger hotels provide business services, but these can be expensive. Web boxes dotted around the second floor of the Parque Arauco Mall (Avenida Kennedy 5413) in Las Condes allow you to access the Internet free of charge.

🔳 Internet Cafés **Cyberia** ✉ Matías Cousino 68, La Alameda ☎ 2/699-7297. **Easy@Net** ✉ Paseo Las Palmas 2213, Providencia ☎ 2/333-7112. **Prolinux** ✉ General Holley 50, Local 12, Providencia ☎ 2/333-9763. **NetAlPaso** ✉ Nueva York 52, Santiago Centro ☎ 2/695-7776 ✉ Mall Paseo Estación, San Francisco de Borja 66, Estación Central ☎ 2/764-2535 ✉ Galería Imperio, Huérfanos 830, Local 889, Santiago Centro ☎ 2/638-7175 ✉ Mall de Centro, Puente 689, Local 900-56, Santiago Centro ☎ 2/633-1669. **Saiber Café** ✉ San Antonio 333, Santiago Centro ☎ no phone.

MAIL & SHIPPING

Correo Central, housed in the ornate Palacio de los Gobernadores, is in Santiago Centro on the north side of the Plaza de Armas. There is a second downtown branch near the Palacio de la Moneda, as well as one in Providencia near the Manuel Montt Metro stop.

For overnight delivery, DHL and Federal Express both have offices in Santiago Centro.

🔳 Overnight Services **DHL** ✉ San Francisco 301, Santiago Centro ☎ 2/124-2121 ✉ Bandera 204, Santiago Centro ☎ 2/697-1081 ✉ Av. 11 de Septiembre 2070, Providencia ☎ 2/234-1516. **Federal Express** ✉ San Camilo 190, Santiago Centro ☎ 2/361-6000 ✉ Providencia 1951, Providencia ☎ 2/233-2564.

🔳 Post Office **Correo Central** ☎ 800/362-236 ⊕ www.correos.cl.

MONEY MATTERS

Unlike other South American countries, Chile rarely accepts U.S. dollars. (The exception is larger hotels, where prices are often quoted only in dollars.) Credit cards and travelers checks are accepted everywhere in Santiago's most touristy areas.

You can exchange money in many places in Santiago Centro, such as Citibank. Banks in Santiago are usually open weekdays 9–2, while *casas de cambio* (currency-exchange offices) are open weekdays 9–2 and 3–6. They normally cluster together; in Providencia, for example, along Pedro de Valdivia, just before La Costanera, there are three or four.

Automatic teller machines only dispense Chilean pesos. To use an ATM issued by a foreign bank, select the "foreign client" option from the menu. Citibank, with the most ATMs in town, has instructions in English, as do most other ATMS, and is linked to both the Plus and Cirrus systems. ATMs belonging to Chilean banks are often only linked to Cirrus. There are two ATMs on the second floor of the airport.

🔳 Banks **American Express** ✉ Av. Andrés Bello 2711, Las Condes ☎ 2/350-6955 ✉ Isidora Goyenechea 3621, Las Condes ☎ 2/350-6700. **Citibank** ✉ Teatinos 180, Santiago Centro ☎ 2/338-8000 ✉ Av. Andrés Bello 2681, Providencia ☎ 2/338-8000 ✉ Av. Apoquindo 5470, Las Condes ☎ 2/338-8000.

SAFETY

Santiago Centro, Providencia, Las Condes, and other areas frequented by tourists are generally very safe. Use the same precautions you would anywhere—don't wear flashy jewelry and watches, keep your camera in a secure bag, and don't handle money in public. Remain alert for pickpockets, especially in crowded markets and parks.

SIGHTSEEING TOURS

Sernatur (⇨ Visitor Information, *below*), the national tourism agency, maintains a listing of experienced individual tour guides who will take you on a half-day tour of Santiago and the surrounding area for about 25,000 pesos. These tours are a great way to get your bearings when you have just arrived in the city. They can also greatly enrich your visit. In museums, for example, they often provide information not generally available to the public and are especially helpful in museums with little or no signage in English.

Altué Expediciones arranges adventure trips such as white-water rafting on nearby rivers and hiking to the mouths of volcanoes.

Chilean Travel Services and Sportstour handle tours of both Santiago and other parts of Chile.

With more than a dozen locations, Turismo Cocha, founded in 1951, is one of the city's biggest private tour operators. It arranges tours of the wineries of the Cajón del Maipo and the beach resorts of Valparaíso and Viña del Mar, in addition to the usual city tours. It also has offices in the domestic and international terminals of the airport as well as in some of the larger hotels.

🚩 Tour Companies **Altué Expediciones** ✉ Encomenderos 83, Las Condes ☎ 2/232-1103 🖶 2/233-6799. **Chilean Travel Services** ✉ Antonio Bellet 77, Office 101, Providencia ☎ 2/251-0400 🖶 2/251-0426 ⊕ www.ia.cl/cts. **Sportstour** ✉ Moneda 970, Santiago Centro ☎ 2/549-5200 🖶 2/698-2981 ⊕ www.sportstour.cl. **Turismo Cocha** ✉ Av. El Bosque Norte 0430, Las Condes ☎ 2/464-1000 🖶 2/464-1010 ✉ Pedro de Valdivia 0169, Providencia ☎ 2/464-1600 🖶 2/464-1699 ✉ Huérfanos 653, Santiago Centro ☎ 2/464-1950 ⊕ www.cocha.com.

SUBWAY TRAVEL

Santiago's excellent subway system is the best way to get around town. The Metro is comfortable, inexpensive, and safe. The system operates Monday–Saturday 6:30 AM–10:30 PM and Sunday 8–10:30 PM. Línea 1 runs east–west along the axis of the Río Mapocho. This is the most popular line, and perhaps the most useful, because it runs past most of the heavily touristed areas. Línea 2 runs north–south; it's rarely used by nonresidents because it heads to residential areas. Línea 5 also runs north–south except at its northern tip, where it bends to the west to connect with the Bellas Artes and Plaza de Armas stations. Every station has an easy-to-read map of all the stations and the adjoining streets. Buy tickets in any station at the glass booths or at the nearby machines. Individual tickets cost 300 to 350 pesos, depending on the time of day. A *boleto inteligente* (smart ticket) or *boleto valor* (value ticket) costs around 3,000 pesos and is good for up to 10 trips; these tickets save you time, if not money. After depositing your ticket in the turnstile, pass through and retrieve it to use again later. Single-ride tickets are not returned.

TAXIS

With some 50,000 taxis in Santiago, you can easily flag one down on most streets. The average ride costs around 2,000 to 3,000 pesos. The driver will turn the taxi meter on when you start your journey; it should read 150 pesos, the minimum charge. Taxi drivers don't always know where they are going and frequently ask directions; it's a good idea to carry a map. Radio-dispatched cabs are slightly more expensive but will pick you up at your door.

Most taxi drivers are willing to be hired for the day. To increase your bargaining power, head for the taxi stand at Calle Huérfanos and Calle MacIver in the heart of downtown, where you can negotiate with more than one driver.

🚩 Taxi Companies **Alborada** ☎ 2/246-4900. **Alto Oriente** ☎ 2/226-2116. **Andes Pacífico** ☎ 2/225-3064 or 2/204-0104. **Apoquindo** ☎ 2/211-6073.

TELEPHONES

When calling Santiago from other parts of the country, use the area code 02; if you are using a carrier, then dial just 2. Within the city, skip the area code and just dial the seven-digit local number.

TRAIN TRAVEL

Chileans once boasted about the country's excellent rail service, but there's little left today aside from the limited service from Santiago to points south. Santiago's Estación Central, in Santiago Centro at the Metro station of the same name, is where you catch trains headed to the Central Valley. Note that you can also purchase tickets for the trains at the Estación Metro Universidad de Chile.

Metrotrens run from Santiago to Nos, Rancagua, and San Fernando. Terrasur operates a service between Santiago and Chillán four times daily. Trains run from Santiago through the larger cities of Rancagua, Curicó, Talca, Chillán, Concepción, and Temuco.

The train from Santiago to Temuco leaves daily at 8:30 PM, stops at several stations on the way, and usually arrives at least 12 hours later at its final destination.

🚆 Train Information **Estación Central** ⊠ Av. O'Higgins 3170, Santiago Centro ☎ 2/ 376–8500 ⊕ www.efe.cl. **Estación Metro Universidad de Chile** ⊠ Local 10, La Alameda ☎ 2/688–3284.

VISITOR INFORMATION

Sernatur, the national tourist service, stocks maps and brochures and has a large and friendly staff that speaks English. The Providencia office, located between the Manuel Montt and Pedro de Valdivia Metro stops, is open daily 9 AM–10 PM.

🚆 Tourist Information **Sernatur** ⊠ Av. Providencia 1550, Providencia ☎ 2/731–8336 or 2/731–8337 ⊕ www.sernatur.cl.

THE CENTRAL COAST

2

FODOR'S CHOICE

Aquí Jaime, seafood restaurant in Concón
Brighton B&B, Valparaíso
Café Turri, Valparaíso
Casa-Museo, Pablo Neruda's home on Isla Negra
El Chiringuito, seafood restaurant in Zapallar
Delicias del Mar, restaurants in Reñaca & Viña del Mar
La Fayette, hotel in Reñaca
Hotel Del Mar, Viña del Mar
Isla Seca, hotel in Zapallar

HIGHLY RECOMMENDED

HOTELS   Altamar Aparthotel, Maitencillo
Der Münchner Hof, El Quisco
Hotel Los Ositos, Reñaca
Hotel Oceanic, Viña del Mar
Hotel Tres Poniente, Viña del Mar
Pao Pao, Algarrobo
Porto Principal, Valparaíso

SIGHTS   Museo de Bellas Artes, Valparaíso
Palacio Vergara, Viña del Mar
La Sebastiana, Pablo Neruda's home in Valparaíso
Zapallar, beach resort

By Michael de Zayas

Updated by David Dudenhoefer

MOST PEOPLE HEAD TO THE CENTRAL COAST for a single reason: the beaches. Yes, some may be drawn by the rough grandeur of the windswept coastline, with its rocky islets inhabited by sea lions and penguins, but those in search of nature generally head south to Chiloé and Patagonia or north to the Atacama Desert. Yet this stretch of coastline west of Santiago has much more than sun and surf.

The biggest surprise is the charm of Valparaíso, Chile's second largest city. Valparaíso shares a bay with Viña del Mar but the similarities end there. Valparaíso is a bustling port town with a jumble of colorful cottages nestled in the folds of its many hills. Viña del Mar has lush parks surrounding neoclassical mansions and a long beach lined with luxury high-rises. Together they form an interesting contrast of working class and wealth at play.

The *balnearios* (small beach towns) to the north of the twin cities have their own character, often defined by coastal topography. Proximity to Santiago has resulted in the development—in some cases overdevelopment—of most of them as summer resorts. At the beginning of the 20th century, Santiago's elite started building vacation homes. Soon after, when trains connected the capital to beaches, middle-class families started spending their summers at the shore. Improved highway access in recent decades has allowed Chileans of all economic levels to enjoy the occasional beach vacation. Late December–mid-March, when schools let out for summer vacation and Santiago becomes torrid, the beaches are packed. Vacationers frolic in the chilly sea by day, and pack the restaurants and bars at night. The rest of the year, the coast is relatively deserted and, though often cool and cloudy, a pleasantly tranquil place to explore. Local *caletas*—literally meaning coves, this is where fishing boats gather to unload their catch, and it's usually the site of local fishing cooperatives—are always colorful and lively.

Exploring the Central Coast

Valparaíso is the only city in the Central Coast capable of holding your attention for long; you could spend a week exploring its winding streets and enjoying its varied nightlife. Viña del Mar has far less character but is still quite pleasant with its tree-lined streets and wide beach. The small towns along the coast, wherever the current has carved out a beach, have few museums or monuments. Most are little more than beaches and a chance to explore the rocky coastline between them—which can be exhilarating. Alternatives to lounging on the beach are horseback riding, golf, and skin diving.

To reach the balnearios south of Valparaíso, take Highway 68 from Santiago to Casablanca, where a road leads to most of the coastal towns. (Quintay is reached via another road a few miles west of Casablanca.) It's a two-hour drive on Highway 68 from Santiago to either Valparaíso or Viña del Mar. Beach towns to the north of Viña del Mar are all accessible by the coastal highway, the *Costanera*, which winds its way past amazing scenery north to Papudo. Los Molles, on the other hand, is best reached by driving on the Pan-American Highway.

About the Restaurants

Dining is one of the great pleasures of visiting the Central Coast. With the exception of major holidays, reservations are almost never required for restaurants here. Most restaurants close between lunch and dinner: from 3 or 4 to 7 or 8.

About the Hotels

Because the central beach resorts were developed by and for the Santiago families who summer here, they are dominated by vacation homes and apartments. There's a shortage of hotels; the most common accommodation is the cabana, which is usually a somewhat rustic cabin with a kitchenette and one or more bedrooms designed to accommodate families on tight budgets. An even more affordable option is a *residencial* (guest house), often just a few rooms for rent in a home. The exceptions to this trend are Viña del Mar and nearby Reñaca, which have dozens of hotels between them.

WHAT IT COSTS In pesos (in thousands)				
$$$$	**$$$**	**$$**	**$**	**¢**
RESTAURANTS over 11	8–11	5–8	2.5–5	under 2.5
HOTELS over 105	75–105	45–75	15–45	under 15

Restaurant prices are for a main course at dinner. Hotel prices are for a double room in high season, excluding tax.

Timing

It seems that all of Chile heads to the coast in the summer months of January and February. This can be a great time to visit, with the weather at its warmest, and the nightlife hopping. It's also a tough time to find a room, especially on weekends. Make reservations as far in advance as possible. The climate is also nice in the spring and fall, when the days are warm and breezy, and the nights cool. December and March are excellent months to visit—the weather is still good, but you can explore the coast's natural wonders in relative solitude.

VIÑA DEL MAR & VALPARAÍSO

Viña del Mar and Valparaíso (Vineyard of the Sea and Paradise Valley, respectively) each maintain an aura that warrants their dreamy appellations. Only minutes apart, these two urban centers are nevertheless as different as twin cities can be. Valparaíso won the heart of Pablo Neruda, who praised its "cluster of crazy houses," and it continues to be a disorderly, bohemian, charming town. Valparaíso's lack of beaches keeps its mind on matters more urban, if not urbane.

Viña del Mar, Valparaíso's glamorous sibling, is a clean, orderly city with miles of beige beach, a glitzy casino, manicured parks, and shopping galore. Viña, together with nearby Reñaca, is synonymous with the best of life for vacationing Chileans. Its beaches gleam, its casino rolls, and its discos sizzle.

Viña del Mar

130 km (85 mi) northwest of Santiago.

Viña del Mar has high-rise apartment buildings that tower above its excellent shoreline. Here are wide boulevards lined with palms, lush parks, and mansions. Miles of beige sand are washed by heavy surf. The town has been known for years as Chile's tourist capital (a title being challenged by several other hot spots), and is currently in the midst of some minor refurbishment.

Viña, as it's popularly known, has the country's oldest casino, excellent hotels, and an extensive selection of restaurants. To some, all this means

Numbers in the text correspond to numbers in the margin and on the Central Coast, Viña del Mar, and Valparaíso maps.

If you have 3 days

Plan to spend at least two nights in the bustling beach town of **Viña del Mar** ❶–❺ ▶, which is central and has the best lodging options. On the first day explore the town, focusing on Plaza José Francisco Vergara, the botanical gardens and museum at Quinta Vergara, and the miles of splendid shoreline. On the second day visit **Valparaíso** ❻–⓲, where you can ride a few funiculars and explore the cobbled neighborhood streets. On the third day, head south. You can overnight at **Algarrobo** ⓳ or **El Quisco** ⓴ so you can visit Pablo Neruda's waterfront home nearby in **Isla Negra** ㉑, or do it as a day trip.

If you have 5 days

Spend the first day in **Viña del Mar** ❶–❺ ▶, and days two and three in **Valparaíso** ❻–⓲, touring the hilltop promenades and exploring its museums. On the fourth day head south to Pablo Neruda's waterfront home in **Isla Negra** ㉑. The fifth day drive north along the coastal highway, stopping for lunch in either **Concón** ㉓ or **Maitencillo** ㉕. From there you can return or continue on to spend a night in either **Zapallar** ㉖ or **Los Molles** ㉘.

---

that Viña del Mar is modern and exciting; to others, it means the city is lacking in character. But there's no denying that Viña del Mar has a little of everything—trendy boutiques, beautiful homes, interesting museums, a casino, varied nightlife, and, of course, one of the best beaches in the country.

a good walk

Downtown Viña del Mar is completely flat and organized on a grid. To make things even easier, almost all of the street names are numbers in sequential order. For the streets running north–south, the numbers start on either side of Avenida Libertad. So you have 1 Poniente (west) and 1 Oriente (east).

Plaza José Francisco Vergara ❶ ▶ is the heart of the city. Just to the south is a smaller square called Plaza Sucre. Grandly filling the east end of the square is the **Club Viña del Mar** ❷. Walking south past Plaza Sucre you reach the **Palacio Vergara** ❸, with the Museo de Bellas Artes and the magnificently landscaped gardens of the Quinta Vergara.

Return to Plaza Vergara and head north across the Estero Marga Marga via the Puente Libertad. Gondolas once floated through the estuary, but today it's nearly dry outside of the rainy season (July–August). Walk north along Avenida Libertad then turn east on 4 Norte. An early-20th-century mansion houses the **Museo de Arqueológico e Historia Francisco Fonck** ❹, renowned for its Easter Island artifacts. Continue east two more blocks until the street ends at a lush park, in the heart of which stands the lovely **Palacio Rioja** ❺.

TIMING The terrain in Viña del Mar is flat, so walking is easy. You can take in all the sights on this tour in a few hours. Save yourself for the beach—it's the main attraction.

What to See

② **Club Viña del Mar.** It would be a shame to pass up a chance to see this private club's magnificent interior. The neoclassical building, constructed in 1901 of materials imported from England, is where wealthy locals come to play snooker. Nonmembers are usually only allowed to enter the grand central hall, but the club hosts occasional art shows, during which you may be able to circumambulate the second-floor interior balcony. ⊠ *Plaza Sucre at Av. Valparaíso* ☎ *32/680–016* ⌑ *Free* ⊙ *Mon.–Sat. 9–9.*

need a break? Even die-hard shoppers may be overwhelmed by the myriad shops along Avenida Valparaíso. Take a load off at **286 Rue Valparaíso** (⊠ Av. Valparaíso 286 ☎ 32/710–140), an Internet café with tables on the sidewalk. Enjoy a cappuccino, a milk shake, or perhaps a crepe.

④ **Museo de Arqueológico e Historia Francisco Fonck.** A 500-year-old stone *moai* (a carved stone head) brought from Easter Island guards the entrance to this archaeological museum. The most interesting exhibits are the finds from Easter Island, which indigenous people call Rapa Nui, such as wood tablets displaying ancient hieroglyphics. The museum, named for ground-breaking archaeologist Francisco Fonck—a native of Viña del Mar—also has an extensive library of documents relating to the island. ⊠ *4 Norte 784* ☎ *32/686–753* ⌑ *1,000 pesos* ⊙ *Tues.–Fri. 9:30–6, weekends 9:30–2.*

⑤ **Palacio Rioja.** This grand palace was built by Spanish banker Francisco Rioja immediately after the earthquake that leveled much of the city in 1906. It contains a decorative arts museum showcasing a large portion of Rioja's belongings and a conservatory, so there's often music in the air. Performances are held in the main ballroom. The beautifully landscaped grounds are great for shady lounging or a picnic. ⊠ *Quillota 214* ☎ *32/689–665* ⌑ *300 pesos* ⊙ *Tues.–Sun. 10–1:30 and 3–5:30.*

▶ ① **Plaza José Francisco Vergara.** Viña del Mar's central square, Plaza Vergara is lined with majestic palms. Presiding over the east end of the plaza is the patriarch of coastal accommodations, the venerable Hotel O'Higgins, which has seen better days. Opposite the hotel is the neoclassical Teatro Municipal, where you can watch a ballet, theater, or music performance. To the west on Avenida Valparaíso is the city's main shopping strip, a one-lane, seven-block stretch with extra-wide sidewalks and numerous stores and sidewalk cafés. You can hire a horse-drawn carriage to take you from the square past some of the city's stately mansions.

★ ③ **Palacio Vergara.** Lose yourself on the paths that wind amid soaring eucalyptus trees on the grounds that contain one of Chile's best botanical gardens, **Quinta Vergara.** An amphitheater here holds an international music festival, *Festival Internacional de la Canción de Viña del Mar,* in February. The neo-Gothic Palacio Vergara, erected after the 1906 earthquake as the residence of the wealthy Vergara family, houses the **Museo de Bellas Artes.** Inside is a collection of classical paintings dating from the 15th to the 19th centuries, including works by Rubens and Tintoretto. ⊠ *Av. Errázuriz 563* ☎ *32/680–618* ⌑ *Gardens free, museum 500 pesos* ⊙ *Gardens daily 7:30–7; museum Tues.–Sun. 10–2 and 3–6.*

Where to Stay & Eat

$–$$$ ✕ **Armandita.** Meat-eaters need not despair in this city of seafood saturation. A seemingly small restaurant half a block west of Avenida San Martín serves almost nothing but grilled meat, including various organs. The menu ranges from the popular *lomo a lo pobre* (flank steak, french

2

Beaches

The rugged Central Coast is Chile's playground, and each summer thousands of Santiaguinos flock here to relax on the region's wide beaches. The Humboldt Current, which flows northward along the coast of Chile, carries cold water to the Central Coast. If you plan to surf or skin dive, you need a wet suit; if you plan to swim, you need thick skin. Because large waves create dangerous undertows at some beaches, pay attention to warning flags: red means swimming is prohibited, whereas green, usually accompanied by a sign reading PLAYA APTA PARA NADAR (beach suitable for swimming), is a go-ahead signal.

Seafood & Other Specialties

"In the turbulent sea of Chile lives the golden conger eel," wrote Chilean poet Pablo Neruda in a simple verse that leaves the real poetry for the dinner table. To many, dining is the principal pleasure of a trip to the Central Coast. Along with that succulent conger eel, *congrio*, menus here typically have *corvina*, (sea bass), a whitefish called *reineta*, and the mild *lenguado*, (sole). The appetizer selection, which is invariably extensive, usually includes *ostiones* (scallops), *machas*, (razor clams), *camarones* (shrimp), and *jaiba* (crab). Because lobster is extremely rare in Chilean waters, it's more expensive here than just about anywhere in the world.

Fish and meat dishes are often served alone, which means that if you want french fries, mashed potatoes, a salad, or *palta* (avocado), you have to order it as an *agregado* (side dish). Bread, a bowl of lemons, and a sauce called *pebre* (a mix of tomato, onion, coriander, parsley, and often chili) are always brought to the table. Valparaíso is known for a hearty, cheap meal called *chorillana*—a mountain of minced steak, onions, and eggs on a bed of french fries.

Shopping

Viña del Mar has, by far, the best shopping on the Central Coast: everything from large department stores and outlet malls to trendy boutiques. Here also are some of the largest markets selling Chilean *artesanías*, or crafts. All summer long, souvenirs are sold in stands on the beaches up and down the coast.

---

fries, and a fried egg) to chateaubriand. The *parrillada especial*, a mixed grill of steak, chicken, ribs, pork, and sausage, serves two or three people. ⊠ *6 Norte 119* ☎ *32/671–607* ⊟ *AE, DC, MC, V.*

$–$$$ ✕ **San Marcos.** More than five decades after Edoardo Melotti emigrated to Chile from northern Italy to open San Marcos, the restaurant maintains a reputation for first-class food and service. A modern dining room with abundant foliage and large windows overlooks busy Avenida San Martín. Farther inside, the two dining rooms in the house the restaurant originally occupied are elegant and more refined. The menu includes the traditional gnocchi and cannelloni, as well as *lasagna di granchio* (crab lasagna) and *pato arrosto* (roast duck). Complement your meal with a bottle from the extensive wine list. ⊠ *Av. San Martín 597* ☎ *32/975–304* ⊟ *AE, DC, MC, V.*

$–$$ ✕ **Delicias del Mar.** Nationally renowned chef Raúl Madinagoitía, who
Fodor'sChoice   has his own television program, runs the show here. The menu lists such
★   seafood delicacies as Peruvian-style ceviche, stuffed sea bass, machas *cu-radas* (steamed clams with dill and melted cheese), and the house's own
version of paella. Oenophiles are impressed by the extensive, almost ex-clusively Chilean wine list. Save room for one of the excellent desserts,
maybe crème brûlée, or cheesecake with a raspberry sauce. ⊠ *San
Martín 459* 🕾 *32/901–837* 🖃 *AE, DC, MC, V.*

¢–$ ✕ **Fogón Criollo.** Hearty food at low prices: this unassuming restaurant
in a residential neighborhood specializes in authentic Chilean cuisine.
Try the *brasero al estilo Fogón Criollo,* a stew of beef, chicken, sausages,
and potatoes. Old photos of Viña del Mar line the walls of this former
home. Weekday lunch specials are a bargain. ⊠ *5 Norte 476* 🕾🕾 *32/
973–312* 🖃 *AE, DC, MC, V.*

★ **$$–$$$**   ✕⛨ **Hotel Oceanic.** Built on the rocky coast between Viña and Reñaca,
this boutique hotel has luxurious rooms with gorgeous ocean views. The
nicest ones have terraces, ideal for watching waves crash against the coast.
The pool area, perched on the rocks below, is occasionally drenched by
big swells. While there's no beach access, the sands of Salinas are a short
walk away. The restaurant is one of the area's best, serving French-in-spired dishes such as shrimp crepes, *filete café de Paris* (tenderloin with
herb butter), and congrio *oceanic* (conger eel in an artichoke mushroom
sauce). ⊠ *Av. Borgoño 12925, north of town* 🕾 *32/830–006* 🖃 *32/830–
390* ⊕ *www.hoteloceanic.cl* 🔄 *22 rooms, 6 suites* ⚫ *Restaurant, room
service, in-room data ports, in-room safes, minibars, cable TV, pool, hot
tub, massage, sauna, bar, business services, meeting rooms; no a/c* 🖃 *AE,
DC, MC, V* 🍴 *BP.*

$$ ✕⛨ **Cap Ducal.** This ship-shaped building on the waterfront is a bit of
an eyesore, but the views from its spacious restaurant and guest rooms
are excellent. Like the building, rooms are oddly shaped, but they are
nicely decorated with plush carpets and pastel wallpaper. Those on the
third floor have narrow balconies. Be sure to ask for a view of Reñaca,
or you may see, and hear, the road. The restaurant serves European cui-sine to top the view. Try the congrio *a la griega* (conger eel with a mush-room, ham, and cream sauce) or *pollo a la Catalana* (chicken with an
olive, mushroom, and tomato sauce). ⊠ *Av. Marina 51* 🕾 *32/828–655*
🖃 *32/665–478* ⊕ *www.capducal.cl* 🔄 *17 rooms, 3 suites* ⚫ *Restau-rant, in-room safes, minibars, cable TV, bar, laundry service; no a/c* 🖃 *AE,
DC, MC, V* 🍴 *BP.*

$$$$ ⛨ **Hotel Del Mar.** Marble floors, fountains, abundant gardens, and im-Fodor'sChoice   peccable service make Hotel Del Mar one of Chile's most luxurious. It
★   occupies a recent annex to the 1930 Casino Viña del Mar. The hotel's
exterior is true to the casino's neoclassical design, but spacious guest
rooms are pure 21st century, with sleek furnishings, original art, and
sliding glass doors that open onto sea-view balconies. An eighth-floor
spa and infinity pool share the view. A stay here includes free access to
the upscale casino, which evokes Monaco rather than Las Vegas. ⊠ *Av.
San Martín 199* 🕾 *32/500–600* 🖃 *32/500–701* ⊕ *www.casino.cl* 🔄 *50
rooms, 10 suites* ⚫ *3 restaurants, café, in-room date ports, in-room safes,
minibars, cable TV, indoor pool, exercise equipment, spa, bar, cabaret,
shop, baby-sitting, laundry service, concierge, Internet, business services,
convention center* 🖃 *AE, DC, MC, V* 🍴 *BP.*

$$ ⛨ **Hotel Alcazar.** Ground-floor rooms (called cabanas here) with giant
windows overlooking a tiny lawn and garden are the best deal. Though
slightly neglected and on the small side, they have a pinch more per-sonality than the more expensive rooms in the main building. Those have
more amenities and large bathrooms with tubs—rooms in front are
brighter, but suffer a bit from street noise. The hotel is south of the train

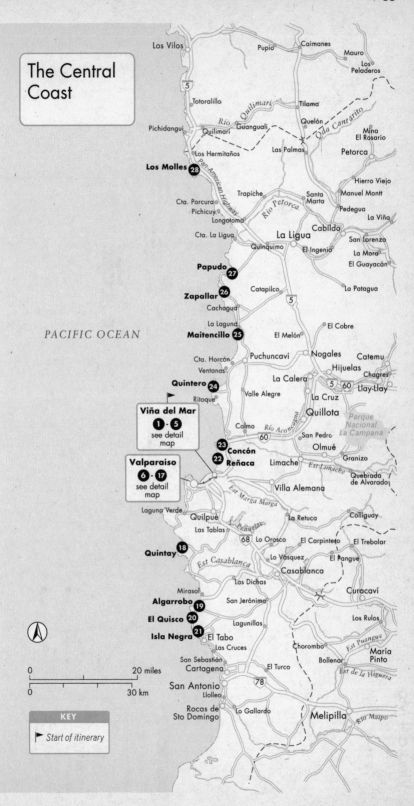

The Central Coast

Viña del Mar

PACIFIC OCEAN

0   400 yards

0   400 meters

KEY

▲ Start of walk

Casino Viña del Mar

Plaza Colombia

Plaza México

Av. Perú

Av. San Martín

Av. Marina

CASTILLO

Berger

Callao

Iberia

Libertad

Balmaceda

Álamos

Av. Marina

RECRERO

Agua Santa

Bellavista

Av. Portales

Von Schroeders

Ecuador

Traslaviña

Villanelo

Echevers

Quinta

Av. Libertad

1 Poniente

2 Poniente

3 Poniente

4 Poniente

5 Poniente

6 Poniente

7 Norte

6 Norte

5 Norte

4 Norte

3 Norte

2 Norte

1 Norte

Oriente

1 Oriente

2 Oriente

4 Oriente

5 Oriente

6 Oriente

Quillota

Av. Los Castaños

Av. Sporting

Valparaíso Sporting Club

Valparaíso Sporting Club

Peñablanca

Batuco

Av. Arlegui

Av. Marina

Av. Valparaíso

Quillota

Estación Viña del Mar

Plaza Sucre

Prieto Nieto

Montana

Errázuriz

Quinta Vergara Anfiteatro

FORESTAL

CHORRILLOS

Limache

Álvarez

Terminal Rodoviario (Bus Station)

Estero Marga-Marga

I Norte

Viana

Álvarez

Av. España

Club Viña del Mar **2**

Museo de Arqueológico e Historia Francisco Fonck **4**

Palacio Rioja **5**

Palacio Vergara **3**

Plaza José Francisco Vergara **1**

tracks. ✉ *Alvarez 646* ☎ *32/685–112* 🖷 *32/884–245* ⬏ *52 rooms, 22 cabanas* ⚲ *Restaurant, in-room safes, minibars, cable TV, bar, laundry service, meeting rooms; no a/c* ▭ *AE, DC, MC, V* ⦿ *BP.*

$$ ⊡ **Hotel Gala.** Modern rooms in this upscale 14-story hotel have panoramic views of the city. The rooms are spacious, and large windows let in lots of light. The bathrooms are crisp and clean and outfitted in white tile. There's a small heated pool next to the bar. One block from the Avenida Valparaíso shopping strip, Gala is near most of the city's attractions. Be sure to pay with pesos, since the dollar rate is considerably higher. ✉ *Arlegui 273* ☎ *32/686–688* 🖷 *32/689–568* ⬏ *64 rooms, 13 suites* ⚲ *Restaurant, in-room data ports, minibars, cable TV, pool, massage, sauna, bar, laundry service, business services, convention center* ▭ *AE, DC, MC, V* ⦿ *BP.*

★ **$** ⊡ **Hotel Tres Poniente.** Come for the personalized service and for many of the same amenities as larger hotels at a fraction of their rates. Rooms are carpeted, nicely furnished, and impeccably clean. Two "apartments," larger rooms in back, are ideal for small families. Complimentary breakfast, and light meals are served at the bright café in front, behind which is a small lounge with armchairs and a sofa. The small hotel is half a block from busy 1 Norte. ✉ *3 Poniente between 1 and 2 Norte* ☎ *32/ 977–833* 🖷 *32/478–576* ⬏ *12 rooms* ⚲ *Café, room service, in-room safe, minibars, cable TV, bar, baby-sitting, laundry service, Internet, no-smoking rooms; no a/c* ▭ *AE, DC, MC, V* ⦿ *BP.*

$ ⊡ **Residencia 555.** A stay in this old wood-frame house, built in 1912, may just make you feel like a local. Antiques fill the high-ceilinged living room, and a wide, curvaceous staircase leads to rooms on the second floor, several with balconies overlooking the garden. Considering the inn's charm, cleanliness, and central location, it's no surprise that Residencia 555 has twice been named the city's top guest house. ✉ *5 Norte 555* ☎ *32/739–035* ⊕ *www.gratisweb.com/residencial555* ⬏ *12 rooms* ▭ *AE, DC, MC, V* ⦿ *BP.*

Nightlife & the Arts

Viña's nightlife varies considerably according to the season, with the most glittering events concentrated in January and February. There are nightly shows and concerts at the Casino and frequent performances at Quinta Vergara. During the rest of the year, things only get going on weekends. Aside from the Casino, late-night fun is concentrated in the area around the intersection of Avenida San Martín and 4 Norte, the shopping strip on Avenida Valparaíso, and the eastern end of the alley called Paseo Cousiño. Viña residents tend to go to Valparaíso to party to live music, since it has a much better selection.

BARS   Though it's surrounded by the dance clubs and loud bars of Paseo Cousiño, **Kappi Kua** (✉ Paseo Cousiño 11-A ☎ 32/977–331) is a good place for a quiet drink. The Mexican restaurant **Margarita** (✉ Av. San Martín 348 ☎ 32/972–110) becomes a popular watering hole late at night. **Rituskuan** (✉ Av. Valparaíso at Von Schroeders ☎ 9/305–0340) is colorful and has excellent beer and electronic music.

CASINO   With a neoclassical style that wouldn't be out of place in a classic James Bond movie, **Casino Viña del Mar** (✉ Av. San Martín 199 ☎ 32/500–600) has a restaurant, bar, and cabaret, as well as roulette, blackjack, and 1,500 slot machines. It's open nightly until the wee hours of the morning most of the year. There's a 3,000-peso cover charge.

DANCE CLUBS   The cabaret on the second floor of the **Casino Viña del Mar** (✉ Av. San Martín 199 ☎ 32/500–600) becomes a chic discotheque after midnight. The popular **El Burro** (✉ Paseo Cousiño 12-D ☎ no phone) only opens Friday and Saturday. **El Mezón con Zeta** (✉ Paseo Cousiño 9 ☎ no phone) has a small dance floor. Viña's most sought-out dance club is **Scratch** (✉ Calle Bohn 970 ☎ 32/978–219), a long block east of Plaza Sucre.

FILM **Cine Arte** (✉ Plaza Vergara 142 ☎ 32/882–998) is an art-house theater on the west side of Plaza Vergara. **Cinemark Marina Arauco** (✉ Av. Libertad 1348 ☎ 32/688–188) has four screens showing American flicks. You can catch newly released American films on eight screens at the **Cinemark Shopping Viña** (✉ Av. 15 Norte 961 ☎ 32/993–388), but it's a little far from the center of town.

Sports & the Outdoors

BEACHES Just north of the rock wall along Avenida Peru is a stretch of sand that draws throngs of people December–March. Viña del Mar really has just one **main beach**, bisected near its southern end by an old pier, though its parts have been given separate names: Playa El Sol and Playa Blanca. South of town, on the far side of Cerro Castillo, the small **Playa Caleta Abarca** receives fewer sun worshippers than the main beach. A short drive north of town is the tiny **Las Salinas**, a crescent of sand that has the calmest water in the area.

GOLF You can play 18 holes Tuesday–Sunday at the **Granadilla Country Club** (✉ Camino Granadilla s/n, ☎ 32/689–249). It's an established course in Santa Inés—a 10-minute drive from downtown. The greens fees are 56,000 pesos, and they rent clubs for 15,000 pesos, but you need to make a reservation.

HORSE RACING **Valparaíso Sporting Club** (✉ Av. Los Castaños 404 ☎ 32/689–393) hosts horse racing every Friday. The Clásico del Derby, Chile's version of the Kentucky Derby, takes place the first Sunday in February. Rugby, polo, cricket, and other sports are also played here.

SOCCER Everton is Viña del Mar's soccer team. Matches are held at the 19,000-seat **Estadio Sausalito** (✉ Laguna Sausalito ☎ 32/978–250), which hosted World Cup matches in 1962.

Shopping

Outside of Santiago, there are more shops in Viña del Mar than anywhere else in Chile. Viña's main shopping strip is **Avenida Valparaíso** between Cerro Castillo and Plaza Vergara, where wide sidewalks accommodate throngs of shoppers. Stores here sell everything from shoes to cameras, and there are also sidewalk cafés, bars, and restaurants. South of Plaza Vergara is the city's largest department store, **Ripley** (✉ Sucre 290 ☎ 32/384–480). **Falabella** (✉ Sucre 250 ☎ 32/264–740) is a popular small department store south of Plaza Vergara. For one-stop shopping, locals head to the mall, **Shopping Viña** (✉ Av. 15 Norte 961 ☎ no phone), on the north end of town.

There are collections of **handicraft stands** on the road to Reñaca, across from the Hotel Oceanic, and in Paseo Cousiño, off the Avenida Valparaíso shopping strip's eastern end. Local crafts are sold at the **Cooperativa de Artesanía de Viña del Mar** (✉ Quinta between Viana and Av. Valparaíso ☎ no phone). On the beach, just off Vergara dock, the **Feria Artesanal Muelle Vergara** is a crafts fair open daily in summer and on weekends the rest of the year.

Valparaíso

10 km (6 mi) south of Viña del Mar, 120 km (75 mi) west of Santiago.

Valparaíso's dramatic topography—45 hills overlooking the ocean—requires the use of winding pathways and wooden *ascensores* (funiculars) to get up many of the grades. The city installed the first ascensor in 1883.

The word means elevator, though only the Ascensor Polanco travels vertically; the rest are pulled up steep inclines at an angle by steel cables. The slopes are covered by colorful houses—there are almost no apartments in the city—most of which have exteriors of corrugated metal peeled from shipping containers decades ago. Valparaíso has served as Santiago's port for centuries. Before the Panama Canal opened, Valparaíso was the busiest port in South America. Harsh realities—changing trade routes, industrial decline—have diminished its importance, but it remains Chile's principal port.

Most shops, banks, restaurants, bars, and other businesses cluster along the handful of streets called *El Plano* (the flat area) that are closest to the shoreline. *Porteños* (locals; the name refers to the port) live in the surrounding hills in an undulating array of colorful homes. At the top of any of the dozens of stairways, the *paseos* (promenades) have spectacular views; many are named after prominent Yugoslavian, Basque, and German immigrants. Neighborhoods are named for the *cerros* (hills) they cover.

With the jumble of power lines overhead and the hundreds of buses that slow down—but never completely stop—to pick up agile riders, it's hard to forget you're in a city. Still, walking is the best way to experience Valparaíso. Be a bit careful where you step though—locals aren't very conscientious about curbing their dogs.

a good walk

Take a taxi, or any bus that has ADUANA written on its windshield, to the Plaza Aduana, at the northwestern end of El Plano. Here is the scarlet Dirección Nacional de Aduana, the 19th-century customs house still in use today. Next door is the Ascensor Artillería, a funicular that carries you up to the **Paseo 21 de Mayo** ⑥ ▶. Behind this promenade with a sweeping view of the bay is the **Museo Naval y Marítimo de Valparaíso** ⑦. Take the funicular back to the plaza, or walk down the stairway that ends near the base of the customs house. Walk southeast along Calle Cochrane, the first block of which has some tawdry bars—note the WELCOME SAILOR signs (avoid this area at night). Follow Cochrane to **Plaza Sotomayor** ⑧, dominated by the stately Comandancia building and the Monumento de los Héroes de Iquique.

North of the monument is **Muelle Prat** ⑨, with the tourist office, the Estación Puerto for trains bound for Viña del Mar, and boats leaving for short tours of the bay. Return to Plaza Sotomayor and cross it, heading to the left of the Comandancia building, where a smaller square lies before the courthouse called the Tribunales de Justicia. On your left is the Ascensor El Peral; take it up to the art nouveau **Museo de Bellas Artes** ⑩ and the lovely neighborhood of Cerro Alegre. Afterwards, return to the base of the hill, turn right on Calle Prat, and walk two blocks southeast to the Ascensor Concepción, at the end of a narrow passage on your right. Ride this up to the neighborhood of **Cerro Concepción** ⑪, with its views of Paseo Gervason.

If you return to Calle Prat and continue right, it becomes Calle Esmeralda; follow this and you'll pass the neoclassical structure that houses the world's oldest Spanish-language newspaper, *El Mercurio de Valparaíso*. Esmeralda then curves south to Plaza Anibal Pinto. Head east on Calle Condell to Calle Ecuador, where you can find some of the city's most popular nightspots. Here are taxis that can take you to **La Sebastiana** ⑫. From there you can walk down the narrow streets of Cerro Bellavista and get a look at a series of murals known as the **Museo a Cielo Abierto** ⑬, near the top of the Ascensor Espíritu Santo. Then ride down to Calle Huito, which in turn leads back to Calle Condell. Turn left, and

Valparaíso

Bahía de Valparaíso

Antonio Varas

Ascensor
Artilleria

Plaza
Advana

Artilleria

Av. Carampangue

Av. Errázuriz

Márquez

Valdivia

San Martín

Clave

Goñi

Serrano

Prat

Estación
Puerto

Estación
Bellavista

Blanco
Cochrane

Esmeralda

Ascensor
Concepción

Ascensor
El Peral

Papudo

Concepción

Uriola

Templeman

Castillo

Tomás Ramos

Monte Alegre

Morrison

Av. Pedro Montt

Munich
Hospital

Cumming

Melgarejo

O'Higgins

Salva

Puteto

Bella Vista

Av. Br

Cor

Cumming

Cementerio
Católico

Cementerio
de Disidentes

Av. Ecuad

Plaza
Bismarck

KEY

▶ Start of walk

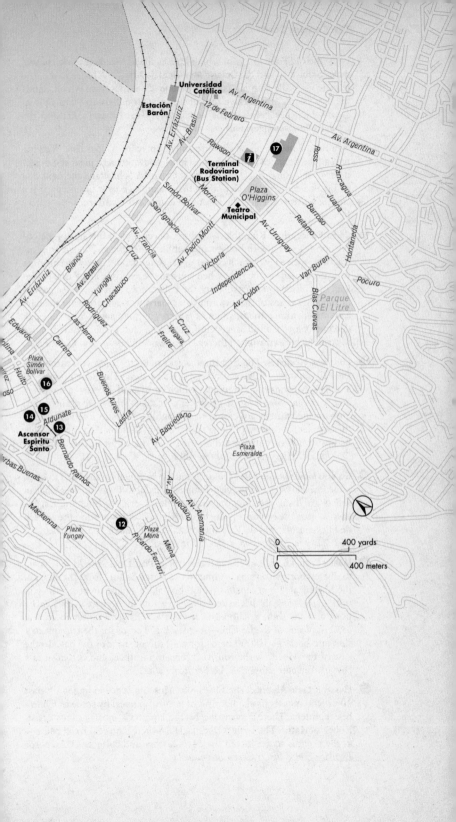

go to the old Palacio Lyon, which houses the **Museo de Historia Natural de Valparaíso** ⁱ⁴ and the **Galería Municipal de Arte** ⁱ⁵. A block east of the Palacio on Calle Condell is **Plaza Victoria** ⁱ⁶, across from which stands the city's cathedral. Take a taxi or bus east from here to Plaza O'Higgins, which lies between the neoclassical Teatro Municipal and the modern **Congreso Nacional** ⁱ⁷.

TIMING   You need a good pair of shoes to fully appreciate Valparaíso. Walking past all the sights, exploring the museums, and enjoying a meal and drinks makes for a long, full day. You might visit La Sebastiana the next day to break up the walk. Definitely bring sunblock or a hat. Even if it's cloudy when you start, the sun often comes out by afternoon.

What to See

🅫 **Cerro Concepción.** Ride the Ascensor Concepción to this hilltop neighborhood covered with houses and cobblestone streets. The greatest attraction is the view, which is best appreciated from Paseo Gervasoni, a wide promenade to the right when you exit the ascensor, and Paseo Atkinson, one block to the east. Over the balustrades that line those paseos lie amazing vistas of the city and bay. Nearly as fascinating are the narrow streets above them, some of which are quite steep. The stairway descent below Calle Concepción, however, should be avoided, since tourists have been robbed there. ⊠ *Ascensor Concepción, Calle Pratt.*

🅭 **Congreso Nacional.** The first three weeks of each month you can watch the 120 *diputados* (representatives) meet Tuesday–Thursday noon–2:30 and 4–6. Meetings of the Senate, which consists of 40 elected members and two *senadores vitalicios* (former presidents who were granted senator-for-life status), are closed to the public. Tours in English explain the bicameral workings of Chile's government. Dictator Augusto Pinochet had this building constructed on the site of one of his boyhood homes. ⊠ *Plaza O'Higgins* 🕾 *no phone* 🎟 *Free* 🕙 *Weekdays 10–6.*

🅯 **Galería Municipal de Arte.** This crypt in the basement of the Palacio Lyon is the finest art space in the city. Temporary exhibits by top-caliber Chilean artists are displayed on stone walls under a series of brick arches. It's easy to miss the entrance, which is on Calle Condell beyond the Museo de Historia Natural de Valparaíso. ⊠ *Calle Condell 1550* 🕾 *32/939-562* 🎟 *Free* 🕙 *Weekdays 10–7, Sat. 10–5.*

🅰 **Muelle Prat.** Though its name translates as Prat Dock, the Muelle is actually a wharf with steps leading to the water. Sailors from the ships in the harbor arrive in *lanchas* (small boats), or board them for the trip back to their vessels. It's a great place to watch the activity at the nearby port, and the ships anchored in the harbor. To get a closer look, you can board one of the lanchas—it costs 2,000 pesos for the trip out to a ship and back, or 10,000 pesos for a 40-minute tour of the bay. To the east of the Muelle is the tourist information office, and behind it is a row of souvenir shops. ⊠ *Av. Errázuriz s/n.*

🅱 **Museo a Cielo Abierto.** The Open Sky Museum is a winding walk past 20 official murals (and a handful of unofficial ones) by some of Chile's best painters. There's even one by the country's most famous artist, Roberto Matta. The path is not marked—there's no real fixed route—as the point is to get lost in the city's history and culture. ⊠ *Ascensor Espíritu Santo up to Cerro Buenavista.*

While exploring Cerro Bellavista, be sure to stop by **Gato Tuerto** (⊠ Calle Hector Calvo Jofré 20 ☎ 32/220–867), the One-Eye Cat. This meticulously restored 1910 Victorian house affords lovely views. It's an Internet café, a book shop, a handicrafts boutique, and a popular night spot.

★ ⑩ **Museo de Bellas Artes.** The art nouveau Palacio Baburizza houses the city's fine arts museum. Former owner Pascual Baburizza donated his large collection of European paintings to the city. The fanciful decorative exterior is reminiscent of the style of Spanish architect Antoni Gaudí. The museum was closed for renovation at press time, but even if it hasn't reopened by the time you visit it's still worth a look at the exterior. ⊠ *Ascensor El Peral to Paseo Yugoslavo* ☎ *32/915–1028* ⊕ *www. museobaburizza.cl.*

⑭ **Museo de Historia Natural de Valparaíso.** Within the Palacio Lyon, one of the few buildings to survive the devastating 1906 earthquake, is this rather outdated natural history museum. Among the more unusual exhibits are a pre-Columbian mummy, newborn conjoined twins in formaldehyde, and stuffed penguins. ⊠ *Calle Condell 1546* ☎ *32/257– 441* 🖺 *600 pesos* ☉ *Tues.–Sat. 10–1 and 2–6, Sun. 10–2.*

❼ **Museo Naval y Marítimo de Valparaíso.** Atop Cerro Artillería is the large neoclassical mansion that once housed the country's naval academy. It now contains a maritime museum, with displays that document the history of the port and the ships that once defended it. Cannons positioned on the front lawn frame the excellent view of the ocean. ⊠ *Ascensor Artillería up to Paseo 21 de Mayo* ☎ *32/437–651* 🖺 *500 pesos* ☉ *Tues.–Sun. 10–5.*

▶ ❻ **Paseo 21 de Mayo.** Ascensor Artillería pulls you uphill to Paseo 21 de Mayo, a wide promenade surrounded by well-tended gardens and stately trees from which you can survey the port and a goodly portion of Valparaíso. It's in the middle of Cerro Playa Ancha, one of the city's more colorful neighborhoods. ⊠ *Ascensor Artillería at Plaza Advana.*

If you can't get enough of the views from Paseo 21 de Mayo, stroll down the stairs that run parallel to the ascensor to the small restaurant, **Poseidon** (⊠ Subida Artillería 99 ☎ 32/346–713). With a terrace superbly perched on a high corner overlooking the city, this makes a great spot for a cool drink, or coffee and a slice of homemade pie.

❽ **Plaza Sotomayor.** Valparaíso's most impressive square, Plaza Sotomayor, serves as a gateway to the bustling port. **Comandancia en Jefe de la Armada,** headquarters of the Chilean navy, is a grand, gray building that rises to a turreted pinnacle over a mansard roof. At the north end of the plaza stands the **Monumento de los Héroes de Iquique,** which honors Arturo Prat and other heroes of the War of the Pacific. In the middle of the square (beware of traffic—cars and buses come suddenly from all directions) is the **Museo del Sitio.** Artifacts from the city's mid-19th century port, including parts of a dock that once stood on this spot, are displayed in the open under Plexiglas. ⊠ *Av. Errázuriz s/n.*

⑯ **Plaza Victoria.** The heart of the lower part of the city is this green plaza with a lovely fountain bordered by four female statues representing the seasons. Two black lions at the edge of the park look across the street to the neo-Gothic **Catedral,** the city's cathedral, and its unusual free-standing bell tower. Directly to the north is **Plaza Simon Bolívar,** which delights children with swings, slides, and simple carnival rides. ⊠ *Calle Condell s/n.*

★ ⑫ **La Sebastiana.** Some say the views from the windows of Pablo Neruda's hillside house are the best in all of Valparaíso. People come to La Sebastiana to marvel at the same ocean that inspired so much poetry. The house is named for Sebastián Collado, a Spanish architect who began it as a home for himself but died before it was finished. The incomplete building stood abandoned for 10 years before Neruda finished it, revising the design (Neruda had no need for the third-floor aviary or the helicopter landing pad) and adding curvaceous walls, narrow stairways, a tower, and a polymorphous character.

A maze of twisting stairwells leads to an upper room where a video shows Neruda enunciating the five syllables of the city's name over and again as he rides the city's *ascensores*. His upper berth contains his desk, books, and some original manuscripts. What makes the visit to La Sebastiana memorable, however, is Neruda's nearly obsessive delight in physical objects. The house is a shrine to his many cherished things, such as the beautiful orange-pink bird he brought back embalmed from Venezuela. His lighter spirit is here also, in the carousel horse and the pink and yellow bar room stuffed with kitsch. ⊠ *Calle Ferrari 692* ☎ *32/256–606* 🖃 *1,800 pesos* ☉ *Jan.–Feb., Tues.–Sun. 10:30–6:50; Mar.–Dec., Tues.–Sun. 10:30–2:30 and 3:30–6.*

Where to Stay & Eat

$$–$$$$ ✕ **Bote Salvavidas.** This restaurant next to Muelle Prat has great views of the harbor and, naturally, specializes in seafood. Dishes such as *congrio margarita* (conger eel with shellfish sauce), *salmón salsa espinaca y nueces* (salmon smothered in a spinach and walnut sauce), and *pastel de jaiba* (crab pie) are among the popular specialties. A three-course *menu ejecutivo* (set lunch), available on weekdays, is quite the deal. ⊠ *Muelle Prat* ☎ *32/251–477* 🖃 *AE, DC, MC, V* ☉ *No dinner Sun.–Mon.*

$$–$$$ ✕ **Café Turri.** Near the top of Ascensor Concepción, this 19th-century
FodorśChoice mansion commands one of the best views of Valparaíso. It also has some
★ of the finest seafood. House specialties such as sea bass or shrimp in almond sauce and ostiones Cleopatra (scallops in a mushroom cream sauce) are alone worth the effort of driving to the coast from Santiago. Outside there's a terrace and inside are two floors of dining rooms. The service is excellent. ⊠ *Templeman 147, at Paseo Gervasoni* ☎ *32/252–091* 🖷 *32/259–198* 🖃 *AE, DC, MC, V.*

$$–$$$ ✕ **La Colombina.** This restaurant is in an old home on Cerro Alegre, one of the city's most beautiful hilltop neighborhoods. Dining rooms on two floors are notable for their elegance, stained-glass windows, and impressive views of the city and sea. Seafood dominates the menu, with such inventive dishes as *albacora del bufón* (swordfish in a caper and mushroom cream sauce) and *trilogía del mar* (salmon, sea bass, and conger eel in a white wine, mushroom, and vegetable sauce). Choose from a list of 80 national wines. ⊠ *Paseo Yugoslavo 15* ☎ *32/236–254* 🖃 *AE, DC, MC, V* ☉ *No dinner Mon.*

$–$$$ ✕ **Coco Loco.** It takes a little more than an hour to turn 360 degrees in this impressive *giratorio* (revolving restaurant), meaning you can savor all the smashing views of the city. The vast menu ranges from *filete de ciervo salsa hongos* (venison in a mushroom sauce) to fettuccine with a squid and mussels sauce. ⊠ *Blanco 1781* ☎ *32/227–614* 🝔 *Reservations essential* 🖃 *AE, DC, MC, V* ☉ *No dinner Sun.*

¢–$ ✕ **Brighton.** Nestled below the eponymous bed-and-breakfast on the edge of Cerro Concepción, this popular restaurant has an amazing view from its black-and-white-tiled balcony. Vintage advertisements hang on the walls of the intimate dining room. A limited menu includes such Chilean standards as machas *a la parmesana* (razor clams Parmesan) and ceviche, as well as several kinds of crepes and a Spanish *tortilla* (egg and potato pie). An extensive wine list and cocktail selection make it a popular night spot, especially on weekends, when there's Latin music. ⊠ *Paseo Atkinson 151* ☎ *32/223–513* 🖃 *AE, DC, MC, V.*

¢–$ ✕ **Casino Social J. Cruz M.** This eccentric restaurant is a Valparaíso institution, thanks to its legendary status for inventing the *chorillana* (minced beef with onions, cheese, and an egg atop french fries), which is now served by most local restaurants. There is no menu—choose either a chorillana for two or three, or *carne mechada* (stewed beef), with a side of french fries, rice, or tomato salad. Glass cases choked with dusty trinkets surround tables covered with plastic cloths in the cramped dining room. You may have to share a table. The restaurant is at the end of a bleak corridor off Calle Condell. ⊠ *Calle Condell 1466* ☎ *32/211–225* 🖃 *No credit cards.*

$ 🛏 **Brighton B&B.** This bright yellow Victorian house enjoys an enviable location at the edge of tranquil Cerro Concepción, within blocks of several restaurants and an ascensor. The house is furnished with antiques chosen by owner Nelson Morgado, who taught architecture for two decades at the University of Barcelona. The terrace of its restaurant and three of its six rooms have vertiginous views of El Plano and the bay beyond it. Only one room has a private balcony. Room size varies considerably—only the so-called suite (just a larger room) is spacious—and those with the best views can be noisy on weekends. Some rooms have cable TV. ⊠ *Paseo Atkinson 151* ☎ *32/223–513* 🖷 *32/598–802* 🖃 *6 rooms* ⚭ *Restaurant, bar, laundry service; no a/c, no room phones* 🖃 *AE, DC, MC, V* ⦿ *CP.*

FodorsChoice
★

$ 🛏 **Hostal Colombina.** The location here is excellent: on a quiet street just up the hill from the Ascensor Concepción, near Paseo 21 de Mayo in the heart of Cerro Concepción. Rooms in this old house may be sparsely furnished, but they are ample, with high ceilings and wooden floors. Most have big windows, though none of them have much of a view. ⊠ *Calle Abtao 575* ☎ *32/236–254 or 32/234–980* 🖃 *8 rooms with shared bath* ⚭ *Dining room, wine bar; no a/c, no room phones, no room TVs* 🖃 *AE, DC, MC, V* ⦿ *CP.*

★ $ 🛏 **Porto Principal.** Though small and fairly basic, this hotel on a side street near Plaza Victoria has comfortable, secure accommodations at a reasonable price. Clean, carpeted rooms with large windows are on the second floor of a two-story building—those in back are slightly quieter. The ground floor has a tiny bar and restaurant, where breakfast is served. ⊠ *Calle Huito 361* ☎ *32/745–629* 🖷 *32/226–738* 🖃 *6 rooms* ⚭ *Restaurant, room service, cable TV, bar, laundry service; no a/c* 🖃 *AE, DC, MC, V* ⦿ *CP.*

$ 🛏 **Puerta de Alcalá.** The rooms surround a five-story atrium flooded with light at this central hotel. They have little personality, but are clean and well equipped, with little extras like hair dryers. Those facing the street are bright, but can be noisy on weekends. If you're a light sleeper, take a room in the back, but try to get on the fourth floor—the lower floors get less sunlight because they are blocked by the building next door. There's a decent restaurant and bar on the ground level. ⊠ *Pirámide 524* ☎ *32/227–478* 🖷 *32/745–642* ⊕ *www.chileinfo.cl/ puertadealcalahotel* 🖃 *21 rooms* ⚭ *Restaurant, room service, in-room data ports, minibars, cable TV, bar, laundry service, meeting room; no a/c* 🖃 *AE, DC, MC, V* ⦿ *CP.*

Nightlife & the Arts

Valparaíso has an inordinate amount of nocturnal establishments, which run the gamut from pubs to tango bars and salsa dance clubs. Thursday–Saturday nights, most places get crowded between 11 PM and midnight. Young people stay out until daybreak. The main concentrations of bars and clubs are on Subida Ecuador, near Plaza Anibal Pinto, and a block of Avenida Errázuriz nearby. Cerro Concepción, Alegre, and Bellavista have quieter options, many with terraces perfect for admiring the city lights.

BARS **Bar Inglés** (⊠ Cochrane 851 ☎ 32/214–625) is dingy but authentic, a short walk east of Plaza Sotomayor. It serves decent food and has the longest bar in town. The huge antique mirrors of **Bar La Playa** (⊠ Serrano 567), just west of Plaza Sotomayor, make it seem historic. Poetry readings are held Wednesday at 11 PM, and it becomes packed with party animals after midnight on weekends January–February. **Valparaíso Eterno** (⊠ 150 Almirante Señoret ☎ 32/228–374), one block from Plaza Sotomayor, is filled with paintings of Valparaíso and floor-to-ceiling graffiti lovingly supplied by patrons. It only opens on weekends.

DANCE CLUBS Among the top dance clubs is **Aché Havana** (⊠ Av. Errázuriz 1042 ☎ 9/521–9872), which plays mostly salsa and other Latin rhythms. Near several other large dance clubs, **Bulevar** (⊠ Av. Errázuriz 1154 ☎ no phone) has eclectic music on weekend nights. The basement **Eterno** (⊠ Calle Blanco 698 ☎ 32/219–024), one block east of Plaza Sotomayor, plays only Latin dance music, and opens weekends only. The four-story **Mr. Egg** (⊠ Calle Ecuador 50 ☎ no phone) has a bar on the ground floor and a dance club above it.

FILM **Cine Hoyts** (⊠ Av. Pedro Montt 2111 ☎ 32/594–709), across from Parque Italia, is a state-of-the-art theater showing American releases on five screens. The restaurant **Valparaíso Mi Amor** (⊠ Papudo 612 ☎ 32/219–891) screens 16-millimeter films about Valparaíso made by owner Nelson Cabrera, as well as European features.

LIVE MUSIC **Brighton** (⊠ Paseo Atkinson s/n ☎ 32/223–513) has live bolero music on Friday and tango on Saturday, starting at 11 PM. Its balcony overlooks the city's glittering lights from Cerro Concepción. **La Colombina** (⊠ Papudo 526 ☎ 32/219–891), on Cerro Alegre, has live Latin music weekend nights and an amazing view. The small restaurant **Color Cafe** (⊠ Papudo 612 ☎ 32/251–183) in Cerro Concepción serves up drinks and live Latin music on weekends. Cerro Bellavista's **Gato Tuerto** (⊠ Calle Hector Calvo Jofré 205 ☎ 32/220–867) hosts live Latin music on weekends in a lovely Victorian mansion with a city view.

Concert fans should check out **La Piedra Feliz** (⊠ Av. Errázuriz 1054 ☎ 32/256–788), which hosts performances by Chile's best bands Tuesday–Saturday. The music starts at 9 PM weeknights and 11 PM weekends. Wednesday is Jazz night. Dance to live tango music weekends at **Cinzano** (⊠ Anibal Pinto 1182 ☎ 32/213–043), on Plaza Anibal Pinto. There's live Latin music weekends at **El Triunfo** (⊠ Calle Ecuador 27 ☎ 32/257–428). Weekends, **Entre Socios** (⊠ Calle Ecuador 75), on the upper end of the Subita Ecuador, plays alternative music.

THEATER Off Plaza O'Higgins, the lovely old **Teatro Municipal de Valparaíso** (⊠ Uruguay 410 ☎ 32/214–654) hosts symphonies, ballet, and opera May–November. **Ex-Cárcel de Valparaíso** (⊠ El Castro s/n ☎ 32/250–891), a crumbling former prison in Cerro Cárcel, is a haunting space used for plays and concerts.

Sports & the Outdoors

BEACHES If it's beaches you're after, head to Viña del Mar. Valparaíso has only one notable beach, **Playa Las Torpederas,** a sheltered crescent of sand east of the port. Though less attractive than the beaches up the coast, it does have very calm water.

BOATING Informal boat operators at **Muelle Prat** take groups on a 40-minute circuit of the bay for 2,000 pesos per person. If you have several people, consider hiring your own boat for 10,000 pesos.

SOCCER Valparaíso's first-division soccer team is the **Valparaíso Wanderers** (⊠ Independencia 2061 ☎ 32/217–210). Matches are usually held Monday at the Estadio Municipal in Playa Ancha.

Shopping

Cooperativa Artesanal de Valparaíso (⊠ Pedro Montt and Calle Las Heras ☎ no phone) is a daily market where you can buy local crafts. The weekend flea market, **Feria de Antigüedades** (⊠ Av. Argentina at Plaza O'Higgins ☎ no phone), has an excellent selection of antiques. **Paulina Acuña** (⊠ Almirante Montt 64 ☎ 9/871–8388), a small boutique up the hill from Plaza Anibal Pinto, sells an unusual collection of handicrafts, including painted glass, candles, jewelry, and clothing.

Chile's major department store chain, **Ripley** (⊠ Calle Condell 1646 ☎ 32/622–531), is across from Plaza Victoria. The fifth floor has a food court.

THE SOUTHERN BEACHES

Once a dominion of solitude and sea, the stretch of coastline south of Valparaíso has seen much development, not all of it well planned, over the past few decades. A succession of towns here caters to the beach-bound hordes January–February. Though none of the towns is terribly attractive, a few of the beaches are quite nice.

The main reason to visit—and it's a great one—is to take a look at poet Pablo Neruda's hideaway at Isla Negra. Here you can see the various treasures he collected during his lifetime.

Quintay

🔟 *30 km (19 mi) south of Valparaíso.*

Not too long ago, migrating sperm whales could still be seen from the beaches at Quintay. The creatures were all but exterminated by the whaling industry that sprung up in Quintay in 1942. Whaling was banned in 1967, and the town went quiet again. Just past the handful of brightly colored fishing boats on the little beach is the nearly abandoned **whaling factory.** Walk around its skeletal remains—parts are now used as an open-air shellfish hatchery.

Escuela San Pedro de Quintay, the town's elementary school, serves as a makeshift museum dedicated to Quintay's whaling past. Jose Daniel Barrios, a former whaler, maintains the humble display; his whaling contract is among the exhibits. Others include photos of the plant, a whale gun, whale teeth, and a harpoon. Also here are some pottery and skeletons from the indigenous Aconcagua people, who inhabited the region around 1300. ⊠ *Calle Escuela San Pedro s/n* ☎ *no phone* 🖃 *Donation* ⏳ *Jan.–Feb., daily 10–noon and 2–6; Mar.–Dec., hrs vary.*

Where to Stay & Eat

$–$$ ✕ **Los Pescadores.** Echoing the colors of the fishing boats below, this seafood restaurant has yellow walls, a bright blue terrace, and wooden floors painted green. Because of the restaurant's proximity to the caleta, the seafood is very fresh. Attentive servers will help you choose from the good wine selection. ⊠ *Costanera s/n* ☎ *32/362–068* ▭ *AE, DC, MC, V.*

Sports & the Outdoors

BEACHES Vacation apartments have replaced the pine forest surrounding **Playa Grande.** There are two ways to reach the beach: through the town, following Avenida Teniente Merino, or through the gated community of Santa Augusta.

DIVING Chile's coastline has several interesting shipwrecks. Two are off the shores of Quintay, including *Indus IV*, a whaling ship that went down in 1947. There are no dive companies in Quintay, but in nearby Algarrobo, Cinco Oceanos dive operator runs trips to both Quintay shipwrecks. The Santiago-based **Poseidon** (⊠ Av. Andrés Bello 2909, Santiago ☎ 2/ 231–3597) arranges dive excursions to the wrecks of Quintay.

Algarrobo

🔟 *35 km (22 mi) south of Quintay.*

The largest town south of Valparaíso, Algarrobo is the first in a string of balnearios spread along the coast to the south. Though Algarrobo isn't the prettiest, it has a winding coastline with several yellow-sand beaches, and consequently attracts throngs of sun worshippers.

Next to Playa San Pedro is the private yacht club, **Club de Yates Algarrobo.** In February, boats from all over the country participate in one of Chile's most important nautical events here: the Regata Mil Millas Náuticas.

The **Cofradía Náutica,** a private marina at the end of a point south of town, harbors some of the country's top yachts. Just offshore from the Cofradía Náutica is a tiny island called **Isla de los Pájaros Niños,** a penguin sanctuary that shelters more than 300 Humboldt and Magellan penguins. The upper crags of the island are dotted with hundreds of little caves dug by the penguins using their legs and beaks. Though only members are allowed in the marina, a path leads to the top of a nearby hill from which you can watch the flightless birds through binoculars.

Where to Stay & Eat

$–$$ ✕ **Restaurante Algarrobo.** The only waterfront restaurant in Algarrobo has a small terrace overlooking a tiny beach. The extensive menu is almost exclusively seafood, including half a dozen types of fish served with an equal number of sauces. Ostiones *pil pil* (spicy scallop scampi) and *loco apanado* (fried abalone) are popular starters. ⊠ *Av. Carlos Alessandri 1505* ☎ *35/481–078* ▭ *No credit cards.*

★ $–$$ ▦ **Pao Pao.** Llamas trim the grass around the cabanas spread here across a forested ridge north of town. The octagonal pine cabanas range from cozy studios to two-bedroom apartments complete with wooden decks and hot tubs. Only some have views of the water at Playa Grande. All of the cabanas have giant windows and well-stocked kitchenettes; most have small fireplaces. The adjacent restaurant only opens on weekends outside of January–February. ⊠ *Camino Mirasol s/n* ☎ *35/482–145 or 35/481–264* ⊕ *www.turismopaopao.cl* ⤵ *21 cabins ⌂ Restaurant, kitchenettes, minibars, cable TV, pool, baby-sitting, playground, laundry service; no a/c* ▭ *AE, DC, MC, V.*

$ ▦ **Hotel Pacífico.** This older hotel in the heart of town, a block from Playa Las Cadenas, has bland but comfortable rooms. The main building dates from the 1940s, with polished wooden floors and a nice lounge with a fireplace. Spacious rooms on the second floor have seen better days, but a few in front overlook the sea. A newer—1960s—annex is stacked against the hillside. Rooms on the upper floors need some fresh paint, but they have nice ocean views. ✉ *Av. Carlos Alessandri 1930* 🕾 *35/482–818* 🖷 *35/481–040* 📞 *79 rooms* ⚭ *Restaurant, cable TV, pool, bar, playground, laundry service, business services, meeting rooms; no a/c* 🖃 *AE, DC, MC, V* ⧖❙ *BP.*

Sports & the Outdoors

BEACHES Algarrobo's nicest beach is **Playa El Canelo,** in a secluded cove south of town. It's an idyllic spot of fine yellow sand, calm blue-green water, and a backdrop of pines. Though quiet most of the year, it can get crowded in January and February. Follow Avenida Santa Teresita south to Avenida El Canelo and the pine forest of Parque Canelo. Guarded parking there costs 2,000 pesos. If you want seclusion, follow the trail that leads southwest from Playa El Canelo, past the guano-splotched outcropping called Peñablanca, to the smaller **Playa Canelillo.**

The second nicest beach in Algarrobo is **Playa Grande.** The beige sand stretches northward from town for several miles. There's usually rough surf, which can make it dangerous for swimming. Massive condominium complexes on either end of this beach spill thousands of vacationers onto it every summer. The most popular beach in town is tiny **Playa San Pedro;** a statue of Saint Peter in the sand next to the wharf marks the spot. It's small, but the waters are surrounded by a rocky barrier that keeps them calm and good for swimming. **Playa Las Cadenas,** on the north end of town, has a waterfront promenade. The name, Chain Beach, refers to the thick metal links lining the sidewalk, which were recovered from a shipwreck off Algarrobo Bay.

DIVING **Cinco Oceanos** (✉ Hotel Pacífico, Av. Carlos Alessandri 1930 🕾 9/720–7960 or 35/482–818) runs boat dives to half a dozen spots, including underwater cliffs and the two shipwrecks off Quintay.

El Quisco

⓴ *2 km (1 mi) south of Algarrobo.*

El Quisco is a gesture of summer, nothing but a long beach of pale sand guarded on either end by stone jetties. In the middle of the beach is a boulder with a 15-ft-high, six-pronged cactus sculpture perched atop it. South of the beach is the blue and yellow caleta, where boats anchored offshore create a picturesque composition. In summer, the beach is packed on sunny days, as visitors outnumber *Quisqueños* (locals) about ten to one.

Where to Stay & Eat

★ $ ✕▥ **Der Münchner Hof.** This German-owned guest house on the north end of the bay stands just across the street from the beach, which gives its restaurant a lovely view. Simple but spotless accommodations are on the second floor, above the spacious dining room. Ask for Room 3, which has a terrace overlooking the beach, or Room 2, the only other room with an ocean view. Though the large restaurant, the best in town, serves mostly seafood, the menu does include a few Bavarian dishes, such as *pernil ahumado* (smoked ham) and strudel. Weekends there's a lunch buffet. ✉ *Costanera 111* 🕾🖷 *35/471–704* 📞 *5 rooms* ⚭ *Restaurant, room service, cable TV, bar, laundry service; no a/c* 🖃 *AE, DC, MC, V.*

$ ▥ **Cabañas El Galeón.** Since El Galeón caters primarily to Chilean families, the suites all have kitchenettes, and most have an extra bedroom with bunk beds. The best choice for a couple is El Faro: a spacious, second-floor room with big windows to let the sun and sea sounds in. This simple hotel has an excellent location south of town—far from the traffic but just a short walk to the beach. Go down the dirt road past the Caleta de Algarrobo. ✉ *Costanera 278* ☎ *35/472–204* ➳ *6 suites* ⚲ *Kitchenettes, cable TV, laundry service; no a/c, no room phones* ⊟ *No credit cards.*

Isla Negra

㉑ *6 km (3 mi) south of El Quisco.*

"I needed a place to work," Chilean poet and Nobel laureate Pablo Neruda wrote in his memoirs. "I found a stone house facing the ocean, a place nobody knew about, Isla Negra." Neruda, who bought the house in 1939, found much inspiration here. "Isla Negra's wild coastal strip, with its turbulent ocean, was the place to give myself passionately to the writing of my new song," he wrote.

Fodor'sChoice   A must-see for Pablo Neruda's ardent admirers, **Casa-Museo Isla Negra** is
★   a shrine to his life, work, and many passions. The house, perched on a bluff overlooking the ocean, displays the treasures—from masks and maps to seashells—he collected over the course of his remarkable life. Although he spent much time living and traveling abroad, Neruda made Isla Negra his primary residence later in life. He wrote his memoirs from the upstairs bedroom; the last pages were dictated to his wife here before he departed for the Santiago hospital where he died of cancer. Neruda and his wife are buried in the prow-shape tomb area behind the house.

Just before Neruda's death in 1973, a military coup put Augusto Pinochet in command of Chile. He closed off Neruda's home and denied all access. Neruda devotees chiseled their tributes into the wooden gates surrounding the property. In 1989 the Neruda Foundation, started by his widow, restored the house and opened it as a museum. Here his collections are displayed as they were while he lived. The living room contains—among numerous other oddities—a number of bowsprits from ships hanging from the ceiling and walls. Neruda called them his "girlfriends."

You can only enter the museum with a guide, but there are excellent English-language tours every half hour. The tour will help you understand Neruda's many obsessions, from the positioning of guests at the dinner table to the east–west alignment of his bed. Objects had a spiritual and symbolic life for the poet, which the tours make evident. ✉ *Camino Vecinal s/n* ☎ *35/461–284* ☞ *3,000 pesos* ⊘ *Tues.–Sun. 10–5.*

Where to Stay & Eat

$–$$ ✕ **El Rincón del Poeta.** Inside the entrance to the Neruda museum, this small restaurant has a wonderful ocean view, with seating both indoors and on a protected terrace. The name translates as Poet's Corner, a theme continued in the small but original menu. Corvina *Neruda* is a sea bass filet in a mushroom, artichoke, and shrimp cream sauce. Congrio *García Lorca* is conger eel topped with tomato, sausage, and melted cheese. The house speciality is *pastel de centolla*, (king crab pie), and they have lighter dishes such as chicken crepes, salmon ceviche, and a spicy squid scampi. ✉ *Casa-Museo Isla Negra, Camino Vecinal s/n* ☎ *35/461–774* ⊟ *No credit cards* ⊘ *Closed Mon.*

$–$$ ✕▦ **La Candela.** Wander along the same rocky shore that Neruda once explored while staying at La Candela. The owner, Chilean folk singer Rosario "Charo" Cofré, was a good friend of the Nerudas—note the photos in the lobby. If there's a crowd, she'll often sing a few songs. Large guest rooms are a bit time-worn, but some of them have fireplaces, and about half overlook the sea through the pines. The restaurant serves a vast selection of clams, sea bass, shrimp, and other seafood in numerous sauces. Prices at this inn are inflated due to its proximity to the Neruda house museum. ⊠ *Calle de la Hostería 67* ☎ *35/461–254* 🖷 *35/462– 531* 🗪 *16 rooms* ♻ *Restaurant, bar, laundry service; no a/c, no room phones, no room TVs* 🖃 *AE, DC, MC, V* ⦿*| CP.*

THE NORTHERN BEACHES

To the north of Viña del Mar, the Pacific collides with the rocky off-shore islands and a rugged coastline broken here and there by sandy bays. The coastal highway runs from Viña del Mar to Papudo, passing marvelous scenery along the way. Between Viña and Concón, it winds along steep rock faces, turning inland north of Concón, where massive sand dunes give way to expanses of undeveloped coastline. The farther north you drive, the greater the distance between towns, each of which is on a significantly different beach. Whether as a day trip from Viña, or on a series of overnights, this stretch of coast is well worth exploring.

Reñaca

㉒ *6 km (3 mi) north of Viña del Mar.*

Thousands of Chileans flock to Reñaca every summer for one, and only one, reason—the beach. You need merely contemplate this wide stretch of golden sand pounded by aquamarine waves, glistening beneath an azure sky, to understand why it's so popular. Contemplate it on a January or February afternoon, though, and you're likely to have trouble discerning the golden sand for the numerous bodies stretched across it. Vacation apartments are stacked up the steep hillside behind the beach, and on summer nights the bars and restaurants are packed. If you're seeking solitude, continue up the coast.

Where to Stay & Eat

$–$$
FodorsChoice
★
✕ **Delicias del Mar.** A branch of the venerable Viña del Mar eatery of the same name, this smaller restaurant serves an identical menu. Start with ceviche or *gratín de jaiba* (crab casserole) as an appetizer, then feast on paella, salmón *gratinado* (salmon covered with asparagus, shrimp, and melted cheese), or corvina *rellena* (sea bass stuffed with crab, spinach, and mushrooms). Nautical paintings hang on colorful walls in the second- and third-floor dining rooms. You can watch through large windows as the waves crash against the rocks across the street. ⊠ *Av. Borgoño 16000* ☎ *32/890–491* 🖃 *MC, V.*

$
✕ **De Picha.** Quality pizza and prices keep De Picha packed with locals despite the surroundings, which are enhanced only by an ocean view. The menu has a few salads and sandwiches, but it's dominated by pizza—from the predictable to such creative combos as artichoke hearts, asparagus, mushrooms, and hearts of palm; or chicken, tomato, and avocado. It's in a shopping center at the southern end of town. ⊠ *Av. Borgoño 13955* ☎ *35/685–072* 🖃 *AE, DC, MC, V.*

$$–$$$
FodorsChoice
★
🎬 **La Fayette.** You can take in some of the best views on the Central Coast from this 10-story hotel built onto the hillside north of the beach. Breakfast is served in a rooftop dining room with a vista to top all. The spacious apartments have two bedrooms, a living room, kitchenette, and large terraces that afford an amazing coastal panorama. Smaller corner rooms have less expansive views, but are still bright, spacious, and well equipped. Though a short walk from the beach, this is a remarkably quiet hotel. ⊠ *Subida el Encanto 280* ☎ *32/832–312* 🖷 *32/832–316* 🗪 *20 rooms, 28 apartments* ♻ *Dining room, in-room safes, kitchenettes, cable TV, laundry service; no a/c* 🖃 *AE, DC, MC, V* ⦿*| BP.*

★ $ ☒ **Hotel Los Ositos.** The rooms here are inexpensive, fairly clean, and just two blocks from the beach, though the hotel has seen better days—the paint is peeling and the carpets are stained. With their large windows overlooking a yard with several trees and a tiny pool, superior rooms are worth the extra money. The pizzeria next door is a popular nightspot. ☒ *Av. Borgoño 14650* ☏☏ *32/831–549* ☎ *30 rooms* ☾ *Restaurant, cable TV, pool, laundry service; no a/c, no room phones* ☐ *No credit cards.*

Nightlife & the Arts

The dance club **Kamikaze** (☒ Av. Vicuña Mackenna 1106 ☏ 32/834–667), west of town, draws a young crowd. The Mexican restaurant **Margarita** (☒ Av. Central 150 ☏ 32/836–398) hosts live music on weekend nights. The bar at **Los Ositos** (☒ Av. Borgoño 14650 ☏ 32/831–549) is a good spot for a quiet drink.

Concón

❷❸   *11 km (6 mi) north of Reñaca.*

How to explain the lovely name Concón? In the language of the Changos, *co* meant water, and the duplication of the sound alludes to the confluence of the Río Aconcagua and the Pacific. When the Spanish arrived in 1543, Pedro de Valdivia created an improvised shipyard here that was destroyed by natives, leading to one of the first clashes between indigenous and Spanish cultures in central Chile.

Today, the town that holds the name is hardly lovely, though it does have decent ocean views. The attraction lies to the north and south: the rugged coastal scenery along the road that connects it to Reñaca, and the sand dunes that rise up behind the beaches north of town.

North of town across from a large wooden restaurant is **Isla de Lobos**, a small rocky island that shelters a permanent population of sea lions, which can be viewed from shore. ☒ *Costanera, 9 km (5 mi) north of Concón.*

Roca Oceánico is a massive promontory covered with scrubby vegetation. Foot paths that wind over it afford excellent views of Viña del Mar and Valparaíso—and of the sea churning against black volcanic rock below. ☒ *Costanera, 1 km (½ mi) north of Isla de Lobos.*

Where to Stay & Eat

$–$$ ✕ **Aquí Jaime.** Owner Jaime Vegas is usually on hand, seating customers
Fodor'sChoice   and scrutinizing the preparation of such house specialties as lenguado
★   *almendrina* (sole in an almond white sauce), the paella-like *arroz a la Valenciana,* and *albacora Portuguesa* (grilled swordfish topped with shrimp-tomato flambé). Perhaps this is why the small restaurant perched on the rocky shore next to the yacht club has one of the best reputations in the region. Large windows let you watch the waves crashing just below, passing boats and seabirds, and the coast that stretches northward. ☒ *Av. Borgoño 21303* ☏ *32/812–042* ☐ *No credit cards* ☯ *No dinner Sun.–Mon.*

$ ✕☒ **Hostería Edelweiss.** Each accommodation in this Swiss-owned inn, nestled in a curve overlooking the rocky coast and sea south of town, consists of two floors: upstairs there's a bedroom, downstairs a sitting area with a wet bar and a small terrace. Breakfast is delivered to your room. The restaurant has one of the best wine lists on the coast, including French and Spanish labels, and an original menu that includes fondues, *salmón a la Florentina* (salmon in a spinach cream sauce), and camarones Bombay (prawns in a curried fruit sauce). ☒ *Av. Borgoño*

19200 ☎ 32/811–043 🖨 32/811–044 ⊕ *www.edelweis.cl* ⤴ *6 rooms*
🖧 *Restaurant, room service, refrigerators, cable TV, pool, bar, laundry service* ⊟ *AE, DC, MC, V* ⅩⅪ *BP.*

$$ ▣ **Mantagua.** In summer, Chilean families flock to these two- and three-bedroom cabanas spread over a farm 3 km (2 mi) north of town. The cabanas are a bit cramped and time-worn, but each one has a terrace in back with a grill and picnic table. It's a short walk through low dunes to the beach. The pool, game rooms, camping areas, and sports facilities make the place seem like a summer camp. ⊠ *Camino Quintero, 3 km (2 mi) north of Concón* ☎☎ *32/811–415* ⊕ *www.mantagua.cl* ⤴ *27 cabins* 🖧 *Restaurant, kitchenettes, miniature golf, pool, horseback riding, soccer, volleyball, bar, recreation room, playground; no a/ c, no room phones* ⊟ *AE, DC, MC, V.*

Sports & the Outdoors

BEACHES The southernmost beach in Concón, **Playa Los Lilenes** is a tiny yellow-sand cove with calm waters. After the wharf is **Playa Las Bahamas,** the beach favored by surfers and windsurfers. At the north end of town is the gray-sand **Playa La Boca.** It was named Mouth Beach because the Río Aconcagua flows into the Pacific here, which makes the water murky. Concón's nicest beach is **Playa Ritoque,** a long, wide, golden strand that starts several miles north of town and stretches northward for several miles. Access is good at Punta de Piedra, 5 km (3 mi) north of town, where guarded parking costs 2,000 pesos per day. You can reenact scenes from *The English Patient* 1 km (½ mi) north of here, where the vast sand dunes that resemble those in the movie rise up behind the beach.

HORSEBACK **Ecoacuatic** (⊠ Camino a Quintero, Km 5 ☎ 32/813–675) has horseback
RIDING excursions on the beach or to the sand dunes that can be combined with kayaking or boat trips on a nearby lake.

Quintero

❷❹ *26 km (16 mi) north of Concón.*

The town of Quintero, with its dusty streets and many dilapidated houses, could easily be skipped if not for its impressive coastal scenery. The town has spread over a bluff that ends in a wind-swept coastline, where several bays hold small, yellow-sand beaches nestled against sheer rock faces. Quintero also has a good hotel, which is well positioned for contemplating the passing pelicans, waves crashing against rocks, and memorable sunsets.

The main strip in town, Avenida Normandie, leads directly to **Muelle Asimar,** a dock where you can watch fishermen unload their catch; you may be able to talk a boat owner into a trip around the bay.

Where to Stay & Eat

$ ✕▣ **Hotel Yachting.** This old hotel's greatest asset is its exquisite view of the rocky coast from all of the guest rooms. The main building sits on the edge of a cliff, giving the restaurant an amazing coastal perspective enhanced by massive windows. Try the veal *cordon bleu* (stuffed with cheese and ham) or corvina *vasca* (sea bass in an onion-tomato sauce). Older, standard rooms are a bargain, opening onto terraces steps from the pool. The added-on superior rooms are more spacious, but only those on the ground floor have terraces. ⊠ *Luís Acevedo 1736* ☎ *32/930– 061* 🖨 *32/931–557* ⤴ *20 rooms, 2 suites* 🖧 *Restaurant, room service, minibars, cable TV, pool, sauna, recreation room, meeting rooms* ⊟ *AE, DC, MC, V* ⅩⅪ *CP or MAP.*

Beaches

Most of Quintero's beaches are in hidden coves and can be hard to find, or may require a bit of a hike to reach. **Playa Los Enamorados,** is a short walk from the Parque Municipal. Surfing is popular at **Playa El Libro,** which is reached from Hermanos Carrera or Balmaceda via concrete stairs. Swimming is prohibited here, but kids play in the little pools that form behind the rocks. If you follow Avenida 21 de Mayo to its end, you come to **Playa Durazno,** a small, unattractive gray-sand beach that does have calm water. **Playa El Caleuche,** beyond the rocks at the end of Playa Durazno, is safe for swimming.

Maitencillo

㉕ *20 km (12 mi) north of Quintero.*

This town is a mass of cabanas and eateries spread out along the 4-km (2 ½-mi) Avenida del Mar. Two long beaches are separated by an extended rocky coastline that holds the local caleta. To complement the abundant sand and surf, there is a decent selection of restaurants, bars, and accommodations.

Spread over the hills just east of Maitencillo is a development complex called Marbella, the name of which is an allusion to the ritzy resort town on the southern coast of Spain. All the houses in the complex are washed an Andalusian white, with Spanish roof tiles. Though it lacks beach access, the development does have an ocean view, and it includes the region's largest golf course and a resort hotel.

Off the coast from Cachagua, several miles north of Maitencillo, is the **Monumento Nacional Isla Cachagua,** a protected island inhabited by Magellan and Humboldt penguins. No one is allowed on the island, but you can ride around in a small boat that can be hired at the Caleta de La Laguna or Caleta de Zapallar. You can also view the island from the beach below Cachagua, though you need binoculars to watch the penguins wobble around.

Where to Stay & Eat

$–$$$$ ✕ **La Tasca de Altamar.** Model ships, bowsprits, and old nautical equipment decorate the interior of this spacious restaurant across the street from the ocean. The ample, almost exclusively marine menu ranges from such Chilean standards as *ostiones a la parmesana* (scallops in melted cheese) and pastel de jaiba to several kinds of ceviche, shrimp and vegetable curry, and exorbitantly priced half lobsters. ✉ *Av. del Mar 3600* ☎ *32/772–132* 🚪 *AE, DC, MC, V* ⊙ *Closed Wed., Mar.–Dec.*

$ ✕ **La Canasta.** Serpentine bamboo tunnels connect rooms, and slabs of wood suspended by chains serve as tables: the scene could be straight from *The Hobbit.* A small menu changes regularly, but includes dishes such as *cordero a la ciruela* (lamb with a cherry sauce) and corvina *queso de cabra* (sea bass with goat cheese). ✉ *Av. del Mar 593* ☎ *32/771–028* 🚪 *No credit cards.*

$$$$ ✕▣ **Marbella.** Golf fairways, pine trees, and ocean vistas surround a four-story white-stucco resort building. Spacious, colorful rooms are decorated with original art, and have large terraces with views of Maitencillo Bay. The circular Mirador restaurant has great views and interesting menu selections, such as salmon-filled ravioli in tomato cream, and *duo de lenguado y salmón* (sole and salmon mixed in a tarragon sauce with artichoke and carrot puree). The only drawback is the distance from the beach—you need a car to stay here. ✉ *Carretera Concón–Zapallar, Km 38* ☎ *32/772–020 or 800/211–108* 🖨 *32/772–030; 2/206–0554 in Santiago* ⇴ *70 rooms, 4 suites* ⚲ *Restaurant, in-room data ports, in-*

room safes, minibars, golf privileges, 4 tennis courts, 2 pools, exercise equipment, hair salon, hot tub, spa, bicycles, horseback riding, bar, recreation room, shop, playground, laundry service, business services, convention center ⊟ AE, DC, MC, V ⦿ BP, FAP, MAP.

★ $–$$ ▣ **Altamar Aparthotel.** All the rooms in this three-story, brick-red building behind the Tasca de Altamar restaurant have ocean views, though those on the third floor have the best ones. They are spotless, bright, and nicely decorated, with sliding glass doors that open onto either a terrace or balcony, most of which are surrounded by flowers. All of them have well-stocked kitchenettes, but they range in size from studios to one-bedroom apartments with sofa beds and large furnished terraces complete with grills. ⊠ Av. del Mar 3600 ☎☎ 32/772–150 ⊕ www.altamaraparthotel.cl ⤺ 18 apartments ⌂ Restaurant, kitchenettes, pool, laundry service, meeting rooms; no a/c ⊟ AE, DC, MC, V.

Sports & the Outdoors

BEACHES On the north side is the largest beach in town, the extra-wide **Playa Larga.** It's often pounded by big surf. The light gray sand of **Playa Aguas Blancas** lies to the south of a rock outcropping, protected from the swells, and consequently is good for swimming.

GOLF The **Marbella Country Club** (⊠ Carretera Concón–Zapallar, Km 35 ☎ 32/772–403) has 27 holes of golf—without a doubt some of the best on the coast—in an exclusive environment. The tennis and paddle-tennis courts are available only to members and to guests of the Marbella resort. Greens fees for hotel guests are 22,000 pesos, whereas nonguests pay 42,000 pesos during the week and 52,000 pesos on weekends.

HANG GLIDING *Parapente*, a seated version of hang gliding, is popular here. **Parapente Aventura** (⊠ South entrance to Maitencillo, veer left ☎ 32/770–019 or 9/332–2426) has classes and two-person trips for beginners.

HORSEBACK In Cachagua, **Club Equestre Cachagua** (⊠ Costanera s/n, Cachagua ☎ 32/
RIDING 689–249) runs horseback tours to scenic overlooks.

Zapallar

★ ㉖ *48 km (30 mi) north of Concón.*

An aristocratic enclave for the past century, Zapallar doesn't promote itself as a vacation destination. In fact, it has traditionally been reluctant to receive outsiders. The resort is the brainchild of Olegario O'Valle, who owned property here. In 1893, following an extended stay in Europe, O'Valle decided to re-create the Riviera on the Chilean coast. He allotted plots of land to friends and family with the provision that they build European-style villas. Today the hills above the beach are dotted with these extravagant summer homes. Above them are the small, tightly packed adobes of a working-class village that has developed to service the mansions.

Zapallar's raison d'être is **Playa Zapallar,** a crescent of golden sand kissed by blue-green waters, with a giant boulder plopped in the middle. Cropped at each end by rocky points and backed by large pines and rambling flower gardens, it may well be the loveliest beach on the Central Coast.

At the south end of Playa Zapallar is a rocky point that holds **Caleta de Zapallar,** where local fisherfolk unload their boats, sell their catch, and settle in for dominoes. The view of the beach from the Caleta and adjacent restaurant, El Chiringuito, is simply gorgeous. On the other side of the point, a trail leads over the rocks to rugged but equally impressive views.

⟳ Up the hill from Caleta de Zapallar is the **Plaza del Mar Bravo.** Rough Sea Square has a park with yet another ocean view and a large playground. In January and February, there are usually mule rides for kids.

Where to Stay & Eat

$–$$ ✕ **El Chiringuito.** Pelicans, gulls, and cormorants linger among the fishing boats anchored near this remarkable seafood restaurant out on an abutment. Since it's next door to the fishermen's cooperative, the seafood is always the freshest. For starters choose from machas (razor clams), camarones (shrimp), or ostiones (scallops) cooked *al pil pil* (with chili sauce and garlic), *a la parmesana* (with cheese), or *a la crema* (with a cream sauce). Then sink your teeth into any of half a dozen types of fish, served with different sauces. ⊠ *Caleta de Zapallar* ☎ *33/741–024* ⊟ *No credit cards* ⊙ *No dinner weekdays, Mar.–Dec.*

FodorsChoice
★

$–$$ ✕ **Restaurante Cesar.** Sip a cool drink or nibble on a snack at tables beneath thatched parasols on a terrace just off the beach. In winter, cozy up to a large fireplace in the dining room. The menu has an ample seafood selection, as well as beef and chicken dishes, and is complemented by an extensive wine list. ⊠ *Playa Zapallar* ☎ *9/824–1845* ⊟ *AE, DC, MC, V.*

$$–$$$ ▦ **Isla Seca.** Bougainvillea and cypress trees surround two identical moss-green buildings with well-appointed, spacious rooms. If you choose those with *terraza y vista al mar,* you get picture windows and narrow balconies with wonderful views of the rocky coast and blue Pacific. Smaller corner rooms with *vista lateral* aren't nearly as nice, and less expensive *turista* rooms are right over the noisy coastal highway. The airy restaurant, with its black-and-white tile floor and original art, has style to rival anything in Miami Beach. Unfortunately the kitchen doesn't match the views. ⊠ *Costanera s/n* ☎ *33/741–224* ⊟ *33/741–228* ⊕ *www. hotelislaseca.cl* ⊅ *34 rooms, 5 suites* ⟡ *Restaurant, in-room safes, minibars, cable TV, 2 pools, bicycles, bar, playground, business services, meeting rooms; no a/c* ⊟ *AE, DC, MC, V.*

FodorsChoice
★

Tennis

Zapallar's **Club de Tenis** (⊠ Costanera s/n ☎ 33/741–55) has 14 clay courts scattered around a forested hillside above town. Nonmembers pay 5,000 pesos per game.

Papudo

➋ *11 km (7 mi) north of Zapallar.*

In a letter dated October 8, 1545, Spanish conquistador Pedro Valdivia wrote: "Of all the lands of the New World, the port of Papudo has a goodness above any other land. It's like God's Paradise: it has a gentle temperate climate; large, resounding mountains; and fertile lands."

Today a jumble of apartment buildings and vacation homes detracts from the view Valdivia once admired, but the beaches and coast north of town remain quite pleasant. For years Papudo was connected to Santiago by a train that no longer runs. You can still find bits of that history in the quiet resort town.

A block from the beach is the **Palacio Recart,** built in 1910. The yellow building, which now holds municipal offices, hosts occasional art and history exhibitions. ⊠ *Costanera s/n* ☎ *no phone.*

Near the south end of town is the lovely **Iglesia Parroquial de Papudo,** a 19th-century church. It was once part of a convent that has been replaced by vacation apartments. ⊠ *Costanera s/n* ☎ *no phone* ⊙ *Jan.–Feb., weekends; closed rest of yr.*

Where to Stay & Eat

$$ ✕ **El Barco Rojo.** In 1913, a French ship called the *Ville de Dijon* sank off the coast of Papudo. The beams, doors, stairways, and other sundry parts were salvaged to build The Red Ship. Poet Pablo Neruda once frequented the spot. The ceiling is papered with love letters to the restaurant written by patrons. Tables and chairs are a delightful hodgepodge of styles and colors, and the tiny bar is eclectically furnished with bric-a-brac. The menu is dominated by seafood, but includes such treats as fried empanadas filled with cheese and basil. ✉ *Av. Irarrazaval 300* ☎ *33/791–488* ▤ *No credit cards* ⊘ *Closed Mon.–Thurs. Mar.–Dec.*

$ ▥ **Hotel Carande.** The only respectable hotel in town, Carande has carpeted rooms devoid of charm but just a short walk from the beach. It's worth paying the extra money for a room on the third floor to have a sea view over the rooftops. There's a restaurant on the second floor, and the lobby has a fireplace that usually has a fire burning in winter. ✉ *Chorillos 89* ☎ *33/791–105* 🖷 *33/791–118* ⇗ *30 rooms* ⚖ *Restaurant, refrigerators, bar; no a/c* ▤ *No credit cards.*

Beaches

Chileans migrate to Papudo from Santiago every summer to play on its beaches. **Playa Chica,** the small beach on the south end of town, is well protected and safe for swimming. Papudo's most popular beach is **Playa Grande,** a wide strand that stretches northward from the Barco Rojo for more than a mile. You have to do a bit of walking to reach **Playa Durazno.** It's an attractive beach north of Playa Grande—past the condominiums— that is lined with pine trees and protected by a rocky barrier offshore.

Los Molles

❷❽ *32 km (20 mi) north of Papudo.*

Upon first inspection, Los Molles seems rather drab: a row of houses on a street leading to the beach. But the nearby landscape—a desert-like collection of cacti and other hearty plants—is truly splendid. Hawks, turtledoves, gulls, and pelicans fly past. Grab your binoculars and follow Avenida Las Jaibas uphill to its end to watch.

A 15-minute walk north of town along the coast brings you within earshot of the **Isla de los Lobos Marinos,** a rocky island filled with boisterous sea lions—off-limits to humans. Hike north from the Isla de los Lobos Marinos, and your ears are likely to be assaulted by the terrifying sound of the ocean water forced up through **Puquén,** a blowhole whose name means Mouth of the Devil. The spray can shoot 50 m (150 ft) in the air on a wavy day. For a simpler natural encounter, follow Avenida Los Pescadores past the north end of the beach to **Las Terrazas.** These terraces of chiseled rock are a great vantage point from which to see the tempestuous swells below.

Where to Stay

$ ▥ **Hostería Kon-Tiki.** Identical cabanas at the mouth of the bay have terraces, full kitchens, and rooms with bunk beds. Across the street, a three-story stucco building has newer, more comfortable rooms with balconies or terraces. The elegant restaurant serves corvina cooked six ways, and has a good selection of Chilean wines. Across the street, a bar in the stone promontory has panoramic views. Reserved for Chilean army officers January–February, this retreat 20 km (12 mi) north of Los Molles is open to everyone the rest of the year. ✉ *Costanera s/n, Pichidangui* ☎ *53/531–103* 🖷 *2/693–5522 in Santiago* ⇗ *32 rooms, 24 cabins* ⚖ *Restaurant, minibars, 2 tennis courts, saltwater pool, massage, bar, meeting rooms* ▤ *No credit cards* ⊘ *Closed Jan.–Feb.* ❍ *CP.*

Diving

Hernan Labarca at **H. L. Divers** (✉ Neruda 11 ☎ 33/791–762 or 9/276–5562), one of only five authorized dive centers in Chile, runs scuba certification classes and dives along submarine cliffs adorned with giant sponges.

CENTRAL COAST A TO Z

To research prices, get advice from other travelers, and book travel arrangements, visit www.fodors.com.

AIR TRAVEL

The Central Coast is served by LanChile via Santiago's Aeropuerto Comodoro Arturo Merino Benítez, an hour and a half from Viña del Mar and Valparaíso.

🔲 Carriers **LanChile** ✉ Esmerelda 1048, Valparaíso ☎ 32/251–441 ✉ Ecuador 76, Viña del Mar ☎ 600/526–2000.

BUS TRAVEL

There is hourly bus service between Santiago and both Valparaíso and Viña del Mar. The two-hour trip costs about 2,100 pesos. Tur-Bus and other companies leave from Santiago's Terminal Alameda. Smaller companies serving the other beach resorts depart from Santiago's Terminal Santiago.

Regular buses between Viña del Mar and Valparaíso cruise the main north-south routes of those cities. Regular city-bus service also connects Viña del Mar, Reñaca, and Concón. Buses to more distant towns along the Central Coast depart from Valparaíso's Terminal Rodoviario, across from the Congreso Nacional, and Viña's Terminal Rodoviario, two blocks east of Plaza Vergara. Pullman Bus serves most coastal towns south of Valparaíso. Tur-Bus heads north to Cachagua, Zapallar, Papudo, and other towns. Sol del Pacífico also runs buses to the northern beaches.

🔲 Bus Depots **Terminal Rodoviario** ✉ Av. Pedro Montt 2800, Valparaíso ☎ 32/213–246. **Terminal Rodoviario** ✉ Av. Valparaíso and Quilpué, Viña del Mar ☎ 32/882–661.
🔲 Bus Lines **Pullman Bus** ☎ 32/24–025. **Tur-Bus** ☎ 32/212–028 in Valparaíso; 32/882–621 in Viña del Mar. **Sol del Pacífico** ☎ 32/213–776.

CAR TRAVEL

Since it's so easy to get around in Valparaíso and Viña del Mar, there's no need to rent a car to explore these cities. But if you want to travel to other towns on the coast, renting a car is advisable. Hertz is the only international chain with an office in the region (Viña del Mar). The Chilean company Rosselot is well represented, as are the smaller local companies Bert and Kovac's.

🔲 Agencies **Bert** ✉ Victoria 2681, Valparaíso ☎ 32/352–365. **Hertz** ✉ Quillota 766, Viña del Mar ☎ 32/381–025 or 32/689–918. **Kovac's** ✉ Colón 2537, Valparaíso ☎ 32/255–505 ✉ 5 Norte 650, Viña del Mar ☎ 32/686–820. **Rosselot** ✉ Victoria 2675, Valparaíso ☎ 32/352–365 ✉ Av. Libertad 892, Viña del Mar ☎ 32/382–373.

FESTIVALS & SEASONAL EVENTS

The annual Festival Internacional de la Canción (International Song Festival) takes place during a week in mid-February in Viña del Mar. The concerts are broadcast live on television. Most towns have colorful processions on the Día de San Pedro on June 29. A statue of St. Peter, patron saint of fisherfolk, is typically hoisted onto a fishing boat and led along a coastal procession. Thousands turn out for the event in Valparaíso.

INTERNET

Valparaíso and Viña del Mar each have dozens of Internet cafés, but many smaller towns on the Central Coast lack them. Internet cafés charge around 800 pesos per hour and stay open until 10 or 11 PM. Valparaíso has several between Plazas Sotomayor and Anibal Pinto, among them the World Next Door and Café Riquet. Viña del Mar's Avenida Valparaíso shopping strip has several per block, including 286 Rue Valparaíso, which sells cheap international calls via computer, and the less expensive OKA Comunicaciones. In Reñaca, try the Centro de Llamado on the south end of town. In El Quisco, Cyber Café Chilecuba is several blocks up from the beach.

Internet Cafés **Café Riquet** ⊠ Plaza Anibal Pinto 1199, Valparaíso ☎ 32/213-171. **Centro de Llamado** ⊠ Av. Borgoño 14417, Reñaca ☎ 32/902-276. **Cyber Café Chilecuba** ⊠ I. Dubournais 350, El Quisco ☎ 35/471-018. **OKA Comunicaciones** ⊠ Av. Valparaíso 242, Viña del Mar ☎ 32/713-712. **286 Rue Valparaíso** ⊠ Av. Valparaíso 286, Viña del Mar ☎ 32/710-140. **World Next Door** ⊠ Blanco 692, Valparaíso ☎ 32/227-148.

MAIL & SHIPPING

Perhaps because it is so close to Santiago, the postal system along the Central Coast is fairly efficient. On average, letters take five to seven days to reach the United States or Europe.

Post Offices **Valparaíso** ⊠ Southeast corner of Plaza Sotomayor. **Viña del Mar** ⊠ North side of Plaza Vergara.

MONEY MATTERS

All but the smallest Central Coast towns have at least one ATM, and both Valparaíso and Viña del Mar have dozens of them, but it's wise to take a fair amount of U.S. dollars, since some hotels require payment in them to discount the 18% tax from your bill. ATMs at well distributed Banco de Chile branches also give cash advances on international credit cards. All but the least expensive restaurants and hotels accept major credit cards.

ATMs **Banco de Chile** ⊠ Cochrane 785, Valparaíso ☎ 32/356-500 ⊠ Av. Valparaíso 667, Viña del Mar ☎ 32/648-760 ⊠ Av. Borgoño 14675, Reñaca ☎ 32/836-938 ⊠ Olegario O'Valle 336, Zapallar ☎ 33/741-613 ⊠ Carlos Alessandri 1666, Algarrobo ☎ 35/482-857. **Citibank** ⊠ 1 Norte 633, Viña del Mar ☎ 32/338-500.

SAFETY

Like most port cities, Valparaíso has its share of street crime. Avoid deserted areas and be on the lookout for suspicious characters. It's best not to walk alone and to avoid sidestreets after dark. In both Valparaíso and Viña del Mar you should always be alert to the possibility of pickpockets in tourist areas. Keep an eye on cameras and other valuables, or keep them in your hotel safe.

Look out for red warning flags on popular beaches, which indicate the sea is unsafe for swimming. If the waves are big and you aren't an experienced ocean swimmer, don't go in any deeper than your waist. Rip currents can be deadly.

TAXIS

In Valparaíso and Viña del Mar you can hail a taxi on busy streets and at plazas. Most smaller towns have a taxi stand on the main road. If you prefer to phone a cab, have your hotel receptionist call a reputable company, such as Radio Taxis Turismo in Valparaíso, and Radio Taxi in Viña del Mar.

Taxi Companies **Radio Taxi** ☎ 32/690-227. **Radio Taxis Turismo** ☎ 32/212-885.

TELEPHONES

There are several different telephone companies in the Central Coast, and each has its own public telephones. Calling cards can be purchased in many shops and newsstands. The card you buy must match the company that owns the individual phone for it to work. You can also place local and international calls, or send faxes, from one of the central Entel or Telefónica offices located throughout the region.

TOURS

You need a tour guide to really get to know the twisting streets of Valparaíso. Claudia Acevedo of Claudia Tours helps you see the city through the eyes of a local. If she's unavailable, contact Enlace Turístico, which has several city tours and trips to the Central Coast's smaller towns. In Viña del Mar, Aguitur and Chile Guías have bilingual guides for city tours, and trips to beaches north and south.

🔳 Tours **Aguitur** ✉ Av. Valparaíso, Viña del Mar ☎ 32/711-052. **Chile Guías** ✉ Errázuriz 670, Viña del Mar ☎ 32/692-580. **Claudia Tours** ✉ Valparaíso ☎ 32/256-854 or 9/665-6333. **Enlace Turístico** ✉ Cerro Bellavista, Valparaíso ☎ 32/232-313, or 9/896-4887.

TRAIN TRAVEL

Merval, a commuter train linking Viña de Mar and Valparaíso, is a fun way to shuttle between the two cities, though service isn't as frequent as abundant city buses. Trains depart about every half hour 6 AM–10 PM; note, however, that there are no trains to Viña for about 90 minutes during the morning rush, and no trains to Valparaíso during the evening rush. The ride costs about 200 pesos. In Valparaíso the main station is at the Muelle Prat. In Viña del Mar, it's south of Plaza Vergara.

🔳 Train Stations **Estación Puerto** ✉ Plaza Sotomayor ☎ 32/217-108. **Estación Viña del Mar** ✉ Plaza Sucre ☎ no phone.

VISITOR INFORMATION

Viña del Mar has the best tourist office on the coast, north of Plaza Vergara. It's open Monday–Saturday 9–2 and 3–7. Valparaíso has two information booths: one at Muelle Prat that is open daily 10–2 and 3–6, and one at the Rodoviario bus terminal, with the same hours except it closes Mondays.

🔳 Tourist Information **Muelle Prat Information Booth** ✉ Muelle Prat, Valparaíso ☎ 32/939-489. **Rodoviario Information Booth** ✉ Av. Pedro Montt 2800, Valparaíso ☎ 32/939-669. **Viña del Mar Central de Turismo** ✉ Av. Libertad and Av. Arlegui, Viña del Mar ☎ 800/800-830.

EL NORTE CHICO

FODOR'S CHOICE
Hotel Rocas de Bahía, Bahía Inglesa
Parque Nacional Fray Jorge, cloud forest

HIGHLY RECOMMENDED

RESTAURANTS El Cisne, Caldera
Donde el Guatón, La Serena
El Plateao, Bahía Inglesa

HOTELS Hotel del Cid, La Serena
Hotel Halley, Vicuña
Hotel La Casona, Copiapó
El Tesoro de Elqui, Pisco Elqui

SIGHTS Museo Gabriela Mistral, Vicuña
Observatorio Cerro Mamalluca, observatory in Vicuña
Parque Nacional Pan de Azúcar
Solar de Pisco Elqui, distillery in Pisco Elqui
Templo Antiguo, church in Andacollo
Valle del Encanto, petroglyphs near Ovalle

By Gregory
Benchwick

FOR HUNDREDS OF YEARS, people have journeyed to El Norte Chico—Chile's Little North—for the riches that lay buried deep within the earth. First came the Incas, who wandered the burnt hills in search of gold. A century later the Spanish arrived on these shores, also seeking this precious metal. Prospectors flocked here in the 19th century when the silver boom afforded great rewards. Today it is yet another metal, copper, that yields the majority of the region's income. No wonder locals once called this "the land of 10,000 mines."

But El Norte Chico's appeal isn't purely metallurgical. The coastline has some of the best beaches in the country. Offshore there are rocky islands that shelter colonies of penguins and sea lions. Shimmering mountain lakes are home to huge flocks of flamingos. Even the parched earth flourishes twice a decade in a phenomenon called *el desierto florido,* or the flowering desert. During these years, the bleak landscape gives way to a riot of colors—flowers of every hue imaginable burst from the normally infertile soil of the plain.

In a land where water is so precious, it's not surprising that the people who migrated here never strayed far from its rivers. In the south, La Serena sits at the mouth of the Río Elqui. El Norte Chico's most important city, La Serena is the region's cultural center as well, with colonial architecture and a European flavor. Nearby, in the fertile Elqui Valley, farmers in tiny villages grow the grapes to make pisco, the potent brandy that has become Chile's national drink. Those in search of the region's history head to Valle del Encanto, a large collection of ancient petroglyphs.

On El Norte Chico's northern frontier is the Río Copiapó. This is the region that grew up and grew rich during the silver boom. The town of Copiapó, this area's most important trade center, makes an excellent jumping-off point for exploring the hinterland. Inland lies Parque Nacional Nevado Tres Cruces, with its snowcapped volcanoes and dazzling white salt flats. Head to the ocean and you'll come to Parque Nacional Pan de Azúcar, where you'll find some of El Norte Chico's most stunning coastal scenery.

Exploring El Norte Chico

El Norte Chico is a vast region spreading some 700 km (435 mi) between Río Aconcagua to Río Copiapó. You'll need more than one base if you want to explore the entire area. In the south, La Serena is a good place to start if you're going to the Elqui Valley. Vallenar, on the Río Huasco, is where you'll want to be if your destination is the flowering desert. Copiapó, near the region's northern border, is a convenient stop if you're headed to Parque Nacional Nevado Tres Cruces.

About the Restaurants

El Norte Chico is not known for its gastronomy, but the food here is simple, unpretentious, and often quite good. Along the coast you'll find abundant seafood. Don't pass up the *merluza con salsa margarita* (hake with butter sauce featuring almost every kind of shellfish imaginable) or *choritos al vapor* (mussels steamed in white wine). Inland you come across country-style *cabrito* (goat), *conejo* (rabbit), and *pinchones escabechadas* (baby pigeons). Don't forget to order a pisco sour, the frothy concoction made with the brandy distilled in the Elqui Valley.

People in El Norte Chico generally eat a heavy lunch at around 2 PM that can last two hours, followed by a light dinner around 10 PM. Reservations are seldom needed, except in the fanciest restaurants. Leave a 10% tip if you enjoyed the service.

Numbers in the text correspond to numbers in the margin and on the El Norte Chico map.

If you have 5 days

Five days won't allow you enough time to explore all of El Norte Chico, so make 🗺 **La Serena** ❶ ⚑ your home base. Spend your first day exploring the whitewashed churches and lively markets of this quaint colonial town. The next morning head inland to **Vicuña** ❷, birthplace of poet Gabriela Mistral. In the afternoon stop by the idyllic village of **Pisco Elqui** ❹. A pisco sour here is almost obligatory. Explore the cloud forest of **Parque Nacional Fray Jorge** ❼ on the fourth day. On your last day, head to **Ovalle** ❻ to see the petroglyphs of the Valle del Encanto. End the day by taking a relaxing dip in the hot springs at the Termas de Socos.

3

If you have 8 days

With a few extra days you'll be able to see much more of El Norte Chico. Use 🗺 **La Serena** ❶ ⚑ as a base for exploring the Elqui Valley and follow the five-day itinerary above. On the sixth day head up to 🗺 **Copiapó** ⓫, perhaps taking a side trip to the **Parque Nacional Llanos de Challe** ❿. Visit the remote mountain lakes of **Parque Nacional Nevado Tres Cruces** ⓯ or the coastal splendor of **Parque Nacional Pan de Azúcar** ⓮ on your seventh day. On your last day, relax on the sandy beaches near **Bahía Inglesa** ⓬.

About the Hotels

The good news is that lodging in El Norte Chico is relatively inexpensive. Your best bet is often the beach resorts, which have everything from nice cabanas to high-rise hotels. The bad news is that away from the areas that regularly cater to tourists you may have to make do with extremely basic rooms with shared baths.

WHAT IT COSTS In pesos (in thousands)					
	$$$$	**$$$**	**$$**	**$**	**¢**
RESTAURANTS	over 11	8–11	5–8	2.5–5	under 2.5
HOTELS	over 105	75–105	45–75	15–45	under 15

Restaurant prices are for a main course at dinner. Hotel prices are for a double room in high season, excluding tax.

Timing

During the summer months of January and February, droves of Chileans and Argentines flee their stifling hot cities for the relative cool of El Norte Chico's beaches. Although it is an exciting time to visit, prices go up and rooms are hard to find. Make your reservations at least a month in advance. For a little tranquility, visit when the high season tapers off in March. Moving inland you'll find the weather is mild all year. The almost perpetually clear skies explain why the region has the largest concentration of observatories in the world. The temperatures drop quite a bit when you head to the mountains.

THE ELQUI VALLEY

It's hard to believe that hidden by the dusty brown hills of El Norte Chico is a sliver of land as lush and green as the Elqui Valley. The people who live along the Río Elqui harvest everything from olives to avocados. The most famous crop are the grapes distilled to make Chile's national drink: pisco. A village named after this lovely elixir, Pisco Elqui, sits high up the valley.

The Elqui Valley is renowned not only for its grapes, but also for its unusually clear skies, which have brought scientists from around the world to peer through the telescopes of the area's many observatories. The stars also attracted many New Agers who decided that the planet's spiritual center had shifted from the Himalayas to the Elqui Valley. Many who came here to check out the vibes decided to stay.

The Elqui Valley has been inhabited for thousands of years. First came the Diaguitas, whose intricate pottery is among the most beautiful of pre-Columbian ceramics. The Molles, who are believed to have carved the fascinating petroglyphs in the Valle del Encanto, followed. The Incas, who came here 500 years ago in search of gold, are relative newcomers. The clues these cultures left behind are part of what makes the Elqui Valley so fascinating.

La Serena

▶ ❶ *270 km (167 mi) north of Santiago.*

La Serena, Chile's second-oldest city, with several old churches and pleasant beaches, got off to a shaky start. Founded by Spanish conquistador Pedro de Valdivia in 1544, La Serena was destroyed by the Diaguitas only four years later. But the Spaniards weren't about to give in, so they rebuilt the city on its original site. Near the mouth of the Río Elqui, La Serena slowly grew until it was visited by British pirate Bartholomew Sharp, who sacked and burned it in a three-day rampage in 1680. Once again the city was rebuilt, and by the time of the silver boom in the late 19th century, it was thriving.

One of the most striking features of La Serena is the number of churches: there are more than 30, and many of them date as far back as the late 16th century. Most have survived fires, earthquakes, and pirate attacks. The largest church is the imposing **Iglesia Catedral,** which faces the beautiful Plaza de Armas. French architect Jean de Herbage built this behemoth in 1844, but it wasn't until the turn of the 20th century that the bell tower was added. On Cordovez stands the **Iglesia Santo Domingo,** a pretty church built in 1673 and then rebuilt after a pirate attack in 1755. One of La Serena's oldest churches, **Iglesia San Francisco,** on Balmaceda and de la Barra, has a baroque facade and thick stone walls. The exact date of the church's construction is not known, as the city archives were destroyed in 1680, but it's estimated that the structure was built sometime between 1585 and 1627.

La Serena's pleasant streets, hidden plazas, and well-preserved colonial buildings are the fruition of one man's dream. Gabriel González Videla, then president of Chile, instituted his "Plan Serena" in 1940. He mandated that all new buildings be in the colonial style. The **Museo Histórico Gabriel González Videla,** his former home, has exhibits about the ex-president as well as showings of works by Chilean artists. ⊠ *Matta 495* ☎ *51/ 215–082* 🖂 *600 pesos* ☉ *Tues.–Sat. 9–1 and 4–7, Sun. 10–1.*

3

Beaches El Norte Chico's seemingly endless beaches lure people from around the world for good reason: the sugary sand, turquoise water, and warm breezes make these beaches among the best in the country. During the summer months of January and February, you may have to fight for a place in the sun. If a little tranquility is what you seek, plan your trip for another part of the year. The weather is fine, the prices are cheaper, and it's not hard to find a stretch of shoreline that's completely deserted. Some of El Norte Chico's beaches are not safe for swimming due to dangerous currents or pollution. These are marked by large signs reading: NO APTA PARA BANARSE.

Shopping El Norte Chico has some items you won't find elsewhere in Chile. The Elqui Valley is known for the beautiful ceramics of the Diaguita people, which often come in zoomorphic shapes with intricate geometric patterns. In La Serena, jewelry and other items crafted from the locally mined marble called *combabalita* are particularly lovely. The best places to shop are usually the *ferias artesanales* (artisan fairs), where locals sell all types of handmade items.

Housing many fascinating artifacts—including an impressive collection of Diaguita pottery—the **Museo Arqueológico** is a must-see for anyone interested in the history of the region. The Archaeology Museum contains one of the world's best collections of precolonial ceramics. Also here is a *moai* (a carved stone head) from Easter Island. ⊠ *Cordovez and Cienfuegos* ☎ *51/224–492* 🖼 *600 pesos* ☉ *Tues.–Fri. 9–1 and 4–7, Sat. 10–1 and 4–7, Sun. 10–1.*

One of the most complete mineral collections in the world can be found at the **Museo Mineralógico.** Exhibits highlight fossils and minerals from the surrounding region. ⊠ *Anfión Muñoz 870* ☎ *51/204–096* 🖼 *Free* ☉ *Weekdays 9:30–12:30.*

A Japanese garden in the heart of Latin America, **Parque Japones** is a pleasant place to pass an afternoon. Here you will find koi-filled ponds, intricate bridges, and a network of paths. The park was built by a mining company as a good-will gesture to its Japanese trading partners. ⊠ *Pedro Pablo Muñoz and Cordovez* ☎ *51/217–013* 🖼 *1,000 pesos* ☉ *Daily 10–8.*

Where to Stay & Eat

★ **$–$$** ✕ **Donde el Guatón.** This European-style steak house, also known as La Cosona del Guatón, serves up everything from shish kebab to steak with eggs. With several intimate dining areas off the main salon, this is a great place to enjoy a romantic, candlelit meal. The service, although friendly, can be overly solicitous. ⊠ *Brasil 750* ☎ *51/211–519* ⌂ *Reservations essential* ▤ *AE, DC, MC, V.*

$–$$ ✕ **El Cedro.** You dine in a courtyard protected from the elements by a glass roof at this pleasant restaurant with an innovative international menu highlighting Middle Eastern fare. A large-screen TV gives the place a sports-bar feel on game day. The service tends to be a bit slow. ⊠ *Prat 572* ☎ *51/219–501* ▤ *AE, DC, MC, V* ☉ *Closed Sun.*

$–$$ ✕ **Restaurant Velamar Beach.** Enjoy a seaside *parrillada* (barbecue) after battling the waves of La Serena's beach. The restaurant literally

El Norte Chico

Parque Nacional
Pan de Azúcar (14)

Altamira

El Salvador

Salar de
Pedernales

Chañaral

Diego de
Almagro

Potrerillos

La Ola

Inca
del Oro

Cerro
Ermitanno ▲

Caldera (13)

Salar de
Maricunga

Bahía Inglesa (12)

Parque Nacional
Nevado Tres Cruces (15)

Copiapó (11)

Los Azules

Tierra
Amarilla

PACIFIC
OCEAN

Cta. del
Medio

La Guardia

Los Loros

Las Juntas

Parque Nacional (10)
Llanos de Challe

Algarrobal

Huasco

Freirina

Vallenar (8)

Alto del (9)
Carmen

Cta. Sarco

Gonay

Domeyko

Cerro del Toro ▲

Cta. Chañaral

Las Breas

La Higuera

Los Hornos

El Romeral

Cerro Las
Tortolas ▲

La Serena (1)

Monte
Grande (3)

Coquimbo

Vicuña (2)

Andacollo (5)

(4) **Pisco**
Elqui

San José
de Jáchal

Tongoy

Quebrada Seca

Ovalle (6)

Monte
Patria

Parque
Nacional (7)
Fray Jorge

Central
Los Molles

ARGENTINA

Punitaque

San Marcos

Tulahuén

Cta. Morritos

Combarbalá

Puerto Oscuro

Rio Choapa

Illapel

Salamanca

0 ____ 50 miles
0 ____ 75 km

KEY

► *Start of itinerary*

sits on the sand, so it's a great place to watch the sunset from inside or on the patio. ✉ *Av. del Mar 2300* ☎ *51/215–461* ▭ *No credit cards* ☉ *Closed Tues.*

$$$ ☒ **Hotel Costa Real.** Despite its neoclassical design, Hotel Costa Real has all the modern touches you might expect from an executive-class hotel—business center, meeting rooms, and Internet access. Wood and glass furniture fill the spotless, homey rooms. The staff is friendly and attentive. ✉ *Av. Francisco de Aguirre 170* ☎ *51/221–010* 🖶 *51/221–122* ⊕ *www. costareal.cl* ↳ *49 rooms, 2 suites* ⚭ *Restaurant, room service, some in-room data ports, in-room safes, minibars, cable TV, pool, bar, laundry service, business services, meeting rooms, free parking; no a/c* ▭ *AE, DC, MC, V* ⦾ *BP.*

$$ ☒ **Hotel Carrera La Serena.** A large beachfront hotel in mauve adobe, this is a good bet for die-hard beachcombers. Yellow and blue comforters brighten up the smallish rooms, and upper-story suites have views of the ocean. There is a large pool with a fountain for kids. ✉ *Avenida del Mar 1000* ☎ *51/221–262* 🖶 *51/217–130* ⊕ *www.carrera.cl* ↳ *49 rooms, 46 suites* ⚭ *Restaurant, in-room safes, minibars, cable TV, 2 tennis courts, pool, bar, laundry service, meeting rooms, free parking; no a/c* ▭ *AE, DC, MC, V* ⦾ *BP.*

★ **$** ☒ **Hotel del Cid.** Relax and catch some rays on a beach chair in the courtyard of this great-value colonial-style bed-and-breakfast run by a Scottish-Chilean couple. The rooms are warm, cozy, and welcoming. Breakfast is served in the courtyard or in the breakfast nook. ✉ *O'Higgins 138* ☎ *51/212–692* 🖶 *51/222–289* ↳ *18 rooms* ⚭ *Cable TV, laundry service, free parking; no a/c* ▭ *AE, DC, MC, V* ⦾ *BP.*

$ ☒ **Hotel Francisco de Aguirre.** A rambling three-story, colonial-style building houses this lovely hotel emanating European charm. This is La Serena's most venerable hotel, and it stands just a block away from the Plaza de Armas. Cool off in the pool tucked away in a lush courtyard, or sweat away your worries in the sauna. ✉ *Cordovez 210* ☎ *51/ 222–991* 🖶 *51/228–506* ↳ *85 rooms* ⚭ *Restaurant, room service, minibars, cable TV, pool, sauna, bar, laundry service, Internet, free parking; no a/c* ▭ *AE, DC, MC, V* ⦾ *BP.*

Nightlife & the Arts

La Serena's nightlife is a little subdued, fitting perfectly with the city's conservative nature. There are very few bars in the city proper—most of La Serena's pubs and discos lie near the beach on glitzy Avenida del Mar. A huge palm dominates the central courtyard at **Café del Patio** (✉ Prat 470 ☎ 51/210–759), a small pub in the center of town. This is a great place to grab a snack and listen to live jazz and blues. **Brooklyn's** (✉ Av. del Mar 2150 ☎ 51/212–891) is a big, impersonal pub with a dance floor. Just off Avenida del Mar is **Kamikaze** (✉ Av. Cuatro Esquinas s/n ☎ 51/ 218–515). Part of a popular chain of Asian-theme discos, it livens things up late at night. There's a Japanese fighter-plane lodged inside.

Beaches

Playa Peñuelas, La Serena's attractive sandy beach, stretches all the way south to the neighboring town of Coquimbo. It's overrun with tourists during high season in summer. **La Herradura,** 2 km (1 mi) south of Coquimbo, has a small but excellent beach. **Playa Totoralillo,** 14 km (9 mi) south of Coquimbo, has beautiful green waters and a white-sand beach.

Shopping

Mercado La Recova, on the corner of Cienfuegos and Cantournet, is a modern market housed in a pleasant neoclassical building. Here you can buy dried fruits and handicrafts. The Diaguita-style ceramics and the trinkets made from *combabalita,* the locally mined marble, are particularly stunning.

Vicuña

② *62 km (38 mi) east of La Serena.*

As you head into the Elqui Valley, the first town you come to is Vicuña, famous as the birthplace of one of Chile's most important literary figures, Gabriela Mistral. Her beautiful, haunting poetry often looks back on her early years in the Elqui Valley. Mistral's legacy is unmistakable as you wander through town. In the Plaza de Armas, for example, there

★ is a chilling stone replica of the poet's death mask. The **Museo Gabriela Mistral** houses various artifacts pertaining to the poet, such as original copies of her books as well as handwritten letters and poems. There's also a replica of the adobe house where Mistral was born. ⊠ *Calle Gabriela Mistral 759* ☎ *51/411–223* 🖃 *600 pesos* 🕐 *Jan.–Feb., daily 10–7; Mar.–Dec., Tues.–Sun. 10–6.*

A huge steeple tops the 1909 **Iglesia de la Inmaculada Concepción,** which faces the central square. **Torre Bauer,** next to the Iglesia de la Inmaculada Concepción, is a wooden tower painted fire-engine red. It was prefabricated in Germany in 1905 and named after a former mayor. On the central square is **Teatro Municipal,** noted for its art-deco flourishes.

The **Casa de los Madariaga** affords a look into a historic, colonial-era home of the region, complete with antique furnishings, including ornate furniture and pictures of the Madariaga family. ⊠ *Calle Gabriela Mistral 683* ☎ *51/411–220* 🖃 *600 pesos* 🕐 *Daily 10–1 and 3–5.*

As this is the Elqui Valley, you'll eventually come across vineyards growing the grapes used to make pisco. **Planta Capel,** a pisco distillery, is just across the Elqui River. Here you can tour the bottling facility and even taste the results. ⊠ *Camino a Peralillo s/n* ☎ *51/411–391* ⊕ *www.piscocapel.com* 🖃 *Free* 🕐 *Jan.–Feb., daily 9:30–6:30; Mar.–Dec. weekdays 9:30–12:30 and 2:30–6, weekends and holidays 9:30–12:30.*

★ Known for its clear skies, the Elqui Valley has many observatories. **Observatorio Cerro Mamalluca** is Chile's only observatory specifically intended for public use. The facility, 9 km (6 mi) north of Vicuña, holds nightly viewings through a 12-inch telescope. ⊠ *Tour office: Calle Gabriela Mistral 260* ☎ *51/411–352* ⊕ *www.mamalluca.org* 🖃 *5,000 pesos* 🕐 *Daily 10–10.*

The **Cerro de la Virgen** is a place of pilgrimage for those devout to the Virgen de Lourdes, the town's patron saint. This hill overlooking the city affords a great view of Vicuña. It's a 2-km (1-mi) hike north of the city via a path on Baquedano between Independencia and Yungay.

Where to Stay & Eat

¢–$ ✕ **Club Social Vicuña.** Specializing in local dishes such as goat and rabbit, the Club Social Vicuña serves decent country food at affordable prices. This is definitely a family place, as the owner's children play their games in the corner where their parents can keep an eye on them. There's also dining in the rather drab courtyard. ⊠ *Calle Gabriela Mistral 445* ☎ *51/411–853* 🖃 *MC, V.*

¢–$ ✕ **Restaurant Halley.** With open-air dining under a straw roof, this restaurant gives you the feeling that you're having a picnic. The menu focuses on hearty country fare. The cabrito is especially succulent. ⊠ *Calle Gabriela Mistral 404* ☎ *51/411–225* 🖃 *AE, DC, MC, V.*

$ ✕🏠 **Hostería Vicuña.** This large hotel's claim to fame is that Gabriela Mistral once slept here. It also has an inviting parlor and bar area complete with piano, and a tree-shaded garden. The restaurant is quite good and serves Elqui Valley specialties such as goat and rabbit as well as international fare. The ambience is a step above most eateries in El Norte Chico—there are even cloth napkins. ⊠ *Sargento Aldea 101* ☎ *51/411–301* 🖷 *51/411–144* ⊕ *www.hosteriavicuna.cl* 🖙 *14 rooms* ⟡ *Restaurant, café, cable TV, tennis court, pool, bar, playground, laundry service, meeting room, free parking; no a/c* ⊟ *AE, DC, MC, V* ⦿⃝ *CP.*

★ $ ⊡ **Hotel Halley.** In a pretty colonial house with wood trim and white walls, this inn has carefully decorated rooms filled with authentic circa-1950s radios and more doilies than you could possibly imagine. There's a small, rather shallow pool in the back. ⊠ *Calle Gabriela Mistral 542* ☎ *51/ 412–070* 🖷 *51/412–070* 🖙 *11 rooms, 1 suite* ⟡ *Restaurant, minibars, cable TV, pool, laundry service, Internet, free parking, no-smoking rooms; no a/c* ⊟ *AE, DC, MC, V* ⦿⃝ *CP.*

Nightlife & the Arts

Pub Kharma (⊠ Gabriela Mistral 417 ☎ 51/419–738) occasionally hosts live music. Otherwise, the bar plays Bob Marley almost exclusively and pays further homage to the reggae legend with posters.

Shopping

You can buy local handicrafts, especially ceramics and jewelry, at the **Poblado Artesenal,** a collection of artisan stands on the Plaza de Armas. It's open daily 10–5.

Monte Grande

❸ *34 km (21 mi) east of Vicuña.*

A tiny village in the rugged Elqui Valley, Monte Grande recalls a time of simpler pleasures. This picturesque village is home to two of the world's purest vices: pisco and poetry. On the neighboring hills and in the valley below, farmers cultivate the grapes used to make pisco. Gabriela Mistral, born in nearby Vicuña, grew up in Monte Grande. Her family lived in the old schoolhouse where her older sister taught. The **Casa Escuela** has been turned into a museum and displays some relics from the poet's life. Her tomb is on a nearby hillside. ⊠ *Central plaza* ☎ *51/451–015* 🖾 *600 pesos* ⊙ *Tues.–Sun. 10–1 and 3–6.*

Where to Eat

$–$$ ╳ **El Meson de Fraile.** This cozy eatery with stone walls and large wooden tables is a good place to stop for lunch on your way to Pisco Elqui. El Meson de Fraile serves basic but tasty food, and the ever-changing menu highlights such local favorites as goat and rabbit. The service is superb. ⊠ *Montegrande s/n* ☎ *51/198–2608* ⊟ *No credit cards.*

Pisco Elqui

❹ *10 km (6 mi) south of Monte Grande, 43 km (27 mi) east of Vicuña.*

Once known as La Unión, this pisco-producing village, perched on a sun-drenched hillside, received its current moniker in 1939. Gabriel González Videla, at that time the president of Chile, renamed the village in a shrewd maneuver to ensure that Peru would not gain exclusive rights over the term "pisco." The Peruvian town of Pisco also produces the heady brandy.

This idyllic village of fewer than 600 residents has two pisco plants. The
★   **Solar de Pisco Elqui** (☎ 51/198–2503), on the main road, is Chile's oldest distillery. It produces the famous Tres Erres brand, perhaps Chile's finest. In the older section of the plant, maintained strictly for show, you can see the antiquated copper cauldrons and wooden barrels. The dis-

tillery arranges free daily tours, followed by tastings where you can sample a pisco sour. About 4 km (2 mi) past Pisco Elqui you come upon the **Los Nichos** distillery (☎ 51/198–2524), which hosts free daily tours and tastings.

Where to Stay & Eat

★ ¢–$ ✕🏠 **El Tesoro de Elqui.** Beautiful gardens with flowers of every imaginable shape and size surround this hotel's nicely decorated cabanas. At the lovely pool you can laze around in the world-famous Elqui Valley sunshine and take in the panoramic view of the Andes. The restaurant, which serves as a meeting place for travelers, has an international menu. The tasty spaghetti Bolognese makes a welcome change from Chilean country cuisine. The owner also makes a mean pisco sour. ⊠ *Prat s/n* ☎ *51/198–2609* ⊕ *www.pisco.de* 🛏 *5 rooms* 🍴 *Restaurant, pool; no a/c, no room phones, no room TVs* 🖃 *AE, MC, V* ⫯⧚ *BP.*

$ 🏠 **Misterios de Elqui.** These six grass-roof cabanas surround a pleasant pool, where you can relax with a pisco sour and enjoy the delightful sunshine. The views of the mountains are outstanding. ⊠ *Prat s/n* ☎☎ *51/451–126* ⊕ *www.valledeelqui.cl* 🛏 *6 cabanas* 🍴 *Restaurant, pool, bar; no a/c, no room phones, no room TVs* 🖃 *DC, MC, V* ⫯⧚ *BP.*

¢ 🏠 **Complejo Turístico Gabriela Mistral.** The cabanas at this hotel are comfortable, although some are a bit dark. The pool is shallow, but can be a great place to wallow after a day of exploring the sun-drenched valley. ⊠ *Prat 59* ☎ *51/451–086* ⊕ *www.valledeelqui.cl* 🛏 *6 cabanas* 🍴 *Restaurant, pool, laundry service; no a/c, no room phones, no room TVs* 🖃 *No credit cards.*

Nightlife & the Arts

There isn't much to do at night in Pisco Elqui but lie on your back and enjoy the brilliant stars. **Restaurante Los Jugos** (☎ no phone), on the corner of the plaza, serves incredible fresh fruit drinks. Try the *jugo de frambuesa* (raspberry juice).

Shopping

Fresh fruit marmalade and preserves are sold in the town's main plaza. You can also head to the pisco distilleries to pick up a bottle of freshly brewed pisco.

Andacollo

❺ *54 km (34 mi) southeast of La Serena.*

The compact town of Andacollo, an important gold and silver mining center since the 16th century, makes a pleasant stopover between Ovalle and La Serena. Here you'll find one of Chile's most famous religious icons. The wooden image of the Virgen de Andacollo, deemed miraculous by the Vatican in 1901 for its putative power to cure disease, draws some 150,000 pilgrims to the town each year from December 23 to 26 for the Fiesta Grande de la Virgen. During the festival, the statue is decorated and paraded through the streets.

★ The Virgen de Andacollo sits on a silver altar in the small **Templo Antiguo,** on Plaza Videla, the town's main square. This church, built in the 17th century, has a museum of the offerings given to the virgin in hopes of her miraculous assistance. The **Basilica,** which was inaugurated in 1893 after nearly 20 years of construction, is by far the largest structure in the town. With a 40-m-high dome and two giant steeples, it towers over everything else.

CHILE'S NATIONAL DRINK

DISTILLED FROM MUSCAT GRAPES grown in the sun-baked river valleys of El Norte Chico, Pisco is indisputably Chile's national drink. This fruity, aromatic brandy is enjoyed here in large quantities—most commonly in a delightful elixir known as a pisco sour, which consists of pisco, lemon juice, and sugar. A few drops of bitters on top is optional. Some bars step it up a notch by adding whipped egg white to give the drink a frothy head. Another concoction made with the brandy is piscola—the choice of many late-night revelers—which is simply pisco mixed with soda. Tea with a shot of pisco is the Chilean answer to the common cold, and it may just do the trick to relieve a headache and stuffy nose. Whichever way you choose to take your pisco, you can expect a pleasant, smooth drink.

Chileans have enjoyed pisco, which takes its name from pisku, the Quechuan word for "flying bird," for more than 400 years. The drink likely originated in Peru—a source of enmity between the two nations. In 1939, Chilean President Gabriel González Videla went so far as to change the name of the town of La Unión to Pisco Elqui in an attempt to gain exclusive rights over the name pisco. But Peru already had its own town south of Lima named Pisco. The situation is currently at a standoff, with both countries claiming they have the better product.

The primary spots for pisco distillation are the Huasco and Elqui valleys; the latter is particularly renowned for the quality of its grapes. The 300 days of sunshine per year here make these lush valleys perfect for cultivating muscat grapes. The distillation process has changed very little in the past four centuries. The fermented wine is boiled in copper stills, and the vapors are then condensed and aged in oak barrels for three to six months—pisco makers call the aging process "resting." The result is a fruity but potent brandy with between 30% and 50% alcohol.

You're welcome to tour many of the region's pisco distilleries. Several of the distilleries are more than 100 years old— Chile's oldest distillery is in the idyllic town of Pisco Elqui in the verdant Elqui Valley. The Solar de Pisco Elqui has been entirely renovated since it began operations, but you can still take a tour of the old plant and learn a bit about how pisco is made. This is where the famous Tres Erres brand, arguably Chile's best pisco, is distilled. In Pisco Elqui you'll also find Los Nichos, a quaint 130-year-old distillery that is open to the public. Nearby Montegrande and Vicuña also have distilleries. To escape the pisco-loving crowds, head north to the Huasco Valley, with its less frequently visited pisco distilleries such as the Planta Pisquera Alto del Carmen. San Felix, a village nestled in the valley, has a 95-year-old plant that produces the Horcón Quemado brand.

Tours generally end with free tastings of different types of pisco, which will let you see why poetic Chileans call pisco "a million years of sunshine in a single drop."

—Gregory Benchwick

Ovalle

6 *34 km (21 mi) south of Andacollo.*

Ovalle, a modern town southeast of La Serena, serves as a good base for trips to the Monumento Natural Pichasca or the Valle del Encanto. The town's shady **Plaza de Armas** is a pleasant place to pass an afternoon. On the Plaza de Armas, the **Iglesia San Vicente Ferrer** is worth a visit. Constructed in 1849, the church was damaged by an earthquake in 1997 and remains in a semi-dilapidated state.

★ Unlike geoglyphs, which are large-scale figures chiseled into the landscape, petroglyphs are small pictures carved onto the rock surface. One of Chile's densest collections of petroglyphs can be found in **Valle del Encanto.** The 30 images in the Valley of Enchantment were most likely etched by the Molle culture between AD 100 and 600. The figures wear ceremonial headdresses hanging low over large, expressive eyes. On occasion a guide waits near the petroglyphs and will show you the best of the carvings for a small fee. To reach the site, take Ruta 45 west from Ovalle. About 19 km (12 mi) from the town head south for 5 km (3 mi) on a rough, dry road. ⊠ *24 km (15 mi) west of Ovalle* 🕾 *no phone* 🖃 *Free* ⊘ *Daily 8–7:30.*

A tourist complex cut from the rough land, **Termas de Socos** is a very pleasant hot springs. The waters, which spout from the earth at 28°C (82°F), are said to have incredible healing powers. Curative or not, the waters here are extremely relaxing. ⊠ *24 km (15 mi) west of Ovalle on Rte. 45* 🕾 *53/236–3336* 🖃 *1,000 pesos* ⊘ *Daily 8–8.*

Heading toward the Andes you come across **Monumento Natural Pichasca,** a forest of petrified tree trunks. These play host to dozens of fossils, such as imprints of leaves and outlines of small animals. Nearby is a cave beneath a stone overhang that housed indigenous peoples thousands of years ago. Inside you'll find some cave paintings by the Molle people. ⊠ *50 km (31 mi) northeast of Ovalle on the Camino Ovalle–Río Hurtado* 🕾 *no phone* 🖃 *1,000 pesos* ⊘ *Daily 8:30–4:30.*

Where to Stay & Eat

$–$$ ✕ **Bavaria.** Because of the country's large number of German immigrants, most Chilean cities have at least one Bavarian-theme restaurant. This one, part of a national chain, evokes the Old Country with wood beams and checkered yellow tablecloths. Entrées like *pollo a la plancha* (grilled chicken) are a bit bland, but wholesome and filling. ⊠ *Vicuña Mackenna 401* 🕾 *53/630–578* 🖃 *AE, MC, V.*

$ ⊡ **Hotel El Turismo.** A pleasant hotel in the center of town, Hotel El Turismo has spacious and well-kept rooms. Ask for a room facing the Plaza de Armas. ⊠ *Victoria 295* 🕾 *53/623–536* 🖶 *53/623–536* ⇗ *30 rooms* ⌂ *Restaurant, minibars, laundry service; no a/c* 🖃 *MC, V* ⦿ *CP.*

$ ⊡ **Hotel Termas de Socos.** This rustic hotel, about 33 km (20 mi) west of Ovalle, allows you unlimited access to the hot springs at Termas de Socos. The rooms have large, comfortable beds, and many have expansive picture windows looking out over the surrounding desert. Also available are relaxing massages and private hot tubs. The service, unfortunately, is a little inattentive. ⊠ *Termas de Socos* 🕾 *53/681–021* 🖶 *02/236–3337* ✎ *termasocos@entelchile.net* ⇗ *28 rooms* ⌂ *Restaurant, room service, cable TV, pool, bar, laundry service, meeting rooms; no a/c* 🖃 *AE, MC, V* ⦿ *BP.*

Parque Nacional Fray Jorge

7 *110 km (68 mi) south of La Serena.*

Fodor'sChoice The thought of a patch of land that is rich with vegetation and animal
★ life in the heart of El Norte Chico's dry, desolate landscape seems to
defy logic. But Parque Nacional Fray Jorge, a UNESCO world biosphere
reserve since 1977, has a small cloud forest similar to those found in
Chile's damp southern regions. The forest, perched 600 m (1,968 ft) above
sea level, receives its life-giving nourishment from the *camanchaca* (fog)
that constantly envelops it. Within this forest you'll come across ferns
and trees found nowhere else in the region. A slightly slippery boardwalk leads you on a half-hour tour. ✛ *At Km 383 of the Pan-American Hwy., take dirt road 18 km (11 mi) west* ☎ *no phone* 🗐 *1,000 pesos*
🕙 *Jan.–Mar., Thurs.–Sun. 8:30–6; Apr.–Dec. weekends 8:30–6.*

THE HUASCO VALLEY

At least twice a decade the desert bursts to life in a phenomena called
el desierto florido. If you are lucky enough to visit the area during these
times, you'll see the desert covered with colorful flowers, some of which
only exist in this region. Parque Nacional Llanos de Challe on the coast
is an excellent place to view the flowering desert. When it occurs you
can see the desierto florido in most of El Norte Chico, but the Huasco
Valley in particular has a lovely and large variety of flora.

The Huasco Valley sees far fewer visitors than the Elqui Valley, giving
you the feeling that you've beaten the crowds. Climbing into the Andes
from Vallenar, the valley's largest city, you reach the Upper Huasco Valley. The Valle del Carmen, part of the Huasco Valley, has several quaint
villages, such as Alto del Carmen and San Felix.

Vallenar

8 *188 km (116 mi) north of La Serena.*

Vallenar, the transportation hub of the Huasco Valley, was founded in
1789 by Ambrosio O'Higgins, who named the town after his home in
Ballinagh, Ireland. There aren't many sights that lure travelers off the
highway—most who stop here are headed to the Parque Nacional
Llanos de Challe. The large **Plaza O'Higgins** is a pleasant place for an
early evening stroll. The **Iglesia Porroquial**, on the main square, is worth
a visit to see its huge copper dome.

On display at the **Museo de Huasco** is a small collection of regional indigenous artifacts like pottery and textiles. There are also pictures of
the flowering desert for those not lucky enough to see it in person. ✉ *Sargento Aldea 742* 🗐 *600 pesos* 🕙 *Weekdays 10–1 and 3–6, Sat. 10–12:30.*

Where to Stay & Eat

$–$$ ✕ **La Casona.** A blue, two-story wooden building houses this comfort-
able restaurant with a cozy bar. Pizzas and pastas round out the menu.
✉ *Serrano 1475* ☎ *51/611–600* 🗖 *No credit cards.*

$–$$ ✕ **Il Boccato.** Opposite the Plaza de Armas, this small, friendly corner
pizza place with a brightly lighted interior is your best bet for a quick
bite. Chose from myriad menu options, including a zesty pollo a la plancha. There's also a wide selection of seafood entrées. ✉ *Plaza de Armas*
☎ *51/614–609* 🗖 *AE, DC, MC, V.*

$–$$ ✗ **Moros y Christianos Restaurant.** This Mediterranean-style restaurant, named for the Spanish festivals commemorating the battle between the Moors and the Christians, serves flavorful Spanish fare. Try the paella for two for an authentic taste of Valencia. ⊠ *Pan-American Hwy. at the entrance to Vallenar* ☎ *51/614–600* ⌕ *Reservations essential* ⊟ *AE, MC, V.*

$ ⌂ **Hostería de Vallenar.** The best lodging in Vallenar, this comfortable hostelry has basic rooms with wood furniture. The staff is friendly and helpful. ⊠ *Alonso de Ercilla 848* ☎ *51/614–195* ☎ *51/614–538* ⌕ *johanacerda@mi.terra.cl* ⇥ *30 rooms* ⌕ *Restaurant, minibars, cable TV, pool, billiards, bar, laundry service, Internet; no a/c* ⊟ *AE, DC, MC, V* ⍥ *CP.*

$ ⌂ **Hotel Cecil.** A pleasant garden with a pool makes Hotel Cecil a good budget lodging choice. The rooms are spotless, but the baths are a bit small. ⊠ *Prat 1059* ☎☎ *51/614–400* ⌕ *hotelcecil@entelchile.net* ⇥ *18 rooms* ⌕ *Cable TV, pool, laundry service, Internet; no a/c* ⊟ *No credit cards* ⍥ *CP.*

Nightlife & the Arts

You can dance to salsa and other Latin rhythms on the town's largest dance floor at **Cubaire** (⊠ Serrano 1398 ☎ no phone). **La Casona** (⊠ Serrano 1475 ☎ 51/611–600) caters to an older crowd and heats up with dancing on the weekends.

Alto del Carmen

❾ *40 km (25 mi) southeast of Vallenar.*

Not far from where the El Transito and El Carmen rivers join to form the Huasco you'll find Alto del Carmen, a quaint town whose inhabitants dedicate themselves to cultivating the muscat grapes used to make pisco. In addition to pisco, the town is famous for making *pajarete*, a sweet wine. **The Planta Pisquera Alto del Carmen,** just outside of town, hosts free tours and tastings daily from 8 AM to 8 PM.

About 26 km (16 mi) east of Alto del Carmen into the Valle del Carmen you'll find the precious town of **San Felix,** whose central plaza, whitewashed church, and pleasant markets shouldn't be missed. There's also a pisco distillery here.

Parque Nacional Llanos de Challe

❿ *78 km (48 mi) northwest of Vallenar, 99 km (61 mi) north of Huasco.*

There is no better place in El Norte Chico to view the desierto florido than this desolate coastal park. Every four or five years it is transformed into a carpet of reds, greens, and blues when there's sufficient rainfall to awaken the dormant bulbs below the dry, cracked earth. The park, spanning 450 square km (174 square mi), was formed to protect the *Garra de León*, a rare plant with an intoxicating red bloom that grows in only a few parts of the Huasco region. There are also a number of unusual species of cactus in the park—pacul, napina, and quisco flourish here. ⊹ *About 17 km (11 mi) north of Vallenar, turn west off the Pan-American Hwy. Take this road 82 km (51 mi) to the coast* ☎ *no phone* ⊠ *Free.*

THE COPIAPÓ VALLEY

The region once known as Copayapu, meaning "cup of gold" in the Quechua language, was first inhabited by the Diaguitas around 1000. The Incas arrived several hundred years later in search of gold. Conquistador Diego de Almagro, who passed this way in 1535, was the first European to see the lush valley. Almagro didn't stop here for long; he continued on to Peru via the Inca Royal Road on his bloody conquest of the region.

During the 19th century the Copiapó Valley proved to be a true cup of gold when prospectors started large-scale mining operations in the region. But today, the residents of the valley make their living primarily from copper.

The northernmost city in the region, Copiapó, lies at the end of the world. Here the semiarid region of El Norte Chico gives way to the Atacama Desert. Continuing north from Copiapó there is little but barren earth for hundreds of miles.

Copiapó

⓫ *145 km (90 mi) north of Vallenar.*

Copiapó was officially founded in 1744 by Don Francisco Cortés, who called it Villa San Francisco de La Selva. Originally a *tambo,* or resting place, Copiapó was where Diego de Almagro recuperated after his grueling journey south from Peru in 1536. The 19th-century silver strikes solidified Copiapó's status as an important city in the region. In the center of Copiapó lies **Plaza Prat,** a lovely park lined with 100-year-old pepper trees. English architect William Rogers built the neoclassical **Iglesia Catedral Nuestra Señora del Rosario,** facing the central square, in the middle of the 19th century. The 1872 **Iglesia San Francisco** is a red-and-white candy cane of a church. The adjacent Plaza Godoy has a statue of goat herd Juan Godoy, who accidently discovered huge silver deposits in nearby Chañarcillo.

The **Museo Mineralógico** offers a geological history of the region and what is perhaps the country's largest collection of rocks and minerals. There are more than 2,000 samples, including some found only in the Atacama Desert. The museum even displays a few meteorites that fell in the area. ⊠ *Colipí and Rodriguez* ☎ *52/206–606* ⌚ *500 pesos* ⊗ *Mon.–Sat. 10–1 and 2:30–7.*

A historic home that once belonged to the wealthy Matta family now houses the **Museo Histórico Regional,** dedicated to the natural history of the area. Regional archives suggest that the house was originally built by mining engineer Felipe Santiago Matta between 1840 and 1850. ⊠ *Atacama 98* ☎ *52/212–313* ⌚ *600 pesos* ⊗ *Mon. 2:30–6, Tues.–Thurs. 9–6, weekends 10–12:45.*

Where to Stay & Eat

$–$$ ✕ **El Corsario.** A babbling fountain and numerous caged birds enliven a pleasant courtyard where you'll find this local favorite. The restaurant has an interesting menu of regional dishes, including *pinchones escabechadas* (baby pigeons). ⊠ *Atacama 245* ☎ *52/215–374* ▭ *No credit cards.*

$–$$ ✕ **El Quincho.** El Quincho serves seafood, but the only reason to come here is for the barbecued meats. The menu has virtually every cut of beef imaginable. The fire-red dining room gives you the feeling that you've descended into a barbecue pit. ⊠ *Atacama 109* ☎ *52/214–647* ▭ *No credit cards.*

$ ✕ **El Cisne.** This locally recommended seafood restaurant specializes in shellfish. The *ostiones a la parmesana* (oysters with grated cheese) is particularly good. Chairs padded with black velvet, and prints of works by the old masters decorate the eclectic dining room. ⊠ *Colipí 220* ☎ *52/ 215–544* ▭ *No credit cards.*

$–$$ ▦ **Hotel Diego de Almeida.** A pleasant tiled entryway leads into an elegantly furnished lobby at this hotel a step above the rest. The Diego provides everything you would expect from a hotel catering to corporate travelers, from meeting rooms to business services. The rooms are pleasant, if a bit bland. Inquire about a room in the back, as those facing the street can be quite noisy. ⊠ *O'Higgins 656* ☎ *52/212–075* 🖷 *52/218– 688* 🖃 *dalmeida@terra.cl* 🖙 *36 rooms* ⌂ *Restaurant, room service, in-room safes, cable TV, pool, sauna, bar, laundry service, business services, meeting rooms; no a/c* ▭ *AE, DC, MC, V* ⦿⊟ *BP.*

$ ▦ **Hotel Chagall.** Although it appears a little run-down on the outside, this business hotel has clean, modern rooms. Ask to see a few before you decide, as some are very dark. The bar, decorated with lots of kelly green, is reminiscent of an Irish pub. You won't find Guinness on tap here, however, so you'll have to settle for a well-made pisco sour. ⊠ *O'Higgins 760* ☎ *52/213–775* 🖷 *52/211–527* 🖃 *chagall@ctcinternet. cl* 🖙 *34 rooms* ⌂ *Restaurant, minibars, cable TV, bar, laundry service; no a/c in some rooms* ▭ *AE, DC, MC, V* ⦿⊟ *BP.*

★ $ ▦ **Hotel La Casona.** Beautiful gardens surround this quaint country inn with a red facade and budget prices. Entering through wooden doors you reach the sunny lobby. To one side is a dining area with oak furniture and blue-and-white-checked tablecloths—an excellent place to enjoy your complimentary pisco sour. The rooms, decorated in blue, can get a little hot in the summer. ⊠ *O'Higgins 150* ☎🖷 *52/217–277* ⊕ *www.lacasonahotel.cl* 🖙 *10 rooms* ⌂ *Restaurant, minibars, cable TV, bar, laundry service; no a/c* ▭ *AE, DC, MC, V* ⦿⊟ *BP.*

$ ▦ **Hotel Miramonte.** This central hotel has clean, modern rooms decorated in the same shade of mauve you'll find in the lobby and hallways. The staff here is friendly and helpful. Arched-back wooden chairs and blue tablecloths fill the the country-style restaurant. The international menu here is heavy on seafood, and includes great merluza and ostiones. ⊠ *Ramón Freire 731* ☎🖷 *52/210–440* ⊕ *www.chilenet.cl/miramonte* 🖙 *47 rooms* ⌂ *Restaurant, in-room safes, minibars, cable TV, bar, recreation room, laundry service; no a/c* ▭ *AE, DC, MC, V.*

Nightlife & the Arts

Because there are lots of students in town, nightlife in Copiapó can get lively, with bars hosting bands, and a few dance clubs that rage all night to salsa beats. **Discoteque Splash** (⊠ Juan Martinéz 46 ☎ 52/215–948) is your best bet for late-night dancing. Outside of town, the **Drive-In Esso Pub** (⊠ Near the exit ramp from the Pan-American Hwy. ☎ 52/211– 535) is perhaps the most innovative bar in northern Chile—it's in a converted gas station. **La Tabla** (⊠ Los Carrera 895 ☎ 52/233–029), near Plaza Prat, has live music, very expensive drinks, and good food.

Shopping

The **Casa de la Cultura** (⊠ O'Higgins 610, on Plaza Prat ☎ 52/210–824) has craft workshops and a gallery displaying works by local artists. On Fridays there is a frenzied **fruit market** in the normally tranquil Plaza Godoy.

Bahía Inglesa

⑫ *68 km (42 mi) northwest of Copiapó.*

Some of the most beautiful beaches in El Norte Chico can be found at Bahía Inglesa, which was originally known as Puerto del Inglés because of the number of English buccaneers using the port as a hideaway. It's not just the beautiful white sand that sets these beaches apart, however:

it's also the turquoise waters, the fresh air, and the fabulous weather. Combine all this with the fact that the town has yet to attract large-scale development and you can see why so many people flock here in the summer. If you are fortunate enough to visit during the low season, you'll likely experience a tranquility rarely felt in Chile's other coastal towns.

Where to Stay & Eat

★ ¢–$ ✕ **El Plateao.** With ocean views and the region's best food, this bohemian bistro is a must for anyone staying in the area. The innovative contemporary menu lists such culinary non sequiturs as curry dishes and *tallarines con mariscos* (a pan-Asian noodle concoction served with shellfish and topped with cilantro). On the sand-covered porch you can sit in a comfy chair and watch the sunset. ⊠ *Av. El Morro 756* ☎ *09/ 679–3016* ▤ *No credit cards.*

$ ▥ **Apart Hotel Playa Blanca.** If you are tired of indistinguishable chain hotels, a cabana at Playa Blanca may just do the trick. These cabins are more like condos, complete with kitchens and living rooms. Relax on a chaise longue by the pool, an asymmetrical beauty. This is a great place for kids, as there is a play area with a slide and jungle gym. ⊠ *Camino de Martín 1300* ☎ *52/316–044* 🖷 *52/316–468* ✍ *olivo.norte@ia.cl* ⇨ *10 cabanas* ⚖ *Kitchens, cable TV, pool, playground; no a/c* ▤ *No credit cards.*

$ ▥ **Hotel Rocas de Bahía.** This sprawling modern hotel, straight from *The Great Gatsby*, has rooms with huge windows facing the sea. You'll also find large beds and Southwestern-style furniture in the rooms. Take a dip in the glistening waters of the bay, or head up to the roof-top pool. ⊠ *Av. El Morro 888* ☎ *52/316–005* 🖷 *52/316–032* ⊕ *www.depetris. cl/rocasdebahia* ⇨ *36 rooms* ⚖ *Restaurant, room service, in-room safes, pool, bicycles, billiards, Ping-Pong, playground, laundry service, meeting rooms; no a/c* ▤ *AE, DC, MC, V* ⌷ *BP.*

FodorsChoice ★

Nightlife & the Arts

There are few true bars in Bahía Inglesa except in the hotels, but outside of the city, on the way north to Caldera, you'll find several discos that are always packed during high season. You can dance at **Discoteque Loreto** (⊠ Camino Bahia Inglesa ☎ no phone), which lies midway between Bahía Inglesa and Caldera. Head to the funky **El Plateao** (⊠ Av. El Morro 756 ☎ 09/679–3016) to listen to reggae and Cuban tunes. **Takeo** (⊠ Camino Bahia Inglesa s/n ☎ no phone) attracts a mature, salsa-dancing crowd.

Sports & the Outdoors

BEACHES There are several easily accessible beaches around Bahía Inglesa. **Playa La Piscina** is the town's main beach. The rocky outcroppings and sugary sand are reminiscent of the Mediterranean. **Playa Las Machas,** the town's southernmost beach, is especially relaxing because few tourists have discovered it.

WATER SPORTS There are all types of water sports in the area. **Morro Ballena Expeditions** (⊠ El Morro s/n, on the south end of the beach ☎ no phone) arranges fishing, kayaking, and scuba-diving trips.

Caldera

⑬ *74 km (46 mi) northwest of Copiapó.*

An important port during the silver era, Caldera today is a slightly run-down town with decent beaches and friendly people. The echoes of piracy still haunt the port—a former pirate hideout—which is used today to export grapes and copper.

Near the beach is the **Estacion Ferrocarril,** once the terminus of Chile's first railroad. There's a tourist-information kiosk here. The large, Gothic-towered **Iglesia de San Vincente de Paul,** on the town's main square, was built in 1862.

Where to Stay & Eat

★ $ ╳ **El Cisne.** This restaurant serves just about every kind of seafood imaginable. Ask your waiter for whatever fish was caught that day, and the kitchen will grill it with lemon and butter or serve it with a succulent salsa margarita sauce. A decent wine list includes Chilean wines. Seating is indoors and outdoors. ⊠ *Edwards 425* ☎ *52/315–626* ▭ *No credit cards.*

$ ╳ **Nuevo Miramar.** Huge windows overlook the pier at this excellent seafood restaurant. One of the most elegant eateries in Caldera, the Nuevo Miramar has tables with fine linens and cloth napkins. Bow-tied waiters, all extremely attentive, will tell you the catch of the day. ⊠ *Gana 90* ☎ *52/315–381* ⌂ *Reservations essential* ▭ *No credit cards.*

$ ▣ **Hostería Puerta del Sol.** These A-frame cabanas have small kitchens and dining areas and a view of the bay. The showers pour out incredibly hot water, a nice touch after a long day of exploring. There is also a pool, which could be quite pleasant if it were filled to the top. ⊠ *Wheelwright 750* ☎ *52/315–205* 🖷 *52/315–507* ↩ *7 cabanas* ⌂ *Kitchenettes, pool, bar, laundry service; no a/c, no room phones* ▭ *AE, DC, MC, V.*

$ ▣ **Motel Portal del Inca.** This string of red cabanas has tennis courts and an inviting pool surrounded by lounge chairs. There's also a playground, making this an excellent choice if you are traveling with children. The rooms are simple, with furnishings that may have been popular back in the 1970s. ⊠ *Carvallo 945* ☎☎ *52/315–252* ↩ *34 cabanas* ⌂ *Coffee shop, kitchenettes, tennis courts, pool, bar, playground, laundry service, business services, meeting rooms; no a/c* ▭ *MC, V.*

Nightlife & the Arts

Many of Caldera's bars are only open during the summer, when the town is packed with vacationing South Americans. The funky **Bartalameo** (⊠ Wheelwright 747 ☎ 52/316–413) plays eclectic music. If you're hungry, chow down on the Asian and Mexican food. **Pub Entre Jotes** (⊠ Wheelwright 485 ☎ no phone), with a terrace overlooking the port, is a good place to enjoy the sunset. The pub hosts live music on weekends, although it's often just a man playing a keyboard.

Beaches

The town's main beach is **Playa Copiapina.** North of the pier, **Playa Brava** stretches as far as you can see. About 4 km (2 mi) to the south of town you come upon the pleasant sandy beach of **Playa Loreto.**

Parque Nacional Pan de Azúcar

★ ☾ ⑭ *91 km (56 mi) north of Caldera.*

Some of Chile's most spectacular coastal scenery is in Parque Nacional Pan de Azúcar, a national park that stretches for 40 km (25 mi) along the coast north of the town of Chañaral. Steep cliffs fall into the crashing sea, their ominous presence broken occasionally by white-sand beaches. These isolated stretches of sand make for excellent picnicking. Be careful if you decide to swim, as there are often dangerous currents.

Within the park you'll find an incredible variety of flora and fauna. Pelicans can be spotted off the coast, as can sea lions and sea otters, cormorants, and plovers (similar to sandpipers but with shorter beaks). There are some 20 species of cacti in the park, including the rare copiapoa. The park also shelters rare predators, including the desert fox. In the pueblo of Caleta Pan de Azúcar, a tiny fishing village, you can get information from the CONAF-run kiosk (CONAF is the national forestry service).

Offshore from Caleta Pan de Azucar is a tiny island that a large colony of Humboldt penguins calls home. You can hire local fisherfolk to bring you here. Negotiate the price, which should be around 7,000 pesos. About 10 km (6 mi) north of the village, Mirador Pan de Azúcar affords spectacular views of the coastline. Another 30 km (19 mi) to the north is Las Lomitas. This 700-m (2,296-ft) cliff is almost always covered with the *camanchaca* (fog), which rolls in from the sea. A huge net here is used to catch the fog and condense it into water. ⊠ *An unpaved road north of the cemetery in Chañaral leads to Caleta Pan de Azúcar* ☎ *no phone* ☜ *1,000 pesos* ⊙ *Park daily, CONAF kiosk daily 8–1 and 2–6.*

Where to Stay & Eat

$ ✕▥ **Hostería Chañaral.** Leaps and bounds above the other places in Chañaral, where you will mostly likely stay the night when visiting the park, the Hostería Chañaral has well-maintained rooms and clean baths with plenty of hot water. A restaurant on the premises serves good seafood. ⊠ *Muller 268* ☎ *52/480–050* 🖷 *52/480–554* ⊸ *34 rooms* ⚫ *Restaurant, bar, laundry service; no a/c* ▤ *MC, V* ⑩ *CP.*

Parque Nacional Nevado Tres Cruces

⑮ *200 km (124 mi) east of Copiapó.*

Heading inland from Copiapó you climb high into the Andes before reaching Parque Nacional Nevado Tres Cruces. The national park lies in the inhospitable altiplano some 4,000 m (13,000 ft) above sea level, and for some time few tourists dared to venture here. Three of the world's four species of flamingos make their home here, and guanacos and vicuñas roam the arid region in search of food.

Two beautiful Andean lakes lie within the park's borders. At Laguna San Francisco, at the main entrance, you'll find flamingos as well as some species of ducks. Along the grassy banks it is not uncommon to come across an occasional Andean fox. Farther into the park you come to Laguna Santa Rosa and the salt flat of El Salar de Maricunga.

Near the border of Argentina are the beautiful waters of Laguna Verde. This shallow lagoon, colored green by microorganisms, is the lifeblood of the region. Many species of birds and animals—including flamingos, guanacos, and desert foxes—live along its banks. On the southern shore of the lake there is a natural hot-springs pool, which is free and open to the public. To the south is Ojos del Salado, the world's highest active volcano. Rising 6,893 meters (22,609 ft) above sea level, it's an awe-inspiring sight.

To visit the park you will need a four-wheel-drive vehicle. Be sure to bring extra fuel, as gas stops are few and far between in this region. An ambitious project to create a linked trail system from Tierra del Fuego to Chile's northernmost tip is underway and scheduled for completion around 2015. Sections of the trail are already in place here. Check with **CONAF** officials (☎ *56/390–000*) for details of the trail in the Tres Cruces region. ✛ *Take Ruta 31 from Copiapó to Paso de San Francisco, then head south on the rough road marked* QUEBRADA CIENAGA REDONDA ☎ *no phone* ☜ *1,000 pesos.*

EL NORTE CHICO A TO Z

To research prices, get advice from other travelers, and book travel arrangements, visit www.fodors.com.

AIR TRAVEL

Because there are no international airports in El Norte Chico, you can't fly here directly from North America, Europe, or Australia. You can fly into Santiago and transfer to an Avant or LanChile flight to La Serena or Copiapó. Round-trip flights from Santiago to El Norte Chico can run up to 140,000 pesos. Round-trip flights between cities in the north range from 28,000 to 105,000 pesos.

✈ Airlines **Avant** ✉ Colipí 510 ☎ 52/217-285 in Copiapó ✉ Aeropuerto La Florido ☎ 51/220-943 in La Serena. **LanChile** ✉ Colipí 101 ☎ 52/213-512 in Copiapó ✉ Balmaceda 400 ☎ 51/221-551 in La Serena.

AIRPORTS

Copiapó's Aeropuerto Chamonate lies 15 km (9 mi) east of the city. In La Serena, Aeropuerto La Florido is 5 km (3 mi) east of the center of town.

✈ Airport Information **Aeropuerto Chamonate** ☎ 51/214-360. **Aeropuerto La Florido** ☎ 51/200-900.

BUS TRAVEL

Every major city in El Norte Chico has a bus terminal, and there are frequent departures to other cities as well as smaller towns in the area. Keep in mind that there may be no bus service to the smallest villages or the more remote national parks.

No bus company has a monopoly, so there are often several bus stations in each city. Because many companies may be running buses along the same route, shop around for the best price. The fare for a 300-km (186-mi) trip usually runs around 3,500–7,000 pesos. For longer trips find a bus that has a *salon semi-cama,* with comfortable seats that make all the difference.

🚌 Bus Stations **Copiapó** ✉ Chañarcillo 680 ☎ 52/213-793. **Ovalle** ✉ Maestranza 443 ☎ 53/626-707. **La Serena** ✉ Av. El Santo and Amunátegui ☎ 51/224-573. **Vallenar** ✉ Av. Matta and Prat.

CAR RENTAL

There are car-rental agencies in La Serena and Copiapó at the airport and in the city, and most hotels will help you arrange for a rental.

🚗 Agencies **Avis** ✉ Rómulo Peña 102, Copiapó ☎ 52/213-966 ✉ Av. Francisco de Aguirre 68, La Serena ☎ 51/227-171. **Budget** ✉ Ramón Freire 466, Copiapó ☎ 52/218-802 ✉ Balmaceda 3850, La Serena ☎ 51/296-879. **Hertz** ✉ Copayapu 173, Copiapó ☎ 52/213-522 ✉ Av. Francisco de Aguirre 225, La Serena ☎ 51/226-171.

CAR TRAVEL

Because of the distances between cities, a car is the best way to truly see El Norte Chico. Many national parks can be visited only by car, preferably a four-wheel-drive vehicle.

Driving can be a little hectic in Copiapó and La Serena, where drivers don't always seem to observe the rules of the road. But once you get out on the open road, driving is considerably easier. Ruta 5, more familiarly known as the Pan-American Highway, bisects all of northern Chile. Ruta 41 snakes along from La Serena through the Elqui Valley to Vicuña. Ruta D485 will take you to Pisco Elqui. Ruta 31 takes you inland from Copiapó.

FESTIVALS & SEASONAL EVENTS

Every town in El Norte Chico celebrates various annual events, such as the days honoring certain patron saints. One fiesta that you should not miss is Andacollo's Fiesta Grande de La Virgen, in which some 150,000 devout pilgrims converge on the small town to celebrate its miraculous statue of the Virgen de Andacollo (December 23–26). Also in Andacollo, the more subdued Fiesta Chica takes place the first Sunday of October.

HEALTH

Altitude sickness—which is marked by difficulty breathing, dizziness, headaches, and nausea—is a danger for visitors to the high elevations of the antiplano. The best way to ward off altitude sickness is to take things slowly. Spend a day or two acclimatizing before undergoing any physical exertion. When hiking or climbing, rest often and drink as much water as possible. If symptoms continue, return to a lower altitude.

The tap water in the major cities and even most smaller communities is drinkable, though quite hard. In general, the water is safer on the coast than in some towns farther inland. To be on the safe side, stick to bottled water.

MAIL & SHIPPING

Although most cities in El Norte Chico have a post office, you'll often encounter long lines that move at a snail's pace. Your best bet is to ask your hotel to post a letter for you. But don't expect your letter to reach its destination quickly. Mail headed out of the country can often take weeks.
🏢 Post Offices **Copiapó** ✉ Los Carreras 691. **Ovalle** ✉ Plaza de Armas. **La Serena** ✉ Prat and Matta. **Vallenar** ✉ Plaza O'Higgins.

SAFETY

El Norte Chico is generally a safe area, with very little violent crime. Nevertheless, you should exercise the same precautions you'd use anywhere else. Women traveling alone should be careful, especially at night. It's best to travel in pairs or in groups.

TAXIS

Taxis are the most efficient way to get around any city in El Norte Chico. They're easy to hail on the streets, but late at night you might want to ask someone at a hotel or restaurant to call one for you. Taxis often function as *colectivos,* meaning they will pick up anybody going in the same direction. The driver will adjust the price accordingly. Almost no taxis have meters, but many have the price posted on the windshield. Make sure you establish the price before getting inside. Prices range from 700–3,500 pesos, depending on the distance traveled and whether the taxi is a colectivo. Prices rise an average of 20% at night. Taxi drivers often will rent out their services for the day for a flat fee.

TELEPHONES

There are several different telephone companies in El Norte Chico, and each has its own public telephones. Calling cards for each company can be purchased in many shops and newsstands. Much easier than calling from the street is to call from one of the many Entel or CTC offices in every city. Here you can dial direct or collect to anywhere in the world.

TOURS

El Norte Chico has travel agencies in most major cities, as well as in some of the smaller ones. Shop around to make sure that you are getting the best itinerary and the best price. In La Serena check out Talinay and Diaguitas Tour for tours to national parks and the interior. In

Copiapó you can arrange trips to the antiplano through Turismo Atacama and Cobre Tour. Ovalle Tour runs trips in the Ovalle area.

🏳 Tour Operators **Cobre Tour** ✉ O'Higgins 640, Copiapó ☎ 52/211-072. **Diaguitas
Tour** ✉ Matta 510, La Serena ☎ 51/214-129. **Ovalle Tour** ✉ Libertad 456, Ovalle
☎ 53/626-696. **Talinay** ✉ Prat 470, La Serena ☎ 51/218-658. **Turismo Atacama**
✉ Carreras 716, Copiapó ☎ 52/212-712.

VISITOR INFORMATION

Every major city in El Norte Chico has an office run by Sernatur, the
Chilean tourism agency. The offices provide informative brochures of
the region and other assistance for travelers. The staff often speaks
some English.

CONAF—the Corporacíon Nacional Forestal de Chile—maintains
Chile's national parks and forests, and can provide information on El
Norte Chico's more remote regions.

🏳 Tourist Information **CONAF** ☎ 56/390-000 🌐 www.conaf.cl. **Copiapó** ✉ Los Carrera 691 ☎ 52/231-510. **La Serena** ✉ Matta 461 ☎ 51/225-199. **Vallenar** ✉ Plaza de
Armas ☎ 51/619-215.

EL NORTE GRANDE

4

FODOR'S CHOICE

Atacama Desert

Casino Español, Spanish restaurant in Iquique

Cerros Pintados, geoglyphs in the Pampa del Tamarugal

Lodge Andino Terrantai, San Pedro de Atacama

Museo Arqueológico de San Miguel de Azapa, Arica

Museo Arqueológico G. Le Paige, San Pedro de Atacama

HIGHLY RECOMMENDED

ESTAURANTS · Café Adobe, San Pedro de Atacama

Restaurant Arriero, Antofagasta

Restaurant La Picada de Don Gato, Pisagua

Taberna Barracuda, Iquique

HOTELS · Hotel Antofagasta, Antofagasta

Hotel Arica, Arica

Hotel Atenas, Iquique

Hotel El Mirador, Calama

Hotel Explora, San Pedro de Atacama

Hotel los Cardenales, Mamiña

Hotel los Emelios, Pica

SIGHTS · Chacabuco, nitrate-era ghost town

Laguna Miscanti, lake near San Pedro de Atacama

Palacio Astoreca, mansion in Iquique

Parque Nacional Lauca

Reserva Nacional Las Vicuñas

Salar de Atacama, salt flat near San Pedro de Atacama

San Pedro de Atacama, tourist base in Atacama Desert

Valle de la Luna, barren valley near San Pedro

By Gregory
Benchwick

A LAND OF ROCK AND EARTH, terrifying in its austerity and vastness, El Norte Grande is one of the world's most desolate regions. Spanning some 1,930 km (1,200 mi), Chile's Great North stretches from the Río Copiapó to the borders of Peru and Bolivia. Here you will find the Atacama Desert, the driest place on earth—so dry that in many parts no rain has ever been recorded.

Yet people have inhabited this desolate land since time immemorial, and indeed the heart of El Norte Grande lies not in its geography but in its people. The indigenous Chinchorro people eked out a meager living from the sea more than 8,000 years ago, leaving behind the magnificent Chinchorro mummies, the oldest in the world. High in the Andes, the Atacameño tribes traded livestock with the Tijuanacota and the Inca. Many of these people still cling to their way of life, though much of their culture was lost during the colonial period.

Although the Spanish first invaded the region in the 16th century, El Norte Grande was largely ignored by Europeans until the 1800s, when huge deposits of nitrates were found in the Atacama region. The "white gold" brought boom times to towns like Pisagua, Iquique, and Antofagasta. Because most of the mineral-rich region lay beyond its northern border, Chile declared war on neighboring Peru and Bolivia in 1878. Chile won the five-year battle and annexed the land north of Antofagasta, a continuing source of national pride for most Chileans. With the invention of synthetic nitrates, the market for these fertilizers dried up and the nitrate barons abandoned their opulent mansions and returned to Santiago. El Norte Grande was once again left on its own.

What you'll see today is a land of both growth and decay. The glory days of the nitrate era are gone, but copper has stepped in to help fill that gap (the world's largest open-pit copper mine is here). El Norte Grande is still a land of opportunity for fortune-seekers, as well as for tourists looking for a less-traveled corner of the world. It is a place of beauty and dynamic isolation, a place where the past touches the present in a troubled yet majestic embrace.

Exploring El Norte Grande

Only if you enjoy the solitude and desolation of the desert should you venture into El Norte Grande. On rare occasions only will you see a swath of green cutting through the empty landscape. The driest desert in the world, the Atacama is barren until it explodes in a riot of color known as *el desierto florido*. The flowering desert takes place every four or five years when unusual amounts of rain awaken dormant bulbs.

Don't worry if you're not lucky enough to see the flowering desert while you're here: there are more mysteries to behold in the desert, along the barren coastline, and among the peaks of the world's longest mountain chain. The *altiplano*, or high plains, rests between two giant branches of the Andes and houses such natural marvels as crystalline salt flats, geysers, and volcanoes. You'll also spot flocks of flamingos and such mammals as the vicuña, a cousin to the llama.

The best bases for exploration of El Norte Grande are San Pedro de Atacama, Iquique, and Arica. San Pedro is close to some of the most breathtaking scenery of the region, and it's within a day's reach of the coastal town of Iquique. Iquique is the best place to stay if you want to visit the the Gigante de Atacama and the nearby hot springs at Pica and Mamiña. From Arica you can head inland to explore the high plains or stay close to the sea, taking in the Chinchorro mummies.

Numbers in the text correspond to numbers in the margin and on the El Norte Grande map.

If you have 5 days

You'll have to hustle to see much of El Norte Grande in less than a week. Start off by spending at least two days in ◧ **San Pedro de Atacama** ❽ ☞, visiting the incredible sights such as the bizarre moonscape of the Valle de la Luna and the desolate salt flats of the Salar de Atacama. On the third day, soak in the hot springs in the tiny town of **Pica** ⓭. Stay in the nearby city of ◧ **Iquique** ⓫. The next day head to the nitrate ghost town of Humberstone. On your last day, take a side trip to the **Gigante de Atacama** ⓰, the world's largest geoglyph.

If you have 7 days

Seven days will allow you to visit El Norte Grande at a more relaxed pace. Follow the five-day itinerary above. On the sixth day cruise up to ◧ **Arica** ⓭, the coastal town that bills itself as the "land of eternal spring." Be sure to visit the Museo Arqueológico de San Miguel de Azapa to see the Chinchorro mummies. On your last day, journey to the altiplano, taking in the flamingos at **Parque Nacional Lauca** ⓴ or the vicuñas, llamas, and alpacas of **Reserva Nacional Las Vicuñas** ㉑.

About the Restaurants

The food of El Norte Grande is simple but quite good. Along the coast you can enjoy fresh seafood and shellfish, including *merluza* (hake), *corvina* (sea bass), *ostiones* (oysters), and *machas* (similar to razor clams but unique to Chile), to name just a few. Ceviche (a traditional Peruvian dish made with marinated fish) is also available in much of El Norte Grande, but make sure the fish is fresh. Fish may be ordered *a la plancha* (grilled in butter and lemon) or accompanied by a sauce such as *salsa margarita* (a butter-based sauce comprising almost every shellfish imaginable). As you enter the interior region you'll come across heartier meals such as *cazuela de vacuno* (beef stew served with corn on the cob and vegetables) and *chuleta con arroz* (beef with rice). More heavily touristed areas, such as San Pedro de Atacama, also serve international fare.

People in the north generally eat a heavy lunch at around 2 PM that can last two hours, followed by a light dinner around 10 PM. Reservations are seldom needed, except in the poshest of places. Leave a 10% tip if you enjoyed the service.

About the Hotels

Lodging in El Norte Grande is relatively inexpensive. Hotels in the larger cities provide all the amenities you might expect from similar establishments back home, such as business centers, laundry service, pools, cable television, and minibars. However, many accommodations that bill themselves as "luxury" hotels haven't been remodeled or painted in years. Ask to look at a room before deciding. Few small towns have hotels, so you will have to make do with guest houses with extremely basic rooms and shared bathrooms.

WHAT IT COSTS In pesos (in thousands)				
$$$$	**$$$**	**$$**	**$**	**¢**
RESTAURANTS over 11	8–11	5–8	2.5–5	under 2.5
HOTELS over 105	75–105	45–75	15–45	under 15

Restaurant prices are for a main course at dinner. Hotel prices are for a double room in high season, excluding tax.

Timing

In the height of the Chilean summer, January and February, droves of Chileans and Argentines mob El Norte Grande's beaches. Although this is a fun time to visit, prices go up and finding a hotel can be difficult. Book your room a month or more in advance. The high season tapers off in March, an excellent time to visit if you're looking for a bit more tranquility. If you plan to visit the altiplano, bring the right clothing. Winter can be very cold, and summer sees a fair amount of rain.

THE NITRATE PAMPA

The vast *pampa salitrera* is an atmospheric introduction to Chile's Great North. Between 1890 and 1925 this region was the site of more than 80 *oficinas de salitre*, or nitrate plants. The invention of synthetic nitrates spelled the end for all but a few. Crumbling nitrate works lay stagnant in the dry desert air, some disintegrating into dust, others remaining a fascinating testament to the white gold that for a time made this one of Chile's richest regions.

Antofagasta

❶ *565 km (350 mi) north of Copiapó.*

Antofagasta is the most important—and the richest—city in El Norte Grande. It was part of Bolivia until 1879, when it was annexed by Chile in the War of the Pacific. The port town became an economic powerhouse during the nitrate boom. With the rapid decline of nitrate production, copper mining stepped in to keep the city's coffers filled.

Most travelers end up spending a night in Antofagasta on their way to the more interesting destinations like San Pedro de Atacama, Iquique, and Arica, but a few sights here are worth a look. Around two in the afternoon the city shuts down most of the streets in the center of town, making for pleasant afternoon shopping and strolling. High above Plaza Colón is the **Torre Reloj,** the clock tower whose face is a replica of London's Big Ben. It was erected by British residents in 1910.

The historic customs house, the town's oldest building, dates from 1866. Housed inside is the **Museo Regional de Antofagasta,** which displays clothing and other bric-a-brac from the nitrate era. ✉ *Bolívar 1888* ☎ *55/227–016* 💰 *600 pesos* 🕐 *Tues.–Sat. 10–1 and 3:30–6:30, Sun. 11–2.*

Where to Stay & Eat

$$–$$$ ✕ **Club de Yates.** This seafood restaurant with nice views of the port caters to yachting types, which may explain why the prices are a bit higher than at other restaurants in the area. The food is quite good, especially the *ostiones a la parmesana* (oysters with Parmesan cheese). The maritime theme is taken to the extreme—the plates, curtains, tablecloths, and every decoration imaginable come in the mandatory navy blue. The service is excellent. ✉ *Balmaceda 2705* ☎ *55/263–942* 🍽 *Reservations essential* ▤ *AE, DC, MC, V.*

4

Beaches

El Norte Grande has some of Chile's best beaches, and during the summer months of January and February they are packed with vacationing South Americans. The stretches of shoreline near Arica and Iquique are pristine, while those around Antofagasta are, for the most part, dirty and overcrowded. Though the Chilean government has done much to clean up polluted waters, many of El Norte Grande's beaches are not safe for swimming. Those with pollution or dangerous currents are marked by large signs saying NO APTA PARA BANARSE (not suitable for swimming). Many locals, however, ignore the warnings.

Shopping

The best places to shop in El Norte Grande are the local *mercados* (markets) and *ferias artesenales* (artisan fairs), where you'll find handmade jewelry and leather goods. Traditional Andean clothing and textiles can be purchased in most cities, but tend to be more authentic farther off the beaten path. It is illegal to export antiques from Chile, so the textiles are never more than 20 years old, and newer ones are often mass-produced in Peru. Though bargaining is acceptable, it is less common than in other parts of South America.

★ **$–$$** ✕ **Restaurant Arriero.** Serving up traditional dishes from Spain's Basque country, Arriero is the place to go for good barbecued meats. The restaurant is in a pleasant Pyrenees-style inn decorated with traditional cured hams hanging from the walls. The restaurant's owners play jazz on the piano almost every evening. ⊠ *Condell 2644* ☎ *55/264–371* ▤ *AE, DC, MC, V.*

$ ✕ **Don Pollo.** This rotisserie restaurant prepares some of the best chicken in Chile—a good thing, because it's the only item on the menu. The thatched-roof terrace is a great place to kick back after a long day of sightseeing. ⊠ *Ossa 2594* ☎ *no phone* ▤ *No credit cards.*

★ **$$** ▥ **Hotel Antofagasta.** Part of the deluxe Panamericana Hoteles chain, this high-rise on the ocean comes with all the first-class luxuries, from an elegant bar with a grand piano to a lovely kidney-shape pool. The rooms are comfortably furnished, and some have ocean views. A semiprivate beach is just steps from the hotel's back door. ⊠ *Balmaceda 2575* ☎ *55/228–811* ☎ *55/268–415* ⊕ *www.hotelantofagasta.cl* ⤻ *145 rooms, 18 suites △ Restaurant, room service, minibars, cable TV, pool, hair salon, health club, billiards, bar, shop, laundry service, business services, meeting rooms* ▤ *AE, DC, MC, V* ✵ *BP.*

$ ▥ **Marsal Hotel.** This modern and clean hotel faces busy Calle Arturo Prat, so be sure to ask for one of the pleasant rooms in the back. The service here is quite friendly—the staff goes out of its way to recommend restaurants and arrange excursions. ⊠ *Arturo Prat 867* ☎☎ *55/268–063* ⤻ *18 rooms △ Minibars, cable TV, laundry service, business services, meeting rooms; no a/c* ▤ *AE, DC, MC, V* ✵ *CP.*

Nightlife & the Arts

Nightlife in El Norte Grande often means heading to the *schoperias*, beer stands where the almost entirely male clientele downs *schops* (draft beers) served by scantily clad waitresses. The drinking generally continues until everyone is reeling drunk. If this is your idea of fun, check out the myriad schoperias in the center of town around the Plaza Colón.

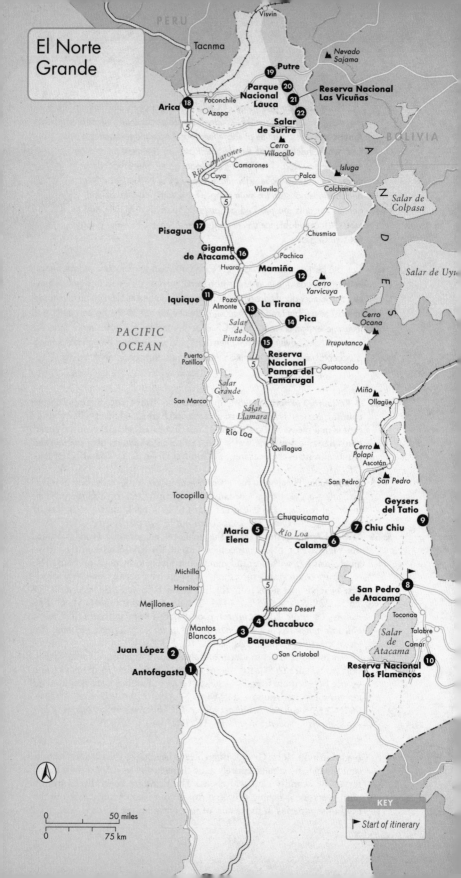

If you're not quite ready for the schoperia experience (and for many these are not the most pleasant places to spend an evening), don't worry: there are also a few bars where you can have a quiet drink. With its swinging saloon-style doors and a great waitstaff donning cowboy hats and blue jeans, the **Country Pub** (✉ Salvador Reyes 1025 ☎ 55/371–751) is lots of fun. The music doesn't go country, however, staying instead on the modern side of pop. The friendly, funky **Nueva Raices** (✉ Condell 3033 ☎ no phone) is steeped in northern Chilean culture. Ask the bartender to show you how to play *cacho*, a dice game popular with locals. Weekends the bar hosts live music. Antofagasta's elite head to **Wally's Pub** (✉ Antonino Toro 982 ☎ 55/223–697), an American-style grill with American-style prices.

Shopping

On the corner of Manuel A. Matta and Maipú you'll find the **Mercado Central**, a fruit and vegetable market with blue and yellow walls. Behind the market is the **Plaza del Mercado,** where artisans sell handmade jewelry and healing crystals, and where the occasional outdoor performance takes place.

Juan López

② *38 km (24 mi) north of Antofagasta.*

Those turned off by the hustle and bustle of Antofagasta will likely be charmed by Juan López, a hodgepodge of pastel-color fishing shacks and a picturesque *caleta* (wharf). In high season, January and February, the beaches are crowded and dirty. The rest of the year you may have the white, silken sand to yourself.

On the coast about 13 km (8 mi) south of Juan López lies **La Portada,** an offshore volcanic rock that the sea has carved into an arch. It's one of the most photographed natural sights in the country.

Where to Stay & Eat

$ ✕ **Restaurant Vitoco.** This restaurant, decorated with native textiles, serves a fixed meal of chicken or grilled fish. The food is good and the kitchen is spotless. ✉ *Manzana 8* ☎ *55/383–071* ▭ *No credit cards.*

¢ ⌑ **Hosteria Sandokan.** An airy garden complete with chirping caged birds surrounds the nicest place to stay in Juan López. Hosteria Sandokan has basic but clean rooms with shared baths. The hotel's terrace restaurant, which serves excellent seafood, affords great views of the pelicans going about their business. ✉ *Fernando Bull s/n* ☎ *55/223–302* ⇆ *6 rooms with shared bath* ⌂ *Restaurant; no a/c, no room phones, no room TVs* ▭ *No credit cards.*

Beaches

People come to Juan López for the beaches, and there are plenty from which to choose, both around town and south of town, where there are several larger beaches easily reached by car. The most popular beach is **Balneario Juan López,** a small strip of white sand near the center of town. Picturesque **Playa Acapulco** is in a small cove north of Balneario Juan López. **Playa Rinconada,** about 5 km (3 mi) south of Juan López, is lauded by locals for its warm water.

Baquedano

③ *72 km (45 mi) northeast of Antofagasta.*

Once an important railway transfer station, Baquedano today sees only a fraction of the freight that passed through during its heyday. With the exception of an open-air railroad museum that hints at the village's past importance, there are few reasons to linger here. The **Museo Ferroviario** is a testament to the greatness of the nitrate era. Old locomotives sit silently, waiting for the next boom. Hop aboard one of these paralyzed monsters and relive the days when they roared across the barren pampa. ⊠ *South of the current depot* ☎ *no phone* ✉ *Free* ☉ *Daily 8–12:30 and 2–7.*

Chacabuco

★ ❹ *26 km (16 mi) northeast of Baquedano.*

In this region locals refer to as the pampa salitrera there were some 80 nitrate plants in operation between 1890 and 1925. Many of the plants, as well as the company towns that housed their workers, still survive. A mysterious dot on the desert landscape, the ghost town of Chacabuco is a decidedly eerie place. More than 7,000 employees and their families lived here when the Oficina Chacabuco was in operation between 1922 and 1944. Today you'll find tiny houses, their tin roofs flapping in the wind and their walls collapsing. You can wander through many of the abandoned buildings and tour a museum with photographs of the town.

Chacabuco did not remain closed forever. During the first years of Augusto Pinochet's military regime, it was used as a concentration camp for political dissidents. The artwork of prisoners still adorns many of the walls. Do not walk around the town's exterior, as land mines from this era are still buried here. ⊠ *26 km (16 mi) northeast of Baquedano on the Pan-American Hwy.* ☎ *no phone* ✉ *1,000 pesos* ☉ *Daily 7 AM–8 PM.*

María Elena

❺ *148 km (92 mi) north of Baquedano.*

Maria Elena, founded by a British company in 1926, is a dusty place that warrants a visit if you want to see a functioning nitrate town. It's home to the employees of the region's last two nitrate plants. The 8,000 people who live in María Elena are proud of their history—nearly every house has a picture of the town hanging inside.

The tiny but informative **Museo Arqueológico,** on the town's run-down main plaza, houses many artifacts from the nitrate boom as well as a few from the pre-Columbian era. ⊠ *Av. Ignacio Carrera Pinto* ☎ *55/639–506* ✉ *600 pesos* ☉ *Daily 10–1 and 3–8.*

Where to Stay

¢ 🏠 **Residencial Chacance.** If you need lodging in Maria Elena, this is the best choice by far. The inn has basic rooms with shared baths. There's also a pleasant, albeit neglected, garden. ⊠ *Claudio Vicuña 437* ☎ *55/639–524* ➦ *10 rooms with shared bath* ⚭ *No a/c, no room phones, no room TVs* 🗖 *No credit cards.*

Calama

❻ *141 km (87 mi) northeast of Baquedano.*

The discovery of vast deposits of copper in the area turned Calama into the quintessential mining town, and therein lies its interest. People from the length of Chile flock to this dusty spot on the map in hopes of striking it rich. A modern-day version of the boomtowns of the 19th-century American West, Calama is rough around the edges, but it does possess a certain energy.

Founded as a *tambo*, or resting place, at the crossing of two Inca trails, Calama still serves as a stopover for people headed elsewhere. Most people traveling to San Pedro de Atacama end up spending the night here. But the town does have a few attractions of its own.

The gleaming copper roof of **Catedral San Juan Bautista** (⊠ Calle Ramírez and Av. Granaderos), on Plaza 23 de Marzo, testifies to the importance of mining in this region.

The **Museo Arqueológico y Etnológico,** a natural history museum in the well-manicured Parque El Loa, depends heavily on dioramas to explain the region's pre-Columbian past. Nearby is a replica of the quaint church in neighboring Chiu Chiu. ⊠ *Parque El Loa, south of town on Av. O'Higgins* ☎ *55/340–112* 💲 *600 pesos* ☉ *Tues.–Sun. 10–1 and 3–7:30.*

One of the world's largest open-pit mines, **Chiquicamata** is the lifeblood of Chile's copper industry. Heavy machinery roars in the bottom of the pit, producing 600,000 metric tons of copper yearly. Chiquicamata's immense size—4 km (2½ mi) long and 3 km (2 mi) wide—is the result of nearly a century of continuous mining. Experts say the mine will continue to yield copper for the next 45 years. There is a small museum at the mine's entrance where you can get a close-up view of the machinery used to make such big holes. Tours are in Spanish, though your guide may speak some English. ⊠ *16 km (10 mi) north of Calama* ☎ *55/322–316* 💲 *1,000 pesos* ☉ *Guided tours begin at 9* AM.

Where to Stay & Eat

$–$$ ✕ **Las Brasas de Juan Luis.** This restaurant with a pleasant country atmosphere is known around the region for its delicious *parrilladas* (barbecued meats). Try a mixed grill, which includes a variety of cuts. ⊠ *Balmaceda 1972* ☎ *55/344–366* ⚵ *Reservations essential* 🖃 *AE, DC, MC, V* ☉ *No dinner Sun.*

$–$$ ✕ **Plaza Restaurant.** Excellent seafood, such as the merluza con salsa margarita, makes this central restaurant a good choice. The grilled meat is also tasty. The atmosphere, though tasteful, is a bit antiseptic. ⊠ *Abaroa 1859* ☎ *55/362–631* 🖃 *No credit cards.*

$$$ 🏨 **Park Hotel Calama.** It's easy to see why international mining consultants frequent this top-notch hotel. The rooms have giant beds made up with luxurious linens, and the steaming showers feel great after a day of exploring the surrounding desert. A pool, a lovely garden, and an excellent restaurant serving international cuisine round out the hotel's attractions. ⊠ *Camino Aeropuerto 1392* ☎ *55/319–900* 🖷 *55/319–901* 🌐 *www.parkplaza.cl* ⤶ *102 rooms* ⚭ *Restaurant, room service, minibars, in-room safes, cable TV, tennis court, pool, health club, bar, piano, laundry service, business services, meeting rooms* 🖃*AE, DC, MC, V* ⧖*BP.*

★ $ 🏨 **Hotel El Mirador.** This friendly bed-and-breakfast around the corner from Plaza 23 de Marzo is a charmer, with cheerful yellow rooms that are both clean and comfortable. A tasteful, antiques-filled salon leads to an enclosed courtyard where you can enjoy the sun while sipping a pisco sour. A Continental breakfast is served at a nearby Bavarian restaurant. ⊠ *Sotomayor 2064* ☎☎ *55/340–329* 🌐 *www.hotelmirador. cl* ⤶ *14 rooms* ⚭ *Cable TV, laundry service, Internet; no a/c, no room phones* 🖃 *AE, DC, MC, V* ⧖ *CP.*

Nightlife & the Arts

Calama is the land of the schoperia—locals say there are more schoperias than people. Come payday at the mine, these drinking halls fill up with beer-swilling workers. The schoperias near Plaza 23 de Marzo are less raucous. On weekends head to **Direccíon Obligada** (⊠ Granaderos 2663 ☎ 55/345–834), an upscale bar that attracts foreigners and locals alike. Pop and cumbia are played here at top volume, so bring your earplugs.

Cine Teatro Municipal (⊠ Ramírez 2034 ☎ 55/342–864) screens recent Hollywood movies. It also stages the occasional play or concert.

Shopping

Locals sell clothing and jewelry at the covered markets off the pedestrian mall of Calle Ramírez. There are also markets on Calle Vargas between Latorre and Vivar.

Chiu Chiu

7 *33 km (20 mi) northeast of Calama.*

In contrast to the nearby, sprawling industrial center of Calama, Chiu Chiu, in a lush valley near the Río Loa, is a vision of the region's agrarian past. Inhabitants still make their living growing carrots and other vegetables in this pastoral town. Across from Chiu Chiu's main square is the **Iglesia de Chiu Chiu.** Built in 1674, it's one of the oldest churches in the altiplano. A cactus-shingle roof tops the squat building's whitewashed adobe walls. No nails were used in its construction—rafters and beams are lashed together with leather straps. On October 4, things get lively when the 500 inhabitants congregate in the nearby central plaza to celebrate the town's patron saint.

San Pedro de Atacama

★ ▶ **8** *100 km (62 mi) southeast of Calama.*

The most popular tourist destination in El Norte Grande (and perhaps all of Chile), San Pedro de Atacama sits in the midst of some of the most Fodor'sChoice breathtaking scenery in the country—the heart of the **Atacama Desert.** A ★ string of towering volcanoes, some of which are still active, stands watch to the east. To the west is La Cordillera de Sal, a mountain range composed almost entirely of salt. Here you'll find such marvels as the Valle de la Luna (Valley of the Moon) and the Valle de la Muerte (Valley of Death), part of the Reserva Nacional los Flamencos. The desolate Salar de Atacama, Chile's largest salt flat, lies to the south. The number of attractions in the Atacama area does not end there: alpine lakes, steaming geysers, colonial villages, and ancient fortresses all lie within easy reach.

The area's history goes back to pre-Columbian times, when the Atacameño people scraped a meager living from the fertile delta of the San Pedro River. By 1450 the region had been conquered by the Incas, but their reign was cut short by the arrival of the Europeans. Spanish conquistador Pedro De Valdivia, who eventually seized control of the entire country, camped here in 1540 while waiting for reinforcements. By the 19th century San Pedro had become an important trading center and was a stop for llama trains on their way from the altiplano to the Pacific coast. During the nitrate era, San Pedro was the main resting place for cattle drives from Argentina.

With its narrow streets lined with whitewashed and mud-color adobe houses, San Pedro centers around a small Plaza de Armas teeming with artisans, tour operators, and others who make their living catering to tourists. The 1744 **Iglesia San Pedro,** to the west of the square, is one of the altiplano's largest churches. It was miraculously constructed without the use of a single nail—the builders used cactus sinews to tie the roof beams and door hinges. ⊠ *Padre Le Paige s/n* ☎ *no phone* ☉ *Daily 8–8.*

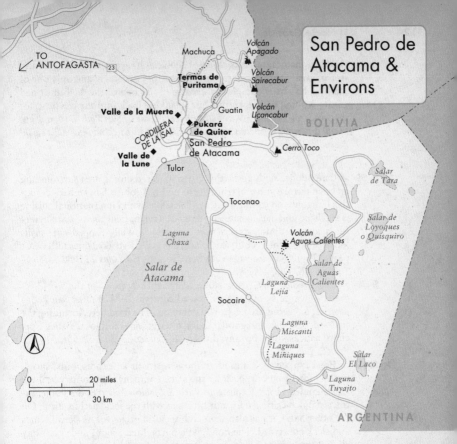

Fodor'sChoice ★ The **Museo Arqueológico Gustavo Le Paige** exhibits an awe-inspiring collection of artifacts from the region, including fine examples of textiles and ceramics. The museum traces the history of the area from pre-Columbian times through the Spanish colonization. The most impressive exhibit is the well-preserved, fetal-positioned Atacameño mummy with her swatch of twisted black hair. Most of the items on display were gathered by the founder, Jesuit missionary Gustavo Le Paige. ☒ *Calle Padre Le Paige and Paseo Artesenal* ☎ *55/851–002* ☒ *2,000 pesos* ☺ *Weekdays 9–noon and 2–6, weekends 10–noon and 2–6.*

need a break? Stop at **Café del Viaje** (☒ Tocopilla 359 ☎ 09/822–4787) for sweet, fresh juices and an excellent vegetarian fixed-menu lunch or dinner. The dining area is in a huge courtyard with chañar trees.

Just 3 km (2 mi) north of San Pedro lies the ancient fortress of **Pukara de Quitor.** This group of stone structures at the entrance to the Valle de Catarpe was built in the 12th century to protect the Atacameños from invading Incas. It wasn't the Incas but the Spanish who were the real threat, however. Spanish conquistador Pedro de Valdivia took the fortress by force in 1540. The crumbling buildings were carefully reconstructed in 1981 by the University of Antofagasta. ☒ *On the road to Valle Catarpe* ☎ *no phone* ☒ *1,200 pesos* ☺ *Daily 8–8.*

The archaeological site of **Tulor,** 9 km (6 mi) southwest of San Pedro, marks the remains of the oldest known civilization in the region. Built around 800 BC, the village of Tulor was home to the Linka Arti people, who lived in small mud huts resembling igloos. The site was only uncovered in the middle of the 20th century, when Jesuit missionary Gustavo Le Paige excavated it from a sand dune. Archaeologists hypothesize that the inhabitants left because of climatic changes and a possible sand storm. Little more about the village's history is known, and only one of the huts has been completely excavated. As one of the well-informed guides will tell you, even this hut is sinking back into the obscurity of the Atacama sand. ⊹ *9 km (6 mi) southwest of San Pedro, then 3 km (2 mi) down the road leading to the Valle de la Luna* ☎*no phone* 🖼*1,500 pesos* ☉ *Daily 8–8.*

Where to Stay & Eat

★ **$-$$** ✕ **Café Adobe.** With an earthy, lattice-covered dining area surrounding an open terrace and a blazing fire at night, Adobe is San Pedro's definitive hangout and its finest eatery. The Chilean and international cuisine is excellent, and the animated (at times downright frenetic) waitstaff makes for a unique dining experience. At night, a white-capped chef grills meat in the center courtyard. Try the grilled steaks, quesadillas, or pasta. There's an Internet café here, too. ✉ *Carcoles 211* ☎ *55/851–132* 🖃 *AE, DC, MC, V.*

$-$$ ✕ **Casa Piedra.** This rustic stone house affords views of the world-famous Atacama skies from its central courtyard. As at most San Pedro eateries, a blazing fire keeps you company. The food here, including the seafood, is simple and good, mixing international and local dishes. Specialty sauces spice up any dinner. ✉ *Caracoles 225* ☎ *55/851–271* 🖃 *AE, DC, MC, V.*

★ **$$$$** 🏨 **Hotel Explora.** Is it a modern monstrosity or an expressionist showpiece? Hotel Explora, built by the same company that constructed the much-lauded Hotel Explora in Parque Nacional Torres del Paine, attracted much criticism for not fitting in with the local architecture. On the other hand, it has also won architectural prizes for its skewed lines and sleek courtyard. The hotel, which has three-, four-, and seven-day all-inclusive stays—with tours, meals, and drinks included—delivers the best service and amenities of any lodging in northern Chile. ✉*Domingo Atienza s/n* ☎*55/851–110* 🖨*55/851–115* ⊕*www.explora. com* ⇆ *52 rooms* ⚘ *Restaurant, fans, in-room safes, 4 pools, massage, sauna, mountain bikes, horseback riding, bar, shop, baby-sitting, laundry service, Internet, meeting rooms, airport shuttle, free parking, nosmoking rooms; no a/c, no room phones, no room TVs* 🖃 *AE, DC, MC, V* ⍾ *All-inclusive.*

$$$ 🏨 **Lodge Andino Terrantai.** An architectural beauty with river-stone walls, the Terrantai has high-ceilinged rooms highlighted by beautiful tile floors and big beds piled with down comforters. Throw open the huge windows to let in the morning breeze. The candlelit restaurant, perfect for a romantic dinner, serves international fare. There's also a tiny, natural-rock plunge pool in the center. The hotel is just a block away from the Plaza de Armas. ✉ *Tocopilla 411* ☎ *55/851–140* 🖨 *55/851–037* ⊕ *www.adex.cl* ⇆ *16 rooms* ⚘ *Restaurant, room service, pool, laundry service; no a/c, no room TVs* 🖃 *AE, DC, MC, V* ⍾ *BP.*

FodorśChoice
★

$$ 🏨 **Hotel Altiplanico.** This boutique hotel just outside the center of San Pedro has the look and feel of an altiplano pueblo. A river-stone walkway leads you from room to room, each with its own private terrace. Muted whites decorate the guest chambers, making them quite welcoming. Some rooms have private watchtowers for stargazing. ✉ *Domingo Atienza 282* ☎ *55/851–212* ⊕ *www.altiplanico.cl* ⇆ *14 rooms, 2 with shared bath* ⚘ *Restaurant, pool, massage, laundry service, Internet, travel services; no a/c, no room phones, no room TVs* 🖃*AE, DC, MC, V* ⍾*BP.*

$$ 🏨 **Hotel Kimal.** The adobe-walled Hotel Kimal has comfortable rooms and a cheery central courtyard dotted with islands of desert shrubbery. The rooms are pleasantly airy, with skylights and reed ceilings. The excellent, small restaurant serves Chilean fare. The pool is ideal for cooling off after your desert exploration. ✉ *Domingo Atienza 452* ☎ *55/ 851–030* 🖨 *55/851–152* 🌐 *www.kimal.cl* ➪ *11 rooms* ⚙ *Restaurant, minibars, pool, shop, laundry service; no a/c, no room TVs* 🖃 *AE, DC, MC, V* 🍴 *BP.*

$ 🏨 **Hotel Tambillo.** A good budget alternative, Hotel Tambillo has simple, rather drab rooms along a long, outdoor walkway. There's also a restaurant. ✉ *Gustavo Le Paige 159* ☎☎ *55/851–078* ✉ *tambillo@sanpedrodeatacama.com* ➪ *15 rooms* ⚙ *Restaurant; no a/c, no room phones, no room TVs* 🖃 *No credit cards.*

Nightlife & the Arts

The bohemian side of San Pedro gets going after dinner and generally ends around 1 AM. Most of the bars are on Caracoles. At night there's seating around a bonfire in the courtyard of **Café Adobe** (✉ Caracoles 211 ☎ 55/851–132), which occasionally hosts live music. During the day the latticed roof around the edges protects you from the sun's rays. **Café Export** (✉ Caracoles and Toconao ☎ 55/851–547) is smaller and more intimate than the other bars in town. There's a small terrace out back. **La Estaka** (✉ Caracoles 259B ☎ 55/851–201) is a hippie bar with funky decor, including a sculpted dragon hanging on one of the walls. Reggae music rules, and the international food isn't half bad either.

Sports & the Outdoors

San Pedro is an outdoors-lover's dream. There are great places for biking, hiking, and horseback riding in every direction. Extreme-sports enthusiasts can try their hand at sand-boarding on the dunes of the Valle de la Muerte. Climbers can take on the nearby volcanoes. The only trouble is the crowds. At the Valle de la Luna, for example, you'll sometimes encounter a caravan of 20 or 30 tourists scurrying towards the top of the large sand dune to watch the sunset.

Whatever your sport, keep in mind that San Pedro lies at 2,400 m (7,900 ft). If you're not acclimated, you'll feel tired much sooner than you might expect. Also remember to slather on the sunscreen and drink plenty of water.

BIKING   An afternoon ride to the Valle de la Luna is unforgettable, as is a quick trip to the ruins of Tulor. You can also head to the Salar de Atacama. Bike rentals can be arranged at most hotels and tour agencies.

HIKING   There are hikes in all directions from San Pedro. Good hikes include trips through the Valle de la Muerte, as well as to the ruins of Pukara de Quitor. **Cosmo Andino Expediciones** (✉ Calle Caracoles s/n, San Pedro de Atacama ☎ 55/851–069 🌐 www.cosmoandino.cl) runs excellent treks with well-informed guides.

HORSEBACK   San Pedro has the feeling of a Wild West town, so why not hitch up your
RIDING   horse and head out on an adventure? Although the sun is quite intense during the middle of the day, sunset is a perfect time to visit Pukara de Quitor or Tulor. An overnight journey to the Salar de Atacama or the Valle de La Luna is a great way to see the region at a relaxed pace. **Herradura** (✉ Tocopilla s/n, San Pedro de Atacama ☎ 55/851–087) provides horses and guides.

Shopping

Just about the entire village of San Pedro is an open-air market. The **Feria Artesenal,** just off the Plaza de Armas, is bursting at the seams with artisan goods. Here, you can buy high-quality knits from the altiplano, such as sweaters and other woolen items. **Galeria Cultural de Pueblos Andinos** (✉ Caracoles s/n, east of town ☎ no phone) is an open-air market selling woolens and crafts. **Mallku** (✉ Caracoles s/n ☎ no phone) is a pleasant store carrying traditional altiplano textiles, some up to 20 years old. **Taller de Artesania Rayo de La Luna** (✉ Caracoles 378 ☏ 09/ 473–9018) sells jewelry made by local artisans.

Geysers del Tatio

❾ *95 km (59 mi) north of San Pedro.*

The world's highest geothermal field, the Geysers del Tatio are a breath-taking natural phenomenon. The sight of dozens of *fumaroles,* or geysers, throwing columns of steam into the air is unforgettable. A trip to El Tatio usually begins at 4 AM, on a guided tour, when San Pedro is still cold and dark (any of the tour agencies in San Pedro can arrange this trip). After a three-hour bus trip on a relentlessly bumpy road you reach the high plateau at about daybreak. The jets of steam are already shooting into the air as the sun slowly peaks over the adjacent cordillera. The rays of light illuminate the steam in a kaleidoscope of chartreuses, violets, reds, oranges, and blues. The vapor then silently falls onto the sulfur-stained crust of the geyser field. As the sun heats the cold, barren land, the force of the geysers gradually diminishes, allowing you to explore the mud pots and craters formed by the escaping steam. Be careful, though—the crust is thin in places and people have been badly burned falling into the boiling-hot water. On your way back to San Pedro, you may want to stop at the **Termas de Puritama** (✉ 5,000 pesos) hot springs. A hot soak may be just the thing to shake off that early morning chill.

Reserva Nacional los Flamencos

❿ *10 km (6 mi) south and east of San Pedro.*

Many of the most astounding sights in El Norte Grande lie within the boundaries of the protected Reserva Nacional los Flamencos. This sprawling national reserve to the south and east of San Pedro encompasses a wide variety of geographical features, including alpine lakes, salt flats, and volcanoes. You can get information about the park at the station run by CONAF, the Chilean forestry service. ✉ *CONAF station near Laguna Chaxa* ☏ *no phone* ✉ *2,000 pesos* ☉ *Daily 8:30–1 and 2:30–6:30.*

About 10 km (6 mi) south of San Pedro you arrive at the edge of the ★ **Salar de Atacama,** Chile's largest salt flat. The rugged crust measuring 3,000 square km (1,158 square mi) formed when salty water flowing down from the Andes evaporated in the stifling heat of the desert. Unlike other salt flats, which are chalkboard-flat surfaces of crystalline salt, the Salar de Atacama is a jumble of jagged rocks. **Laguna Chaxa,** in the middle of Salar de Atacama, is a very salty lagoon that is home to three of the world's four species of flamingos. The elegant pink and white birds are mirrored by the lake's glassy surface. Near Laguna Chaxa, beautiful plates of salt float on the calm surface of **Laguna Salada.**

It's possible to take a three- to five-day, four-wheel-drive excursion from San Pedro into Bolivia's massive and mysterious **Salar de Uyuni.** Beware: the accommodations—usually clapboard lodgings in small oasis towns—are rustic to say the least, but sailing along the world's largest salt flat, which is chalkboard flat, is a treat. Around the Salar de Uyuni are geysers, small Andean lagoons, and islands of cactus that sit in sharp contrast to the sea-like salt flat. The number of tour agencies in San Pedro can be a bit overwhelming: shop around, pick a company you feel comfortable with, ask questions, and make sure the company is willing to cater to your needs.

★ One of the most impressive sights in Reserva Nacional los Flamencos is the 4,350-m-high (14,270-ft-high) **Laguna Miscanti**, an awe-inspiring blue lake that merits a few hours of rest and repose. **Laguna Miñeques**, a smaller lake adjacent to Laguna Miscanti, is spectacular. Here you will find vicuña and huge flocks of flamingos.

★ Very few places in the world can compare to the **Valle de la Luna** (⊠ 14 km [9 mi] west of San Pedro). This surreal landscape of barren ridges, soaring cliffs, and pale valleys could be from a canvas by Salvador Dalí. Originally a small corner of a vast inland sea, the valley rose up with the Andes. The water slowly drained away, leaving deposits of salt and gypsum that were folded by shifting of the earth's crust and then worn away by wind and rain. It's best to visit Valle de la Luna in the late afternoon to take advantage of the incredible sunsets visible from atop the immense sand dune. Not far from the Valle de la Luna are the reddish rocks of the **Valle de la Muerte.** Jesuit missionary Gustavo Le Paige, the first archaeologist to explore this desolate area, found many human bones. He hypothesized that people may have come here to die.

IQUIQUE AREA

The waterside town of Iquique itself is rather dreary, but the area holds many sights that merit a visit. A stone's throw from Iquique, nitrate ghost towns like Humberstone sit in eternal silence. Farther inland you encounter the charming hot spring oases of Pica and Mamiña and the enigmatic Gigante de Atacama, the world's largest geoglyph.

Iquique

⑪ *390 km (242 mi) northwest of Calama.*

Iquique is the capital of Chile's northernmost region, but it wasn't always so important. For hundreds of years it was a tiny fishing community. After the arrival of the Spanish the village grew slowly, eventually becoming a shipping port. The population, however, never totaled more than 100. It was not until the great nitrate boom of the 19th century that Iquique became a major port. Many of those who grew rich on nitrate moved to the city and built opulent mansions, almost all of which still stand today. Many of the old mansions are badly in need of repair, however, giving the city a rather worn-down feeling. The boom went bust, and those who remained turned again to the sea to make a living. Today Iquique is the world's largest exporter of fish meal.

At the base of a coastal mountain range, Iquique is blessed with year-round good weather. This may explain why it's popular with vacationing Chilean families, who come for the long stretches of white beaches as well as the *zona franca*, or duty-free zone. Life in the city revolves around the **Plaza Prat**, where children ride bicycles along the sidewalks and adults chat on nearly every park bench. The 1877 **Torre Reloj**, with its gleaming white clock tower and Moorish arches, stands in the center of the plaza.

Leading out from Plaza Prat is **Calle Baquedano**, a pedestrian mall with wooden sidewalks. This is a great place for an afternoon stroll past some of Iquique's salitrera-era mansions, or a leisurely cappuccino in one of the many sidewalk cafés. An antique trolley runs the length of the mall.

Unlike most cities, Iquique does not have a cathedral on the main plaza. Here instead you'll find the sumptuous **Teatro Municipal**, built in 1890 as an opera house. The lovely statues on the Corinthian-columned facade represent the four seasons. If you're lucky you can catch a play or musical performance here. ⊠ *Plaza Prat* ☎ *57/411–292* ☒ *Tickets 1,500–5,000 pesos* ⊙ *Daily 8–7.*

★ For a tantalizing view into the opulence of the nitrate era, visit the Georgian-style **Palacio Astoreca**. This palace, built in 1903, include such highlights as the likeness of Dionysus, the Greek god of revelry; a giant billiards table; and a beautiful skylight over the central hall. An art and natural history museum on the upper level houses modern works by Chilean artists and such artifacts as pottery and textiles. ⊠ *O'Higgins 350* ☎ *57/425–600* ☒ *Free* ⊙ *Tues.–Fri. 10–1 and 4–7:30, Sat. 10–1:30, Sun. 11–2.*

Along the historic Calle Baquedano is the **Museo Regional**, a natural history museum of the region. It showcases pre-Columbian artifacts such as deformed skulls and arrowheads, as well as an eclectic collection from the region's nitrate heyday. ⊠ *Baquedano 951* ☎ *57/411–214* ☒ *Free* ⊙ *Mon.–Sat. 9:30–1 and 3–6:30.*

Inside **Museo Naval**, in the old customs house, are displays about the Battle of Iquique in 1879, when the Chileans claimed Iquique from their neighbors to the north. Here you can get a glimpse at what the soldiers wore during the war and at the antiquated English arms used by Chilean soldiers. ⊠ *Sotomayor and Anibal Pinto* ☎ *57/402–121* ☒ *Free* ⊙ *Weekdays 9:30–12:30 and 3–6.*

Where to Stay & Eat

$$–$$$ ✕ **Casino Español.** This venerable gentleman's club on Plaza Prat has been
Fodor'sChoice transformed into a palatial Spanish restaurant, with beautiful Moorish
★ architecture that calls to mind the Alhambra in Granada. The service is good, though rather fussy, and the food is extravagant in the traditional Andalucian style. The paella *Valenciana* is quite good. ⊠ *Plaza Prat 584* ☎ *57/423–284* ⚱ *Reservations essential* ▤ *AE, DC, MC, V.*

$$–$$$ ✕ **Restaurant Nautico Cavancha.** Located away from the center of the city, this seafood restaurant treats you to views of Playa Cavancha. It's very stylish, right down to the cloth napkins (a rarity in El Norte Grande). Try the paella for two, served by friendly bow-tied waiters. ⊠ *Los Rieles 110* ☎ *57/432–896* ⚱ *Reservations essential* ▤ *DC, MC, V.*

★ **$$** ✕ **Taberna Barracuda.** An immensely popular bar and grill, Taberna Barracuda serves everything from Spanish tapas to rib-eye steak. The wine list is good, making this an ideal place to sample some of Chile's labels. A general sense of joviality and merriment here harken to the decadent days of the nitrate boom. Antiques ranging from brass instruments to time-stained photos decorate the labyrinthine, salitrera-era house. ⊠ *Gorostiaga 601* ☎ *57/427–969* ⚱ *Reservations essential* ▤ *AE, DC, MC, V* ⊙ *Closed Sun. mid-June–early Sept.*

$–$$ ✕ **Boulevard.** Excellent seafood is served in a variety of ways at this intimate, candlelit restaurant. The cuisine is an interesting mélange of French and international recipes—try hake served in a creamy sauce or the *tagine,* a savory Moroccan stew. There's live music on weekends. ⊠ *Baquedano 790* ☎ *57/413–695* ⚱ *Reservations essential* ▤ *MC, V.*

$ ✕ **Restaurant Protectora.** A soaring molded ceiling and a huge chandelier overlook this elegant contemporary restaurant next to the Teatro Municipal. The international menu includes such succulent items as lamb cooked in mint sauce and merluza con salsa margarita. The service, though a bit doting, is top-notch. ⊠ *Thompson 207* ☎ *57/421–923* ▤ *AE, DC, MC, V.*

$$ ▥ **Sunfish.** On Playa Cavancha, Sunfish has very large, very modern rooms, many with views of the beach. Though the hotel lacks character, the royal blue exterior will certainly catch your eye. There's a small roof-top pool, but it's surrounded by a tacky artificial-grass terrace. ⊠ *Amunategui 1990* ☎ *57/419–000* ⚏ *57/419–001* ⊕ *www.sunfish.cl* ⬫ *45 rooms*

⚐ *Restaurant, in-room safes, minibars, cable TV, pool, bar, laundry service, business services, meeting rooms* ▭ *AE, DC, MC, V* ¶◎¶ *BP.*

$$ ⊞ **Terrado Suites.** A skyscraper at the southern end of Playa Cavancha, the Terrado is Iquique's most upscale hotel. A marble entryway chaperones you down to the comfortable lounge and restaurant area. Overstuffed sofas, Andean prints, and hardwood accents decorate the large suites, which have private balconies. The pool and underground sauna are a delight after a day in the desert. ⊠ *Los Rieles 126,* ☎ *57/437–878* ᕰ *57/437–755* ⊕ *www.terrado.cl* ⤸ *91 suites* ⚐ *2 restaurants, room service, in-room data ports, in-room safes, minibars, cable TV, 2 pools, gym, hot tub, massage, sauna, bar, baby-sitting, laundry service, business services, meeting rooms, airport shuttle, car rental; no a/c in some rooms* ▭ *AE, DC, MC, V* ¶◎¶ *BP.*

$–$$ ⊞ **Hotel Arturo Prat.** The only thing this luxury hotel in the heart of Iquique's historic district lacks is access to the ocean. To make up for this, it has a very pleasant roof-top pool area decorated with white umbrellas and navy-blue sails. The rooms are all comfortable and modern, though some look out onto the parking lot. Ask for one of the newer rooms, which are several steps above the rooms in the older section of the hotel. The Arturo faces the central square, and the restaurant, which serves good but somewhat uninspired fare, sits right on Plaza Prat. ⊠ *Anibal Pinto 695* ☎ *57/427–000* ᕰ *57/429–088* ⊕ *www. hotelarturoprat.cl* ⤸ *83 rooms, 9 suites* ⚐ *Restaurant, room service, in-room safes, minibars, cable TV, pool, exercise equipment, sauna, billiards, bar, laundry service, business services, meeting rooms; no a/c in some rooms* ▭ *AE, DC, MC, V* ¶◎¶ *BP.*

★ $ ⊞ **Hotel Atenas.** Housed in a venerable nitrate-era mansion on the beach, Hotel Atenas is truly a taste of the city's history. Antiques and wood furnishings fill most of the rooms. There are more modern rooms in the back, but these are not nearly as charming. The honeymoon suite has a giant tub where you can imagine the nitrate barons bathing in champagne. There's also a pleasant pool in the garden. ⊠ *Los Rieles 738* ☎ *57/431–100* ᕰ *57/431–100* ⊕ *www.iquiqueonline.cl/atenas* ⤸ *40 rooms* ⚐ *Restaurant, room service, fans, in-room safes, minibars, cable TV, pool, hot tub, laundry service, Internet; no a/c* ▭ *AE, DC, MC, V* ¶◎¶ *CP.*

$ ⊞ **Hotel Carlos Condell.** A beautiful nitrate-era mansion complete with wrought-iron balconies and a rickety elevator, this restored landmark is a decent budget alternative. This friendly B&B has lots of character, from the model sailboats in the reception area to the flower-print comforters in the rooms. The rooms are quite dark, however, and can be a bit oppressive until you head out onto the terraces. It's clean, although the baths are a bit small and run-down. ⊠ *Baquedano 964* ☎ *57/313–028* ᕰ *57/313–027* ✉ *j-aragon@entelchile.net* ⤸ *29 rooms* ⚐ *Fans, minibars, cable TV, laundry service; no a/c* ▭ *No credit cards* ¶◎¶ *CP.*

Nightlife & the Arts

Iquique really gets going after dark. Young vacationers stay out all night and then spend the next day lazing around on the beach.

BARS Bars, most of which feature folk and jazz performances, get crowded around midnight. **Bar Sovia** (⊠ Tarapaca 173 ☎ 57/517–015), perhaps the North's only microbrewery, is a relaxed place for a frothy brew. For sunset drinks and excellent empanadas head to **Choza Bambu** (⊠ Arturo Prat s/n, Playa Cavancha ☎ 57/519–002). One of the city's most popular bars is **Circus Pub** (⊠ Thompson 123 ☎ 57/316–827), where the walls are decorated with cheesy art deco murals. It has live music, a very friendly staff, and—in keeping with its name—occasional trapeze shows.

At about 2 AM the beachfront discos start filling with a young, energetic crowd. Check out the dance clubs along Playa Brava and just south of town. **Kamikaze** (✉ Bajo Molle, Km 7 ☎ no phone), part of a popular chain of discos, is jam-packed on weekends with young people dancing to salsa music. **Timber House** (✉ Bolívar 553 ☎ 57/422–538) has a disco upstairs and an Old West–style saloon downstairs.

Beaches

Just south of the city center on Avenida Balmaceda is **Playa Cavancha**, a long stretch of white, sandy beach that's great for families. You can stroll along the boardwalk and pet the llamas and alpacas at the small zoo. Because it's so close to town, the beach is often crowded. If you crave solitude, follow the coast south of Playa Cavancha for about 3 km (2 mi) on Avenida Balmaceda to reach **Playa Brava**, a pretty beach that's often deserted. The currents here are quite strong, so swimming is not recommended. **Playa Blanca**, 13 km (8 mi) south of the city center on Avenida Balmaceda, is a sandy spot that you can often have all to yourself.

Shopping

Many Chileans come to Iquique with one thing on their minds—shopping. About 3 km (2 mi) north of the city center is the **Zona Franca**—known to locals as the Zofri—the only duty-zone in the country's northern tip. This big, unattractive mall is stocked with cheap cigarettes, alcohol, and electronic goods. Remember that large purchases, such as personal computers, are taxable upon leaving the country. ✉ *Av. Salitrera Victoria* ☎ *57/515–100* ☺ *Mon. 4–9, Tues.–Fri. 10–9, Sat. 10–2 and 5–9.*

en route One of the last nitrate plants in the region, **Humberstone** closed in 1960 after operating for nearly 200 years. Now it's a ghost town where ancient machines creak and groan in the wind. You can wander through the central square and along the streets of the company town, where almost all of the original buildings survive. The theater, with its rows of empty seats, is particularly eerie. ✉ *45 km (28 mi) east of Iquique on the Pan-American Hwy.* ☎ *57/324–642* ✑ *1,000 pesos* ☺ *Daily 9–5.*

Mamiña

 125 km (78 mi) east of Iquique.

An oasis cut from the brown desert, the tiny village of Mamiña has hundreds of hot springs. Renowned throughout Chile for their curative powers, these springs draw people from around the region. Every hotel in the town has the thermal water pumped into its rooms, so you can enjoy a soak in the privacy of your own *tina*, or bathtub. The valley also has several public pools fed by thermal springs. The town itself is perched on a rocky cliff above the terraced green valley where locals grow alfalfa.

If you'd like to wallow in the mud, try a soothing mud bath in a secluded setting at **Barros El Chino** (✉ near the Mamiña bottler ☎ no phone ✑ 1,000 pesos). After your bath you can bake in the sun on one of the drying racks. Leap into one of the plunge pools to wash the stinky brown stuff off your skin. **Baños Ipla** (✉ near the Mamiña bottler ☎ no phone ✑ 1,000 pesos) lets you soak in large public tinas. A fountain near the Baños Ipla called the **Vertiente del Radium**, with slightly radioactive spring water, is said to cure every type of eye malady.

The simple, charming **Iglesia Nuestra Señora del Rosario** in the central plaza dates to 1632. The church's twin bell towers are unique in Andean Chile. A garish electric sign mars the front of the building.

A two-hour hike from Mamiña will bring you to **Pukara del Cerro Inca,** a great place to watch the sunset. Here you'll find interesting petroglyphs left by the Incas and an excellent view of the valley. To find it, head west on the trail a block west of the bottler.

Where to Stay & Eat

★ **$$** ✕▦ **Hotel los Cardenales.** Two highlights of this hotel are its lovely garden and pool covered to protect you from the fierce rays of the sun. All rooms have private tubs that fill with spring water—most tubs are on the small side, but the one in the honeymoon suite is big enough for two. At the pleasant restaurant terrace you can enjoy views of the valley. A fixed menu includes a soup or cazuela, and grilled meat. ⊠ *Camino Barros El Chino s/n* ☎ *09/553–0934* ☞ *10 rooms* ♨ *Restaurant, pool; no a/c, no room phones, no TV in some rooms* ⊟ *No credit cards* ❢❢ *All-inclusive.*

$$ ✕▦ **Hotel Refugio del Salitre.** You reach the Hotel Refugio del Salitre, on the hill in the northern part of the valley, by a series of flower-lined walkways. Although the rooms here have seen better days, the tubs are big and the king-size towels are luxurious. The views of the alfalfa-laden valley from your bath are also quite nice. Your stay includes all meals, usually grilled fish or meat, which are served in the wood-floor restaurant. ⊠ *Av. El Tambo 1* ☎ *57/751–203* 🖷 *57/751–203* ☞ *40 rooms* ♨ *Restaurant, pool, bar; no a/c, no room phones* ⊟ *No credit cards* ❢❢ *All-inclusive.*

La Tirana

⓭ *72 km (45 mi) southeast of Iquique.*

Bushlike tamarugo trees and a hodgepodge of adobe and concrete houses make up this town in the forbidding Atacama Desert. La Tirana, a village of 250 people, is usually a quiet place. The sleepy town awakens each year from July 12 to 18, when 80,000 people in colorful masks and costumes converge here, filling the square with riotous dancing. The object of all this merriment is one of Chile's most important religious icons, the Virgen del Carmen (also known as the Virgen de la Tirana). The statue is found inside the rather run-down **Santuario de la Tirana,** on the main plaza.

The **Museo del Salitre,** on Tirana's main plaza, is a family-run museum that houses artifacts from the nitrate era, including ice-cream makers and a film projector. There are also other odd items, such as a stuffed condor. ⊠ *Opposite the Santuario de la Tirana on the main plaza* ☎ *no phone* ☞ *Free* ⊙ *Mon.–Sat. 8:30–1 and 3–8.*

Pica

⓮ *42 km (26 mi) southeast of La Tirana, 114 km (71 mi) southeast of Iquique.*

From a distance, Pica appears to be a mirage. This oasis cut from the gray and brown sand of the Atacama Desert is known for its fruit—the limes used to make pisco sours are grown here. The town's chief pleasure is sitting in the Plaza de Armas and sipping a *jugo natural,* fresh-squeezed juice of almost any fruit imaginable, including mangoes, oranges, pears, and grapes.

Most people come to Pica not for the town itself but for the incredible hot springs at **Cocha Resbaladero.** Tropical green foliage surrounds this lagoonlike pool cut out of the rock, and nearby caves beckon to be explored. It is quite a walk, about 2 km (1½ mi) north of town, but well worth the effort. You can also drive here. ⊠ *Calle Gen. Ibañez* ☎ *no phone* 🖃 *1,000 pesos* ☉ *Daily 8–8.*

Where to Stay & Eat

$$–$$$ ✕ **El Eden de Pica.** Pica's only upscale restaurant, El Eden del Pica has an innovative menu. It should, as the chef has published his own book on the cuisine of the region. Ask him to recommend an entrée and he'll claim they're all his favorites. The lamb is a good choice, though. The straw-mat roof gives the restaurant a rather musty odor, but the tranquil surroundings more than make up for this. ⊠ *Riquelme 12* ☎ *57/ 741–332* 🖃 *No credit cards.*

¢–$ ✕ **San Andres.** Locals speak highly of this family-style restaurant at the Hotel San Andres serving a fixed lunch. The northern Chilean fare, which usually includes a cazuela and chicken or beef entrée, is delicious. ⊠ *Balmaceda 197* ☎ *57/741–319* 🖃 *No credit cards.*

★ ¢ 🏨 **Hotel los Emelios.** Birds chirping in the garden and a refreshing plunge pool make this comfortable, homey, family-owned B&B your best bet in Pica. The small rooms have nice linens on the somewhat lumpy beds. Breakfast is served on the terrace in the back, where you'll enjoy bread with marmalade and tea or coffee. ⊠ *L. Cochrane 213* ☎ *57/741–126* 🖨 *57/741–126* 🛏 *7 rooms* ♻ *Restaurant, pool, laundry service; no a/c, no room phones* 🖃 *No credit cards* ❏ *CP.*

Reserva Nacional Pampa del Tamarugal

⑮ *96 km (60 mi) southeast of Iquique.*

The tamarugo tree is an anomaly in the almost lifeless desert. These bushlike plants survive where most would wither because they are especially adapted to the saline soil of the Atacama. Over time they developed extensive root systems that search for water deep beneath the almost impregnable surface. Reserva Nacional Pampa del Tamarugal has dense groves of tamarugos, which were almost wiped out during the nitrate era when they were felled for firewood. At the entrance is a CONAF station. ⊠ *24 km (15 mi) south of Pozo Almonte on the Pan-American Hwy.* ☎ *57/751–055* 🖃 *Free.*

Fodor$Choice The amazing **Cerros Pintados** (Painted Hills), within the Reserva Nacional
★ Pampa del Tamarugal, are well worth a detour. Here you'll find the largest group of geoglyphs in the world. These figures, which scientists believe ancient peoples used to help them navigate the desert, date from AD 500 to 1400. They are also enormous—some of the figures are decipherable only from the air. Drawings of men wearing ponchos were probably intended to point out the route to the coast to the llama caravans coming from the Andes. More than 400 figures of birds, animals, and geometric patterns adorn this 4-km (2½-mi) stretch of desert. There is a CONAF kiosk on a dirt road 2 km (1 mi) west of the Pan-American Highway. ⊠ *45 km (28 mi) south of Pozo Almonte* ☎ *57/751–055* 🖃 *1,000 pesos* ☉ *Daily 9:30–6.*

Gigante de Atacama

⑯ *84 km (52 mi) northeast of Iquique.*

The world's largest geoglyph, the Gigante de Atacama, measures an incredible 86 m (282 ft). The Atacama Giant, thought to represent a chief of an indigenous people or perhaps created in honor of Pachamama

THE GEOGLYPHS OF EL NORTE GRANDE

OR WHATEVER REASON THEY WERE CONSTRUCTED, the geoglyphs of El Norte Grande are a beautiful testament to the sophistication and aesthetic sensibility of the indigenous cultures that created them more than 1,000 years ago. Huge pictures drawn on the sides of mountains with stone, these geoglyphs are sometimes so big that they can only be seen properly from the air.

The motive behind the creation of these immense geoglyphs still remains a mystery, but some invaluable clues can be found from the region's history. Chile's extreme north has been inhabited for thousands of years. Nearly 8,000 years ago, the Chinchorro people lived in coastal villages around Arica and Iquique, dedicating themselves primarily to fishing. Later, two of the world's great ancient civilizations, the Tijuanacota and the Inca, were building pyramids high in the Andes. These people of the altiplano kept up commerce with the coastal villages, and the two cultures flourished, exchanging both ideas and material goods. This intercultural exchange left a lasting impression on the region, and long trade routes were established through the mountains down to the coast. On the sides of some of these mountains along the trade routes the ancients constructed huge figures representing animals, people, and geometric designs.

Various theories exist to explain the purpose of these figures. They may have been built, for example, as offerings to the gods; many of the geoglyphs do seem to depict high priests within the cultures. Or perhaps they were used as giant road signs for navigation along the trade routes—as landmarks in the vast wasteland of the Atacama Desert. Other, slightly wilder theories have been forwarded: some say that aliens visited the ancient cultures and that the geoglyphs were built in their honor—not quite so far-fetched when you consider the all too E.T.-esque face of the Gigante de Atacama, located inland from Iquique.

In addition to the Gigante de Atacama, the world's largest geoglyph at 86 m (282 ft) high, there are geoglyphs throughout El Norte Grande. The rock art at Cerros Pintados comprises the largest collection of geoglyphs in South America. More than 400 images adorn this hill in Reserva Nacional Pampa del Tamarugal. Figures representing birds, animals, people, and geometric patterns appear to dance along the hill. Farther north, the Tiliviche geoglyphs decorate a hill sitting not far from the modern-day marvel of the Pan-American Highway. These geoglyphs, most likely constructed between AD 1,000 and 1,400, during the Inca reign, depict a large caravan of llamas. All of these llamas are headed in the same direction—towards the sea—a testament, perhaps, to the geoglyphs' navigational use during the age when llama trains brought silver down to the coast in exchange for fish.

—Gregory Benchwick

(Mother Earth), looks a bit like a space alien. It is adorned with a walking staff, a cat mask, and a feathered headdress that resembles rays of light bursting from his head. The exact age of the figure is not known, but it certainly hails from before the arrival of the Spanish, perhaps around AD 900. The geoglyph, which is on a hill, is best viewed just before dusk, when the long shadows make the outline clearer. ⊠ *Cerro Unita, 13 km (8 mi) west of the turnoff to Chusmiza* ☎ *no phone* 🎫 *Free.*

Pisagua

🔟 *132 km (82 mi) north of Iquique.*

Pisagua, one of the region's most prominent ports during the nitrate era, at one time sustained a population of more than 8,000 people. Many of the mansions built at that time are still standing, although others have fallen into disrepair. During Pinochet's regime Pisagua was the site of a concentration camp, now used as a hotel. Today, there are only around 100 inhabitants in Pisagua—fisherfolk and guano harvesters primarily. The echoes of the Pinochet massacres and the bygone era of decadence still permeate the oceanfront village, giving it a hauted air.

The town's most famous sight, the **Torre Reloj**, built in 1887 from Oregon pine, stands on a hill overlooking the city, its blue and white paint peeling in the hot coastal sun. This clock tower, which some insist was constructed by Gustave Eiffel, is an excellent place to catch views of the town and its port.

The **Teatro Municipal** testifies to the wealth the town once possessed. Built in 1892 at the height of the nitrate boom, the once-lavish theater has grand touches, such as the painted cherubs dancing across the ceiling. The theater sits right on the edge of the sea, and waves crash against its walls, throwing eerie echoes through the empty, forgotten auditorium. Get the key to the theater and a very informative free tour from a woman in the tourist kiosk opposite the theater.

Where to Stay & Eat

★ ¢–$ ✕ **Restaurant La Picada de Don Gato.** This terrace restaurant, recommended by locals, serves simple but exquisite seafood. The shellfish dishes, especially the ostiones a la parmesana, are particularly delicious. Don't let the plastic chairs, which look like they belong in a bus station, distract you from the great food. ⊠ *Prat 127* ☎ *57/731–511* ▤ *No credit cards.*

$ 🛏 **Hotel Pisagua.** In the two-story warden's residence at the former prison, the wood-frame Hotel Pisagua has a bit of a sinister feeling. Despite this, the hotel is still the nicest place to stay in town. The restaurant serves excellent seafood, and all meals are included in your stay. ⊠ *At the entrance to town* ☎ *57/731–509* ⇩ *11 rooms with shared bath* ⚭ *Restaurant; no a/c, no room phones, no room TVs* ▤ *No credit cards* ⦿ *All-inclusive.*

ARICA AREA

At the very tip of Chile, Arica is the country's northernmost city. This pleasant community on the rocky coast once belonged to Peru. In 1880, during the War of the Pacific, Chilean soldiers stormed El Morro, a fortress set high atop a cliff in Arica. Three years later, much of the land north of Antofagasta that was once part of Peru and Bolivia belonged to Chile. Though the Arica of today is fervently Chilean, you can still see the Peruvian influence in the streets and market stalls of the city. Indigenous women still sell their goods and produce in the town's colorful markets.

Inland from Arica, the Valle Azapa cuts its way up into the mountains, a strip of green in a land of brown. Here, the excellent Museo Arqueológico de San Miguel de Azapa contains the world's oldest mummies. They were left behind by the Chinchorro people who inhabited Chile's northern coast during pre-Hispanic times. Ascending farther up the mountains towards the Bolivian border you pass through the pleasant indigenous communities of Socoroma and Putre. These towns, though far from picturesque, are good resting points if you're planning to make the journey to the 4,000-m-high (13,120-ft-high) Parque Nacional Lauca and the neighboring Reserva Nacional Las Vicuñas. The beautiful Lago Chungará, part of Parque Nacional Lauca, lies near Bolivia, creating what is probably the country's most impressive border crossing.

Arica

⑱ *301 km (187 mi) north of Iquique.*

Arica boasts that it is "the land of the eternal spring," but its temperate climate and beaches are not the only reason to visit this small city. On Plaza Colón is the **Iglesia de San Marcos,** constructed entirely from iron. Gustave Eiffel, designer of that famed eponymous Parisian tower, had the individual pieces cast in France before erecting them in Arica in 1876. Across from Parque General Baquedano, the **Aduana de Arica,** the city's former customs house, is one of Eiffel's creations. It currently contains the town's cultural center, where you can find exhibits about northern Chile, old photographs of Arica, and works by local painters and sculptors. ☎ *No phone* ✉ *Free* ⊙ *Daily 10–6.*

North of Parque General Baquedano is the defunct **Estación Ferrocarril,** the train station for the Arica–La Paz railroad. Though trains no longer run across the mountains to the Bolivian capital, this 1913 building houses a small museum with a locomotive and other remnants of the railroad. ☎ *No phone* ✉ *Free* ⊙ *Daily 10–6.*

Hanging over the town, the fortress of **El Morro de Arica** is impossible to ignore. This former Peruvian stronghold was the site of one of the key battles in the War of the Pacific. The fortress now houses the **Museo de las Armas,** which commemorates that battle. As you listen to the proud drumroll of military marches you can wander among the uniforms and weapons of past wars. ✉ *Reached by footpath from Calle Colón* ☎ *58/254–091* ✉ *500 pesos* ⊙ *Daily 8–8.*

Fodor'sChoice ★ The **Museo Arqueológico de San Miguel de Azapa,** a short drive from Arica, is a must for any visitor to El Norte Grande. In an 18th-century olive-oil refinery, this museum houses an impressive collection of artifacts from the cultures of the Chinchorros (a coastal people) and Tijuanacotas (a group that lived in the antiplano). Of particular interest are the Chinchorro mummies, the oldest in the world, dating to 6,000 BC. The incredibly well-preserved mummies are arranged in the fetal position, which was traditional in this area. To look into their wrinkled, expressive faces is to get a glimpse at a history that spans more than 8,000 years. ✉ *12 km (7 mi) south of town on the route to Putre* ☎ *58/205–555* ✉ *1,000 pesos* ⊙ *Daily 10–6.*

Where to Stay & Eat

$–$$ ✕ **Maracuyá.** Wicker furniture enhances the cool South Pacific atmosphere of this pleasant, open-air restaurant that literally sits above the water on stilts. The international menu focuses on seafood. The food, lauded by locals, is always fresh; ask the waiter what fish was caught that day. ✉ *Av. Comandante San Martin 0321* ☎ *58/227–600* ⊟ *AE, DC, MC, V.*

¢–$ ✕ **Casino La Bomba.** In the old fire station, Casino La Bomba is more of a cultural curiosity than a culinary one. That said, the traditional food isn't bad, and the service is friendly. You'll have to maneuver around the parked fire trucks to get inside, where you are greeted by wagon-wheel furnishings and a menu heavy on grilled fish. ✉ *Colon 357* ☎ *58/231–312* ⊟ *No credit cards.*

¢–$ ✕ **Club de Deportes Náuticos.** This old yacht club with views of the port serves succulent seafood dishes in a relaxed terrace setting. One of the friendliest restaurants in town, this former men's club is a great place to meet the old salts of the area. Bring your fish stories. ✉ *Thompson 1* ☎ *58/234–396* ⊟ *MC, V.*

¢–$ ✕ **El Rey de Mariscos.** Locals call this the best seafood restaurant in town, for good reason. The merluza con salsa margarita is a winner. The dreary fluorescent lights and tacky furnishings give this restaurant on the second story of a cement-block building an undeserved down-at-the-heel air. ⊠ *Colon 565* ☎ *58/229–232* ⊟ *AE, MC, V.*

★ **$$–$$$** ✕⌷ **Hotel Arica.** The finest hotel in Arica, this first-class establishment sits on the ocean between Playa El Laucho and Playa Las Liseras. The rooms, which are elegant if a bit dated, have views of the ocean and great showers with plenty of hot water. The courteous and attentive staff can help set up sightseeing tours or book a table at a local eatery. The hotel's tony restaurant ($–$$), which looks onto the ocean, serves fresh seafood cooked to order. ⊠ *Av. Comandante San Martin 599* ☎ *58/254–540* 🖷 *58/231–133* ⊕ *www.panamericanahoteles.cl* ⥱ *108 rooms, 13 suites, 20 cabanas* ♿ *Restaurant, room service, in-room safes, mini-bars, cable TV, tennis court, pool, gym, bar, shop, children's programs (ages 2–10), laundry service, business services, convention center, meeting rooms, car rental* ⊟ *AE, DC, MC, V* ⦾ *BP.*

$ ⌷ **Hotel El Paso.** This modern lodging in the center of Arica surrounds a landscaped courtyard and a pool with a swim-up bar. Though not on the ocean, it's a short walk from any of the city's beaches. There are plenty of diversions here, including a petting zoo that kids love. The superior rooms, with newer furnishings and larger televisions, are a far better value than the standard ones. ⊠ *Av. General Velasquez* ☎ *58/230–808* 🖷 *58/231–965* ⊕ *www.hotelelpaso.cl* ⥱ *71 rooms, 10 suites* ♿ *Restaurant, in-room safes, minibars, cable TV, tennis court, pool, bar, laundry service, Internet, free parking* ⊟ *AE, DC, MC, V* ⦾ *BP.*

$ ⌷ **Hotel Plaza Colon.** The central Plaza Colon is a good budget option if you don't mind being so far from the beach. The pink-walled rooms are small but clean. ⊠ *San Marcos 261* ☎ *58/254–424* 🖷 *58/231–244* 📧 *hotel_plaza_colon@entelchile.net* ⥱ *39 rooms* ♿ *Restaurant, room service, minibars, cable TV, baby-sitting, laundry service, free parking; no a/c* ⊟ *AE, DC, MC, V* ⦾ *CP.*

$ ⌷ **Hotel Sainte Georgette.** Although it's quite a hike from Arica's city center, this pleasant ocean-front hotel is great for weary travelers who simply want to relax on the beach. Some of the rooms and common areas feel a bit run-down, but the hotel is still a good value. Many rooms have their own hot tubs. ⊠ *Av. Comandante San Martin 1020* ☎ *58/257–697* 🖷 *58/229–187* ⊕ *www.hotelsaintegeorgette.cl* ⥱ *28 rooms, 8 suites* ♿ *Restaurant, some kitchenettes, cable TV, indoor-outdoor pool, exercise equipment, massage, billiards, bar, dance club, Internet, airport shuttle, free parking* ⊟ *AE, DC, MC, V* ⦾ *CP.*

Nightlife & the Arts

You can join the locals for a beer at one of the cafés lining the pedestrian mall of 21 de Mayo. These low-key establishments, many with outdoor seating, are a great place to spend an afternoon watching the passing crowds. An oddity in Arica is the attire of the servers in various tranquil cafés and tea salons: women serve coffee and tea dressed in lingerie. If this offends you, you might just want to check out the uniform of your server before you sit down and commit yourself to a café. The waitstaff dresses conventionally at the cafés of 21 de Mayo.

In the evening you won't have trouble finding the city's many watering holes. For a more refined setting, try the lively, funky **Barrabas** (⊠ 18 de Septiembre 520 ☎ 58/230–928), a bar and adjoining disco that attracts Arica's younger set. **Discoteca SoHo** (⊠ Buenos Aires 209 ☎ 58/215–892), near Playa Chinchorro, livens things up weekends with the sounds of pop and cumbia. The beachfront **Puesta del Sol** (⊠ Raul Pey 2492 ☎ 58/216–150) plays '80s tunes and appeals to a slightly older crowd. Weekends you can enjoy live music on the pleasant terrace.

Beaches

Part of the reason people flock to Arica is the beaches. South of El Morro, **Playa El Laucho** is the closest to the city, and thus the most crowded. South of Playa El Laucho you'll find **Playa Brava,** with a pontoon that keeps the kids occupied. At the somewhat secluded white-sand **Playa Chinchorro,** 2 km (1 mi) north of the city, you can rent Jet Skis in high season.

Shopping

Calle 21 de Mayo is a good place for window-shopping. **Calle Bolognesi,** just off Calle 21 de Mayo, is crowded with artisan stalls selling hand-made goods. The **Feria Internacional** on Calle Máximo Lira sells everything from bowler hats (worn by Aymara women) to blankets to batteries. The Terminal Pesquero next door offers an interesting view of fishing, El Norte Grande's predominant industry. Located outside of the city in the Azapa Valley, the **Poblado Artesenal** (✉ Calle Hualles ☎ 58/222–683) is an artisan cooperative designed to resemble an altiplano community. This is a good place to pick up traditionally styled ceramics and leather.

Putre

⑲ *145 km (90 mi) east of Arica.*

In a valley protected by two snowcapped mountains, Putre can be described only as *tranquilo*—tranquil. As tourism has yet to take root in this Andean village, it's still possible to witness traditional Aymara culture, such as women wearing traditional hats and shawls. On an ancient Inca trail later used by the Spanish to transport gold from Bolivia, Putre is still a stop along the road for people heading elsewhere, such as to Parque Nacional Lauca and Reserva Nacional de Las Vicuñas. Worth a visit is the lovely **Iglesia de Putre,** on the northeast corner of the main plaza. The church was built in 1670 but had to be reconstructed in 1871 after an earthquake destroyed the interior.

Where to Stay & Eat

¢ ✕ **Pub Kuchu Marka.** The funky, eclectic Pub Kuchu Marka is a nice place to pass an evening playing a game of cacho or sipping a *mate de coca* (medicinal tea made with leaves from the coca plant). Grab a cold beer and plan your excursion for the next day. The pub serves local specialty dishes such as cazuela and, on certain days, llama steaks. ✉ *Calle Baquedano* ☎ *no phone* ☐ *No credit cards.*

$$ ✕ **Hotel Las Vicuñas.** This row of older buildings, originally used as a miners' camp, is the best lodging in town. The rooms are clean and basic and have space heaters, which are essential because it gets chilly in the Andes. With Andean textiles serving as tablecloths, the restaurant (¢) serves typical fare for the region: expect a fixed menu with cazuela followed by a meat dish. Breakfast and your choice of lunch or dinner are included. ✉ *Calle Baquedano* ☎ *58/228–564* ✉ *ukg@entelchile.net* ⤴ *112 rooms* ⌂ *Restaurant, Ping-Pong, bar; no a/c, no room phones, no room TVs* ☐ *No credit cards* ⏺ *MAP.*

$ **Casa Barbarita.** Comfy flannel sheets and heaters keep you warm on chilly nights at this friendly B&B, and the baths have steaming hot showers. You can get the scoop on the area from the owner, naturalist Barbara Knapton, and you can prepare your own food in the kitchen. ✉ *Calle Baquedano 294* ☎☎ *58/300–013* ⎙ *58/222–735* ⊕ *www. birdingaltoandino.com* ⤴ *2 rooms* ⌂ *Kitchen; no a/c, no room phones, no room TVs* ☐ *No credit cards* ⏺ *BP.*

Parque Nacional Lauca

★ ⓴ *47 km (29 mi) southeast of Putre.*

On a plateau more than 4,000 m (13,000 ft) above sea level, the magnificent Parque Nacional Lauca shelters flora and fauna found in few other places in the world. Cacti, grasses, and a brilliant emerald-green moss called *llareta* dot the landscape. Playful vizcacha—rabbitlike rodents with long tails—laze in the sun, and llamas, graceful vicuñas, and alpacas make their home here as well. About 10 km (6 mi) into the park you come upon a CONAF station with informative brochures. ⊠ *Off Ruta 11* ☎ *58/250–570 in Arica* ☒ *Free.*

Within the park, off Ruta 11, is the altiplano village of **Parinacota**, one of the most beautiful in all of Chile. In the center of the village sits the whitewashed **Iglesia Parinacota**, dating from 1789. Inside are murals depicting sinners and saints and a mysterious "walking table," which parishioners have chained to the wall for fear that it will steal away in the night. Opposite the church you'll find crafts stalls run by Aymara women in the colorful shawls and bowler hats worn by many altiplano women. Only 18 people live in the village, but many more make a pilgrimage here for annual festivals such as the Fiesta de las Cruces, held on May 3, and the Fiesta de la Virgen de la Canderlaria, a three-day romp that begins on February 2.

About 8 km (5 mi) east of Piranacota are the beautiful **Lagunas Cotacotani**, which means "land of many lakes" in the Quechua language. This string of ponds—surrounded by a desolate moonscape formed by volcanic eruptions—attracts many species of bird, including Andean geese.

Lago Chungará sits on the Bolivian border at an amazing altitude of 4,600 m (15,100 ft) above sea level. Volcán Parinacota, at 6,330 m (20,889 ft), casts its shadow onto the lake's glassy surface. Hundreds of flamingos make their home here. There is a CONAF-run office at Lago Chungará on the highway just before the lake. ⊹ *From Ruta 11, turn north on Ruta A-123* ☎ *no phone* ☒ *Free* ☽ *CONAF office daily 8–8.*

Reserva Nacional Las Vicuñas

★ ㉑ *121 km (75 mi) southeast of Putre.*

Although it attracts far fewer visitors than neighboring Parque Nacional Lauca, Reserva Nacional Las Vicuñas contains some incredible sights—salt flats, high plains, and alpine lakes. And you can enjoy the vistas without running into buses full of tourists. The reserve, which stretches some 100 km (62 mi), has a huge herd of graceful vicuñas. Although quite similar to their larger cousins, llamas and alpacas, vicuñas have not been domesticated. Their incredibly soft wool, among the most prized in the world, led to so much hunting that these creatures were threatened with extinction. Today it is illegal to kill vicuña. Getting to this reserve, unfortunately, is quite a challenge. There is no public transportation, and the roads are only passable in four-wheel-drive vehicles. Many people choose to take a tour out of Arica. ⊠ *From Ruta 11, take Ruta A-21 south to park headquarters* ☎ *58/250–570 in Arica.*

Salar de Surire

㉒ *126 km (78 mi) southeast of Putre.*

After passing through the high plains, where you'll spot vicuña, alpaca, and the occasional desert fox, you'll catch your first glimpse of the sparkling Salar de Surire. Seen from a distance, the salt flat appears to be a giant white lake. Unlike its southern neighbor, the Salar de Atacama, it's completely flat. Three of the world's four species of flamingos live in the nearby lakes. ⊠ *South from Reserva Nacional Las Vicuñas on Ruta A-235* ☎ *58/250–570* ⊠ *Free.*

EL NORTE GRANDE A TO Z

To research prices, get advice from other travelers, and book travel arrangements, visit www.fodors.com.

AIR TRAVEL

Since there are no international airports in El Norte Grande, you can't fly here directly from the United States, Canada, Europe, or Australia. You must fly into Santiago and transfer to a flight headed to Antofagasta, Calama, Iquique, or Arica. Avant and LanChile fly from Santiago to El Norte Grande. Round-trip flights can run up to 210,000 pesos.

You can also get here from other South American countries. LanChile runs direct flights between El Norte Grande and neighboring Bolivia and Peru.

Since the cities in El Norte Grande are far apart, taking planes between them can save you both time and a lot of hassle. Both Avant and LanChile offer service between the major cities. Prices range from 28,000 to 105,000 pesos.

🛦 Airlines **Avant** ☎ 55/452–050 in Antofagasta. **LanChile** ☎ 55/265–151 in Antofagasta; 55/313–927 in Calama; 57/427–600 in Iquique; 58/251–641 in Arica.

AIRPORTS

Antofagasta's Aeropuerto Cerro Moreno lies 25 km (16 mi) north of the city. Calama's Aeropuerto El Loa is 5 km (3 mi) south of the city center. Iquique's Aeropuerto Diego Aracena is a little far from the center of the city, about 40 km (25 mi) to the south. Arica's Aeropuerto Internacional Chacalluta lies 18 km (11 mi) north of the center.

🛦 Airport Information **Aeropuerto Cerro Moreno** ☎ 55/269–077 in Antofagasta. **Aeropuerto El Loa** ☎ 55/312–348 in Calama. **Aeropuerto Diego Aracena** ☎ 57/407–000 in Iquique. **Aeropuerto Internacional Chacalluta** ☎ 58/211–116 in Arica.

BUS TRAVEL

Getting around by bus in El Norte Grande is easy. There is a terminal in every major city with frequent departures to the other cities as well as smaller towns in the area. Keep in mind that there may be no bus service to the smaller villages or the more remote national parks.

No bus company has a monopoly, so there are often several bus stations in each city. Because many companies may be running buses along the same route, shop around for the best price. The fare for a 300-km (186-mi) trip usually runs around 7,000 pesos. For longer trips find a bus that has a *salon semi-cama,* with comfortable seats that make all the difference.

CAR RENTAL

You can rent cars in Antofagasta, Calama, Iquique, and Arica at both the airport and downtown. Most hotels will also help you arrange a rental. Avis, Budget, and Hertz have offices in most major cities in northern Chile. The best deals are probably in Iquique. However, cars rented here cannot be taken out of the Iquique area.

🛦 Agencies **Avis** ⊠ Balmaceda 2556, Antofagasta ☎ 55/319–797 ⊠ Latorre 1498, Calama ☎ 55/319–797 ⊠ Manuel Rodriguez 734, Iquique ☎ 57/472–392. **Budget** ⊠ Baquedano 300, Antofagasta ☎ 55/283–667 ⊠ Granaderos 2875, Calama ☎ 55/346–868 ⊠ Bolívar 615, Iquique ☎ 57/416–332. **Hertz** ⊠ Balmaceda 2566, Antofagasta ☎ 55/

269-043 ✉ Latorre 1510, Calama ☎ 55/341-380 ✉ Anibal Pinto 1303, Iquique ☎ 57/510-136 ✉ Hotel El Paso, Baquedano 999, Arica ☎ 58/231-487.

CAR TRAVEL

A car is definitely the best way to see El Norte Grande. If you want to get far off the beaten path, there is no other way to travel. Driving in the cities can be a little hectic, but once you get on the highway it is usually smooth sailing. The roads of the north are generally well maintained. The farther from major population centers you travel—such as the remote national parks like Parque Nacional Lauca and Reserva Nacional Las Vicuñas—the worse the roads become. Destinations like these require a four-wheel-drive vehicle. Ruta 5, more familiarly known as the Pan-American Highway, bisects all of Northern Chile. Ruta 1, Chile's answer to California's Highway 101, is a beautiful coastal highway running between Antofagasta and Iquique. Calama is reached by Ruta 25.

FESTIVALS & SEASONAL EVENTS

Every town in the region celebrates the day honoring its patron saint. Most are small gatherings attended largely by locals, but a few are huge celebrations that attract people from all over the country. One fiesta not to be missed takes place in La Tirana from July 12 to 18. During this time some 80,000 pilgrims converge on the town to honor the Virgen del Carmen with riotous dancing in the streets.

HEALTH

Because of El Norte Grande's extremely varied topography, you should be prepared for many different weather conditions. If you're heading up into the Andes, remember to bring along warm clothes, even during the warmer months. A weather phenomenon called Bolivian winter, which actually takes place in the summer, brings rains and even snow to the Andes. The Atacama Desert, where some areas have never recorded any rainfall, can take its toll on unsuspecting tourists. Bring sunblock, a wide-brimmed hat, and plenty of water.

Altitude sickness—which is marked by difficulty breathing, dizziness, headaches, and nausea—is a danger for visitors to the high elevations of the antiplano. The best way to ward off altitude sickness is to take things slowly. Spend a day or two acclimatizing before any physical exertion. When hiking or climbing, rest often and drink as much water as possible. If symptoms continue, return to a lower altitude.

The tap water in the major cities and even most smaller communities is drinkable. In general, the water is safer on the coast than in some towns farther inland. To be on the safe side, stick to bottled water.

MAIL & SHIPPING

Mailing letters and packages from El Norte Grande is a formidable task. Although most cities have a post office, you often are faced with long lines that move at a snail's pace. Your best bet is to ask your hotel to post a letter for you. But don't expect your letter to reach its destination quickly. Mail headed out of the country can often take weeks.

🖪 Post Offices **Antofagasta** ✉ Washington 2613. **Arica** ✉ Arturo Prat 305. **Calama** ✉ Mackenna and Granaderos. **Iquique** ✉ Bolívar 485.

SAFETY

El Norte Grande experiences very little crime. Nevertheless, you should use the same precautions as anywhere else. Women traveling alone should be careful, especially at night. It's best to travel in pairs or groups.

TAXIS

Taxis are the most efficient way to get around any city in El Norte Chico. They're easy to hail on the streets, but late at night you might want to ask someone at a hotel or restaurant to call one for you. Taxis often function as *colectivos,* meaning they will pick up anybody going in the same direction. The driver will adjust the price accordingly. Almost no taxis have meters, but many have the price posted on the windshield. Make sure you establish the price before getting inside. Prices range from 700–2,800 pesos, depending on the distance traveled and whether the taxi is a colectivo. Prices rise an average of 20% at night. Taxi drivers often will rent out their services for the day for a flat fee.

TELEPHONES

There are several different telephone companies in El Norte Grande, and each has its own public telephones. Calling cards for each company can be purchased in many shops and newsstands. Much easier than calling from the street is to call from one of the many Entel or CTC offices in every city. Here you can dial direct or collect to anywhere in the world.

TOURS

Tours can be arranged in the major cities and a number of the smaller towns. It's a good idea to shop around to make sure that you're getting the best itinerary and the best price.

In Antofagasta, Desertica Expediciones arranges trips into the interior, including excursions to Parque Nacional Pan de Azucar.

There are myriad tour agencies in San Pedro de Atacama. Cosmo Andino Expediciones offers excellent tours with well-informed guides. Herradura runs horseback tours.

In Arica and Iquique, a well-respected agency called Geotour arranges trips to Parque Nacional Lauca, the Salar de Surire, and the Reserva Nacional las Vicuñas.

In Putre, Birding Alto Andino has an Alaskan naturalist who leads birding expeditions.

Tour Operators Birding Alto Andino ⊠ Calle Baquedano, Putre ☎ 58/300-013. **Cosmo Andino Expediciones** ⊠ Calle Caracoles s/n, San Pedro de Atacama ☎ 55/851-069. **Desertica Expediciones** ⊠ La Torre 2732, Antofagasta ☎ 55/386-877. **Geotour** ⊠ Bolognesi 421, Arica ☎ 58/253-927 ⊠ Baquedano 982, Iquique ☎ 57/428-984. **Herradura** ⊠ Tocopilla s/n, San Pedro de Atacama ☎ 55/851-087.

VISITOR INFORMATION

Most major cities in El Norte Grande have an office of Sernatur, Chile's tourism agency. Here you'll find helpful information about the region, including maps and brochures. Some staff members speak English.

Sernatur Offices Antofagasta ⊠ Maipú 240 ☎ 55/264-044. **Arica** ⊠ San Marcos 101 ☎ 58/252-054. **Calama** ⊠ Latorre and Vicuña ☎ 55/364-176. **Iquique** ⊠ Anibal Pinto 436 ☎ 57/312-238. **San Pedro de Atacama** ⊠ Toconao and Gustavo Le Paige ☎ 55/851-420.

THE CENTRAL VALLEY

5

FODOR'S CHOICE

Hacienda Los Lingues, ranch lodging in San Fernando

Rubén Tapío, Latin restaurant in Talca

HIGHLY RECOMMENDED

RESTAURANTS Canto de Luna, San Pedro

Los Varietales, Santa Cruz

HOTELS Gran Hotel Termas de Chillán, Termas de Chillán

Hotel Santa Cruz Plaza, Santa Cruz

Parador Jamón, Pan y Vino, Termas de Chillán

SIGHTS Casa del Arte, art museum in Concepción

Museo de Colchagua, Santa Cruz

Museo San José del Carmen de El Huique, Santa Cruz

By Michael de Zayas

Updated by David Dudenhoefer

A QUIET NOBILITY is maintained by the people of the Central Valley. Perhaps it is because they have had to work so hard to cultivate the arid region, irrigating their farmland with the runoff from distant Andean snow. Perhaps it's because their tradition of industriousness has paid off—the region produces wine to rival that of any nation. Though it has ties to other great wine regions, the area has a personality all its own. If Bordeaux has its châteaux, the Central Valley has its haciendas. Here the traditional hacienda—the main structure on a farm—has become more than an economic and agricultural center; it is a manifestation of a family's honor. Some of these grand manor houses have been preserved as museums, and one of them is a luxury hotel.

The Central Valley is also home to the *huaso,* a cousin of the Argentine gaucho and a distant relation of the American cowboy. Chilean rodeo began here, and you're likely to see horses being ridden in the countryside and sometimes even in the area's major cities.

As you head south, or east into the mountains, the relatively dry foliage gives way to pine forests and more verdant pastures. Follow any of various valleys into the high country, and you'll encounter gorgeous mountain scenery, patches of which are protected in nature reserves, and one corner of which holds one of the country's best ski areas: Termas de Chillán.

Exploring the Central Valley

Bordered on the east by the volcanic cones of the Andes and on the west by smaller mountain ranges running along the Pacific coast, the Central Valley is a straight shot down the Pan-American Highway. The landscape in between is unpredictably hilly. It's about a six-hour drive from Santiago south to Concepción, although most people choose to stop somewhere along the way.

About the Restaurants

Even the most informal meal in the Central Valley is likely to be centered around an excellent local wine. Lunch in Santa Cruz may be accompanied by a cabernet from Viña Santa Laura, while dinner in Curicó might mean a merlot from Viña San Pedro. Knowing a handful of wine-related words will doubtless come in handy. *Vino* is the Spanish word for wine; red is *tinto* (never *rojo*) and white is *blanco*. *Desgustación* and *cata* both refer to a formal wine tasting.

Cuisine in the Central Valley is not unlike what you'll find in other parts of the country. Though much of the region is ranching country, seafood forms an integral part of most menus, even in the mountain resorts. Although most restaurants in the region serve uninspired food, enough of them stand apart from the crowd to provide some memorable dining experiences. Note that many restaurants don't open for dinner until 8 or so.

About the Hotels

Each sizeable town in this region has one or two respectable hotels, usually near the central square. But with the notable exception of Hacienda Los Lingues outside of Rancagua, the lodgings in the Central Valley can't match those you'll find in Santiago. It may be an unfair comparison, however, as hotels here often have a charm all their own.

WHAT IT COSTS In pesos (in thousands)				
	$$$$	**$$$**	**$$**	**$**	**¢**
RESTAURANTS	over 11	8–11	5–8	2.5–5	under 2.5
HOTELS	over 105	75–105	45–75	15–45	under 15

Restaurant prices are for a main course at dinner. Hotel prices are for a double room in high season, excluding tax.

Timing

There is no real high season in the Central Valley except in the Termas de Chillán, where snow attracts skiers from June to September. The activities here shift to hiking and horseback riding from December to April. Most people head to the Central Valley for its wineries. Grapes are picked in February and March, which is the best time to visit a vineyard, since you can see everything from crushing to bottling. The Fiesta de la Vendimia, the annual harvest festival, is celebrated with particular zest in Santa Cruz and Curicó. The four-day fiesta, which takes place the first weekend in March, includes grape-stomping contests and the selection of a queen, whose weight is measured out in grapes on a massive scale. In the religious festival called the Fiesta de San Francisco, held October 4 in the small town of Huerta de Maule, 38 km (24 mi) southwest of Talca, more than 200 huasos gather from all over Chile for a day of horseback events, including races around the central square.

THE WINE COUNTRY

Within the vast Región del Valle Central are the four subregions that you'll most commonly find on a bottle of Chilean wine: Valle del Maipo (south of Santiago), Valle del Rapel (west of Rancagua), Valle de Curicó (around Curicó), and Valle del Maule (south of Talca). These four subregions are further subdivided, but save for moments of inspired snobbery these aren't found on labels. An exception is the Valle del Rapel, which is divided into the Valle del Cachapoal and the Valle de Colchagua.

The Pan-American Highway bisects the Central Valley, passing through most of the wine-growing areas. Just south of Santiago is the Valle del Rapel, where you'll find some of the area's most prestigious wineries. After exploring the valley's vineyards, you can head into the mountains and relax in the hot springs at the Termas de Cauquenes.

Don't overlook the wineries along the banks of the Río Maule—the Valle de Curicó and the Valle del Maule. Also here are the pleasant city of Talca and such wonderful protected areas as the Reserva Nacional Radal Siete Tazas.

Rancagua

 87 km (54 mi) south of Santiago.

The Rancagua region was first settled by the indigenous Picunche people and then by the Incas. A hanging bridge built over the Río Cachapoal by the Incas was later used by Spanish colonists led by José Antonio Manso de Velasco. He founded Villa Santa Cruz de Triana, later renamed Rancagua, here in 1745.

In 1814, the hills around the city were the site of a battle in the War of Independence known as the *Desastre de Rancagua* (Disaster of Rancagua). Chilean independence fighters, including Bernardo O'Higgins, held off the powerful Spanish army for two days before being captured. In a resulting blaze, much of the town was destroyed.

5

Numbers in the text correspond to numbers in the margin and on the Central Valley map.

If you have 3 days

If you can afford it, spend at least one night at Hacienda Los Lingues. The restored ranch near **Rancagua** ❶ ⚑ gives you a sense of what life was like for the aristocrats who lived here centuries ago. Otherwise head to 🏙 **Santa Cruz** ❷, where you can explore another perfectly preserved hacienda outside of town at the Museo San José del Carmen de El Huique. There are plenty of vineyards around Santa Cruz, in the Valle de Colchagua. You could easily stay put the second night or head south, through **Curicó** ❸, to the lovely city of 🏙 **Talca** ❺, from which you can visit the wineries of Domaine Oriental and Balduzzi, the rodeo at San Clemente, and the nearby mountains.

If you have 5 days

Spend your first three days as described above. On the fourth day, continue south to 🏙 **Chillán** ❽, with its markets selling handicrafts from all over the country. Drive east to 🏙 **Termas de Chillán** ❾, which has hot springs, skiing during the winter, hiking during the summer, and amazing mountain scenery year-round. On the fifth day, head to **Concepción** ❿, the region's biggest city, which has a couple of nice museums, fine dining, and regular flights to Santiago.

Today's Racagüinos spend their evenings in the city's central square, the **Plaza de los Héroes.** A block north of the plaza along Calle Estado is **Iglesia de la Merced,** a church that has been declared a national monument. It was in this bell tower that O'Higgins waited in vain for reinforcements during the battle for independence.

The three rooms of the **Museo Regional de Rancagua** re-create a typical 18th-century home, complete with period furniture and religious artifacts. It's a few blocks south of Plaza de los Héroes. ⊠ *Estado and Ibieta* ☎ *72/230–976* 💲 *500 pesos* ☉ *Tues.–Sun. 10–5.*

Casa de Pilar de Esquina, across the street from the Museo Regional de Rancagua, is the house that belonged to independence fighter Fernando Errázuriz Aldunate. ⊠ *Estado and Ibieta* ☎ *no phone* 💲 *500 pesos* ☉ *Tues.–Sun. 10–5.*

Numerous trails lead through thick forests of cypress trees at **Reserva Nacional Río los Cipreses,** a 15,000-acre national reserve 54 km (33 mi) east of Rancagua. Occasionally you'll reach a clearing where you'll be treated to great views of the mountains above. CONAF, the national parks service, has an office here with informative displays and maps. Just south of the park is the spot where a plane carrying Uruguayan university students crashed in 1972. The story of the group, part of which survived three months in a harsh winter by resorting to cannibalism, was told in the book and film *Alive.* ⊠ *Carretera del Cobre* ☎ *72/297–505* 💲 *1,700 pesos* ☉ *Dec.–Mar., daily 8:30–8; Apr.–Nov., daily 8:30–6.*

On the southern banks of the Río Cachapoal about 31 km (19 mi) east of Rancagua, the **Termas de Cauquenes** spout mineral-rich water that has been revered for its medicinal properties since colonial days. The Spanish discovered the 48°C (118°F) springs in the late 1500s, and basic visitor facilities have existed since the 1700s. José de San Martín, who masterminded the defeat of Spanish forces in Chile, is said to have relaxed here before beginning his campaign. Naturalist Charles Darwin, who visited in 1834, wrote that the springs were situated in "a quiet, solitary spot, with a good deal of wild beauty." The current bathhouse, which resembles a church, was built in 1867. It holds about two dozen rooms with small marble tubs that are filled with spring water for 20-minute baths. There's a hotel here, and its guests have exclusive access to a naturally heated swimming pool outside that is considerably cooler. To reach the springs, take Ruta 32 to Coya and then head south. ⊠ *Carretera del Cobre* ☎ *72/899–010* ☜ *3,500 pesos* ☉ *Daily 8–6:30.*

Mina El Teniente, in the mountains north of Termas de Cauquenes, 60 km (37 mi) northeast of Rancagua, is the world's largest subterranean copper mine. The mine can be visited on guided tours arranged by Hacienda los Lingues and the Rancagua tour operator **VTS** (☎ 72/210–290).

Where to Stay & Eat

$$$$
Fodor'sChoice
★

✕⊞ **Hacienda Los Lingues.** One of Chile's best preserved colonial haciendas, this estate southeast of Rancagua has remained in the same family for four centuries. Staying here is a bit like traveling back in time: 17th- and 18th-century adobe buildings hold spacious rooms furnished with antiques and heated by wood stoves. The hacienda is part of a 20,000-acre working ranch with extraordinary horses and miles of trails through the foothills. Manicured gardens, timeless porticos, and plush living rooms provide idyllic spots for relaxation. Four-course Continental dinners, served in the garden or sumptuous dining room, make use of fine china, crystal, and silverware and are complemented by the definitive Chilean wine list. ⊠ *Panamericana Sur Km. 124, San Fernando* ☎ *2/235–5446* 🖷 *2/235–7604* ⊕ *www.loslingues.com* ☜ *17 rooms* ♿ *Restaurant, room service, in-room safes, tennis court, pool, fishing, mountain bikes, horseback riding, bar, recreation room, shop, laundry service, travel services; no a/c, no room TVs* ⊟ *AE, DC, MC, V* ⧖ *BP, FAP, MAP.*

$$

✕⊞ **Hotel Termas de Cauquenes.** The main attractions of this hotel are the mineral baths, surrounding nature, a thermal swimming pool, and one of the region's best restaurants, serving Continental and Chilean dishes. Despite its great location overlooking the Río Cachapoal, the hotel doesn't have much of a view. Only the restaurant and a few rooms in the *pabellón del río* (river building) afford glimpses of the boulder-strewn river. Dating from the 1960s, the pabellón's rooms are smallish and slightly spartan. Rooms in the older *patio central* building are spacious but lack views. Everything is timeworn, and the decor is uninspired. ⊠ *Carretera del Cobre* ☎ *72/899–010* 🖷 *72/899–009* ☜ *50 rooms* ♿ *Restaurant, room service, some minibars, pool, hot tubs, massage, bar, recreation room, playground, laundry service; no a/c* ⊟ *AE, DC, MC, V* ⧖ *BP, FAP, MAP.*

Horseback Riding

A working ranch with more than 200 horses, **Hacienda los Lingues** (☎ 02/235–5446) offers mountain rides on world-class steeds.

Santa Cruz

❷ *104 km (64 mi) southwest of Rancagua.*

Reminiscent of many small towns in the grape-growing regions of Spain, Santa Cruz has a central square surrounded by a mix of modern and traditional architecture, a few streets lined with shops, and vineyards radiating out in all directions. In the center of the palm-lined **Plaza de**

Rodeos From September to April, San Clemente, a town 16 km (10 mi) southeast of Talca, hosts the best rodeo in the region. Besides riding and roping, you'll find food, dances, and beauty-queen competitions. Beyond San Clemente there are important *medialunas* (corrals) in Talca, Pelarco, Curicó, Molina, Pencahue, Los Niches, and Linares.

Wineries Chile recognizes five distinct wine regions. By far the most important of these, in terms of quality and quantity, is the Región del Valle Central, which begins near Santiago and extends for 300 km (186 mi) to the south. The wineries of this sprawling region grow mostly cabernet sauvignon, merlot, sauvignon blanc, and chardonnay. However, two increasingly popular red varietals are malbec and carmenère—a grape only grown in Chile. When visiting *viñas* (vineyards) you're likely to come across these Spanish words: *barrica* (barrel), *fundo* (estate), *botella* (bottle), and *bodega* (cellar). The phrase *ruta del vino* refers to a region where you can tour various vineyards.

5

Armas is a colonial-style bell tower with a carillon that chimes every 15 minutes; inside the tower you'll find the town's tourist office. Facing the central square is the fortresslike **Iglesia Parroquial**, an imposing white stucco structure built in 1817.

★ The attractive **Museo de Colchagua,** built in colonial style at the end of the 20th century, focuses on the history of the region. It's the largest private natural history collection in the country, and second only in size to Santiago's Museo Nacional de Historia Natural. Exhibits include pre-Columbian mummies; extinct insects set in amber, which are viewed through special lenses; the world's largest collection of silver work by the indigenous Mapuche; and the only known original copy of Chile's proclamation of independence. A few early vehicles and wine-making implements surround the building. The museum is the creation of Santa Cruz native Carlos Cardoén, who has made made millions from the global arms trade. The placards are only in Spanish, but a video provides some information in English about the museum's collection. ✉ *Av. Errázuriz 145* ☎ *72/821–050* ⊕ *www.museocolchagua.cl* ✍ *2,500 pesos* ⊗ *Tues.–Sun. 10–6.*

★ **Museo San José del Carmen de El Huique,** a 2,600-acre country estate, is one of Chile's most important national monuments. Built in 1756, the hacienda belonged to the Errázuriz family until the government turned it into a museum in 1975. The rooms are preserved exactly as they were when Federico Errázuriz Echaurren, president of Chile from 1896 to 1901, lived here. Sumptuous suites contain collections of opal glass, lead crystal, bone china, and antique furniture as well as photographs and family portraits evoking aristocratic life in Chile a century ago. Today's tour guides know a lot about the estate, as they are descendents of the hundreds of people who worked for the Errázuriz family. A highlight of a tour of the grounds is the 1852 chapel, which has Venetian blown-glass balustrades ringing the altar and the choir loft. Sunday morning mass is held here at 11:30. Call ahead to arrange for an English-speaking guide. ✛ *16 km (10 mi) north of Santa Cruz; follow road to Pichidegua and make a right onto dirt road leading to museum* ☎ *72/ 933–083* ✍ *2,000 pesos* ⊗ *Wed.–Sun. 11–5.*

Unlike most other small towns in the Central Valley, Santa Cruz has capitalized on the burgeoning interest in the region's viticulture. The **Ruta del Vino** office provides basic information about Colchagua's 12 vineyards and arranges guided tours in English to 10 of them. Though most vineyards have their own guides, few of them speak English, and some only accept visits arranged by Ruta del Vino. The office arranges tours to two or three vineyards, which cost 28,000–49,000 pesos per person and can include lunch at a vineyard; reserve at least one day in advance. One of the best times to visit the area is in early March, when the Fiesta de la Vendimia celebrates the harvest. Around that time of year, you can see much of the process of turning the grapes into wine. ⊠ *Plaza de Armas 298* 🖼 *72/823–199* ⊕ *www.colchaguavalley.cl* ⊘ *Weekdays 9–1 and 3–6, Sat. 9–1.*

One of the most attractive wineries in the Valle de Colchagua is **Viña Bisquertt**, where a 200-year-old farmhouse with a Spanish-tile roof makes you feel as though you've stepped back in time. The property once belonged to Federico Errázuriz Zañartu, Chile's president from 1871 to 1876, and his carriage is part of a beautiful collection of 19th-century coaches here. This family-run business oversees 1,200 acres of plantings. A tour will take you through the cellars, which hold 16 15-ft-tall wooden casks dating from the 1940s. The guides here lead tours in Spanish only, so you may want to arrange for an English-language tour through the Ruta del Vino office. ⊠ *Camino a Lihueimo s/n* 🖼 *72/821–692* ⊕ *www.bisquertt.cl* ▦ *7,000 pesos* ⊘ *Wed–Mon. 9–6.*

Viña Santa Laura is a small winery on lands where grapes have been grown for more than a century. The likeness of Laura Hartwig, the elegant owner of the estate, is beautifully drawn on the winery's labels by the famous Chilean artist Claudio Bravo. Hartwig's brother owns Viña Bisquertt, a family tie not uncommon among Chilean wineries. After a tour of the facilities, you should have a chance to sample the carmenère, a type of wine grown only in Chile. It has more character than merlot but is not as full-bodied as cabernet sauvignon. Also worth trying is the malbec, which has a lasting finish, a sensation compared by a winery guide to "kissing Sean Connery." Tours must be arranged through the Ruta del Vino office. ⊠ *Camino Barreales s/n* 🖼 *72/823–179* ⊕ *www.bisquertt. cl* ⊘ *Daily 10–1 and 3–6.*

Where to Stay & Eat

$–$$ ✕ **Club Social de Santa Cruz.** This simple restaurant overlooking the town's main square is known for its meat dishes. The house specialties are *conejo salsa alcachofa* (rabbit in an artichoke sauce) and *codornicez salsa cazador* (quail in a bacon and mushroom sauce), but there are also plenty of beef and chicken dishes. In summer, the courtyard fills with locals lunching under the shady pergola. Note that there's no English menu. ⊠ *Plaza de Armas 178* 🖼 *72/824–548* ▭ *DC, MC, V.*

★ **$–$$** ✕ **Los Varietales.** The lovely Hotel Santa Cruz Plaza houses the best restaurant in town. The name refers to varieties of grapes, a motif reflected in the magnums above the fireplace mantel, and on the wine list, which includes all the Valle de Colchagua's labels. You have a choice of meat dishes, seafood, and sandwiches. Try the *ajiaco* (beef and potato soup), *gambas al pil pil* (spicy shrimp scampi), rack of lamb, or grilled corbina with a seafood sauce. In warmer months, the trellised terrace in back is a great spot for lunch. ⊠ *Plaza de Armas 286* 🖼 *72/821–010* ▭ *AE, DC, MC, V.*

★ **$$$** ▥ **Hotel Santa Cruz Plaza.** This beautiful, colonial-style hotel on the Plaza de Armas may look historic, but it's less than a decade old. Behind the yellow facade adorned with wooden columns are Spanish-style

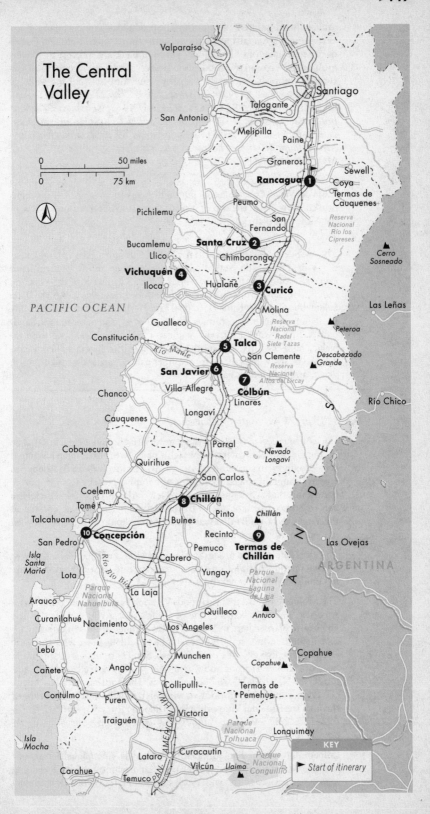

The Central Valley

0 ——————————— 50 miles

0 ——————————— 75 km

PACIFIC OCEAN

Valparaíso

Talagante

Santiago

San Antonio

Melipilla

Paine

Graneros

Sewell

Rancagua ①

Coya

Termas de Cauquenes

Peumo

San Fernando

Reserva Nacional Río los Cipreses

Pichilemu

Cerro Sosneado

Bucamlemu

Santa Cruz ②

Llico

Chimbarongo

Vichuquén ④

Hualañe

Iloca

Curicó ③

Molina

Gualleco

Las Leñas

Reserva Nacional Radal Siete Tazas

Constitución

Peteroa

Río Maule

Talca ⑤

San Clemente

Descabezado Grande

San Javier ⑥

Reserva Nacional Altos del Lircay

Villa Allegre

⑦

Chanco

Colbún

Río Chico

Linares

Longaví

Cauquenes

Parral

Cobquecura

Nevado Longaví

Quirihue

San Carlos

Coelemu

Chillán ⑧

Tomé

Bulnes

Pinto

Chillán

Concepción ⑩

Recinto

San Pedro

Pemuco

Termas de Chillán ⑨

Las Ovejas

Isla Santa María

Cabrero

ARGENTINA

Lota

Río Bío Bío

Yungay

Parque Nacional Laguna de Laja

Arauco

5

Parque Nacional Nahuelbuta

La Laja

Copahue

Curanilahué

Nacimiento

Quilleco

Copahue

Lebú

Los Angeles

Antuco

Cañete

Munchen

Copahue

Contulmo

Puren

Collipulli

Termas de Pemehue

Angol

Traiguén

Victoria

Isla Mocha

Parque Nacional Tolhuaca

Lonquimay

Lataro

Curacautín

Parque Nacional Conguillío

KEY

Carahue

Vilcún

Llaima

Temuco

▶ Start of itinerary

PAN AMERICAN HIGHWAY

arches, hand-painted tiles, antique reproductions, and stained glass. Guest rooms are small but charming, with orange stucco walls and French doors that open onto balconies. Those in back are quieter; they overlook a creek crossed by wooden footbridges, and a curvaceous pool surrounded by lush foliage. The nearby wine shop sells all the Valle de Colchagua wines. ✉ *Plaza de Armas 286* ☎ *72/821–010; 2/242–1030 in Santiago* 📠 *72/823–445; 2/242–1044 in Santiago* 🌐 *www. hotelsantacruzplaza.cl* ➷ *41 rooms, 3 suites* ♿ *Restaurant, room service, in-room data ports, in-room safes, cable TV, pool, sauna, bar, babysitting, laundry service, business services, meeting rooms* ☰ *AE, DC, MC, V* ❏ *BP, FAP.*

Horseback Riding

Punta del Viento Cabalgatas (✉ Fundo El Arrayán ☎ 09/728–4784) runs horseback tours to the top of a peak that affords a panoramic view of the Valle de Colchagua.

Shopping

The **Asociación de Artesanos** (✉ Av. Rafael Casanova ☎ no phone), near the Viña La Posada, sells high-quality leather goods, embroidered tapestries, and clay figurines. About 5 km (3 mi) west of the plaza on the road to San Fernando is a colorful adobe house that holds the **Doña Selina** boutique (✉ Ruta I-50 ☎ 072/931–166), where you can buy local jams, straw hats, ceramics, wood carvings, and other unique handicrafts. If you want a souvenir you can't find elsewhere, head to **La Lajuela,** a hamlet 8 km (5 mi) southeast of Santa Cruz. Residents here weave *chupallas,* straw hats made from a fiber called *teatina* that is cut, dyed, dried, and braided by hand.

Curicó

❸ *113 km (71 mi) south of Rancagua.*

Curicó, founded in 1743, is the gateway to the Valle de Curicó. The bustling industrial town has a few sights of its own, but its main attraction is its proximity to surrounding vineyards. The lovely **Plaza de Armas** has a pretty fountain ringed by statues of nymphs. Nearby is an elaborate bandstand that was constructed in New Orleans in 1904. The **Iglesia San Francisco,** five blocks east of the central plaza, houses a statue of the Virgen de la Velilla that was brought from Spain in 1734. It has been named a national monument.

The local **Ruta del Vino** office (✉ Merced 341 ☎ 75/328–972 🌐 www. rvvc.cl) provides basic information and arranges tours with English-speaking guides to a dozen nearby wineries.

The Molina Vineyard that surrounds **Viña San Pedro** is the largest in Latin America. Viña San Pedro is one of Chile's oldest wineries, as the first vines were planted here in 1701. It's also among the most modern, with 28 half-million-liter stainless-steel tanks producing more wine than any other competitor except Concha y Toro. San Pedro makes the premium lines of Cabo de Horbos and Castillo de Molino as well as the ubiquitous Gato Negro and Gato Blanco brands. The bottling plant has a sleek glass dome and a second-floor viewing platform. Tours can be arranged through the Ruta del Vino office in Curicó. ✉ *Ruta 5 S, Km 205* ☎ *75/ 492–770; 2/235–9144 in Santiago* 🌐 *www.vinosdechile.cl* ☉ *Weekdays 9:30–5:30.*

Immediately off the Pan-American Highway is **Viña Miguel Torres,** one of Chile's most visitor-savvy vineyards. An orientation video providing a glossy overview of the winery all but nominates owner Don Miguel

Torres for sainthood. The Spanish vintner may actually deserve the honor, as he single-handedly started the wine revolution in Chile. When he set up shop here in 1972, he had to import from Spain all the equipment needed to make wine. Now the methods he introduced to the region are taken for granted. Also from his native country came the idea for an annual fiesta: Torres established the wine harvest festival that takes place in Curicó's main square each year. ⊠ *Ruta 5 S, Km 195, Curicó* ☎ *75/564–100* ⊕ *www.migueltorres.cl* ⊠ *Free* ⊘ *Daily 10–7.*

A 13,000-acre national reserve 70 km (43 mi) southeast of Curicó, **Reserva Nacional Radal Siete Tazas** is famous for the unusual "Seven Teacups," a series of pools created by waterfalls along the Río Claro. From the park entrance, where you'll find a CONAF station, the falls are a short hike away. Farther along the trail are two other impressive cascades: the Salto Velo de la Novia (Bride's Veil Falls) and Salto de la Leona (Lioness Falls). Visible throughout the park is the *loro tricahue*, an endangered species that is Chile's largest and most colorful parrot. Camping is permitted in the park, which is snowed over in winter. October–March is the best time to visit. ⊠ *Camino Molina–Parque Inglés* ☎ *71/228–029* ⊠ *1,000 pesos* ⊘ *Daily 8:30–1 and 2–5:30.*

Vichuquén

❹ *112 km (69 mi) west of Curicó.*

An hour's drive from Curicó, this once isolated community was a popular country retreat for Santiago business executives rich enough to helicopter in for the weekend. There is now a paved road almost all the way to the lake; nevertheless, the town retains a remote feeling, with just a few streets and very little traffic. Black-necked swans are a common sight on meandering Lago Vichuquén and nearby Laguna Torca, which is a protected area. Popular pastimes include swimming, windsurfing, boating, and fishing.

The **Museo Colonial de Vichuquén** displays ceramics, stone tools, and other artifacts collected from pre-Hispanic peoples. ⊠ *Av. Manuel Rodríguez s/n* ☎ *75/400–045* ⊠ *700 pesos* ⊘ *Tues.–Sun. 8:30–10 and 1–8.*

Where to Stay & Eat

$ ✕⚄ **Hotel Playa Aquelarre.** This two-story structure of native woods affords unmatched views of Lago Vichuquén, with many rooms overlooking the lake from private decks. The hotel has excellent water-sports facilities, plus Jet Ski classes. The discotheque is a popular night spot, and the restaurant is the best on the lake—many people arrive by motorboat. ⊠ *Sector Aquelarre, Lago Vichuquén* ☎☎ *75/400–018* ⊕ *www. lagovichuquen.cl* ⊃ *12 rooms* ⚲ *Restaurant, boating, jet skiing, bicycles, bar, dance club, laundry service; no a/c, no room TVs* ⊟ *AE, DC, MC, V* ⎟◎⎥ *BP.*

$ ⚄ **Marina Vichuquén.** The comfortable Marina Vichuquén has an enviable location right on the shore as well as its own marina. Many rooms have nice views of the lake and the surrounding pine forests. There are plenty of opportunities for water sports, including a sailing school for children. If you want to explore the nearby countryside, you can rent horses or mountain bikes. ⊠ *Sector Aquelarre, Lago Vichuquén* ☎ *75/ 400–265* 🖶 *75/400–274* ⊕ *www.marinavichuquen.cl* ⊃ *18 rooms* ⚲ *Restaurant, tennis court, pool, exercise equipment, boating, jet skiing, marina, bicycles, horseback riding, volleyball, bar, recreation room, shop, baby-sitting, playground, laundry service, Internet; no a/c, no room TVs* ⊟ *AE, DC, MC, V* ⎟◎⎥ *BP.*

Talca

⑤ *56 km (35 mi) south of Curicó.*

Straddling the banks of the Río Claro, Talca is one of the most attractive towns in the Central Valley. Founded in 1692, it is laid out on a regimented grid pattern extending out from the Plaza de Armas. It's divided into quadrants—*poniente* means west and *oriente* east; *sur* means south and *norte* north. You can make out the city's orderly colonial design from **Cerro de la Virgen,** a hill that affords a panoramic view of Talca and the vineyards in the distance. One of the most pleasant stretches of green is **Avenida O'Higgins,** a cedar-lined boulevard popular with joggers, skaters, and strolling couples. At its western tip is the Balneario Río Claro, where you can hire a boat to paddle down the river.

The **Museo O'Higgiano,** one block east of the Plaza de Armas, is a pink colonial mansion that belonged to Albano Pereira, a tutor of national hero Bernardo O'Higgins. As Chile's first president, O'Higgins signed the country's proclamation of independence in this house in February 1818. Declared a national monument in 1971, it now houses the city's fine arts museum, which has a collection of more than 500 paintings by local artists. ⊠ *1 Norte and 2 Oriente* ☎ *71/227–330* ☒ *Free* ☉ *Tues.–Fri. 10–7, weekends 10–2.*

Talca is the capital of the Valle del Maule, one of Chile's most important wine-producing regions, and a dozen wineries are scattered along the Maule River valley between Talca and San Javier. The **Valle del Maule Ruta del Vino** office, east of town, arranges visits to nearly a dozen wineries. They can provide transportation and an English-speaking guide, which simplifies and enriches a visit. The office is in the **Villa Cultural Huilquilem,** a hacienda built in 1850 that also holds a small museum of religious art and a restaurant. ⊠ *Camino a San Clemente, Km 7* ☎ *71/246–460* ⊕ *www.chilewineroute.com* ☉ *Weekdays 10–1 and 3–7, Sat. 10–1.*

The **Domaine Oriental** winery was named for its location east of the city. A five-minute drive east out of Talca on a dirt road takes you to a massive iron gate bearing the winery's initials, beyond which stands a red hacienda with a barrel-tile roof. The vineyards themselves climb up into the Andean foothills. It is also known as Casa Donoso, since the Donoso family owned the estate for many generations before it was purchased in 1989 by four Frenchmen. The oenological work is done by a skilled Chilean staff, and the results are auspicious. The Casa Donoso label's blend of cabernet sauvignon, which lends the structure, and carmenère, which brings out the soft edges, is one of Chile's most promising reserves. ⊠ *Camino a Palmira, Km 3.5* ☎ *71/242–506* ⊕ *www.domaineoriental. cl* ☒ *Free* ☉ *Wed.–Sun. 8:30–1:30 and 3–6:30.*

There may be no better way to get to know the Central Valley than by taking a ride on Chile's only remaining *ramal* (branch-line railroad), which runs from Talca to the coastal city of Constitución. The 100-km (62-mi) **Ramal Talca–Constitución** makes a slow trip to the coast—it's 2½ hours each way—stopping for about 15 minutes at each of the small towns en route. In Constitución you'll be able to admire the coastal cliffs and rock formations. The train departs Talca's Estación de Tren daily at 7:30 AM, returning at 6 PM. In high season (December–April) a train also leaves at 11 and returns at 9. A good option is to arrange a tour on which you take the train to Constitución, then board a van to visit nearby sand dunes and other natural attractions. Contact **Turismo Ruta Verde** (☎ 71/674–824 ⊕ www.rutaverde.cl) for more information on the train tour.

The town of **San Clemente**, 16 km (10 mi) southeast of Talca, hosts the best rodeo in the region September–April, with riding, roping, dances, and beauty-queen competitions. The events take place weekends 11–6. The national championship selections are held here toward the end of the season.

Where to Stay & Eat

$ ✕ **Rubén Tapío.** One of the best restaurants in the Central Valley, Rubén
Fodor'sChoice   Tapío is renowned for its refined service and outstanding cuisine. The
★   elegant dining rooms make you feel like a guest in someone's home. The spacious bar, which displays most local wines, is a nice spot for a cocktail. Signature dishes include a *caldillo de congrio dorado* (conger eel stew) that is reputed to be Pablo Neruda's recipe, curried salmon, *lomo estilo corralero* (tenderloin in a shellfish sauce), and *chupe de locos* (abalone casserole topped with shredded cheese). ☒ *2 Oriente 1339* ☎*71/ 237–875* ☰ *AE, DC, MC, V* ⊘ *Closed Sun.*

$ ✕ **Vivace.** Hardwood, tiles, and brick decorate the warm dining room, and window tables overlook the lovely tree-lined boulevard at Vivace, one of Talca's most popular restaurants. The Italian menu includes the familiar, such as lasagna Bolognese, but also original entrees, such as *conejo mediterraneo* (rabbit with vegetables in a sherry sauce), fettuccine *con ragú de ciervo* (with a venison sauce), and fettuccine *con ragú de cordero* (with a curried lamb and pistachio sauce). The restaurant occupies a refurbished home half a block northwest of the Plaza de Armas, on the diagonal road. ☒ *Isodoro del Solar 50* ☎ *71/238–337* ☰ *AE, DC, MC, V* ⊘ *Closed Sun.*

$ ⌂ **Hostal del Puente.** This quiet, family-run hotel, at the end of a dusty street several blocks west of the Plaza de Armas, is quite a bargain. Simple carpeted rooms have small desks and windows that open onto a portico or overlook the parking area in back. Try to get one of the older rooms, in front, where a narrow garden holds níspero and cherry trees. The owners provide inexpensive breakfasts and free travel advice. ☒ *1 Sur 407* ☎☎ *71/220–930* ↩ *14 rooms* ♦ *Dining room, cable TV, no-smoking rooms; no a/c, no room phones* ☰ *No credit cards.*

$ ⌂ **Hotel Terrabella.** Talca's most comfortable accommodations are in a remodeled house half a block west of the Plaza de Armas. Though neither especially bright nor spacious, the rooms are tasteful and spotless. The ground floor holds a small lounge and a restaurant enclosed in glass walls with a view of the backyard and swimming pool. The shady lawn hemmed by gardens, and the friendly staff make this a pleasant, if not luxurious, place to stay. ☒ *1 Sur 641* ☎☎ *71/226–555* ↩ *29 rooms, 2 suites* ♦ *Restaurant, in-room data ports, in-room safes, cable TV, pool, laundry service, business services, meeting room; no a/c* ☰ *AE, DC, MC, V* ⊘❙ *BP.*

Nightlife

Pura Candela (☒ Isidoro del Solar 38 ☎ 41/236–505), in a colorful house just northwest of the Plaza de Armas, draws a young professional crowd Tuesday–Saturday. There's live Latin music on Friday and Saturday evenings, as well as a cover charge.

Horseback Riding

Horseback-riding tours are an excellent way to explore the amazing mountain scenery east of Talca. **Achibueno Expediciones** (☒ Ruta L-45, Km 8, Linares ☎☎ 73/375–098) runs two- to ten-day horseback trips through the Andes that pass waterfalls, hot springs, and mountain lakes. **Expediciones Quizapu** (☒ Casilla 421, Talca ☎ 71/621–592) arranges three- to seven-day horseback expeditions that combine camping and overnight stays in rustic farmhouses.

The **Centro Artesanal Antumapu** (⊠ 1 Sur 1330, Galería Bavaria ☎ no phone) sells work by 17 local artisans, including ceramics, jewelry, leather, and woolen goods. The **Mercado Central** (⊠ 1 Sur, between 4 and 5 Oriente ☎ no phone) is undergoing incremental reconstruction following a fire years ago, but stands still operate along its periphery, including several that sell ceramics, copperware, baskets, and other handicrafts.

San Javier

❻ *21 km (13 mi) south of Talca.*

The small, bustling town of San Javier serves as the gateway to half a dozen Valle del Maule vineyards. Most of these wineries are family-run establishments, where the owners hand-label each bottle. In San Javier itself is **Viña Balduzzi.** Albano Balduzzi, who came from generations of wine makers in Italy, built the 40-acre estate here in 1906. His grandson, Jorge Balduzzi, still lives here, making a million liters of wine each year. The premium label features varietals such as cabernet sauvignon, sauvignon blanc, carmenère, merlot, and a sweet late-harvest chardonnay. The winery accepts individual visits, but the guides don't speak English very well. Tours include a peek at the cellars that stretch underneath the property, and the collection of antique machinery, as well as a tasting. ⊠ *Av. Balmacaeda 1189* ☎ *73/322–138* ⊕ *www.balduzzi.cl* ✉ *5,000 pesos* ◐ *Mon.–Sat. 9–6.*

Colbún

❼ *50 km (31 mi) southeast of Talca.*

The tiny town of Colbún sits near a 93-square-km (36-square-mi) lake formed after a hydroelectric dam was built on the Río Maule in 1985. The largest such plant in Chile, it produces half the country's electrical power. The lake, stocked with trout, is an especially popular destination for fly-fishing aficionados. You can also rent motorboats and Jet Skis.

Hikers love the **Reserva Nacional Alto de Lircay,** with its lengthy trails that cut through native oak forest on their way to the volcanic cones of the Andes. To reach the CONAF-administered park, head east on Ruta 115, which is called the Camino Internacional Paso Pehuenche. Turn left at the signs past the hamlet of Corralones. About 25 km (16 mi) farther is the reserve. The park is snowed over July–September. ☎ *71/228–029* ✉ *1,700 pesos* ◐ *Daily 8:30–5:30.*

$ ▥ **Casas el Colorado.** Fields of grazing horses surround this lovingly restored 19th-century hacienda, not far from Colbún's lake. On the grounds is the simple wood-and-brick chapel of Santa Teresita de los Andes, where mass is still said on Sundays. It was constructed over the foundations of a Jesuit church dating from 1790; you can visit the ruins in the basement. The restaurant here is the best in the area; grilled salmon and filet mignon are house specialties. If you're going to spend some time here, pay for the full meal plan—otherwise there are additional charges for use of the spa and other facilities. ⊠ *Km 46, Colorado* ☎☎ *71/221–750* ⊕ *www.hotelcasaselcolorado.cl* ⮑ *25 rooms* ⚫ *Restaurant, 6-hole golf course, tennis court, pool, exercise equipment, spa, horseback riding, bar, recreation room, shop, meeting rooms, helipad; no a/ c* ▭ *AE, DC, MC, V* ⎯⎯ *BP, FAP.*

RÍO BÍO BÍO

The mighty Río Bío Bío empties into the Pacific Ocean at the regional capital of Concepción, a pleasant city of about 500,000 people with an important university but few attractions. The area's other major community, Chillán, is known for its attractive handicrafts market. It is also the gateway to the mountains of Termas de Chillán. Here, skiing rules in winter, hiking and horseback riding are possible in summer, and hot springs draw people year-round.

Chillán

8 *157 km (97 mi) south of Talca.*

Friendly, tranquil Chillán isn't much to look at, but it's worth a stop for its colorful market. At the sprawling **Feria de Chillán** (⊠ Av. 5 de Abril between Calles Maipón and Arturo Prat) dozens of vendors sell crafts from all over Chile, including woven clothing, pottery, jewelry, and handicrafts. It's open daily until sunset. Across the street is the main market, where vendors sell locally produced sausages called *longaniza*, which you'll see hanging from stalls. The sight of thousands of these dangling rings of pork makes it clear that this delicacy is a staple of the local diet.

The heart of Chillán is the verdant **Plaza de Armas,** the city's pretty main square. A plaque honors Bernardo O'Higgins, who was born here in 1778. The modern **Catedral de Chillán,** on the east side of the main square, is constructed of nine parabolic arches. All ornamentation is eschewed inside and out, except for a crucifix above the altar, the stations of the cross in the spaces between the arches, and the mosaic above the entrance. A huge cement cross, even taller than the church itself, stands outside.

After an earthquake devastated Chillán in 1939, prompting a major reconstruction effort in the city, Pablo Neruda, then Chile's ambassador to Mexico, arranged a visa allowing Mexican painter David Alfaro Siqueiros to travel to Chile. He painted an incendiary mural in the **Escuela México** (⊠ Av. O'Higgins and Vega de Saldias), about five blocks from the Plaza de Armas. The mural depicts indigenous peoples being murdered by the Spanish conquistadors. Neruda lost his job because of the resulting scandal, but the mural remains.

Where to Stay & Eat

$–$$ ✕ **Centro Español.** The narrow dining room of this small restaurant on the Plaza de Armas curves gracefully, as if reacting to the sinuous form of the adjacent cathedral, and its large widows overlook the plaza's massive trees. The menu has a good selection of local seafood and meat dishes as well as such traditional Spanish favorites as paella and *arroz a la valenciana*, a comparable seafood and rice dish. The building here also houses the Spanish Friends Society. ⊠ *Calle Arauco 555* ☎ *42/242–121* ⊟ *AE, DC, MC, V* ✹ *Closed Sun.*

$ ⊡ **Hotel Las Terrazas.** The carpeted rooms here are on the small side, with tiny desks, but they have large baths and picture windows—those on the east side of the building afford memorable views of the Andes. The lounge has pillowy furniture that invites you to linger over the pisco sour that greets you when you arrive. Steps from the Plaza de Armas, Las Terrazas occupies the fifth and sixth floors of a small shopping center. ⊠ *Constitución 664, 5th floor* ☎ *42/227–000* 🖷 *42/227–001* ⊕ *www. lasterrazas.cl* ⮂ *35 rooms, 2 suites* ⟡ *Restaurant, room service, in-room safes, minibars, cable TV, laundry service, Internet, meeting room; no a/c* ⊟ *AE, DC, MC, V* ⊦⊙⊧ *BP.*

Termas de Chillán

❾ *78 km (49 mi) east of Chillán.*

Billed as the continent's "most complete ski resort," Termas de Chillán has a mountainside location that rivals Valle Nevado and Portillo. Nine lifts carry skiiers to 28 groomed runs, including one that is the longest in South America. There are snowmobiling and snowboarding, as well as more unusual activities such as Alaskan malamute sledding. Come summertime the activities switch to hiking and horseback riding. Ski lifts are still used to take people to the top of the mountain, from which they can hike down. Year-round, you can soak in the waters of the hot springs for which the resort was named—they are funneled into several swimming pools.

Where to Stay

During the ski season, rooms at the two resort hotels here can only be arranged in three-, four-, and seven-night packages, which include half-board (breakfast and dinner), lift tickets, use of the hot springs, and transportation from Chillán or Concepción. They also offer nightly rates when available. Rates change weekly during the ski season, varying considerably over the course of four months and peaking in mid-July. Hotels in nearby Las Trancas rent rooms by the night year-round.

★ **$$$$**   **Gran Hotel Termas de Chillán.** This impressive deluxe facility offers skiing June–October, hiking and other outdoor activities December–April, and a state-of-the-art spa year-round. A stepped, seven-story building contains colorful, carpeted rooms with picture windows that take in either the ski hill and granite peaks, or a tree-lined mountainside. Rooms on the seventh floor are slightly cramped, but cost less. The spacious lobby and bar overlook the thermal pool and forested grounds. The restaurant serves mostly buffets, since meals are included in the rates. Activities for all ages make this a fun summer destination. ⊠ *Termas de Chillán* ☎ *42/223–887 or 42/366–8726; 2/233–1313 in Santiago* ⊕ *www.termaschillan.cl* ⇗ *109 rooms* ♻ *Restaurant, room service, in-room safes, minibars, cable TV, 2 tennis courts, 1 indoor pool, 2 outdoor pools, gym, hair salon, spa, mountain bikes, hiking, horseback riding, squash, downhill skiing, ski shop, bar, dance club, recreation room, shop, baby-sitting, children's programs, laundry service, Internet, meeting rooms* ▤ *AE, DC, MC, V* ⦿❘ *All-inclusive.*

$$$$ **Hotel Pirigallo.** Though dwarfed by the nearby Gran Hotel and lacking its sweeping views, the Pirigallo provides access to the same outdoor diversions for a little less money. Guest rooms and the restaurant surround a pool fed by the hot springs. Rooms are on the small side, but have large windows overlooking either the pool or surrounding forest; a few of them have tiny balconies. Room rates cover meals, lift tickets, spa service, and summer activities. ⊠ *Termas de Chillán* ☎ *42/223–887; 2/233–1313 in Santiago* ⊕ *www.skichillan.com* ⇗ *48 rooms* ♻ *Restaurant, room service, cable TV, some minibars, pool, spa, downhill skiing, bar, baby-sitting, laundry service* ▤ *AE, DC, MC, V* ⦿❘ *MAP, all-inclusive.*

★ **$**   **Parador Jamón, Pan y Vino.** Though 6 km (4 mi) short of the Termas proper, in the community of Las Trancas, this small lodge has a great location near the mountains and an impressive waterfall. Wooden buildings give the place a frontier feel, especially the lobby and restaurant, with their fireplace and various wood stoves. Guest rooms are rustic but spacious and have wood stoves and a porch overlooking verdant grounds. Three-bedroom cabins are perfect for small groups. The restaurant serves a good selection of seafood and a few meat dishes; try the house specialty, *jamón serrano* (smoked ham). ⊠ *Km 70, Termas de Chillán*

☎ 42/222–682 🖨 42/221–054 🛏 *15 rooms, 6 cabins* ♨ *Restaurant, pool, hot tub, sauna, billiards, bar, recreation room, laundry service* ⊟*AE, DC, MC, V.*

Concepción

🔟 *112 km (70 mi) southwest of Chillán.*

Earthquakes have devastated this coastal city since it was founded in 1551. The latest few, in 1939 and 1960, destroyed pretty much any historic building still standing. The regional capital is a mishmash of modern buildings, many in disrepair and most aesthetically awry. The city straddles the Río Bío Bío, with two mile-long bridges (Puente Viejo and Puente Nuevo) crossing to the other side. **Plaza de la Independencia**, also called Plaza de Concepción, is the heart of the city, with pedestrian shopping streets radiating from its borders. To the west of the plaza stands the **Catedral de Concepción**, a massive grey structure built in the 1940s to replace a church destroyed by the 1939 earthquake.

Cerro Caracol, or Conch Hill, overlooks the city from the southeast, and is popular with joggers, hikers, and mountain bikers. You can reach the pine-tree-covered hill by heading south on Calle Tucapel. Park along the mossy cobblestone streets and wander among the many footpaths that lead into the woods.

The **Museo de la Historia de Concepción** depicts regional history through a dozen dioramas, including the 1939 earthquake that devastated the city; battles between the Spanish invaders and the indigenous Mapuche people; and Alonso de Ercilla writing the epic poem *La Auraucana* in 1557. Rooms upstairs are dedicated to changing art exhibitions. The museum is in Parque Ecuador, at the foot of Cerro Caracol. ⊠ *Lamas and Lincyán* ☎ *41/231–830* 🖾 *Free* ☉ *Tues.–Sun. 10–1:30 and 3–6.*

★ The **Casa del Arte**, at the Universidad de Concepción, contains the country's largest, and arguably best, collection of classical Chilean paintings. The museum is most famous for the striking mural by Mexican artist Jorge González Camarena. Unaware of the presence of a protruding staircase until he saw the room, González incorporated it into the work. It now bears the snaky form of Quetzalcoatl, a symbol of Aztec culture. Climb Quetzalcoatl to the galleries displaying selections from the collection of more than 1,600 works, including major canvases by Alfredo Valenzuela Puelma. Past exhibits in the three halls downstairs have included works by Picasso and the promising young painter, sculptor, and designer José Fernández Covich. ⊠ *Av. Chacabuco at Av. Paicavi* ☎ *41/204–126* 🖾 *Free* ☉ *Tues.–Fri. 10–6, Sat. 10–4, Sun. 10–1.*

Where to Stay & Eat

\$\$ ✕ **El Faro Belén.** While it may not appear like much from the outside, this nautically themed restaurant serves some of the best seafood in Concepción. A towering wooden mermaid surveys the dining room, which overflows with locals on weekday afternoons. If you're a big eater, try the *plato americano*, a selection of seven seafood dishes including sea bass, shrimp, salmon, and clams, all served cold. A more intimate dining room is tucked away upstairs. ⊠ *Av. Bulnes 382* ☎ *41/243–430* ⊟ *AE, DC, MC, V* ☉ *No dinner Sun.*

★ \$–\$\$ ✕ **Canto de Luna.** This popular restaurant is perched over the water on Laguna Chica, a small lake in San Pedro, on the south side of the river. Giant windows and a wraparound deck overlook the surrounding lake, hemmed in by forested hills. The food rivals the view, with an enticing mix of grilled meat and seafood and an eclectic collection of European dishes such as *risotto de mariscos* (seafood risotto) and salmon *al pa-*

pillote (baked in paper). The wine list is extensive. There's a buffet at night and at lunch on Sundays, when reservations are a must. ✉ *Av. Costanera 825, San Pedro* ☎ *41/284–545* ▭ *AE, DC, MC, V* ☺ *No dinner Sun.*

$–$$ ✕ **Solo Carne.** Serious carnivores enjoy this popular *parrillada*, which serves everything from steak to lamb to *jabalí* (wild boar). Complement your grilled meat with any of a dozen fresh sauces, including sauces made from pesto, Roquefort, pepper, and capers. The name, which translates as "Meat Only," isn't entirely accurate: the restaurant also serves inexpensive pastas, including spinach or crab cannelloni, as well as seafood starters such as ceviche. Dining is in several rooms with high wooden ceilings and paintings on the walls. It's a 10-minute drive from downtown, behind the Holiday Inn. ✉ *Av. San Andres 78, Lomas de San Andrés* ☎ *41/480–199* ▭ *AE, DC, MC, V* ☺ *Closed Sat.*

$$ ▦ **Hotel El Araucano.** Though a bit run-down, Hotel El Araucano is still a good choice for its excellent location next to the Plaza de la Independencia. The bathrooms are on the small side and the minibars are clearly relics from an earlier era, but the rooms have large windows with great city views—those on the upper floor on the west side overlook the Río Bío Bío. Because the hotel primarily serves business travelers, rooms here are half price on weekends. ✉ *Caupolicán 521* ☎ *41/740–606* 🖷 *41/740–623* ⊕ *www.hotelcarrera.cl* ⇗ *138 rooms, 6 suites* ⚑ *Restaurant, room service, in-room safes, minibars, cable TV, indoor pool, sauna, shops, laundry service, business services, meeting rooms, airport shuttle, free parking, no-smoking rooms; no a/c* ▭*AE, DC, MC, V* ¹⁰¹*BP.*

$ ▦ **Hotel Terrano.** From Avenida Bernardo O'Higgins, this hotel looks small and uninviting, but don't be fooled. It's actually quite spacious, with a taller wing hidden in the back that provides room for a restaurant and even a cavernous convention hall. Inside are bright and cheerful rooms with comfortable beds. The baths are fairly large, with extras like hair dryers and phones. Windows in upper-floor rooms overlook the surrounding hills. ✉ *Av. O'Higgins 340* ☎☎ *41/240–078* ⊕ *www.hotelterrano.com* ⇗ *68 rooms, 2 suites* ⚑ *Restaurant, room service, in-room safes, minibars, cable TV, exercise equipment, billiards, bar, laundry service, business services, convention center, free parking; no a/c* ▭*AE, DC, MC, V* ¹⁰¹ *BP.*

¢–$ ▦ **Hotel San Sebastian.** This hotel, spread over several floors in an old building on busy Calle Rengo, behind the Catedral, is quite likely Concepción's best lodging deal. Simple, clean rooms have large windows, high ceilings, and prints of modern art on the walls. Some have private bathrooms, but most share baths. There's a comfortable lounge next to the reception. ✉*Rengo 463* ☎☎ *41/243–412* ⇗*10 rooms, 5 with shared bath* ⚑ *Cable TV, laundry service; no a/c* ▭ *AE, DC, MC, V* ¹⁰¹ *BP.*

Nightlife

Nearly all this city's bars and dance clubs are clustered in the Barrio de la Estación, several blocks along Arturo Prat across from the Estación Ferrocarriles. Within walking distance of the train station are dozens of nocturnal lairs, which run the gamut from cozy pubs to crowded discotheques. **Treinta y Tantos** (✉ Arturo Prat 402 ☎ 41/251–516), one of the Barrio de la Estación's more bohemian spots, is famous for its extensive selection of empanadas, which make it a good option for a light dinner or late-night snack.

Shopping

The best selection of handicrafts and other gift items can be found in the gallery of small shops surrounding the Hotel El Araucano. Head to the underground **Artesanias Yanara** (✉ Caupolicán 521, Local 64 ☎ 41/242–617) for various souvenirs, including wool sweaters, decorative copper plates, mugs, jewelry, and knickknacks. **El Carro** (✉ Caupolicán 521, Local 43 ☎ 41/232–543) carries ceramics, copper work, and jewelry made of local lapis lazuli and *piedra cruz* set in silver. The jewelry store **Itacolor** (✉ Caupolicán 521, Local 36-A ☎ 41/229–178) sells lapis lazuli, jade, and other semiprecious stones set in silver and gold.

THE CENTRAL VALLEY A TO Z

To research prices, get advice from other travelers, and book travel arrangements, visit www.fodors.com.

AIR TRAVEL
LanChile runs half a dozen flights per day from Santiago to Concepción.
🚹 Carrier **LanChile** ✉ Barros Arana 600, Concepción ☎ 41/521-092 or 41/229-138.

AIRPORT
Concepción's Aeropuerto Carriel Sur—5 km (3 mi) northwest of town—is the only major airport in the region. It's a good choice if you plan to explore the area around the Río Bío Bío. Otherwise it may be more convenient to fly into Santiago.
🚹 Airport Information **Aeropuerto Carriel Sur** ☎ 41/732-000.

BUS TRAVEL
The two big bus companies in the region, Pullman Bus and Tur-Bus, offer hourly departures during the day between Santiago and Rancagua, Talca, Curicó, Chillán, and Concepción. There is less frequent service to Santa Cruz.
🚹 Bus Lines **Pullman Bus** ☎ 2/779-2026. **Tur-Bus** ☎ 2/270-7500.
🚹 Bus Terminals **Chillán Terminal María Teresa** ✉ Av. O'Higgins 10 ☎ 42/272-149. **Concepción Terminal Puchucay** ✉ Terminal Principal Collao, Calle Tegualda 860 ☎ 41/311-511. **Rancagua Terminal Sur** ✉ Dr. Salinas 1165 ☎ 72/230-340. **Talca Terminal de Buses** ✉ 12 Oriente and 2 Sur ☎ 71/243-270.

CAR RENTALS
Most visitors to the Central Valley who rent a vehicle do so in Santiago. If you find you need a car while traveling in the region, you can rent one from Avis or Hertz, both of which have offices in Aeropuerto Carriel Sur and downtown Concepción. The Chilean company Rosselot has agencies in Concepción and Talca.
🚹 Agencies **Avis** ✉ Aeropuerto Carriel Sur ☎ 41/480-089 ✉ Av. Chacabuco 726, Concepción ☎ 41/235-837. **Hertz** ✉ Aeropuerto Carriel Sur ☎ 41/480-088 ✉ Av. Arturo Prat 248, Concepción ☎ 41/230-341. **Rosselot** ✉ Aeropuerto Carriel Sur, Concepción ☎ 41/732-010 ✉ Av. San Miguel 2710, Talca ☎ 71/247-979.

CAR TRAVEL
The Central Valley is sliced in half by Chile's major highway, the Pan-American Highway. With the exception of Concepción, it passes through all of the major towns in the region. Since so many of the sights are off the beaten path, traveling by car is often the most convenient way to see the region. The speed limit here is 100 kph (62 mph). Be aware that road conditions vary greatly. Many of the secondary roads in the region remain unpaved.

INTERNET
In the major cities in the Central Valley, there are always one or two Internet cafés. In smaller towns, however, they are much harder to find. Cyber Planet Café, across from the tourist information office in Talca, is open daily 9:30 AM–11:30 PM. Concepción has various Internet cafés, among them Cyber C@fé, a block north of the Catedral, which is open

daily 9:30 AM–midnight. Also here is Moonblass Café, which is open Monday–Saturday 9:30 AM–10:30 PM and Sunday 4 PM–9 PM.

🖪 Internet Cafés **Cyber C@fé** ✉ Caupolican 588, Concepción ☎ 41/238-394. **Cyber Planet Café** ✉ 1 Poniente 1282, Talca ☎ 71/210-775. **Moonblass Café** ✉ Aureliano Manzano 538, Concepción ☎ 41/910-233.

MAIL & SHIPPING
There's at least one post office in every town in the Central Valley. Because of the proximity to Santiago, mail service is quicker here than in other regions.

🖪 Post Offices **Chillán** ✉ Calle Libertad 505 ☎ 42/223-272. **Concepción** ✉ Calle Colo Colo 417 ☎ 41/235-666. **Curicó** ✉ Carmen s/n ☎ 75/310-000. **Rancagua** ✉ Calle Campos at Calle Cuevas ☎ 72/230-413. **Talca** ✉ 1 Oriente 1150 ☎ 71/227-271.

MONEY MATTERS
Traveler's checks can be used at nearly all hotels and many restaurants. Every town has at least one bank with an ATM on its central plaza or main commercial street, and ATMs are also common in shopping centers, bus stations, large gas stations, and other spots where people congregate. The following are central banks in major towns.

🖪 Banks **Banco Concepción** ✉ Constitución 550, Chillán ☎ 42/221-306. **Banco del Estado** ✉ 1 Sur 971, Talca ☎ 71/223-285. **Banco Sudamericano** ✉ Independencia at Bueras, Rancagua ☎ 72/230-413. **BCI** ✉ Plaza de Armas 286-A, Santa Cruz ☎ 72/825-059. **Citibank** ✉ Av. O'Higgins 499, Concepción ☎ 41/233-870.

TOURS
In addition to the Ruta del Vino offices, which specialize in vineyard tours, there are several operators in the region that arrange day trips and overnight excursions. Casa Chueca, a guesthouse and outdoor outfitter near Talca, runs day trips to Constitución and the Reserva Nacional Radal Siete Tazas, white-water rafting trips, and hiking expeditions. Maule Ando Tours arranges various city tours of Talca. Tursimo Ruta Verde, in Constitución, arranges the train tour between Ramal Talca and Constitución, horseback riding, and trips to various sites near Talca.

RAM offers tours of Concepción and environs as well as excursions to Chillán, the waterfall and protected area of Salto del Laja, and the upper Río Bío Bío. Ecoturismo Puelche, in Chillán, runs one- to seven-day horseback tours in the nearby mountains.

🖪 Tour Operators **Casa Chueca** ✉ Talca ☎ 71/370-096 ⊕ www.trekkingchile.com. **Ecoturismo Puelche** ✉ Vegas de Saldía 688, Chillán ☎ 42/224-829. **Maule Ando Tours** ✉ 1 Poniente 1282, Talca ☎ 71/210-775. **RAM** ✉ Martinez de Roca 869-E, Concepción ☎ 41/733-007. **Turismo Ruta Verde** ✉ Constitción ☎ 71/674-824 ⊕ www.rutaverde.cl.

TRAIN TRAVEL
Although service in much of the rest of the country has been gutted, the train remains an excellent way to travel among towns in the Central Valley. Express trains from Santiago to the cities of Rancagua, Curicó, Talca, Chillán, and Concepción are faster than taking the bus or driving. Local trains are slower, but they stop in the smaller towns along that route.

🖪 Train Stations **Chillán** ✉ Av. Brasil at Libertad ☎ 42/222-424. **Concepción** ✉ Av. Arturo Prat at Calle Barros Arana ☎ 41/226-925. **Curicó** ✉ Maipú 567 ☎ 75/310-028. **Rancagua** ✉ Av. Viña del Mar at Carrera Pinto ☎ 72/225-239. **Talca** ✉ 11 Oriente and 2 Sur ☎ 71/232-721.

VISITOR INFORMATION
Sernatur has outstanding offices with English-speaking staff in Concepción, Rancagua, and Talca. The offices are open weekdays 8:30–6.

🖪 **Concepción** ✉ Anibal Pinto 460, Plaza de Armas ☎ 41/227-976. **Rancagua** ✉ German Riesco 277, Offices 2 and 3 ☎ 72/230-413. **Talca** ✉ 1 Poniente 1281 ☎ 71/226-940.

THE LAKE DISTRICT

6

By Jeffrey Van Fleet

AS YOU TRAVEL THE WINDING ROADS of the Lake District, the snow-capped shoulders of volcanoes emerge, mysteriously disappear, then materialize again, peeping through trees or towering above broad valleys. The sometimes difficult journey through breathtaking mountain passes is inevitably rewarded by views of a glistening lake, vibrant and blue. You might be tempted to belt out "The hills are alive . . . ," but this is southern Chile, not Austria. With densely forested national parks, a dozen large lakes, easy access to transportation and facilities, and predominantly small, family-run lodgings, this area has come pretty close to perfecting tourism.

The Lake District is the historic homeland of Chile's indigenous Mapuche people, who revolted against the early Spanish colonists in 1598, driving them out of the region. They kept foreigners out of the area for nearly three centuries. Though small pockets of the Lake District were controlled by Chile after it won its independence in 1818, most viewed the forbidding region south of the Río Bío Bío as a separate country. After a treaty ended the last Mapuche war in 1881, Santiago began to recruit waves of German, Austrian, and Swiss immigrants to settle the so-called empty territory and offset indigenous domination. The Lake District took on the Bavarian sheen still evident today.

Exploring the Lake District

The Lake District's altitude descends sharply from the towering peaks of the Andes on the Argentine border, to forests and plains, and finally to sea level, all in the space of about 200 km (120 mi). The Pan-American Highway (Ruta 5) runs straight down the middle, making travel to most places in the region relatively easy. It connects the major cities of Temuco, Osorno, and Puerto Montt, but bypasses Valdivia by 50 km (30 mi). A drive from Temuco to Puerto Montt should take less than four hours. Flying between the hubs is a reasonable option. A Temuco–Puerto Montt ticket, for example, costs 15,000 pesos.

About the Restaurants

Meat and potatoes characterize the cuisine of this part of southern Chile. The omnipresent *cazuela* (a plate of rice and potatoes with beef or chicken) and *pastel de choclo* (a corn, meat, and vegetable casserole) are solid, hearty meals. Though more associated with Chiloé, the southern Lake District dishes up its own *curanto*, a fish stew served with lots of bread.

Arguably the greatest gifts from the waves of German immigrants were their tasty *küchen*, rich fruit-filled pastries. (Raspberry is a special favorite here.) Sample them during the late afternoon *onces*, the coffee breaks locals take to tide them over until dinner. The Germans also brought their beer-making prowess to the New World; Valdivia, in particular, is recognized as Chile's brewing center, home to the popular Kunstmann brand.

About the Hotels

If you've traveled in Europe, you may feel at home in the Lake District, where most of the lodgings resemble old-world hotels. Many hostelries, even the newly built ones, are constructed in Bavarian-chalet style echoing the region's Germanic heritage. A handful of lodgings—Temuco's Hotel Continental, Pucón's Hotel Antumalal, and Puerto Octay's Hotel Centinela—are also historic landmarks that shouldn't be missed. The owners of many smaller places are couples in which one

6

Numbers in the text correspond to numbers in the margin and on the Lake District map.

If you have 3 days

Fly directly to 🚉 **Temuco** ❶ 🛫 and spend the afternoon shopping for Mapuche handicrafts at the city's Mercado Municipal. Rise early the next morning and drive to 🚉 **Villarrica** ❹ or 🚉 **Pucón** ❺, where you can spend the day exploring a beautiful area, maybe taking a dip in one of the nearby thermal springs. The next day take a hike up Volcán Villarrica.

If you have 5 days

Spend your first day in 🚉 **Temuco** ❶ 🛫. On your second day head south to 🚉 **Valdivia** ❾, where you can spend the afternoon visiting the modern art and history museums on Isla Teja. Catch an evening cruise along the Río Valdivia. Rise early the next day and drive to the Bavarian-style village of 🚉 **Frutillar** ⓮ on Lago Llanquihue. Visit the Museo Colonial Alemán and wind up the afternoon partaking of the Chilean *onces* ritual with a cup of coffee and küchen. Head for 🚉 **Puerto Varas** ⓯ the next day for a thrilling rafting excursion on the nearby Río Petrohué. Save **Puerto Montt** ⓱ for the final day, and spend the afternoon shopping for handicrafts in the Angelmó market stalls. Finish with a seafood dinner at one of the market's lively restaurants.

---

spouse is Chilean and the other is German, combining what one such pair calls "the best of both worlds: Chilean warmth and Germanic efficiency."

Central heating is a much-appreciated feature in most lodgings here during the winter and on brisk summer evenings. Air-conditioning is unheard of, but then it's rarely necessary this far south. Rates usually include a Continental breakfast of coffee, cheese, bread, and jam. Although most of the places listed here stay open all year, call ahead to make sure the owners haven't decided to take a well-deserved vacation during the March–November off-season.

WHAT IT COSTS In pesos (in thousands)				
	$$$$	**$$$**	**$$**	**$**	**¢**
RESTAURANTS	over 11	8–11	5–8	2.5–5	under 2.5
HOTELS	over 105	75–105	45–75	15–45	under 15

Restaurant prices are for a main course at dinner. Hotel prices are for a double room in high season, excluding tax.

Timing

Seemingly everyone heads here during southern Chile's glorious summer, between December and February. Visiting during the off-season is no hardship, though, and lodging prices drop dramatically. An increasing number of smog-weary Santiaguinos flee the capital in the winter to enjoy the Lake District's brisk, clear air. Just be prepared for rain and some snow at higher elevations.

LA ARAUCANÍA

The tourism industry uses "Lake District" to denote the 400-km (240-mi) stretch of land beginning in Temuco and running south to Puerto Montt, but Chileans only call the southern part of this region *Los Lagos* (The Lakes). To the north is the fiercely proud La Araucanía, whose regional government seems to emblazon its name on everything possible.

La Araucanía is the historic home of the Araucano, or Mapuche, culture. The Spanish both feared and respected the Mapuche. This nomadic society, always in search of new terrain, was a moving target that the Spaniards found impossible to defeat. Beginning with the 1598 battle against European settlers, the Mapuche kept firm control of the region for 300 years. After numerous peace agreements failed, a treaty signed near Temuco ended hostilities in 1881 and paved the way for the German, Swiss, and Austrian immigration that would transform the face of the Lake District.

It may not be called Los Lagos, but La Araucanía contains some of Chile's most spectacular lake scenery. Several volcanoes, among them Villarrica and Llaima, two of South America's most active, loom over the region. Burgeoning Pucón, on the shore of Lago Villarrica, has become the tourism hub of southern Chile. Other quieter alternatives exist, however. Lago Calafquén, farther south, begins the seven-lake Siete Lagos chain that stretches across the border to Argentina.

Temuco

▶ ❶ *675 km (405 mi) south of Santiago.*

The south's largest city, and Chile's fastest-growing metropolis, Temuco has a more Latin flavor than the communities farther south. (It could be the warmer weather and the palm trees swaying in the pleasant central park.) This northern gateway to the Lake District is an odd juxtaposition of modern architecture and indigenous markets, of traditionally clad Mapuche women darting across the street and business executives talking on cell phones, but oddly enough, it all works. This is big-city life Chilean style, and it warrants a visit of a day or two.

Bustling **Plaza Aníbal Pinto,** Temuco's central square, is ringed with imported palm trees—a rarity in this part of the country. A monument to the 300-year struggle between the Mapuche and the Spaniards sits in the center. The small subterranean **Galería de Arte** displays rotating exhibits by Chilean artists. ✉ *Plaza Aníbal Pinto* ☎ *45/236–785* 🎫 *Free* ⊙ *Mon.–Sat. 10–1 and 3–8; Sun. 10–1.*

The city's modern **Catedral de Temuco** sits on the northwest corner of the central square, flanked by an office tower emblazoned with a cross.

Lined with lime and oak trees, a shady secondary square called **Plaza Teodoro Schmidt** lies six blocks north of the Plaza Aníbal Pinto. It's ruled over by the 1906 Iglesia Santa Trinidad, an Anglican church that is one of the city's oldest surviving structures.

Housed in a 1924 mansion, the **Museo Regional de la Araucanía** covers the history of the area. It has an eclectic collection of artifacts and relics, including musical instruments, utensils, and the country's best collection of indigenous jewelry. Upstairs, exhibits document the Mapuche people's three-century struggle to keep control of their land. The presentation could be more evenhanded: the rhetoric glorifies the Central European colonization of this area as the *pacificación de la Araucanía*

Beaches Despite its long coastline, this part of southern Chile historically looks inward rather than to the sea. Development is sparse along the coast, except for a couple of beach communities near Valdivia and Puerto Montt. Most tourists seeking fun in the sun concentrate on the inland lakes. Chileans from the north flock to the gray-sand beaches on Lago Llanquihue, Lago Villarrica, and others.

6

Nightlife An early-to-bed, early-to-rise ethic brought by the Germans, combined with years of curfews under the former government, didn't infuse the region with a wild nightlife. That said, the streets are still lively on summer evenings, with everyone out dining, strolling, shopping—and enjoying the glorious sunsets that don't fade until 10 PM. Businesses keep much later hours during the December–February high season.

Sports & the Outdoors Awash in rivers, mountains, forests, gorges, and its namesake lakes, this part of the country is Chile's outdoor capital. Outfitters traditionally have concentrated in the northern resort town of Pucón and the southern Puerto Varas, but firms up and down this 400-km-long (240-mi-long) slice of Chile can rent you equipment, or guide your excursions.

You can—take a deep breath—go white-water rafting, canoeing, kayaking, mountain biking, fishing, volcano climbing, rappelling, canyoning, horseback riding, skiing, snowshoeing, snowboarding, waterskiing, bird-watching, hiking, swimming, sailing, and skydiving. The most recent addition to the activities mix is the canopy tour: you can make like a bird and glide through the treetops, courtesy of zip lines, helmets, and a very secure harness.

Shopping The Lake District is one of the best places to purchase traditional wares of two of Chile's strongest regional cultures, one native to this part of the country, the other not. The best selection of woolen blankets and ponchos of the indigenous Mapuche people is sold in the markets of Temuco, most notably in the Mercado Municipal. Chilote woolens come from nearby Chiloé, but the best place to buy these handicrafts is not the island itself, but at the market stalls of Caleta Angelmó near Puerto Montt.

(taming of the Araucanía territories). But the museum gives you a reasonably good Spanish-language introduction to Mapuche history, art, and culture. ⊠ *Av. Alemania 84* ☎ *45/211–108* 🖃 *500 pesos* ☉ *Weekdays 9–5, Sat. 11–5, Sun. 11–1.*

The imposing **Monumento Natural Cerro Ñielol** is the hillside site where the 1881 treaty between the Mapuche and the Chilean army was signed, allowing for the city of Temuco to be established. Trails bloom with bright red *copihues* (a bell-like flower with lush green foliage), Chile's national flower, in autumn (March–May). The monument, not far from downtown, is part of Chile's national park system. ⊠ *Av. Prat, 5 blocks north of Plaza Teodoro Schmidt* 🖃 *700 pesos* ☉ *Jan.–Mar., daily 8 AM–11 PM; Apr.–Nov., daily 8:30–12:30 and 2:30–6.*

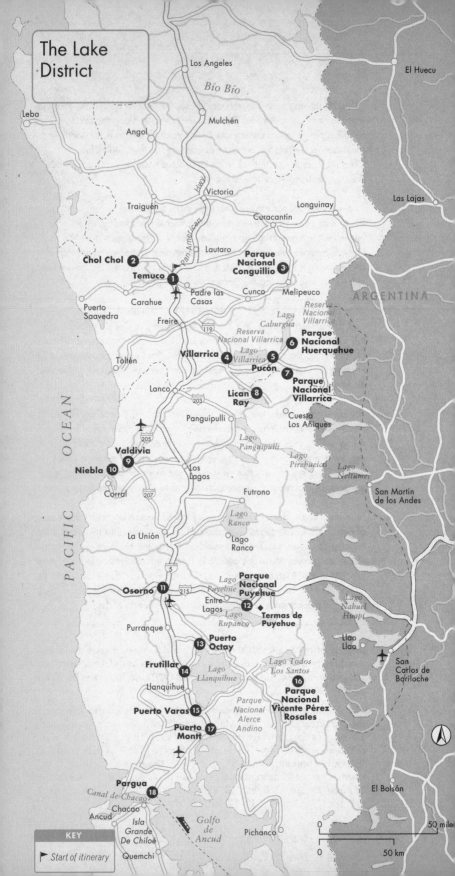

The Lake District

KEY

▶ Start of itinerary

Where to Stay & Eat

$$-$$$ ✕ **El Fogón.** Decorated with primary colors—yellow walls, red tablecloths, and blue dishes—this place certainly stands out in pastel-hue Temuco. The Chilean-style *parrillada*, or grilled beef, is the specialty of the house. Barbecue here has subtler spices than its better-known Argentine counterpart. The friendly owners will gladly take the time to explain the menu to the uninitiated. Even though this is close to downtown, you should splurge on a cab if you're coming to this dark street at night. ⊠ *Aldunate 288* ☎ *45/952–163* ☱ *AE, DC, MC, V.*

$$-$$$ ✕ **La Estancia.** The Ranch restaurant occupies a rustic wooden house with reindeer heads on the walls and cured hams hanging from the ceiling. You can dine out in the garden during the summer. It serves good southern beef in the form of steaks, roasts, and barbecues. ⊠ *Rudecindo Ortega 02340-A Interior* ☎ *45/220–287* ☱ *AE, DC, MC, V* ☉ *No dinner Sun.*

$$-$$$ ✕ **La Pampa.** The wealthy professionals of this bustling city frequent this upscale modern steak house for its huge, delicious cuts of beef and the best *papas fritas* (french fries) in Temuco. Although most Chilean restaurants douse any kind of meat with a creamy sauce, this is one of the few exceptions: the entrées are served without anything but the simplest of seasonings. ⊠ *Caupolicán 0155* ☎ *45/329–999* ⚑ *Reservations essential* ☱ *AE, DC, MC, V* ☉ *No dinner Sun.*

$-$$ ✕ **Centro Español.** The basement dining room of Centro Español, an association that promotes Spanish culture in Temuco, is open to all for lunch and dinner. You have your choice of four or five rotating prix-fixe menus. There will always be something Spanish, something seafood, and something meaty to choose from. *Jamón de Serrano*, a salty type of ham, is a specialty. ⊠ *Brunes 483* ☎ *45/217–700* ☱ *AE, DC, MC, V.*

$-$$ ✕ **Confitería Central.** Coffee and homemade pastries are the specialties of this café, but sandwiches and other simple dishes are also available. Piping-hot empanadas are served on Sundays and holidays. ⊠ *Bulnes 442* ☎ *45/210–083* ☱ *DC, MC, V.*

$-$$ ✕ **Mercado Municipal.** In the central market around the produce stalls are small stands offering such typical Chilean meals as cazuela and pastel de choclo. Many have actually taken on the trappings of sit-down restaurants, and a few even have air-conditioning. The complex closes at 8 in the summer and 6 the rest of the year, so late-night dining is not an option. ⊠ *Manuel Rodríguez 960* ☎ *no phone.*

★ $ ✕▥ **Hotel Continental.** If you adore faded elegance and don't mind an uneven floorboard or two and few conveniences, the 1890 Continental is for you. Checkered in black-and-white tiles, the lobby has leather furniture, antique bronze lamps, and handsome *alerce* and *raulí* (native wood) trims. Rooms, painted in ash-blue and cream tones, have hardwood floors and lofty ceilings. The hotel has hosted Nobel laureates Pablo Neruda and Gabriela Mistral, and former president Salvador Allende. The restaurant serves delicious French cuisine. Good choices include the steak au poivre and the salade Niçoise. ⊠ *Antonio Varas 708* ☎ *45/238–973* 🖷 *45/233–830* ⊕ *www.turismochile.cl/continental/* ⇨ *40 rooms, 18 with bath* ⚐ *Restaurant; bar, meeting room; no a/c, no room TVs* ☱ *AE, DC, MC, V* ▯⊖ *CP.*

$ ✕▥ **Hotel Frontera.** This lovely old hotel is really two in one, with *nuevo* (new) and *clásico* (classic) wings facing each other across Avenida Bulnes. Tastefully decorated rooms have double-paned windows to keep out the street noise. Opt for the less expensive rooms in the newer wing—they're nicer anyway. La Taberna, the downstairs restaurant on the clásico side, has excellent steak and seafood dining. An orchestra plays and people dance on weekends. ⊠ *Bulnes 733–726* ☎ *45/200–400* 🖷 *45/200–401* ⊕ *www.hotelfrontera.cl* ⇨ *60 rooms, 2 suites*

CloseUp

THE PEOPLE OF THE LAND

THE MAPUCHE PROFOUNDLY AFFECTED the history of southern Chile. For almost 300 years this indigenous group fought to keep colonial powers out of their land. The Spanish referred to these people as the Araucanos, from a word in the Quechua language meaning "brave and valiant warriors." In their own Mapudungun language, today spoken by some 400,000 people, the word Mapuche means "people of the land." In colonial times only the Spanish missionaries, who were in close contact with the Mapuche, seemed to grasp what this meant. "There are no people in the world," one of them wrote, "who so love and value the land where they were born."

Chilean schoolchildren learning about the Mapuche are likely to read about Lautaro, a feared and respected young chief whose military tactics were instrumental in driving out the Spanish. He cunningly adopted a know-thy-enemy strategy that proved tremendously successful in fending off the colonists. Students are less likely to hear about the tightly knit family structure or nomadic lifestyle of the Mapuche. Even the region's two museums dedicated to Mapuche culture, in Temuco and Valdivia, traditionally focused on the three-century war with the Spaniards. They toss around terms like pacificación (meaning "to pacify" or "to tame") to describe the waves of European immigrants who settled in the Lake District at the end of the 1800s, the beginning of the end of Mapuche dominance in the region.

Life has been difficult for the Mapuche since the signing of a peace treaty in 1881. Their land was slowly taken by the Chilean government. Some 200,000 Mapuche today are living on 3,000 reducciones (literally meaning "reductions"), operated much like reservations in the United States. Other Mapuche have migrated to the cities, in particular fast-growing Temuco, in search of employment. Many have lost their identity in the urban landscape, scraping together a living as handicraft vendors.

A resurgence in Mapuche pride these days takes several forms, some peaceful, some militant. Mapuche demonstrations in Temuco are now commonplace, many calling attention to deplorable conditions on the reducciones. Some are seeking the return of their land, although others are fighting against the encroachment of power companies damming the rivers and logging interests cutting down the forests. News reports occasionally recount attacks and counterattacks between indigenous groups and farmers in remote rural areas. The courts have become the newest battleground as the Mapuche seek legal redress for land they feel was wrongfully taken.

Awareness of Mapuche history is rising. (Latest census figures show that about 1 million of Chile's population of 15 million can claim some Mapuche ancestry.) Both major museums have devoted more of their space to the art, language, and culture of this people. Both institutions spend ample time these days discussing the group's distinctive textiles, with their bold rhomboid, triangular, and zigzagging lines. Both museums also devote considerable space to traditional animal-shape pottery.

There is also a newfound interest in the Mapuche language and its seven dialects. Mapudungun poetry movingly describes the sadness and dilemma of integration into modern life and of becoming lost in the anonymity of urban life. Never before really understood by others who shared their land, the Mapuche may finally make their cause known.

—Jeffrey Van Fleet

                ♿ *Restaurant, minibars, bar, convention center, meeting room; no a/c*
                🚭 *AE, DC, MC, V* ❑❘ *BP.*

$$–$$$ 🏨 **Hotel Terraverde.** Temuco's most luxurious lodging combines all the comforts of a modern hotel with the style of a hunting lodge. The dramatic, glass-enclosed spiral staircase has a view of Cerro Ñielol. Cheerful rooms have lovely wood furnishings. Rates include a huge breakfast buffet, a nice change from the roll and coffee served at many other lodgings in the region. It's part of Chile's Panamericana Hoteles chain. ✉ *Av. Prat 220* 🕾 *45/239–999; 2/234–9610 in Santiago* 🖷 *45/239–455; 2/234–9608 in Santiago* 🌐 *www.panamericanahoteles.cl* 🛏 *64 rooms, 9 suites* ♿ *Restaurant, in-room safe, minibars, pool, piano bar, convention center, meeting rooms, no-smoking rooms* 🚭 *AE, DC, MC, V* ❑❘ *BP.*

$$ 🏨 **Holiday Inn Express.** This hotel is one of four of the chain's outlets in Chile. It comes complete with U.S.-style amenities, including the do-it-yourself breakfast for which the chain is known. It's adjacent to a shopping mall on the northern outskirts of town. ✉ *Av. Rudecindo Ortega 1800* 🕾 *45/223–300* 🖷 *45/224–100* 🌐 *www.hiexpress.com* 🛏 *62 rooms* ♿ *Dining room, pool, hot tub, gym, laundry facilities, business services, no-smoking rooms* 🚭 *AE, MC, V* ❑❘ *CP.*

$ 🏨 **Don Eduardo Hotel.** Orange inside and out, this pleasant nine-story hotel is made up entirely of cozy furnished apartments. All have two or three bedrooms and kitchenettes. The many business travelers who frequent the place appreciate the work area. An eager-to-please staff tends to your needs. ✉ *Bello 755* 🕾 *45/214–133* 🖷 *45/215–554* 🛏 *33 apartments* ♿ *Business services; no a/c* 🚭 *AE, DC, MC, V.*

$ 🏨 **Hotel Aitué.** The exterior is unimposing, but this small, pleasant business-class hotel has bright, airy rooms with a tan and lavender color scheme. They come complete with minibars and music systems. ✉ *Antonio Varas 1048* 🕾 *45/212–512* 🖷 *45/212–608* 🌐 *www.hotelaitue.cl* 🛏 *34 rooms* ♿ *Coffee shop, minibars, bar, business services, meeting rooms, laundry service; no a/c* 🚭 *AE, DC, MC, V.*

$ 🏨 **Nuevo Hotel Turismo.** Originally established as a budget accommodation, this three-story hotel retains its bland facade. The interior has been upgraded, with a comfortable lobby and rooms with their own music systems. A lime-green color scheme permeates throughout. ✉ *Av. Lynch 563* 🕾 *45/213–151* 🖷 *45/232–902* 🌐 *www.nuevohotelturismo.cl* 🛏 *30 rooms* ♿ *Restaurant, bar, laundry service; no a/c* 🚭 *AE, DC, MC, V.*

¢–$ 🏨 **Hotel Espelette.** The large and airy rooms at this simple hotel surround a spacious lobby overflowing with knickknacks. The decor throughout— flowers all over the wallpaper and drapes—echoes the Basque origins of the owners. Soft beds compensate for hard pillows the size of watermelons. The hotel is a few blocks from the main square. ✉ *Claro Solar 492* 🕾🖷 *45/234–805* 🛏 *9 rooms, 4 with bath* ♿ *No a/c, no TV in some rooms* 🚭 *AE, DC, MC, V.*

Shopping

Casa de la Mujer Mapuche (✉ Arturo Prat 283 🕾 45/233-886), an indigenous women's center, lets you shop for textiles, ponchos, and jewelry in its display room, with a minimum of fuss. (The organization even handles catalogue sales.) Proceeds support social development programs. It's open weekdays 9:30–1 and 3–6.

A little more rough-and-tumble than the Mercado Municipal is the **Feria Libre** (✉ Barros Arana and Miraflores). You can bargain hard with the Mapuche vendors who sell their crafts and produce in the blocks surrounding the railroad station and bus terminal. Leave the camera behind, as the vendors aren't happy about being photographed. It's open until 2 Monday–Saturday.

The **Mercado Municipal** (✉ Manuel Rodríguez 960 ☎ no phone) is one of the best places in the country to find Mapuche woolen ponchos, pullovers, and blankets. The interior of the 1930 structure has been extensively remodeled, opening it up. The low-key artisan vendors share the complex with butchers, fishmongers and fruit sellers. There is no bargaining, but the prices are fair. It's open daily, but closes around 3 on Sundays

Across the Río Cautín from Temuco is the suburb of **Padre Las Casas** (✉ 2 km [1 mi] southeast of Temuco), a Mapuche community whose center is populated by artisan vendors selling locally crafted woodwork, textiles, and pottery under the auspices of the town's rural development program. You can purchase crafts here weekdays 9–5.

Sports & the Outdoors

CONAF (✉ Bilbao 931 ☎ 45/298–221) administers Chile's national parks and provides maps and other information about them. In the summer it also organizes hikes in Parque Nacional Conguillío. The agency is strict about permits to ascend the nearby volcanoes, so expect to show evidence of your ability and experience.

Chol Chol

❷ *29 km (18 mi) northwest of Temuco.*

The Chol Chol experience begins the moment you board the bus in Temuco. Expect to share space with Mapuche vendors and their enormous sacks and baskets of fruits and vegetables, all returning from market. A trip in your own vehicle is much less wearing, but infinitely less colorful, too. Regardless of your chosen mode of transport, you'll arrive to the sight of *rucas,* traditional indigenous thatch huts, plus claptrap wooden houses, horsedrawn carts, and artisan vendors lining the dusty streets—selling their wares from 9 until about 6. Photo opportunities are plentiful, but be unobtrusive and courteous with your camera. Locals dislike being treated as merely part of the scenery.

The small **Museo de Chol Chol** exhibits a collection of animal-shape ceramics and textiles with bold rhomboid and zigzag designs—both are distinctively Mapuche specialties—as well as old black-and-white photographs. A *fogón,* the traditional cooking pit, graces the center of the museum. ✉ *Balmaceda s/n* ☎ *45/611–034* 💲 *300 pesos* ☉ *Tues.–Sun. 9–6.*

Parque Nacional Conguillío

❸ *91 km (54 mi) east of Temuco.*

Volcán Llaima, which erupted as recently as 1994 and showed increasing activity in 2002, is the brooding centerpiece of Parque Nacional Conguillío. The 3,125-m (10,200-ft) monster, one of the continent's most active volcanoes, has altered the landscape—much of the park's southern portion is a moonscape of hardened lava flow. But in the 610-square-km (235-square-mi) park's northern sector there are thousands of umbrella-like araucaria pines, often known as monkey puzzle trees.

The Sierra Nevada trail is the most popular for short hiking. The three-hour trek begins at park headquarters on Laguna Conguillío, continuing northeast to Laguna Captrén. One of the inaugural sections of the Sendero de Chile, a hiking and biking trail, passes through the park. Modeled on the Appalachian Trail in the United States, the project will eventually span the length of the country.

Heavy snow can cut off the area in winter, so November to March is the best time to visit the park's eastern sector. Conguillío's western sector, Los Paraguas, comes into its own in winter because of a small ski center. ⊠ *Entrances at Melipeuco and Curacautín* ☎ *45/298–221 in Temuco* ☎ *2,500 pesos* ⊙ *Dec.–Mar., daily 8 AM–10 PM; Apr.–Nov., daily 8–5.*

Where to Stay

$–$$ ⊞ **Cabañas Conguillío.** The only accommodation available close to the park, Cabañas Conguillío rents basic four- or six-person cabins built around the trunks of araucaria trees. All come with kitchen utensils, stove, and cooking fuel. Also here are an on-site restaurant and a small store where you can stock up on provisions. ⊠ *Laguna Conguillío* ☎ *45/272–402* ⇌ *10 cabins* △ *Restaurant, grocery; no a/c, no room phones, no room TVs* ⊟ *No credit cards* ⊙ *Closed Apr.–Nov.*

Villarrica

❹ *87 km (52 mi) southeast of Temuco.*

Villarrica was founded in 1552, but the Mapuche wars prevented extensive settlement of the area until the early 20th century. Today, the pleasant town on the lake of the same name is in one of the loveliest, least spoiled areas of the southern Andes. Villarrica lives in the shadow of Pucón, its flashier neighbor a few miles down the road. Many travelers drive through without giving Villarrica a glance, but they're missing out. Villarrica has some wonderful hotels that won't give you high-season sticker shock. Well-maintained roads and convenient public transportation make Villarrica a good base for exploring the area.

The municipal museum, **Museo Histórico y Arqueológico de Villarrica**, displays an impressive collection of Mapuche ceramics, masks, leather, and jewelry. A replica of a ruca graces the front yard. It's made of thatch so tightly entwined that it's impermeable to rain. ⊠ *Pedro de Valdivia 1050* ☎ *45/413–445* ☎ *100 pesos* ⊙ *Jan.–Feb., Mon.–Sat. 9–1 and 4–10; Mar.–Dec., Mon.–Sat. 9–1 and 3–7:30.*

Where to Stay & Eat

$–$$$ ✕ **The Travellers.** This restaurant's owners met by happenstance and decided to open a place serving food from their far-flung homelands. The result is a place that serves one or two dishes from Thailand, Italy, Mexico, and many countries in between. While you chow down on an enchilada, your companions might be having spaghetti with meatballs or sweet-and-sour pork. Dining on the front lawn under umbrella-covered tables is the best option on a summer evening. ⊠ *Valentín Letelier 753* ☎ *45/412–830* ⊟ *AE, DC, MC, V.*

$–$$ ✕ **Café 2001.** For a filling sandwich, a homemade küchen, and an espresso or cappuccino brewed from freshly ground beans, this is the place to stop in Villarrica. Pull up around a table in front or slip into one of the quieter booths by the fireplace in the back. The *lomito completo* sandwich—with a slice of pork, avocado, sauerkraut, tomato, and mayonnaise—is one of the best in the south. ⊠ *Camillo Henríquez 379* ☎ *45/411–470* ⊟ *AE, DC, MC, V.*

$$$$ ⊞ **Villarrica Park Lake Hotel.** The Park Lake captures the perfect mix of plushness and clean, uncluttered design—a sumptuous old European spa with thoroughly modern touches. There's ample use of hardwood in the bright, spacious common area and the rooms—each with its own balcony—that descend down a hill toward Lago Villarrica. ⊠ *13 km (8 mi) east of Villarrica* ☎ *45/45–0000; 2/207–7070 in Santiago* 🖷 *45/45–0202; 2/207–7020 in Santiago* ⊕ *www.villarrica.com/parklake/*

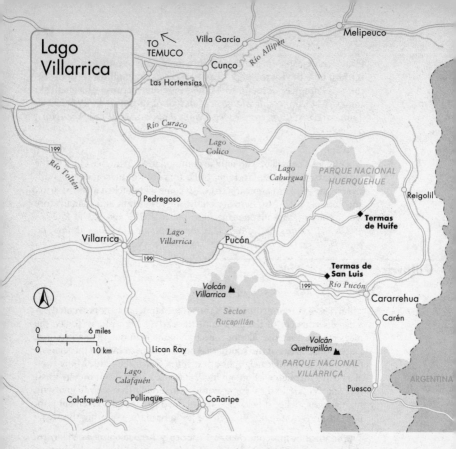

📇 *61 rooms, 10 suites* ⚒ *Restaurant, in-room data ports, in-room safes, minibars, 2 pools, indoor pool, gym, hair salon, hot tub, sauna, spa, 3 bars, baby-sitting, dry cleaning, laundry service, business services, meeting rooms* ▭ *AE, DC, MC, V.*

$$–$$$

Fodor'sChoice ★

🏨 **Hostería de la Colina.** The friendly American owners of this hostería, Glen and Beverly Aldrich, provide attentive service as well as special little touches like homemade ice cream. Rooms in the half-century-old main house are a mix of large and small, carpets and hardwood floors, all tastefully decorated with wood furnishings. Two bright, airy hillside cottages are carpeted and wood-paneled and have private patios. There's a hot tub heated by a wood-burning stove and a serene *vivero* (greenhouse) and garden that attracts birds. The terrace has stupendous views of Lago Villarrica. ✉ *Las Colinas 115* ☎ *45/411–503* ⊕ *www. hosteriadelacolina.com* 📇 *8 rooms, 2 cabins* ⚒ *Dining room, hot tub, Ping-Pong, bar; no a/c, no room phones, no room TVs* ▭ *AE, DC, MC, V* ⎟⊙⎟ *BP.*

$$

🏨 **El Parque.** You can take in the commanding views of Lago Villarrica from just about anywhere at this 70-year-old rustic, quaint retreat—from the plush lobby, the sitting area, the restaurant, and the rooms. Warm earth tones color the guest rooms. Eleven modern cabins amble down the hill to a private beach and dock. Each cabin, which accommodates 2–10 people, comes with a kitchen, fireplace, and terrace. ✉ *Camino Villarrica–Pucón, Km 2.5* ☎ *45/411–120* 🖶 *45/411–090* ⊕ *www. hotelelparque.cl* 📇 *8 rooms, 11 cabins* ⚒ *Restaurant, tennis court, pool, meeting room* ▭ *AE, MC, V* ⎟⊙⎟ *BP.*

$$

🏨 **Hotel El Ciervo.** Villarrica's oldest hotel is an unimposing house on a quiet street, but inside are elegant details such as wrought-iron fixtures and wood-burning fireplaces. Spacious rooms, some with their own fireplaces, have huge beds and sparkling bathrooms. Just outside is a lovely pool and a secluded patio. Rates include an enormous German breakfast with loads of fruit, muesli, and fresh milk. El Ciervo also has all-inclusive seven-day tour packages. ⊠ *General Körner 241* ☎ *45/411–215* 🖷 *45/410–925* ⊕ *www.hotelelciervo.cl* 🖘 *12 rooms* ♧ *Restaurant, pool, laundry service, meeting rooms; no a/c* ⊟ *AE, DC, MC, V* ⦿ *BP.*

$ ⊞ **Montebianco Hotel.** The owner makes many of the wood furnishings that fill this central lodging. The pleasant rooms upstairs all have small balconies. The tiled bathrooms are clean and bright, but the showers are tiny, with barely enough room to turn around. ⊠ *Pedro de Valdivia 1011* ☎ *45/411–798* 🖷 *45/411–536* ⊕ *http://hotelmontebianco.cl* 🖘 *12 rooms* ♧ *Restaurant, bar, meeting room; no a/c* ⊟ *AE, DC, MC, V* ⦿ *CP.*

Horseback Riding

The friendly, knowledgeable folks at **Flor del Lago** (⊠ Camino a Pedregoso, Km 9 ☎ 45/415–455 ⊕ www.flordellago.cl) will take you on half- or full-day horseback-riding excursions in the forests surrounding Lago Villarrica.

Pucón

❺ *25 km (15 mi) east of Villarrica.*

The trendy resort town of Pucón, on the southern shore of Lago Villarrica, attracts wealthy, fashionable Chileans. Like their counterparts in the Colorado ski resort of Vail, they come to enjoy their luxurious vacation homes, stroll along the main strip, and flock to the major night spots. For every fan, Pucón has a detractor who laments the town's growth. A stream of ugly billboards appears at the turnoff from the Pan-American Highway and continues until you reach town. But many don't seem to mind, and Pucón remains one of Chile's top tourist draws.

Where to Stay & Eat

$$–$$$$ ✕ **La Maga.** Argentina claims to prepare the perfect parrillada, or grilled beef, but here's evidence that Uruguayans just might do it best. Watch the beef cuts or salmon turn slowly over the wood fire at the entrance. That, rather than charcoal, is the key, says the owner, a transplant from Punta del Este. The end product is a wonderfully smoked, natural taste, accented with a hint of spice in the mild *chimichurri* (a tangy steak sauce) ⊠ *Fresia 125* ☎ *45/444–277* ⊟ *No credit cards.*

$$–$$$$ ✕ **¡Viva Perú!** As befits the name, Peruvian cuisine reigns supreme at this restaurant in a thatch-roof house with rustic wooden tables. Try the *ají de gallina* (hen stew with cheese, milk, and peppers) or the ceviche, thoroughly cooked but served cold. You can dine on the porch or order to carry out. ⊠ *O'Higgins 761* ☎ *45/444–285* ⊟ *AE, DC, MC, V.*

$$–$$$ ✕ **En Alta Mar.** The best seafood in Pucón is served here, so don't be frightened off by the nondescript dining room: basic wooden tables and the ubiquitous nautical theme. You'll receive a free welcoming pisco sour when you arrive. ⊠ *Fresia and Urrutia* ☎ *45/442–294* ⊟ *AE, DC, MC, V.*

¢–$ ✕ **Arabian Restaurant.** The dishes served here reflect the friendly owner's Palestinian roots. Try the tasty falafel or *shawarma* (a pita-bread sandwich filled with spicy beef or lamb). Most everyone opts for the outdoor tables over the tiny indoor dining area. ⊠ *Fresia 354* ☎ *45/443–469* ⊟ *No credit cards.*

¢   ✕⊞ **¡école!** It's part hostel and part beach house—and takes its name from a Chilean expression meaning "Great!" Cozy two-, three-, and four-person rooms can be shared or private. The vegetarian restaurant ($–$$), a rarity in the Lake District, merits a trip in itself. Choose among truly international options, such as lasagna, burritos, and moussaka. Eat in the sunny courtyard or small dining room. The environmentally conscious staff can organize hiking and horseback-riding trips and expeditions to volcanoes and hot springs, as well as arrange for Spanish lessons and massages. ☒ *General Urrutia 592* ☎☎ *45/441–675* ⊕ *www.ecole. cl* ⤶ *23 rooms, 9 with bath* ☖ *Restaurant, bar, travel services; no a/c, no room phones, no room TVs* ☱ *AE, DC, MC, V.*

$$$$ 🏨 **Gran Hotel Pucón.** This imposing hotel, Pucón's largest, has wonderful views of Lago Villarrica. Its location right on the shore provides direct access to the beach. The rooms, however, are somewhat plain. ☒ *Clemente Holzapfel 190* ☎ *45/441–001; 2/353–0000 in Santiago* ☎ *2/207–4586 in Santiago* ⊕ *www.granhotelpucon.cl* ⤶ *145 rooms* ☖ *2 restaurants, 2 pools, massage, sauna, squash, bar, travel services; no a/c* ☱ *AE, DC, MC, V* ⭥ *BP, MAP.*

$$$$ 🏨 **Hotel Antumalal.** Perched atop a cliff overlooking Lago Villarrica, this
★ Frank Lloyd Wright–inspired masterpiece is easily one of the best hotels in Chile. Queen Elizabeth, Neil Armstrong, and Jimmy Stewart are just a few who thought so. This family-run hotel, just outside of Pucón, has the feel of a country inn. The cozy rooms have fireplaces and huge windows overlooking the spectacularly landscaped grounds. If you tire of relaxing with a refreshing pisco sour on the wisteria-shaded deck, just ask owner Rony Pollak to arrange an adventure for you. Favorites include fly-fishing, white-water rafting, and volcano cave tours. ☒ *Casilla 84* ☎ *45/441–011* ☎ *45/441–013* ⊕ *www.antumalal.com* ⤶ *16 rooms, 2 suites* ☖ *Restaurant, pool, 2 tennis courts, bar, travel services* ☱ *AE, DC, MC, V* ⭥ *BP.*

$$$$ 🏨 **Hotel del Lago.** Short on charm, this glitzy hotel has everything else you could hope for—an indoor pool, a health spa, even a movie theater. Enter through the five-story atrium lobby, then let one of the glass elevators whisk you upstairs. The rooms are simple and elegant, with blond wood and crisp white linens. The hotel is known as "the Casino" for its Las Vegas–style ground floor, complete with rows of one-arm bandits and tables for roulette and poker. ☒ *Miguel Ansorena 23* ☎ *45/ 291–000; 2/462–1900 in Santiago* ☎ *45/291–200; 2/370–5942 in Santiago* ⊕ *www.hoteldellago.cl* ⤶ *81 rooms, 2 suites* ☖ *Restaurant, snack bar, minibars, 2 pools, gym, hair salon, massage, sauna, bar, casino, business services, meeting room; no a/c* ☱ *AE, DC, MC, V* ⭥ *BP, MAP.*

$$–$$$$ 🏨 **Termas de San Luis.** The famous San Luis hot springs are the main attraction of this hideaway east of Pucón. Here you can rent a rustic cabin that sleeps up to six people. Rates include all meals and free use of the baths. If you're not staying, 6,000 pesos gets you a day of soaking in the thermal springs. ☒ *Carretera Internacional, Km 27, Catripulli* ☎☎ *45/412–880* ⊕ *www.termasdesanluis.cl* ⤶ *6 cabins* ☖ *2 restaurants, 2 pools, massage, sauna; no a/c* ☱ *No credit cards* ⭥ *FAP.*

$$$ 🏨 **Hotel Huincahue.** The elegant Huincahue is close to the center of town and has the attentive service that only a small hotel can offer. Lots of windows brighten the lobby of the German-style building, which is warmed by a roaring fire. Rates for the airy rooms include a hearty American breakfast. ☒ *Pedro de Valdivia 375* ☎☎ *45/443–540* ⊕ *www. hotelhuincahue.cl* ⤶ *20 rooms* ☖ *Coffee shop, pool, bar, laundry service; no a/c* ☱ *AE, DC, MC, V* ⭥ *BP.*

$$ 🏨 **Del Volcán.** In keeping with the region's immigrant heritage, the furnishings of this chalet-style hotel look like they come straight from Germany. Checked fabrics cover carefully fluffed duvets in the guest apartments. Many of the generously proportioned apartments also have balconies. Each unit in this central hotel sleeps up to six people. ☒ *Fresia 420* ☎ *45/442–055* ☎ *45/442–053* ⊕ *www.aparthoteldelvolcan.cl* ⤶ *18 apartments* ☖ *Dining room, in-room safes, kitchenettes, gym, free parking; no a/c* ☱ *AE, DC, MC, V* ⭥ *BP.*

$$ ☒ **Hotel Munich.** The Bavarian-style Hotel Munich stands out because the owner is a stickler for good service. Each of the rooms, furnished in native woods and decorated in soft pastels, is unique. The buffet breakfast is enormous. ⊠ *Gerónimo de Alderete 275* ☎☎ *45/444–595* ⊕ *www.pucon.com/munich* ↝ *14 rooms* ⚲ *Café, bar, laundry service; no a/c* ⊟ *No credit cards* †⦿† *BP.*

¢ ☒ **Kila Leufu.** Part of a growing agro-tourism trend in Chile, a Mapuche family has opened its red farmhouse, 15 minutes from Pucón, to temporary urban refugees anxious to partake of rural life. You can bake bread and milk the cows if you like, or just relax and read. Horseback-riding excursions cost an extra 14,000 pesos. ⊠ *Camino a Curarrehe, Puente Cabedane* ☎ *09/711–8064* ⊕ *www.kilaleufu.homestead.com* ↝ *5 rooms, 2 with bath* ⚲ *Dining room, horseback riding; no a/c, no room phones, no room TVs* ⊟ *No credit cards* †⦿† *FAP.*

Nightlife

As suits a resort town, there's plenty of nightlife activity in Pucón, but many places are on the rowdy side. Feel welcome to make an appearance at the friendly **Mamas & Tapas** (⊠ O'Higgins 597 ☎ 45/449–002). It's de rigueur among the expat crowd. Light Mexican dining morphs into DJ-generated or live music lasting into the wee hours.

Sports & the Outdoors

At first glance Pucón's myriad outfitters look the same and sell the same slate of activities and rentals; quality varies, however. The firms listed below get high marks for safety, professionalism, and friendly service. Pucón is the center for rafting expeditions in the northern Lake District.

BICYCLING **Pedal Aventura** (⊠ General Urrutia 592 ☎ 45/441–675) specializes in mountain-bike rental during the summer. **Anden Sport** (⊠ O'Higgins 535 ☎ 45/441–048) is a good bet for bikes and snowboards, snowshoes, and skis.

HORSEBACK **Huepil Malal** (⊠Km 27, Carretera a Huife ☎09/643–2673 ⊕www.huepil-
RIDING malal.cl) arranges horseback riding in the nearby Cañi mountains, with everything from half-day to six-day excursions.

WHITE-WATER Friendly **Aguaventura** (⊠ Palguín 336 ☎ 45/444–246 ⊕ www.
RAFTING aguaventura.com) outfits for rafting, as well as canoeing, kayaking, snowshoeing, and snowboarding. **Politur** (⊠ O'Higgins 635 ☎ 445/441–373 ⊕ www.politur.com) can take you rafting on the Río Trancura, trekking in nearby Parque Nacional Huerquehue, on ascents of the Volcán Villarrica, and skydiving. William Hatcher of **Sol Y Nieve** (⊠ O'Higgins and Lincoyan ☎☎ 45/441–070 ⊕ www.chile-travel.com/solnieve.htm) runs rafting trips and hiking and skiing expeditions. **Trawen** (⊠O'Higgins 311 ☎ 45/442–024 ⊕ www.trawenchile.com) specializes in kayaking—with standard and inflatable kayaks, otherwise known as duckies—on the Río San Pedro. It also leads snow trekking or canyoning excursions in the nearby Cañi mountains.

Parque Nacional Huerquehue

❻ *35 km (21 mi) northeast of Pucón.*

Unless you have a four-wheel-drive vehicle, this 124-square-km (48-square-mi) park is accessible only during the summer. (And even then, a jeep isn't a bad idea.) It's worth a visit for the two-hour hike on the Lago Verde trail beginning at the ranger station near the park entrance. You head up into the Andes through groves of araucaria pines, eventually reaching three startlingly blue lagoons with panoramic views of the whole area, including distant Volcán Villarrica. ☎ 45/298–221 *in Temuco* ✉ *2,200 pesos* ⊙ *Dec.–Mar., daily 8 AM–10 PM; Apr.–Nov., daily 8–6.*

Where to Stay

$$$ ⬚ **Termas de Huife.** Just outside Parque Nacional Huerquehue, this resort lets you relax in two steaming pools set beside an icy mountain stream. At the spa you can enjoy an individual bath, a massage, or both. The complex includes a handful of luxurious cabins, all of which have enormous tubs you can fill with water from the hot springs. Those just visiting for the day pay 6,500 pesos for entry. There's also a country house past the spa where you can soak in privacy. ✉ *33 km (20 mi) from Pucón on the road to Caburga* ☎☎ *45/441–222* ⊕ *www.termashuife.cl* ↪ *11 cabins* ⚘ *Restaurant, minibars, pool, massage, hot tub, sauna, bar; no a/c* ➡ *AE, DC, MC, V* ⊙⟊ *BP.*

Parque Nacional Villarrica

❼ *15 km (9 mi) south of Pucón.*

Fodor'sChoice   One of Chile's most popular national parks, Parque Nacional Villarrica has skiing, hiking, and many other outdoor activities. The main draw, however, is the volcano that gives the 610-square-km (235-square-mi) national park its name. You don't need to have any climbing experience to reach the 3,116-m (9,350-ft) summit of Volcán Villarrica, but a guide is a good idea. The volcano sits in the park's Sector Rucapillán, a Mapuche word meaning "house of the devil." That name is apt, as the perpetually smoldering volcano is one of South America's most active. CONAF closes off access to the trails at the slightest hint of volcanic activity. It's a steep uphill walk to the snow line, and then crampons and ice axes are needed. That equipment will be supplied by any of the Pucón outfitters that organize day-long excursions for about 3,000 pesos per person. Your reward for the six-hour climb is the rare sight of an active crater, which continues to release clouds of sulfur gases and explosions of lava. You're also treated to superb views of the nearby volcanoes, the less-visited Quetrupillán and Lanín. ✉ *15 km (9 mi) south of Pucón* ☎ *45/298–221 in Temuco* ✉ *1,100 pesos* ⊙ *Daily 8–6.*

Where to Stay

$ ⛰ **Volcán Villarrica.** This camping area run by CONAF is in the midst of a forest of *coigüe*, Chile's massive red oaks. The site charges 8,800 pesos per person and provides very basic toilets. ✉ *Sector Rucapillán* ☎ *45/298–221 in Temuco* ➡ *No credit cards.*

Skiing

The popular **Ski Pucón** (✉ Parque Nacional Villarrica ☎ 45/441–001; 2/353–0000 in Santiago ♖ 2/207–4586 in Santiago), in the lap of Volcán Villarrica, is one of the best-equipped ski areas in southern Chile, with 20 runs for varying levels of experience, nine rope tows, three double-chair tows, and equipment rental. There's also a restaurant and coffee shop. Information about the facility can be obtained from the Gran Hotel Pucón.

Lican Ray

❽ *30 km (18 mi) south of Villarrica.*

In the Mapuche language, Lican Ray means "flower among the stones." This pleasant, unhurried resort town is on Lago Calafquén, the first of a chain of seven lakes that spills over into Argentina. You can rent rowboats and sailboats along the shore. Lican Ray lacks Pucón's perfect manicure. With but one paved street, a lot of dust gets kicked up on a dry summer day.

Where to Stay & Eat

$$–$$$$ ✕ **Cábala Restaurant.** Impeccable service is the hallmark of this Italian restaurant on Lican Ray's main street. The brick-and-log building has plenty of windows where you can watch the summer crowds stroll by as you enjoy pizza and pasta. ⊠ *General Urrutia 201* ☎ *45/431–176* ⊟ *AE, DC, MC, V* ⊘ *Closed Apr.–Nov.*

$–$$$ ✕ **The Ñaños.** Hearty meats and stews are the offerings at Lican Ray's most popular eatery. Most people partake of cazuela on the plain terrace on the main street, but the wood-trimmed dining room is a lot cozier. ⊠ *General Urrutia 105* ☎ *45/431–021* ⊟ *DC, MC, V.*

$ 🏨 **Hostal Hoffman.** An attentive German woman watches over this little house just outside town. You can get lost in the plush chairs as you read a book in the sitting room. Equally plush and comfy are the bright, airy rooms with lots of pillows and thick, colorful quilts on the beds. Rates include a huge breakfast with lots of homemade breads and pastries. ⊠ *Camino a Coñaripe 100,* ☎☎ *45/431–109* ⌘ *4 rooms* ⌂ *Dining room; no a/c, no room phones, no room TVs* ⊟ *No credit cards* ⊙❘ *BP.*

$ 🏨 **Hotel Inaltulafquen.** This rambling old house sits in a garden on a quiet street fronting Playa Grande. The rooms are simple, but bright and airy and filled with plants. The cozy restaurant serves Chilean dishes. There's soft music playing in the background, but someone is bound to sit down at the piano and encourage the crowd to sing along. Credit cards are only accepted in January and February. ⊠ *Punulef 510* ☎ *45/431–115* ⌘ *8 rooms, 6 with bath* ⌂ *Restaurant, bar; no a/c, no room phones, no room TVs* ⊟ *DC, MC, V.*

Beaches

The peninsula on which Lican Ray sits has two gray-sand beaches. **Playa Chica,** the smaller of the beaches near Lican Ray, is south of town. It's popular for swimming. **Playa Grande,** to the west of Lican Ray, has rough water.

LOS LAGOS

Los Lagos, the southern half of the Lake District, is a land of snowcapped volcanoes, rolling farmland, and, of course, the shimmering lakes that give the region its name. This landscape is literally a work in progress, as it's part of the so-called Ring of Fire encircling the Pacific Rim. Most of Chile's 55 active volcanoes are here.

For a region so conscious of its heritage, history is not much in evidence. Some of Chile's oldest colonial cities are in Los Lagos, yet you may be disappointed if you come looking for colonial grandeur. Wars with indigenous peoples kept the Spaniards from building here for 300 years. An earthquake in 1960, the largest recorded in history, was centered near Valdivia and destroyed many older buildings in the region.

Anxious to fill its *tierras baldías* (uncultivated lands), Chile worked tirelessly to promote the country's virtues to German, Austrian, and Swiss immigrants looking to start a new life. The newcomers quickly set up shop, constructing breweries, foundries, shipyards, and lumberyards. By the early part of the last century, Valdivia had become the country's foremost industrial center, aided in large part by the construction of a railroad from Santiago. To this day the region retains a distinctly Germanic flare, and you might swear you've taken a wrong turn to Bavaria when you pull into towns such as Frutillar or Puerto Octay.

Valdivia

9   *120 km (72 mi) southwest of Villarrica.*

One of the Lake District's oldest and most beautiful cities, Valdivia gracefully combines Chilean wood-shingle construction with the architectural style of the well-to-do German settlers who colonized the area in the late 1800s. But the historic appearance is a bit of an illusion, as the 1960 earthquake destroyed all but a few old riverfront buildings. The city painstakingly rebuilt its downtown area, seamlessly mixing old and new buildings. Today you can enjoy evening strolls through its quaint streets and along its two rivers, the Valdivia and the Calle Calle.

Valdivia's imposing modern **Catedral de Nuestra Señora del Rosario** faces the west side of the central plaza. A small museum inside documents the evangelization of the region's indigenous peoples from the 16th through 19th centuries. ⊠ *Independencia 514* ☎ *63/232–040* ⊠ *Free* ☉ *Dec.–Mar., Tues.–Sun. 10–1 and 3–7; Apr.–Nov., Tues.–Fri. 10–1 and 3–7.*

The awning-covered **Mercado Fluvial,** in the southern shadow of the bridge leading to Isla Teja, is a perfect place to soak up the sights, sounds, and smells of a real fish market. ⊠ *Arturo Prat and Libertad* ☎ *no phone* ☉ *Mon.–Sat. 8–3.*

For a historic overview of the region, visit the **Museo Histórico y Antropológico Maurice van de Maele,** on neighboring Isla Teja. The collection focuses on the city's colonial period, during which it was settled by the Spanish, burned by the Mapuche, and invaded by Dutch corsairs. Downstairs, rooms re-create the interior of the late-19th-century Anwandter mansion that belonged to one of Valdivia's first immigrant families; the upper floor delves into Mapuche art and culture. ⊠ *Los Laureles, Isla Teja* ☎ *63/212–872* ⊠ *1,200 pesos* ☉ *Dec.–Feb., Tues.–Sun. 10–1 and 2–6; Mar.–Nov., Tues.–Sun. 10–1 and 2–8.*

Fondly known around town as the "MAC," the **Museo de Arte Contemporáneo** is one of Chile's foremost modern art museums. This Isla Teja complex was built on the site of the old Anwandter brewery destroyed in the 1960 earthquake. The minimalist interior, formerly the brewery's warehouses, contrasts sharply with ongoing construction of a modern glass wall fronting the Río Valdivia, a project slated for completion by 2010. ⊠ *Los Laureles, Isla Teja* ☎ *63/221–968* ⊕ *www.macvaldivia. uach.cl* ⊠ *Free* ☉ *Tues.–Sun. 10–1 and 3–7.*

The **Jardín Botánico,** north and west of the Universidad Austral campus, is awash with 1,000 species of flowers and plants native to Chile. It's a lovely place to walk whatever the season, but it's particularly enjoyable in spring and summer. ⊠ *Isla Teja* ☎ *63/216–964* ⊠ *Free* ☉ *Dec.–Feb., daily 8–8; Mar.–Nov., daily 8–4.*

Valdivia means beer to many Chileans, and **Cervecería Kunstmann** brews up the country's beloved lager. The Anwandter family immigrated from Germany a century-and-a-half ago, bringing along their beer-making know-how. The *cervecería* (brewery), on the road to Niebla, hosts interesting guided tours by prior arrangement. Also here are a small museum and a souvenir shop where you can buy the requisite caps, mugs, and T-shirts, plus a pricey restaurant serving German fare. ⊠ *Ruta 350 No. 950* ☎ *63/222–560* ⊠ *Free* ☉ *Restaurant and museum, daily noon–midnight.*

off the
beaten
path

Isla Huapi. Some 20% of Chile's 1 million Mapuche live on *reducciones*, or reservations. One of the most welcoming communities is on Isla Huapi, a leafy island in the middle of deep-blue Lago Ranco. It's out of the way—about 80 km (48 mi) southeast of Valdivia—but worth the trip for those interested in Mapuche culture. A boat departs from Futorno, on the northern shore of the lake, at 7 AM Monday, Wednesday, and Friday, returning at 5 PM. The pastoral quiet of Isla Huapi is broken once a year in January or February with the convening of the island council, in conjunction with the Lepún harvest festival. You are welcome during the festival, but be courteous and unobtrusive with your camera.

Where to Stay & Eat

$$–$$$$ ✕ **Camino de Luna.** The Way of the Moon floats on the Río Valdivia just north of the Pedro de Valdivia bridge. As the city is only a few miles from the ocean, it's no surprise that seafood is a speciality here. The *congrío calle calle* (conger eel in a cheese-and-tomato sauce) is particularly good. Tables by the windows offer views of Isla Teja. ⊠ *Av. Prat Costanera s/n* ☎ *63/213–788* ▤ *AE, DC, MC, V.*

$$–$$$$ ✕ **Salón de Té Entrelagos.** This swanky café caters to Valdivian business executives. The specialties are sandwiches such as the Isla Teja—a grilled chicken sandwich with tomato, artichoke hearts, asparagus, olives, and red peppers—decadent crepes, and sweet-tooth goodies. ⊠ *Vicente Pérez Rosales 640* ☎ *63/218–333* ▤ *AE, DC, MC, V.*

$–$$$ ✕ **Café Haussmann.** Take advantage of the fact that Valdivia was a center of German immigration by sampling the excellent *crudos* (steak tartare) and German-style sandwiches here. Don't forget delicious küchen for dessert. The place is small—a mere four tables and a bar, but worth a stop. ⊠ *O'Higgins 394* ☎ *63/213–878* ▤ *AE, DC, MC, V* ☉ *Closed Sun.*

$–$$$ ✕ **La Calesa.** Head to this central, well-known restaurant for a good introduction to Peruvian cuisine. Try the *ají* (chicken stew with cheese, milk, and peppers), but be careful not to burn your mouth. Peruvian dishes, particularly the stews, are spicier than their Chilean counterparts. ⊠ *Yungay 735* ☎ *63/225–467* ▤ *AE, DC, MC, V* ☉ *Closed Sun. No lunch Sat.*

$$$
Fodor'sChoice
★
Hotel Pedro de Valdivia. This pink palace near Valdivia's central square is, in a word, magnificent. With pleasant views of the Río Calle Calle, the historic hotel is most notable for its elegant appointments and excellent service. All the tasteful rooms have lovely wood furniture, and some have small terraces. ⊠ *Carampague 190* ☎ *63/212–931* 🖷 *63/203–888* ⊕ *www.hotelpedrodevaldivia.telsur.cl* ⤴ *77 rooms, 17 suites, 8 apartments* ♨ *Restaurant, in-room data ports, pool, bar, laundry service, concierge, business services, meeting rooms, airport shuttle; no a/c* ▤ *AE, DC, MC, V* ❘⊙❘ *CP.*

$$$ **Hotel Puerta del Sur.** Expect lavish pampering at a highly regarded lodging if you stay here. Spacious rooms, all with views of the river, are decorated in soft lavender tones. Play a few games of tennis, then hit the pool or relax in the hot tub. ⊠ *Los Lingues 950, Isla Teja* ☎ *63/224–500; 2/633–5101 in Santiago* 🖷 *63/211–046; 2/633–6541 in Santiago* ⊕ *www.hotelpuertadelsur.com* ⤴ *40 rooms, 2 suites* ♨ *Restaurant, in-room safes, tennis court, pool, outdoor hot tub, sauna, dock, volleyball, 2 bars, meeting room, travel services* ▤ *AE, DC, MC, V* ❘⊙❘ *BP.*

$$ **Hotel Naguilán.** Here, you can relax in the garden by a pool while watching the boats pass by on the Río Valdivia. Ask for one of the rooms in the newer building of this charming hotel seven blocks south of the city center; they are bigger, with balconies and more modern furnishings. The older rooms are a bit dated, but cheaper. All are great value.

⊠ *General Lagos 1927* ☎ *63/212–851* 🖷 *63/219–130* ⊕ *www. hotelnaguilan.com* ↩ *33 rooms, 3 suites* ↻ *Restaurant, pool, dock, bar, baby-sitting, laundry service, meeting room* ⊟ *AE, DC, MC, V.*

$ 🏨 **Hostal Centro Torreón.** Originally constructed in 1918 for a family of German settlers, Centro Torreón now has basic lodgings inside this architecturally appealing German-style home set back from the street. A stairway of *pellín* (oak) twists up to the bright second-story rooms. José Retamales Prelle, the hotel's amiable proprietor, gives discounts to Hosteling International members. ⊠ *Vicente Pérez Rosales 783* ☎ *63/ 212–622* 🖷 *63/203–217* ✒ *hctorreon@entelchile.net* ↩ *13 rooms* ↻ *Café, travel services; no a/c* ⊟ *No credit cards* ⏀ *BP.*

$ 🏨 **Hostal Prat.** The friendly, eager-to-please owner and the reasonable rates make this one of those terrific finds that you want to keep to yourself. Rooms in this lodging near the bus station are mostly tan, but a few splashes of color liven things up. ⊠ *Prat 595* ☎ *63/222–020* ↩ *10 rooms* ↻ *Dining room; no a/c, no room phones* ⊟ *No credit cards* ⏀ *CP.*

$ 🏨 **Hotel Isla Teja.** This affordable hotel doubles as student housing for the nearby Universidad Austral, though a section is always open for non-university guests. The rooms are quiet and comfortable, with modern amenities. ⊠ *Las Encinas 220, Isla Teja* ☎ *63/215–014* 🖷 *63/214–911* ⊕ *www.hotelislateja.cl* ↩ *95 rooms* ↻ *Restaurant, bar, meeting room, travel services; no a/c* ⊟ *AE, DC, MC, V* ⏀ *CP.*

¢ ⚠ **Complejo Turístico Isla Teja.** The campsites at this facility sit in the middle of an apple orchard with an attractive view of the Río Valdivia. There's electricity and hot showers. ⊠ *Los Cipreses 1125, Isla Teja* ☎ *63/213– 584* 🖷 *63/225–855.*

Sports & the Outdoors

Valdivia-based tour operator **Jumping Chile** (⊠ Pasaje 11 No. 50 ☎ 63/ 217–810) organizes marvelous fly-fishing trips for two to six people on the nearby rivers. An astonishing variety of wetland birds inhabits this part of the country. **Hualamo** (☎ 63/215–135 ⊕ www.hualamo.com) lets you get a close look if you join its bird-watching and natural-history tours based out of a lodge 20 km (12 mi) upriver from Valdivia.

Niebla

➓ *18 km (11 mi) southwest of Valdivia.*

To protect the all-important city of Valdivia, the Spanish constructed a series of strategic fortresses at Niebla, where the Valdivia and Torna-galeones rivers meet. Portions of the 1671 **Fuerte de Niebla** and its 18 cannons have been restored. The old commander's house serves as a small museum documenting the era's military history. ⊠ *1 km (½ mi) west of Niebla* ☎ *no phone* 🎟 *Free* ⊙ *Nov.–Mar., daily 9–8; Apr.–Oct., Tues.–Sun. 10–5.*

Across the estuary from the Fuerte de Niebla, the 1645 **Castillo San Sebastián de la Cruz** is large and well preserved. In the January–February summer season, historic reenactments of Spanish military maneuvers take place daily at 4 and 6. ⊠ *1 km (½ mi) north of Corral* 🎟 *Free* ⊙ *Dec.–Mar., daily 8:30 AM–10 PM; Apr.–Nov., daily 9–5.*

Beaches

Just north of Niebla is the green-blue water of the popular **Playa Los Molinos.** A few miles past the villages of Loncollén and Calfuco is **Playa Curiñanco.** The waves can be a bit strong, so be cautious.

Osorno

① *107 km (65 mi) southeast of Valdivia.*

Workaday Osorno is the least visited of the Lake District's four major cities. It's one of the oldest in Chile, but the Mapuche prevented foreigners from settling here until the late 19th century. Like other communities in the region, it bears the imprint of the German settlers who came here in the 1880s. Osorno, situated in a bend of the Río Rahue, makes a convenient base for exploring the nearby national parks.

Osorno's friendly **tourist office** arranges free daily tours in summer. Each day has a different focus: walks around the city, fruit orchards, or nearby farms are a few of the offerings. ⊠ *North side of Plaza de Armas* ☎*64/264–250* ✉*Free* ☉*Office: Dec.–Feb., daily 8–8; Mar.–Nov., weekdays 9–1 and 2:30–6. Tours: daily 10:30.*

The 1960 earthquake left Osorno with little historic architecture, but a row of **19th-century houses** miraculously survived on Calle Juan Mackenna between Lord Cochrane and Freire. Their distinctively sloped roofs, which allow adequate drainage of rain and snow, are replicated in many of Osorno's newer houses.

The modern **Catedral de San Mateo Apostol** fronts the Plaza de Armas and is topped with a tower resembling a bishop's mitre. "Turn off your cell phone," the sign at the door admonishes those who enter. "You don't need it to communicate with God." ⊠ *Plaza de Armas* ☎*no phone* ☉ *Mass Mon.–Sat. 7:15 PM; Sun. 10:30, noon, and 8:15.*

The **Museo Municipal Osorno** contains a decent collection of Mapuche artifacts, Chilean and Spanish firearms, and exhibits devoted to the German settlement of Osorno. Housed in a pink neoclassical building dating from 1929, this is one of the few older structures in the city center. ⊠ *Manuel Antonio Matta 809* ☎ *64/238–615* ✉ *Free* ☉ *Mon.–Thurs. 9:30–5:30, Fri. 9:30–4:30, Sat. 2:30–6.*

Where to Stay & Eat

$–$$$ ✕ **Club Alemán.** This was the first in a network of German associations in southern Chile. Established in 1862, it predated the first big waves of European immigration. Despite the exclusive-sounding name, anyone can dine here. Options are limited, however. There's usually a choice of four or five rotating prix-fixe menus for lunch and dinner, often including a seafood stew or a hearty cazuela, and lots of tasty küchen and other pastries for dessert. ⊠ *O'Higgins 563* ☎ *64/232–784* ▭ *AE, DC, MC, V.*

$–$$ ✕ **Café Central.** Dig into a hearty American-style breakfast in the morning, and burgers and sandwiches the rest of the day. This diner, swathed in orange, sits on the Plaza de Armas next to the Gran Hotel Osorno. The friendly, bustling staff speaks no English, but if it's clear you're North American an English menu will be presented with great fanfare. ⊠ *O'Higgins 610* ☎ *64/257–711* ▭ *DC, MC, V.*

$$ ▦ **Hotel García Hurtado de Mendoza.** This stately hotel two blocks from the Plaza de Armas is one of Osorno's nicest lodgings. Classical lines grace the traditional furnishings and complement the subdued fabrics of the bright and airy guest rooms. ⊠ *Juan Mackenna 1040* ☎ *64/237–111* ▤*64/237–115* ⊕*www.hotelgarciahurtado.cl* ➹*31 rooms* ⟳ *Restaurant, in-room VCRs, sauna, bar, meeting room; no a/c* ▭ *AE, DC, MC, V* ❙❂❙ *BP.*

$ ▦ **Gran Hotel Osorno.** Osorno's grande dame, built in the era when art deco was all the rage, has stood the test of time. The five-story hotel has an unbeatable location on the Plaza de Armas. The rooms, although a tad dark, are clean and comfortable. Mercifully, the hotel's Power Disco has closed, though the neon sign still blinks out front. ⊠ *O'Higgins 615* ☎ *64/232–171* 🖷 *64/239–311* 🛏 *57 rooms* ♿ *Restaurant, bar, laundry service, meeting room; no a/c* ⊟ *AE, DC, MC, V.*

$ 🖳 **Hotel Innsbruck.** Osorno's most Germanic hotel, the Innsbruck has half-timbered walls and cheery flower boxes in the windows. The vaulted ceilings make the simply furnished rooms seem spacious. ⊠ *Manuel Rodríguez 941* 🖷🖷 *64/242–000* ✉ *hinnsbruck@telsur.cl* 🛏 *20 rooms* ♿ *Restaurant, coffee shop, bar; no a/c* ⊟ *MC, V* 🍴 *CP.*

$ 🖳 **Hotel Lagos del Sur.** Warm golds and greens make a splash in sparkling white guest rooms. The color scheme echoes the building's dark green exterior. Doubles include a small sitting room off to one side. This quiet lodging is near the Plaza de Armas. ⊠ *O'Higgins 564* ☎ *64/243–244* 🖷 *64/243–696* ⊕ *www.hotelagosdelsur.cl* 🛏 *20 rooms* ♿ *Coffee shop, bar, laundry service; no a/c* ⊟ *AE, DC, MC, V* 🍴 *CP.*

Shopping

Osorno's city government operates the **Centro de Artesanía Local** (⊠ Juan MacKenna and Ramón Freire), a complex of 46 artisan vendors' stands built in the style of the Calle MacKenna houses. Woodwork, leather, and woolens abound. Prices are fixed but fair. It's open January–February, daily 9 AM–10 PM, and March–December, daily 10–8.

en route An Osorno business executive's love for tail fins and V-8 engines led him to establish the **Auto Museum Moncopulli.** His particular passion is the little-respected Studebaker, which accounts for 40 of the 50 vehicles on display. Elvis and Buddy Holly bop in the background to put you in the mood. ⊠ *Ruta 215, Puyehue,, 25 km (16 mi) east of Osorno* ☎ *64/204–200* 🎟 *1,500 pesos* ⊙ *Dec.–Mar., daily 10–8; Apr.–Nov., Tues.–Sun. 10–6:30.*

Parque Nacional Puyehue

⑫ *81 km (49 mi) east of Osorno.*

Chile's most popular national park, Parque Nacional Puyehue draws crowds who come to bask in its famed hot springs. Most never venture beyond them, and that's a shame. A dozen miles east of the Aguas Calientes sector lies a network of short trails leading to evergreen forests with dramatic waterfalls. Truly adventurous types attempt the five-hour hike to the summit of 2,240-m (7,350-ft) Volcán Puyehue. As with most climbs in this region, CONAF rangers insist on ample documentation of experience before allowing you to set out. Access to the 1,070-square-km (413-square-mi) park is easy: head due east from Osorno on the highway leading to Argentina. ⊠ *Ruta 215* ☎ *64/374–572* 🎟 *800 pesos* ⊙ *Nov.–Mar., daily 8 AM–9 PM; Apr.–Oct., daily 8–7.*

Where to Stay

$$–$$$ 🖳 **Gran Hotel Termas de Puyehue.** Probably Chile's most famous hot springs resort, this grandiose stone-and-wood lodge sits on the edge of Parque Nacional Puyehue. The compound has all sorts of outdoor activities, from skiing to horseback riding to sportfishing. Most people come for a soak in the thermal pools. All-day use of the springs is 10,000 pesos for nonguests. The rooms and common areas here mix starkly modern and 19th-century Germanic features: chrome, hardwoods, and even some modern art happily share the same space. ⊠ *Ruta 215, Km 76, Puyehue* ☎ *64/232–881; 2/234–3440 in Santiago* 🖷 *64/236–988; 2/333–2370 in Santiago* ⊕ *www.puyehue.cl* 🛏 *132 rooms* ♿ *3 restaurants,*

2 pools, gym, sauna, fishing, horseback riding, downhill skiing, shop, laundry service, meeting room, travel services; no a/c, no room TVs ☐ *AE, DC, MC, V.*

Puerto Octay

🔟 *80 km (48 mi) southwest of Parque Nacional Puyehue, 50 km (30 mi) southeast of Osorno.*

The story goes that a German merchant named Ochs set up shop in this tidy community on the northern tip of Lago Llanquihue. A phrase uttered by customers looking for a particular item, "¿*Ochs, hay . . . ?*" ("Ochs, do you have . . . ?"), gradually became "Octay." With spectacular views of the Osorno and Calbuco volcanoes, the town was the birthplace of Lake District tourism: a wealthy Santiago businessman constructed a mansion outside of town in 1912, using it as a vacation home to host his friends. (That structure is now the area's famed Hotel Centinela.) Puerto Octay doesn't have the frenetic energy of neighboring Frutillar and Puerto Varas, but its many fans enjoy its less frenzied, more authentic nature.

The small **Museo El Colono** displays great old photographs and maps documenting the town's turn-of-the-last-century German settlers. An annex in a barn outside of town at the turnoff to Centinela exhibits farm machinery. ☒ *Independencia 591* 🕿 *64/391–523* 💲 *500 pesos* 🕙 *Dec.–Mar., daily 9:30–1 and 3–7; Apr.–Nov., Tues.–Sun. 9:30–1 and 3–7.*

Where to Stay & Eat

$–$$ ✕ **Restaurant Baviera.** Because it's on the Plaza de Armas, this is a popular lunch stop for tour groups. Baviera serves solid German fare—schnitzel, sauerkraut, sausage, and küchen are among the favorites. Beer steins and other Bavarian paraphernalia on the walls evoke the Old Country. ☒ *German Wulf 582* 🕿 *64/391–460* ☐ *No credit cards.*

★ **$–$$$** ▥ **Hotel Centinela.** Simple and elegant, the venerable 1912 Hotel Centinela remains one of Chile's best-known accommodations. This imposing wood-shingled lodge with a dramatic turret sits amid 20 forested acres at the tip of Península Centinela jutting into Lago Llanquihue. Britain's Edward VII, then Prince of Wales, was the most famous guest (but there's some mystery as to whether his future wife, American divorcée Wallis Simpson, accompanied him). Imposing beds and armoires fill the huge rooms in the main building. The cabins, whose rates include three meals a day delivered to the door, are more modern than the rooms in the lodge. ☒ *Península de Centinela* 🕿 *64/391–326* 🌐 *www.hotelcentinela.cl* ⇆ *11 rooms, 1 suite, 18 cabins* ♧ *Restaurant, sauna, bar; no a/c, no TV in some rooms* ☐ *AE, DC, MC, V* ❙◯❙ *BP, FAP.*

★ **$** ▥ **Zapato Amarillo.** Backpackers make up the majority of the clientele here, but this is no scruffy youth hostel. This modern alerce-shingled house with wood-panel rooms affords a drop-dead gorgeous view of Volcán Osorno outside of town. The eager-to-please Chilean-Swiss couple that owns it will arrange guided horseback-riding, hiking, and cycling tours, as well as a cheese-fondue evening. Rates include a Continental breakfast that's a cut above the rest, tossing in fruit and local dairy products. You also have access to the kitchen. ☒ *2 km (1 mi) north of Puerto Octay on road to Osorno* 🕿 *64/391–575* 🌐 *zapatoamarillo.8k.com* ⇆ *4 rooms with shared bath* ♧ *Dining room, horseback riding, library, laundry facilities, Internet, travel services; no a/c, no room phones, no room TVs* ☐ *No credit cards* ❙◯❙ *BP.*

Frutillar

⑭ *30 km (18 mi) southwest of Puerto Octay.*

Halfway down the western edge of Lago Llanquihue lies the small town of Frutillar, one of the destinations of European immigrants in the late 19th century. The town—actually two adjacent hamlets joined, Frutillar Alto and Frutillar Bajo—is known for its perfectly preserved German architecture. Don't be disappointed if your first look at the town is the nondescript neighborhood on the top of the hill; head down to the charming streets that face the lake. Each January and February, the town hosts *Semanas Musicales de Frutillar,* an excellent series of mostly classical concerts (and a little jazz) outdoors.

★ You step into the past when you step into one of southern Chile's best museums, the **Museo Colonial Alemán.** Besides displays of the 19th-century agricultural and household implements, this open-air museum has full-scale reconstructions of buildings—a smithy and barn, among others—used by the original German settlers. Exhibits at this complex administered by Chile's Universidad Austral are labeled in Spanish and, *natürlich,* German, but there are also a few signs in English. A short walk from the lake up Avenida Arturo Prat, the museum also has beautifully landscaped grounds and great views of Volcán Osorno. ⊠ *Vicente Pérez Rosales at Arturo Prat* ☎ *65/421–142* ⊠ *1,600 pesos* ⊙ *Dec.–Feb., daily 10–8; Mar.–Nov., Tues.–Sun. 10–2 and 3–6.*

Where to Stay & Eat

$$ ✕ **Club Alemán.** One of the German clubs that dot the Lake District, this restaurant in the center of town has a selection of four or five rotating prix-fixe menus. There will always be a meat and seafood option—often steak and salmon—with soup, salad, and dessert. Don't forget the küchen. ⊠ *Philippi 747* ☎ *65/421–249* ▤ *AE, DC, MC, V.*

$–$$ ✕ **Selva Negra.** Friendly, attentive service and good, solid German food are the hallmark of the casual semicircular restaurant just up the hill from the beach road. As you'd expect at any dining place called the "Black Forest," bratwurst, sauerkraut, smoked pork chops, and cabbage abound, but seafood is an option if you're looking for something a bit less Teutonic. A special summer-only treat is a mixed seafood platter served in a pineapple half. ⊠ *Antonio Varas 24* ☎ *65/421–164* ▤ *No credit cards.*

$$ ✕▥ **Hotel Salzburg.** Rooms at this Tyrolean-style lodge command excellent views of the lake. Cozy cabins and slightly larger bungalows, all made of native woods, are fully equipped with kitchens and private terraces. The staff will gladly organize fishing trips. The restaurant serves some of the best smoked salmon in the area. ⊠ *Costanera Norte* ☎ *65/ 421–569* 🖨 *65/421–599* ⊕ *www.salzburg.cl* ⇨ *31 rooms, 9 cabins, 5 bungalows* ⚥ *Restaurant, pool, sauna, billiards, Ping-Pong, volleyball, bar, laundry service, meeting rooms, travel services; no a/c, no room TVs* ▤ *AE, DC, MC, V.*

— ★ **$$** ▥ **Hotel Elun.** From just about every vantage point—the lobby, the library, and, of course, the guest rooms—you have a spectacular view of Lago Llanquihue. Each room has huge bay windows framing Volcán Osorno. The blue of the facade is repeated in the rooms, which have polished wood furniture. Add the exceptionally attentive owners to the mix, and you have a real find just south of town. ⊠ *Costanera Sur* ☎ *65/ 420–055* 🖨 *65/420–170* ⊕ *www.hotelelun.cl* ⇨ *14 rooms* ⚥ *Restaurant, in-room safes, sauna, bar, meeting rooms, no-smoking rooms; no a/c, no TV in some rooms* ▤ *AE, DC, MC, V* ⑩ *BP.*

$$ ▥ **Hotel Volcán Puntiagudo.** This redwood lodge sits on a hillside a mile north of town. Decorated in soft earth tones, the rooms have views of

Lago Llanquihue and Volcán Osorno. Rates, which drop for stays over three days, include a large breakfast. ✉ *Camino Fundo las Piedras* ☎ *65/421–646* 🖷 *65/421–640* 🌐 *www.hotelvolcanpuntiagudo.com* 🛏 *10 rooms* ♨ *Restaurant, tennis court, pool, bar, meeting room; no a/c, no room phones* 🖃 *DC, MC, V* ⊘ *Closed May–Nov.* ⟐ *BP.*

$ 🖫 **Hotel Frau Holle.** The friendly owner of the 1930s German-style house is not exactly Frau Holle, a character out of the Grimm brothers' fairy tales, but she will provide you with attentive service and serve fruit for breakfast from the orchard on the property. Rooms are bright and cheery with hardwood floors and period furnishings. A few have views of Lago Llanquihue and both volcanoes. ✉ *Antonio Varas 54* ☎🖷 *65/421–345* ✉ *frauholle@frutillarsur.cl* 🛏 *8 rooms* ♨ *Dining room, laundry service; no a/c, no room phones, no room TVs* 🖃 *AE, DC, MC, V* ⟐ *CP.*

$ 🖫 **Hotel Klein Salzburg.** Gingerbread cutouts and swirls adorn a cozy 1911 home-turned-inn. Flowered bedspreads and curtains decorate the tasteful wood-panel rooms. The German breakfast is quite filling. And you couldn't ask for a much better location—the property is right on the lake. ✉ *Av. Philippi 663* ☎ *65/421–201* 🖷 *65/421–750* 🌐 *www. salzburg.cl* 🛏 *8 rooms* ♨ *Restaurant, coffee shop; no a/c, no TV in some rooms* 🖃 *AE, DC, MC, V* ⟐ *BP.*

$ 🖫 **Hotel Serenade.** Names of the rooms here reflect musical compositions—*Fantasia* or the *Wedding March,* for example—and the doors display the first few measures of the work. Inside are plush quilts and comforters, hardwood floors, and throw rugs. Enjoy the fireplace in the cozy sitting room of this 1940 house on a quiet side street. You could stay at this musical-theme lodging during the Semanas Musicales de Frutillar in late January, but any time of year will do. ✉ *Pedro Aguirre Cerda 50* ☎ *65/ 420–332* 🛏 *6 rooms* ♨ *Meeting room; no a/c, no room TVs* ⟐ *CP.*

Beaches

Packed with summer crowds, the gray-sand **Playa Frutillar** stretches for 15 blocks along Avenida Philippi. From this point along Lago Llanquihue you have a spectacular view due east of the conical Volcán Osorno, as well as the lopsided Volcán Puntiagudo.

Puerto Varas

⑮   *27 km (16 mi) south of Frutillar.*

A small resort town on the edge of Lago Llanquihue, Puerto Varas is known for the stunning rose arbors that bloom from December to March. Often described as the "Lucerne of Chile," the town has ice cream shops, cozy cafés, and trendy restaurants. The view of the Osorno and Calbuco volcanoes graces dozens of postcards and travel brochures for the Lake District. The town isn't quite there yet, but it could someday soon mount a serious challenge to Pucón as the region's top vacation spot.

Where to Stay & Eat

$$–$$$$ ✕ **Merlin.** Often called the best restaurant in southern Chile, this charming establishment combines fish and vegetables in unusual ways. Specialities include razor clams with vegetable strips in a curry vinaigrette and beef tenderloin in a morel-mushroom sauce. For dessert, try peaches packed with almond cream. ✉ *Imperial 605* ☎ *65/233–105* 🖃 *AE, DC, MC, V* ⊘ *No lunch.*

$$–$$$ ✕ **Kika.** These folks get going early in the morning, cranking out rich German pastries for breakfast, and don't quit until well into the evening when they serve seafood for dinner. Try the *rollitos de salmón* (salmon rolls). Kika operates out of a cozy house near the center of town. ✉ *Walker Martínez 584* ☎ *65/234–703* 🖃 *AE, DC, MC, V.*

$–$$$ ✕ **Pim's.** This restaurant just a couple of blocks from the center of town captures the essence of an old-style American bar and the good food you can often find at such places. There's nothing particularly southwestern about the decor, but expect to chow down on good, filling Tex-Mex cuisine—the portions are enormous—in front of a fireplace. ⊠ *San Francisco 712* ☎ *65/233–998* ⊟ *AE, DC, MC, V.*

$–$$ ✕ **Restaurant Aníbal.** Although the dining room in this Italian restaurant is plain, the food is anything but. The friendly staff dishes up pasta with a tangy Argentine flavor. Instead of tomato or marinara on your spaghetti, you might get a tangy Argentine chimichurri sauce. ⊠ *Del Salvador at Santa Rosa* ☎ *65/235–222* ⊟ *MC, V.*

$$$ ▥ **Hotel Cabañas del Lago.** It's the pine-panel cabins that make this spot special. Hidden in carefully tended gardens, each A-frame unit is decorated with lace curtains and floral-pattern bedding. The cabins, which can accommodate five people, have wood stoves and full kitchens. Most rooms in the main hotel are cozy and have lovely views of Volcán Osorno. ⊠ *Klenner 195* ☎ *65/232–291* 🖷 *65/232–707* ⊕ *www. cabanasdellago.cl* ⇆ *63 rooms, 13 cabins, 2 suites* ⌕ *Restaurant, indoor pool, massage, sauna, billiards, bar, baby-sitting, meeting rooms; no a/c* ⊟ *AE, DC, MC, V.*

$$ ▥ **Hotel Bellavista.** This hotel, an eclectic mix of traditional Bavarian and modern architectural styles, sits right on the lake. Most of the bright rooms have views of the nearby volcanoes, and some have their own balconies. Stylish contemporary furnishings are upholstered in tailored stripes. ⊠ *Vicente Pérez Rosales 60* ☎ *65/232–011* 🖷 *65/232–013* ⊕ *www.hotelbellavistachile.com* ⇆ *51 rooms* ⌕ *Restaurant, sauna, bar, laundry service; no a/c* ⊟ *AE, DC, MC, V* ⫶⊙⫶ *BP.*

➤ **$$** ▥ **Hotel Colonos del Sur.** This five-story building, with peaked gables that give it a Germanic look, dominates the waterfront in Puerto Varas. The views from the upper floors are magnificent. Warm alerce and pine dominate the interior, including the paneled guest rooms. ⊠ *Del Salvador 24* ☎ *65/233–369* 🖷 *65/233–394* ⊕ *www.colonosdelsur.cl* ⇆ *64 rooms* ⌕ *Restaurant, coffee shop, minibars, indoor pool, sauna, bar, meeting room; no a/c* ⊟ *AE, DC, MC, V* ⫶⊙⫶ *BP.*

$$ ▥ **Hotel Licarayén.** Ask for a room with a balcony overlooking Lago Llanquihue at this rambling Bavarian-style chalet. Those rooms without views of the lake overlook the garden. There's a fireplace in the common sitting room. ⊠ *San José 114* ☎ *65/232–305* 🖷 *65/232–955* ⇆ *23 rooms* ⌕ *Dining room, gym, sauna; no a/c* ⊟ *AE, DC, MC, V* ⫶⊙⫶ *CP.*

★ **$** ▥ **The Guest House.** The aroma of fresh coffee greets you all day long, and little homemade chocolates await on your pillow at this central B&B, a restored 1926 mansion. Period furnishings and antiques fill the rooms, which are bright and cheery. The exuberant American owner, a longtime resident of Chile and a fount of information, truly treats you like a valued guest. ⊠ *O'Higgins 608* ☎ *65/231–521* 🖷 *65/232–240* ⊕ *www.vicki-johnson.com* ⇆ *10 rooms* ⌕ *No a/c, no rooms TVs, nosmoking* ⊟ *No credit cards* ⫶⊙⫶ *BP.*

Nightlife

The flashy **Casino de Puerto Varas** (⊠ Del Salvador 21 ☎ 65/346–600) dominates the center of town these days. There are all the Vegas-style trappings, from slot machines to roulette.

Cozy, intimate café by day, seafood restaurant by evening, **Barómetro** (⊠ San Pedo 418 ☎ 65/346–100) becomes a live music venue by night—well into the night. Expect a DJ most of the year, but live music during the peak summer season.

Sports & the Outdoors

Al Sur Expediciones (⊠ Del Salvador 100 ☎ 65/232–300 ⊕ www. alsurexpeditions.com) is known for rafting and kayaking trips on the Class III Río Petrohué. It also runs horseback-riding and fly-fishing trips. **Aqua Motion** (⊠ San Francisco 328 ☎ 65/232–747 ⊕ www.aqua-motion. com) leads rafting and kayaking excursions on the nearby Río Petrohué, as well as trekking, horseback riding, helicopter rides, bird-watching, and fly-fishing tours. Based in nearby Cochamó, **Campo Aventura** (⊠ Valle Cochamó ☎ 65/232–910) leads one- to ten-day horseback and trekking expeditions to its base camp in Parque Nacional Vicente Pérez Rosales.

Tranco Expediciones (⊠ San Pedro 422 ☎ 65/311–311 ⊕ www. trancoexpediciones.cl) leads photo hikes up Volcánes Osorno and Calbuco, in addition to rafting trips on the Río Petrohué, and bike excursions. **Pachamagua** (⊠ San Pedo 418 ☎ 65/346–100) specializes in half- and full-day canyoning and rappelling trips near Volcán Calbuco, in addition to kayaking and horseback-riding excursions.

Parque Nacional Vicente Pérez Rosales

16 *50 km (30 mi) east of Puerto Varas.*

Chile's oldest national park, Parque Nacional Vicente Pérez Rosales was established in 1926. South of Parque Nacional Puyehue, the 2,538-square-km (980-square-mi) preserve includes the Osorno and lesser-known Puntiagudo volcanoes, as well as the deep blue Lago Todos los Santos. The visitor center opposite the Hotel Petrohué provides access to some fairly easy hikes. The Rincón del Osorno trail hugs the lake; the Saltos de Petrohué trail runs parallel to the river of the same name. Rudimentary campsites are available for 10,000 pesos per person. ☎ 65/290–711 🎫 *1,000 pesos* ⊗ *Dec.–Feb., daily 9–8; Mar.–Nov., daily 9–6.*

Where to Stay

$$–$$$ ⌂ **Hotel Petrohué.** This upscale rustic chalet, with vaulted ceilings and huge fireplaces, is quite comfortable. Rooms are a mix of dark woods and stone and have brightly colored drapes and spreads. The hotel's tour office can set you up with cruises on nearby lakes or take you to scale Volcán Osorno if you're an experienced climber. ⊠ *Petrohué s/n* ☎ *65/258–042* ⊕ *www.petrohue.com* ↪ *28 rooms* ⌂ *Restaurant, bicycles, horseback riding, bar, shop, laundry service, travel services; no a/c, no room TVs* ⊟ *AE, DC, MC, V.*

Sports & the Outdoors

Make like Tarzan (or Jane) and swing through the treetops in the shadow of Volcán Osorno with **Canopy Chile** (☎ 65/233–121 or 09/750–1040 ⊕ www.canopychile.com). A helmet, a very secure harness, 2 km (1 mi) of zip line strung out over 12 platforms, and experienced guides give you a bird's-eye view of the forest below.

Puerto Montt

17 *20 km (12 mi) south of Puerto Varas.*

For most of its history, windy Puerto Montt was the end of the line for just about everyone traveling in the Lake District. Now the Carretera Austral carries on southward, but for all intents and purposes Puerto Montt remains the region's last significant outpost, a provincial city that is the hub of local fishing, textile, and tourist activity. Today the town consists of low clapboard houses perched above its bay, the Seno de Reloncaví. If it's a sunny day, head east to Playa Pelluco or one of the city's other beaches. If you're more interested in exploring the countryside, drive along the shore for a good view of the surrounding hills.

The **Museo Juan Pablo II**, east of the city's bus terminal, has a collection of crafts and relics from the nearby archipelago of Chiloé. Historical photos of Puerto Montt itself give a sense of the area's slow and often difficult growth and the impact of the 1960 earthquake, which virtually destroyed the port. Pope John Paul II, for whom the museum was renamed, celebrated mass on the grounds during his 1987 visit. One exhibit documents the event. ⊠ *Av. Diego Portales 991* ☎ *65/344–457* ▨ *250 pesos* ☉ *Daily 9–7.*

About 3 km (2 mi) west of downtown along the coastal road lies the **Caleta Angelmó,** Puerto Montt's fishing cove. This busy port serves small fishing boats, large ferries, and cruisers carrying travelers and cargo southward through the straits and fjords that form much of Chile's shoreline. On weekdays small launches from Isla Tenglo and other outlying islands arrive early in the morning and leave late in the afternoon. The fish market here has one of the most varied selections of seafood in all of Chile.

Barely a stone's throw from Puerto Montt, the mountainous 398-square-km (154-square-mi) **Parque Nacional Alerce Andino,** with more than 40 small lakes, was established to protect some 20,000 endangered alerce trees. Comparable to California's hardy sequoia, alerce grow to average heights of 40 m (130 ft), and can reach 4 m (13 ft) in diameter. Immensely popular for construction of houses in southern Chile, they are quickly disappearing from the landscape. Many of these are 3,000–4,000 years old. ⊠ *Carretera Austral, 35 km (21 mi) east of Puerto Montt* ☎ *65/ 212–036* ▨ *1,000 pesos* ☉ *Daily 9–6.*

Where to Stay & Eat

★ **$–$$$** ✕ **Balzac.** One of Puerto Montt's finest restaurants, Balzac specializes in seafood prepared with a French flair. Try the *jaiba de chardonnay* (a stew of king crab, Parmesan cheese, and white wine). The owner's father—an endearing gentleman and a rich source of Chilote history—passes his time downstairs chewing the fat with friends. Don't worry about waking the child sleeping on the stairs inside the door—it's a doll. ⊠ *Urmeneta 305* ☎ *65/313–251* ▤ *No credit cards* ☉ *Closed Sun. Apr.–Oct.*

$–$$$ ✕ **Club Alemán.** As befitting an old German association, Club Alemán serves delicious küchen and other pastries, but the rest of the menu doesn't recall Deutschland. Seafood—delicious clams, oysters, and lobster—as well as freshwater trout are the specialties here. ⊠ *Antonio Varas 264* ☎ *65/252–551* ▤ *AE, DC, MC, V* ☉ *No dinner Sun.*

$–$$$ ✕ **Club de Yates.** There are no yachts here, despite the tony-sounding name, and prices are reasonable—you can feast on lobster for just a few dollars. The arresting yellow exterior contrasts sharply with the subdued elegance of the interior, complete with crisp linens and candlelight. You can't miss this place, as it sits on a high pier jutting out into the bay. ⊠ *Av. Juan Soler Manfredini 1* ☎ *65/276–888* ▤ *AE, DC, MC, V* ☉ *No dinner Sun.*

$–$$$ ✕ **Feria Artesanal Angelmó.** Several kitchens here prepare *mariscal* (shellfish soup) and *caldillo* (seafood chowder), as well as *almejas* (clams), *machas* (razor clams), and *ostiones* (scallops) with Parmesan cheese. Separate tables and counters are at each kitchen in this enclosed market, which is 3 km (2 mi) west of Puerto Montt along the coast road. ⊠ *Caleta Angelmó* ☎ *no phone* ▤ *No credit cards.*

$–$$$ ✕ **New Harbor Café.** When you step into this café decorated with pale woods and chrome, you might think it's a bit too trendy. In reality it's a fun, friendly place serving sandwiches and other light meals—a great destination for late-night noshing. ⊠ *San Martín 85* ☎ *65/293–980* ⊟ *AE, DC, MC, V.*

$–$$ ✕ **Café Central.** This old-style café in the heart of Puerto Montt retains the spirit of the 1920s and 1930s. It's a good place for a filling afternoon tea, with its menu of sandwiches, ice cream, and pastries. ⊠ *Rancagua 117* ☎ *65/254–721* ⊟ *No credit cards.*

$–$$ ✕ **Restaurant Kiel.** Hospitable German-born proprietor Helga Birkir stands guard at this Chilean-Teutonic seafood restaurant on the coast west of Puerto Montt. Fresh produce from her well-kept garden makes lunch here a delight. ⊠ *Camino Chinquihue, Km 8, Chinquihue* ☎ *65/ 255–010* ⊟ *AE.*

$$–$$$ ▥ **Hotel Don Luis.** This modern lodging next to the cathedral, a favorite among upscale business travelers, has panoramic views of the Seno de Reloncaví. There's a small salon for the big American-style breakfast included in the rate. ⊠ *Urmeneta and Quillota* ☎ *65/259–001* ☎ *65/ 259–005* ⊕ *www.hoteldonluis.com* ⇝ *60 rooms, 1 suite* ⬙ *Restaurant, coffee shop, snack bar, gym, sauna, bar, laundry service, meeting rooms; no a/c* ⊟ *AE, DC, MC, V.*

$$ ▥ **Gran Hotel Don Vicente.** The grandest of Puerto Montt's hotels underwent a much needed remodeling and face-lift in 2002–2003 and, more than ever, it retains its Gstaad-by-the-sea glory. Its Bavarian-style facade resembles that of countless other Lake District lodgings, but the lobby's huge picture window overlooking the Seno de Reloncaví lets you know this place is something special. ⊠ *Diego Portales and Guillermo Gallardo* ☎ *65/432–900; 2/953–5037 in Santiago* ☎ *65/437–699; 2/953– 5900 in Santiago* ⊕ *www.granhoteldonvicente.cl* ⇝ *71 rooms* ⬙ *Restaurant, coffee shop, minibars, bars, laundry service, concierge, business services, travel services, meeting rooms, airport shuttle; no a/c* ⊟ *AE, DC, MC, V* ⫿⊙⫿ *BP.*

$$ ▥ **O'Grimm.** This four-story lodging is in the heart of Puerto Montt, but O'Grimm's warmth and charm would make it equally appropriate to a small town in Germany. The helpful staff makes you feel right at home. Muted shades of gray, rose, and green decorate the simple rooms. ⊠ *Guillermo Gallardo 211* ☎ *65/252–845* ☎ *65/258–600* ⊕ *www. ogrimm.com* ⇝ *27 rooms, 1 suite* ⬙ *Restaurant, minibars, bar, laundry service, meeting rooms; no a/c* ⊟ *AE, DC, MC, V* ⫿⊙⫿ *BP.*

$$ ▥ **Viento Sur.** An old Victorian house sits proudly on a hill, offering a majestic view of both the city and the sea. Rooms are comfortably furnished with generous use of native Chilean woods. The restaurant serves excellent Chilean seafood. ⊠ *Ejército 200* ☎ *65/258–701* ☎ *65/314– 732* ⇝ *27 rooms, 2 suites* ⬙ *Restaurant, sauna, bar, laundry service, business services; no a/c* ⊟ *AE, DC, MC, V* ⫿⊙⫿ *BP.*

$ ▥ **Hostal Pacífico.** European travelers favor this solid budget option up the hill from the bus station. The rooms are small, but they have comfy beds with lots of pillows. Look at a few before you pick one, as some of the interior rooms have skylights rather than windows. The staff is exceptionally friendly and helpful. ⊠ *Juan J. Mira 1088* ☎☎ *65/256– 229* ⇝ *22 rooms* ⬙ *Dining room, travel services; no a/c* ⊟ *No credit cards* ⫿⊙⫿ *CP.*

$ ▥ **Hotel Gamboa.** The floors creak, the rooms are very plain, and the bright yellow exterior looks strangely out of place in staid downtown Puerto Montt. But the sweetly fussy owner makes this second-story lodging a good budget choice. ⊠ *Pedro Montt 157* ☎ *65/252–741* ⇝ *8 rooms, 4 with bath* ⬙ *No a/c, no room phones, no room TVs* ⊟ *No credit cards.*

¢ ⚠ **Los Alamos.** Camp within sight of fine views of the Seno de Reloncaví and Isla Tenglo. Sites have electricity and water, and hot showers are nearby. Rent a boat here to explore and then park it at Los Alamos' dock. To get there, go 11 km (7 mi) west of Caleta Angelmó. ⊠ *Costanera* ☎ *65/264–666* ▤ *No credit cards.*

¢ ⚠ **Chinquihue.** This campground is 7 km (4½ mi) west of Caleta Angelmó and has showers and views of the beach. ⊠ *Costanera* ☎ *65/262–950* ▤ *No credit cards.*

¢ ⚠ **El Ciervo.** Campsites here have electricity, and there are hot showers and a boat rental facility. It's 1 km (½ mi) west of Angelmó. ⊠ *Costanera* ☎ *65/255–271* ▤ *No credit cards.*

¢ ⚠ **Paredes.** A pretty beach and a playground make this campground attractive, but don't come looking for shade—there isn't much. Hot showers are available. To get here drive 6 km (4 mi) west of Caleta Angelmó. ⊠ *Costanera* ☎ *65/258–394* ▤ *No credit cards.*

Nightlife & the Arts

The **Casa de Arte Diego Rivera** (⊠ Quillota 116 ☎ 65/261–859) a gift of the government of Mexico, commemorates the famed muralist of the same name. It hosts art exhibitions in the gallery, as well as evening theater productions and occasional music and film festivals.

Shopping

An excellent selection of handicrafts is sold at the best prices in the country in the **Feria Artesanal Angelmó,** on the coastal road near Caleta Angelmó. Chileans know there's a better selection of crafts from Chiloé for sale here than in Chiloé itself. Baskets, ponchos, figures woven from different kinds of grasses and straws, and warm sweaters of raw, handspun and hand-dyed wool are all offered. Much of the merchandise is geared toward tourists, so look carefully for more authentic offerings. Haggling is expected. It's open daily 9–dusk.

Pargua

18 *63 km (39 mi) southwest of Puerto Montt.*

Pargua is the Lake District's end of the line, the jumping-off point for ferries to nearby Chiloé. This is where you catch the boats leaving every 30 minutes to Chacao on the northern tip of Chiloé.

THE LAKE DISTRICT A TO Z

To research prices, get advice from other travelers, and book travel arrangements, visit www.fodors.com.

AIR TRAVEL

LanChile and its domestic partner LanExpress have flights from Santiago to the four major cities within the Lake District—Temuco, Valdivia, Osorno, and Puerto Montt. Some flights to Puerto Montt continue south to Balmaceda and Punta Arenas. Sky Airline connects Temuco and Puerto Montt to Santiago and south to Balmaceda. Aeromet flies daily between Puerto Montt and Chaitén.

✈ Airlines **Aeromet** ⊠ Guillermo Gallardo 55, Puerto Montt ☎ 65/299-400. **LanChile/ LanExpress** ⊠ Manuel Antonio Matta 862, Osorno ☎ 64/204-119 ⊠ San Martin 200, Puerto Montt ☎ 65/253-315 ⊠ Bulnes 687, Temuco ☎ 45/211-339 ⊠ Maipú 271, Valdivia ☎ 63/213-042. **Sky Airline** ⊠ Bulnes 655, Temuco ☎ 45/747-300 ⊠ San Martín 189, Puerto Montt ☎ 65/437-555.

AIRPORTS

Osorno's Aeropuerto Carlos Hott Siebert is 7 km (4 mi) east of the city. Puerto Montt's Aeropuerto El Tepual is 16 km (10 mi) west of the city center. Temuco's Aeropuerto Maquehue is 6 km (4 mi) south of the city. Valdivia's Aeropuerto Pichoy lies 29 km (18 mi) north of the city.

Airport Information **Aeropuerto Carlos Hott Siebert** ⊠ Osorno ☎ 64/318-855.
Aeropuerto El Tepual ⊠ Puerto Montt ☎ 65/294-159. **Aeropuerto Maquehue**
⊠ Temuco ☎ 45/337-703. **Aeropuerto Pichoy** ⊠ Valdivia ☎ 63/272-224.

BOAT & FERRY TRAVEL

To drive much farther south than Puerto Montt, you've got to take a
boat or ferry. Cruz del Sur operates a ferry connecting the mainland town
of Pargua with Chacao on the northern tip of Isla Grande de Chiloé.
Boats run every 30 minutes from early morning until late at night. The
trip takes about half an hour.

Navimag operates a cargo and passenger fleet throughout the region.
The M/N *Evangelistas,* a 324-passenger ferry, sails round-trip from
Puerto Montt to the popular tourist destination of Laguna San Rafael,
stopping in both directions at Puerto Chacabuco on the Southern Coast.
The 200-passenger M/N *Alejandrina* and M/N *Puerto Edén* sail from
Puerto Montt to Chaitén, Quellón, and Puerto Chacabuco before mak-
ing the trip in reverse.

Transmarchilay operates a cargo and passenger ferry service similar to
that of Navimag, with ships that start in Puerto Montt and sail to
Chaitén. From early January through late February, Transmarchilay's
M/N *El Colono* sails weekly from Puerto Montt into Laguna San Rafael
and back to Puerto Montt.

If it's speed you're after, Catamaranes del Sur provides twice-weekly cata-
maran service between Puerto Montt and Chaitén at a relatively quick
4½ hours. During January and February you can continue on from
Chaitén for three more hours to Castro, on the island of Chiloé.
Boat & Ferry Companies **Catamaranes del Sur** ⊠ Diego Portales and Guillermo
Gallardo, Puerto Montt ☎ 65/267-533 ⊕ www.catamaranesdelsur.cl. **Cruz del Sur**
⊠ Puerto Montt ☎ 64/254-731. **Navimag** ⊠ Angelmó 2187, Puerto Montt ☎ 65/432-
300 ⊕ www.navimag.cl. **Transmarchilay** ⊠ Angelmó 2187, Puerto Montt ☎ 65/270-
421 ⊕ www.transmarchilay.cl.

BUS TRAVEL

There's no shortage of bus companies traveling the Pan-American Highway (Ruta 5) from Santiago south to the Lake District. The buses aren't
overcrowded on these long routes, and seats are assigned. Tickets may
be purchased in advance, always a good idea if you're traveling during
summer. Cruz del Sur and Tur-Bus connect the major cities. Buses JAC
connects the resort towns of Pucón and Villarrica with Temuco and Valdivia. Buses Vía Octay runs between Osorno and Puerto Octay.

In Temuco, there's no central bus terminal, but several companies are
close together along Vicuña Mackenna and Lagos. Osorno, Puerto
Montt, and Valdivia have their own central terminal.
Bus Depots **Osorno** ⊠ Errázuriz 1400 ☎ 64/234-149. **Puerto Montt** ⊠ Av. Diego
Portales ☎ no phone. **Valdivia** ⊠ Anfión Muñoz 360 ☎ 63/212-212.
Bus Lines **Buses JAC** ⊠ Vicuña Mackenna 798, Temuco ☎ 45/210-313 ⊠ Bilbao
610, Villarrica ☎ 45/411-447 ⊠ Anfión Muñoz 360, Valdivia ☎ 63/212-925. **Buses Vía
Octay** ⊠ Errázuriz 1400, Osorno ☎ 64/237-043. **Cruz del Sur** ⊠ Vicuña Mackenna 671,
Temuco ☎ 45/210-701 ⊠ Anfión Muñoz 360, Valdivia ☎ 63/213-840 ⊠ Errázuriz 1400,
Osorno ☎ 64/232-777 ⊠ Av. Diego Portales, Puerto Montt ☎ 65/254-731. **Tur Bus**
⊠ Lagos 538, Temuco ☎ 45/239-190.

CAR RENTAL

For a drop-off charge, a few rental-car companies, including Hertz, will
allow you to rent a car in one city and return it in another.
Agencies **Autovald** ⊠ Portales 1330, Puerto Montt ☎ 65/256-355 ⊠ Vicente
Pérez Rosales 660, Valdivia ☎ 63/212-786. **Avis** ⊠ Urmeneta 783, Puerto Montt ☎ 65/

253-307 ✉ Aeropuerto El Tepual, Puerto Montt ☎ 65/255-155 ✉ Vicuña Mackenna 448, Temuco ☎ 45/238-013 ✉ Aeropuerto Maquehue, Temuco ☎ 45/337-715. **Hertz** ✉ Antonio Varas 126, Puerto Montt ☎ 65/259-585 ✉ Aeropuerto El Tepual, Puerto Montt ☎ 65/268-944 ✉ Las Heras 999, Temuco ☎ 45/318-585 ✉ Aeropuerto Maquehue, Temuco ☎ 45/337-019 ✉ Picarte 640, Valdivia ☎ 63/218-316 ✉ Aeropuerto Pichoy, Valdivia ☎ 63/272-273.

CAR TRAVEL

It's easier to see more of the Lake District if you have your own vehicle. The Pan-American Highway through the region is a well-maintained four-lane toll highway. You pay tolls of 1,400 pesos each at Pua (Km 623), Quepe (Km 695), Lanco (Km 775), La Unión (Km 888), and Purranque (Km 961). Tollbooths at many exits levy a 400-peso charge as well.

Once you're this far south, driving is easy because there's little traffic, even on the major highways. Roads to most of the important tourist centers are paved, but many of the routes through the mountains are gravel or dirt, so a four-wheel-drive vehicle is ideal.

EMERGENCIES

🆘Emergency Services **Ambulance** ☎131. **Fire (Bomberos)** ☎132. **Police (Carabineros)** ☎133.

🆘 Hospitals **Hospital Base Osorno** ✉ Dr. Guillermo Bühler, Osorno ☎ 64/235-571. **Hospital Base Puerto Montt** ✉ Seminario s/n, Puerto Montt ☎ 65/261-100. **Hospital Regional Valdivia** ✉ Simpson 850, Valdivia ☎ 63/297-000. **Hospital de Temuco** ✉ Manuel Montt, Temuco ☎ 45/296-100.

FESTIVALS & SEASONAL EVENTS

Summer, with its better weather and ample presence of vacationers, means festival season in the Lake District. In late January and early February, Semanas Musicales de Frutillar brings together the best in classical music. Verano en Valdivia is a two-month-long celebration centered around the February 9 anniversary of the founding of Valdivia. Villarrica hosts a Muestra Cultural Mapuche in January and February that shows off Mapuche art and music.

HEALTH

The tap water is fine to drink in most places, although many people opt for bottled water. As far as food goes, the standards of hygiene are generally high. The Ministry of Health has beefed up its warnings about eating raw shellfish, citing the risk of contracting intestinal parasites.

INTERNET

You can check your e-mail at hotels in the larger towns and cities. Most towns also have Internet cafés, which are generally open until at least 10 PM, charging 700–1,400 pesos per hour.

🆘Internet Cafés **Café Phonet** ✉ Libertad 127, Valdivia ☎ 63/341-054. **Ciber City** ✉ Prat 350, Temuco, ☎45/272-027. **Comunicaciones** ✉ Camilo Henríquez 590, Villarrica ☎45/410-961. **Cyber Centro** ✉ Av. Gramado and Av. San Jose, Puerto Varas ☎ 65/311-901. **Cybercafé Mundosur** ✉ San Martín 232, Puerto Montt ☎ 65/344-773. **Gea.com** ✉ Juan Mackenna 1140, Osorno ☎ 64/207-700. **Unid@d G** ✉ O'Higgins 415, Pucón ☎ 45/444-918

LANGUAGE

The English-speaking world lies a long way from southern Chile. Those in the tourism industry speak English, but the person on the street likely knows little. Despite the region's history of Central European immigration, few people here speak German anymore. The unfamiliar-sounding language most heard is Mapudungun, the indigenous Mapuche language, today spoken by 400,000 people in Chile. Communities cluster around Temuco and Villarrica.

MAIL & SHIPPING

Reasonably efficient, Correos de Chile has post offices in most towns. They are generally open weekdays 9–7 and Saturday 9–1. Mail posted from the Lake District's four hub cities takes up to two weeks to reach North America and three to reach Europe. Anything of value (or valuable looking) should be sent via courier. DHL has offices in Temuco and Puerto Montt.

🖪 Post Offices **Correos de Chile** ✉ Av. O'Higgins 645, Osorno ✉ Av. Rancagua 126, Puerto Montt ✉ Av. Diego Portales at Av. Prat, Temuco ✉ Av. O'Higgins 575, Valdivia. 🖪 Courier Company **DHL** ✉ Bello 765, Temuco, ☎ 45/218–720 ✉ O'Higgins 175, Puerto Montt ☎ 65/268–740.

MONEY MATTERS

All of the major cities in the Lake District have several banks that will exchange U.S. dollars. Most banks will not touch traveler's checks, which are best cashed at a *casa de cambio* (exchange office). Many larger hotels will also exchange currency and a few will exchange traveler's checks. ATMs at Banco Santander and Banco de Chile, part of the omnipresent Redbanc network, accept both Cirrus- and Plus-affiliated cards. The district's four main airports have ATMs and casas de cambio.

SAFETY

Volcano climbing is a popular pastime here, with Volcán Villarrica the most popular because of its easy ascent and proximity to Pucón. But Villarrica is also one of South America's most active. CONAF cuts off access to any volcano at the slightest hint of out-of-normal activity. Check with CONAF before heading out on any hike in this region.

TAXIS

As elsewhere in Chile, solid black or solid yellow cabs operate as *colectivos,* or collective taxis, following fixed routes and picking up up to four people along the way. A sign on the roof shows the general destination. The cost is little more than that of a city bus. A black cab with a yellow roof will take you directly to your requested destination for a metered fare. Hail these in the street.

TELEPHONES

Entel, CTC, and Telefónica del Sur have call centers throughout the region. All allow you to place calls and send faxes. Each company also has its own network of public telephones. Phone booths use calling cards, which you can purchase at many shops and newsstands. Each works only in that company's telephones, so make sure you have the right one.

TOURS

The Lake District is the jumping-off point for luxury cruises. Many companies that offer trips to the fjords of Chilean Patagonia are based in Puerto Montt. Skorpios, with a trio of luxurious ships, has first-class cruises from Puerto Montt to the Laguna San Rafael. The ships carry between 70 and 130 passengers.

A number of companies offer cruises on the region's lakes. Andina del Sud operates between Puerto Varas and San Carlos de Bariloche, and traverses the Lago Todos los Santos.

🖪 Boat Tours **Andina del Sud** ✉ Del Salvador 72, Puerto Varas ☎ 65/232–811. **Skorpios** ✉ Augosto Leguia Norte 118, Santiago ☎ 2/231–1030 ⊕ www.skorpios.cl.

TRAIN TRAVEL

Chile's State Railway Company, the Empresa de los Ferrocarriles del Estado, has daily service southward from Santiago as far as Temuco. It's a far cry from the journey Paul Theroux recounted in *The Old Patagonian Express*. Trains run daily all year; the overnight trip takes about 12 hours. Prices range from 14,000 pesos for an economy-class seat to 70,000 pesos for a sleeper with all the trimmings. If you prefer to rent a vehicle in Santiago, you can use the auto-train service from there to Temuco. The price is an extra 70,000 pesos each way, with surcharges assessed for vehicles longer than 5 m (16 ft).

🚆 Train Information **Empresa de los Ferrocarriles del Estado** ☎ 2/376-8500 in Santiago; 45/233-522 or 45/233-416 in Temuco ⊕ www.efe.cl.

🚆 Train Stations **Estación de Ferrocarriles** ⊠ Av. Barros Arana, Temuco ☎ 45/233-416.

VISITOR INFORMATION

The Lake District's four major cities have offices of Sernatur, Chile's national tourist office, which can help you book travel arrangements. City tourist offices, run by the government or a chamber of commerce, are in most communities catering to tourists. They are valuable resources but cannot book rooms or tours.

🚆 Tourist Information **Frutillar Tourist Office** ⊠ Philippi at San Martín ☎ 65/420-198. **Lican Ray Tourist Office** ⊠ General Urrutia 310 ☎ 45/431-201. **Osorno Tourist Office** ⊠ Plaza de Armas ☎ 64/264-250. **Pucón Tourist Office** ⊠ O'Higgins 483 ☎ 45/293-002. **Puerto Montt Tourist Office** ⊠ San Martín at Diego Portales ☎ 65/261-700. **Puerto Octay Tourist Office** ⊠ La Esperanza 55 ☎ 64/391-491. **Puerto Varas Tourist Office** ⊠ Costanera at San José ☎ 65/233-315. **Sernatur** ⊠ O'Higgins 667, Osorno ☎ 64/237-575 ⊠ Av. de la Décima Región 480, Puerto Montt ☎ 65/254-850 ⊠ Claro Solar and Bulnes, Temuco ☎ 45/211-969 ⊠ Arturo Prat 555, Valdivia ☎ 63/342-300. **Temuco Tourist Office** ⊠ Mercado Municipal ☎ 45/216-360. **Valdivia Tourist Office** ⊠ Terminal de Buses, Anfión Muñoz 360 ☎ 63/212-212. **Villarrica Tourist Office** ⊠ Pedro de Valdivia 1070 ☎ 45/206-618.

CHILOÉ

FODOR'S CHOICE

Hostería Ancud, hotel and restaurant in Ancud

Iglesia Santa María de Loreto, church on Isla Quinchao

Museo Regional de Castro, Castro

HIGHLY RECOMMENDED

Hotel Unicornio Azul, Castro

By Jeffrey Van
Fleet

STEEPED IN MAGIC, SHROUDED IN MIST, the 41-island archipelago of Chiloé is that proverbial world apart, isolated not so much by distance from the mainland—it's barely more than 2 km (1 mi) at its nearest point—but by the quirks of history. Some 130,000 people populate 35 of these rainy islands, with most of them living on the 8,394-square-km (3,241-square-mi) Isla Grande de Chiloé. Almost all are descendants of a seamless blending of colonial and indigenous cultures, a tradition that entwines farming and fishing, devout Catholicism and spirits of good and evil, woolen sweaters and wooden churches.

Originally inhabited by the indigenous Chono people, Chiloé was gradually taken over by the Huilliche. Though Chiloé was claimed as part of Spain's empire in the 1550s, colonists dismissed the archipelago as a backwater. The 1598 rebellion by the Mapuche people on the mainland drove a contingent of Spanish settlers to the isolated safety of Chiloé. Left to their own devices, Spaniards and Huilliche lived and worked side by side. Their society was built on the concept of *minga,* a help-thy-neighbor spirit in the best tradition of the barn raisings and quilting bees in pioneer America. The outcome was a culture neither Spanish nor indigenous, but Chilote, a quintessential mestizo society.

Isolated from the rest of the continent, islanders had little interest in or awareness of the revolutionary fervor sweeping Latin America in the early 19th century. In fact, the mainland Spaniards recruited the Chilote to help put down rebellions in the region. When things got too hot in Santiago, the Spanish governor took refuge on the island, just as his predecessors had done two centuries earlier. Finally defeated, the Spaniards abandoned Chiloé in 1826, and the island soon joined the new nation of Chile.

These days, the isolation is more psychological than physical. Some 40 buses per day and frequent ferries make the half-hour crossing between Chiloé and Puerto Montt in the Lake District on the mainland. The long-discussed but controversial Puente Bicentenario de Chiloé, a projected 2½ km (1½ mile) bridge spanning the Gulf of Ancud and connecting Isla Grande with the mainland, was on hold at press time. Santiago is pushing hard to implement the $306 million project, but many islanders maintain the funds could be better used to improve infrastructure within Chiloé itself.

Exploring Chiloé

If you're like most people, you'll explore Chiloé by car. The Pan-American Highway (Ruta 5) that meanders through northern Chile ends at the Golfo de Ancud and continues again on Isla Grande. It connects the major cities of Ancud, Castro, and Chonchi before coming to its anticlimactic end in Quellón. Paved roads also connect the Pan-American to Quemchi, Dalcahue, and Achao on Isla Quinchao.

About the Restaurants

As befits an island culture, seafood reigns in Chiloé. The signature Chilote dish is *curanto,* a hearty stew of fish and shellfish with chicken, beef, pork, and lamb thrown in. It's served with plenty of potato bread. Most restaurants here serve curanto, though not every day of the week. *Salmón ahumado* (smoked salmon) is another seafood favorite.

The archipelago is also known for its tasty fruit liqueurs, usually from the central Chiloé town of Chonchi. Islanders take mangoes, grapes, and apples and turn them into the *licor de oro* that often greets you as you check into your hotel.

*Numbers in the text correspond to numbers in the margin and o
map.*

If you have
3 days

After crossing the Golfo de Ancud on the morning ferry, drive south
to ☒ **Ancud** ❶ ☞. Soak up the port town's atmosphere that afternoon. Head to **Dalcahue** ❺ the next day. If it's Sunday you can
wander among the stalls of the morning market. Take the short
ferry ride to **Isla Quinchao** ❻ and visit the colorful church of
Santa María de Loreto. Back on Isla Grande, head to ☒ **Castro** ❼.
Spend the next day visiting the capital's historical and modern art
museums and the lovely cathedral.

If you have
5 days

With five days you have time to head to the more remote corners of Chiloé.
After visiting Castro, head south to **Chonchi** ❽, known to locals as the "City
of Three Stories." From there it's an easy drive to the sparsely populated Pacific coast to visit the **Parque Nacional Chiloé** ❿, where you can enjoy one
of the short hikes through the forest. On your last day head to Chiloé's southernmost town, ☒ **Quellón** ⓬.

About the Hotels

There are three or four good hotels on Chiloé, but none would pass for
luxury lodgings on the mainland. That said, the islands have perfectly
acceptable, reasonably priced hotels. Castro and Ancud have the most
varied choices; Chonchi, Achao, and Quellón less so. As in the Lake District to the north, a number of the hotels look as if they were transplanted
from Germany. Many are sided with shingles made from a type of local
wood called *alerce*. Much appreciated central heating and a light breakfast are standard in most better hostelries. Few places here are equipped
to handle credit cards, but with ATM machines readily available in Castro and Ancud, paying in cash isn't as inconvenient as you might expect.

Outside the major cities, the pickings are slim. *Hospedaje* signs seem to
sprout in front of every other house in Castro and Ancud during the
summer as home owners rent rooms to visitors. Quality varies, so inspect the premises before agreeing to take a room from someone who
greets you at the bus station.

WHAT IT COSTS In pesos (in thousands)				
$$$$	**$$$**	**$$**	**$**	**¢**
RESTAURANTS over 11	8–11	5–8	2.5–5	under 2.5
HOTELS over 105	75–105	45–75	15–45	under 15

Restaurant prices are for a main course at dinner. Hotel prices are for a double
room in high season, excluding tax.

Timing

When best to visit Chiloé? In one word, summer. The islands get only
60 days of sunshine a year, most during December–February. Chiloé receives some 157 inches of rain annually, and most of that falls between
April and November. You should be prepared for rain any time of year,

igh-season crowds are never overwhelming, and they make festive. Off-season Chiloé is beguilingly forlorn. Though or everyone, the mist and fog and sunless days deepen e island.

outhwest of Puerto Montt.

ess you're one of those rare visitors who approaches the archipelago from the south, Ancud is the first encounter you'll have with Chiloé. Founded in 1769 as a fortress city on the northern end of Isla Grande, Ancud was repeatedly attacked during Chile's war for independence. It remained the last stronghold of the Spaniards in the Americas, and the seat of their government-in-exile after fleeing from Santiago, a distinction it retained until Chiloé was finally annexed by Chile in 1826.

Although it's the largest city in Chiloé, Ancud seems like a smaller town than perpetual rival Castro. Both have their fans. Castro has more activities, but Ancud, with its hills, irregular streets, and commanding ocean views, gets raves for its quiet charm.

Statues of mythical Chilote figures, such as the Pincoya and Trauco, greet you on the terrace of the fortresslike **Museo Regional de Ancud,** just uphill from the Plaza de Armas. The ship *La Goleta Ancud,* the museum's centerpiece, carried Chilean settlers to the Strait of Magellan in 1843. Inside is a collection of island handicrafts. ⊠ *Libertad 370* ☎ *65/622–413* 🖾 *600 pesos* 🕑 *Jan.–Feb., daily 10:30–7:30; Mar.–Dec., weekdays 9:30–5:30, weekends 10–2.*

Northwest of downtown Ancud, the 16 cannon emplacements of the **Fuerte de San Antonio** are nearly all that remain of Spain's last outpost in the New World. The fort, constructed in 1786, was a key component in the defense of the Canal de Chacao, especially after the Spanish colonial government fled to Chiloé during Chile's war for independence. ⊠ *Lord Cohrane at San Antonio* ☎ *no phone* 🖾 *Free.*

Where to Stay & Eat

$$–$$$ ✕ **Restaurant La Pincoya.** According to Chilote legend, the presence of the spirit La Pincoya signals an abundant catch. La Pincoya does serve up abundant fresh fish and usually whips up curanto on the weekends. This friendly waterfront restaurant is nothing fancy—plain wooden tables and chairs—but the views are stupendous. ⊠ *Arturo Prat 61* ☎ *65/622–613* 🖃 *No credit cards.*

$$–$$$ ✕ **Retro's Pub.** This cozy, intimate place makes a nice break from Chiloé's ubiquitous seafood. Instead, chow down on fajitas, burritos, and nachos. Portions are ample. The dining room is dark and casual. Around the corner on Pudeto, the same owners operate Cafe Retro's, which is much brighter with lighter sandwich-and-dessert fare. ⊠ *Maipú 615* ☎ *65/626–410* 🖃 *AE, DC, MC, V.*

$$ ✕🖾 **Hostería Ancud.** Ancud's finest hotel—some say the best in Chiloé—

Fodor'sChoice sits atop a bluff overlooking the Fuerte de San Antonio. It's part of the ★ Panamericana Hoteles chain, but that doesn't mean it lacks individuality. The rooms in the rustic main building, for example, have log-cabin walls. The wood-panel lobby, with a huge fireplace inviting you to linger, opens into the town's loveliest restaurant, which feels spacious thanks to its vaulted ceilings and picture windows. Try the *salmón del caicavilú* (salmon stuffed with chicken, ham, cheese, and mushrooms). ⊠ *San Antonio 30* ☎ *65/622–340* 🖶 *65/622–350* ⊕ *www.hosteriancud. com* 🛌 *24 rooms* 🖒 *Restaurant, coffee shop, bar, meeting room, travel services, no-smoking rooms; no a/c* 🖃 *AE, DC, MC, V.*

7

Architecture

Nothing symbolizes Chiloé more than the 150 wooden churches that dot the eastern half of the main island. Built by Jesuit missionaries who came to the archipelago after the 1598 Mapuche rebellion on the mainland, the chapels were an integral part of the effort to convert the indigenous peoples. Pairs of missionaries traveled the region by boat, making sure to celebrate mass in each community at least once a year. Franciscan missionaries continued the tradition after Spain expelled the Jesuits from its New World colonies in 1767.

The architectural style of the churches calls to mind those in rural Germany, the home of many of the missionaries. The complete lack of ornamentation is offset only by a steep roof covered with wooden shingles called *tejuelas* and a three-tier hexagonal bell tower. An arched portico fronts most of the churches. Getting to see more than the outside of many of the churches can be a challenge. Many stand alone on the coast, forlorn in their solitude and locked most of the year; others are open only for Sunday services. The exceptions: Castro's orange-and-lavender Iglesia de San Francisco, dating from 1906, opens its doors to visitors. Achao's Iglesia de Santa María de Loreto gives daily guided Spanish-language tours.

A nonprofit support organization, the Fundación de Amigos de las Iglesias de Chiloé, raises funds for restoration of the archipelago's churches, many of which are in urgent need of repair. A March 2002 storm toppled the tower of Chonchi's Iglesia de San Carlos, prompting studies, underway at press time, to evaluate the structural integrity of several other churches.

Next to its wooden churches, *palafitos* are the best-known architectural symbol of Chiloé. These shingled houses—built on stilts and hanging over the water—are all along the island's coast. The Pedro Montt coastal highway is the best place to see palafitos in Castro. Many of these ramshackle structures have been turned into restaurants and artisan markets.

Folklore

As the southernmost outpost of Spain's empire, Chiloé was also the "end of Christendom," as naturalist Charles Darwin wrote after his 1834 visit. But Chilote Catholicism was also tied up in magic and legend. Much of what is identified as Chilean folklore originated here, though the rest of the country happily embraces it as its own. Mythical creatures are thought to populate the coasts of these foggy green islands. On the beach you might spot the beautiful blonde *Pincoya*, signaling good fishing that day. Beware the troll-like *Trauco*, seducer of young women. Don't go poking around caves for fear of stumbling upon a *brujo*, or witch; that encounter could bode good or evil. And don't gaze too intently out at the ocean on a foggy night, lest you catch a glimpse of the *Caleuche*, the ill-fated ghost ship that sank on its maiden voyage and forever cruises the dark waters looking for its passengers lost at sea.

These days, your encounter with such characters will more likely take the form of a woven-straw figure for sale in a market in Castro or Dalcahue. But you just might run into a self-proclaimed brujo in that same market offering an herbal cure for whatever ails you.

Sports & the Outdoors

Chiloé doesn't have quite the extensive adventure tourism infrastructure of the neighboring Lake District. Hiking, especially in Parque Nacional Chiloé, sea kayaking in the channels east of Isla Grande, and horseback riding around the island are the three most popular activities. What the archipelago lacks in sheer number of outfitters, it makes up in the high quality of services offered by those that are here.

Shopping

Baskets, ponchos, figurines woven from different kinds of grasses and straws, and sweaters of raw, hand-spun, and hand-dyed wool all come from Chiloé. Chilote wool processing retains the natural oils, making the sweaters and ponchos wonderfully warm and water-resistant. Castro's waterfront Feria Artesanal is the most popular place to shop for traditional goods, and Dalcahue's Sunday-morning market also draws the shop-'til-you-drop crowd. But the best selection of Chilote handicrafts is not here in the archipelago at all; it's in the stalls of the Caleta Angelmó market in Puerto Montt, on the mainland in the Lake District.

$ ▨ **Hostal Lluhay.** Don't judge a book by its cover: if you did you'd pass by this hillside hostal because of its drab exterior, missing the lobby filled with knickknacks and the dining room dominated by a 200-year-old rosewood piano. Rooms are plain, but pleasant considering the reasonable rates. The amiable owners include a buffet breakfast in the price. ⊠ *Lord Cochrane 458* ☎🖷 *65/622–656* ✉ *lluhay@entelchile.net* ⇨ *14 rooms* ♨ *Bar, travel services; no a/c, no room phones, no room TVs* ▭ *AE, DC, MC, V* ❍ *BP.*

$ ▨ **Hotel Galeón Azul.** Formerly a Catholic seminary, the Blue Galleon is actually painted bright yellow. Perched like a ship run aground on a bluff overlooking Ancud's waterfront, this modern hotel has pleasantly furnished rooms with big windows and great views of the sea. It's owned by the same folks who own the Hotel Unicornio Azul in Castro, and it has the same personalized service. ⊠ *Libertad 751* ☎ *65/622–567* 🖷 *65/622–543* ⇨ *16 rooms* ♨ *Restaurant, bar; no a/c* ▭ *No credit cards* ❍ *CP.*

¢ ▨ **Hospedaje O'Higgins.** The nicest of the many hospedajes in Ancud, this 60-year-old home sits on a hillside overlooking the bay. You have your pick of eight bright rooms. The furniture in the common areas is a bit worn, but the whole place has a cozy, lived-in feel. The friendly service will make you overlook any inadequacies. ⊠ *O'Higgins 6* ☎ *65/622–266* ⇨ *8 rooms, 2 with bath* ♨ *Laundry service; no a/c, no room phones, no room TVs* ▭ *No credit cards.*

Quemchi

❷ *62 km (37 mi) southeast of Ancud.*

On the protected inside of the Golfo de Ancud, Quemchi is a small, picturesque fishing village with a church in one of the best structural conditions on the island. The **Iglesia de San Antonio de Padua,** on the Plaza de Armas, was constructed in the late 19th century, replacing the original Jesuit structure, and painstakingly restored in 1996. Sunday-morning mass is the only time to get a glimpse inside.

A block uphill from the church is a typical old Chilote **cemetery,** almost a town in miniature. Each tomb is a small mausoleum, topped and sided with alerce shingles and made to look like a little house, with a door and windows.

Some 4 km (2½ mi) east of Quemchi is the tiny **Isla de Aucar,** a forested islet reached only by a wooden pedestrian bridge. The Jesuit chapel here dates from 1761.

Quicaví

❸ *25 km (15 mi) southeast of Quemchi.*

The center of all that is magical and mystical about Chiloé, Quicaví sits forlornly on the eastern coast of Isla Grande. More superstitious locals will strongly advise you against going anywhere near the coast to the south of town, where miles of caves extend to the village of Tenaún. They believe that witches, and evil ones at that, inhabit them. On the beaches are mermaids—not the beautiful and benevolent Pincoya—that lure fishermen to their deaths. And many a Quicaví denizen claims to have glimpsed Chiloé's notorious ghost ship, the *Caleuche,* roaming the waters on foggy nights, searching for its doomed passengers. Of course, a brief glimpse of the ship is all anyone dares admit, as legend holds that a longer gaze could spell death.

In an effort to win converts, the Jesuits constructed the enormous **Iglesia de San Pedro,** on the Plaza de Armas. The original structure survives from colonial times, though it underwent extensive remodeling in the early 20th century. It's open for services the first Sunday of every month at 11 AM, which is the only time you can get a look inside.

Tenaún

❹ *12 km (7 mi) south of Quicaví.*

A small fishing village, Tenaún is notable for its 1861 neoclassical **Iglesia de Tenaún,** on the Plaza de Armas, which replaced the original 1734 structure built by the Jesuits. The style differs markedly from that of other Chilote churches, as the two towers flanking the usual hexagonal central bell tower are painted a striking deep blue. You can see the interior during services on Sundays at 9:30 AM and the rest of the week at 5 PM.

Dalcahue

❺ *40 km (24 mi) west of Tenaún, 74 km (44 mi) southeast of Ancud.*

Most days travelers in Dalcahue stop only long enough to board the ferry that deposits them 15 minutes later on Isla Quinchao. But everyone lingers in Dalcahue if it's a Sunday morning, when they can visit the weekly artisan market. Dalcahue is a pleasant coastal town—one that deserves a longer visit.

The 1850 **Iglesia de Nuestra Señora de los Dolores,** modeled on the churches constructed during the Jesuit era, sits on the main square. A portico with nine arches, an unusually high number for a Chilote church, fronts the structure. The church, which is on Plaza de Armas, holds a small museum and is open daily 9–6.

A *fogón*—a traditional indigenous cooking pit—sits in the center of the small palafito housing the **Museo Histórico de Dalcahue,** which displays historical exhibits from this part of the island. ✉ *Pedro Montt 105* ☎ *65/642–375* ✍ *Free* ⊘ *Daily 8–6.*

Where to Stay

$ ⌂ **Hotel La Isla.** One of Chiloé's nicest lodgings, the wood-shingled Hotel La Isla greets you with a cozy sitting room and big fireplace off the lobby. Huge windows and vaulted ceilings make the wood-panel rooms bright and airy. Comfortable mattresses with plush pillows and warm

comforters invite you to sleep tight. ⊠ *Mocopulli 113* 🖼 *65/641–241*
🛏 *16 rooms* ♦ *Bar, laundry service; no a/c* ▭ *No credit cards* ⑩ *BP.*

Shopping

Dalcahue's Sunday-morning art market, **Feria Artesanal,** on Avenida Pedro
Montt near the waterfront municipal building, draws crowds who come
to shop for Chilote woolens, baskets, and woven mythical figures.
Things get underway at about 8 AM and begin to wind down about noon.
Bargaining is expected, though the prices are already quite reasonable.
There's fun to be had and bargains to be found, but the market is more
touristy than the ramshackle daily market in nearby Castro.

Isla Quinchao

❻ *1 km (½ mi) southeast of Dalcahue.*

For many visitors, the elongated Isla Quinchao, the easiest to reach of
the islands in the eastern archipelago, defines Chiloé. Populated by
hardworking farmers and fisherfolk, Isla Quinchao provides a glimpse
into the region's past. Head to Achao, Quinchao's largest community,
to see the alerce-shingle houses, busy fishing pier, and colonial church.

Fodor's Choice On Achao's Plaza de Armas, the town's centerpiece is its 1706 **Iglesia**
★ **Santa María de Loreto,** the oldest remaining house of worship on the
archipelago. In addition to the alerce so commonly used to construct
buildings in the region, the church also uses wood from cypress and *mañío*
trees. Its typically unadorned exterior contrasts with the deep-blue ceiling embellished with gold stars inside. Rich baroque carvings grace the
altar. Mass is celebrated Sunday at 11 AM and Tuesday at 7 PM, but do-
cents give guided tours in Spanish while the church is open. An informative Spanish-language museum behind the altar is dedicated to the
period of Chiloé's Jesuit missions. All proceeds go to much-needed
church restoration—termites have taken their toll. ⊠ *Delicias at Amunategui* ☎ *65/661–881* 🎫 *500 pesos* ☉ *Daily 10:30–1 and 2:30–7.*

About 10 km (6 mi) south of Achao is the archipelago's largest church,
the 1869 **Iglesia de Nuestra Señora de Gracia.** As with many other Chilote
churches, the 200-ft structure sits in solitude near the coast. The church
has no tours, but may be visited during Sunday mass at 11 AM.

Where to Stay & Eat

$–$$ ✕ **Mar y Velas.** Scrumptious oysters and a panoply of other gifts from
the sea are served in this big wooden house at the foot of Achao's dock.
You might not pick it out as a restaurant at first, as there's sometimes
laundry hanging outside the windows, but the place has the friendliest
service in town. ⊠ *Serrano 2, Achao* ☎ *65/661–375* ▭ *No credit
cards.*

$–$$ ✕ **Restaurant La Nave.** On the beach, Restaurant La Nave serves seafood
in a rambling building that arches over the street. The matter-of-fact
staff dishes up curanto most days during the January–March high season, but usually only weekends the rest of the year. ⊠ *Arturo Prat at
Sargento Aldea, Achao* ☎ *65/661–219* ▭ *No credit cards.*

¢ 🏠 **Hostal La Plaza.** This cozy private home is close to the hubbub of the
Plaza de Armas, but being down an alley and behind a chocolate shop
affords it a degree of privacy and quiet. Simply furnished rooms have
private baths, which is surprising considering the very reasonable rates.
The owners are warm and friendly. ⊠ *Amunategui 20, Achao* 🖼 *65/
661–283* 🛏 *8 rooms* ♦ *Dining room; no a/c, no room phones* ▭ *No
credit cards* ⑩ *CP.*

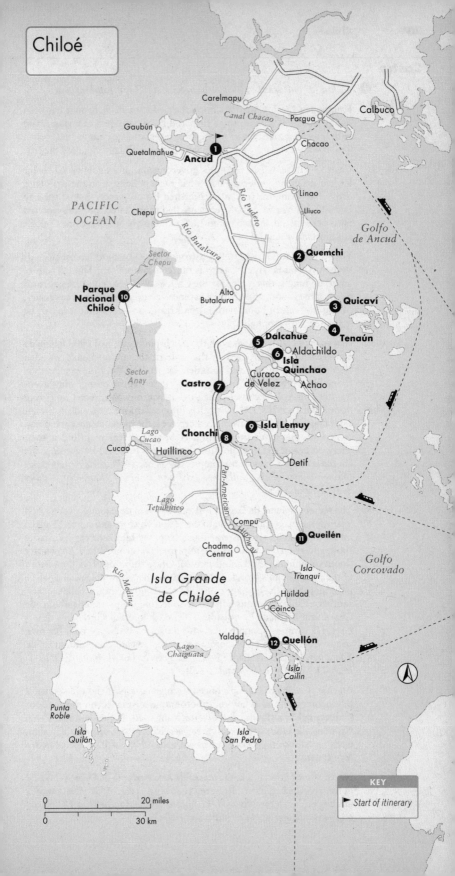

Castro

❼ *45 km (27 mi) southeast of Achao, 88 km (53 mi) south of Ancud.*

Founded in 1567, Castro is Chile's third-oldest city. Its history has been one of destruction, with three fires and three earthquakes laying waste to the city over four centuries. The most recent disaster was in 1960, when a tidal wave caused by an earthquake on the mainland engulfed the city.

Castro's future as Isla Grande's governmental and commercial center looked promising after the 1598 Mapuche rebellion on the mainland drove the Spaniards to Chiloé, but then Dutch pirates sacked the city in 1600. Many of Castro's residents fled to the safety of more isolated parts of the island. It wasn't until 1982 that the city finally became Chiloé's administrative capital.

With a population of 20,000, Castro is Chiloé's second-largest city. Although Ancud is larger, Castro is more cosmopolitan. Though hardly an urban jungle, this is big-city life Chiloé style. Residents of more rural parts of the island who visit the capital—no more often than necessary, of course—return home with tales of traffic so heavy that it has to be regulated with stoplights.

Any tour of Castro begins with the much-photographed 1906 **Iglesia de San Francisco,** constructed in the style of the archipelago's wooden churches, only bigger and grander. Depending on your perspective, terms like "pretty" or "pretty garish" describe the orange-and-lavender exterior, colors chosen when the structure was spruced up before Pope John Paul II's 1987 visit. It's infinitely more reserved on the inside. The dark-wood interior's centerpiece is the monumental carved crucifix hanging from the ceiling. A Spanish firm installed a soft, energy-efficient external illumination system in 2002; by evening, the church is one of Chiloé's most impressive sights. ⊠ *Plaza de Armas* ☎ *no phone* ☉ *Dec.–Feb., daily 9–12:30 and 3–11:30; Mar.–Nov., daily 9–12:30 and 3–9:30.*

Fodor'sChoice
★

The **Museo Regional de Castro,** just off the Plaza de Armas, gives a good Spanish-language introduction to the region's history and culture. Packed into a fairly small space are artifacts from the Huilliche era (primarily rudimentary farming and fishing implements) through the 19th century (looms, spinning wheels, and plows). One exhibit displays the history of the archipelago's wooden churches; another shows black-and-white photographs of the damage caused by the 1960 earthquake that rocked southern Chile. The museum has a collection of quotations about the Chiloé culture made by outsiders: "The Chilote talks little, but thinks a lot. He is rarely spontaneous with outsiders, and even with his own countrymen he isn't too communicative," wrote one ethnographer. ⊠ *Esmeralda 205* ☎ *65/635–967* ☑ *Free* ☉ *Jan.–Feb., daily 9:30–8; Mar.–Dec., daily 9:30–1 and 3–6:30.*

All that remains of Chiloé's once thriving Castro–Ancud rail service is the locomotive and a few old photographs displayed on the outdoor **Plazuela del Tren** down on the waterfront road. Nobel laureate Pablo Neruda called the narrow-gauge rail service "a slow, rainy train, a slim, damp mushroom." Service ended with the 1960 earthquake. ⊠ *Pedro Montt s/n.*

Northwest of downtown, the **Museo de Arte Moderno de Chiloé** is housed in five refurbished barns. Referred to locally as the MAM, the complex in a city park exhibits works by Chilote artists. ⊠ *Pasaje Díaz 181* ☎ *65/635–454* ☑ *Free* ☉ *Jan.–Mar., daily 10–7.*

Conozca Castro Caminando, or "Get to Know Castro Walking," runs two-hour historical walking tours in English, Spanish, or German, at least four times weekly December–February and at other times by request. The folks here are quite flexible about accommodating your schedule. ⊠ *Plaza de Armas* ☎ *09/411–6198* ✆ *7,000 pesos.*

Where to Stay & Eat

$–$$$ ✕ **Octavio.** A devoted tourist clientele flocks to waterside Octavio for its well-known curanto, seafood stews, and some of the most attentive service around. And unlike at other restaurants in town, you can also chow down on steak and pork chops here. Enjoy the great views from this alerce-shingled palafito-style building—one that is much nicer and in better shape than most of the palafitos in town. ⊠ *Pedro Montt 261* ☎ *65/632–855* ✄ *No credit cards.*

$–$$ ✕ **Café la Brújula del Cuerpo.** Next to the fire station on the Plaza de Armas, this little place bustles with all the commotion of a big-city diner. Sandwiches are standard fare—burgers and clubs are favorites. Don't leave without trying one of the mouthwatering ice-cream sundaes or banana splits. ⊠ *O'Higgins 308* ☎ *65/633–229* ✄ *No credit cards.*

$–$$ ✕ **1 Palafito Restaurant.** This is the first of five palafitos on Castro's downtown waterfront that have been converted into seafood restaurants. You really can't go wrong with the other four, but locals swear this one is the best. This is no place to escape the crowds: the cavernous restaurant can easily seat a few hundred on a bright summer night. The portions are huge; it's a hard task to finish the tasty curanto. If you have a light appetite order something smaller, such as clams or salmón ahumado. ⊠ *Eusebio Lillo 30* ☎ *65/635–476* ✄ *No credit cards.*

★ **$$** ▦ **Hotel Unicornio Azul.** Taking its name from a popular song by Cuban singer Silvio Rodríguez, the Blue Unicorn is actually pink, though its roof is bright blue. The rambling hotel, dating from 1910, climbs the hill from the waterfront. There are lots of stairs, and many twists and turns as it makes its ascent, but you'll find a sitting room and reading alcove at every landing and big windows to catch the view. Furnishings in the bright rooms echo the facade's pastel hues. ⊠ *Pedro Montt 228* ☎ *65/632–359* ✆ *65/632–808* ✑ *hotelunicornioazul@hotmail.com* ✎ *18 rooms* ⚬ *Restaurant, bar; no a/c* ✄ *No credit cards* ⊚ *CP.*

$ ▦ **Hostal Kolping.** Great inexpensive lodging is yours in an alerce-shingled building with a big porch in the center of town. Paneled rooms are bright, sunny, spacious, and sparkling clean, with comfortable beds and lots of pillows. ⊠ *Chacabuco 217* ☎☎ *65/633–273* ✎ *11 rooms* ⚬ *Dining room; no a/c, no room phones* ✄ *No credit cards* ⊚ *CP.*

$ ▦ **Hostería de Castro.** Looming over downtown Castro, Hostería de Castro is near the estuary. Its sloped chalet-style roof has a long skylight, making the interior seem bright and airy even on a cloudy day. Nice modern rooms have simple furnishings and cheery flowered bedspreads. The downstairs seafood restaurant has huge windows with great views of the Golfo de Corcovado. ⊠ *Chacabuco 202* ☎ *65/632–301* ✆ *65/635–688* ⊕ *www.hosteriadecastro.cl* ✎ *29 rooms* ⚬ *Restaurant, bar, laundry service; no a/c* ✄ *AE, DC, MC, V* ⊚ *BP.*

$ ▦ **Hotel Esmeralda.** This hot-pink storefront hotel sits just off the bustling Plaza de Armas. The compact four-story building has lots of windows and all the amenities that you would expect from such a modern place. It's popular among corporate travelers because of its meeting rooms and business services. ⊠ *Esmeralda 266* ☎ *65/637–900* ✆ *65/637–910* ⊕ *www.bosquemodelochiloe.cl/chwb/hotelesmeralda/* ✎ *32 rooms, 2 suites* ⚬ *Restaurant, pool, bar, recreation room, laundry service, business services, meeting rooms; no a/c* ✄ *AE, DC, MC, V* ⊚ *BP.*

¢–$ 🔲 **Hostal Quelcun.** An unpromising alley between two downtown store-fronts opens onto a green, leafy courtyard around which you'll find this two-story wooden building, one of Castro's nicest budget lodgings. Some of the wood-panel rooms have improbable layouts, requiring a bit of maneuvering to get into the second bed, but all are pleasantly furnished. The staff here is friendly and eager to please. ✉ *San Martín 581* 📠 *65/632–396* ➰ *16 rooms* ♿ *Dining room, travel services; no a/c, no room phones* ▭ *No credit cards* ¶◯¶ *CP.*

Shopping

The city's **Feria Artesanal,** a lively, often chaotic artisan market on Eusebio Lillo, is regarded by most as the best place on the island to pick up the woolen sweaters, woven baskets, and the straw figures for which Chiloé is known. Prices are already quite reasonable, but vendors expect a bit of bargaining. The stalls share a ramshackle collection of palafitos with several seafood restaurants. It's open daily 9–dusk.

Chonchi

8   *23 km (14 mi) south of Castro.*

The colorful wooden houses of Chonchi are on a hillside so steep that it's known in Spanish as the *Ciudad de los Tres Pisos* (City of Three Stories). The town's name means "slippery earth" in the Huilliche language, and if you tromp up the town's steep streets on a rainy day you'll understand why. Arranged around a scenic harbor, Chonchi wins raves as Chiloé's most picturesque town.

The town's centerpiece is the **Iglesia de San Carlos,** on the Plaza de Armas. Started by the Jesuits in 1754, it was left unfinished until 1859. Rebuilt in the neoclassical style, the church is now a national monument. An unusually ornate arcade with five arches fronts the church, and inside are an intricately carved altar and wooden columns. The church contains Chonchi's most prized relic, a statue of the Virgen de la Candelaria. According to tradition, this image of the Virgin Mary protected the town from the Dutch pirates who destroyed neighboring Castro in 1600. Townspeople celebrate the event every February 2 with fireworks and gunpowder symbolizing the pirate attack. A March 2002 storm felled the church's tower; fund-raising for reconstruction has been painfully slow, but the building remains open for mass on Sunday at 11 AM.

The small **Museo de las Tradiciones Chonchinas** documents life in Chonchi through furnishings and photos in a 19th-century house. ✉ *Centenario 116* 🕾 *no phone* 📧 *Free* ◷ *Sept.–May, weekdays 9–7; June–Aug., weekdays 9–1.*

Where to Eat

$ ✕ **El Trébol.** This seafood restaurant is on the second floor inside Chonchi's waterfront market. The decorations are basic, and there's no view—this is the market, after all. But the food is good, and the prices are very reasonable. You have a better chance of getting curanto or salmón ahumado if you're here in high season. ✉ *Irarrázaval s/n* 🕾 *65/671–203* ▭ *No credit cards.*

Isla Lemuy

9   *3 km (2 mi) east of Chonchi.*

Though easily reached by a 15-minute ferry ride from Chonchi, Isla Lemuy seems miles away from anything. It's the third-largest of Chiloé's islands, just slightly smaller than Isla Quinchao to the north. Jesuit churches dominate three of its villages—Ichuac, Aldachildo, and Detif—none of which is more than a handful of houses. Ichuac's church is in a sorry state of disrepair, as funds for restoration are in short supply. The Aldachildo chapel is locked most of the year, though the folks in the local telephone office can help track down someone who can open it up for you. Detif's church, open only for Sunday-morning mass, is noteworthy for its "votive boats," small wooden ship models hung in thanksgiving for a safe journey. From here there's a stunning view of Volcán Michinmahuida on the mainland.

Where to Stay

$ 🏠 **Lidia Pérez.** The Pérez family of Puchilco operates one of the nicer lodgings in Red Agroturismo Chiloé, the 19-member agro-tourism network. The only accommodation on Isla Lemuy, it's just a wooden farmhouse painted a distinctive orange and green, but it gives you a chance to see rural Chilote life up close—in this case, life on a sheep farm. Rooms are spartan, but pleasantly furnished with cheery green bedspreads and drapes. ⊠ *Puchilco* ☎ *09/444–0252; 65/628–333 in Ancud* ➪ *3 rooms without bath* ⟁ *Dining room; no a/c, no room phones, no room TVs* ⊟ *No credit cards* ⊙ *BP.*

Parque Nacional Chiloé

⑩ *35 km (21 mi) west of Chonchi.*

The 430-square-km (166-square-mi) Parque Nacional Chiloé hugs Isla Grande's sparsely populated Pacific coast. During his 1834 visit, Charles Darwin, the park's most famous visitor, marveled at the indigenous families who scratched out a living from this inhospitable land.

The park's two sections differ dramatically in terms of landscape and access. Heavily forested with evergreens, Sector Anay, to the south, is most easily entered from the coastal village of Cucao. An unpaved but passable road heads west to the park from the Pan-American Highway at Notuco, just south of Chonchi. Sector Anay is popular among backpackers, who hike the short El Tepual trail, which begins at the Chanquín Visitor Center 1 km (½ mi) north of the park entrance. The longer Dunas trail also begins there and leads through the forest to the beach dunes near Cacao. You stand the best chance of seeing the Chiloé fox, native to Isla Grande, in your hike through the park. More reclusive is the *pudú,* a miniature deer found throughout southern Chile. Some 3 km (2 mi) north of the Cucao entrance is a Huilliche community on the shore of Lago Huelde. Unobtrusive visitors are welcome.

Only accessible during the drier months of January through March, the northern Sector Chepu of Chiloé National Park is primarily wetlands created by the tidal wave that rocked the island in 1960. The sector now shelters a large bird population (most notably penguins) as well as a sea lion colony. Reaching the park is difficult—take a gravel road turnoff at Coipomó, about 20 km (12 mi) south of Ancud on the Pan-American Highway, to Chepu on the Pacific coast. From there, it's about a 90-minute hike to the park's northern border. ⊠ *North of Cucao and south of Chepu* ☎ *65/637–266 in Castro* ⊠ *Each sector, 1,000 pesos* ⊙ *Daily 7–5.*

Queilén

⑪ *47 km (33 mi) southeast of Chonchi.*

This town named for the red cypress trees that dot the area sits on an elongated peninsula and, as such, is the only town on Isla Grande with two seafronts. Two of Isla Grande's best bathing beaches are the town's central **Playa de Queilén,** and the **Playa Lelbun,** 15 km (9 mi) northwest of the city.

The **Refugio de Navegantes** serves as the town's cultural center and contains a small museum with artifacts and old black-and-white photographs. Nothing is too colorful here—the muted tones of the pottery, the fabrics, and the farm implements reflect the stark life of colonial Chiloé. ⊠ *Pedro Aguirre Cerda s/n* ☎ *no phone* ⊠ *Free* ⊙ *Weekdays 9–12:30 and 2:30–6.*

Uphill on Calle Presidente Kennedy is a **mirador.** The observation point has stupendous views of the Golfo de Ancud, the smaller islands in the archipelago, and, on a clear day, the Volcán Corcovado on the mainland.

Quellón

🔟 *99 km (60 mi) south of Castro.*

The Pan-American Highway, which begins in Alaska and stretches for most of the length of North and South America, ends without fanfare here in Quellón, Chiloé's southernmost city. The Carretera Austral continues south on the mainland. Quellón was the famed "end of Christendom" described by Charles Darwin during his 19th-century visit. Just a few years earlier it had been the southernmost outpost of Spain's empire in the New World. For most visitors today, Quellón is also the end of the line. But if you're truly adventurous, it's the starting point for ferries that head to the Southern Coast.

Taking its name from a Huilliche phrase meaning "from our past," the **Museo Inchin Cuivi Ant** stands apart from other museums in Chiloé because of its "living" exhibitions: a Chilote woman spins woolens on her loom or makes empanadas in a traditional fogón. A botanical garden with herbs, plants, and trees native to Chiloé was taking root at press time. ⊠ *Ladrilleros 225* ☎ *no phone* ⊠ *500 pesos* ⊙ *Daily 9–1 and 2:30–8.*

Where to Stay & Eat

$–$$ ✕ **Hostería Romeo Alfa.** This imposing seafood restaurant, which resembles a Bavarian chalet, sits right on Quellón's pier. Choose one of the tables along the window and watch all the comings and goings while you dine on the delectable curanto. The white tablecloths and candles make the dining room appear quite elegant, but the whole affair is really quite informal and very friendly. ⊠ *Capitán Luis Alcazar 554* ☎ *65/680–177* ⊟ *No credit cards.*

$ 🏨 **Hotel Los Suizos.** The owners pride themselves on providing Swiss-style service to their lodgers, which means you can expect efficiency and friendliness. The bright upstairs rooms have light-wood paneling. The intimate downstairs restaurant serves Swiss cuisine as well as seafood. ⊠ *Ladrilleros 399* ☎ *65/681–787* 🖨 *65/680–747* ⊘ *doberlin@enterlchile.net* ⇄ *6 rooms* ⚐ *Restaurant, bar, laundry service; no a/c, no room phones* ⊟ *No credit cards.*

¢–$ 🏨 **Hotel Tierra del Fuego.** This rambling alerce-shingle house is on Quellón's waterfront. The owners added a dozen rooms, and you definitely know when you've crossed the border between old and new. Opt for one of the wood-paneled rooms in the newer wing, which have sunlight streaming in through big windows. Everyone in town seems to stop by for lunch at the bustling restaurant downstairs. ⊠ *Pedro Montt 445* ☎🖨 *65/682–079* ⇄ *24 rooms, 12 with bath* ⚐ *Restaurant, bar; no a/c, no room phones* ⊟ *No credit cards.*

Shopping

Quellón's **Feria Artesanal Llauquil**, on Avenida Gómez García, doesn't have the hustle and bustle of similar artisan markets in Castro and Dalcahue, but there are some good buys at this restored complex of artisan shops. Don't bother to bargain, as the prices are already too reasonable. It's open daily until 7 December–February, and Monday–Saturday until 6 the rest of the year.

CHILOÉ A TO Z

To research prices, get advice from other travelers, and book travel arrangements, visit www.fodors.com.

AIR TRAVEL

Chiloé has a small military airstrip, but there's no airport for either national or international flights. Most people flying to the region head to Aeropuerto El Tepual, 90 km (54 mi) northeast of Ancud in Puerto Montt. LanChile and its domestic partner LanExpress maintain an office in Castro.

◻ Airlines **LanChile/LanExpress** ✉ Blanco 299, Castro ☎ 65/632-866.

BOAT & FERRY TRAVEL

Since Chiloé is an archipelago, the only way to drive here is by taking one of the frequent ferries across the Golfo de Ancud. Most people arrive by crossing from the mainland to the tiny town of Chacao in the north. Cruz del Sur operates the frequent ferry service connecting mainland Pargua with Chacao on the northern tip of Isla Grande. Boats leave twice an hour from early morning until late at night, and trips take about 30 minutes (8,000 pesos for a car, no passenger fee).

Many fewer arrive via Quellón in the south. Navimag connects Quellón with Chaitén eight times a month during the January–February summer season, less frequently the rest of the year. Departure time varies. The cost is 50,000 pesos for a vehicle less than 4 m (13 ft) in length. Each passenger pays 10,000 pesos for the crossing.

Catamaranes del Sur provides twice-weekly catamaran service during January and February between Castro and mainland Chaitén at a relatively quick 3 hours, with continuing service to Puerto Montt. Pehuén Expediciones is the sales agent in Castro.

◻ Boat & Ferry Information **Catamaranes del Sur** ✉ Pehuén Expediciones, 299 Blanco, Castro ☎ 65/632-361 ✉ Diego Portales and Guillermo Gallardo, Puerto Montt ☎ 65/267-533 ⊕ www.catamaranesdelsur.cl. **Cruz del Sur** ✉ Chacabuco 672, Ancud ☎ 65/622-265. **Navimag** ✉ Pedro Montt 457, Quellón ☎ 65/682-207 ⊕ www.navimag.cl.

BUS TRAVEL

Cruz del Sur and its subsidiary Transchiloé operate some 30 buses per day between Ancud and the mainland, usually terminating in Puerto Montt. Many of the routes continue north to Temuco, and a few travel all the way to Santiago. Bus service is timed to coincide with the company's frequent ferries between Pargua and Chacao. Buses arriving from the mainland provide *very* local service once they reach the island, making frequent stops.

Cruz del Sur and Transchiloé also operate hourly service along the Pan-American Highway between Ancud, Castro, Chonchi, and Quellón. Queilén Bus has service between Chiloé's major cities about 10 times daily. It also makes twice daily runs between Castro and Quemchi.

Many other companies operate small buses or comfortable minivans. Dalcahue Expreso connects Castro with Dalcahue every half hour during the week, less often on weekends. Buses Gallardo runs buses between Castro and Isla Lemuy three times a day during the week, less often on weekends. Buses Arroyo has twice-a-day service between Castro and Cucao, the gateway to Parque Nacional Chiloé.

🚍 Bus Information **Buses Arroyo** ✉ San Martín s/n, Castro ☎ 65/635-604. **Buses Gallardo** ✉ San Martín 667, Castro ☎ 65/634-521. **Cruz del Sur** ✉ Chacabuco 672, Ancud ☎ 65/622-265 ✉ San Martín 486, Castro ☎ 65/632-389 ✉ Av. Portales at Lota, Puerto Montt ☎ 64/254-731. **Dalcahue Expreso** ✉ Ramírez 233, Castro ☎ 65/635-164. **Queilén Bus** ✉ San Martín 667, Castro ☎ 65/632-173.

CAR TRAVEL

Rather than terminating in Puerto Montt, the Pan-American Highway skips over the Golfo de Ancud and continues through Ancud, Castro, and Chonchi before stopping in Quellón. The Carretera Austral continues on down the mainland Southern Coast. Paved roads also lead to Quemchi, Dalcahue, and Achao on Isla Quinchao. You can reach a few other communities by *ripios,* rough gravel roads. Plan ahead, as it's often slow going during the long rainy season. Most of the western half of the island is inaccessible by car.

Most visitors who rent a vehicle do so on the mainland, but if you decide you need wheels after your arrival, try the local firm of ADS Rent-a-Car in Castro.

🚗 Agency **ADS Rent-a-Car** ✉ Esmeralda 260, Castro ☎ 65/637-373.

EMERGENCIES

Chiloé has no hospital for emergency attention. The nearest such facility is in mainland Puerto Montt.

🚑 Emergency Services **Ambulance** ☎131. **Fire (Bomberos)** ☎132. **Police (Carabineros)** ☎ 133.

🏥 Hospitals **Hospital Base Puerto Montt** ✉ Seminario s/n, Puerto Montt ☎ 65/261-100.

FESTIVALS & SEASONAL EVENTS

As elsewhere in southern Chile, Chiloé's festivals usually take place in summer, when there's the best chance of good weather. Fiestas Costumbritsas, which celebrate Chilote customs and folklore, take place over several weekends during January and February in Ancud and Castro. Ancud hosts a small open-air film festival the first few days in February. Every community celebrates its patron saint's day. Although they are local affairs, outsiders are always welcome.

HEALTH

Chiloé shares Chile's generally high standard of hygiene, so eating and drinking shouldn't cause you too much concern. The government continues to warn against eating raw or steamed shellfish, citing the risk of intestinal parasites. Though some visitors drink tap water here, most stick to bottled water, especially outside Castro.

INTERNET

Internet access is not as common here as on the mainland. Chiloé Virtual in Castro charges 800 pesos per hour.

💻 Internet Cafés **Chiloé Virtual** ✉ Esmeralda 232, Castro ☎ 65/533-427.

LANGUAGE

People in the tourism industry likely speak some English; the person on the street, very little. Most speak only Spanish; few speak the indigenous Huilliche language these days.

LODGING

Following a trend seen elsewhere in Chile, Chiloé has developed a system of so-called agro-tourism lodgings called the Red Agroturismo Chiloé, headquartered in the northern community of Ancud. The network of 19 farms, most of them on Isla Grande, gives the adventurous Spanish-speaking traveler a chance to partake of rural life, helping to milk the cows, churn the butter, or just relax. Rates run 10,000–12,000 pesos per person including breakfast. Accommodations are in no-frills farmhouses, but plenty of smog- and traffic-weary Santiago residents are lapping up the experience.

🖪 **Red Agroturismo Chiloé** ✉ Eleuterio Ramírez 207, Ancud ☎ 65/628–333 ⊕ www. portalsur.cl/rural/INDEX.HTM.

MAIL & SHIPPING

Mail sent from Chiloé can take a few weeks to reach North America or Europe. Posting from mainland Puerto Montt is a quicker option. You can find a Correos de Chile office in most larger cities. They are generally open weekdays 9–6 and Saturdays 9–noon.

🖪 Post Offices **Correos de Chile** ✉ O'Higgins 388, Castro ✉ Pudeto and Blanco Encalada, Ancud ✉ 22 de Mayo and Ladrilleros, Quellón.

MONEY MATTERS

With few businesses equipped to handle credit cards, Chiloé is primarily a cash-and-carry economy. Banks will gladly change U.S. dollars for Chilean pesos, but most will not touch traveler's checks. The situation is not as frustrating as it sounds; ATMs are popping up everywhere in larger cities like Castro and Ancud. You can use your Plus- or Cirrus-affiliated card to get cash at the going rate at any of the ATMs on the Redbanc network.

SAFETY

Crimes against travelers are almost unheard of in pastoral Chiloé, but the standard precautions about watching your possessions apply.

TAXIS

As is true elsewhere in the region, solid black or solid yellow cabs operate as *colectivos,* or collective taxis. They follow fixed routes with fixed stops, picking up up to four people along the way. A sign on the roof shows the general destination. The cost (less than 700 pesos within town) is little more than that of a city bus. Black cabs with yellow roofs take you directly to your requested destination for a metered fare. You can hail them on the street.

Colectivos also operate between many of Isla Grande's communities. They may look like a regular cabs, or they may be minivans. They have fixed stops, often near a town's central bus station.

TELEPHONES

Chiloé shares Puerto Montt's area code of 65. Anywhere in the archipelago or the southern Lake District you can drop the area code and dial the six-digit number. CTC, Entel, and Telefónica del Sur are the three most prominent telephone companies. Their *centros de llamados* (call centers) are the place to make calls and send faxes. Each company also has its own network of public telephones. Make sure you have the right company's calling card to match the phone booth. Calling cards can be purchased in many shops and newsstands.

TIPPING

As elsewhere in Chile, you should add a 10% tip to your restaurant bill. Most other workers don't expect tips.

TOURS

Highly regarded Dalcahue sea kayaking expert Francisco Valle is the local contact for Santiago tour operator Altue. He leads kayakers on two- to nine-day tours through the region. The two- and four-day excursions focus on Chiloé itself; longer tours incorporate travel into the mainland fjords.

Austral Adventures, the region's best tour operator, runs intimate guided tours of Chiloé and neighboring Patagonia. The agency's own 15-m (50-ft) vessel, the *Cahuella,* plies the archipelago and the Chilean fjords in three-, four-, and eight-day tours. Austral Adventures can custom-design tours of Chiloé itself, whether your tastes run to sea kayaking, church visits, farmstays, or hikes in Chiloé National Park.

Pehuén Expediciones has guided tours of the archipelago, in particular land tours to Dalcahue and Isla Achao and the island churches, as well as horseback riding and hiking in Parque Nacional Chiloé.

A few of Skorpios' luxury cruises from Puerto Montt to the Laguna San Rafael call at Castro on their return trip.

🚩 Tour Operators **Altue** ✉ Encomenderos 83 Santiago 📠 2/232-1103 ⊕ www.seakayakchile.com. **Austral Adventures** ✉ Lord Cochrane 432, Ancud 📠 65/625-977 ⊕ www.austral-adventures.com. **Pehuén Expediciones** ✉ Blanco 299, Castro ☎ 65/632-361. **Skorpios** ✉ Augosto Leguia Norte 118, Santiago ☎ 2/231-1030 ⊕ www.skorpios.cl.

VISITOR INFORMATION

Sernatur, Chile's national tourist office, operates a friendly, well-staffed information office on the Plaza de Armas in Ancud. It's open January–February, daily 9–8; March–December, Monday–Saturday 9–noon and 2–6.

For more information about the islands' churches, contact the Fundación de Amigos de las Iglesias de Chiloé, a nonprofit organization that raises funds for their restoration.

🚩 Tourist Information **Fundación de Amigos de las Iglesias de Chiloé** ✉ Victoria Subercaseaux 69, Santiago ☎ 2/632-1141. **Sernatur** ✉ Libertad 665, Ancud ☎ 65/622-800.

THE SOUTHERN COAST

8

FODOR'S CHOICE

Parque Nacional Laguna San Rafael, glacier

Parque Pumalín, temperate rain forest

Termas de Puyuhuapi, resort near Puerto Puyuhuapi

HIGHLY RECOMMENDED

RESTAURANT   La Casona Restaurante, Coihaique

HOTELS   Cabañas Caleta Gonzalo, near Parque Pumalín

Hostal Belisario Jara, Coihaique

Puma Verde, Chaitén

By Pete Nelson

Updated by Michael de Zayas

THE SLIVER OF LAND known as the Southern Coast stretches for more than 1,000 km (620 mi) in the administrative district of Aisén (locally spelled Aysen). Sandwiched between the tranquil valleys of the Lake District and the wondrous ice fields of Patagonia, it largely consists of heavily forested mountains, some of which rise dramatically from the shores of shimmering lakes, others directly out of the Pacific Ocean. Slender waterfalls and nearly vertical streams, often seeming to emerge from the rock itself, tumble and slide from neck-craning heights. Some dissipate into misty nothingness before touching the ground, others flow into the innumerable rivers—large and small, wild and gentle—heading westward to the sea. Chile has designated vast tracts of this truly magnificent landscape as national parks and reserves, but most are accessible only on foot. The few roads available to vehicles are slightly widened trails or the occasional logging route navigable only by the most rugged of four-wheel-drive vehicles.

The Southern Coast is one of the least populated areas remaining in South America: the population density here is said to be lower than that of the Sahara Desert. The infrequent hamlets scattered along the low-lying areas of this rugged region exist as fishing villages or small farming centers. The gradual increase of boat and ferry service to some of these towns and the expansion of the major highway called the Carretera Austral have begun to encourage migration to the region. Coihaique, the only town here of any size, with a population of 50,000, has lots of dining, lodging, and shopping. Meanwhile, a few intrepid entrepreneurs have established world-class accommodations in remote locations near spectacular mountain peaks, ancient volcanoes, and glaciers, with their concomitant fjords and lakes.

Planning a visit to the region's widely separated points of interest can be challenging, as getting from place to place is often difficult. Creating a logical itinerary in southern Chile is as much about choosing how to get here as it is about choosing where you want to go. The most rewarding mode of transport through this area is a combination of travel by boat and by plane, with an occasional car rental if you want to journey a little deeper into the hinterlands.

Exploring the Southern Coast

The Southern Coast is an expansive region covered with vast national parks and reserves. By and large, this is territory for adventurous types who come for the unparalleled fishing, kayaking, and white-water rafting. The region rewards intrepid explorers with relatively untrammeled trails and rarely viewed vistas.

Part of the challenge of traveling within this region of Chile is the country's narrow north–south orientation. The distances between sights can be daunting. Circuits, per se, are virtually impossible. Traveling by air is a good option if your time is limited. Ferries are slow and not always scenic, particularly if skies are the least bit clouded. There are, however, a few firms offering sightseeing cruises.

The key to enjoying the Southern Coast is knowing that your trip probably won't always go as planned. Itineraries cannot be too tight as schedules are not always reliable. Meet with a professional tour operator familiar with the region and focus on your priorities.

About the Restaurants

The Southern Coast's ecology means that fish and shellfish can be found just about anywhere. Lamb and beef dishes are almost as common. Rice

Numbers in the text correspond to numbers in the margin and on the Southern Coast map.

If you have 7 days

Unless you fly, the only way to reach the Southern Coast is by boat or ferry. On your first day head to the port town of 🚢 **Chaitén ❶ ⚑**. Devote a day to visiting **Parque Pumalín ❷**, which has some of the most pristine landscape in the region. The third day, take the Carretera Austral to 🚢 **Puerto Puyuhuapi ❹**. A stay at Termas de Puyuhuapi, a resort accessible only by boat, is a must. Head out the next morning to see the famous "hanging glacier" of **Parque Nacional Queulat ❺**. On your fifth day travel down to 🚢 **Coihaique ❻**, the only city of any size in the region. The next morning head to **Puerto Chacabuco ❼**, where you can board a boat bound for the unforgettable **Parque Nacional Laguna San Raphael ❽**. On your last day make your way back up the highway.

If you have 10 days

Follow the above itinerary, but add a day or so to explore the national parks surrounding Coihaique. Then consider spending a few days on one of the boats that run along the coast.

8

is usually available as an alternative to the ubiquitous french fries. By and large, entrées are simple and hearty. Locally grown vegetables and fruits abound. The variety on most menus is extensive, so many dishes are prepared from scratch when you order. Just sit back and sip your wine or beer while you wait.

Having food and drink on hand when driving along the Carretera Austral is necessary because of the distances between points of interest. The tiniest rural town has at least one *supermercado*. These markets are rarely "super," but the shelves typically sag under all manner of canned and packaged foods and bottled drinks. Bread of one type or another is rarely out of stock, and many stores carry a small selection of deli meats and cheeses.

Traveling by road throughout the region, you may see crudely printed signs with an arrow pointing to a nearby farmhouse advertising *küchen* (rich, fruit-filled pastries)—clear evidence of the many pockets of German influence.

About the Hotels

This region offers a surprisingly wide choice of accommodations, including some of the finest resorts in the country. What you won't find is the blandness of chain hotels. Most of the region's establishments reflect the distinct personalities and idiosyncrasies of their owners.

Some of the most humble homes in villages along the Carretera Austral have supplemented their family income by becoming bed-and-breakfasts. A stay in one of these *hospedajes* is an ideal way to meet the people and experience the culture. These accommodations are not regulated, so inquire about the availability of hot water and confirm that breakfast is included. Don't hesitate to ask to see the room—you may even get a choice.

WHAT IT COSTS In pesos (in thousands)				
$$$$	**$$$**	**$$**	**$**	**¢**
RESTAURANTS	over 11	8–11	5–8	2.5–5	under 2.5
HOTELS	over 105	75–105	45–75	15–45	under 15

Restaurant prices are for a main course at dinner. Hotel prices are for a double room in high season, excluding tax.

Timing

Mid-summer—late November to early February—is considered high season in southern Chile; demand for accommodations is keen, and advance reservations at high-end lodgings are vital. In spring (September into November) and fall (March to May) the weather is delightfully cool and hotel rooms are easier to come by. However, ferry service is reduced and sometimes even cancelled.

Chaitén

▶ ❶ *201 km (125 mi) south of Puerto Montt.*

A century ago, Chaitén wasn't even on the map. Today it's a small port town, with a population of barely more than 3,000. Although it's not really a destination itself, Chaitén serves as a convenient base for exploring the area, including Parque Pumalín and Reserva Nacional Futaleufú.

Getting there is fairly easy: both Navimag and Transmarchilay operate regular ferry service between Chaitén and Puerto Montt in the Lake District and Quellón on Chiloé. Flying is also an option; a few small airlines offer flights between Chaitén and Puerto Montt.

It's also possible to drive to Chaitén from Puerto Montt via the Carretera Austral, but you have to make use of two car ferries. The first is fine, as Transmarchilay ferries make nine daily trips between La Arena and Puelche all year. The second leg is tougher because Transmarchilay's ferries between Hornopirén and Caleta Gonzalo only operate in January and February.

Isla Puduguapi, home to some 150 noisy sea lions, is an hour-long boat ride away. Toninas, a resident dolphin, may escort your boat. Half-day tours are the only way to see the island. Try Chaitur Excursions (⇨ Tour Operators *in* The Southern Coast A to Z).

The emerald-green **Lago Yelcho,** one of the best places in the region to fish for brown trout, runs along the Carretera Austral south of Chaitén. Just past the village of Puerto Cárdenas is Puente Ventisquero Yelcho (Glacier Bridge), the beginning of a challenging two-hour hike to Ventisquero Cavi (Hanging Glacier). ⊠ *Off Carretera Austral, 2 km (1½ mi) past Puerto Cardenas.*

The much-lauded **Termas de Amarillo,** a modest hot springs about 25 km (16 mi) southeast of Chaitén, offers a nice respite for weary muscles. The setting, along a river running through a heavily forested valley, is lovely. ⊠ *Off Carretera Austral, 6 km (4 mi) inland from Puerto Cardenas* 🕾 *no phone* 🖃 *1,500 pesos* ☉ *Daily 8 AM–9 PM.*

Where to Stay & Eat

$–$$ ✕ **Corcovado.** Here's one place where you won't leave hungry: the portions of the seafood dishes and *asado a la brasa* (mixed grilled meats), served with a baked potato and salad, are huge, but the prices are small. This wooden building sits near the water, so you are treated to great views. ⊠ *Pedro Aguirre Cerda 5* 🕾 *65/731–221* 🖃 *No credit cards.*

8

Fishing

Fly-fishing enthusiasts, among the first to explore the area thoroughly, found an abundance of fish—from brown and rainbow trout to silver and steelhead salmon—in the region's icy rivers and streams. At numerous mountain lodges you can step right outside your door for great fishing. A short boat trip will bring you to isolated spots where you won't run into another soul for the entire day.

Shopping

A small artisans' market in Coihaique sells locally produced handicrafts such as leather goods and pottery. Interesting regional items to be on the lookout for are the pottery bowls and small jugs with animal skin shrunken onto their bases to keep liquids from seeping out. Woolen items are sold everywhere.

$-$$ ✕ **Restaurant Brisas del Mar.** This cheerful little eatery overlooks the sea from its perch on the second floor. The sheer number of items on the menu is astounding. Try excellent fish dishes such as *salmón en mantequilla* (salmon braised in butter). ⊠ *Corcovado 278* ☎ *65/731–284* ▤ *No credit cards.*

$ ⊡ **Hotel Shilling.** Of the town's numerous family-run hospedajes, Hotel Shilling is the most professional and hospitable. It's just across from the ocean. ⊠ *Corcovado 230* ☎ *65/731–295* ➪ *12 rooms* ♦ *Dining room, laundry service; no a/c, no room phones* ▤ *No credit cards* ⦿ *CP.*

★ $ ⊡ **Puma Verde.** This adorable, wood-shingled B&B is run by Parque Pumalín, which explains why it's in a class of its own. Locally crafted furniture sits atop polished wood floors. Woolen blankets and piles of pillows add to the coziness. Puma Verde has three rooms (one double, one shared hostel-style triple, and one apartment). The large five-person apartment rents for a bargain 60,000 pesos without breakfast. ⊠ *O'Higgins 54* ☎ *65/731–184* ⊕ *www.parquepumalin.cl* ➪ *2 rooms, 1 apartment* ♦ *Restaurant* ▤ *MC, V* ⦿ *BP.*

Parque Pumalín

❷ *56 km (35 mi) north of Chaitén.*

Fodor'sChoice ★ The privately owned Parque Pumalín is an extraordinary venture that began when conservationist Doug Tompkins bought a 1,000-acre *araucaria* (an indigenous evergreen tree) forest south of Puerto Montt. Since 1988, he has spent more than $15 million to purchase the 800,000 acres that make up Parque Pumalín. The region shelters one of the last remaining temperate rain forests in the world.

Tompkins, an American who made his fortune founding the clothing company Esprit, owns two strips of land that stretch from one side of the country to the other. He tried to buy the parcel between the two halves that would have connected them, but the sale was fiercely opposed by some government officials who questioned whether a foreigner should own so much of Chile. Tompkins still hopes to work with the government to make Parque Pumalín part of the national system. The Pan-American Highway, which trundles all the way north to Alaska, is interrupted here. No public roads, with their accompanying pollution, pass through the preserve.

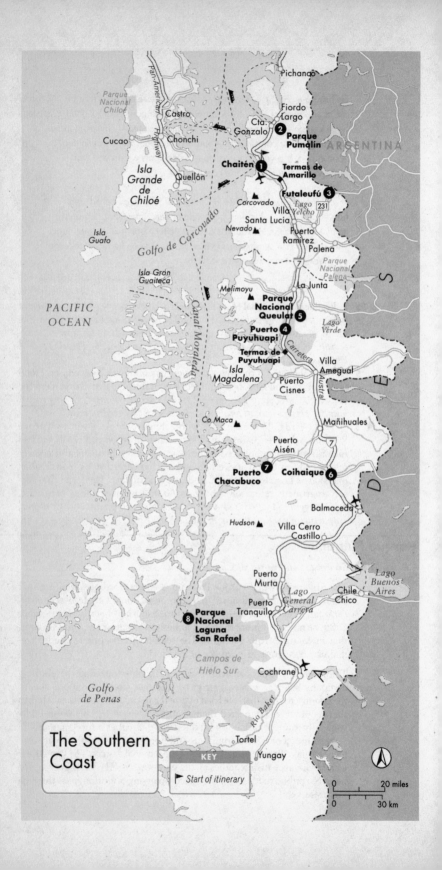

The Southern Coast

KEY

▶ *Start of itinerary*

0 — 20 miles

0 — 30 km

Parque Pumalín encompasses some of the most pristine landscape in the region, if not the world. There are a dozen or so trails that wind past lakes and waterfalls. Stay in log cabins at traditional or covered campsites, or put up your tent on one of the local farms scattered across the area that welcome travelers. The entrance to the park is at Caleta Gonzalo, where the ferries from Hornopirén arrive. Buses run from Chaitén January–February. ⊠ *Information centers: Buín 356, Puerto Montt* ☎ *65/250–079* 🖷 *65/255–145* ⊠ *O'Higgins 62, Chaitén* ☎ *65/731–341* ⊕ *pumalinproject.org* 🖘 *Free* ☉ *Daily.*

Where to Stay & Eat

★ **$$** ⊞ **Cabañas Caleta Gonzalo.** Nine gray-shingled cabanas, each designed to be distinct from its neighbor, sit high on stilts against the backdrop of the misty mountains. Broad front porches and tall windows let in lots of light. The interiors are rustic yet luxurious, with handcrafted furniture and handwoven woolen blankets. The complex includes an attractive visitor center and handicraft shop stocking books, guides, and maps, as well as organic honey and jams. A copper-hooded corner fireplace welcomes you at the adjacent café for meals from early morning until midnight year-round. ⊠ *Caleta Gonzalo* ☎ *65/731–364* 🖷 *65/731–184* 🖘 *9 rooms* ⚲ *Café, shop* ⊟ *MC, V* ⚭ *BP.*

Futaleufú

❸ *159 km (99 mi) east of Chaitén.*

Near the town of Villa Lucia, Ruta 231 branches east from the Carretera Austral and winds around Lago Yelcho. About 159 km (98 mi) later, not far from the Argentine border, it reaches the tiny town of Futaleufú. Despite being barely five square blocks, Futaleufú is on many travelers' itineraries. World-class adventure sports await here, where the Río Espolón and the Río Futaleufú collide. It's the staging center for serious river and sea kayaking, white-water rafting, and mountain biking, as well as fly-fishing, canyon hiking, and horseback riding. Day-long trips for less-experienced travelers are available.

Where to Stay

$$$$ ⊞ **Hostería Río Grande.** The biggest and best lodging in Futaleufú, this sleek wooden hotel is adventure-travel headquarters for the area. It hosts the Futaleufú Adventure Center, operated by former U.S. Olympic paddler Chris Spelius. December–March it offers four- to seven-night packages that include kayaking, rafting, and hiking trips throughout the region. There is cable TV in the salon. For an additional 35,000 pesos per couple, all meals can be included. ⊠ *Calle O'Higgins 397* ☎ *65/721–320; 888/488–9082 in the U.S.* ⊕ *www.expedicioneschile.com* 🖘 *12 rooms* ⚲ *Restaurant, room service, boating, fishing, hiking, bar, Internet; no room TVs* ⊟ *AE, MC, V* ⚭ *BP.*

Puerto Puyuhuapi

❹ *196 km (123 mi) south of Chaitén*

This mossy fishing village of about 500 residents is one of the oldest along the Carretera Austral. It was founded in 1935 by German immigrants fleeing the economic ravages of post–World War I Europe. As in much of Patagonia, Chile offered free land to settlers with the idea of making annexation by Argentina more difficult. Those early immigrants ventured into the wilderness to clear the forests to make way for farms.

Today this sleepy town is a convenient stopover for those headed farther south in the region. It has a few modest guest houses, as well as some markets and a gas station.

Most people headed to Puerto Puyuhuapi stop at the dock, where a courtesy phone (and attendants in summer) dials up the hot-springs resort of **Termas de Puyuhuapi,** the coast's most prestigious hotel. The resort's private catamaran ferries you 20 minutes down Seno Ventisquero (Glacier Sound) to its thermal waters. The Termas has a full-service spa offering thalassotherapy and other treatments. ⊠ *Carretera Austral, 13 km (8 mi) south of Puerto Puyuhuapi* ☎ *2/225–6489 in Santiago.*

Where to Stay & Eat

$$$ ✕ **Termas de Puyuhuapi.** The restaurant at this hot springs resort is worth a visit for nonguests—explore the grounds, and enjoy the complimentary 20-minute boat ride required to get here. The dining room of the lovely, peaceful place has terrific placid views of the fjord. The food itself is good if not spectacular—typical Chilean fare, centering on fish. Digest by taking a stroll around one of three trails that circle the mammoth grounds. If you come for breakfast or lunch you might opt for one of numerous daily trips to area sights run by the hotel, including the Ventisquero Colgante in Parque Nacional Queulat. ⊠ *Carretera Austral, 13 km (8 mi) south of Puerto Puyuhuapi* ☎ *2/225–6489 in Santiago* ⌕ *Reservations essential* ▭ *AE, DC, MC, V.*

$$$$ 🛏 **Termas de Puyuhuapi.** If you arrive at night, your catamaran pulls past
Fodor'sChoice a dark fjord to a spectacular welcome—drums, bonfires along the shore,
★ and fireworks illuminating the grounds. Accessible only by water, Puyuhuapi Hot Springs is profoundly secluded. Once on land, you are invited to don a bathrobe and take a dip in the many indoor and outdoor hot springs, some of which have falls tumbling into them. Carefully landscaped walkways lead to the low-roofed redwood buildings that hold spacious rooms with decks extending over the water to take full advantage of the views. There's a TV with a VCR in the lounge. ⊠ *Carretera Austral, 13 km (8 mi) south of Puerto Puyuhuapi* ☎ *2/ 225–6489 in Santiago* ⎙ *2/274–8111 in Santiago* ⊕ *www.patagonia-connection.com* ⇝ *28 rooms, 2 cabins* ⌕ *Restaurant, 3 pools, saltwater pool, health club, sauna, spa, boating, waterskiing, fishing, hiking, bar, lounge, recreation room, shop, laundry service, Internet; no room TVs.* ▭ *AE, DC, MC, V* ⦿| *BP.*

$ 🛏 **Hosteria Alemana.** The home of Ursula Flack, last of the town's original German settlers, is a great choice for budget-minded travelers who want to explore the beautiful countryside. Flack moved here in 1958, ten years after her husband, who built this large Bavarian-style home with gardens in the middle of town. Rooms with functional baths are simple but charming. Fresh flowers fill the quaint dining room. Ursula also runs the best eatery in town, Café Rossbach, just a 5-minute walk down the road, next to the carpet workshop run by her son, Helmut. ⊠ *Puerto Puyuhuapi s/n* ☎ *67/325–118* ⇝ *6 rooms* ⌕ *Laundry facilities; no room phones, no room TVs* ▭ *No credit cards* ⦿| *BP.*

Shopping

Carpets at **Alfombras de Puyuhuapi** (⊠ Calle E. Ludwig s/n ☎ 67/325–131 ⊕ www.puyuhuapi.com) are hand-woven by three generations of women from Chiloé who use only natural wool thread and cotton fibers. The rustic vertical looms, designed and built specifically for this shop, allow the weavers to make carpets with a density of 20,000 knots per square meter. Trained by his father and grandfather, who opened the shop here in the 1940s, proprietor Helmut E. Hopperdietzel proudly

CHILE'S ROAD TO RICHES

THE PAN-AMERICAN HIGHWAY, which snakes its way through the northern half of Chile, never quite makes it to the Southern Coast. To connect this remote region with the rest of the country, former President Agusto Pinochet proposed a massive public works project to construct a highway called the Carretera Austral. But the $300 million venture had another purpose as well. Pinochet was afraid that without a strong military presence in the region, neighboring Argentina could begin chipping away at Chile's territory. The highway would allow the army easier access to an area that until then was accessible only by boat.

Ground was broken on the Carretera Austral in 1976, and in 1982 the first section, running from Chaitén to Coihaique, opened to great fanfare. The only trouble was that you still couldn't get there from the mainland. It took another five years for the extension from Chaitén north to Puerto Montt to be completed. An extension from Coihaique south to Cochrane was finished the following year.

The word "finished" is misleading, as construction continues to this day. Although the Carretera Austral is nicely paved near Puerto Montt, it soon reveals its true nature as a two-lane gravel surface that crawls inexorably southward for 1,156 km (718 mi) toward the outpost of Villa O'Higgins. And the highway isn't even contiguous. In places the road actually ends abruptly at water's edge (ferries link these broken stretches of highway), and it is interrupted by Parque Pumalín, a preserve where the road is not allowed to pass. The segment from Chaitén to Coihaique should be paved by 2006.

The Carretera Austral is lauded in tourism brochures as "a beautiful road studded with rivers, waterfalls, forests, lakes, glaciers, and the occasional hamlet." This description is accurate —you may live the rest of your life and never see anything half as beautiful as the scenery. However, the highway itself is far from perfection. The mostly unpaved road has dozens of single-lane, wide-board bridges over streams and rivers. Shoulders are nonexistent or made of soft, wheel-grabbing gravel. Periodically, traffic must wend its way through construction, amid heavy equipment and workers.

As you drive south along the Carretera Austral, Chile's southernmost reaches seem to simply disintegrate into a tangle of sounds and straits, channels and fjords. Here you'll find lands laden with lush vegetation or layered in fields of ice. The road struggles valiantly along this route, connecting tiny fishing towns and farming villages all the way from Puerto Montt to Villa O'Higgins. There, the huge Campo de Hielo Sur (Southern Ice Field) forces it to a halt.

Navigating the Carretera Austral requires some planning, as communities along the way are few and far between. Some parts of the highway, especially in the southernmost reaches, are deserted. Check out your car thoroughly, especially the air in the spare tire. Make sure you have a jack and jumper cables. Bring along enough food in case you find yourself stuck far from the nearest restaurant.

What the Carretera Austral offers adventurous travelers is a chance to see a part of the world where few have ventured. The views from the highway are truly amazing, from the conical top of Volcán Corcovado near Chaitén to the sprawling valleys around Coihaique. Here you'll find national parks where the trails are virtually deserted, such as Parque Nacional Queulat and Reserva Nacional Río Simpson. The region's crowning glory, of course, is the vast glacier at Laguna San Raphael. It may be a tough journey today, but when it is eventually finished, the Carretera Austral could rival the most spectacular scenic roadways in the world.

—Pete Nelson

displays the extensive stock of finished carpets of various sizes and designs. Carpets can be shipped. The shop is closed in June.

Fishing

More than 50 rivers are within easy driving distance of Puerto Puyuhuapi, making this a cherished destination among fishing enthusiasts. Here are rainbow and brown trout, silver and steelhead salmon, and local species such as the robalo. The average size is about 6 pounds, but it's not rare to catch monsters twice that size. Daily trips are organized by the staff at the resort hotel, Termas de Puyuhuapi.

Parque Nacional Queulat

5 *175 km (109 mi) south of Chaitén.*

The rugged 350,000-acre Parque Nacional Queulat begins to rise and roll to either side of the Carretera Austral some 20 km (12 mi) south of the town of La Junta. Rivers and streams that crisscross dense virgin forests attract fishing aficionados from all over the world. At the higher altitudes brilliant blue glaciers can be found in the valleys between snowcapped peaks.

Less than 1 km (½ mi) off the east side of the Carretera Austral you are treated to a close-up view of the hanging glacier, **Ventisquero Colgante.** This sheet of ice slides forward between a pair of gentle rock faces. Several waterfalls cascade down the cliffs to either side of the glacier's foot. There is an easy 15-minute walk leading to one side of the lake below the glacier, which is not visible from the overlook. Another longer hike takes you deeper into the park's interior.

A short drive farther south, where the Carretera Austral makes one of its sharp switchback turns as it climbs higher, a small sign points into the undergrowth, indicating the trailhead for the **Salto de Padre García.** There is no parking area, but you can leave your car on the shoulder. This short hike through dense forest is well worth attempting for a close-up view of this waterfall of striking proportions.

There are two CONAF stations (the national forestry service), one at the Ventisquero Colgante overlook, the other a few miles north of the southern park gateway. ⊠ *Carretera Austral, 20 km (12 mi) south of La Junta* 🕾🕾 *67/231–065 or 67/232–599* 🕾 *1,500 pesos* ☉ *Daily 8:30–6:30.*

Where to Stay & Eat

$$ 🏨 **Hotel El Pangue.** Follow the driveway to the sprawling complex of reddish buildings on the sheltered shores of Lake Risopatrón. Several shingle-roofed cabanas, all with central heating and ample hot water, were constructed by local craftspeople from native wood. The clubhouse has a fireplace and a panoramic view of the lake. The dining room serves barbecued lamb prepared on a traditional *quincho* (grill). Activities include trolling and fly-fishing on the lake and nearby rivers. Canoes, mountain bikes, and horses are available for exploring the lake and park trails. It's 5 km (3 mi) south of the entrance of Parque Nacional Queulat. ⊠ *Carretera Austral, Km 240* 🕾🕾 *67/325–128* 🛏 *15 cabanas* ⚐ *Restaurant, pool, lake, hot tub, sauna, boating, fishing, hiking, horseback riding, bar* 🖃 *AE, MC, V* 🍴 *BP.*

Coihaique

6 *224 km (140 mi) south of Puerto Puyuhuapi.*

Where Río Simpson and Río Coihaique come together you'll find Coihaique, the only community of any size on the Carretera Austral.

Calling itself "the capital of Patagonia," Coihaique has some 50,000 residents—more than half of the region's population. Locals spell the city name Coyaique.

Ten streets radiate from the central plaza. Horn, one of the most colorful, holds the crafts stands of the Feria Artesenal. Balmaceda connects the central square with the smaller Plaza Prat. Navigating the area around the plaza is confusing at first, but the streets, bearing those traditional names used throughout the country, soon yield to a simple grid system.

The pentagonal **Plaza de Armas** is the center of town and the nexus for its attractions, including the town **Catedral** and **Intendencia**, the govenrment building.

The Carretera Austral leads into the northeastern corner of town and to the **Monumento al Ovejero.** On the broad median of the Avenida General Baquedano a solitary shepherd with his horse and his dog lean motionless into the wind behind a plodding flock of sheep. ⊠ *Av. General Baquedano.*

The **Museo Regional de la Patagonia** is worth the small fee for the black-and-white photos of early-20th-century pioneering in this region, as well as for the collections of household, farming, and early industrial artifacts from the same era. A visit is a reminder of how recently many parts of southern Chile began to develop. ⊠ *Av. Baquedano 310* 🕾 *no phone* 🎟 *1,000 pesos* ⊘ *Daily 8:30–1 and 2:30–6:30.*

The 5,313-acre **Reserva Nacional Coihaique,** about 4 km (2½ mi) north of Coihaique, provides hikers with some stunning views when the weather cooperates. If it's raining you can drive a 9-km (5-mi) circuit through the park. ✛ *54 km (34 mi) east of Coihaique* 🕾 *no phone* 🎟 *3,500 pesos* ⊘ *Jan.–Feb., daily 8 AM–9 PM; Mar.–Dec., daily 8:30–5.*

The evergreen forests of **Reserva Nacional Río Simpson,** just north of Reserva Nacional Coihaique, are filled with waterfalls tumbling down steep canyons walls. A lovely waterfall called the Cascada de la Virgen is a 1-km (½-mi) hike from the information center, while another called the Velo de la Novia is 8 km (5 mi) farther. ⊠ *Carretera Austral, Km 32* 🕾 *no phone* 🎟 *3,500 pesos* ⊘ *Jan.–Feb., daily 8 AM–9 PM; Mar.–Dec., daily 8:30–5.*

The only skiing in northern Patagonia can be had 32 km (20 mi) outside of town at **El Fraile.** You can rent equipment for the three trails here. There are no accommodations and it's wise to bring food and water with you. The season runs May–September. ⊠ *Camino Lago Pollux* 🕾 *67/210–210.*

Where to Stay & Eat

$–$$ ✕ **Cafetería Alemana.** Whether you're seated in one of the dining rooms or outside at a table on the sidewalk, Cafetería Alemana is a great place for people-watching. The menu lists light fare, including tiny *empanaditas* (small meat-filled pies). Challenge your dietary willpower by taking a look at the case full of authentic küchen. ⊠ *Condell 119* 🕾 *67/231–731* 🖃 *AE, MC, V.*

★ $–$$ ✕ **La Casona Restaurante.** A fire crackles in the corner wood-burning stove in this tidy little restaurant. Vases filled with fresh flowers adorn tables covered with white linen. The place is run by a small family—the mother cooks, her husband and son serve—who exude a genuine warmth to everyone who walks in the door. There's plenty of traditional fare on the menu, but the *centolla* (king crab) and *langostino* (lobster) are the standouts. ⊠ *Obispo Vielmo 77* 🕾 *67/238–894* 🖃 *No credit cards.*

$–$$ ✕ **Restaurant Histórico Ricer.** Operated by the same family for decades, this popular restaurant is a Coihaique institution. The stairs in the back lead to a wooden dinner parlor; the walls are covered with fascinating sepia photos from the town's archives. An upper loft here makes a cozy place for tea. Among the most popular items on the extensive menu are salmon, rabbit, and grilled leg of lamb. Lighter fare includes excellent empanadas filled with *locate* (a local mollusk). The pottery and crocheted hangings that decorate the restaurant were created by the family's matriarch. ⊠ *Horn 40 and 48* ☎ *67/232–920 or 67/237–950* ⊟ *AE, DC, MC, V.*

$ ✕ **La Olla.** Starched linen tablecloths lend an unmistakable aura of European gentility to this modest restaurant, operated by a courtly Spaniard and his son. Among the specialties are a fine paella and a hearty *estofado de cordero* (lamb stew). ⊠ *Av. Prat 176* ☎ *67/234–700* ⊟ *AE, MC, V.*

★ $$ ⊞ **Hostal Belisario Jara.** You realize how much attention has been paid to the detail here when the proprietor points out that the weather vane on the peak of the single turret is a copy of one at Chilean poet Pablo Neruda's home in Isla Negra. In the quaint lodging's various nooks and crannies, wide windows and natural woods are abundant. The artwork on the walls is created by the proprietor himself during the low season. In the small but tasteful rooms, terra-cotta floors complement the rustic carved-pine beds, spread with nubby cream linens. ⊠ *Francisco Bilbao 662* ☎ *67/234–150* ⊕ *www.belisariojara.itgo.com* ⇨ *8 rooms* ⚲ *Dining room, bar* ⊟ *No credit cards* ⧈ *BP.*

$$ ⊞ **Hotel Coihaique.** This nicely landscaped lodging is in a quiet corner of town, but it's within easy walking distance of the Plaza de Armas. Rooms are a bit motel-like, with flat pale-green comforters and drapes, a bed, a TV, and not much else. But they are clean and spacious. ⊠ *Magallanes 131* ☎ *67/231–137 or 67/231–737* ⊕ *www.hotelsa.cl* ⇨ *40 rooms* ⚲ *Restaurant, room service, minibars, cable TV, pool, bar, laundry service, Internet, convention center, airport shuttle* ⊟ *AE, MC, V* ⧈ *CP.*

$ ⊞ **El Reloj.** Simple, very clean, wood-panel rooms contain just the basic pieces of furniture. But the salon is warmly decorated with antiques and wood furnishings, and it has a large fireplace. Request a second-floor room for a view of the Coihaique River. ⊠ *Baquedano 828* ☎ *67/231–108* ⇨ *9 rooms* ⚲ *Restaurant, cable TV, bar, laundry service, Internet* ⊟ *No credit cards* ⧈ *CP.*

Nightlife & the Arts

The outrageous stylishness of **Piel Roja** (⊠ Moraleda 495 ☎ 67/237–832) is refreshingly amplified, given its remote location. The bar-disco, whose name translates into "Red Skin," opens relatively early, at 7 pm. Nosh on pizza and explore the four levels of sculptural decor, several bars, a large dance floor, and a private nook. The furnishings are oversized and slightly surreal, a mix of motifs from art nouveau to Chinese. The weekend cover price of 6,000 pesos for men and 3,000 pesos for women is credited toward drinks or food.

Shopping

The **Feria Artesenal** (⊠ Plaza de Armas between Dussen and Horn ☎ no phone) has stalls selling woolen clothing, small leather items, and pottery.

Puerto Chacabuco

❼ *68 km (43 mi) northwest of Coihaique.*

It's hard to imagine a drive more beautiful—anywhere in the world—than the one from Coihaique to Puerto Chacabuco. The mist hangs low over farmland, adding a dripping somnolence to the scenery. Dozens of waterfalls and rivers wend their way through mountain formations. Yellow poplars surround charming rustic lodges. And sheep and cattle graze on mossy, vibrant fields. The picture of serenity terminates at the sea, where the nondescript port town of Chacabuco, Coihaique's link to the ocean, sits, a conduit to further beauty. This harbor ringed by snowcapped mountains is where you board the ferries that transport you north to Puerto Montt in the Lake District and Quellón on Chiloé, as well as boats headed south to the spectacular Laguna San Raphael.

A hanging bridge leads from Chacabuco to **Puerto Aisén,** founded in 1928 to serve the region's burgeoning cattle ranches. Devastating forest fires that swept through the interior in 1955 filled the once-deep harbor with silt, making it all but useless for transoceanic vessels. The busy main street is a good place to stock up on supplies for boat trips to the nearby national parks.

Where to Stay & Eat

$$$ ✕⌂ **Hotel Loberías del Sur.** On a hill overlooking the port, Hotel Loberías del Sur is a luxurious hotel in an unlikely place. The owner also runs catamaran service to the San Rafael glacier, and needed a place to pamper foreign vacationers for the night (running a nice tab in the process). Completed in spring 2003, the hotel provides real comforts after a blustery day at sea, such as firm queen-size beds and separate showers and bath tubs. The restaurant, as you might expect, has the finest service in town. ⊠ *Carrera 50, Puerto Chacabuco* ☎ *67/351–112* 🖷 *67/351–188* ⊕ *www.loberiasdelsur.cl* ⤴ *60 rooms* ⚭ *Restaurant, room service, cable TV, pool, gym, sauna, bar, lounge, recreation room, shop, laundry service, Internet, business services, convention center* ⊟ *AE, DC, MC, V* ⏗ *BP.*

Parque Nacional Laguna San Rafael

❽ *5 hours by boat from Puerto Chacabuco.*

Fodor'sChoice Nearly all of the 101,000-acre Parque Nacional Laguna San Rafael is
★ fields of ice, totally inaccessible. But only a handful of the people who come here ever set foot on land. Most travel by boat from Puerto Chacabuco or Puerto Montt through the maze of fjords along the coast to the expansive San Rafael Lagoon. Floating on the surface of the brilliant blue water are scores of icebergs that rock from side to side as boats pass. Most surprising is the variety of forms and colors in each iceberg, including a shimmering, translucent cobalt blue.

Massive Ventisquero San Rafael extends 4 km (2½ mi) from end to end. The glacier is receding about 600 ft a year: paint on a bordering mountain marks the location of the glacier in past years. It's a noisy beast, roaring like thunder as the sheets of ice shift. If you're lucky you'll see huge pieces of ice calve off, causing violent waves that should make you glad your boat stayed at a safe distance.

Several different companies make the trip to Laguna San Raphael. The cheapest are Navimag and Transmarchilay, which offer both two-night trips from Puerto Chacabuco and four-night trips from Puerto Montt. More luxurious are the three-night cruises from Puerto Chacabuco and the six-night cruises from Puerto Montt run by Skorpios. For those with less time, Patagonia Connection has day trips from Chacabuco on a deluxe catamaran.

THE SOUTHERN COAST A TO Z

To research prices, get advice from other travelers, and book travel arrangements, visit www.fodors.com.

AIR TRAVEL

LanChile and its domestic subsidiary LanExpress have flights to the regions from Santiago, Puerto Montt, and Punta Arenas. They arrive at the Southern Coast's only major airport, 55 km (34 mi) south of Coihaique in the town of Balmaceda. Areomet flies from Puerto Montt to a small airfield near Chaitén.

Booking air travel through a good tour company or travel agency can be invaluable. Unforeseen delays may occur when traveling this challenging region, and an informed agent is best equipped to rearrange your plans at the last minute.

🛪 Airlines **Areomet** ⊠ O'Higgins 67, Chaitén ☎ 65/731-429. **LanChile** ⊠ General Parra 215, Coihaique ☎ 67/231-188 ⊕ www.lanchile.com.

TRANSFERS A minivan ride from Balmaceda airport to Coihaique using Transfer Valencia costs 2,500 pesos.

🛪 **Transfer Valencia** ⊠ Balmaceda Airport, Coihaique ☎ 67/233-030.

BOAT & FERRY TRAVEL

Ferry lines operating in southern Chile sail the interwoven fjords, rivers, and lakes of the region. Fares in high season (January and February) are dramatically higher than other times.

Navimag (short for "Navegación Magallanes") operates a rather inelegant, but highly serviceable, cargo and passenger fleet throughout the region. The M/V *Evangelistas,* a 324-passenger ferry, sails round-trip from Puerto Montt to the Laguna San Raphael, stopping in both directions in Coihaique's port of Puerto Chacabuco. The 200-passenger M/V *Alejandrina* sails from Puerto Montt to Chaitén, Quellón on Chiloé, and Puerto Chacabuco before making the trip in reverse.

Transmarchilay operates a cargo and passenger ferry fleet similar to that of Navimag, with ships that start in Puerto Montt and sail either to Chaitén or Puerto Chacabuco. It also sails between Quellón and Chaitén. Transmarchilay operates the ferry M/V *El Colono* from early January through late February, sailing weekly from Puerto Montt into Laguna San Rafael and back to Puerto Montt. Tour companies offer more luxurious transport to similar destinations.

🛥 Boat & Ferry Information **Navimag** ⊠ Presidente Ibáñez 347, Coihaique ☎ 67/233-306 ⊕ www.navimag.cl. **Transmarchilay** ⊠ Corcovado 266, Chaitén ☎ 65/731-272 ⊠ O'Higgins s/n, Puerto Chacabuco ☎ 67/351-144 ⊠ General Parra 86, Coihaique ☎ 67/231-971 ⊕ www.transmarchilay.cl.

BUS TRAVEL

Service between Puerto Montt and Cochrane is by private operators such as Turbus. Travel along the Carretera Austral is often agonizingly and inexplicably slow, so don't plan on getting anywhere on schedule.

🚌 Bus Information **Turbus** ⊠ Baquedano 1171, Coihaique ☎ 67/231-333.

CAR RENTAL

Renting a car in the Southern Coast can be expensive, and driving the Carretera Austral can be a hassle. But if you want to see the parts of the Southern Coast that are off the beaten path, there's no better way than in your own four-wheel-drive vehicle: you can stop in any of the little fishing villages and farming communities that the tour buses whiz past. A four-wheel-drive vehicle runs about 60,000 pesos, including tax and insurance. A car costs less than 40,000 pesos.

At Balmaceda airport there are three rental agencies, Budget, AGS Rent A Car, and Int'l Rent A Car. Automotriz Los Carrera and Happylandia both rent four-wheel-drive vehicles. Make certain to understand the extent of your liability for any damage to the vehicle, including routine events such as a chipped or cracked windshield. If you want to visit one of the more popular parks, check out prices of tours. They might prove far cheaper than driving yourself.

🚗 Agencies **AGS Rent A Car** ✉ Balmaceda Airport, Coihaique ☎ 67/231–511. **Automotriz Los Carrera** ✉ Carrera 330, Coihaique ☎ 67/231–457. **Budget** ✉ Balmaceda Airport, Coihaique ☎ 67/255–177. **Happylandia** ✉ Condell 149, Coihaique ☎ 67/234–730. **Int'l Rent A Car** ✉ Balmaceda Airport, Coihaique ☎ 67/214–770.

INTERNET

Some hotels offer Internet access, either for free or for a small fee. Internet access is often available at telephone company offices such as CTC, but this is generally a more expensive option. Usually cheaper are the Internet cafés that have sprung up around Coihaique as well as in smaller towns. In Coihaique, Aysenet is friendly, helpful, and patient with visitors.

🌐 Internet Cafés **Aysenet** ✉ Prat 470, Coihaique ☎ 67/231–752.

MAIL & SHIPPING

Mail service is poky here, so you might want to save that letter for home until you get to a bigger city. The post office in Coihaique is on the south side of the Plaza de Armas. It's open weekdays 9–12:30 and 2:30–6, Saturday 8:30–noon.

✉ Post Offices **Post office** ✉ Cochrane 202, Coihaique.

MONEY MATTERS

Converting cash can be a bureaucratic headache, particularly in smaller towns like Chaitén. A better option is using your ATM card at numerous local banks connected to Cirrus or Plus networks.

When you're anticipating smaller purchases, try to have coins and small bills on hand at all times, even though your pockets and purses will seem to bulge a bit. Small vendors do not always have change for large bills.

TELEPHONES

Public phones are plentiful in larger towns and are becoming more and more common in smaller villages. Some accept phone cards. Entel and CTC have offices throughout the region and both have fax and international-call capabilities.

TOURS

Willy Stone in Coihaique also takes up a small charter plane for tours of San Rafael and the surrounding countryside: reservations required.

Austral Adventures offers a personalized approach to seeing the waterways of the northern Southern Coast, especially the fjords around Parque Pumalín. Three- to seven-day tours include trips to natural and hidden hot springs. The deluxe catamaran *Patagonia Express* is operated by Patagonia Connection, the same company that owns the beautiful Termas de Puyuhuapi resort. During the peak season months of January and February, the vessel operates a full-day tour to the Laguna San Rafael from Puerto Chacabuco daily. Out of season the boat makes the same trip on Fridays. Service is excellent. Catamaranes del Sur also offers luxury catamaran trips to San Rafael from Puerto Chacabuco, as well as trips to other coastal destinations.

If it's Laguna San Raphael you want to see, there are several different types of boats to take you there, but most do not operate during the winter months of June, July, and August. Skorpios' trio of luxurious ferries carry between 70 and 130 passengers in first-class style to the Laguna San Rafael. You can sail round-trip either from Puerto Chacabuco or Puerto Montt.

In Coihaique, Andes Patagónicos is adjacent to the Restaurant Histórico Ricer and owned by the same family. Gregarious Patricia Chiblé and her staff are knowledgeable and helpful. Among the regional tours they offer are flights over Laguna San Rafael and its glacier. American-born Nicholas La Penna runs Chaitur Excursions, the best place in Chaitén for tours, trekking, and general information about the region. Among his itineraries are full-day trips into Parque Pumalín as well as a half-day trip to the sea lion colony on Isla Puduguapi.

In Santiago, SportsTour has more than 30 years of experience. It puts together individual itineraries, as well as offering half- and full-day city tours and multiday excursions throughout the Southern Coast and the rest of the country. Most staff members speak excellent English.

A knowledgeable tour operator or travel agent is a must for travel to the Southern Coast. In the United States, a number of companies are experienced with travel here. Among them is the Georgia-based Lost World Adventures, whose staff specializes in tailoring itineraries around your specific interests.

 Air Tours **Willy Stone** ☎ 9/817–2172.

 Boat Tours **Austral Adventures** ✉ Lord Cochrane 432, Chiloé ☎ 2/225–6489 ⊕ www.austral-adventures.com. **Catamaranes del Sur** ✉ Carrera 50, Puerto Chacabuco ☎ 67/351–112 ⊕ www.catamaranesdelsur.cl. **Patagonia Connection** ✉ Puerto Puyuhuapi ☎ 2/225–6489 ⊕ www.patagoniaconnex.cl. **Skorpios** ✉ Augosto Leguia Norte 118, Santiago ☎ 2/231–1030 ⊕ www.skorpios.cl.

 Regional Tours **Andes Patagónicos** ✉ Horn 40 and 48, Coihaique ☎📠 67/232–920 or 67/237–950 ⊕ www.patagoniachile.cl/ap. **Chaitur Excursions** ✉ Diego Portales 350, Chaitén ☎ 65/731–439. **SportsTour** ✉ Moneda 790, 14th floor, Santiago ☎ 2/549–5200 📠 2/698–2981 ⊕ www.chilnet.cl/sportstour.

 U.S.-based Tours **Lost World Adventures** ✉ 112 Church St., Decatur, GA ☎ 404/373–5820 or 800/999–0558 📠 404/377–1902 ⊕ www.lostworldadventures.com.

VISITOR INFORMATION

Sernatur, the national tourist office, is one-stop shopping (so to speak) for all information: you can pick up brochures, book tours, and get general advice. The area is so rich in natural beauty that you're sure to learn something new. Stop in before exploring.

 Sernatur ✉ O'Higgins 254, Chaitén ☎ 65/731–281 ✉ Bulnes 35, Coihaique ☎ 67/231–752.

PATAGONIA & TIERRA DEL FUEGO

9

FODOR'S CHOICE

Los Ganaderos, restaurant in Punta Arenas

Hotel Explora, in Parque Nacional Torres del Paine

Hotel José Nogueira, Punta Arenas

Museo Regional de Magallanes, Punta Arenas

Parque Nacional Torres del Paine

El Rincón del Tata, restaurant in Puerto Natales

HIGHLY RECOMMENDED

RESTAURANTS Indigo, Puerto Natales

Restaurant Edén, Puerto Natales

Sotito's, Punta Arenas

La Taberna, Punta Arenas

HOTELS Hostal Oro Fueguino, Punta Arenas

Indigo, Puerto Natales

SIGHTS Palacio Sara Braun, mansion in Punta Arenas

By Pete Nelson

Updated by
Michael de
Zayas

TRADITIONAL BOUNDARIES CANNOT DEFINE Patagonia. This vast stretch of land east of the Andes is mostly a part of Argentina, but Chile shares its southern extremity. Geographically and culturally it has little in common with either country. Patagonia, isolated by impenetrable mountains and endless fields of ice, is really a region unto itself.

Navigating the channel that today bears his name, conquistador Hernando de Magallanes arrived on these shores in 1520, claiming the region for Spain. Although early attempts at colonization failed, the forbidding landscape continued to fascinate explorers. Naturalist Charles Darwin, who sailed through the Estrecho de Magallanes in 1833 and 1834, called it a "mountainous land, partly submerged in the sea, so that deep inlets and bays occupy the place where valleys should exist."

Because of the region's remote location, much of what Darwin described is still relatively undisturbed. North from Punta Arenas the land is flat and vast; this terrain gave rise to the book of poems *Desolation* by Nobel Prize–winning, Chilean poet Gabriela Mistral. The road peters out to the north at Parque Nacional Torres del Paine, a natural wonder. The snow-covered pillars of stone seem to rise vertically from the plains below. To the south is Tierra del Fuego, the storm-lashed island at the continent's southernmost tip. This bleak wilderness, which still calls out to explorers today, is literally the end of the earth.

Exploring Patagonia & Tierra del Fuego

The intriguing part of Patagonia is the fact that you can't travel any farther south without boarding a boat. South Africa's Cape of Good Hope lies near the 35th parallel, about the same latitude as Montevideo, Uruguay. The southernmost New Zealand territory touches the 47th parallel. Contrast those with Punta Arenas, located near the 53rd parallel. The southernmost town on the globe, Puerto Williams, is just above the 55th. It's closer to the South Pole than to the northern border of Chile.

Working out a rewarding itinerary can be relatively easy. Fly into Punta Arenas, the region's principal city, unless you want to spend days driving south through Argentina. From there you can travel to most of the other destinations by bus or car. (Take the ferry from Punta Arenas to Tierra del Fuego). A few remote spots, such as Isla Magdalena or Puerto Williams, are reached by boat or airplane.

About the Restaurants

The aura of sophistication that lingers in Punta Arenas, the region's largest city, is reflected in the variety of restaurants you can find here. Service is courteous and careful even in informal eateries. In Puerto Natales, too, you can dine well for several days without returning to the same place.

Menus tend to be extensive, although two items in particular might be considered specialties: succulent *centolla* (king crab) and tender and moist *cordero asado* (grilled lamb). King crab is always expensive, but it's worth the splurge. Lamb is often prepared in the manner that has been used for generations: roasted whole on a vertical spit. Look for these grills positioned in a restaurant's front window to tempt passersby.

Don't relegate hotel cuisine to second-class status until you've studied the menu. Hotels also often have tantalizing breakfast spreads that, if you choose to indulge, will carry you comfortably well past noon. Be warned: many restaurants close for several hours in the afternoon and early evening (3–8).

Numbers in the text correspond to numbers in the margin and on the Patag-onia and Tierra del Fuego and Punta Arenas maps.

9

If you have
5 days

With such a limited amount of time you should head to the moun-tains as soon as possible. Factor in the weather and dedicate days that promise sunshine to Torres del Paine park. Assuming the weather is clear each day, spend your first day driving from ⬚ **Punta Arenas** ❶–❽ ⌐ north to ⬚ **Puerto Natales** ⓫, where you can spend the night. Head another three hours (a slow drive along gravel roads) north to see the magnificent soaring peaks of **Par-que Nacional Torres del Paine** ⓬ on your second, third, and fourth days. On your last day head back to Punta Arenas, stopping, if time per-mits (don't get caught after dark along these roads) at the **Pingüinera de Seno Otway** ❿.

If you have
7 days

If you have a little longer, you have time to explore the faded elegance of ⬚ **Punta Arenas** ❶–❽. Use one day to take in the city's major sights, and another to see nearby points of interest such as **Puerto Hambre** ❾ and **Pingüin-era de Seno Otway** ❿. On your third day, head three hours north to ⬚ **Puerto Natales** ⓫, where you can spend the night. In the morning head to **Parque Nacional Torres del Paine** ⓬ for the fourth, fifth, and sixth days, then head back to Punta Arenas.

If you have
11 days

If you have more time to spend, consider seeing more of the region by boat. From ⬚ **Punta Arenas** ❶–❽, the *Terra Australis* sails round-trip to **Puerto Williams** ⓯, stopping along the way at breathtaking glaciers and colonies of elephant seals and penguins. The cruise takes seven nights, leaving you plenty of time to visit ⬚ **Puerto Natales** ⓫ and **Parque Nacional Torres del Paine** ⓬.

About the Hotels

Because of its prosperous past, Punta Arenas has many historic hotels offering luxurious amenities and fine service. A night or two in one of them should be part of your trip. For its size, Puerto Natales has a sur-prising number of options: though most tend to be small, subpar inns, many are not without their own particular charms. There are also sev-eral good resorts, and one excellent lodge, within Parque Nacional Tor-res del Paine. Rates can be half-price out of peak season. Some hotels in the park turn off electricity during night hours, such as midnight–6 AM. Almost absent in the region are foreign chains.

The terms *hospedaje* and *hostal* are used interchangeably in the region, so don't make assumptions based on the name. Many hostals are fine hotels—not youth hostels with multiple beds—just very small. By con-trast, some hospedaje are little more than a spare room in someone's home.

WHAT IT COSTS In pesos (in thousands)				
$$$$	**$$$**	**$$**	**$**	**¢**
RESTAURANTS over 11	8–11	5–8	2.5–5	under 2.5
HOTELS over 105	75–105	45–75	15–45	under 15

Restaurant prices are for a main course at dinner. Hotel prices are for a double room in high season, excluding tax.

Timing

Late November to early March—summer in the southern hemisphere— is considered high season in Patagonia. Demand for accommodations is highest in January and February, so advance reservations are vital. Summer weather in these latitudes is by no means warm, but rather pleasantly cool. Bring an extra layer or two, even when the sun is shining. Windbreakers are essential. On or near these antarctic waters, stiff breezes can be biting. In spring (September to November) and fall (March to May) the weather is usually delightfully mild, but can also feel downright cold. The region goes into virtual hibernation in the winter months of June, July, and August.

PATAGONIA

Patagonia held little appeal for the earliest explorers. Discouraged by the inhospitable climate, they continued up the coast of South America in search of gold among the Aztec and Inca civilizations. The first Spanish settlements, given only halfhearted support from the crown, were soon abandoned. The newly formed nation of Chile showed little interest in Patagonia until 1843, when other countries began to eye the region. President Manuel Bulnes sent down a ragtag group of soldiers to claim it for Chile. Five years later the town of Punta Arenas was founded.

And it was not a moment too soon, for Punta Arenas was to become a major stop on the trade route around the tip of South America. Steam navigation intensified the city's commercial importance, leading to its short-lived age of splendor from 1892 to 1914, when its population rose from approximately 2,000 to 20,000. The opening of the Panama Canal all but bumped Punta Arenas off the map. By 1920 many of the founding families decided to move on, leaving behind the lavish mansions and the impressive public buildings they'd built.

Massive ranches once dominated the area around Punta Arenas. The vast flocks of sheep that dot the landscape still contribute to the local economy, but not as before. Today exploration for oil and natural gas is making the region prosperous again. Another source of income is tourism, as more and more people are drawn to this beautiful land at the bottom of the earth.

Punta Arenas

Founded a little more than 150 years ago, Punta Arenas (Sandy Point) was Chile's first permanent settlement in Patagonia. This port, no longer an important stop on trade routes, exudes an aura of faded grandeur. Great development in cattle-keeping, mining, and wood production carried out by European immigrants led to an economic and social boom at the end of the 19th century. Plaza Muñoz Gamero, the central square, is surrounded by evidence of that prosperity: buildings whose then-opulent brick exteriors recall a time when this was one of Chile's wealthiest cities.

9

Cruises

Patagonia's unusual topography encourages travel by water. A number of medium-size vessels take passengers on journeys ranging from a day or two to a week or more. The vistas, such as the fantastic Avenue of the Glaciers, are breathtaking. Along this stretch of the Beagle Channel you pass six tremendous glaciers in rapid succession. Most sightseeing boats traversing these waters also visit colonies of elephant seals and penguins.

Shopping

Wool may no longer be king of the economy, but vast flocks of sheep still yield a high-quality product that is woven into the clothing here. Leather products are also common, but the prices are not necessarily low.

The newer houses here have colorful tin roofs, best appreciated when seen from a high vantage point such as the Mirador Cerro la Cruz. Although the city as a whole may not be particularly attractive, look for details: the pink-and-white house on a corner, the bay window full of potted plants, parking attendants wearing the regional blue and yellow colors, and school children in identical naval pea coats that remind you that the city's fate is tied to the sea.

Although Punta Arenas is 3,141 km (1,960 mi) from Santiago, daily flights from the capital make it an easy journey. As the transportation hub of southern Patagonia, Punta Arenas is within reach of Chile's Parque Nacional Torres del Paine (about a six-hour drive) and Argentina's Parque Nacional los Glaciares. It's also a key point of embarkation for travel to Antarctica. But don't overlook Punta Arenas as a worthy destination unto itself.

Numbers in the text correspond to numbers in the margins and on the Punta Arenas map.

a good walk

Get an idea of the layout of the city at **Mirador Cerro la Cruz** ➊ ▶, an observation deck with a stunning view of the city. Head down the stairs and continue for three blocks to reach the cedar-lined **Plaza Muñoz Gamero** ➋, the center of the city. Here you'll find a monument honoring explorer Hernando de Magallanes. In deference to the many historical and political figures they honor, streets change their names as they pass by this square. The venerable **Palacio Sara Braun** ➌ overlooks Plaza Muñoz Gamero. A block east is the **Museo Regional de Magallanes** ➍, commonly known as the Braun-Menéndez Palace for the family that built and occupied the mansion that houses the museum. Farther along Pedro Montt is the **Museo Naval y Marítimo** ➎, with its overview of the all-important role of the Chilean Navy in the region's history.

A block north you reach Avenida Colón, one of four intersecting avenues designed to accommodate large flocks of sheep. Today the parks that run down the centers make pleasant places to stroll. Head north on Calle Bories for four blocks to reach the **Museo Salesiano de Maggiorino Borgatello** ➏. Three blocks north on Avenida Bulnes is the main entrance to the **Cementerio Municipal** ➐. Here among the manicured gardens and tall cypress trees are the grand mausoleums the town's wealthiest citizens erected in memory of themselves. Farther north on Avenida Bulnes is the **Museo de Recuerdo** ➑.

TIMING   The walk itself will take at least 1½ hours, but budget in extra time if you wish to explore the museums. Remember that most of the museums, as well as many businesses, close for lunch about noon and reopen a few hours later. You might want to save a visit to Cerro la Cruz or the Cementerio Municipal for these times.

What to See

❼ Cementerio Municipal. The fascinating history of this region is chiseled into stone at the Municipal Cemetery. Bizarrely ornate mausoleums honoring the original families are crowded together along paths lined by sculpted cypress trees. In a strange effort to recognize Punta Arenas's indigenous past, there's a shrine in the northern part of the cemetery where the remains of the last member of the Selk'nam tribe are buried. Local legend says that rubbing the statue's left knee brings good luck. ⊠ *Av. Bulnes 949* ☎ *no phone* ✉ *Free* ☉ *Daily dawn–dusk.*

Isla Magdalena. Punta Arenas is the launching point for a boat trip to see the more than 100,000 Magellanic penguins at the **Monumento Natural Los Pingüinos** on this island. A single trail, marked off by rope, is accessible to humans. The trip to the island, in the middle of the Estrecho de Magallanes, takes about two hours. To get here, you must take a tour boat: Comapa and Cruceros Australis (⇨ Tour Operators *in* Patagonia and Tierra del Fuego A to Z) have service. However you get here, make sure to bring along warm clothing, even in summer; the island can be chilly, particularly if a breeze is blowing across the water.

▶ **❶ Mirador Cerro la Cruz.** From a platform beside the white cross that gives this hill lookout its name, you have a panoramic view of the city's colorful corrugated rooftops leading to the Strait of Magellan. Stand with the amorous local couples gazing out toward the flat expanse of Tierra del Fuego in the distance. ⊠ *Fagnano and Señoret* ☎ *no phone* ✉ *Free* ☉ *Daily.*

❽ Museo de Recuerdo. In the gardens of the Instituto de la Patagonia, part of the Universidad de Magallanes, the Museum of Memory is an enviable collection of machinery and heavy equipment used during the late-19th- and early-20th-century pioneering era. There are exhibits of rural employment, such as a carpenter's workshop, and displays of typical home life. ⊠ *Av. Bulnes* ☎ *61/207–056* ✉ *Free* ☉ *Weekdays 8:30–12:30 and 2:30–6, Sat. 8:30–12:30.*

❺ Museo Naval y Marítimo. The Naval and Maritime Museum extols Chile's high seas prowess, particularly concerning Antarctica. Its exhibits are worth a visit by anyone with an interest in ships and sailing, merchant and military alike. The second floor is designed in part like the interior of a ship, including a map and radio room. Aging exhibits include an account of the 1908 visit to Punta Arenas by an American naval fleet. Ask for a tour or an explanatory brochure in English. ⊠ *Pedro Montt 989* ☎ *61/205–558* ✉ *700 pesos* ☉ *Oct.–May, weekdays 9:30–5, Sat. 10–1, Sun. 3–6; June–Sept., weekdays 9:30–12:30 and 2–5, Sat. 10–1, Sun. 3–6.*

❹ Museo Regional de Magallanes. Housed in what was once the mansion of the powerful Braun-Menéndez family, the Regional Museum of the Magallanes is an intriguing glimpse into the daily life of a wealthy provincial family at the beginning of the 20th century. Lavish Carrara marble hearths, English bath fixtures, and cordovan leather walls are among the original accoutrements. The museum also has an excellent group of displays depicting Punta Arenas's past, from the moment of European contact to its decline with the opening of the Panama Canal. The museum is half a block north of the main square. ⊠ *Magallanes*

FodorśChoice
★

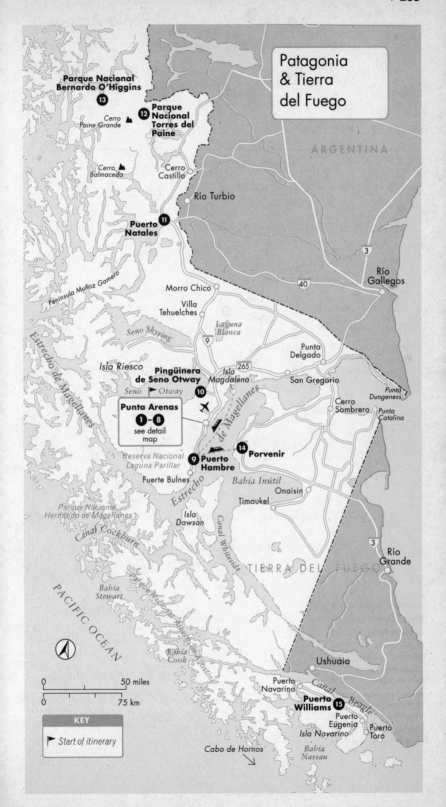

Patagonia & Tierra del Fuego

Parque Nacional Bernardo O'Higgins ⑬

Parque Nacional Torres del Paine ⑫

Cerro Paine Grande ▲

Cerro Balmaceda ▲

Cerro Castillo

Río Turbio

Puerto Natales ⑪

ARGENTINA

Río Gallegos

Península Muñoz Gamero

Morro Chico

Villa Tehuelches

Laguna Blanca

Seno Skyring

9

40

Punta Delgado

Isla Riesco

Pingüinera de Seno Otway

Seno ► Otway ⑩

265

Isla Magdalena

San Gregorio

Punta Dungeness

Cerro Sombrero

Punta Catalina

Estrecho de Magallanes

Punta Arenas
①-⑧
see detail map

Estrecho de Magallanes

Reserva Nacional Laguna Parillar

⑨ **Puerto Hambre**

Fuerte Bulnes

⑭ **Porvenir**

Bahía Inútil

Onaisin

Timaukel

Parque Nacional Hernando de Magallanes

Canal Cockburn

Isla Dawson

Canal Whiteside

TIERRA DEL FUEGO

Río Grande

3

Bahía Stewart

PACIFIC OCEAN

Parque Nacional Alberto de Agostini

Bahía Cook

Ushuaia

0 ——— 50 miles

0 ——— 75 km

Puerto Navarino

Canal Beagle

Puerto Williams ⑮

Puerto Eugenia

Puerto Toro

Isla Navarino

Cabo de Hornos ↓

Bahía Nassau

KEY

► *Start of itinerary*

Punta Arenas

Angamos

Bulnes

Maipu

Jorge Montt

Quillota

Sarmiento

Croacia

Bories

Chiloé

Armando Sanhueza

Magellanes

Mejicana

Navarro

O'Higgins

Carrera Pinto

Av. Colón

Señoret

Av. España

José Menéndez

Post
Office

Waldo Seguel

Pedro Montt

Cathedral

Roca

Fagnano

Chiloé

José Noguiera

21 de Mayo

Navarro

Armando Sanhueza

Errázuriz

Balmaceda

Port

Av. Indepencia

Estrecho de Magellanes

KEY

▶ Start of walk

PATAGONIA'S PENGUINS

AS THE FERRY SLOWLY APPROACHES Isla Magdalena, you begin to make out thousands of black dots along the shore. You catch you breath, knowing that this is your first look at the 120,000 residents of Monumento Natural Los Pingüinos, one of the continent's largest penguin sanctuaries.

But the squat little birds are much closer than you think. You soon realize that on either side of the ferry are large groups of penguins catching their breakfast. They are amazingly agile swimmers, leaping almost entirely out of the water before diving down below the surface once again. A few swim alongside the boat, but most simply ignore the intrusion.

Several different types of penguins, including the Magellanic penguins found on the gentle hills of Isla Magdalena, make their homes along the Chilean coast. Although most favor cooler climates, small colonies can be found in the warmer waters north of Santiago. But for the thrill of seeing tens of thousands in one place, nothing beats Monumento Natural Los Pingüinos. At this reserve, a two-hour trip by boat from Punta Arenas, the birds can safely reproduce and raise their young.

Found only along the coast of Chile and Argentina, Magellanic penguins are named for Spanish explorer Hernando de Magallanes, who spotted them when he arrived on these shores in 1520. They are often called jackass penguins because of the braying sound they make when excited. Adults, with the characteristic black-and-white markings, are easy to distinguish from the adolescents, which are a mottled gray. Also gray are the chicks, which hide inside their burrows when their parents are searching for food. A good time to get a look at the fluffy little fellows is when their parents return to feed them regurgitated fish.

A single trail runs across Isla Magdalena, starting at the dock and ending on a hilltop at a red-and-white lighthouse. Ropes on either side keep humans from wandering too far afield. The penguins, however, have the run of the place. They waddle across the path, alone or in small groups, to get to the rocky beach. Familiar with the boatloads of people arriving two or three times a week, the penguins usually don't pay much attention to the camera-clutching crowds. A few of the more curious ones will walk up to people and inspect a shoelace or pants leg. If someone gets too close to a nest, however, they cock their heads sharply from side to side as a warning.

An easier way to see penguins in their natural habitat is to drive to Pingüinera de Seno Otway, on the mainland about an hour northwest of Punta Arenas. Founded in 1990, the reserve occupies 2 km (1 mi) of coastline. There are far fewer penguins here—only about 7,500—but the number is still astounding. The sanctuary is run by a nonprofit group, which can provide English-language guides. Travel companies from Punta Arenas arrange frequent tours to the reserve.

—Pete Nelson

949 ☎ 61/244–216 ⊠ 1,000 pesos ⊙ Oct.–Apr., Mon.–Sat. 10:30–5,
Sun. 10:30–2; May–Sept., daily 10:30–2.

⑥ Museo Salesiano de Maggiorino Borgatello. Commonly referred to simply as "El Salesiano," the museum is operated by Italian missionaries whose order arrived in Punta Arenas in the 19th century. The Salesians, most of whom spoke no Spanish, proved to be daring explorers. Traveling throughout the region, they collected the artifacts made by indigenous tribes that are currently on display. They also relocated many of the indigenous people to nearby Dawson Island, where they died by the hundreds. The museum contains an extraordinary collection of everything from skulls and native crafts to stuffed animals. ⊠ Av. Bulnes 398 ☎ 61/241–096 ⊠ 1,500 pesos ⊙ Tues.–Sun., 10–12:30 and 3–5.

★ ③ Palacio Sara Braun. This resplendent 1895 mansion, a national landmark and architectural showpiece of southern Patagonia, was designed by French architect Numa Meyer at the behest of Sara Braun. Materials and craftsmen were imported from Europe during the home's four years of construction. The city's central plaza and surrounding buildings soon followed, ushering in the region's golden era. The Club de la Unión, a social organization that now owns the building, opens its doors to nonmembers for tours of some of the rooms and salons that remain in their original state (a good portion of the mansion is leased to a hotel). Noteworthy are the lavish bedrooms, magnificent parquet floors, marble fireplaces, and hand-painted ceilings. Don't miss portraits of Braun and her husband José Nogueira in the music room. Afterwards head to the cellar for a drink or snack in the warm public tavern. ⊠ Plaza Muñoz Gamero 716 ☎ 61/241–489 ⊠ 1,000 pesos ⊙ Tues.–Fri. 10:30–1 and 6:30–8:30, Sat. 10:30–1 and 8–10, Sun. 11–2.

② Plaza Muñoz Gamero. A canopy of conifers shades this square, which is surrounded by splendid baroque-style mansions from the 19th century. A bronze sculpture commemorating the voyage of Hernando de Magallanes dominates the center of the plaza. Local lore has it that a kiss on the shiny toe of Calafate, one of the Fuegian people at the base of the monument, will one day bring you back to Punta Arenas. ⊠ José Nogueira and 21 de Mayo.

Where to Stay & Eat

$–$$$ ✕ **La Pergola.** In what was once the sun room and patio garden of Sara Braun's turn-of-the-20th-century mansion, La Pergola has one of the city's most refined settings. A 100-year-old vine festoons the glass windows and ceiling. Choose from mainly Chilean seafood and meat specialties on the photo-illustrated menu: you might start with fried calamari and then have white fish in garlic sauce. The service is formal and attentive as in the rest of the Hotel José Nogueira. ⊠ Bories 959 ☎ 61/248–840 ▭ AE, DC, MC, V.

$–$$ ✕ **El Remezón.** Even among the many fine restaurants in Punta Arenas, this cheerful little place stands out because of its deliciously seasoned grilled fish and meats. The dining room is unpretentious and homey. The restaurant is near the port, but the terrific food and potent pisco sours—brandy mixed with lemon, egg whites, and sugar—make it worth the walk. ⊠ 21 de Mayo 1469 ☎ 61/241–029 ▭ AE.

$–$$ ✕ **Los Ganaderos.** Feel at home on the range in this restaurant resembling a rural *estancia* (ranch). The manager and waiters, dressed in authentic gaucho costumes, serve up tasty *corderos al ruedo* (spit-roasted lamb) cooked to perfection in the *salón de parilla* (grill room). Wash down your meal with something from the long list of Chilean wines. Interesting black-and-white photographs of past and contemporary ranch life are displayed along the walls. The restaurant is several blocks

FodorśChoice
★

north of the center of town, but it's worth the long walk or very short taxi ride. ⊠ *Bulnes 0977* ☎ *61/214–597* ▭ *AE, MC, V* ⊘ *Closed Sun.*

$–$$ ✕ **Restaurant Asturias.** Rough-hewn wood beams and white stucco walls conjure up the Asturias region of Spain. The *salmón papillote* (salmon poached in white wine with cured ham, cream cheese, and tomatoes) combines smoky aromas with flavors from the sea. The *paella castellana* varies from the traditional dish because it includes meats, and the *congrio a la vasca* (with pepper and garlic) is an imaginative rendition of Chile's ubiquitous white fish. ⊠ *Lautaro Navarro 967* ☎ *61/243–763* ▭ *AE, DC, MC, V.*

★ **$–$$** ✕ **Sotito's.** A longtime favorite among locals, Sotito's is a virtual institution in Punta Arenas. The dining room is warm and cozy, with exposed-brick walls and wood-beam ceilings. More importantly, it serves some of the best king crab in the area. It's prepared a half dozen ways, including in an appetizer called *centolla con palta* (king crab with avocado). The restaurant is near the water a few blocks east of Plaza Muñoz Gamero. ⊠ *O'Higgins 1138* ☎ *61/243–565* ▭ *AE, DC, MC, V.*

$ ✕ **El Estribo.** Centered around a large fireplace used to grill the meats, this narrow restaurant is filled with intimate little tables covered with white tablecloths. The name means The Stirrup, and the walls are adorned with tastefully arranged bridles, bits, lariats, and—of course—all manner of stirrups. The success of this longtime favorite, however, is due to its excellent regional food, including lamb, salmon, and king crab. For dessert try rhubarb pie—uncommon in these parts. ⊠ *Ignacio Carrera Pinto 762* ☎ *61/244–714* ▭ *No credit cards.*

$ ✕ **El Quijote.** Red neon inside and out boldly announces El Quijote restaurant. The kitchen dishes out delicious soups and sandwiches, as well as meat and seafood dishes, making it a reliable local hangout. Stop by for the espresso drinks as well as the *liquados* (fruit and milk shakes). ⊠ *Lautaro Navarro 1087* ☎ *61/241–225* ▭ *AE, DC, MC, V.*

★ **$** ✕ **La Taberna.** A jovial, publike atmosphere prevails in this labyrinthine cellar redoubt down the side stairway of Sara Braun's old mansion. A series of nearly hidden rooms are walled in cozy stone and brick, and black-and-white photos of historical Punta Arenas adorn the walls. You're likely to hear ragtime and jazz on the stereo while enjoying beers served cold in frosted mugs, tapas-style meat and cheese appetizers, sandwiches, tacos, pizza, fajitas, and even carpaccio. The owners belong to the elite Club de la Union headquartered upstairs, and many members relax down here. ⊠ *Plaza Muñoz Gamero 716* ☎ *61/241–317* ▭ *AE, DC, MC, V* ⊘ *Closed Sun.*

¢–$ ✕ **Calipso.** The strong espresso and fresh pastries served here are certain to revive you after a day of strolling the broad avenues of Punta Arenas. More substantial fare includes moderately priced hamburgers with all the trimmings, as well as more expensive salmon and crab dinners. ⊠ *Bories 817* ☎ *61/241–782* ▭ *DC, MC, V.*

¢–$ ✕ **Lomit's.** A fast-moving but friendly staff serves Chilean-style blue-plate specials at this bustling deli. In addition to traditional hamburgers you can eat the ubiquitous *completos*—hot dogs buried under mounds of toppings, from spicy mayonnaise to guacamole. Locals come here from morning to midnight. ⊠ *José Menéndez between Bories and Magallanes* ☎ *61/243–399* ▭ *No credit cards.*

¢–$ ✕ **La Mamá.** Massive plates of lovingly prepared pasta, such as gnocchi and lasagna, have made this restaurant very popular with budget travelers. The hosts' warmth makes up for the unsightly red plastic furniture and low stucco ceiling. A bulletin board in the corner is plastered with raves from every corner of the globe. ⊠ *Armando Sanhueza 720* ☎ *61/225–127* ▭ *No credit cards.*

$$ ✕⊠ **Hotel Los Navegantes.** This unpretentious, older hotel a block from the Plaza de Armas has spacious burgundy and green rooms. The nautical-theme restaurant, in a simple but comfortable dining room with a bright garden at one end, serves delicious grilled salmon and roast lamb. Don't pass up the shellfish appetizers. ⊠ *José Menéndez 647* ☎ *61/244–677* 🖨 *61/247–545* ⊕ *www.hotel-losnavegantes.com* ⤴ *50 rooms, 2 suites* ♢ *Restaurant, in-room safes, minibars, bar, airport shuttle, travel services* ⊟ *AE, DC, MC, V.*

$$$$ ⊠ **Hotel Finis Terrae.** A Best Western affiliate, this modern interpretation of an alpine-style hotel has a very professional staff. Rooms are comfortable, with traditional floral-print bedcovers and overstuffed chairs, and the baths are spacious and modern. Head up to the sixth floor for panoramic views from the restaurant and bar. ⊠ *Av. Colón 766* ☎ *61/228–200* 🖨 *61/248–124* ⊕ *www.hotelfinisterrae.com* ⤴ *60 rooms, 4 suites* ♢ *Restaurant, in-room safes, minibars, cable TV, 2 bars, Internet, business center, airport shuttle* ⊟ *AE, DC, MC, V.*

$$$$ ⊠ **Hotel José Nogueira.** Originally the home of Sara Braun, wealthy
FodorśChoice widow of wool baron José Nogueira, this opulent 19th-century man-
★ sion also contains a museum. Carefully restored over many years, the building retains the original crystal chandeliers, marble floors, and polished bronze accents that were imported from France. Rooms are rather small, but compensate with high ceilings, thick carpets, English wallpaper, period furniture, and marble sinks. Suites have hot tubs and in-room faxes. ⊠ *Bories 959* ☎ *61/248–840* 🖨 *61/248–832* ⊕ *www.hotelnogueira.com* ⤴ *25 rooms, 3 suites* ♢ *Restaurant, in-room data ports, in-room safes, minibars, cable TV, salon, pub, laundry service, business services* ⊟ *AE, DC, MC, V.*

$$$ ⊠ **Hotel Cabo de Hornos.** You can look out from this imposing eight-story hotel over the adjacent Plaza Muñoz Gamero park on one side and to the Estrecho de Magallanes on the other. Rooms and suites have contemporary beds and multicolor-striped drapes that match the flowers on the bedspread—think slightly bland, European conservative in style. Botanical prints line the halls. The fine restaurant, Navarino, serves international cuisine. ⊠ *Plaza Muñoz Gamero 1025* ☎☎ *61/242–134* ⊕ *www.hch.co.cl* ⤴ *90 rooms, 1 suite* ♢ *Restaurant, room service, in-room safes, minibars, cable TV, sauna, bar, baby-sitting, Internet, business services, convention center, airport shuttle, travel services, no-smoking floors* ⊟ *AE, DC, MC, V.*

$$$ ⊠ **Hotel Isla Rey Jorge.** Lofty wood windows let lots of light into the intimate rooms, decorated in mint and deep rose, at this English-style hotel with impeccable service. The hotel's richly toned *linga* and *coigué* woodwork in the lobby continues down into the popular basement pub, El Galeón. The hotel is just one block from Plaza Muñoz Gamero. ⊠ *21 de Mayo 1243* ☎☎ *61/248–220* ⊕ *www.islareyjorge.com* ⤴ *25 rooms, 4 suites* ♢ *Restaurant, cable TV, bar, Internet, airport shuttle, travel services* ⊟ *AE, DC, MC, V.*

$ ⊠ **Hostal de la Avenida.** The rooms of this pea-green guest house all overlook the garden, lovingly tended by its owner, a local of Yugoslav origin. Flowers spill out from a wheelbarrow and a bathtub, birdhouses hang from trees, and a statue of Mary rests in a shrine with a grotto. The rooms offer modest comforts for those on a budget. The ones beyond the garden are the newest. Beside them is a funky bar (Chilean poet Pablo Neruda would have approved) that seems hunkered down for blustery winters. ⊠ *Av. Colón 534* ☎ *61/247–532* ⤴ *10 rooms, 6 with bath* ♢ *Dining room, in-room safes, minibars, cable TV, bar, laundry service* ⊟ *AE, DC, MC, V* ⧖ *CP.*

★ $ ⊠ **Hostal Oro Fueguino.** On a slightly sloping cobblestone street near the observation deck at Cerro la Cruz, this funky little hostelry—tall, narrow, and rambling—welcomes you with lots of color. The first thing you notice is the facade, painted bright orange and blue. Inside are wall hangings and lamp shades made of eye-catching fabrics from as far off as India that create a hominess. The dining and living rooms are cheerful, and there's a wealth of tourist information. The warmth is enhanced by the personal zeal of the proprietor, Dinka Ocampo. ⊠ *Fagnano 365* 🕾🕾 *61/249–401* ⊕ *www.orofueguino.cl* ⚲ *12 rooms* ⚭ *Dining room, cable TV, laundry service, Internet* ☰ *AE, DC, MC, V* ⍟ *BP.*

$ 🖭 **Hotel Condor de Plata.** The idiosyncratic decor at the Silver Condor includes scale models of ships and photographs of old-fashioned airplanes that once traversed the region. Like a handful of other small hotels on this busy, tree-lined avenue, it offers basic amenities for those on a budget—simple, clean rooms that have a bed and a TV. ⊠ *Av. Colón 556* 🕾 *61/247–987* 🕾 *61/241–149* ⚲ *14 rooms* ⚭ *Cafeteria, in-room safes, minibars, bar, laundry service* ☰ *AE, DC, MC, V.*

$ 🖭 **Residencial Sonia Kuscevic.** The only Punta Arenas inn affiliated with Hosteling International, Residencial Sonia Kuscevic is named for its gentle, hospitable owner. Rooms are small and clean, if slightly tacky, and have gas heaters and mountains of blankets to keep you warm. An annex in the house next door offers greater independence, especially for those in large groups. ⊠ *Pasaje Darwin 175, off Angamos between Chiloé and Sanhueza* 🕾🕾 *61/248–543* ⊕ *www.hostalsk.50megs.com* ⚲ *11 rooms* ⚭ *Lounge, library; no room TVs* ☰ *No credit cards.*

Nightlife & the Arts

Because Punta Arenas is so far south, the sun doesn't set until well into the evening. That means that locals don't think about hitting the bars until midnight. If you can't stay up late, try the hotel bars, such as Hotel Tierra del Fuego's **Pub 1900** (⊠ Av. Colón 716 🕾 61/242–759), which attract an early crowd. If you're in the mood for dancing, try **Abracadabra** (⊠ Bories 546 🕾 61/224–144), where the younger set goes to party until dawn.

Shopping

About 3 km (2 mi) north of town is the **Zona Franca** (⊠ Av. Bulnes s/n 🕾 no phone). This duty-free zone is where people from all around the region come for low-priced electronics and other consumer items. It's open Monday–Saturday 9–8.

Almacén de Antaño (⊠ Colón 1000 🕾 61/227–283) offers a fascinatingly eclectic selection of pewter, ceramics, mirrors, and graphics frames. **Dagorret** (⊠ Bories 587 🕾 61/228–692), a Chilean chain with other outlets in Puerto Montt and Puerto Natales, carries top-quality leather clothing, including *gamuza* (suede) and *gamulán* (buckskin), some with wool trim. **Quilpue** (⊠ José Nogueira 1256 🕾 61/220–960) is a shoe-repair shop that also markets *huaso* (cowboy) supplies such as bridles, bits, and spurs. Pick up some boots for folk dancing.

Puerto Hambre

❾ *50 km (31 mi) south of Punta Arenas.*

In an attempt to gain a foothold in the region, Spain founded Ciudad Rey Don Felipe in 1584. Pedro Sarmiento de Gamboa constructed a church and homes for more than 100 settlers. But just three years later, British navigator Thomas Cavendish came ashore to find all but one person had died of hunger. He renamed the town Port Famine. Today a tranquil fishing village, Puerto Hambre still has traces of the original settlement, a sobering reminder of the often unbridled zeal of early European explorers.

About 2 km (1 mi) west of Puerto Hambre is a small white **monolith** that marks the geographical center of Chile, the midway point between northernmost Arica and the South Pole.

In the middle of a Chilean winter in 1843, a frigate under the command of Captain Juan Williams Rebolledo sailed southward from the island of Chiloé carrying a ragtag contingent of 11 sailors and eight soldiers. In October, on a rocky promontory called Santa Ana overlooking the Estrecho de Magallanes, they built a wooden fort, which they named **Fuerte Bulnes,** thereby founding the first Chilean settlement in the southern reaches of Patagonia. Much of the fort has been restored. ⊠ *5 km (3 mi) south of Puerto Hambre* ☎ *no phone* ⊠ *Free* ☉ *Daily.*

The 47,000-acre **Reserva Nacional Laguna Parillar,** west of Puerto Hambre, is centered around a shimmering lake in a valley flanked by hills. It's a great place for a picnic, if the weather cooperates. There are a number of well-marked paths that offer sweeping vistas over the Estrecho de Magallanes. ⊠ *Off Ruta 9* ☎ *no phone* 🕮 *650 pesos* ☉ *Mid-Oct.–mid-Mar., weekdays 8:30–5:30, weekends 8:30–8:30.*

Pingüinera de Seno Otway

🔟 *50 km (31 mi) northwest of Punta Arenas.*

Magellanic penguins, which live up to 20 years in the wild, return to their birthplace to mate with the same partner. For about 2,000 penguin couples—no singles make the trip—home is this desolate and windswept land off the Otway Sound. In late September the penguins begin to arrive from the southern coast of Brazil and the Falkland Islands. They mate and lay their eggs in early October, and brood their eggs in November. Offspring are hatched mid-November through early December. If you're lucky, you may catch sight of one of the downy gray chicks that stick their heads out of the burrows when their parents return to feed them. Otherwise you might see scores of the ungainly adult penguins waddling to the ocean from their nesting burrows. They swim for food every eight hours and dive up to 100 ft deep. The penguins depart from the sound in late March.

The road to the sanctuary begins 30 km (18 mi) north of Punta Arenas, where the main road, Ruta 9, diverges near a checkpoint booth. A gravel road then traverses another fierce and winding 30 km (18 mi), but the rough trip (mud will be a problem if there's been a recent rain) should reward you with the sight of hundreds of sheep, cows, and birds, including, if you're lucky, rheas and flamingos. The sanctuary is a 1-km (½-mi) walk from the parking lot. It gets chilly, so bring a windbreaker. ⊠ *Off Ruta 9* 🕮 *1,200 pesos* ☉ *Sept.–Apr., daily 8:30–8:30.*

Puerto Natales

⓫ *242 km (150 mi) northwest of Punta Arenas.*

The land around Puerto Natales held very little interest for Spanish explorers in search of riches. A not-so-warm welcome from the indigenous peoples encouraged them to continue up the coast, leaving only a name for the channel running through it: Seno Última Esperanza (Last Hope Sound).

In the late 1800s Hermann Eberhard, a German entrepreneur, founded a sheep farm at nearby Puerto Prat. The town of Puerto Natales wasn't founded until 1911. Today this town of fading fishing and meat-packing enterprises is rapidly emerging as the staging center for visits to Parque Nacional Torres del Paine, Parque Nacional Bernardo

O'Higgins, and other remote sites. The town, with 15,000 friendly and hospitable residents, is still unspoiled by tourism.

On a clear day, an early morning walk along Avenida Pedro Montt, which follows the shoreline of the Seno Última Esperanza (or Canal Señoret, as it is called on some maps), can be a soul-cleansing experience. The rising sun gradually casts a glow on the mountain peaks to the west.

A few blocks east of the shore is the not-quite-central **Plaza de Armas.** An incongruous railway engine sits prominently in the middle of the square. ☒ *Arturo Prat and Eberhard.*

Across from the Plaza de Armas is the squat little **Iglesia Parroquial.** The ornate altarpiece in this church depicts the town's founders, indigenous peoples, and the Virgin Mary all in front of the Torres del Paine.

A highlight in the small but interesting **Museo Historico Municipal** is a room of photos of indigenous peoples. Another room is devoted to the exploits of German-born Hermann Eberhard, considered the region's first settler. ☒ *Bulnes 285* ☎ *61/411–263* ☒ *Free* ☉ *Weekdays 8:30–12:30 and 2:30–6, weekends 2:30–6.*

In 1896, Hermann Eberhard stumbled upon a gaping cave that extended 200 m (650 ft) into the earth. Venturing inside, he discovered the bones and dried pieces of hide of an animal he could not identify. It was later determined that what Eberhard had discovered were the extraordinarily well-preserved remains of a prehistoric herbivorous mammal, about twice the height of a man, which they called a *milodón.* The cave and a somewhat kitschy life-size fiberglass rendering of the creature are at the **Monumento Natural Cueva de Milodón.** ☒ *Off Ruta 9, 28 km (17 mi) northwest of Puerto Natales* ☎ *no phone* ☒ *1,000 pesos* ☉ *Daily 8:30–6.*

Where to Stay & Eat

★ **$$–$$$** ✕ **Restaurant Edén.** Grilled lamb sizzles prominently near the entrance while Chilean folk music plays softly in the background. This expansive venue, with tables generously spaced on the white terrazzo floor, has floor-to-ceiling windows on two sides that give you the feeling of dining alfresco. ☒ *Blanco Encalada 345* ☎ *61/414–120* ▤ *AE, MC, V.*

$–$$ ✕ **Centro Español.** Tables swathed in bright red, and hardwood floors that would be perfect for flamenco dancing create this restaurant's subtly Spanish style. It's a bit formal, but never stuffy. There's a wide selection of simply prepared meat and fish entrées, including succulent squid, served in ample portions. ☒ *Magallanes 247* ☎ *61/411–181* ▤ *AE, MC, V.*

$–$$ ✕ **Don Pepe.** Creative seafood preparations draw a large crowd here, especially in summer. Try the salmon with a crab and cream sauce, a house specialty, and you likely won't mind that the place isn't much to look at. ☒ *Ladrilleros 172* ☎ *61/412–189* ▤ *DC, MC, V.*

★ **$–$$** ✕ **Indigo.** Eco-friendly vibes waft from this bright café, setting it apart from nearly every other eatery in Patagonia. Fossils collected from the nearby fjord, piles of National Geographics and informational brochures about area attractions, Internet access, and an English-speaking staff make Indigo a de facto tourist office, museum, and library. The homemade pizzas are good—ask which toppings are fresh and which are canned— as are the sandwiches served on homemade wheat bread. The corner spot, overlooking the water and a backdrop of snowy peaks, makes this a pleasant place to visit, even if you come just for a cup of coffee. ☒ *Ladrilleros 105* ☎ *61/413–609* ▤ *MC, V.*

$–$$ ✕ **Restaurant Última Esperanza.** Named for the strait on which Puerto Natales is located, Last Hope Restaurant sounds as if it might be a bleak place. It's known, however, for its attentive service and top-quality entrées that include meats and fish. *Salmón a la plancha* (grilled salmon) is a specialty. ⊠ *Av. Eberhard 354* ☎ *61/411–391* ▭ *No credit cards.*

$ ✕ **El Rincón del Tata.** In the evenings a strolling guitarist entertains with Chilean folk songs, encouraging diners to join in at this funky little spot. Artifacts, mainly household items, from the town's early days fill the dining room, including a working wood-burning stove to keep you warm. More expensive restaurants can't match the *salmón à la mantequilla* (salmon baked in butter and black pepper), and the grilled lamb with garlic sauce is a Patagonian highlight. ⊠ *Arturo Prat 236* ☎ *61/413–845* ▭ *AE, DC, MC, V.*

¢–$ ✕ **Café Melissa.** The best espresso in town is found at Café Melissa, which also serves pastries and cakes baked on the premises. In the heart of downtown, this is a popular meeting place for residents and visitors alike. ⊠ *Blanco Encalada 258* ☎ *61/411–944* ▭ *No credit cards.*

$$$–$$$$ ▥ **Hotel CostAustralis.** The peaked green roof of this venerable three-story hotel—complete with turret—dominates the waterfront. Designed by a local architect, it's considered one of the finest hotels in Peurto Natales. Rooms have wood-paneled entryways and Venetian and Czech furnishings. Some have a majestic view of the Seno Última Esperanza and the snowcapped mountain peaks beyond, while others look out over the city. ⊠ *Pedro Montt and Bulnes* ☎ *61/412–000* 🖷 *61/411–881* ⊕ *www.australis.com* ⥱ *50 rooms, 2 suites* ⌂ *Restaurant, café, room service, in-room safes, minibars, cable TV, bar, laundry service, Internet, travel services* ▭ *AE, DC, MC, V.*

$$$ ▥ **Hotel Martín Gusinde.** Part of Chile's modern AustroHoteles chain, this intimate inn possesses an aura of sophistication that contrasts with the laid-back atmosphere of Puerto Natales. The hotel is named after the Austrian ethnologist who studied the natives inhabitants of Tierra del Fuego. Rooms are decorated with wood furniture and colorfully patterned wallpaper. It's across from the casino, a block south of the Plaza de Armas. ⊠ *Carlos Bories 278* ☎ *61/412–770; reservations 61/229–512* 🖷 *61/412–820* ⊕ *www.austrohoteles.cl* ⥱ *20 rooms* ⌂ *Restaurant, room service, in-room safes, cable TV, bar* ▭ *AE, MC, V.*

$$ ▥ **Hostal Lady Florence Dixie.** Named after an aristocratic English immigrant and tireless traveler, this modern hostel with an alpine-inspired facade is on the town's main street. Its bright, spacious lounge is a great people-watching perch. Guest rooms are a bit spartan—mostly just a bed. ⊠ *Bulnes 659* ☎ *61/411–158* 🖷 *61/411–943* ⊕ *www.chileanpatagonia.com/florence* ⥱ *18 rooms* ⌂ *In-room safes* ▭ *AE, MC, V* ⦿ *CP.*

$$ ▥ **Hotel Alberto de Agostini.** The Agostini is one of the modern hotels that have cropped up in Puerto Natales in the past few years. Small rooms—some with hot tubs—are unremarkable in decor. A comfortably furnished lounge on the second floor looks out over the Seno Última Esperanza. ⊠ *Calle O'Higgins 632* ☎ *61/410–060* 🖷 *61/410–070* ⥱ *21 rooms* ⌂ *Restaurant, room service, minibars, sauna, bar* ▭ *AE, MC, V.*

$$ ▥ **Hotel Glaciares.** An enduring choice in Puerto Natales, the cheery Hotel Glaciares is half a block from the Seno Última Esperanza. Rooms have lots of windows letting in the sun. The hotel also offers tours of Parque Nacional Torres del Paine in its own fleet of minivans. ⊠ *Eberhard 104* ☎🖷 *61/411–452* ⊕ *www.hotelglaciares.co.cl* ⥱ *15 rooms* ⌂ *Restaurant, laundry service, travel services* ▭ *DC, MC, V.*

$ ▥ **Hostal Francis Drake.** Toss a coin in the wishing well out front before you enter this half-timbered house near the center of town. The proprietor is a delightful European lady who dotes on her guests and carefully maintains cleanliness. Rooms are small and basic. The beds are not the world's most comfortable. ⊠ *Philippi 383* ☎ *61/411–553* ⊕ *www. chileaustral.com/francisdrake* ⇝ *12 rooms* ♨ *Cable TV, lounge* ⊟ *DC, MC, V.*

★ $ 🖃 **Indigo.** Rooms in this restored old home have amazing views down the Canal Señoret stretching as far as the Mt. Balmaceda glacier and the Paine Grande. Ask for one of the corner rooms, which have windows along two walls. The walls are sponge-painted in bright reds, yellows, and blues, and hung with local art. The funky and friendly café downstairs has an eclectic collection of artifacts. English is spoken well, as exhibited in the nightly slide shows about Torres del Paine park. ⊠ *Ladrilleros 105* ☎ *61/413–609* ⊕ *www.conceptoindigo.com* ⇝ *7 rooms* ♨ *Restaurant, laundry service, Internet, travel services; no room phones, no room TVs* ⊟ *MC, V.*

Parque Nacional Torres del Paine

⑫ *125 km (75 mi) northwest of Puerto Natales.*

FodorsChoice
★

Some 12 million years ago, lava flows pushed up through the thick sedimentary crust that covered the southwestern coast of South America, cooling to form a granite mass. Glaciers then swept through the region, grinding away all but the ash-gray spires that rise over the landscape of one of the world's most beautiful natural phenomena, now the Parque Nacional Torres del Paine (established in 1959). Snow formations dazzle along every turn of road, and the sunset views are spectacular.

Among the 2,420-square-km (934-square-mi) park's most beautiful attractions are its lakes of turquoise, aquamarine, and emerald green waters. Another draw is its unusual wildlife. Creatures like the guanaco (a woollier version of the llama) and the *ñandú* (resembling a small ostrich) abound. They are used to visitors, and don't seem to be bothered by the proximity of automobile traffic and the snapping of cameras. Predators like the gray fox make less frequent appearances. You may also spot the dramatic aerobatics of a falcon and the graceful soaring of the endangered condor. The beautiful puma, celebrated in a National Geographic video filmed here, is especially elusive, but sightings have grown more and more common. Pumas follow the guanaco herds and eat an estimated 40% of their young.

Although considerable walking is necessary to take full advantage of Parque Nacional Torres del Paine, you need not be a hard-core backpacker. Many people take five or six days to hike El Circuito, a route that leads around the entire park, spending the nights in tents or the dozen or so *refugios* (shelters) found along the trails. Others prefer to stay in one of the comfortable lodges and hit the trails for the morning or afternoon. Glaciar Grey, with its fragmented icebergs, makes a rewarding and easy hike. Driving is another way to enjoy the park: most of the more than 100 km (62 mi) of roads leading to the most popular sites are safe and well maintained, though unpaved.

The vast majority of visitors come during the summer months, which means the trails can get congested. Early spring, when wildflowers add flashes of color to the meadows, is an ideal time to visit because the crowds have not yet arrived. The park is open all year, and trails are almost always accessible. Storms can hit without warning, however, so be prepared for sudden rain or snow. The sight of the Paine peaks in clear weather is stunning; if you have any flexibility in your itinerary, be sure to visit the park on the first clear day.

There are three entrances: Laguna Amarga, Lago Sarmiento, and Laguna Azul. You are required to sign in when you arrive at the park. *Guarda-*

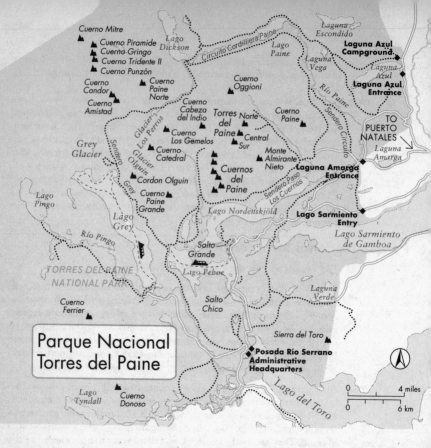

Parque Nacional Torres del Paine

parques (park rangers) staff six stations around the reserve. They request that you inform them when setting out on a hike. CONAF, the national forestry service, has an office at the northern end of Lago del Toro with a scale model of the park, and numerous exhibits (some in English) about the flora and fauna. ✛ *CONAF station in southern section of the park past Hotel Explora* ☎ *61/691–931* ✉ *8,000 pesos* ☉ *Ranger station: Nov.–Feb., daily 8–8; March–Oct., daily 8–12:30 and 2–6:30.*

Where to Stay & Eat

$$ ✕🏠 **Posada Río Serrano.** A welcoming staff will show you a selection of rooms, including those with bunk beds and those with regular beds. Rooms are small, but clean, and have colorful bedspreads. A few actually have lake views. A surprisingly warm salon with a fireplace makes a nice place to relax. Don't expect pampering—besides camping this is the cheapest dining and lodging in the park. The restaurant serves filling fish dishes *a lo pobre* (with fried eggs and french fries), as well as lamb. The inn also has a general store where you can find basic necessities such as batteries and cookies. ⊠ *Lago Toro* ☎ *61/411–129 for reservations (Puerto Natales)* 🍴 *20 rooms, 4 with bath* ⚐ *Restaurant, grocery; no a/c, no room phones, no room TVs* ▤ *No credit cards* ¶❅ *CP.*

$$$$ 🏠 **Hostería Lago Grey** The panoramic view past the lake to the glacier beyond is worth the journey here, which doesn't change the fact that this older hotel is overpriced and not very attractive. Rooms are comfortable, but the materials are inexpensive, and baths small. There's a TV with a VCR in the lounge. The view—and it's one you're not likely to forget—can also be enjoyed at dinner (a 16,800 pesos per person prix fixe with wine) or at the hotel's large breakfast. The hotel operates its own sightseeing vessel, the *Grey II*, for close-up tours to Glaciar Grey. ⊠ *Lago Grey* ☎📠 *61/229–512 or 61/225–986* ⊕ *www.lagogrey.com*

🛏 *20 rooms* ⚒ *Restaurant, boating, fishing, hiking, horseback riding, bar, lounge, laundry service; no room TVs* ⊟ *AE, DC, MC, V* ⦿⧀ *BP.*

$$$$ ⊡ **Hosteria Pehoé.** Cross a 30-m (100-ft) footbridge to get to this hotel on its own island in the middle of glistening Lake Pehoé, across from the beautiful Torres del Paine mountain peaks. Upon seeing the setting, nonguests are often tempted to cancel other reservations. Unfortunately, rooms at Pehoé—built in 1970 as the first hotel in the park—are dark, poorly furnished, and windowless, and they face an interior lawn. Management built a new wing (completed in early 2003) with newly obstructed views. However, it is a delight to walk over the footbridge and have a drink at the ski lodge–like bar, where the views are jaw-dropping. ⊠ *Lago Pehoé* ☎ *61/411–390* 🛏 *20 rooms* ⚒ *Restaurant, bar, laundry service; no room TVs, no room phones* ⊟ *AE, DC, MC, V* ⦿⧀ *CP.*

$$$$ ⊡ **Hosteria Tyndall.** A boat ferries you from the end of the road the few minutes along the Serrano River to this wooden lodge. The simple rooms in the main building are small but cute, with attractive wood paneling. The lodge can be noisy, a problem solved by renting a log cottage (a great value for groups). Owner Christian is a wildlife enthusiast and bird-watcher; ask him for a tour of the grassy plain looking out toward the central cluster of snowy peaks. Or fish for a river salmon—they'll cook it for you for free. The prix-fixe dinner costs 11,900 pesos. ⊠ *Lago Toro (Reservations: Av. Croacia 731, Punta Arenas)* ☎☎ *61/235–457 in Punta Arenas* ⊕ *www.hosteriatyndall.com* 🛏 *24 rooms, 6 cottages* ⚒ *Restaurant, boating, fishing, hiking, horseback riding, lounge, laundry service; no room phones, no room TVs* ⊟ *AE, DC, MC, V.*

$$$$ ⊡ **Hotel Explora.** On the southeast corner of Lago Pehoé, this lodge is
FodorsChoice one of the most luxurious—and one of the most expensive—in Chile.
★ While there may be some debate about the aesthetics of the hotel's low-slung minimalist exterior, the interior is impeccable: it's Scandinavian in style, with local woods used for ceilings, floors, and furniture. No expense has been spared—even the bed linens were imported from Spain. A dozen full-time guides (for a maximum of 60 guests) tailor all-inclusive park outings to guests' interests. A three-night minimum stay is required. Nonguests may also enjoy the 42,000-peso prix-fixe dinner, with wine. ⊠ *Lago Pehoé* ☎ *2/206–6060 in Santiago* 🖷 *2/228–4655 in Santiago* ⊕ *www.explora.com* 🛏 *26 rooms, 4 suites* ⚒ *Restaurant, indoor pool, gym, outdoor hot tub, massage, sauna, boating, hiking, horseback riding, piano bar, library, gift shop, baby-sitting, laundry service, Internet, business services, meeting rooms, airport shuttle; no room TVs* ⊟ *AE, DC, MC, V* ⦿⧀ *All-inclusive.*

Parque Nacional Bernardo O'Higgins

⑬ *Southwest of Parque Nacional Torres del Paine.*

Bordering the Parque Nacional Torres del Paine on the southwest, Parque Nacional Bernardo O'Higgins is composed primarily of the southern tip of the vast Campo de Hielo Sur (Southern Ice Field). As it is inaccessible by land, the only way to visit the park is to take a boat up the Seno Última Esperanza. The Puerto Natales tour company Turismo 21 de Mayo (⇨ Tours *in* Patagonia & Tierra del Fuego A to Z) operates two boats here, the *21 de Mayo* and the *Alberto de Agostini*. On your way to the park you approach a cormorant colony with nests clinging to sheer cliff walls, venture to a glacier at the foot of Mt. Balmaceda, and finally dock at Puerto Toro for a 1-km (½-mi) hike to the foot of the Serrano Glacier. On the trip back to Puerto Natales the crew treats you to a pisco sour served over a chunk of glacier ice. As with many full-day tours, you must bring your own lunch. Warm clothing, including gloves, is recommended year-round, particularly if there's even the slightest breeze.

TIERRA DEL FUEGO

Tierra del Fuego, a vaguely triangular island separated from the southernmost tip of South America by the twists and bends of the Estrecho de Magallanes, is indeed a world unto itself. The vast plains on its northern reaches are dotted with trees bent low by the savage winds that frequently lash the coast. The mountains that rise in the south are equally forbidding, traversed by huge glaciers slowly making their way to the sea.

The first European to set foot on this island was Spanish explorer Hernando de Magallanes, who sailed here in 1520. The smoke that he saw coming from the fires lit by the native peoples prompted him to call it Tierra del Humo (Land of Smoke). King Charles V of Spain, disliking that name, rechristened it Tierra del Fuego, or Land of Fire.

Tierra del Fuego is split in half. The island's northernmost tip, well within Chilean territory, is its closest point to the continent. The only town of any size here is Porvenir. Its southern extremity, part of Argentina, points out into the Atlantic toward the Falkland Islands. Here is Ushuaia, on the shores of the Canal Beagle. Farther south is Cape Horn, the southernmost bit of land before you reach Antarctica.

Porvenir

🄯 *30 km (18 mi) by boat from Punta Arenas.*

A short trip eastward across the Estrecho de Magallanes, Porvenir is the principal town on Chile's half of Tierra del Fuego. It's not much to speak of, as its population is just more than 6,000. Located at the eastern end of narrow Bahia Porvenir, it was born during the gold rush of the 1880s. After the boom went bust, it continued to be an important port for the burgeoning cattle and sheep industries.

Porvenir's small **Museo Provincial Fernando Cordero Rusque** includes collections of memorabilia about subjects as eclectic as early Chilean filmmaking and the culture of the indigenous peoples. There are interesting photos of the gold rush and the first sheep ranches. The museum is the only sight of particular interest in this otherwise quiet port of entry to Tierra del Fuego. ✉ *Plaza de Armas* ☎ *no phone* 💲 *Free* ⊙ *Weekdays 9–5, weekends 11–5.*

Puerto Williams

🄯 *75-minute flight from Punta Arenas.*

On an island southeast of the Argentine city of Ushuaia, the town of Puerto Williams is the southernmost permanent settlement in the world. Originally called Puerto Luisa, it was renamed in 1956 in honor of the military officer who took possession of the Estrecho de Magallanes for the newly founded nation of Chile in 1843. Most of the 2,500 residents are troops at the naval base, but there are several hundred civilians in the adjacent village. A tiny community of indigenous peoples makes its home in the nearby Ukika.

For a quick history lesson on how Puerto Williams evolved and some insight into the indigenous peoples, visit the **Museo Martin Gusinde,** named for the renowned anthropologist who traveled and studied in the region between 1918 and 1924. ✉ *Aragay 1* ☎ *no phone* 💲 *500 pesos* ⊙ *Weekdays 10–1 and 3–6, weekends 3–6.*

Weather permitting, **Aerovís DAP** (☎ 61/223–340 ⊕ www.aeroviasdap.cl) offers charter flights over **Cabo de Hornos**, the southernmost tip of South America. Although the water looks placid from the air, strong westerly winds make navigating around Cape Horn treacherous. Hundreds of ships met their doom here trying to sail to the Pacific.

Where to Stay & Eat

When you arrive in Puerto Williams, your airline or ferry company will recommend a few of the hospedajes available, then take you around to see them. All are rustic inns that also serve meals.

¢ ▦ **Hostal Pusaki.** Run with Chilean hospitality, this humble hospedaje has comfortable rooms with up to four beds (including bunks). The dining room serves fine local fare. Dinner is especially pleasant if the fresh *ensalada de centolla* (king crab salad) is on the changing menu. ⊠ *Piloto Pardo 242* ☎ *61/621–020* 🖷 *61/621–116* ⬎ *3 rooms with shared bath* ⚲ *Restaurant; no a/c, no room phones, no room TVs* ▭ *No credit cards* ¶○¶ *CP.*

Nightlife

Permanently moored at the dock is a small Swiss freighter listing slightly to port called the *Micalvi*. It's home to the rustic **Club de Yates** (⊠ Dockside ☎ 61/621–041). Sailors stop off here for good company, strong spirits, and hearty food as they travel between the Atlantic and Pacific around Cape Horn. Stop by and mingle with whomever is there at the time. You might meet Aussies, Brits, Finns, Russians, Swedes, or even the occasional American.

A world away from the cosmopolitan clubs of Santiago, **Pub El Pingüino** (⊠ Centro Commercial ☎ no phone) is a watering hole patronized by the town's civilians. Hours are irregular, but closer to the weekend it opens earlier and closes later.

Hiking

A hike to the top of nearby **Cerro Bandera** is well worth the effort if you have the stamina. The trail is well marked, but very steep. The view from the top toward the south to the Cordón Dientes del Perro (Dog's Teeth Range) is impressive, but looking northward over the Beagle Channel to Argentina—with Puerto Williams nestled below and Ushuaia just visible to the west—is truly breathtaking.

PATAGONIA & TIERRA DEL FUEGO A TO Z

To research prices, get advice from other travelers, and book travel arrangements, visit www.fodors.com.

AIR TRAVEL

LanChile and its subsidiary Ladeco operate a number of flights daily between Punta Arenas and Santiago, Coihaique, and Puerto Montt. Another domestic airline, Aerovís DAP, has regularly scheduled flights between Punta Arenas, Porvenir, Puerto Williams, and the Argentine city of Ushuaia.

It's a good idea to make air-travel arrangements through a reliable tour company, if possible. That way you can rely on the company if you need to make last-minute changes in your itinerary.

🖪 Airlines **Aerovís DAP** ⊠ Bernardo O'Higgins 891, Punta Arenas ☎ 61/223–340 ⊕ www.aeroviasdap.cl. **LanChile/Ladeco** ⊠ Lautaro Navarro 999, Punta Arenas ☎ 61/241–232 ⊕ www.lanchile.com.

AIRPORTS

Punta Arenas' Aeropuerto President Ibañez is 20 km (13 mi) north of town. Porvenir's airport is 5 km (3 mi) north of town. The airstrip in Puerto Williams is on the western edge of town. There is a small airport near Puerto Natales, but it is not open to commercial air traffic.

TRANSFERS Public bus service from the airport into Punta Arenas is 1,500 pesos. Private transfers by small companies running minivans out of the airport (with no other pick up points or call-in service) run 2,500 pesos per person.

BOAT & FERRY TRAVEL

Comapa runs a ferry three times a week between Punta Arenas and Porvenir. Navimag operates an inelegant, but highly serviceable, cargo and passenger ferry fleet between Puerto Montt and Puerto Natales. These are boats designed for transportation, not touring, but they are comfortable enough for all but the most finicky travelers.

🛥 Boat & Ferry Lines **Comapa** ✉ Independencia 803, Punta Arenas ☎ 61/224-256. **Navimag** ✉ Av. El Bosque Norte 0440, Santiago ☎ 2/442-3120 🖷 2/203-5025 ⊕ www. navimag.cl.

BUSINESS HOURS

Most shops in the region close for a few hours in the afternoon, usually noon–3. Grocery stores are the exception. Most restaurants close between lunch and dinner, which means most don't serve meals from 3–8 or even later.

BUS TRAVEL

The four-hour trip between Punta Arenas and Puerto Natales is serviced by small, private companies. One of the best is Buses Fernández, which has a fleet of first-class coaches and its own terminals in both towns.

🚌 Bus Information **Buses Fernández** ✉ Armando Sanhueza 745, Punta Arenas ☎ 61/ 221-429 ✉ Eberhard 555, Puerto Natales ☎ 61/411-111 ⊕ www.busesfernandez.com.

CAR RENTAL

Renting a car in Patagonia is not cheap—most companies charge about 70,000 pesos per day. Compare rental rates to the cost of tours; you may find a tour is far cheaper than driving yourself. Make sure you don't rent a more expensive car than you need. Four-wheel-drive vehicles are popular and readily available, but they often aren't necessary if you're not leaving the major roads. Make certain to understand the extent of your liability for any damage to the vehicle, including routine accidents such as a chipped or cracked windshield. Puerto Williams is a 12-hour drive from Punta Arenas and some agencies have daily surcharges (typically 21,000 pesos a day) for a foreign licence, so flying to southern Tierra del Fuego is an attractive option.

Of the international chains, Budget, Avis, and Hertz have officess in Punta Arenas. At the Punta Arenas airport, there are four rental agencies: Avis, Budget, Hertz, and Int'l Rent A Car. Check prices with each, as any one may be considerably lower than the other three. Avis also has a branch in Puerto Natales. Additional drivers are free. Reputable local companies in Punta Arenas include RUS and Payne.

🚗 Agencies **Avis** ✉ Roca 1044, Punta Arenas ☎ 61/241-182 ✉ Aeropuerto President Ibañez, Punta Arenas ☎ 61/210-861 ✉ Bulnes 632, Puerto Natales ☎ 61/410-775. **Budget** ✉ O'Higgins 964, Punta Arenas ☎ 61/241-696 ✉ Aeropuerto President Ibañez, Punta Arenas ☎ 61/241-696. **Hertz** ✉ O'Higgins 987, Punta Arenas ☎ 61/248-742 ✉ Aeropuerto President Ibañez, Punta Arenas ☎ 61/210-096. **Int'l Rent A Car** ✉ Aeropuerto President Ibañez, Punta Arenas ☎ 61/212-401. **Payne** ✉ José Menéndez 631, Punta Arenas ☎ 61/240-852. **RUS** ✉ Colón 614, Punta Arenas ☎ 61/221-529.

CAR TRAVEL

Driving in Patagonia isn't as difficult as you might think. Highways are paved. Secondary roads, including those in the more popular parks, are well maintained. Be careful of gravel roads—broken windshields are common.

HEALTH

As with other parts of the country, the tap water is safe to drink. If you want to be on the extra-safe side, stick to bottled water. Because of the thin ozone layer, the sun is particularly strong here. Make sure to slather yourself with sunscreen before going outdoors.

INTERNET

Some hotels offer Internet access for a small fee. Some telephone company offices also offer Internet services, but it's generally more expensive. Your best bet is usually the Internet cafés that are springing up around Punta Arenas and Puerto Natales.

In Punta Arenas, one of the most welcoming Internet cafés is Calafate, on Avenida Magallanes. It's open 24 hours. Rates are about 2,100 pesos per hour. Another Internet site in Punta Arenas is Cyber Café. In Puerto Natales, El Rincón del Tata has one computer terminal; Indigo has two.

🚹 Internet Cafés **Calafate** ⊠ Magallanes 922, Punta Arenas ☎ 61/241-281. **Cyber Café** ⊠ Av. Colón 778, 2nd floor, Punta Arenas ☎ 61/200-610. **El Rincón del Tata** ⊠ Arturo Prat 23, Puerto Natales ☎ 61/413-845. **Indigo** ⊠ Ladrilleros 105, Puerto Natales ☎ 61/413-609.

MAIL & SHIPPING

Mail takes weeks and weeks to get from the end of the earth to the United States or the United Kingdom. It's best to send it from the airport in Santiago.

MONEY MATTERS

There are a number of banks in Punta Arenas and Puerto Natales where you can exchange cash, and withdraw money from ATMs that accept cards on the Cirrus or Plus systems. Do not count on banking services outside of these two cities. In Puerto Natales, ChileExpress on the main square has Western Union services.

When you're anticipating smaller purchases, try to have coins and small bills on hand at all times. Many vendors do not always have appropriate change for large bills.

🚹 Currency Exchange **ChileExpress** ⊠ Av. Tomas Rogers, Puerto Natales ☎ 61/411-3000.

TAXIS

Taxis are readily available in Punta Arenas and Puerto Natales. Ordinary taxis, with yellow roofs, are the easiest. *Colectivos,* with black roofs, run on fixed routes. They cost less, but figuring them out can be tricky if you're not a fluent Spanish speaker. You can flag down one of these along the set route, but stops are unmarked. Ask at your hotel to find out which car number to look for.

TELEPHONES

Public telephones, plentiful in larger towns, are becoming more common in smaller villages. Some accept phone cards that can be purchased at nearby shops. Entel and CTC have offices throughout the region where you can send faxes and make international calls.

TOURS

Air tours are often a little more expensive than cruises, but they provide an entirely different perspective, and may take you farther than you could otherwise go. Aerovís DAP operates charter flights over Cape Horn for about 12,600 pesos per person. DAP was the first airline to have regular commercial flights to the Antarctic, beginning in 1987. In the austral summer (December–February) they fly small groups to comfortable refuges in the Chilean Antarctic, where you can stay in a lodge for up to three nights. DAP staffs a resident guide in Antarctica, and visits include trips to the air force bases of Russia, China, and Chile. Single-day visits begin at U.S.$2,500. The flight is 3½ hours. DAP also has helicopter service across Patagonia.

Boat tours are a popular way to see otherwise inaccessible parts of Patagonia and Tierra del Fuego. The *Barcaza Melinka,* run by Comapa, makes thrice-weekly trips to Isla Magdalena. Cruceros Australis operates the elegant *Terra Australis,* a 55-cabin ship that sails round-trip between Punta Arenas and Ushuaia. On the way, the ship stops at a number of sights, including the Garibaldi Glacier, a breathtaking mass of blue ice. You also ride smaller motorboats ashore to visit Isla Magdalena's colony of 120,000 penguins, and Ainsworth Bay's family of elephant seals. The cruises include lectures in English, German, and Spanish on the region's geography and history, flora and fauna.

Turismo 21 de Mayo operates two ships, the *21 de Mayo* and the *Alberto de Agostini,* to the Balmaceda and Serrano glaciers in Parque Nacional Bernardo O'Higgins. Passengers on these luxurious boats are treated to lectures about the region as the boat moves up the Seno Última Esperanza.

With offices in both cities, Comapa offers numerous tours all over Patagonia and Tierra del Fuego. In Santiago, SportsTour puts together individual itineraries. It also offers half- and full-day city tours and multiday excursions throughout the region. Most staff members speak excellent English. In Puerto Natales, TourExpress operates a fleet of small vans for comfortable tours into Parque Nacional Torres del Paine. The bilingual guides are well versed not only on the area's culture and history but on its geology, fauna, and flora. In Punta Arenas, one of the best companies is Ventistur. Operated by Gonazalo Tejeda, who studied in the United States, Ventistur offers expert advice on travel throughout the region.

A region-knowledgeable tour operator or travel agent is a must for travel to Patagonia and Tierra del Fuego. In the United States, a number of companies have experience. Among them is the Georgia-based Lost World Adventures, whose staff specializes in tailoring itineraries around your specific interests. There are many good companies in Chile as well.

🛪 Air Tours **Aerovís DAP** ✉ O'Higgins 891, Punta Arenas ☎ 61/223-340 🌐 www.aeroviasdap.cl.

🛥 Boat Tours **Comapa** ✉ Independencia 803, Punta Arenas ☎ 61/224-256. **Cruceros Australis** ✉ Av. El Bosque Norte 0440, Santiago ☎ 2/442-3110 🖶 2/203-5173 🌐 www.australis.com. **Turismo 21 de Mayo** ✉ Ladrilleros 171, Puerto Natales ☎ 61/411-176.

🚐 Regional Tours **Comapa** ✉ Independencia 803, Punta Arenas ☎ 61/200-202 ✉ Pedro Montt 262 ☎ 61/414-300 🌐 www.comapa.com. **SportsTour** ✉ Moneda 790, 14th floor, Santiago ☎ 2/549-5200 🖶 2/698-2981 🌐 www.chilnet.cl/sportstour. **Tour-Express** ✉ Bulnes 769, Puerto Natales ☎ 61/410-734. **Ventistur** ✉ José Menéndez 647, Punta Arenas ☎ 61/241-463 🖶 61/229-081 🌐 www.chileaustral.com/ventistur.

🛫 U.S.-based Tours **Lost World Adventures** ✉ 112 Church St., Decatur, GA 30030 ☎ 404/373-5820 or 800/999-0558 🖶 404/377-1902 🌐 www.lostworldadventures.com.

VISITOR INFORMATION

Sernatur, the national tourism agency, has offices in Punta Arenas and in Puerto Natales. The Punta Arenas office is open daily 8–5, and the small Puerto Natales office is open Monday–Thursday 8:15–6 and Friday 8:15–5. The Punta Arenas City Tourism Office, in an attractive kiosk in the main square, is quite helpful. It's open December–March, Monday–Saturday 8–8 and Sunday 9–3; April–November, Monday–Thursday 8–5 and Friday 8–4. They offer a free Internet connection.

🚩 **Punta Arenas City Tourism** ✉ Plaza Muñoz Gamero, Punta Arenas ☎ 61/200-610 🌐 www.puntaarenas.cl. **Sernatur** ✉ Magallanes 960, Punta Arenas ☎ 61/241-330 ✉ Puerto Montt s/n, Puerto Natales ☎ 61/412-125.

EASTER ISLAND

10

FODOR'S CHOICE
Ranu Raraku, quarry for *moais* (stone statues)

HIGHLY RECOMMENDED

HOTELS   Aloha Nui
Hotel Gomero
Hotel Otai
Tadeo and Lili

SIGHTS   Ahu Tongariki, archaeological site with moais
Orongo, 17th-century ceremonial village
Playa Anakena, beach with moais

By Mark
Sullivan

Updated by
Cheryl Stanton

BELCHING OUT GREAT COLUMNS OF SMOKE, the volcano pushed its way out of the Pacific Ocean about 2.5 million years ago. Poike's anger had barely subsided when it was joined by two fiery siblings, Rano Kau and Terevaka. The triangular landmass that formed between the trio is what is known today as Easter Island.

The most isolated island in the world—2,985 km (1,850 mi) from its nearest populated neighbor—was uninhabited until around 1,500 years ago. That's when, according to local legend, King Hotu Matu'a and his extended family landed on a beach on the northern shore. Exactly where they came from is still a mystery. Norwegian archaeologist Thor Heyerdahl, asserting that the fine masonry found on the island resembles that of the Incas, believed they came from South America. To prove the journey was possible, Heyerdahl set sail in 1947 from Peru in a balsa wood boat called the *Kon-Tiki*. Most archaeologists, however, believe the original inhabitants were of Polynesian descent, citing similarities in language and culture.

Its earliest inhabitants called the island Te Pito O Te Henua—the navel of the world. They cleared vast forests for cultivation and fished the surrounding waters for tuna and swordfish. As the population grew, they moved from the caves along the shore into tight-knit communities of *hare paengas,* or boat-shape houses. To communicate they created *rongo-rongo,* a beautiful script and the only written language in all of Polynesia. But their greatest achievement was the hundreds of sad-eyed stone statues called *moais* they erected to honor their ancestors.

Dutch explorer Jacob Roggeveen, the first European to encounter the island, gave it the name most people recognize when he landed here on Easter Sunday in 1722. Here he found a thriving community of thousands. But when British Captain James Cook anchored here in 1774, he found only several hundred people so impoverished they could barely afford to part with a few sweet potatoes. What's more, many of the moais had been toppled from their foundations. What happened during those 50 years? Archaeologists believe overpopulation and overdevelopment devastated the island. Warfare broke out between clans, who knocked down the moais belonging to their opponents.

This period pales in comparison to the devastation the island suffered in 1862, when slave traders from Peru captured more than 1,000 islanders. Forced to work in guano mines on the mainland, most of them died of hunger or disease. Religious leaders interceded, and the few that remained alive were returned to their island. They spread smallpox to the rest of the population, killing all but 110 people. Everyone who could read the rongo-rongo script died, and to this day no one has been able to decipher the language.

With the collapse of Spanish influence in South America, several countries began to covet Easter Island. In 1888 a Chilean ship raced westward and claimed the island before France or Britain could do so. Chile leased the entire island to a British sheep company, which restricted the islanders from venturing outside the little town of Hanga Roa. The sheep company left in 1953, but life didn't really begin to improve for islanders until an airport was constructed in 1967. The promise of large-scale tourism encouraged the Chilean government to make much-needed improvements on the island.

Tourism is now the biggest industry on Rapa Nui—the name locals give the island (known as Isla de Pascua by mainland Chileans). Most of the 3,500 residents are involved in this endeavor in some way. The residents, most of whom are descended from the original inhabitants, are extremely proud of the island's past. Ask anyone here about Poike, the volcano that poked its head out of the Pacific so long ago, and they'll probably tell you the whole tale.

EXPLORING EASTER ISLAND

An adventurous spirit is a prerequisite for visiting Easter Island. It's possible to sign up for a package tour, but you'd visit only a handful of the sights. To fully experience the island, hire a private guide. Even better, rent a four-wheel-drive vehicle or a mountain bike and head out on your own. Tour buses often bypass fascinating destinations that are off the beaten path. Even in the height of the high season you can find secluded spots.

It's nearly impossible to get lost on Easter Island which is just 22 km (14 mi) from end to end. Two major thoroughfares—a gravel road that winds its way around the coastline past most of the major archaeological sites, and a paved road that leads across the island to the beaches—traverse the island; both meet near Playa Anakena.

About the Restaurants

If you spot an unassuming place filled with Rapa Nui residents, chances are you'll find delicious and inexpensive food. Barbecue of all types, especially lamb, is extremely popular. As this is an island, seafood appears on nearly every menu. Don't hesitate to ask which type is the freshest—the tuna may have been caught that morning. Meals are often accompanied by fresh fruit, especially bananas, papayas, and intensely sweet pineapples, or *camote* (sweet potato).

Hotels on the island include breakfast in the room rate and sometimes lunch and dinner. However, if you plan to spend your days exploring the island, ask your hotel to prepare a picnic for you or drop by a *supermercado* (supermarket) for provisions.

About the Hotels

Easter Island has two types of accommodations: *hoteles* and *residenciales*. A hotel is built specifically to house many tourists, while a residencial is often a private home with a few rooms added to accommodate guests. If you can't get by without amenities such as a swimming pool, opt for a hotel. You'll miss out, however, on the chance to stay with a local family at a residencial—the best way to learn about life on Rapa Nui.

All accommodations on the island will arrange for someone to welcome you at the airport with a garland of flowers. It's a good thing, as most places would be hard to find because Hanga Roa doesn't post the street names. Breakfast and airport transfer are included almost everywhere. Most places accept credit cards, but many add a surcharge (around 4%) because it often takes months for them to be reimbursed. It's best to settle on a rate beforehand and bring travelers checks. It's often possible to negotiate significant discounts off-season, including the shoulder months of November, December, and March.

Although it's possible to show up on the island without a reservation—owners of residenciales with spare rooms crowd the airport—it's best to reserve in advance, especially in January and February. Many flights arrive late in the evening, and the last thing you'll want to do is search for a place to stay.

Numbers in the text correspond to numbers in the margin and on the Easter Island and Hanga Roa maps.

If you have
3 days

In three days, you won't see everything on Easter Island, but you can visit the major sights. Spend your first full day in **Hanga Roa** ❶–❺ ►, stopping by the Iglesia Hanga Roa, the Cementerio, and the Museo Antropológico Sebastián Englert. Finish the day with sunset at Tahai. On your second day visit the volcano of **Rano Kau** ❼, where you'll find the ceremonial village of **Orongo** ❽. In the afternoon head inland to the small quarry of **Puna Pau** ⓫ and the seven moais of **Ahu Akivi** ⓬. Tour the coastal road on your last day, visiting the hundreds of moais in the quarry at **Ranu Raraku** ⓲ and the 15-moai lineup at **Ahu Tongariki** ⓳.

10

If you have
5 days

Follow the first day and the morning of the second day of the itinerary above. In the afternoon check out the cave paintings of Ana Kai Tangata, then take the airport road out to Ahu Vinapu and ponder its Inca-like stonework. On the third day follow the coastal route to **Ahu Akivi** ⓬ and **Puna Pau** ⓫. Save the southern coast for your fourth day: visit **Ahu Vaihu** ⓯, **Ahu Akahanga** ⓰, and **Ahu Hanga Tetenga** ⓱ before heading out to **Ranu Raraku** ⓲ and **Ahu Tongariki** ⓳. On your final day visit the beaches of **Playa Ovahe** ㉒ and **Playa Anakena** ㉓, home of some of the island's most striking moais.

If you have
7 days

If you're lucky enough to have a week here you can travel far off the beaten path. Follow the five-day itinerary above, and then reserve a day for snorkeling around the spectacular islets of Motu Nui and Motu Iti, just off the southwestern coast. If you'd rather stay on dry land, consider a hike around the island's northern coast. Another day should be set aside for a little spelunking—visit the hidden garden of **Ana Te Pahu** ⓭ and the eerie **Ana O Keke and Ana O Neru** ⓴, where young women were sequestered until their weddings.

WHAT IT COSTS In pesos (in thousands)				
$$$$	**$$$**	**$$**	**$**	**¢**
RESTAURANTS over 11	8–11	5–8	2.5–5	under 2.5
HOTELS over 105	75–105	45–75	15–45	under 15

Restaurant prices are for a main course at dinner. Hotel prices are for a double room in high season, excluding tax.

Timing

Most people visit in summer, between December and March. Many time their visit to coincide with Tapati Rapa Nui, a two-week celebration with music and dancing that starts at the end of January. Temperatures can soar above 27°C (81°F) in summer. In winter, temperatures reach an average of 22°C (72°F), although brisk winds can often make it feel much cooler. Be sure to bring a light jacket. The wettest months are June and July.

Hanga Roa

Hugging the coast on the southwest side of the island is the village of Hanga Roa. About 3,500 people, many of Polynesian descent, make this tangle of streets their home. Few live outside the village because the bulk of the island forms the Rapa Nui National Park. The population is beginning to spread out, however, as the Chilean government cedes more land to the locals.

The two main roads in Hanga Roa intersect a block from the ocean at a small plaza. Avenida Atamu Tekena, which runs the length of the village, is where you'll find most of the tourist-oriented businesses. Avenida Te Pito O Te Henua begins near the fishing pier and extends two blocks uphill to the church. These two roads are paved, but most others in town are gravel.

Buildings are not numbered and signs are nonexistent (street names are sometimes painted on curbstones), so finding a particular building can be frustrating at first. Locals will give directions from landmarks, so it's not a bad idea to take a walk around town as soon as you arrive so you can get your bearings.

a good tour

Start at the **Iglesia Hanga Roa** ❶ ⌐, the squat colonial church near the center of Hanga Roa. Peek inside to see the carved wooden statues that put a Polynesian spin on traditional Christian iconography. Walk two blocks downhill on Avenida Te Pito O Te Henua to reach the **Caleta Hanga Roa** ❷, the town's little fishing pier. To the north along the coast is the colorful **Cementerio** ❸. Head east on Petero Atamu for a block, then turn left and walk north on Avenida Atamu Tekena. On your left is the **Museo Antropológico Sebastián Englert** ❹, a museum that takes a fascinating look at the island's history. From here it's a short walk to **Tahai** ❺, a ceremonial site where impressive moais stand with their backs to the sea.

TIMING   If you decide to walk, this tour will take most of the day. If you drive, you can take in all these sights in two or three hours. Either way, try to plan your tour so you arrive at Tahai in time to watch the sunset.

What to See

❷ **Caleta Hanga Roa.** Colorful fishing boats bob up and down in the water at Hanga Roa's tiny pier. Here you may see fisherfolk hauling in the day's catch of tuna, or a boatload of divers returning from a trip to the neighboring islets. Nearby is **Ahu Tautira**, a ceremonial platform with two restored moais. ⊠ *Av. Policarpo Toro at Av. Te Pito O Te Henua.*

❸ **Cementerio.** Hanga Roa's colorful walled cemetery occupies a prime position overlooking the Pacific and is unlike any other in the world. Its overgrown flower beds and brightly painted tombstones lend the cemetery a cheerful feeling. The central cross is erected on a *pukao*, the reddish headdress that once adorned a moai. ⊠ *Av. Policarpo Toro at Petero Atamu.*

⌐ ❶ **Iglesia Hanga Roa.** Missionaries brought Christianity to Rapa Nui, but the Rapa Nui people brought their own beliefs to Christianity. In this colonial church you'll find the two religions intertwined. The figure on the cross above the altar is obviously Christ, but it looks surprisingly similar to many ancient carvings found on the island. A bird in the hand of the statue of St. Francis of Assisi strongly resembles the god Make-Make. Try to visit on Sunday morning, as the hymns have a distinctly Polynesian flavor. ⊠ *Av. Te Pito O Te Henua.*

❹ **Museo Antropológico Sebastián Englert.** The museum, named for a German priest who dedicated his life to improving conditions on Rapa Nui,

Archaeology

Even if Easter Island held not a single moai, there would still be plenty to see. Hundreds of well-preserved petroglyphs stand on the cliffs near the ancient village of Orongo, and a few are near the ceremonial sights of Ahu Tongariki and Ahu Te Pito Kura. Cave paintings can be viewed at Ana Kai Tangata. More than 300 of the stone platforms called *ahus* line the coast, and many are worth exploring.

10

Shopping

Local handicrafts such as miniature moais, shell jewelry, carved wooden bowls, and masks are sold on Easter Island. Your first opportunity to shop comes the minute you step into the airport, where dozens of vendors hawk miniature moais in the form of paperweights or earrings. Just outside the airport is a minimarket with lots of souvenir stalls. There are also plenty of shops in Hanga Roa along Avenida Atamu Tekena and Avenida Te Pito O Te Henua. Bargaining is expected, but don't expect to knock much off the price.

---

focuses on daily life on the island. Explanations on how the islanders caught fish and cultivated the land accompany exhibits of ancient tools. Displays describe the various theories about how the moais were transported and set upright. Here, too, is the only female moai on the island, as well as a coral eye found during the reconstruction of an ahu at Playa Anakena. Most of the text is in Spanish, but a guide will be happy to explain the displays. ⊠ *Tahai s/n* ☎ *32/551–020* ⊕ *www.museorapanui.cl* ✉ *1,000 pesos* ☉ *Weekdays 9:30–12:30 and 2–5:30, weekends 9:30–12:30.*

❺ **Tahai.** The ancient ceremonial center of Tahai, where much of the annual Tapati Rapa Nui festival takes place, was restored in 1968 by archaeologist William Mulloy, who is buried nearby. Tahai consists of three separate ahus facing a wide plaza that once served as a community meeting place. You can still find the foundations of the boat-shape dwellings where religious and social leaders once lived. In the center is Ahu Tahai, which holds a single weathered moai. To the left is Ahu Vai Uri, where five moais, one little more than a stump, cast their stony gaze over the island. Also here is Ahu Kote Riku, holding a splendid moai with its red topknot intact; this is the only moai on the island to have had its gleaming white eyes restored. These are the only moais standing on the western coast, so this is an especially good place to come to see the blazing yellow sunsets. ⊠ *On the coast near Museo Antropológico Sebastián Englert.*

The Western Circuit

On the western tip of the island are the cave paintings of Ana Kai Tangata and the petroglyphs near the ceremonial village of Orongo. You'll also be treated to a spectacular view of the crater lake inside the long-dormant volcano of Rano Kau.

a good tour

Heading south from Hanga Roa you'll soon reach **Ana Kai Tangata** ❻ ►, a shallow cave in a protected cove on the coast. Look up to the cave ceiling to see the remains of reddish paintings of birds. Continue south and the road suddenly winds uphill to the crater of **Rano Kau** ❼. On its rim is the partially restored ceremonial village of **Orongo** ❽, where islanders worshiped the god Make-Make and where you'll see petroglyphs

Easter Island

PACIFIC OCEAN

KEY

▲ Start of itinerary

Ahu Te Peu ⑭

Ana Te Pahu ⑬

Ahu Akivi ⑫

Maunga Terevaka ▲

Maunga Kuma ▲

Maunga Ohu'u ▲

Puna Pau ⑪

⑩ Ahu Huri a Urenga

Maunga Orito ▲

⑨ Ahu Vinapu

Hanga Roa ▲ ① – ⑤ *see detail map*

Ana Kai Tangata ▲

⑥

Rano Kau ▲

Orongo ⑧

⑦

Motu Nui

Maunga Pui ▲

Maunga Ana Marama ▲

Playa Anakena ㉓

Playa Ovahe ㉒

Ahu Te Pito Kura ㉑

Ana O Keke and Ana O Neru ⑳

Puakatiki ▲

Ranu Raraku ⑱

Ahu Tongariki ⑲

Ahu Hanga Tetenga ⑰

Ahu Akahanga ⑯

Ahu Vaihu ⑮

0 — 2 miles
0 — 3 km

of birdlike creatures carved into the rock. Take the Avenida Hotu Matu'a southeast to **Ahu Vinapu** ⑨, which has some of the best stonework on the island. Head back toward town, then turn northeast on the paved road leading across the island. You'll soon pass **Ahu Huri a Urenga** ⑩, a solitary moai noted for its four hands. A sign on the left marks the turnoff to **Puna Pau** ⑪, the small quarry where the rust-color topknots for the moais were carved. Several miles farther north is **Ahu Akivi** ⑫, where seven moais stare toward the sea. Continuing down the same road you'll have to look hard for the entrance to the cave dwellings of **Ana Te Pahu** ⑬. Finally, as you reach the coast, you'll come to the ruins of the boat-shape houses at **Ahu Te Peu** ⑭.

TIMING   Because much of this tour is over rough gravel roads, it will take most of the day. Consider stopping for lunch in Hanga Roa after visiting Ahu Vinapu, or pack a lunch and picnic on the rim of Ranu Rao and take in its unmatched views of the crater.

What to See

⑫ **Ahu Akivi.** These seven stoic moais—believed to represent explorers sent on a reconnaissance mission by King Hotu Matu'a—are among the few that gaze out to sea. Researchers say they actually face a ceremonial site. Archaeologists William Mulloy and Gonzalo Figueroa restored the moais in 1960. ⊠ *Past Puna Pau on a gravel road branching north from the paved road to Playa Anakena.*

⑩ **Ahu Huri a Urenga.** One of the few ahus to be erected inland, Ahu Huri a Urenga appears to be oriented toward the winter solstice. Its lonely moai is exceptional because it has two sets of hands, the second carved above the first. Researchers believe this is because the lower set was damaged during transport to the ahu. ⊠ *3 km (2 mi) from Av. Hotu Matu'a on the paved road to Playa Anakena.*

⑭ **Ahu Te Peu.** As at Ahu Vinapu, the tightly fitting stones at the unrestored Ahu Te Peu recall the best work of the Incas. The foundations for several boat-shape houses, including one that measures 40 m (131 ft) from end to end, are clearly visible. From here you can begin the six-hour hike around the island's northern coast to Playa Anakena. ⊠ *Past Ana Te Pahu on a gravel road branching north from the paved road to Playa Anakena.*

⑨ **Ahu Vinapu.** The appeal of this crumbled ahu isn't apparent until you notice the fine masonry on the rear wall. Anyone who has seen the ancient Inca city of Machu Picchu in Peru will note the similar stonework. This led Norwegian archaeologist Thor Heyerdahl to theorize that Rapa Nui's original inhabitants may have sailed here from South America. Most others disagree, believing that the first settlers were Polynesian. The moais here still lay where they were toppled, one staring sadly up at the sky. ⊠ *Southeast of Hanga Roa on Av. Hotu Matu'a.*

▶ ⑥ **Ana Kai Tangata.** A small sign just past the entrance of Hotel Iorana points toward Ana Kai Tangata, a seldom-visited cavern on the coast that holds the island's only cave paintings. Directly over your head are images of red and white birds in flight. Dramatic cliffs shelter the cave from the crashing surf. ⊠ *South of Hanga Roa.*

⑬ **Ana Te Pahu.** A grove of banana trees marks the entrance to these underground caverns that once served as dwellings. Partly shielded from the blazing sun, a secret garden of tropical plants thrives in the fissure where the caves begin. Below ground is a passage leading to a second cave where the sunlight streams through a huge hole. ⊠ *Past Ahu Akivi on a gravel road branching north from the paved road to Playa Anakena.*

★ **8** **Orongo.** The 48 oval huts of this ceremonial village, constructed in 1600 and used by locals until 1866, were occupied only during the ceremony honoring the god Make-Make. The high point of the annual event was a competition in which prominent villagers designated servants to paddle small rafts to Motu Nui, the largest of three islets just off the coast. The first servant to find an egg of the sooty tern, a bird nesting on the islets, would swim back with the prize tucked in a special headdress. His master would become the *tangata manu,* or birdman, for the next year. He was honored by being confined to a cave until the following year's ceremony. Dozens of petroglyphs depicting birdlike creatures cover nearby boulders along the rim of Rano Kau. There's a ranger station at the entrance to Orongo, where you pay admission to the Rapa Nui National Park. ⊠ *South of Hanga Roa on Rano Kau* 🖾 *750 pesos.*

11 **Puna Pau.** Scoria, the reddish stone used to make the topknots for the moais, was once excavated at this quarry. About two dozen finished topknots can still be found here. The views of the island from the top of the hill are well worth the climb. ⊠ *Off a gravel road branching north from the paved road to Playa Anakena.*

7 **Rano Kau.** This huge volcano on the southern tip of the island affords wonderful views of Hanga Roa. The crater, which measures a mile across, holds a lake nearly covered over by bright green reeds. The opposite side of the crater has crumbled a bit, revealing a crescent of the deep blue ocean beyond. ⊠ *South of Hanga Roa.*

The Southeastern Circuit

Most of the archaeological sites on the island line the southeastern coast. Driving along the coast you'll pass many ahus, all of them completely untouched. Busloads of tourists hurry past most of these on their

MYSTERIES OF THE MOAIS

WHEN EUROPEAN EXPLORERS **FIRST SPOTTED** Easter Island in 1722, they were bewildered by the dozens of massive stone heads that lined the coast. Just how the small band of islanders he encountered could have constructed these monoliths mystified Dutch explorer Jacob Roggeveen. "The stone images at first caused us to be struck with astonishment," Roggeveen wrote in his log, "because we could not comprehend how it was possible that these people, who are devoid of heavy thick timber for making any machines, as well as strong ropes, nevertheless had been able to erect such images."

When British captain James Cook anchored here in 1774, he was also impressed by the "stupendous figures" that had been "erected in so masterly a manner." But he noted in his journal of the expedition that many had been knocked from their pedestals. By the time French admiral Abel Dupetit-Thouars visited in 1838, almost all had been toppled. Now the question was not only how and why the massive carvings had been erected, but also how and why they had been destroyed.

After hundreds of years of study, we still know very little about these stone statues called moais. Archaeological evidence suggests that most of these statues, apparently memorials to ancestors, were constructed during a period of fevered activity between 1400 and 1600. Most were erected on ahus, or stone platforms, along the coast. All but a few come from Ranu Raraku, the quarry where 397 moais can still be seen today. By studying those left behind archaeologists know that most were carved in a horizontal position, and that once finished they were moved to a nearby trench where they stood until moved to their ahus.

But how were they transported? The more than 90 moais that were abandoned en route provide few clues. Many are broken, but most are intact. Most are facedown, but a few gaze up at the sky. Although theories abound, most archaeologists believe they were either dragged on wooden platforms or rolled along on top of tree trunks. It's not clear, though, how they could have been moved several miles without damaging the delicate features that were carved at the quarry.

Once they arrived at their ahus, how were the moais lifted into place? In 1955, Norwegian archaeologist Thor Heyerdahl and a team of a dozen men were able to raise the single moai on Ahu Ature Huki in 18 days. In 1960 archaeologists William Mulloy and Gonzalo Figueroa and their men raised the seven moais at Ahu Akivi. They struggled for a month to lift the first, but the last took only a week. Both teams used the same method—lifting them with a stone ramp and wooden poles. This technique would be unwieldy for lifting the larger moais, however. It also fails to explain how the pukaos, or topknots, were placed on many of the heads.

And why were the moais destroyed? The reason, ironically enough, may have been that creating the moais required a tremendous amount of natural resources. Most of the palm trees that had once covered the island were felled to move the moais. This had a devastating effect on the island—there soon was little wood for constructing dwellings or boats. Fuel for fires was increasingly hard to find. Crops were ruined as erosion washed away the soil. Archaeological evidence suggests internecine battles developed between clans that had once worked together peacefully. Bloody battles ensued, during which members of one clan toppled the moais belonging to another. In a period of about 100 years, the islanders themselves laid waste to their greatest artistic achievement. The battles eventually ended, but no more moais were ever erected.

—Mark Sullivan

way to Ranu Raraku, the quarry where 397 moais wait in stony silence, and Ahu Tongariki, where 15 moais stand in line.

The coastal road starts out paved but soon disintegrates into dusty gravel, so make sure you rent a four-wheel-drive vehicle. Heading east on the road you'll soon encounter a string of unrestored ahus—including **Ahu Vaihu** ⑮ ▶, **Ahu Akahanga** ⑯, and **Ahu Hanga Tetenga** ⑰—all worth exploring. From miles away the dome-shape volcano of **Ranu Raraku** ⑱ is visible. As you approach, look for scores of unfinished moais covering its upper reaches. From Ranu Raraku you can see the 15 stern-faced moais of **Ahu Tongariki** ⑲. The coastal road veers north, soon passing the bare slopes of the volcano Poike. A dirt path meandering over the hill leads to **Ana O Keke and Ana O Neru** ⑳, the Caves of the Virgins. The largest moai ever erected on an ahu lies shattered at **Ahu Te Pito Kura** ㉑, on the northern coast. At the end of the road you reach the island's two beaches, **Playa Ovahe** ㉒ and **Playa Anakena** ㉓.

TIMING   Depending on how many sights you visit, this tour will take at least a day. If you have time you might want to break it into two separate tours, visiting the sights on the southern coast on one day and those on the northern coast the next. If you want to spend more time at the beach, consider starting the tour at Playa Anakena and working your way backward.

What to See

⑯ **Ahu Akahanga.** Tradition holds that this is the burial site of Hotu Matu'a, the first of the island's rulers. The 12 moais lying facedown on the ground once stood on the four long stone platforms. ⊠ *2 km (1 mi) east of Ahu Viahu on the coastal road.*

⑰ **Ahu Hanga Tetenga.** The largest moai ever transported to a platform, measuring nearly 10 m (33 ft), lies here in pieces. The finishing touches were never made to its eye sockets, so researchers believe it fell while being erected. ⊠ *3 km (2 mi) east of Ahu Akahanga on the coastal road.*

㉑ **Ahu Te Pito Kura.** The largest moai ever successfully erected—a fraction of an inch shorter than the one at Ahu Hanga Tetenga—stands at Ahu Te Pito Kura. Also here is the perfectly round stone (believed to represent the navel of the world) that Hotu Matu'a is said to have brought with him when he arrived on the island. ⊠ *9 km (6 mi) north of Ahu Tongariki on the coastal road.*

★ ⑲ **Ahu Tongariki.** One of the island's most breathtaking sights is Ahu Tongariki, where 15 moais stand side by side on a 60-m-long (200-ft-long) ahu, the longest ever made. Tongariki was painstakingly restored after being destroyed by a massive tidal wave in 1960. The moais here, some whitened with a layer of sea salt, have holes in their extended earlobes that might have once been filled with obsidian. They face an expansive ceremonial area where you can find petroglyphs of turtles and fish. ⊠ *2 km (1 mi) east of Ranu Raraku on the coastal road.*

▶ ⑮ **Ahu Vaihu.** Eight fallen moai lay facedown in front of this ahu, the first you'll encounter on the southern coastal road. Three reddish topknots are strewn around them. Even after the ahu was destroyed this continued to be a burial chamber, evidenced by the rocks piled on the toppled moais. ⊠ *11 km (7 mi) southeast of Hanga Roa on the coastal road.*

⑳ **Ana O Keke and Ana O Neru.** Legend has it that young women awaiting marriage were kept here in the Caves of the Virgins so that their skin would remain as pale as possible. You need an experienced guide to find the caverns, which are hidden in the cliffs along the coast. Take a flashlight to see the haunting petroglyphs of flowers and fish thought to have been carved by these girls. ✉ *Reached via a dirt road through a ranch on Poike.*

★ ㉓ **Playa Anakena.** Here, beside the swaying palm trees, stand the island's best-preserved moais on **Ahu Nau Nau**. Buried for centuries in the sand, these five statues were protected from the elements. The minute details of the carving—delicate lips, flared nostrils, gracefully curved ears—are still visible. On their backs, fine lines represent belts. It was here during the 1978 restoration that a white coral eye was found, leading researchers to speculate that all moais once had them; the eye is now on display at the Museo Antropológico Sebastián Englert.

Staring at Ahu Nau Nau is a solitary moai on nearby **Ahu Ature Huki.** This statue was the first moai to be replaced on his ahu. Thor Heyerdahl conducted this experiment in 1955 to see if the techniques islanders said were used to erect the moais could work. It took 12 islanders nearly three weeks to lift the moai into position using rocks and wooden poles. ✉ *1 km (½ mi) west of Playa Ovahe.*

㉒ **Playa Ovahe.** This beautiful stretch of pinkish sand is the island's best-kept secret, passed over by most tourists in favor of nearby Playa Anakena. The pile of volcanic rocks jutting out into the water is actually a ruined ahu. ✉ *10 km (6 mi) north of Ahu Tongariki on the coastal road.*

⑱ **Ranu Raraku.** When it comes to moais, this is the mother lode. Some 397 moais have been counted at the quarry of this long-extinct volcano, both on the outer rim and clustered inside the crater. More than 150 are unfinished, some little more than faces in the rock. Among these is El Gigante, a monster measuring 22 m (72 ft). It's twice the height of the second tallest, which crumbled while being erected at Ahu Hanga Tetenga. Also here is Moai Tukuturi, the only moai in a kneeling position; it's thought to predate most others. ✉ *5 km (3 mi) east of Ahu Hanga Tetenga on the coastal road.*

Fodor'sChoice
★

WHERE TO EAT

$$$$ ✕ **La Taverne du Pêcheur.** The dishes at this quaint little French eating house occupying a prime position on the corner of Caleta Hanga Roa are undoubtedly some of the most innovative on the island—and the most expensive. Try the *atún con salsa Roquefort* (tuna with Roquefort sauce) or *ostiones gratinado* (scallops au gratin). Catch the French owner in a good mood and he'll be more than happy to discuss his wine list. ✉ *Caleta de Hanga Roa* ☎ *32/100–619* ▤ *No credit cards.*

$$$–$$$$ ✕ **Cuerito Regalon.** The friendly proprietor Luis will happily tell you about the dishes made from the day's fresh catches—perhaps a tasty grilled tuna steak or *rape rape* (a small lobster). Just across the street from the Feria Municipal, this plant-filled restaurant fronts a supermarket; neatly laid out tables afford great views of Hanga Roa's busiest street. ✉ *Av. Atamu Tekena s/n* ☎ *32/551–232* ▤ *No credit cards.*

$$–$$$ ✕ **Orongo.** When the owner Raul is around, this small seafood restaurant, alongside the hotel of the same name and set back from the island's main thoroughfare, is exceedingly popular (when he's out of town, the restaurant closes, so you may want to call ahead). He whips up all the local fresh catches of the day—toremo and kana kana (both are meaty white fish), and tuna—and serves them with fragrant sauces of his own invention. The sauce you order might include caramel, cassava, or white wine, among other ingredients. ✉ *Av. Atamu Tekena s/n* ☎ *32/100–294* ▤ *No credit cards.*

$$–$$$ ✕ **Playa Pea.** With its dazzling view of the bay, this seafood restaurant is a great place to catch the sunset. Much of the fish is bought at the nearby *caleta* (fishing pier), so it couldn't be fresher. The standout on the menu is the lemony atún *con salsa alcaparras* (tuna with caper sauce). ⊠ *Av. Policarpo Toro s/n* ☎ *32/100–382* ▭ *No credit cards.*

$$ ✕ **Iorana.** A large carved wooden fish adorns the entrance to this simple restaurant; you can't miss it. The service is a little slow but the seafood dishes are wholesome, tasty, and large—so a good appetite is essential. Ask for the special of the day, and you can't go too far wrong. ⊠ *Av. Atamu Tekena s/n* ☎ *32/100–265* ▭ *No credit cards.*

$$ ✕ **KopaKavana.** Twice a week (usually Tuesdays and Fridays, but call ahead) this large, airy restaurant hosts the dance group Polinesia, so while you enjoy a tasty fish steak, you can marvel at the flexible limbs of these Rapa Nui (note that there's a cover charge of $15 to see the performance). The menu, written in Japanese, Spanish, and English, includes seafood dishes, fried bananas, and sweet potatoes. Ornate shell lamp shades hang from the ceiling, adding a Polynesian touch. ⊠ *Av. Te Pito O Te Henua s/n* ☎ *32/100–447 or 32/551–176* ▭ *No credit cards.*

$$ ✕ **La Tinita.** Little more than a handful of tables on a shady front porch, this restaurant near Plaza Policarpo Toro is a pleasant place to stop for lunch. The dishes are simple but good. Try the atún *a la plancha* (grilled tuna) or *pollo asado* (roast chicken). ⊠ *Av. Te Pito O Te Henua s/n* ☎ *32/100–813* ▭ *No credit cards.*

$–$$ ✕ **Avarei Pua.** You won't leave here hungry—the portions are big enough for two. The barbecue dishes are simple but extremely satisfying. Delicious dishes such as grilled pork or tuna are served with a mixed salad flavored with lemon juice. From the terrace near the dock you can sip a pisco sour while watching the locals saunter by, against the backdrop of the crashing waves of the Pacific. ⊠ *Av. Policarpo Toro s/n* ☎ *32/100–431* ▭ *No credit cards.*

WHERE TO STAY

$$$$ ▥ **Hotel Taha Tai.** Open and airy, this hotel seems to have sunlight streaming in from everywhere. The intimate bar has a view of the ocean, as does the expansive dining room, which has a tropical feeling lent by its soaring arched ceiling and lazily spinning fans. Guests gather here or in the garden to share the sunset. Rooms in the newer building are larger than the older ones in the bungalows, but all are clean and comfortable. ⊠ *Av. Apina Nui s/n* ☎ *32/551–192, 32/551–193, or 32/551–194* ⊕ *www.hotel-tahatai.co.cl* ⋌ *40 rooms* ⌂ *Restaurant, room service, some in-room safes, pool, bar, laundry service, Internet, airport shuttle, car rental, travel services; no TV in some rooms* ▭ *AE, DC, MC, V* ⍉ *BP.*

$$$–$$$$ ▥ **Hotel Hanga Roa.** Part of the Panamericana Hoteles chain, this hotel— one of the oldest on the island—attracts lots of tour groups. The common areas, from the spacious lobby to the more intimate bar, are comfortable. The newer bungalows, with private terraces overlooking the ocean, are clean and bright. The older rooms, however, have seen better days. Make sure you ask for a room with a sea view. ⊠ *Av. Pont s/n* ☎ *32/100–299* ☎ *32/100–695* ⊕ *www.panamericanahoteles.cl* ⋌ *90 rooms, 1 suite* ⌂ *Restaurant, fans, some in-room safes, some minibars, pool, bar, laundry service, Internet, airport shuttle, car rental; no a/c* ▭ *AE, DC, MC, V* ⍉ *BP.*

$$$–$$$$ ▥ **Hotel Hotu Matua.** Set well back from the coast is this secluded accommodation that played host to former Chilean president Eduardo Frei. A small sitting area in each guest room overlooks the pool and surrounding tropical vegetation. The owner's collection of artifacts rivals that of the island's museum. ⊠ *Av. Pont s/n* ☎ *32/100–242* ⊟ *32/100–445* ⋌ *65*

rooms, 5 suites ⚖ *Dining room, minibars, pool, bar, recreation room, shops, laundry service, airport shuttle, car rental, travel services* ▤ *AE, DC, MC, V* ❡ *BP.*

$$$–$$$$ ▦ **Hotel Iorana.** Perched high on a cliff that juts into the ocean, this hotel entices its visitors with unmatched views. From your private terrace you can hear the sound of the waves crashing on the rocks. The rooms are simply furnished and have generously proportioned baths. Masses of ruby-red hibiscus flowers grow at one end of the small triangular pool, making this the perfect place to relax with a fruity cocktail. The hotel, which is popular with tour groups, is some 2 km (1 mi) south of town, so you may feel a little isolated. ⊠ *Av. Ana Magaro s/n* ☎ *32/100–608* 🖷 *32/100–312* ⊕ *www.ioranahotel.com* ⌦ *50 rooms, 2 suites* ⚖ *Restaurant, some fans, in-room safes, some minibars, tennis court, pool, bar, laundry service, meeting room, airport shuttle, car rental, travel services; no a/c in some rooms, no TV in some rooms* ▤ *AE, DC, MC, V* ❡ *BP.*

★ **$$** ▦ **Aloha Nui.** One of the most charming accommodations on Easter Island, Aloha Nui begins to feel like home even before you can unpack. The genial owner, Maria Reina Pacomio Paoa, makes you feel very welcome, and though you'll start out in the dining room, it probably won't be long before you're in the kitchen having breakfast with the family. The generously proportioned rooms, in a separate building behind the main house, look out on the palm-shaded gardens. ⊠ *Av. Atamu Tekena s/n* ☎ *32/100–274* ⌦ *6 rooms* ⚖ *Dining room, bar, airport shuttle, car rental, travel services; no a/c, no room phones, no room TVs* ▤ *MC, V* ❡ *CP.*

$$ ▦ **Chez Maria Gorretti.** The beautiful garden and lovely airy, plant-filled dining room are the main attractions of this guest house on the northern edge of town. All the rooms have sliding doors that open onto clumps of banana trees and lush vines that wrap around the trunks of papaya trees. ⊠ *Av. Atamu Tekena s/n* ☎ *32/100–459* ⌦ *18 rooms* ⚖ *Dining room, bar, horseback riding, laundry service, Internet, airport shuttle, car rental, travel services; no a/c, no room phones, no room TVs* ▤ *DC, MC, V* ❡ *BP.*

★ **$$** ▦ **Hotel Gomero.** A long drive lined by palm and papaya trees leads to this charming small hotel. Guests gather in the comfortable dining room, which has rattan furniture and beautifully carved wooden columns. The guest rooms, some with handcrafted furnishings, have private terraces overlooking a beautifully attended garden. The owners, a multilingual Austrian–Rapa Nui couple, run a tight ship, so everything is spotless. ⊠ *Av. Tu'u Koihu s/n* ☎ *32/100–313* 🖷 *32/100–591* ⊕ *www.hotelgomero.com* ⌦ *13 rooms* ⚖ *Dining room, fans, minibars, pool, bar, laundry service, Internet, airport shuttle, car rental, travel services; no a/c, no room phones, no room TVs* ▤ *DC, MC, V* ❡ *BP.*

$$ ▦ **Hotel Manavai.** This friendly lodging's comfortable, spacious rooms, with large bathrooms, have been ingeniously constructed with walls of chipboard, making them rustic and cozy. Rooms open out onto a garden of flourishing vegetation and a small pool. Hotel Manavai sits on one of Hanga Roa's main thoroughfares. ⊠ *Av. Te Pito o Te Henua* ☎ *32/100–670* 🖷 *32/100–658* ⌦ *30 rooms* ⚖ *Dining room, fans, pool, bar, shop, airport shuttle, car rental, travel services; no a/c, no room phones, no room TVs* ▤ *AE, DC, MC, V* ❡ *CP.*

$$ ▦ **Hotel Manutara.** Palm trees tower over this low-slung resort on the southern edge of Hanga Roa. The hotel invites you to relax, whether reclining in a lounge chair by the bean-shape pool or reading in one of the overstuffed sofas in the sunny lobby. Especially nice is the shaded dining room, which has rattan tables covered with tropical-print tablecloths. The homey rooms overlook the lush gardens overflowing with red and orange hibiscus. ⊠ *Av. Hotu Matu'a s/n* ☎ *32/100–297* 🖷 *32/100–768* ⌦ *26 rooms* ⚖ *Dining room, room service, fans, pool, bar,* *lounge, shop, laundry service, car rental, travel services; no a/c ▣ DC, MC, V* ⍩ *BP.*

★ **$$** ▦ **Hotel Otai.** Although the hotel is right in the center of town, its beautiful gardens make you feel like you're miles from anywhere. From the flower-scented deck surrounding the pool you can catch a glimpse of the sea. Pretty wicker furniture fills the spacious rooms, which open out onto shady wooden verandas. The wood-ceilinged dining room is cool and quiet. ⊠ *Av. Te Pito O Te Henua s/n* ☎ *32/100–250* 🖷 *32/100–482* 🛏 *35 rooms* ⟡ *Restaurant, fans, pool, bar, airport shuttle, car rental, travel services; a/c in some rooms, no room TVs* ▣ *AE, DC, MC, V* ⍩ *BP.*

$$ ▦ **Hotel Victoria.** Fabulous views of the Pacific are what make this hotel special. The rooms in the low-slung main building are a bit spartan, but that hardly matters when you can just sit on the covered terrace or in the leafy garden and enjoy the sliver of blue on the horizon. Shops and restaurants are a short walk away. ⊠ *Av. Pont s/n* ☎ *32/100–272* 🛏 *7 rooms* ⟡ *Dining room, airport shuttle, car rental, travel services; no a/c, no room phones, no room TVs* ▣ *V* ⍩ *CP.*

$$ ▦ **Martín and Anita.** Papaya and banana trees surround this little hostelry with clean, spacious rooms that open onto plant-lined terra-cotta pathways. Owner Martín Hereveri also runs several different tours of the island. ⊠ *Av. Simon Paoa s/n* 🖷☎ *32/100–593* ⊕ *www.hostal.co.cl* 🛏 *13 rooms* ⟡ *Dining room, bar, laundry service, Internet, airport shuttle, car rental, travel services, no-smoking rooms; no a/c, no room phones, no room TVs* ▣ *AE, DC, MC, V* ⍩ *BP.*

$$ ▦ **Vai Moana.** The name of this lovely lodging means "blue sea," and you'll soon discover why. A long stretch of azure can be seen from just about everywhere, from the glass-enclosed dining room to the umbrella-shaded veranda. Little white cabanas strewn around the grounds are simply furnished, with wood-beamed ceilings and wide windows. The effusive staff speaks English and French. ⊠ *Av. Atamu Tekena s/n* 🖷☎ *32/100–626* ⊕ *www.vai-moana.cl* 🛏 *14 rooms* ⟡ *Dining room, fans, minibars, bar, lounge, laundry service, Internet, car rental, travel services, no-smoking rooms; no a/c, no room phones, no room TVs* ▣ *AE, MC, V* ⍩ *BP.*

★ **$** ▦ **Tadeo and Lili.** Individual bungalows fronted in black volcanic rock form part of this lovely guesthouse on the coast with unspoilt views of Hanga Roa and the rolling surf of the Pacific. Lili is French and Tadeo Rapa Nui. Together they created these attractive cabins, each with a stamp of individuality. Lili is also a renowned guide. ⊠ *Av. Policarpo Toro s/n* 🖷☎ *32/100–422* 🛏 *6 bungalows* ⟡ *Dining room, Internet, airport shuttle, travel services; no a/c, no room phones, no room TVs* ▣ *MC, V* ⍩ *CP.*

NIGHTLIFE & THE ARTS

The Arts

For a taste of the excitement of the annual Tapati Rapa Nui festival, take in a performance by the folk troupe Kari Kari or Polinesia. In a dance called the *sau sau*, the men and women spin wildly as the music gets faster and faster. The exuberant movements of the dancers are punctuated by shouts of joy. Another dance called the *hoko* incorporates birdlike movements. Shows start at around 11,500 pesos each. **Kari Kari** (☎ 32/100–595) performs at various hotels. The dance group **Polinesia** (☎ 32/100–447) performs at the restaurant KopaKavana on Avenida Te Pito O Te Henua.

Nightlife

You're in for a late night if you want to sample the scene in Hanga Roa. Locals don't hit the bars until around midnight. The most popular place to stop for a beer is the **Banana Pub** (⊠ Av. Atamu Tekena s/n 🕾 no phone), a laid-back bar on the main road. **Aloha** (⊠ Av. Atamu Tekena s/n 🕾 no phone), a bar-restaurant with a palm tree growing through its front porch, plays both Rapu Nui and international music. **Tavake** (⊠ Av. Atamu Tekena s/n 🕾 no phone) is a small, popular bar with a front porch and plastic tables along the main thoroughfare.

On weekends, the younger set heads to **Toroko** (⊠ Av. Policarpo Toro s/n 🕾 no phone), a dance club a stone's throw from the beach. You won't need directions—just follow the thumping disco beat. **Piditi** (⊠ Av. Hotu Matu'a s/n 🕾 no phone), a dance club close to the airport, blares music into the wee hours of the morning.

SPORTS & THE OUTDOORS

Haka pei, or sliding down hillsides on banana trunks, is one of the more popular activities during the Tapati Rapa Nui festival. Another is racing across the reed-choked lake that's hidden inside the crater of Ranu Raraku. Visitors who take to the water usually prefer swimming at one of the sandy beaches or snorkeling near one of the offshore islets. Another option is to hike out to isolated spots on the northern coast.

Beaches

Easter Island's earliest settlers are believed to have landed on idyllic **Playa Anakena.** Legend has it that the caves in the cliffs overlooking the beach are where Hotu Matu'a, the island's first ruler, dwelled while constructing his home. It's easy to see why Hotu Matu'a might have selected this spot: on an island ringed by rough volcanic rock, Playa Anakena is the widest swath of sand. Ignoring the sun-worshipping tourists are the five beautifully carved moais standing on nearby Ahu Nau Nau. On the northern coast of the island, Playa Anakena is reachable by a paved road that runs across the island, or by the more circuitous coastal road.

A lovely strip of pink sand, **Playa Ovahe** isn't as crowded as neighboring Playa Anakena. But the fact that most tourists pass it by is what makes this secluded beach so appealing. Families head here on weekends for afternoon cookouts. The cliffs that tower above the beach were once home to many of the island's residents. Locals proudly point out caves where relatives were born.

The only beach in Hanga Roa is **Playa Pea,** a tiny stretch of sand near the caleta. It's a popular spot among families with small children.

Diving

The crystal-clear waters of the South Pacific afford great visibility for snorkelers and divers. Dozens of types of colorful fish flourish in the warm waters surrounding the island's craggy volcanic rocks. Some of the most spectacular underwater scenery is at Motu Nui and Motu Iti, two adjoining islets just off the coast. **Orca Diving Center** (⊠ Caleta de Hanga Roa 🕾 32/550–877 or 32/550–375 🖷 32/550–448) provides a boat, a guide, and all your diving gear for 45,000 pesos per person. You can rent a snorkeling mask and fins for 1,000 pesos. **Rapu Nui Dive Center** (⊠ Caleta de Hanga Roa 🕾 32/551–055) arranges night dives for 45,500 pesos and various excursions for around 75,000 pesos.

Hiking

The breezes that cool the island even in the middle of summer make this a perfect place for hikers. Be careful, though, as the sun is much stronger than it feels. Slather yourself with sunblock and bring along plenty of water.

You can take numerous hikes from Hanga Roa. A short walk takes you to Ahu Tahai. More strenuous is a hike on a gravel road to the seven moais of Ahu Akivi, about 10 km (6 mi) north of town. One of the most rewarding treks is along a rough dirt path on the northern coast that leads from Ahu Te Peu to Playa Anakena. The six-hour journey around Terevaka takes you past many undisturbed archaeological sites that few tourists ever see. If you're planning on heading out without a guide, pick up a copy of the *Easter Island Trekking Map* at any local shop.

Horseback Riding

One popular way to see the island is on horseback, which typically costs up to 210,000 pesos per day. Many locals rent out their horses, and you can also often rent horses and guides from tour operators and car-rental agencies. Also try asking your hotel to arrange this for you.

Mountain Biking

Mountain biking is a great way to get around and see the sights of Easter Island. Most car-rental agencies also rent mountain bikes for up to 14,000 pesos per day.

SHOPPING

Souvenir shops line Hanga Roa's two main streets, Avenida Atamu Tekena and Avenida Te Pito O Te Henua. **Feria Municipal** (⊠ Av. Atamu Tekena s/n ☎ no phone), an open-air market, has good buys on hand-made jewelry. **Hotu Matu'a's Favorite Shop** (⊠ Av. Atamu Tekena s/n ☎ no phone) sells the widest selection of T-shirts on the island. Next to the church is the **Mercado Artesenal** (⊠ Av. Ara Roa Rakei s/n ☎ no phone), a large building filled with craft stands. Here, local artisans whittle wooden moais and string together seashell necklaces. It's open Monday–Saturday 9 AM–8 PM and Sunday 9 AM–12:30 PM.

EASTER ISLAND A TO Z

To *research prices, get advice from other travelers, and book travel arrangements, visit www.fodors.com.*

AIR TRAVEL

LanChile operates all flights from Santiago to the east and Tahiti to the west. Three or four flights a week arrive from Santiago during the high season between December and March, two the rest of the year; two flights a week arrive from Tahiti. The planes are often full in January and February, so it's best to book far ahead and reconfirm your flights.

Tickets to Easter Island are expensive—up to U.S.$750 for a round-trip flight from Santiago. However, you'll get a better deal if you combine it with a flight to Santiago.

🛪 Airline **LanChile** ⊠ Av. Atamu Tekena s/n ☎ 32/100-279 or 32/100-920.

AIRPORT

Easter Island's shoe-box-size Aeropuerto Internacional Mataveri is on the southern edge of Hanga Roa.

🛪 Airport Information **Aeropuerto Internacional Mataveri** ⊠ Av. Hotu Matu'a s/n ☎ 32/100-277 or 32/100-278.

BUSINESS HOURS

Almost all of Easter Island's businesses, including those catering to tourists, close for a few hours in the afternoon. Most are open 9 to 1 and 4 to 8, but a few stay open late into the evening. Many are closed Sunday.

CAR RENTAL

None of the international car-rental chains have offices on Easter Island, but you have many reputable local agencies from which to choose. Most charge about 37,500 pesos for eight hours, or 67,500 pesos per day for a four-wheel-drive vehicle. If you plan on visiting during January and February, call a few days ahead to reserve a car.

You can also rent cars at many restaurants, souvenir shops, and possibly the guest house where you're staying. If you ask around, you may find a significantly cheaper rate than what the rental companies charge. ◻Agencies **Aku Aku** ⊠ Av. Tu'u Koihu s/n ☎ 32/100-770. **Insular** ⊠ Av. Atamu Tekena s/n ☎ 32/100-480 or 32/551-276. **Kia Koe** ⊠ Av. Atamu Tekena s/n ☎ 32/100-282. **Oceanic Rapa Nui** ⊠ Av. Atamu Tekena s/n ☎ 32/100-985 or 32/551-392. **Toki** ⊠ Av. Atamu Tekena s/n ☎ 32/551-157.

CAR TRAVEL

To see many of Easter Island's less traveled areas, a four-wheel-drive vehicle is a necessity. Except for the well-maintained roads leading to Rano Kau and Playa Anakena, the best you can hope for are gravel roads. The most isolated spots are reached by dusty dirt roads or no roads at all.

FESTIVALS & SEASONAL EVENTS

The annual Tapati Rapa Nui festival, a two-week celebration of the island's heritage, takes place every year from late January through early February. The normally laid-back Hanga Roa bursts to life in a colorful festival that includes much singing and dancing. The Dia de la Lengua (Day of the Tongue), which usually takes place toward the end of November, celebrates the Rapa Nui language.

HEALTH

The tap water in Easter Island, which comes straight from the lake inside the crater of Rano Kau, is safe to drink but has a mineral taste. Bottled water is available everywhere.

LANGUAGE

Almost all residents speak Spanish, but a good number also speak Rapa Nui. Those who work in the tourist industry also generally speak English, French, German, and a smattering of other languages.

MAIL & SHIPPING

Correos de Chile, the island's tiny post office, is on Avenida Te Pito O Te Henua across from Hotel Otai. Postage is the same as in the rest of Chile. Bear in mind that mail is sent via LanChile flights, so you're likely to travel back to the mainland on the same plane as the letter you posted. If you want an Easter Island postmark, you might want to bring your own stamps. The post office here sometimes runs out.

MONEY MATTERS

The official currency is Chilean pesos, but U.S. dollars are accepted just about everywhere, and most restaurants and hotels will present your bill in U.S. dollars.

The only bank on the island is the Banco del Estado de Chile, on Avenida Tuumaheke. It's open weekdays 8 to noon. You can exchange U.S. dollars and travelers checks, or get a cash advance on your Visa card.

ATMS There is one ATM on the island, where you can withdraw cash with MasterCard, Visa, and Cirrus cards. It's near the Sernatur office on Avenida Tuumaheke, but it's still a good idea to bring cash before you arrive just in case the ATM breaks down.

CREDIT CARDS Few restaurants or shops accept credit cards. Almost all hotels and guest houses do, but charge a fee because it takes them months to get reimbursed. It's best to negotiate a rate for your lodging in advance and bring enough cash or travelers checks to cover it.

TAXIS

Taxis have become extremely popular among residents, so it's never difficult to find one during the day. Most trips to destinations in Hanga Roa should cost less than 1,000 pesos. After 8 or 9 PM, the price doubles.

TELEPHONES

A handful of public phones, which take only Entel phone cards (tickets), are scattered around Hanga Roa. You can also place local and international calls from the office of Entel, across from the Banco del Estado de Chile. Because Easter Island is part of the same governmental region as the Central Coast, Valparaíso and Viña del Mar are local calls. If you need to call Easter Island from mainland Chile you have to use Carrier 123.

TIPPING

Tour guides generally expect a tip of about 10%. Locals don't tip the restaurant staff, but most tourists leave about 10%. Taxi drivers do not expect a tip.

TOURS

Rapa Nui is filled with companies selling tours of the island. Most run similar half-day and full-day excursions to major archaeological sites, although a few offer "adventure" tours to lesser-known areas. Make sure to settle on the itinerary before booking a tour. If you know exactly where you want to visit, consider a private tour guide. Haumaka Tours' Josefina Nahoe Mulloy and Ramón Edmunds Pacomio, both English speakers, can show you sights not on any tour-bus itinerary.

Kia Koe, Mahinatur, and Manu Iti are all reputable tour agencies. Kia Koe attracts a lot of street traffic, so its tours are often crowded. Mahinatur generally books tours in advance, so the groups are often smaller. Both have friendly, knowledgeable guides.

🖪 Tour Agencies **Haumaka Tours** ⊠ Av. Hotu Matu'u s/n 🖼🖼 32/100-274 or 32/100-411. **Kia Koe** ⊠ Av. Atamu Tekena s/n ☎ 32/100-282. **Mahinatur** ⊠ Av. Atamu Tekena and Av. Hotu Matu'a ☎ 32/100-220. **Manu Iti** ⊠ Av. Tuukoihu s/n ☎ 32/100-313.

VISITOR INFORMATION

The local office of Sernatur, the Chilean tourism agency, is run by the genial Francisco Edmunds Paoa. He used to teach local history, so he knows just about everything about the island. He and his staff can provide you with maps and lists of local businesses. It's open weekdays 8:30–1 and 2:30–6, and Saturdays 8:30–1.

🖪 Tourist Information **Oficina de Tourismo** ⊠ Av. Tuumaheke s/n ☎ 32/100-255.

SPANISH VOCABULARY

Words and Phrases

	English	Spanish	Pronunciation
Basics			
	Yes/no	Sí/no	see/no
	Please	Por favor	pore fah-**vore**
	May I?	¿Me permite?	may pair-**mee**-tay
	Thank you (very much)	(Muchas) gracias	(**moo**-chas) **grah**-see-as
	You're welcome	De nada	day **nah**-dah
	Excuse me	Con permiso	con pair-**mee**-so
	Pardon me	¿Perdón?	pair-**dohn**
	Could you tell me?	¿Podría decirme?	po-dree-ah deh-**seer**-meh
	I'm sorry	Lo siento	lo see-**en**-to
	Good morning!	¡Buenos días!	**bway**-nohs **dee**-ahs
	Good afternoon!	¡Buenas tardes!	**bway**-nahs **tar**-dess
	Good evening!	¡Buenas noches!	**bway**-nahs **no**-chess
	Goodbye!	¡Adiós!/¡Hasta luego!	ah-dee-**ohss/ah**-stah-**lwe**-go
	Mr./Mrs.	Señor/Señora	sen-**yor**/sen-**yohr**-ah
	Miss	Señorita	sen-yo-**ree**-tah
	Pleased to meet you	Mucho gusto	**moo**-cho **goose**-to
	How are you?	¿Cómo está usted?	**ko**-mo es-**tah** oo-**sted**
	Very well, thank you.	Muy bien, gracias.	**moo**-ee bee-**en**, **grah**-see-as
	And you?	¿Y usted?	ee oos-**ted**
	Hello (on the telephone)	Diga	**dee**-gah

Numbers

	1	un, uno	oon, **oo**-no
	2	dos	dos
	3	tres	tress
	4	cuatro	**kwah**-tro
	5	cinco	**sink**-oh
	6	seis	saice
	7	siete	see-**et**-eh
	8	ocho	**o**-cho
	9	nueve	new-**eh**-vey
	10	diez	dee-**es**
	11	once	**ohn**-seh
	12	doce	**doh**-seh

13	trece	**treh**-seh
14	catorce	ka-**tohr**-seh
15	quince	**keen**-seh
16	dieciséis	dee-**es**-ee-**saice**
17	diecisiete	dee-**es**-ee-see-**et**-eh
18	dieciocho	dee-**es**-ee-**o**-cho
19	diecinueve	**dee**-es-ee-**new**-**ev**-ah
20	veinte	**vain**-teh
21	veinte y uno/veintiuno	**vain**-te-**oo**-noh
30	treinta	**train**-tah
32	treinta y dos	train-tay-**dohs**
40	cuarenta	kwah-**ren**-tah
43	cuarenta y tres	kwah-**ren**-tay-**tress**
50	cincuenta	seen-**kwen**-tah
54	cincuenta y cuatro	seen-**kwen**-tay **kwah**-tro
60	sesenta	sess-**en**-tah
65	sesenta y cinco	sess-**en**-tay **seen**-ko
70	setenta	set-**en**-tah
76	setenta y seis	set-**en**-tay **saice**
80	ochenta	oh-**chen**-tah
87	ochenta y siete	oh-**chen**-tay see-**yet**-eh
90	noventa	no-**ven**-tah
98	noventa y ocho	no-**ven**-tah-**o**-choh
100	cien	see-en
101	ciento uno	see-en-toh **oo**-noh
200	doscientos	doh-see-**en**-tohss
500	quinientos	keen-**yen**-tohss
700	setecientos	set-eh-see-**en**-tohss
900	novecientos	no-veh-see-**en**-tohss
1,000	mil	meel
2,000	dos mil	dohs meel
1,000,000	un millón	oon meel-**yohn**

Colors

black	negro	**neh**-groh
blue	azul	ah-**sool**
brown	café	kah-**feh**
green	verde	**ver**-deh
pink	rosa	**ro**-sah
purple	morado	mo-**rah**-doh
orange	naranja	na-**rahn**-hah
red	rojo	**roh**-hoh
white	blanco	**blahn**-koh
yellow	amarillo	ah-mah-**ree**-yoh

Days of the Week

Sunday	domingo	doe-**meen**-goh
Monday	lunes	**loo**-ness
Tuesday	martes	**mahr**-tess
Wednesday	miércoles	me-**air**-koh-less

Thursday	jueves	hoo-**ev**-ess
Friday	viernes	vee-**air**-ness
Saturday	sábado	**sah**-bah-doh

Months

January	enero	eh-**neh**-roh
February	febrero	feh-**breh**-roh
March	marzo	**mahr**-soh
April	abril	ah-**breel**
May	mayo	**my**-oh
June	junio	**hoo**-nee-oh
July	julio	**hoo**-lee-yoh
August	agosto	ah-**ghost**-toh
September	septiembre	sep-tee-**em**-breh
October	octubre	oak-**too**-breh
November	noviembre	no-vee-**em**-breh
December	diciembre	dee-see-**em**-breh

Useful Phrases

Do you speak English?	¿Habla usted inglés?	**ah**-blah oos-**ted** in-**glehs**
I don't speak Spanish	No hablo español	no **ah**-bloh es-pahn-**yol**
I don't understand (you)	No entiendo	no en-tee-**en**-doh
I understand (you)	Entiendo	en-tee-**en**-doh
I don't know	No sé	no seh
I am American/ British	Soy americano (americana)/ inglés(a)	soy ah-meh-ree-**kah**-no (ah-meh-ree-**kah**-nah)/ in-**glehs** (**ah**)
What's your name?	¿Cómo se llama usted?	koh-mo seh **yah**-mah oos-**ted**
My name is . . .	Me llamo . . .	may **yah**-moh
What time is it?	¿Qué hora es?	keh **o**-rah es
It is one, two, three . . . o'clock.	Es la una. . . . Son las dos, tres	es la **oo**-nah/sohn lahs dohs, tress
Yes, please/No, thank you	Sí, por favor/No, gracias	**see** pohr fah-**vor**/no **grah**-see-us
How?	¿Cómo?	**koh**-mo
When?	¿Cuándo?	**kwahn**-doh
This/Next week	Esta semana/ la semana que entra	**es**-teh seh-**mah**-nah/lah seh-**mah**-nah keh **en**-trah
This/Next month	Este mes/el próximo mes	**es**-teh mehs/el **proke**-see-mo mehs
This/Next year	Este año/el año que viene	**es**-teh **ahn**-yo/el **ahn**-yo keh vee-**yen**-ay
Yesterday/today/ tomorrow	Ayer/hoy/mañana	ah-**yehr**/oy/mahn-**yah**-nah
This morning/ afternoon	Esta mañana/ tarde	**es**-tah mahn-**yah**-nah/**tar**-deh

Tonight	Esta noche	es-tah no-cheh
What?	¿Qué?	keh
What is it?	¿Qué es esto?	keh es es-toh
Why?	¿Por qué?	pore keh
Who?	¿Quién?	kee-yen
Where is . . . ?	¿Dónde está . . . ?	dohn-deh es-tah
the train station?	la estación del tren?	la es-tah-see-on del train
the subway station?	la estación del Tren subterráneo?	la es-ta-see-on del trehn soob-tair-ron-a-o
the bus stop?	la parada del autobus?	la pah-rah-dah del oh-toh-boos
the post office?	la oficina de correos?	la oh-fee-see-nah deh koh-reh-os
the bank?	el banco?	el bahn-koh
the hotel?	el hotel?	el oh-tel
the store?	la tienda?	la tee-en-dah
the cashier?	la caja?	la kah-hah
the museum?	el museo?	el moo-seh-oh
the hospital?	el hospital?	el ohss-pee-tal
the elevator?	el ascensor?	el ah-sen-sohr
the bathroom?	el baño?	el bahn-yoh
Here/there	Aquí/allá	ah-key/ah-yah
Open/closed	Abierto/cerrado	ah-bee-er-toh/ser-ah-doh
Left/right	Izquierda/derecha	iss-key-er-dah/dare-eh-chah
Straight ahead	Derecho	dare-eh-choh
Is it near/far?	¿Está cerca/lejos?	es-tah sehr-kah/leh-hoss
I'd like . . . a room	Quisiera . . . un cuarto/una habitación	kee-see-ehr-ah oon kwahr-toh/oo-nah ah-bee-tah-see-on
the key	la llave	lah yah-veh
a newspaper	un periódico	oon pehr-ee-oh-dee-koh
a stamp	un sello de correo	oon seh-yo deh koh-reh-oh
I'd like to buy . . .	Quisiera comprar . . .	kee-see-ehr-ah kohm-prahr
cigarettes	cigarrillos	ce-ga-ree-yohs
matches	cerillos	ser-ee-ohs
a dictionary	un diccionario	oon deek-see-oh-nah-ree-oh
soap	jabón	hah-bohn
sunglasses	gafas de sol	ga-fahs deh sohl
suntan lotion	loción bronceadora	loh-see-ohn brohn-seh-ah-do-rah
a map	un mapa	oon mah-pah
a magazine	una revista	oon-ah reh-veess-tah
paper	papel	pah-pel
envelopes	sobres	so-brehs

a postcard	una tarjeta postal	**oon**-ah tar-**het**-ah post-**ahl**
How much is it?	¿Cuánto cuesta?	**kwahn**-toh **kwes**-tah
It's expensive/ cheap	Está caro/barato	es-**tah kah**-roh/ bah-**rah**-toh
A little/a lot	Un poquito/ mucho	oon poh-**kee**-toh/ **moo**-choh
More/less	Más/menos	mahss/**men**-ohss
Enough/too much/too little	Suficiente/ demasiado/ muy poco	soo-fee-see-**en**-teh/ deh-mah-see-**ah**-doh/**moo**-ee **poh**-koh
Telephone	Teléfono	tel-**ef**-oh-no
Telegram	Telegrama	teh-leh-**grah**-mah
I am ill	Estoy enfermo(a)	es-**toy** en-**fehr**-moh(mah)
Please call a doctor	Por favor llame a un medico	pohr fah-**vor ya**-meh ah oon **med**-ee-koh
Help!	¡Auxilio! ¡Ayuda! ¡Socorro!	owk-**see**-lee-oh/ ah-**yoo**-dah/ soh-**kohr**-roh
Fire!	¡Incendio!	en-**sen**-dee-oo
Caution!/Look out!	¡Cuidado!	kwee-**dah**-doh

On the Road

Avenue	Avenida	ah-ven-**ee**-dah
Broad, tree-lined boulevard	Bulevar	boo-leh-**var**
Fertile plain	Vega	**veh**-gah
Highway	Carretera	car-reh-**ter**-ah
Mountain pass, Street	Puerto Calle	poo-**ehr**-toh **cah**-yeh
Waterfront promenade	Rambla	**rahm**-blah
Wharf	Embarcadero	em-bar-cah-**deh**-ro

In Town

Cathedral	Catedral	cah-teh-**dral**
Church	Templo/Iglesia	**tem**-plo/ee-**glehs**-see-ah
City hall	Casa de gobierno	kah-sah deh go-bee-**ehr**-no
Door, gate	Puerta portón	poo-**ehr**-tah por-**ton**
Entrance/exit	Entrada/salida	en-**trah**-dah/sah-**lee**-dah
Inn, rustic bar, or restaurant	Taverna	tah-**vehr**-nah
Main square	Plaza principal	plah-thah prin-see-**pahl**
Market	Mercado	mer-**kah**-doh

Neighborhood	Barrio	**bahr**-ree-o
Traffic circle	Glorieta	glor-ee-**eh**-tah
Wine cellar, wine bar, or wine shop	Bodega	boh-**deh**-gah

Dining Out

A bottle of . . .	Una botella de . . .	**oo**-nah bo-**teh**-yah deh
A cup of . . .	Una taza de . . .	**oo**-nah **tah**-thah deh
A glass of . . .	Un vaso de . . .	oon **vah**-so deh
Ashtray	Un cenicero	oon sen-ee-**seh**-roh
Bill/check	La cuenta	lah **kwen**-tah
Bread	El pan	el pahn
Breakfast	El desayuno	el deh-sah-**yoon**-oh
Butter	La mantequilla	lah man-teh-**key**-yah
Cheers!	¡Salud!	sah-**lood**
Cocktail	Un aperitivo	oon ah-pehr-ee-**tee**-voh
Dinner	La cena	lah **seh**-nah
Dish	Un plato	oon **plah**-toh
Menu of the day	Menú del día	meh-**noo** del **dee**-ah
Enjoy!	¡Buen provecho!	bwehn pro-**veh**-cho
Fixed-price menu	Menú fijo o turistico	meh-**noo fee**-hoh oh too-**ree**-stee-coh
Fork	El tenedor	el ten-eh-**dor**
Is the tip included?	¿Está incluida la propina?	es-**tah** in-cloo-**ee**-dah lah pro-**pee**-nah
Knife	El cuchillo	el koo-**chee**-yo
Large portion of savory snacks	Raciónes	rah-see-**oh**-nehs
Lunch	La comida	lah koh-**mee**-dah
Menu	La carta, el menú	lah **cart**-ah, el meh-**noo**
Napkin	La servilleta	lah sehr-vee-**yet**-ah
Pepper	La pimienta	lah pee-me-**en**-tah
Please give me	Por favor déme	pore fah-**vor deh**-meh
Salt	La sal	lah sahl
Savory snacks	Tapas	**tah**-pahs
Spoon	Una cuchara	**oo**-nah koo-**chah**-rah
Sugar	El azúcar	el ah-**thu**-kar
Waiter!/Waitress!	¡Por favor Señor/Señorita!	pohr fah-**vor** sen-**yor**/sen-yor-ee-tah

INDEX